Insurance Handbook for the Medical Office

Student Workbook

SEVENTH EDITION

Marilyn Takahashi Fordney, CMA-AC, CMT

Formerly Instructor of Medical Insurance, Medical Terminology, Medical Machine Transcription, and Medical Office Procedures

Ventura College

Ventura, California

W.B. Saunders Company

An Imprint of Elsevier Science

Philadelphia London New York St. Louis Sydney Toronto

W.B. SAUNDERS COMPANY
An Imprint of Elsevier Science
The Curtis Center
Independence Square West
Philadelphia, Pennsylvania 19106

Editor-in-Chief: Andrew Allen
Acquisitions Editor: Adrianne Williams
Developmental Editor: Rae L. Robertson
Project Manager: Tina Rebane
Illustration Specialist: John S. Needles, Jr.
Book Designer: Gene Harris

Student Workbook for the
INSURANCE HANDBOOK FOR THE MEDICAL OFFICE ISBN 0-7216-9519-1

Printed in the United States of America

Last digit is the print number: 9 8 7 6 5 4 3 2

Acknowledgments

This edition of the *Student Workbook for the Insurance Handbook for the Medical Office* has had considerable input from many medical professionals. Expert consultation has been necessary due to the complexities of the managed care environment, intricacies of procedural and diagnostic coding, impact of technology on insurance claims processing, and the more sophisticated role the insurance billing specialist has in today's work force. I wish to express an immense debt of gratitude to Linda French, CMA-C, NCICS, who acted as a technical collaborator and contributor, and helped me enhance many sections of the *Student Workbook* to assist the learner as well as the instructor using the material.

Thank you to my assistant, Nina Janis, who enthusiastically and competently did the typing, filing, and many other tasks necessary to meet the deadlines.

Lastly, and most importantly, I express overwhelming gratitude to the professional consultants who provided vital information to make this Workbook better than previous editions, and they are:

Deborah Emmons, CMA
President
S.T.A.T. Transcription Service
Port Hueneme, California

Ronna Jurow, M.D.
Active Staff and Attending Physician in Obstetrics, Gynecology and Infertility
Community Memorial Hospital
Ventura, California

Lucille M. Loignon, M.D., F.A.C.S.
Diplomate, American Board of Ophthalmology
Oxnard, California

Maria Reyes
Ventura Anesthesia Medical Group
Ventura, California

Walter A. Shaff
President
CPR
Lake Oswego, Oregon

Lita Starr
Office Manager and wife of William E. Starr, M.D.
Oxnard, California

Paul Wertlake, M.D.
Medical Director and Chief Pathologist
Unilab Corporation
Tarzana, California

Shirley Wertlake, CLS
Technical Specialist
Clinical Laboratories
UCLA Medical Center
Los Angeles, California

Editorial Review Board

Contents

Instruction Guide to the *Workbook*

LEARNING OBJECTIVES

The student will be able to

- Define and spell key terms for each chapter.
- Answer self-study review questions for each chapter of the handbook.
- Complete assignments to enhance and develop better critical thinking skills.
- Define abbreviations as they appear on a patient record.
- Abstract subjective and objective data from patient records.
- Review documentation on patient records.
- Prepare legally correct medicolegal forms and letters.
- Code professional services properly, using the *Current Procedural Terminology* (CPT) Code Book or Appendixes A and B.
- Select diagnostic code numbers, using the *International Classification of Diseases (9th Revision) Clinical Modification (ICD-9-CM)*.
- Locate errors on insurance claims before submission to insurance companies.
- Locate errors on returned insurance claims.
- Complete an insurance claim tracer form.
- Carry out collection procedures on delinquent accounts.
- Execute financial management procedures for tracing managed care plans.
- Abstract information necessary to complete insurance claim forms from patient records and billing statement/ledger cards.
- Complete insurance claim forms commonly used in medical offices.
- Post payments, adjustments, and balances to patients' statement/ledger cards when submitting insurance claims.
- Compute mathematic calculations for Medicare and TRICARE cases.
- Analyze insurance claims in both hospital inpatient and outpatient settings.
- Prepare a cover letter, résumé, job application, and follow-up letter when searching for employment.
- Access the Internet and visit web sites to research and/or obtain data.

Instructions to the Student

This seventh edition of *Insurance Handbook for the Medical Office Student Workbook* has been prepared for those who use the textbook, *Insurance Handbook for the Medical Office* (hereafter referred to as the *Handbook*). It is designed to assist the learner in a practical approach to doing insurance billing and coding. It will also develop a better understanding of the differences between the insurance programs when completing the HCFA-1500 health insurance claim form.

The key terms are repeated for quick reference when studying. Each chapter's outline will serve as a lecture guide to use for note taking. Self-study review questions in the form of short answer, true/false, multiple choice, and matching are presented to reinforce learning of key concepts for each topic. Answers are found in Appendix D.

Some assignments give students hands-on experience in typing claim forms for optical character recognition (OCR) scanning equipment, which is used in many states for insurance claims processing and payment. Insurance claim forms and other sample documents that are easily removable are included for typing practice.

Current procedural and diagnostic code exercises are used throughout to facilitate and enhance coding skills for submitting a claim or making up an itemized billing statement.

Icons appearing throughout the workbook are used to indicate assignment types. An illustration of each icon, along with its description, is outlined below.

Self-study assignments encompass important points from each chapter and allow you to study at your own pace.

Critical thinking assignments require skills that help prepare you for real-world scenarios encountered in insurance billing.

The **Student Software Challenge** CD-ROM found in the back of the *Handbook* is required for completing assignments that indicate this icon.

Internet assignments point you to the World Wide Web for resources.

The 20-minute **video, The HCFA Files: A case for Medical Billing Accuracy** illustrating HCFA-1500 claim form tragedies is required viewing for assignments that indicate this icon.

Key Terms

Key terms are presented for each chapter, and definitions may be located in the Glossary at the end of the textbook. It is suggested that you make up 3″ by 5″ index cards for each term and write in the definitions as you encounter them while reading each chapter in the *Handbook*. This will reinforce your knowledge and help you learn the words. Your instructor may wish to select certain words to study for "pop" quizzes.

Note Taking

Taking notes is an important key to success in studying and learning. Note taking helps an individual pay attention during class and retain information. Each chapter has a study outline for organizational purposes, and this may be used as a guide for writing down key points during lectures or when studying or reviewing from the textbook for tests. Use file cards, note pads, or a notebook for taking notes. Underline or highlight important words or phrases. To improve the usefulness of notes, try this format:

1. On a notepad sheet or file card draw a margin 3 inches from the left.
2. Use the left side for topic headings and the right side for notes.
3. Skip a few lines when there is a change in topic.
4. Write numbers or letters to indicate subideas under a heading.
5. Be brief; do not write down every word except when emphasizing a quote, rule, or law. Write notes in your own words, since that is what you will understand.
6. Use abbreviations that you know how to translate.
7. Listen carefully to the lecture.
8. After the lecture, reread your notes. Highlight the word(s) on the left side of the page to identify the topic of the notes on the right.
9. For study purposes, cover the right side and see if you can explain to yourself or someone else the topic or word.
10. Remember—learning is by doing, and doing is up to you. So take notes for better understanding.

Self-Study Assignments

Review questions have been designed to encompass important points for each chapter to assist you in studying insurance billing and coding theory. Answers are located in Appendix D. With this edition, they have been made as self-study assignments so students and instructors will have more time in class to cover other important issues related to billing and coding.

Simulation Assignments

Assume that you have been hired as an insurance billing specialist and that you are working in a clinic setting for an incorporated group of medical doctors, other allied health specialists, and a podiatrist. You will be asked to complete various assignments. These doctors will be on the staff of a nearby hospital. Appendix A details this clinic's policies and procedures, which you must read completely before beginning the competency-based assignments. Within each chapter, the simulation assignments progress from easy to more complex. Some assignments are given with critical thinking problems, which the instructor may use for class discussion.

Always read the assignment entirely before beginning to complete it. There are 119 *Workbook* assignments. Table 1 is a reference guide that lists chapter numbers and titles, along with the corresponding assignment numbers.

Medical Terminology and Abbreviations

An abbreviation list is provided in Appendix A to help you learn how to abstract and read doctors' notes. Decode any abbreviations that you do not understand or that are unfamiliar to you. To reinforce learning these abbreviations, write their meanings on the assignment pages. If you do not have a background in medical terminology, it might be wise to use a good medical dictionary as a reference or, better yet, enroll in a terminology course if you do not have that skill mastered.

Patient Records

Patient records, ledgers, and encounter forms are presented as they might appear in a physician's office, so the learner may have the tools needed to extract information to complete claim forms. Patient records have been abbreviated due to space and page constraints. They contain pertinent data for each type of case, but it was necessary to omit a lengthy physical examination. Because detailed documentation is encouraged in medical practices, the records all appear typewritten rather than in handwritten notes. The doctor's signature will appear after each dated entry on the record.

All the materials included in the assignments have been altered to prevent identification of the cases or parties involved. The names and addresses are fictitious, and no reference to any person living or dead is intended. No evaluation of medical practice or medical advice is to be inferred from the patient records, nor is any recommendation made toward alternative treatment methods or prescribed medications.

Financial Records

Ledger card assignments will provide you with experience in posting, totaling the fees, and properly recording appropriate information on the ledger when the insurance claim is submitted. Statement/ledger cards are also included for the purpose of typing practice. Refer to Appendix A to obtain doctors' fees for posting to the statement/ledger cards.

TABLE 1

***Workbook* Assignments**

Handbook Chapter	Corresponding *Workbook* Chapter	Assignments
1	Role of an Insurance Billing Specialist	1–1 through 1–4
2	Basics of Health Insurance	2–1 through 2–6
3	Medical Documentation	3–1 through 3–6
4	Diagnostic Coding	4–1 through 4–10
5	Procedural Coding	5–1 through 5–13
6	The Health Insurance Claim Form	6–1 through 6–6
7	Electronic Data Interchange (EDI)	7–1 through 7–5
8	Receiving Payments and Insurance Problem Solving	8–1 through 8–7
9	Office and Insurance Collection Strategies	9–1 through 9–7
10	Managed Care Systems	10–1 through 10–6
11	Medicare	11–1 through 11–9
12	Medicaid and Other State Programs	12–1 through 12–4
13	TRICARE and CHAMPVA	13–1 through 13–5
14	Workers' Compensation	14–1 through 14–6
15	Disability Income Insurance and Disability Benefit Program	15–1 through 15–6
16	Hospital Billing	16–1 through 16–9
17	Seeking a Job and Attaining Professional Advancement	17–1 through 17–8

HCFA-1500 Claim Form

If you have access to a computer, use the CD-ROM that accompanies the *Handbook* to complete each assignment and print it out for evaluation. To complete the HCFA-1500 claim form properly for each type of program, refer to the section in Chapter 6 of the *Handbook* that describes in detail the correct information to be put in each block. Also view the templates found at the end of Chapter 6 for each insurance type.

Complete all insurance forms in OCR style, since this is the format in which insurance carriers process claims most expediently. Chapter 6 gives instructions on OCR do's and don'ts. If you do not have access to a computer, type or neatly write in the information on the insurance form as you abstract it from the patient record.

Performance Evaluation Checklist

This seventh edition features a competency-based format for each assignment indicating performance objectives to let you know what is to be accomplished. The task (job assignment), conditions (elements needed to perform and complete the task), and standards (time management), as well as directions for the specific task, are included. Use of a checklist assists in scoring the assignments and helps you develop the skill of speed in completing tasks.

A two-part performance evaluation checklist used when completing an HCFA-1500 claim form is presented on the following pages (see Figs. 1 and 2). Reproduce these sheets only for the assignments that involve completing the HCFA-1500 claim form. Your instructor will give you the number of points to be assigned for each step.

Appendixes

Refer to Table 2, which shows what is included in each of the appendixes.

Student Reference Notebook

A *student reference notebook* is recommended so you can access information quickly to help you complete the *Workbook* assignments. Before beginning the assignments, tear out Appendix A and place it in a three-ring binder with chapter indexes. Appendix A includes the clinic policies and guidelines, data about the clinic staff, medical and laboratory abbreviations, and mock fee schedule used while working as an insurance billing specialist for the College Clinic.

Besides these suggestions, you may wish either to tear out or make photocopies of other sections of the textbook for your personal use. In addition, your instructor may give you handouts from time to time, pertaining to regional insurance program policies and procedures, to place in your notebook.

Content Suggestions from *Workbook*

- ✔ Appendix A: College Clinic policies, data about staff physicians, medical and laboratory abbreviations, and mock fee schedule
- ✔ Appendix B: HCPCS codes
- ✔ HCFA-1500 claim form (photocopy if extra copies are needed for making rough drafts or retyping an assignment)

Content Suggestions from *Handbook*

- ✔ Evaluation and Management CPT codes: Tables 5–1 and 5–2

TABLE 2

Appendix	Contents
A	College Clinic Staff (Provider) Information College Clinic and Contract Facilities Information Medical Abbreviations and Symbols Laboratory Abbreviations College Clinic Mock Fee Schedule
B	Medicare Level II HCFA Common Procedure Code System (HCPCS) Codes
C	Medi-Cal Abbreviations Medi-Cal Self-Study Review Questions
D	Answers to Self-Study Review Questions for Chapters

PERFORMANCE EVALUATION CHECKLIST

Assignment No. ____________

Name:____ Date:____________________________

Performance Objective

Task: Given access to all necessary equipment and information, the student will complete a HCFA-1500 health insurance claim form.

Standards: Claim Productivity Management
Time __________ minutes
Note: Time element may be given by instructor.

Directions: See assignment.

NOTE TIME BEGAN__________ **NOTE TIME COMPLETED**__________

PROCEDURE STEPS	ASSIGNED POINTS	STEP PERFORMED SATISFACTORY	COMMENTS
1. Assembled HCFA-1500 claim form, patient record, E/M code slip, ledger card, typewriter or computer, pen or pencil, and code books.	______	______	______
2. Posed ledger card correctly.	______	______	______
3. Proofread form for spelling and typographical errors while form remained in typewriter or on computer screen.	______	______	______
4. Points earned for correct completion of HCFA-1500 block-by-block data.	______	______	______

Figure I–1

- ✔ Insurance form templates from Chapter 6: Figures 6–6 through 6–15
- ✔ Medical Terminology (lay and medical terms): Table 3–1
- ✔ Terminology used in coding procedures: Table 3–2 HCFA-1500 block-by-block claim form instructions from Chapter 6
- ✔ Glossary

Tests

Tests are provided at the end of the *Workbook* to provide a complete, competency-based educational program.

BLOCK	INCORRECT	MISSING	NOT NEEDED	REMARKS	BLOCK	INCORRECT	MISSING	NOT NEEDED	REMARKS
					18				
1A					19				
2					20				
3					21				
4									
5					22				
6					23				
7					24A				
8					24B				
					24C				
9					24D				
9A									
9B									
9C					24E				
9D									
					24F				
10A					24G				
10B					24H, 24I				
10C					24J				
10D					24K				
11					25, 26				
11A					27				
11B					28				
11C					29				
11D									
12					30				
13									
14					31				
15									
16					32				
17									
17A					33				
					Reference Initials				

TOTAL POINTS EARNED: ________ TOTAL POINTS POSSIBLE: ________

Evaluator's signature ______________________________ NEED TO REPEAT: ____________

Figure I–2

Reference Material

To do the assignments in this *Workbook* and gain expertise in coding and insurance claims completion, an individual must have access to the books listed here. Addresses for obtaining these materials are given in parentheses. Additional books and booklets on these topics as well as Medicaid, Medicare, TRICARE and more are listed in Appendix B of the *Handbook*.

Dictionary

Dorland's Illustrated Medical Dictionary, 29th edition, W.B. Saunders Company, 2000 (6277 Sea Harbor Drive, Orlando, FL 32821–9989; 1–800–545–2522).

Code Books

Current Procedural Terminology, American Medical Association, published annually (515 North State Street, Chicago, IL 60610; 1-800-621-8335).

International Classification of Diseases (9th Revision) Clinical Modification (an inexpensive soft cover generic physician version of Volumes 1–3 is available from Channel Publishing Limited, 4750 Longley Lane, Suite 100, Reno, NV 89502; 1-800-248-2882).

Word Book

Medical Abbreviations and Eponyms by Sheila Sloane, W.B. Saunders Company, 1997 (6277 Sea Harbor Drive, Orlando, FL 32821–9989; 1–800–545–2522).

Pharmaceutical Book

Optional for drug names and descriptions might be either drug books used by nurses, e.g., Mosby's Gen RX, *Harcourt Health Sciences*, published annually (11830 Westline Industrial Drive, St. Louis, MO 63146; 1-800-325-4177; www.harcourthealth.com), or ones used by physicians, e.g., *Physician's Disk Reference (PDR)*, Medical Economics Company, published annually (5 Paragon Drive, Montvale, NJ, 07645; 1-800-432-4570).

Employee Insurance Procedural Manual

If you are presently working in a medical office and taking this course, you may custom design an insurance manual for your physician's practice as you complete insurance claims in this *Workbook*. Obtain a three-ring binder with indexes and label them group plans, private plans, Medicaid, Medicare, managed care plans, State Disability, TRICARE, and Workers' Compensation. If many of your patients have group plans, complete an insurance data or fact sheet (Figure 3) for each plan and organize them alphabetically by group plan. For managed care plans, type a form as shown in Chapter 10, Figure 10-5 of the *Handbook*.

An insurance manual with fact sheets listing benefits can keep you up-to-date on policy changes and ensure maximum reimbursement. Fact sheets can be prepared from information obtained when patients bring in their benefit booklets. Obtain and insert a list of the procedures that must be performed on an outpatient basis and those that must have second opinions for each of the insurance plans.

As you complete the assignments in this *Workbook*, place them in the insurance manual as examples of completed claims for each particular program.

STUDENT SOFTWARE CHALLENGE CD-ROM FOR WINDOWS

Since many medical practices use computer technology to perform financial operations, user-friendly computer software has been developed to accompany the *Handbook* and *Workbook*. It is designed to create a realistic approach to completing the HCFA-1500 insurance claim form. All relevant documents appear on screen and may be printed for 10 patient cases that escalate in difficulty. Key terms are integrated into the cases, and definitions may be accessed from a glossary.

The main objective is to complete the HCFA-1500 insurance claim form for each case and insert accurate data, including diagnostic and procedural code numbers. This mimics real office claims processing. The HCFA-1500 form has been created in an open-entry format, making it easy to move between the related patient forms and corresponding blocks on the HCFA form. By working through the cases, the student will challenge both computer skills and critical thinking skills.

An ongoing summary of scores achieved on completed cases may be brought up on screen to keep the student and instructor informed of progress made. Detailed scoring reports may be printed so that the instructor has access to the information from time to time. The software also allows the user to complete the HCFA-1500 claim form for all assignments in the *Workbook* and print it out for evaluation. This method of learning will help the student produce perfect completed insurance claims in a fun and challenging way. Getting started is easy. . . .

SPECIAL FEATURES

1

▶ **On-Line Help**. If you get stuck, just click on one of the Help files, which will give you instructions.

Help accessed from the Button Bar provides program software instructions for every screen of the Student Software Challenge CD-ROM. Use the Contents button or Search button to find information in **Help. Block Help** found in claim completion provides formatting details and reviews specific insurance guidelines for:

INSURANCE DATA

1. Employer's name ____________________
2. Address ____________________ Telephone Number ____________________
3. Insurance Company Contact Person ____________________
4. Insurance Carrier ____________________
5. Address ____________________ Telephone Number to Call for Benefits ____________________
6. Group Policy Number ____________________
7. Group Account Manager ____________________ Telephone Number ____________________
8. Insurance Coverage:
   Annual Deductible ____________________ Patient Copayment Percentage ____________________
   Noncovered Procedures ____________________
   Maximum Benefits ____________________
9. Diagnostic Coverage:
   Limited Benefits ____________________
   Maximum Benefits ____________________
   Noncovered Procedures ____________________
10. Major Medical:
   Annual Deductible ____________________ Patient Copayment Percentage ____________________
   Limited Benefits ____________________
   Maximum Benefits ____________________
   Noncovered Procedures ____________________

Mandatory Outpatient Surgeries ____________________

Second Surgical Opinions ____________________

Preadmission Certification Yes ______ No ______ Authorized Labs ____________________

Payment Plan:

UCR ______________ Schedule of Benefits ______________ CPT ______________ RVS ______________

Send claims to: ____________________

____

Date Entered ____________________ Date Updated ____________________

Figure I–3

Private insurance claims
Medicare claims
TRICARE claims

► **Zoom In/Zoom Out** is available while viewing the Patient Information Form, Encounter Form, Medical Record, and Physician Information. All forms may be printed.

► **Scroll** is a feature that allows vertical and horizontal movement of the document on screen. It is available while working on the

Patient Information, Encounter Form, Medical Record, Physician Information, and HCFA-1500 screens.

▶ **Bookmark** keeps track of where you are each time you exit the program. When you start the program subsequently, the bookmark dialog box displays if you were working on a case that was not completed. You can either review and continue the previous work from where you left off or restart the case.

▶ **Print** capabilities allow all documents to be printed for easy reference. The HCFA-1500 insurance claim form may be printed from two screens. Printing from the Patient Case screen allows the student to see all errors made on the first and second tries. Printing from the Report screen (Print Preview) allows the student to see all the correct answers.

2 ▶ **Glossary.** A comprehensive list of 200 key terms and abbreviations can be *accessed from all screens* in the software except the log-on sequence. It includes a Find text entry field that searches on multiple characters and then displays its definition. A simple click on a term or abbreviation highlighted in green in a patient's Medical Record links automatically to the glossary for quick reference.

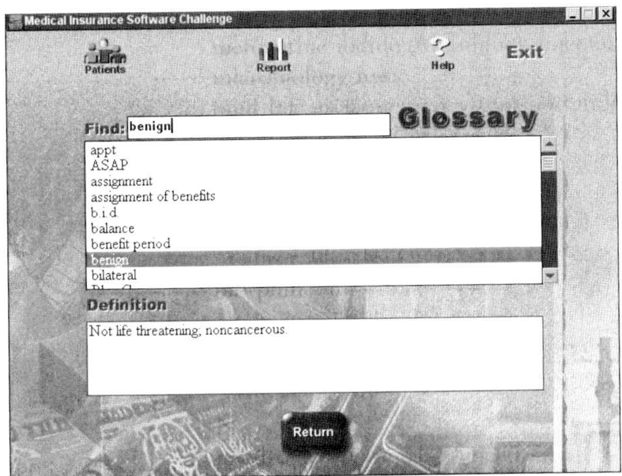

3 ▶ **Button Bars.** Buttons at the top of the screen allow you to access the following: **Patients** to go to the Patient Cases menu, **Glossary** to look up a word, **Reports** to view scores of your work, **Print** to produce hard copy of information forms or an HCFA-1500 claim form, **Help** to obtain information on the currently displayed screen, and **Exit** to quit the program.

4 ▶ **Patient Cases Screen.** Five basic insurance cases may be chosen by name or number in order of difficulty. Cases one through five are completed using general third party payer guidelines.

▶ Five advanced insurance cases may be chosen by name or insurance type (Blue Plan, TRICARE, Medicare, Medicare/Medigap, and Medi-Medi). These cases, 6 through 10, are numbered in order of difficulty and completed using specific program guidelines.

▶ The Other Patient file may be chosen to complete the HCFA-1500 insurance claim form for a case the instructor may choose, or for any case in the *Workbook*.

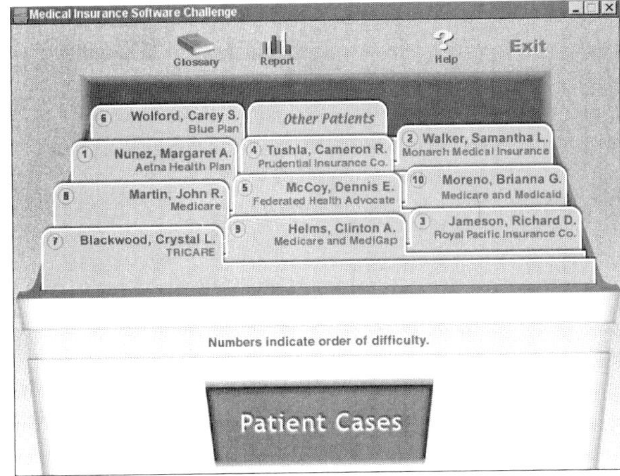

▶ Buttons at the bottom of the screen are: **Score Block**, which may be clicked to receive immediate feedback on your entry for a specific block. You will have two chances to complete the block correctly.

▶ **Score Form** may be clicked after you have completed the form. You will see all errors highlighted and will have an opportunity to correct the errors.

5 **Scenario-based Cases.** Documents needed to complete the claims for each case are:

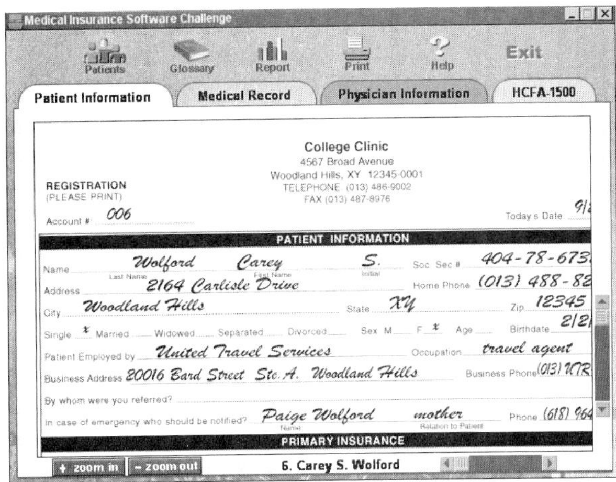

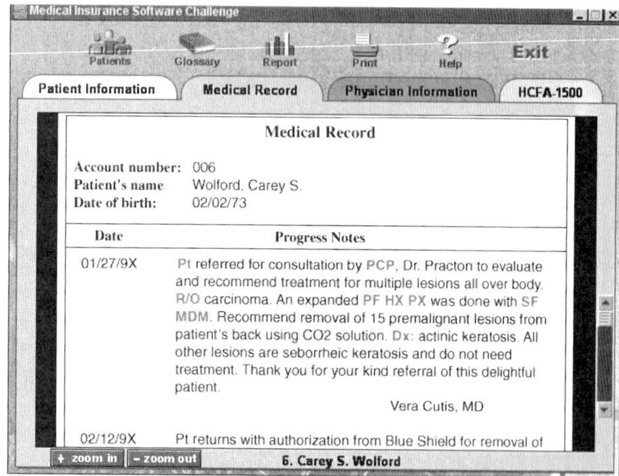

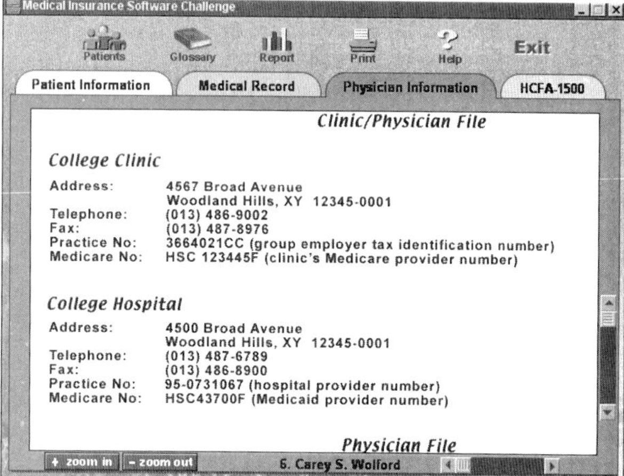

► **Patient Information Form.** This data is needed to complete the top portion of the HCFA-1500 insurance claim form.

► **Encounter Form.** This form is used for Cases 1 through 5.

► **Medical Record.** This form is used for Cases 6 through 10. This document gives you realistic medical history and progress notes about the patient. Information is extracted directly from the chart note to code diagnoses and procedures when completing the HCFA-1500 insurance claim form.

► **Physician Information File.** The clinic/physician file contains important data about the clinic physicians and the demographic information and reference numbers needed to complete the HCFA-1500 insurance claim form.

► These documents may be viewed by placing the cursor in the form, clicking and holding down the mouse button, and dragging the form until the part you are looking for is in view.

6 ► **HCFA-1500 Claim Form.** Information may be entered by keyboard and mouse, and in any order on the claim form.

OR

Scroll the HCFA-1500 claim form horizontally or vertically to locate different sections of the form.

OR

Click in a block to enter information, or tab from one block to the next to enter information.

► **Block Help.** Click on this button if you are unsure of what information goes in a block on the HCFA-1500 claim form.

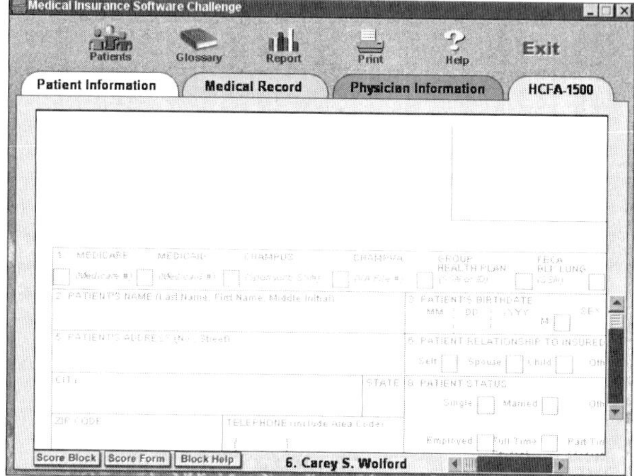

► Blocks completed incorrectly will display the correct answer marked in **blue, bold text** (first try errors that were corrected on second attempt), or ***blue, bold italic text*** (second try errors or first try errors that were never corrected).

7 ► **Report Screen.** Each completed case will be indicated by a check (✓)mark. Each attempt on a patient case will be scored and reflected as a percentage. The data are stored in the Report.

8 ► **Print Preview.** This function may be accessed when viewing the HCFA-1500 claim form screen. Click Report from the top menu. Scroll and highlight the name of the case. Then click the HCFA-1500 form button at the bottom right of the screen, which takes you to the Print Preview screen.

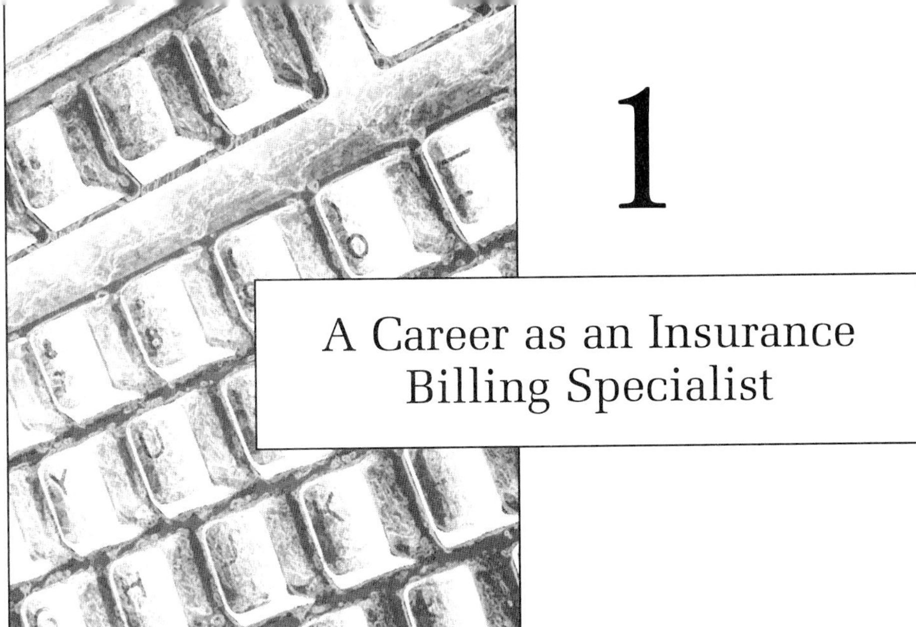

1

A Career as an Insurance Billing Specialist

KEY TERMS

Your instructor may wish to select some specific words pertinent to this chapter for a test. For definitions of the terms, further study, and/or reference, the words, phrases, and abbreviations may be found in the Glossary at the end of the Handbook. *Key terms for this chapter follow.*

abuse
American Health Information Management Association (AHIMA)
American Medical Association (AMA)
blanket-position bond
bonding
cash flow
churning
claims assistance professional (CAP)
confidential communication
embezzlement
ethics
etiquette
fraud
insurance billing specialist
list service (listserv)
multiskilled health practitioner (MSHP)
nonprivileged information
personal bond
phantom billing
ping-ponging
position-schedule bond
privileged information
reimbursement specialist
respondeat superior
yo-yoing

PERFORMANCE OBJECTIVES

The student will be able to

- Define and spell the key terms for this chapter, given the information from the handbook Glossary, within a reasonable period of time and with enough accuracy to obtain a satisfactory evaluation.
- Answer the self-study review questions, after reading the chapter, with enough accuracy to obtain a satisfactory evaluation.
- Use critical thinking to write one or two grammatically correct paragraphs with sufficient information to obtain a satisfactory evaluation.

STUDY OUTLINE

Role of the Insurance Billing Specialist
- Job Responsibilities
- Educational and Training Requirements
- Career Advantages
- Qualifications
  - Attributes
  - Skills
  - Personal Image
  - Behavior

Medical Etiquette

Medical Ethics

Confidential Communication
- Privileged Information
- Nonprivileged Information
  - Right to Privacy and Exceptions

Professional Liability
- Employer Liability
  - Fraud
  - Internet
  - Abuse
- Employee Liability
  - Scope of Practice
- Embezzlement
  - Precautions for Financial Protection
  - Bonding

Future Challenge

SELF-STUDY 1–1 ▶ REVIEW QUESTIONS

Review the objectives, key terms, and chapter information before completing the following review questions.

1. Identify three career opportunities (job titles) available after training in diagnostic and procedural coding and insurance claims completion.

   a. Insurance billing specialist, medical biller, reimbursement specialist, insurance counselor, collection manager, coding specialist

   b. Electronic claims professional

   c. claims assistance professional

2. List the duties an insurance billing specialist might perform.

   a. Review diagnostic and procedural codes for correctness and completeness

   b. Submit insurance claims promptly

   c. collect data from hospitals, laboratories, and other physicians involved in a case

   d. Discuss patient's treatment plan and insurance coverage and negotiate a payment plan

   e. answer routine inquiries related to account balances and insurance submission dates

   f. assist patients in budgeting

   g. Follow-up on delinquent accounts by tracing denied, adjusted, or unpaid claims.

3. List the duties of a claims assistance professional.

   a. Help patients organize, file, and negotiate health insurance claims of all types

b. Assist the consumer in obtaining maximum benefits from insurance companies

c. Tell the patient what checks to write to providers to elminate overpayment.

4. Skills required for an insurance billing specialist are:

a. Knowledge of medical terminology

b. Knowledge of insurance terminology

c. proficiency in completing insurance claims

d. Knowledge of procedural and diagnostic coding

e. Knowledge of anatomy and physiology, disease and treatment (surgical, drug, and laboratory terms).

f. computer skills; basic typing/and or keyboarding.

g. medicolegal knowledge

h. Knowledge of insurance carriers and Medicare policies and regulations

i. Basic math and use of calculator

j. Billing and collection techniques K. Precise reading skills L. Proficiancy in assessing information via the internet M. Expert in legalities of collection on accounts n. Use of photocopy and facsimile equipment

5. Standards of conduct by which an insurance billing specialist determines the propriety of his or her behavior in a relationship are known as Medical Ethics.

6. Complete these statements with either the words *illegal* or *unethical*.

a. To report incorrect information to the Aetna Casualty Company is unethical

b. To report incorrect information to a Medicare fiscal intermediary is illegal.

c. It is unethical for two physicians to treat the same patient for the same condition.

7. A confidential communication that may be disclosed only with the patient's permission is known as

priviledged communication.

8. Exceptions to the right of privacy are those records involving

a. industrial cases

b. reports of communicable diseases

c. child abuse

d. gunshot wounds

e. stabbings

f. ailments of newborns and infants

g. workers compensation - Medical information obtained by a Medicare insurance carrier

9. When a physician is legally responsible for an employee's conduct performed during employment, this is known as vicarious liability or respondeat superior.

10. Indicate whether the situation is one of *fraud* or *abuse* in the following situations.

a. Billing a claim for services not medically necessary. Fraud - abuse

b. Changing a figure on an insurance claim form to get increased payment. Fraud

c. Dismissing the copayment owed by a Medicare patient. Fraud

d. Neglecting to refund an overpayment to the patient. abuse

e. Billing for a complex fracture when the patient suffered a simple break. Fraud

11. A claims assistance professional neglects to submit an insurance claim to a Medicare supplemental insurance carrier within the proper time limit. What type of insurance is needed for protection against this loss for the client?

Errors and omissions insurance

12. State three bonding methods.

a. Position-schedule bond

b. Blanket-position bond

c. Personal-Bond

To check your answers to this self-study assignment, see Appendix D.

CRITICAL THINKING

To enhance your critical thinking skills, problems will be interspersed throughout the *Workbook*. Thinking is the goal of instruction and a student's responsibility. When trying to solve a problem by critical thinking, it is desirable to have more than one solution and take time to think out answers. Remember that an answer may be changed when additional information is provided in a classroom setting.

ASSIGNMENT 1–2 ▶ CRITICAL THINKING

Performance Objective

Task: Describe why you are training to become an insurance billing specialist.

Conditions: Use one or two sheets of white typing paper and pen or pencil.

Standards: Time: ________________ minutes

Accuracy: ________________

(Note: The time element and accuracy criteria may be given by your instructor.)

Directions: Write one or two paragraphs describing why you are training to become an insurance billing specialist. Or, if enrolled in a class that is part of a medical assisting course, explain why you are motivated to seek a career as a medical assistant. Make sure grammar, punctuation, and spelling are correct.

ASSIGNMENT 1–3 ▶ FRAUD AND ABUSE DECISION MAKING

Performance Objective

Task: Make a decision after reading each scenario, whether it is considered fraud, abuse, or neither.

Conditions: Use pen or pencil.

Standards: Time: ________________ minutes

Accuracy: ________________

(Note: The time element and accuracy criteria may be given by your instructor.)

Directions: Read through each scenario and circle whether it is a fraud (F) issue, practice of abuse (A), or neither (N).

Scenarios

1. Dr. Pedro Atrics has a friend and his child needs elective surgery. He agrees to do the surgery and bill as an "insurance only" case.

F A N

2. A patient, Carl Skinner, calls the office repeatedly about his prescriptions. When seen in the office the next time, Dr. Input bills a higher level of E & M service to allow for the additional time.

F A N

3. Dr. Skeleton sets a simple fracture and puts a cast on Mr. Davis. He bills for a complex fracture.

F A N

4. A patient, Maria Gomez, asks a friendly staff member to change the dates on the insurance claim form.

F A N

5. A patient, Roberto Loren, asks the physician to restate a diagnosis so the insurance company will pay since payment would be denied based on the present statement.

F A N

6. Dr. Rumsey sees a patient twice on the same day but bills as though the patient were seen on two different dates.

F A N

7. A Medicare patient, Joan O'Connor, is seen by Dr. Practon, and the insurance claim shows a charge to the Medicare fiscal intermediary at a higher and different fee schedule rate than that of non-Medicare patients.

F A N

8. A patient, Hazel Plunkett, receives a service that is not medically necessary to the extent rendered and an insurance claim is submitted.

F A N

9. A patient, Sun Cho, paid for services that were subsequently declared not medically necessary, and Dr. Cardi failed to refund the payment to the patient.

F A N

10. Dr. Ulibarri told the insurance biller not to collect the deductible and copayments from Mrs. Gerry Coleman.

F A N

ASSIGNMENT 1–4 ▶ VISIT WEB SITES

Performance Objective

Task: Access the Internet and visit several web sites of the World Wide Web.

Conditions: Use a computer with printer and/or pen or pencil to make notes.

Standards: Time: ________________ minutes

Accuracy: ________________

(Note: The time element and accuracy criteria may be given by your instructor.)

Directions: If you have access to the Internet, visit the World Wide Web and do the following three site searches.

1. Access an Internet server and find one of the web search engines (Yahoo, Excite, Alta Vista). Begin a web search, e.g., key in "Yahoo insurance billers" to search for information about insurance billers or go to web site: http://www.careerpath.com. List three to five web sites found. Go to one or more of those resources and list the benefits those sites might have for a student in locating job opportunities or networking with others for professional growth and knowledge. Bring the web site addresses to share with the class.
2. Site-search information on patient confidentiality by visiting the web site of the American Medical Association (http://www.ama-assn.org/). Under "Ethics, Education, Science, Public Health, Quality, and Accreditation," click on "Legal Issues of Physicians." Then click on "Patient-Physician Relationship Issues." Then click on "Patient Confidentiality." Make notes or print out a hard copy of the pages while remaining online.
3. Site-search information on patient confidentiality by visiting the web site of the American Health Information Management Association (http://www.ahima.org). Click on Site Search at that web site. Key in "patient confidentiality." Then click on "Search for Matching Documents." List a recent question asked about this topic and record the answer and/or print out a hard copy of all the questions with answers while remaining online.
4. Site search for information on fraud and/or abuse by visiting one or more of the federal web sites. See what you can discover and either print out or take notes and bring back information to share with the class for discussion. Try one or more of these web site addresses:

   www.hcfa.gov
   http://www.hcfa.gov/medicare/fraud/DEFINI2.HTM
   http://www.hcfa.gov/medicaid/mbfraud.htm
   http://www.gov/medicaid/medicaid.htm

2

Basics of Health Insurance

KEY TERMS

Your instructor may wish to select some words pertinent to this chapter for a test. For definitions of the terms, further study, and/or reference, the words, phrases, and abbreviations may be found in the Glossary at the end of the Handbook. *Key terms for this chapter follow.*

applicant
assignment
blanket contract
capitation
CHAMPVA
claim
coinsurance
Competitive Medical Plan (CMP)
conditionally renewable
contract
day sheet
deductible
disability income insurance
electronic signature
eligibility
emancipated minor
encounter form
exclusions
exclusive provider organization (EPO)
expressed contract
extend
foundation for medical care (FMC)
guaranteed renewable
guarantor
health insurance
health maintenance organization (HMO)
high risk
implied contract
indemnity
independent or individual practice association (IPA)
insured
ledger card
major medical
Maternal and Child Health Programs (MCHP)
Medicaid (MCD)
Medicare (M)
Medicare/Medicaid (Medi-Medi)
member
noncancelable policy
nonparticipating provider (nonpar)
optionally renewable
participating provider (par)
patient registration form
personal insurance
point-of-service (POS) plan
post
preauthorization
precertification
predetermination
preferred provider organization (PPO)

premium
running balance
subscriber
TRICARE
Unemployment Compensation Disability (UCD) or State Disability Insurance (SDI)
Veterans' Affairs (VA) outpatient clinic
workers' compensation (WC) insurance

PERFORMANCE OBJECTIVES

The student will be able to

- Define and spell the key terms for this chapter, given the information from the textbook Glossary, within a reasonable period of time and with enough accuracy to obtain a satisfactory evaluation.
- Answer the self-study review questions after reading the chapter with enough accuracy to obtain a satisfactory evaluation.
- Use critical thinking to list the basic steps in processing an insurance claim from submission to payment, given data from the textbook, within a reasonable period of time, and with enough accuracy to obtain a satisfactory evaluation.

STUDY OUTLINE

History
- Insurance in the United States

Legal Principles of Insurance
- Insurance Contracts

Physician/Patient Contracts and Financial Obligation
- Private Patients
- Guarantor
- Emancipated Minor
- Managed Care Patients
- Employment and Disability Examinations
- Workers' Compensation Patients

The Insurance Policy
- Policy Application
- Policy Renewal Provisions
- Policy Terms
- Coordination of Benefits
- General Policy Limitations
  - Case Management Requirements and Preapproval

Choice of Health Insurance
- Group Contract
  - Conversion Privilege
  - Income Continuation Benefits
  - Medical Savings Accounts
- Individual Contract
- Prepaid Health Plan

Types of Health Insurance Coverage
- CHAMPVA
- Competitive Medical Plan
- Disability Income Insurance
- Exclusive Provider Organization
- Foundation for Medical Care
- Health Maintenance Organization
- Independent or Individual Practice Association
- Maternal and Child Health Program
- Medicaid
- Medicare
- Medicare/Medicaid
- Point-of -Service Plan
- Preferred Provider Organization
- TRICARE
- Unemployment Compensation Disability
- Veterans' Affairs Outpatient Clinic
- Workers' Compensation Insurance

Examples of Insurance Billing

Procedure: Handling and Processing Insurance Claims
- Preregistration—Patient Registration Form
- Insurance Identification Card
- Patient's Signature Requirements
  - Release of information
  - Assignment of Benefits
  - Signature Guidelines
- Encounter Form
- Physician's Signature
- Determine Fees
- Bookkeeping—Ledger Card

SELF-STUDY 2–1 ▶ REVIEW QUESTIONS

Review the objectives, key terms, glossary definitions to key terms, chapter information, and figures before completing the following review questions.

1. A/an insurance contract policy is a legally enforceable agreement or contract.

2. List five health insurance policy renewal provisions.
   a. cancelable
   b. optionally renewable
   c. conditionally renewable
   d. guaranteed renewable
   e. noncancelable

3. Insurance reimbursement or payment is also called indemnity.

4. Name two general health insurance policy limitations.
   a. exclusions
   b. waiver or rider

5. The act of finding out whether treatment is covered under an individual's health insurance policy is called precertification.

6. The steps to obtain permission for a procedure before it is done, to see whether the insurance program agrees it is medically necessary, is termed preauthorization.

7. Determining the maximum dollar amount the insurance company will pay for a procedure before it is done is known as predetermination.

8. Name three ways an individual may obtain health insurance.
   a. Take out insurance through a group plan (contract or policy)
   b. Pay the premium on an individual basis
   c. enroll in a prepaid health plan

9. List four ways a physician's practice may use to submit insurance claims to insurance companies.

   a. manual claims submission

   b. in-office electronic filing by fax or computer

   c. contracting with an outside service bureau to submit claims manually or electronically

   d. Telecommunications networking system via modem/telephone line/computer

10. A patient service slip personalized to the practice of the physician and used as a communications/billing tool during routing of the patient is also known as a/an

    a. encounter or routing form

    b. transaction slip

    c. charge slip

    d. fee ticket E. communicator F. Multipurpose billing form G patient service slip H. superbill

11. Match the insurance terms in the first column with the definitions in the second column. Write the correct letters in the blanks.

adjuster	E	a. An insurance company takes into account benefits payable by another carrier in determining its own liability.
assignment	C	b. Benefits paid by an insurance company to an insured person.
carrier	J	c. Transfer of one's right to collect an amount payable under an insurance contract.
coordination of benefits	A	d. Time that must elapse before an indemnity is paid.
deductible	G	e. Acts for insurance company or insured in settlement of claims.
exclusions	I	f. Periodic payment to keep insurance policy in force.
indemnity	B	g. Amount insured person must pay before policy will pay.
premium	F	h. Period of time in which a claim must be filed.
subscriber	K	i. Certain illnesses or injuries listed in a policy that the insurance company will not cover.
time limit	H	j. Insurance company that carries the insurance.
waiting period	D	k. One who belongs to an insurance plan.

12. An individual promising to pay for medical services rendered is known as a/an guarantor.

13. A document signed by the insured directing the insurance company to pay benefits directly to the physician is known as a/an assignment of benefits.

14. Electronic access to computer data may consist of the following verification or access methods.

 a. series of numbers d. voice

 b. series of letters e. fingerprint transmission

 c. electronic writing (signatures or initials) f. computer key

15. Guidelines for avoiding unauthorized use and preventing problems when a medical practice uses a facsimile signature stamp are:

 a. Make only one stamp

 b. allow only long-term, trusted, bonded staff members to have access to the stamp

 c. Keep the stamp in a location with a secure lock

 d. Limit access to the stamp

To check your answers to this self-study assignment, see Appendix D.

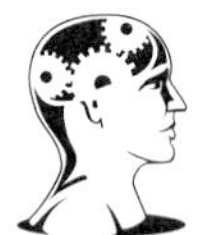

ASSIGNMENT 2–2 ▸ CRITICAL THINKING

Performance Objective

Task: Describe and/or explain your response to five questions.

Conditions: Use one or two sheets of white typing paper and pen or pencil.

Standards: Time: ______________ minutes

Accuracy: ______________

(Note: The time element and accuracy criteria may be given by your instructor.)

Directions: Respond verbally or in writing to these five questions.

1. Write down the basic steps in processing an insurance claim form from the physician's office, to the insurance company, and after payment is received.

2. What is the difference between a blanket contract and an individual contract?

3. What is the difference between a participating provider and a nonparticipating provider for a commercial insurance company or a managed care plan? Medicare program?

4. What is the difference between an implied contract and an expressed contract?

5. Explain the birthday rule, and when it is used.

ASSIGNMENT 2-3 ► PREPARE A LEDGER CARD

Performance Objective

Task: Prepare a ledger card and post entries. If you have access to copy equipment, make a photocopy.

Conditions: Use one ledger form (Figure 2–1).

Standards: Time: ______________ minutes

Accuracy: ______________

(Note: The time element and accuracy criteria may be given by your instructor.)

Directions: Type a ledger card (Figure 2–1) using the form and information provided. Post the charges, date the insurance claim was submitted, payment received, and adjustment. Examples of how a ledger card should be completed are shown in the Textbook in Chapter 2, Figure 2–17; Chapter 9, Figure 9–2; and Chapter 11, Figure 11–16. A good bookkeeping practice is to take a red pen and draw a line across the ledger card from left to right to indicate the last entry billed to the insurance company. There are abbreviations at the bottom of the ledger card that pertain to Evaluation and Management CPT codes and types of professional services. Physicians have this section personalized to their practice, and these abbreviations may vary from practice to practice.

Scenario: A new patient, Miss Carolyn Wachsman, of 4590 Ashton Street, Woodland Hills, XY 12345, was seen by Dr. Practon; her account number is 2001. She is insured by Blue Cross.

Miss Wachsman was seen on March 24 of the current year for a Level III evaluation and management office visit ($______). She also received an ECG ($______). Locate the fees in the Mock Fee Schedule in Appendix A of this *Workbook*.

An insurance claim form was sent to Blue Cross on March 25. On May 15 Blue Cross sent an explanation of benefits stating the patient had previously met her deductible. Check No. 433 for $76 was attached to the EOB and $19 was indicated as the adjustment to be made by the provider. On May 25, the patient was billed for the balance.

After the instructor has returned your work to you, either make the necessary corrections and place it in a 3-ring notebook for future reference, or, if you received a high score, place it in your portfolio for reference when applying for a job.

ASSIGNMENT 2-4 ► ABSTRACT DATA FROM AN INSURANCE IDENTIFICATION CARD

Performance Objective

Task: Answer questions in reference to an insurance identification card for Case A.

Conditions: Use an insurance identification card (Figure 2–2) and the questions presented.

Standards: Time: ______________ minutes

Accuracy: ______________

(Note: The time element and accuracy criteria may be given by your instructor.)

Directions: An identification card provides much of the information needed to establish a patient's insurance coverage. You have photocopied the front and back sides of three patients' cards and placed copies in their patient records, returning the originals to the patients. Answer the questions by abstracting and/or obtaining the data from the cards.

Case A

1. Name of patient covered by the policy. Linda L Field
2. Provide the insurance policy's effective date. 05-01-93
3. List the telephone number for preauthorization. (800) 274-7767
4. State name and address of insurance company. Blue Cross of California P.O. Box 9027 Oxnard CA 93031-9027
5. List the telephone number to call for provider access. (800) 810-Blue
6. Name the *type* of insurance plan. Prudent Buyer Plan
7. List the insurance identification number (a.k.a. subscriber, certificate, or member numbers). XPS-564-00-9044
8. Furnish the group number. C54628 Plan or coverage code. 5031B
9. State the copay requirements. $20.00
10. Does the card indicate the patient has hospital coverage? yes

ASSIGNMENT 2-5 ► ABSTRACT DATA FROM AN INSURANCE IDENTIFICATION CARD

Performance Objective

Task: Answer questions in reference to the insurance identification card for Case B.

Conditions: Use an insurance identification card (Figure 2–3) and the questions presented.

Standards: Time: ______ minutes

Accuracy: ______

(Note: The time element and accuracy criteria may be given by your instructor.)

Case B

1. Patient's name covered by the policy. M T Fordham
2. Provide the insurance policy's effective date. 0101 20XX
3. List the telephone number for preauthorization. 1800-343-1691
4. State name of insurance company. Blue Shield of California
5. List the telephone number to call for patient benefits and eligibility. (800)-331-2001

STATEMENT

College Clinic
4567 Broad Avenue
Woodland Hills, XY 12345-0001
Telephone: 013-486-9002
Fax: 013-487-8976

DATE	PROFESSIONAL SERVICE DESCRIPTION	CHARGE	CREDITS		CURRENT BALANCE
			PAYMENTS	ADJUSTMENTS	
9/14/02	99212 PF	45.00		0	35.00
9/12/02	99212 PF		20.00	15.00	0.00

Due and payable within 10 days. **Pay last amount in balance column** 

Key: PF:	Problem-focused	SF:	Straightforward	CON:	Consultation	HCD:	House call (day)
EPF:	Expanded problem-focused	LC:	Low complexity	CPX:	Complete phys exam	HCN:	House call (night)
D:	Detailed	MC:	Moderate complexity	E:	Emergency	HV:	Hospital visit
C:	Comprehensive	HC:	High complexity	ER:	Emergency dept.	OV:	Office visit

Figure 2–1

CALIFORNIA CARE
HEALTH PLANS

Type of Insurance: **PRUDENT BUYER PLAN** ®'

GROUP: C54G28

PPO ®

XDS - 564 - 00 - 9044

EFFECTIVE DATE: 05-01-95
PLAN CODE: 5031B

LINDA L FIELD

PLAN 040: MEDICAL - WELLPOINT PHARMACY

CLAIMS & INQUIRIES: P.O. BOX 9072 OXNARD CA 93031-9072
CUSTOMER SERVICE: 1-800-627-8797

COPAY $20 OFFICE

This is your employer health plan Identification Card. Present it to the provider of health care when you or your eligible dependents receive services. See your certificate(s) or booklet(s) for a description of your benefits, terms, conditions, limitations, and exclusions of coverage. When submitting inquiries always include your member number from the face of this card. Possession or use of this card does not guarantee payment.

Wellpoint Pharmacy	(800) 700-2541
BlueCard Provider Access	(800) 810-BLUE

FOR BLUE CROSS AND BLUE SHIELD PROVIDERS NATIONWIDE:
Please submit claims to your local Blue Cross and/or Blue shield plan. To ensure prompt claims processing, please include the three-digit alpha prefix that precedes the patient's identification number listed on the front of this card.

TO THE PROVIDER:
For pre-authorization or Pre-Service Review call: (800) 274-7767
* An Independent License of the Blue Cross Association.
® Registered Mark of the Blue Cross Association.
®' Registered Mark of WellPoint Health Networks Inc.
Hospital coverage: Yes

Figure 2–2

6. Name the *type* of insurance plan. Preferrd Plan

7. List the insurance identification number (aka subscriber, certificate, or member numbers).
AJC 557469969

8. Furnish the group number. 00P1901 Plan or coverage code. 542

9. State the copay requirements, if there are any. none

10. List the Blue Shield web site. www.blueshieldca.com

PPO ®

Preferred Plan

SUBSCRIBER NAME:
M T FORDHAM

EFFECTIVE DATE:
010120XX

SUBSCRIBER ID NUMBER
AJC557469969

GROUP NUMBER
00P1901

PLAN CODE
542

CUSTOMER SERVICE
(800) 331-2001

07/16/20XX

Use Blue Shield of California Preferred Physicians and Hospitals to receive maximum benefits.

Carry the Blue Shield Identification Card with you at all times and present it whenever you or one of your covered dependents receives medical services. Read your employee booklet/Health Services Agreement which summarizes the benefits, provisions, limitations and exclusions of your plan. Your health plan may require prior notification of any hospitalization and notification, within one business day, of an emergency admission. Review of selected procedures may be required before some services are performed. To receive hospital pre-admission and pre-service reviews, call 1-800-343-1691. Your failure to call may result in a reduction of benefits.

For questions, including those related to benefits, and eligibility, call the customer service number listed on the front of this card.

The PPO logo on the front of this ID Card identifies you to preferred providers outside the state of California as a member of the Blue Card PPO Program.

When you are outside of California call 1-800-810-2583 to locate the nearest PPO Provider. Remember, any services you receive are subject to the policies and provisions of your group plan.

ID-23200-PPO REVERSE www.blueshieldca.com

Figure 2–3

ASSIGNMENT 2–6 ▶ ABSTRACT DATA FROM AN INSURANCE IDENTIFICATION CARD

Performance Objective

Task: Answer questions in reference to the insurance identification card for Case C.

Conditions: Use an insurance identification card (Figure 2–4) and the questions presented.

Standards: Time: ______ minutes

Accuracy: ______

(Note: The time element and accuracy criteria may be given by your instructor.)

Case C

1. Patient's name covered by the policy. Linda L Flores
2. Provide the insurance policy's effective date, if there is one. none
3. List the number to call for out-of-network preauthorization. 800-842-5751
4. State name and address of insurance company. United healthcare P.O Box 30990, Salt Lake City, UT 84130-0990

UNITEDhealthcare

LINDA L. FLORES
Member # 52170-5172

CALMAT

Group # 176422
COPAY: Office Visit $10 ER $50
Urgent $35

Electronic Claims Payor ID 87726

POS PCP Plan
WITH RX D - UHC
and MH/CD
PCP: G. LOMAN
805-643-9973

MTH

Call 800-842-5751 for Member Inquiries

This identification card is not proof of membership nor does it guarantee coverage. Persons with coverage that remains in force are entitled to benefits under the terms and conditions of this group health benefit plan as detailed in your benefit description.

IMPORTANT MEMBER INFORMATION
In non-emergencies, call your Primary Care Physician to receive the highest level of benefits. If you have an emergency and are admitted to a hospital, you are required to call your Primary Care Physician within two working days.
For out of network services that require authorization, call the Member Inquiries 800 number on the front of this card.

Claim Address: P.O. Box 30990, Salt Lake City, UT 84130-0990

Figure 2–4

5. List the telephone number to call for member inquiries. 800 - 842 - 5751

6. Name the *type* of insurance plan. POS PCP Plan with Rx UHC and MH/CP

7. List the insurance identification number (aka subscriber, certificate, or member numbers).

52170-5172

8. Furnish the group number. 176422

9. State the copay requirements, if there are any. Office visit $10 ER 50 Urgent $35

10. Who is the patient's primary care physician? G. Loman

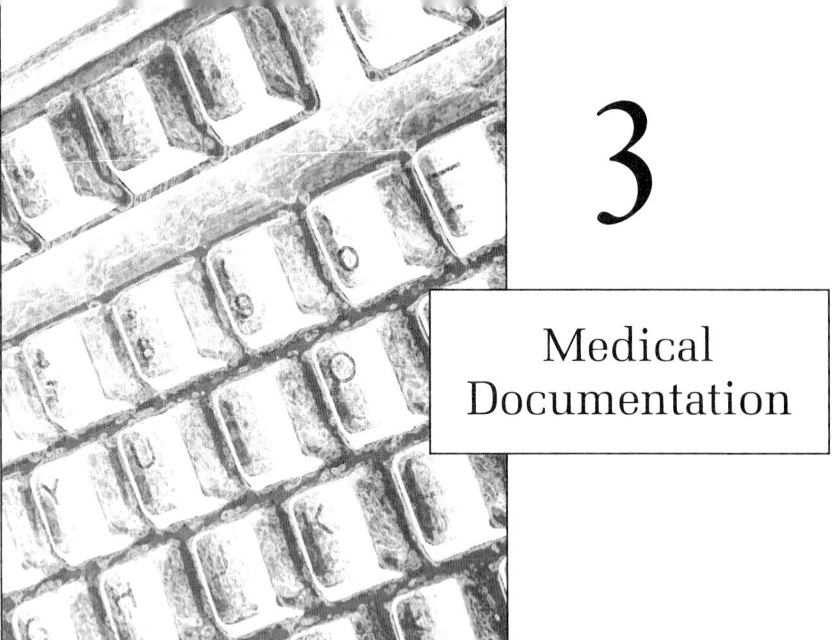

3

Medical Documentation

KEY TERMS

Your instructor may wish to select some words pertinent to this chapter for a test. For definitions of the terms, further study, and/or reference, the words, phrases, and abbreviations may be found in the Glossary at the end of the Handbook. *Key terms for this chapter follow.*

acute
attending physician
breach of confidential communication
chief complaint (CC)
chronic
comorbidity
compliance program
comprehensive (C)
concurrent care
consultation
consulting physician
continuity of care
counseling
critical care
detailed (D)
documentation
emergency care
eponym
established patient
expanded problem focused (EPF)
external audit
facsimile (fax)
family history (FH)
high complexity (HC)
history of present illness (HPI)
internal review
low complexity (LC)
medical necessity
medical record
medical report
moderate complexity (MC)
new patient (NP)
ordering physician
past history (PH)
physical examination (PE)
problem focused (PF)
prospective review
referral
referring physician
retrospective review
review of systems (ROS)
social history (SH)
subpoena
subpoena duces tecum
treating or performing physician

PERFORMANCE OBJECTIVES

The student will be able to

- Define and spell the key terms for this chapter, given the information from the handbook Glossary, within a reasonable period of time and with enough accuracy to obtain a satisfactory evaluation.
- Answer the self-study review questions after reading the chapter.
- Abstract subjective and objective data from patient records, within a reasonable period of time and with enough accuracy to obtain a satisfactory evaluation.
- Review a patient record and obtain answers to questions about the documentation presented, within a reasonable period of time and with enough accuracy to obtain a satisfactory evaluation.
- Select the correct medicolegal form letters and properly prepare them for the physician's signature, given the patients' chart notes and ledger cards, within a reasonable period of time and with enough accuracy to obtain a satisfactory evaluation.

STUDY OUTLINE

The Documentation Process
- Medical Record
- Documenters
- Reasons for Documentation

General Principles of Medical Record Documentation
- Medical Necessity
- External Audit Point System
- Enforcement of Medical Record Keeping

Documentation Guidelines for Evaluation and Management Services

Contents of a Medical Report
- Documentation of History
  - Chief Complaint
  - History of Present Illness
  - Review of Systems
  - Past, Family, and Social Histories
- Documentation of Examination
  - Physical Examination
    - Organ Systems/Body Areas—Elements of Examination
    - Types of Physical Examination
- Documentation of Medical Decision Making Complexity

Documentation Terminology
- Terminology for Evaluation and Management Services
  - New Versus Established Patients
  - Consultation
  - Referral
  - Concurrent Care
  - Continuity of Care
  - Critical Care
  - Emergency Care
  - Counseling
- Diagnostic Terminology and Abbreviations
- Directional Terms
- Surgical Terminology

Review and Audit of Medical Records
- Internal Reviews
  - Prospective Review
  - Retrospective Review
- External Audit
  - Audit Prevention

Legalities of Medical Records
- Patient Confidentiality
- Principles for Release of Information
  - Faxing Documents
  - Sensitive Information
  - Medicare Guidelines
  - Financial Data
  - Legal Documents
  - Subpoena
- Retention of Records
  - Medical Records
  - Financial Documents
- Termination of a Case
- Prevention of Legal Problems

SELF-STUDY 3–1 ► REVIEW QUESTIONS

Review the objectives, key terms, glossary definitions to key terms, chapter information, and figures before completing the following review questions.

1. Written or graphic information about patient care is termed a/an Medical record.

2. Documentation is written or dictated to record chronologic facts and observations about a patient's health.

3. Match the terms in the first column with the definitions in the second column. Write the correct letters on the blanks.

attending physician	C	a. Renders a service to a patient.
consulting physician	D	b. Directs selection, preparation, and administration of tests, medication, or treatment.
ordering physician	B	c. Legally responsible for the care and treatment given to a patient.
referring physician	E	d. Gives an opinion regarding a specific problem that is requested by another doctor.
treating or performing physician	A	e. Sends the patient for tests or treatment or to another doctor for consultation.

4. Performance of services or procedures consistent with the diagnosis, done with standards of good medical practice and a proper level of care given in the appropriate setting is known as Medical Necessity.

5. If a medical practice is audited by Medicare officials and intentional miscoding is discovered, fines & penalties may be levied and providers may be excluded from the program

6. A list of all staff members' names, job titles, signatures, and their initials is known as a/an signature log.

7. How should an insurance billing specialist correct an error on a patient's record? Use legal copy pen, cross out wrong entry with a single line, write the correct entry, date, and initial entry

8. Name the five documentation components of a patient's history.

a. Chief complaint

b. History of Present illness

c. Past history

d. Family history

e. Social history

9. An inventory of body systems by documenting responses to questions about symptoms that a patient has experienced is called a/an Review of Systems.

10. Define the following terms in relationship to billing.

a. New patient— one who has not received any professional services from the physician or another physician of the same specialty who belongs to the same group practice within the past 3 years

b. Established patient— one who has received professional services from the physician or another physician of the same specialty who belongs to the same group practice, within the past three years.

11. Explain the difference between a consultation and the referral of a patient.

a. Consultation— services rendered by a physician whose opinion or advice is requested by another physician or agency in the evaluation or treatment of a patient's illness or a suspected problem

b. Referral— Transfer of the total or specific care of a patient from one physician to another for known problems.

12. Medical care for a patient who has received treatment for an illness and is referred to a second physician for treatment of the same condition is a situation called continuity of care.

13. If two doctors see the same patient on the same day, one for the patient's heart condition and the other for a diabetic situation, this medical care situation is called concurrent care.

14. What is (are) the exception(s) to the Right of Privacy and Privileged Communication?

a. When the physician examines a patient at the request of a third party who is paying the bill as in workers comp

b. When the patient is suing someone, such as an employer, who must protect himself

c. When the patients records are subpoenaed or there is a search warrant

d. When the patient is a member of a MCO and the physician has signed a contract with the MCO that has a clause that allows the MCO access to the medical records of their

15. When faxing a patient's medical records, a signed document for patients authorizing release of information via the fax machine must be obtained from the patient.

16. Action to take when a faxed medical document is misdirected is telephone or fax a request to destroy the information erroneously sent.

17. What must the former physician have from the patient before a record can be given to a new physician? A written request from the patient or a signed authorization or release of information form

18. What must an insurance billing specialist do if he or she receives a request from another physician for certain records? Obtain a written request from the patient or a signed authorization or release of information form.

19. What must a physician have from the patient before he or she can give information to an attorney? an authorization or release of information form signed by the patient or a subpoena.

20. Indicate either *indefinite retention* or *number of years* for keeping records in the following situations.

    a. Computerized payroll records 7 years

    b. Insurance claim for Medicare patient 7 years

    c. Medical record of a deceased patient 5 years

    d. Active patient medical records Indefinite retention

    e. Letter to a patient about balance due after insurance paid 1-5 years

21. Can an insurance billing specialist receive a subpoena for his or her physician?

    Yes, if the physician gives him or her this authority

22. Can a physician terminate a contract with a patient? Yes If so, how?

    By sending a letter of withdrawl of care, registered or certified with return signature.

23. This question is presented for critical thinking. A patient comes into the office for treatment. He does not return, because he is dissatisfied with Dr. Practon's treatment. Is it necessary to keep his records when he obviously will not return?

    Yes Why? Records must be kept as required by state law for a certain period of time. Records of a dissatisfied patient should be kept indefinitely because of the possibility of a lawsuit at a later date or to prevent a lawsuit.

To check your answers to this self-study assignment, see Appendix D.

SELF-STUDY 3–2 ▸ REVIEW QUESTIONS

Diagnostic Terminology and Abbreviations

In the *Handbook*, review Tables 3–1 and 3–2 and anatomic figures, as well as Appendix A in the *Workbook*, which has a list of abbreviations and symbols.

1. Match the terms in the first column with the definitions in the second column. Write the correct letters on the blanks.

acute	C	a. Pertaining to both sides
chronic	F	b. Decubitus ulcer
menopause	D	c. Condition that runs a short but severe course
bilateral	a	d. Change of life
bed sore	b	e. Tinnitus
ringing of ear	e	f. Condition persisting over a long period of time

2. Write in the meaning for these abbreviations and/or symbols commonly encountered in a patient's medical record.

RLQ Right lower quadrant

DC discharge

WNL within normal limits

R/O Role out

UPI Upper respiratory infection

$\bar{C}$ with

\+ positive

3. When documenting incisions, the unit of measure length should be listed in Contimeters CM ______.

Multiple Choice: Circle the letter that gives the best answer to each question.

4. If a physician called and asked for a patient's medical record STAT, what would he or she mean?

a. The physician wants a statistic from a patient's record.

b. The physician wants the record delivered on Tuesday.

c. The physician wants the record delivered immediately.

5. If a physician asks you to locate the results of the last UA, what would you be searching for?

a. a urinalysis report

b. an x-ray report of the ulna

c. uric acid test results

6. If a physician telephoned and asked for a copy of the last H&P to be faxed, what is he requesting?

a. heart and pulmonary findings

b. H_2 antagonist test results

c. a history and physical

7. If a hospital nurse telephoned and asked you to read the results of the patient's last CBC, what would you be searching for?

   a. carcinoma basal cell report

   b. complete blood count

   c. congenital blindness, complete report

8. If you were asked to make a photocopy of the patient's last CT, what would you be searching for?

   a. chemotherapy record

   b. connective tissue report

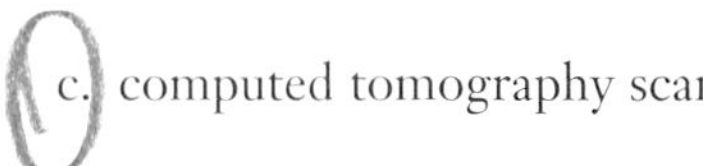

   c. computed tomography scan

To check your answers to this self-study assignment, see Appendix D.

ASSIGNMENT 3–3 ▸ ABSTRACTING SUBJECTIVE OBSERVATIONS AND OBJECTIVE FINDINGS FROM PATIENT RECORDS

Performance Objective

Task: List subjective observations and objective findings for four scenarios.

Conditions: Use a pencil and four case studies.

Standards: Time: ________________ minutes

Accuracy: ________________

(Note: The time element and accuracy criteria may be given by your instructor.)

Scenario 1: Mrs. Smith is 25 years old and was brought into the emergency department of College Hospital with complaints of difficulty in breathing and chest pain. Her vital signs show an elevated temp. of 101°F and pulse of 90. Respirations are labored and 30/min. BP is 140/80. Her skin is warm and diaphoretic (perspiring). She states, "This condition has been going on for the past 3 days."

Subjective observations: Mrs Smith is 25 years old and was brought into the emergency department of college hospital with complaints of difficulty in

Objective findings: breathing and chest pain

____

Scenario 2: Mr. Jones is 56 years old and was admitted to the hospital with chest pains, elevated pulse and blood pressure. His skin is cold and clammy.

Subjective observations: Mr Jones is 56 years old and was admitted to the hospital with chest pains, elevated pulse and blood pressure

Objective findings: His skin is cold and clammy

Scenario 3: You are assisting the radiology technician with Sally Salazar, a 6-year-old Hispanic girl, who was brought into the pediatrician's office with a suspected fracture of the right arm. Sally states she was "running at school, tripped on my shoelace, and fell." She tells you her "arm hurts," points out how "funny my arm looks," and starts to cry. You notice her arm looks disfigured and is covered with dirt. Sally is cradling her arm against her body and is unwilling to let go because "it's going to fall off."

Subjective observations: running at school, tripped on my shoelace and fell. says her arm hurts

Objective findings: arms looks disfigured and is covered with dirt.

Scenario 4: You are working in the Business Office of College Hospital. A former patient in your hospital comes in complaining of his billing. He states he was never catheterized, never had any of the medications listed on his itemized bill, and has "never been in this hospital for that length of time." His face is red, his voice is gradually getting louder, and you notice he is standing with the aid of crutches because his left leg is in a full cast.

Subjective observations: Patient complains about bill / never was catheterized, never had any of the medications listed on his itemized bill and has never been in this

Objective findings: hosp for that length of time

Pt face is red, his voice is gradually getting louder, and see that he is standing with the aid of crutches because his left leg is in a full cast

ASSIGNMENT 3–4 ▶ REVIEW OF A PATIENT RECORD

Performance Objective

Task: Answer questions after reviewing a patient's record.

Conditions: Use a pencil, internal record review sheet, medical dictionary, abbreviation reference list, drug reference book, i.e., *Mosby's GenRx* or *Physician's Desk Reference*, and laboratory reference book.

Standards: Time: ________________ minutes

Accuracy: ________________

(Note: The time element and accuracy criteria may be given by your instructor.)

Directions: In many instances, when developing the skill of reviewing a patient record, you may need critical thinking in addition to efficient use of reference books. Answer only those questions you feel can be justified by the documentation presented in the patient's record. Since each record content is variable, you may or may not have answers to all eight questions.

Answer the questions by recording on the blank the documentation found identifying the components from the patient's record. Check your answers in Appendix D to see if you obtained the correct data.

If your answers vary, perhaps you have a reason for them which may or may not be valid. List your reasons in the response section. Differences may be reviewed with your instructor privately or via class discussion.

Patient Record

10-21-20xx HPI This new pt is an 80-year-old white male who has had problems with voiding since 9-5-20xx. During the night the pt had only 50 cc output and was catheterized this morning because of his poor urinary output (200 cc). He was thought to have a distended bladder. He has not had any gross hematuria. He has voiding difficulty especially lying down and voiding in the supine position. His voiding pattern is improved while standing and sitting. However, the pt has developed a wound to his 1t lateral malleolus and is able to ambulate only with assistance.

Gene Ulibarri, MD

mtf

Check off:

__________ 1. Location: In what part of the body is the sign or symptom occurring?

Urinary system

__________ 2. Quality: Is the symptom or pain burning, gnawing, stabbing, pressure-like, squeezing, fullness?

fullness

__________ 3. Severity: How would you rank the symptom or pain (slight, mild, severe, persistent)?

persistent

__________ 4. Duration: How long has symptom been present or how long does it last?

since 9-5-20xx

__________ 5. Timing: When do (does) sign(s) or symptom(s) occur (AM, PM, after or before meals)?

Voiding difficulty when lying down and when voiding in the supine position

__________ 6. Context: Is the pain/symptom associated with big meals, dairy products, etc.?

No

__________ 7. Modifying factors: What actions make symptoms worse or better?

symptoms are worse when laying down/ are better while standing and sitting

__________ 8. Associated signs and symptoms: What other system or body area produces complaints when the presenting problem occurs? (Example: chest pain leads to shortness of breath.)

wound to his lt latural malleolus and is able to ambulate only with assistance

_____Total check marks

ASSIGNMENT 3–5 ▶ KEY A LETTER OF WITHDRAWAL

Performance Objective

Task: Key letter for the physician's signature.

Conditions: Use one sheet of letterhead (Figure 3–1), U.S. Postal Service forms for Certified mail with return receipt requested (Figure 3–2), Authorization for Release of Information form (Figure 3–3), and a number 10 envelope.

Standards: Time:_____________ minutes

Accuracy: _________________

(Note: The time element and accuracy criteria may be given by your instructor.)

Directions: Mrs. Mclean is negligent about following Dr. Ulibarri's advice after she received surgery. Refer to *Workbook* Assignment 6–3 for information from the patient record of Mrs. Merry M. Mclean. Use a letterhead and type in modified block style an appropriate letter to Mrs. Mclean advising her of the doctor's withdrawal from the case (see *Handbook* Figure 3–21). Date the letter June 30 of the current year. Dr. Ulibarri will be available to this patient for 30 days after receipt of this letter.

This letter must be prepared for Dr. Ulibarri's signature as it is a legal document. Type Mrs. Mclean's address on a number 10 envelope, referring to *Workbook* Figure 3–4. Send the letter by certified mail with return receipt requested, referring to *Handbook* Figure 3–22, and enclose a completed Authorization for Release of Information form WB Figure 3–3.

After the instructor has returned your work to you, either make the necessary corrections and place it in a 3-ring notebook for future reference, or, if you receive a high score, place it in your portfolio for reference when applying for a job.

College Clinic
4567 Broad Avenue
Woodland Hills, XY 12345-0001
Telephone: 013-486-9002 Fax: 013-487-8976

Figure 3–1

UNITED STATES POSTAL SERVICE

First-Class Mail
Postage & Fees Paid
USPS
Permit No. G-10

• Sender: Please print your name, address, and ZIP+4 in this box •

SENDER: *COMPLETE THIS SECTION*

- Complete items 1, 2, and 3. Also complete item 4 if Restricted Delivery is desired.
- Print your name and address on the reverse so that we can return the card to you.
- Attach this card to the back of the mailpiece, or on the front if space permits.

1. Article Addressed to:

COMPLETE THIS SECTION ON DELIVERY

A. Received by (*Please Print Clearly*) | B. Date of Delivery

C. Signature
☐ Agent
X ☐ Addressee

D. Is delivery address different from item 1? ☐ Yes
If YES, enter delivery address below: ☐ No

3. Service Type
☐ Certified Mail ☐ Express Mail
☐ Registered ☐ Return Receipt for Merchandise
☐ Insured Mail ☐ C.O.D.

4. Restricted Delivery? *(Extra Fee)* ☐ Yes

2. Article Number *(Copy from service label)*

PS Form 3811, July 1999 Domestic Return Receipt 102595-00-M-0952

PLACE STICKER AT TOP OF ENVELOPE TO THE RIGHT OF RETURN ADDRESS. FOLD AT DOTTED LINE

CERTIFIED MAIL

7000 0520 0020 3886 3112
7000 0520 0020 3886 3112

U.S. Postal Service
CERTIFIED MAIL RECEIPT
(Domestic Mail Only; No Insurance Coverage Provided)

Postage	$
Certified Fee	
Return Receipt Fee (Endorsement Required)	
Restricted Delivery Fee (Endorsement Required)	
Total Postage & Fees	**$**

Postmark Here

Recipient's Name *(Please Print Clearly) (To be completed by mailer)*

Street, Apt. No.; or PO Box No.

City, State, ZIP+4

PS Form 3800, February 2000 **See Reverse for Instructions**

Figure 3–2

AUTHORIZATION FOR RELEASE OF INFORMATION

Section A: Must be completed for all authorizations.

I hereby authorize the use or disclosure of my individually identifiable health information as described below.
I understand that this authorization is voluntary. I understand that if the organization to receive the information is not a health plan or health care provider, the released information may no longer be protected by federal privacy regulations.

Patient name: ____________________ **ID Number:** ____________________

Persons/organizations providing information:
____
____
____

Persons/organizations receiving information:
____
____
____

Specific description of information [including date(s)]: ____________________
____

Section B: Must be completed only if a health plan or a health care provider has requested the authorization.

1. The health plan or health care provider must complete the following:
   a. What is the purpose of the use or disclosure? ____________________
   ____
   b. Will the health plan or health care provider requesting the authorization receive financial or in-kind compensation in exchange for using or disclosing the health information described above? Yes ____ No ____
2. The patient or the patient's representative must read and initial the following statements:
   a. I understand that my health care and the payment of my health care will not be affected if I do not sign this form. Initials: ____________
   b. I understand that I may see and copy the information described on this form if I ask for it, and that I get a copy of this form after I sign it. Initials: ____________

Section C: Must be completed for all authorizations.

The patient or the patient's representative must read and initial the following statements:

1. I understand that this authorization will expire on ____/____ /____ (DD/MM/YR). Initials: ____________
2. I understand that I may revoke this authorization at any time by notifying the providing organization in writing, but if I do not it will not have any effect on actions they took before they received the revocation. Initials: ____________

____________________ ____________________
Signature of patient or patient's representative **Date**
(Form MUST be completed before signing)

Printed name of patient's representative: ____________________

Relationship to patient: ____________________

YOU MAY REFUSE TO SIGN THIS AUTHORIZATION
You may not use this form to release information for treatment or payment except when the information to be released is psychotherapy notes or certain research information.

Figure 3–3

ASSIGNMENT 3-6 ▶ KEY A LETTER TO CONFIRM DISCHARGE BY THE PATIENT

Performance Objective

Task: Key letter for the physician's signature.

Conditions: Use one sheet of letterhead (Figure 3–5), number 10 envelope, and U.S. Postal Service forms for Certified mail with return receipt requested (Figure 3–6).

Standards: Time:__________ minutes

Accuracy: ______________

(Note: The time element and accuracy criteria may be given by your instructor.

Directions: Mr. Walter J. Stone telephones on June 3, sounding extremely upset and irrational. He says that he is unable to return to work on June 22 and that he does not want to be seen by Dr. Input again. Type a letter to confirm this discharge by the patient (see *Handbook* Figure 3–23). Suggest that he contact the local medical society for the names of three internists for further care. This letter must be prepared for Dr. Input's signature as it is a legal document. Refer to Assignment 6–5 for infor-

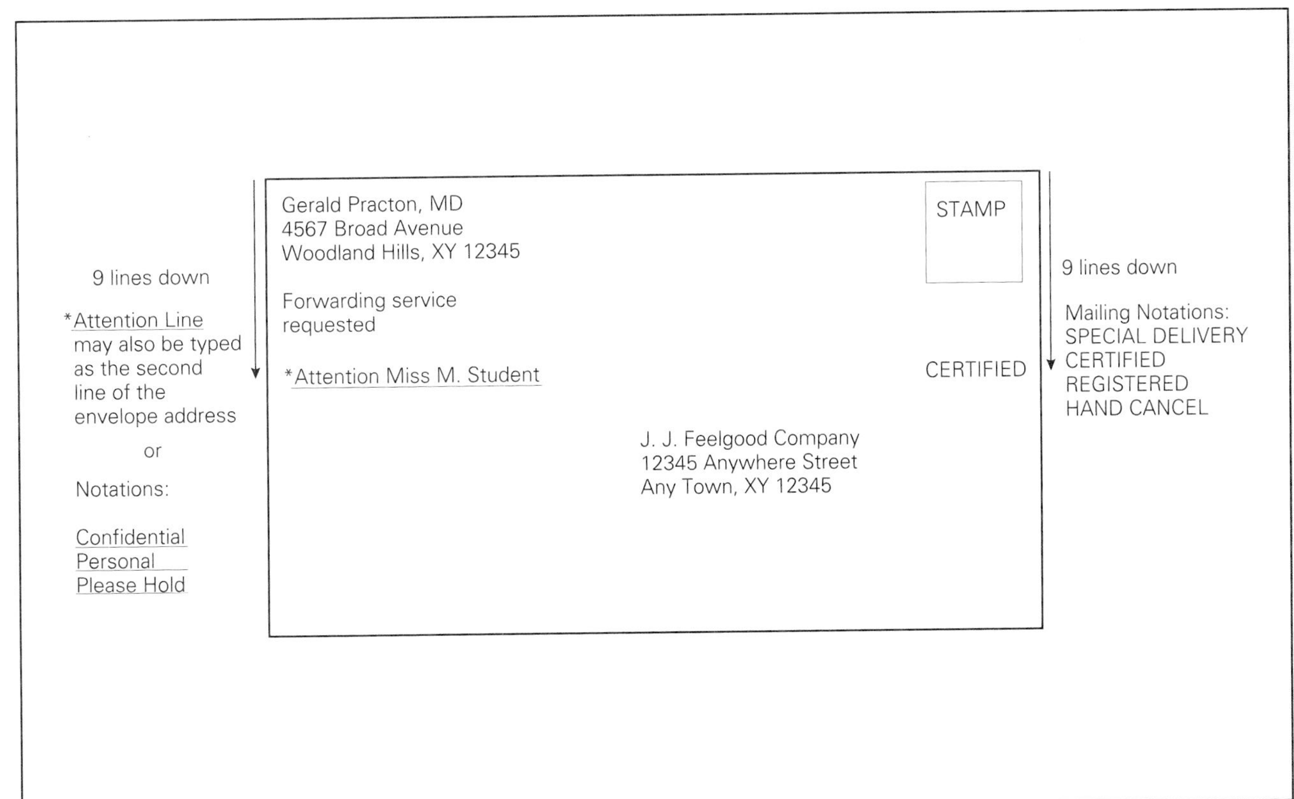

Figure 3–4

mation from the patient record. Use a letterhead and key in modified block style as shown in *Handbook* Figure 3–23. Use current date. Key Mr. Stone's address on a number 10 envelope, referring to *Workbook* Figure 3–4. Send the letter by certified mail with return receipt requested, referring to *Handbook* Figure 3–22.

After the instructor has returned your work to you, either make the necessary corrections and place it in a 3-ring notebook for future reference, or, if you receive a high score, place it in your portfolio for reference when applying for a job.

COLLEGE CLINIC
4567 Broad Avenue
Woodland Hills, XY 12345-0001
Telephone: 013-486-9002 Fax: 013-487-8976

Figure 3–5

United States Postal Service

First-Class Mail
Postage & Fees Paid
USPS
Permit No. G-10

• Sender: Please print your name, address, and ZIP+4 in this box •

SENDER: *COMPLETE THIS SECTION*

- Complete items 1, 2, and 3. Also complete item 4 if Restricted Delivery is desired.
- Print your name and address on the reverse so that we can return the card to you.
- Attach this card to the back of the mailpiece, or on the front if space permits.

1. Article Addressed to:

COMPLETE THIS SECTION ON DELIVERY

A. Received by *(Please Print Clearly)* B. Date of Delivery

C. Signature
X ☐ Agent ☐ Addressee

D. Is delivery address different from item 1? ☐ Yes
If YES, enter delivery address below: ☐ No

3. Service Type
☐ Certified Mail ☐ Express Mail
☐ Registered ☐ Return Receipt for Merchandise
☐ Insured Mail ☐ C.O.D.

4. Restricted Delivery? *(Extra Fee)* ☐ Yes

2. Article Number *(Copy from service label)*

PS Form 3811, July 1999 Domestic Return Receipt 102595-00-M-0952

PLACE STICKER AT TOP OF ENVELOPE TO THE RIGHT OF RETURN ADDRESS. FOLD AT DOTTED LINE

CERTIFIED MAIL

7000 0520 0020 3886 2559
7000 0520 0020 3886 2559

U.S. Postal Service
CERTIFIED MAIL RECEIPT
(Domestic Mail Only; No Insurance Coverage Provided)

Postage	$
Certified Fee	
Return Receipt Fee (Endorsement Required)	
Restricted Delivery Fee (Endorsement Required)	
Total Postage & Fees	**$**

Postmark Here

***Recipient's Name** (Please Print Clearly) (To be completed by mailer)*

Street, Apt. No.; or PO Box No.

City, State, ZIP+4

PS Form 3800, February 2000 **See Reverse for Instructions**

Figure 3–6

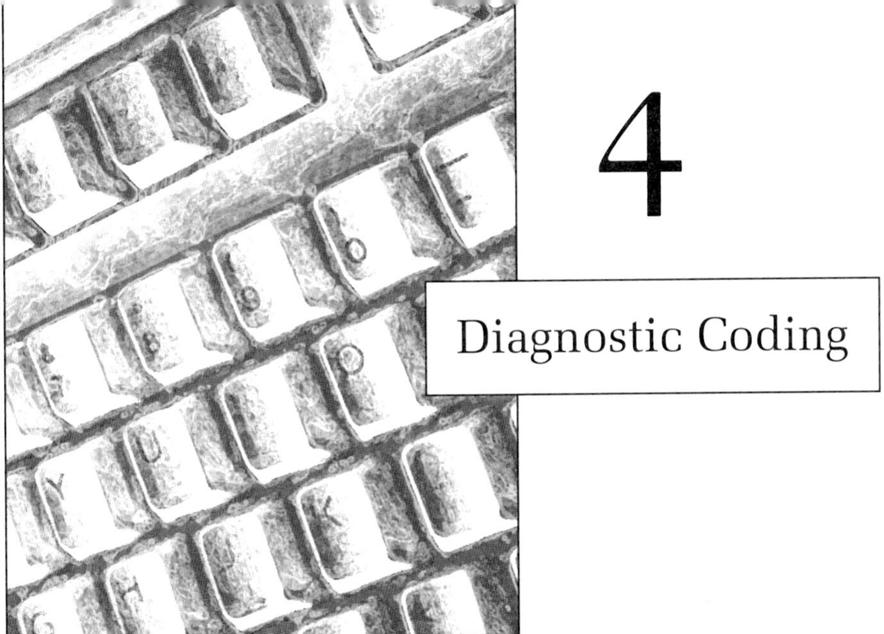

4

Diagnostic Coding

KEY TERMS

Your instructor may wish to select some words pertinent to this chapter for a test. For definitions and further study of words, phrases, and abbreviations, refer to the Glossary at the end of the Handbook. *The words for this chapter follow.*

adverse effect
benign tumor
chief complaint (CC)
combination code
complication
E codes
etiology
in situ
International Classification of Diseases, Ninth Revision, Clinical Modification (ICD-9-CM)
intoxication
italicized code
late effect
malignant tumor
not elsewhere classifiable (NEC)
not otherwise specified (NOS)
physician's fee profile
poisoning
primary diagnosis
principal diagnosis
secondary diagnosis
slanted brackets
V codes

PERFORMANCE OBJECTIVES

The student will be able to

- Define and spell the key terms for this chapter, given the information from the *Handbook* Glossary, within a reasonable period of time and with enough accuracy to obtain a satisfactory evaluation.
- Answer the self-study review questions after reading the chapter with enough accuracy to obtain a satisfactory evaluation.
- Assignment 4–3: Indicate main terms, subterms, subterms to subterms, and carry-over lines, given a section of a page from the *ICD-9-CM* code book, with enough accuracy to obtain a satisfactory evaluation.
- Assignment 4–4: Answer questions given a section of a page from the *ICD-9-CM* code book with enough accuracy to obtain a satisfactory evaluation.
- Assignment 4–5: Select the correct diagnostic code numbers, given a series of diagnoses using Volumes 1 and 2 of the *ICD-9-CM* code book, with enough accuracy to obtain a satisfactory evaluation.

- Assignments 4–6 through 4–13: Select the correct diagnostic code numbers, given a series of scenarios and diagnoses using Volumes 1 and 2 of the *ICD-9-CM* code book, with enough accuracy to obtain a satisfactory evaluation.

STUDY OUTLINE

The Diagnostic Coding System
- Types of Diagnostic Codes
- Reasons for the Development and Use of Diagnostic Codes
- Physician's Fee Profile

History of Coding Diseases

International Classification of Diseases
- History
- Organization and Format
- Contents

How to Use the Diagnostic Code Books Properly
- Coding Instructions
- Procedure: Basic Steps in Coding
  - Special Points to Remember in Volume 1
  - Special Points to Remember in Volume 2
  - Handy Hints in Diagnostic Coding
  - V Codes
  - E Codes

Rules for Coding
- Signs, Symptoms, and Ill-Defined Conditions
- Sterilization
- Neoplasms
- Circulatory System Conditions
  - Hypertension
  - Myocardial Infarctions
  - Chronic Rheumatic Heart Disease
  - Arteriosclerotic Cardiovascular Disease and Arteriosclerotic Heart Disease
- Diabetes Mellitus
- Pregnancy, Delivery, or Abortion
- Admitting Diagnoses
- Burns
- Injuries and Late Effects

***ICD-10-CM* Diagnosis and Procedure Codes**

SELF-STUDY 4–1 ▶ *ICD-9-CM* REVIEW QUESTIONS

Review the objectives, key terms, and chapter information before completing the following review questions.

1. The system for coding and billing diagnoses is found in a book entitled International Classification of Diseases 9th Revision, Clinical Modification.

2. For retrieving types of diagnoses related to pathology by an institution within an institution, the coding system is found in a book entitled Systematized Nomenclature of Human and Veterinary Medicine.

3. Why is it important that diagnostic *ICD-9-CM* coding become routinely used in the physician's office? Diagnostic coding should be routinely used in the physician's office to assure accuracy of reporting patient's diagnosis and so the physician's future profiles reflect more realistic payments

4. The abbreviation *ICD-9-CM* means International Classification of Diseases 9th revision Clinical Modification.

5. The coding in *ICD-9-CM* varies from ___3___ to ___5___ characters.

6. Volume 1, Diseases, is a/an ___tabular or numerical___ listing of code numbers.

7. Volume 2, Diseases, is a/an ___alphabetic___ index or listing of code numbers.

8. The abbreviation NEC appearing in the *ICD-9-CM* code book means ___not elsewhere classifiable___.

9. To code using Volume 2, the Alphabetic Index, the ___condition___ is looked up rather than the anatomic part.

10. E codes are a supplementary classification of coding for ___external causes of injury___ rather than disease and of coding for ___adverse reactions to medications.___.

To check your answers to this self-study assignment, see Appendix D.

SELF-STUDY 4–2 ▸ *ICD-10* REVIEW QUESTIONS

Directions: Multiple Choice. Circle the letter that gives the best answer to each statement.

1. *ICD-10* was created by:

   a. National Center for Health Statistics
   b. World Health Organization
   c. Centers for Disease Control
   d. Health Care Financing Administration

2. *ICD-10-CM* was developed by:

   a. National Center for Health Statistics
   b. World Health Organization
   c. Centers for Disease Control
   d. Health Care Financing Administration

3. *ICD-10-PCS* (Procedure Coding System) was created by:

   a. National Center for Health Statistics
   b. World Health Organization
   c. Centers for Disease Control
   d. Health Care Financing Administration

4. The disease codes in *ICD-10-CM* have a maximum of:

   a. 3 digits
   b. 4 digits
   c. 5 digits
   d. 6 digits

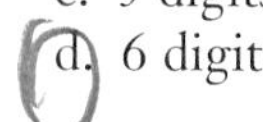

5. Reason(s) the Clinical Modification was developed is/are:

   a. Removal of procedural codes
   b. Removal of unique mortality codes
   c. Removal of multiple codes
   d. Only a and c
   e. Only b
   f. All of the above

6. *ICD-10-PCS* procedure codes have:

   a. 4 digits
   b. 5 digits
   c. 6 digits
   d. 7 digits

7. The first 3 digits of a 7-digit *ICD-10-PCS* code are the:

   a. Code category
   b. Surgical approach
   c. Specific anatomic body part
   d. Type of medical and/or prosthetic device used

8. One of the reasons for *ICD-10-PCS* is that:

   e. *ICD-9-CM* was not capable of necessary expansion
   f. *ICD-9-CM* was not as comprehensive as it should be
   g. *ICD-9-CM* included diagnostic information
   h. All of the above

9. The letters "I" and "O" are (were) used in:

   a. *ICD-9-CM*
   b. *ICD-10-CM* Diseases
   c. *ICD-10-PCS*
   d. None of the above

To check your answers to this self-study assignment, see Appendix D.

ASSIGNMENT 4–3 ▶ IDENTIFY FORMAT COMPONENTS OF *ICD-9-CM*, VOLUME 2

Performance Objective

Task: Identify seven format components of *ICD-9-CM*, Volume 2.

Conditions: Use the abstracted section from *ICD-9-CM*, Volume 2, and pen or pencil.

Standards: Time: ____________ minutes

Accuracy: ____________

(Note: The time element and accuracy criteria may be given by your instructor.)

Directions: Label the line indicated as either main term, subterm, subterm of subterm, or carry-over line. Refer to Chapter 4 in the *Handbook*, section on "Rules for Coding Diabetes Mellitus" and locate Figure 4–13, which graphically illustrates the format components.

1. main term ➤ **Saccharomyces infection** (*see also*
2. carry-over line ➤ Candidiasis) 112.9

Sacroiliitis NEC 720.2

Sacrum—*see* condition

Saddle

3. Subterm ➤ back 737.8

embolus, aorta 444.0

nose 738.0

4. Subterm to subterm ➤ congenital 754.0

due to syphilis 090.5

5. main term ➤ **Salicylism**

correct substance properly administered 535.4

Salmonella choleraesuis (enteritidis)

6. carry-over line ➤ (gallinarum) (suipestifer) (typhimurium) (*see also* Infection Salmonella) 003.9

7. Subterm ➤ arthritis 003.23

carrier (suspected) of V02.3

ASSIGNMENT 4–4 ▶ ANSWER QUESTIONS PERTAINING TO A SECTION FROM *ICD-9-CM*, VOLUME 2

Performance Objective

Task: Answer questions pertaining to categories 320 and 321 of *ICD-9-CM*, Volume 2.

Conditions: Use abstracted section from *ICD-9-CM*, Volume 2 (Figure 4–1) and pen or pencil.

Standards: Time: ____________ minutes

Accuracy : ____________

(Note: The time element and accuracy criteria may be given by your instructor.)

Directions: Refer to a section from a page of *ICD-9-CM*, Volume 2 (Figure 4–1) and answer questions pertaining to categories 320 and 321.

6. DISEASES OF THE NERVOUS SYSTEM AND SENSE ORGANS (320-389)

INFLAMMATORY DISEASES OF THE CENTRAL NERVOUS SYSTEM (320-326)

320 Bacterial meningitis
Includes: arachnoiditis, leptomeningitis, meningitis, meningoencephalitis, meningomyelitis, pachymeningitis } bacterial

320.0 *Haemophilus* meningitis
Meningitis due to *Haemophilus influenzae* [*H. Influenzae*]

320.1 Pneumococcal meningitis

320.2 Streptococcal meningitis

320.3 Staphylococcal meningitis

320.7 Meningitis in other bacterial diseases classified elsewhere

Code first underlying diseases as:
actinomycosis (039.8)
listeriosis (027.0)
typhoid fever (002.0)
whooping cough (033.0-033.9)

Excludes: *meningitis (in):*
epidemic (036.0)
gonococcal (098.82)
meningococcal (036.0)
salmonellosis (003.21)
syphilis:
NOS (094.2)
congenital (090.42)
meningovascular (094.2)
secondary (091.81)
tuberculous (013.0)

320.8 Meningitis due to other specified bacteria

320.81 Anaerobic meningitis
Gram-negative anaerobes
Bacteroides (fragilis)

320.82 Meningitis due to gram-negative bacteria, not elsewhere classified
Aerobacter aerogenes
Escherichia coli [E. coli]
Friedländer bacillus
Klebsiella pneumoniae
Proteus morganii
Pseudomonas

Excludes: *gram-negative anaerobes (320.81)*

320.89 Meningitis due to other specified bacteria
Bacillus pyocyaneus

320.9 Meningitis due to unspecified bacterium
Meningitis: bacterial NOS, purulent NOS
Meningitis: pyogenic NOS, suppurative NOS

321 Meningitis due to other organisms
Includes: arachnoiditis, leptomeningitis, meningitis, pachymeningitis } due to organisms other than bacteria

321.0 Cryptococcal meningitis
Code first underlying disease (117.5)

Figure 4–1

1. Locate the section title Inflammatory Disease of the Central Nervous System and Sense Organs

2. Refer to the INCLUSION TERMS listed under category code 320, entitled "Bacterial meningitis." Place an "X" in front of each of the following diagnostic statements that are included in category 320.

____ purulent meningitis

X bacterial meningomyelitis

X meningitis

X meningoencephalitis

_____ pyogenic meningitis

_____ meningococcal

3. Refer to the EXCLUSION TERMS located under code 320.7, entitled "Meningitis in other bacterial diseases classified elsewhere." Place an "X" in front of the following code number(s) which are excluded.

X secondary syphilis 091.81

_____ acquired syphilis 097.9

X gonococcal meningitis 098.82

X congenital syphilis 090.42

_____ primary syphilis 091.2

_____ gram-negative anaerobes 320.81

4. Place an "X" in front of each of the following diagnostic statements included in category code 320 and its subcategories.

_____ leptomeningitis

X meningitis due to *E. coli*

X pyogenic meningitis

_____ epidemic meningitis

_____ tuberculous meningitis

5. Write the code numbers for category 320 that require fifth digits.

320.82 320.89

ASSIGNMENT 4–5 ▶ OBTAIN GENERAL DIAGNOSTIC CODES FOR CONDITIONS

Performance Objective

Task: Locate the correct diagnostic code for each diagnosis listed.

Conditions: Use pen or pencil and *ICD-9-CM* diagnostic code book.

Standards: Time: ______________ minutes

Accuracy: ______________

(Note: The time element and accuracy criteria may be given by your instructor.)

Directions: Using the *International Classification of Diseases, 9th Revision, Clinical Modification* code book, read each diagnosis and locate the *condition* in Volume 2, the alphabetical index. Look at the diagnostic statement and see whether the main term specifically describes the disease; if not, look at the subterms listed under the main term. Try and find a more specific code. Continue to look at sub-subterms (words or phrases listed under the subterm) if a more specific definition is needed. Read all the cross references or notes. Then locate the code chosen in Volume 1, the tabular index. Match the definition to the written description as close as possible and assign the correct code, entering it on the blank line.

1. Breast mass 611.72
2. *Klebsiella* pneumonia 482.0
3. Acute lateral wall myocardial infarction; initial episode 410.51
4. Acute cerebrovascular accident 436
5. Arteriosclerotic cardiovascular disease 429.2
6. Dyspnea, R/O cystic fibrosis 786.09
7. Ileitis 558.9
8. Arthritis of elbow 716.98
9. Ringing in the ears 388.30
10. Acute exacerbation of chronic asthmatic bronchitis 491.21

ASSIGNMENT 4–6 ▶ CODE DIAGNOSES FROM MEDICAL RECORDS

Performance Objective

Task: Locate the correct diagnostic code for each case scenario.

Conditions: Use pen or pencil and *ICD-9-CM* diagnostic code book.

Standards: Time: ______________ minutes

Accuracy: ______________

(Note: The time element and accuracy criteria may be given by your instructor.)

Directions: This exercise will give you experience in basic diagnostic coding for physicians' insurance claims. First list the *ICD-9-CM* code for the diagnosis, condition, problem, or other reason for the admission and/or encounter (visit) shown in the medical record to be *chiefly responsible* for the services provided. Then list additional diagnostic codes that describe any coexisting conditions that *affect* patient care. Always assign codes to their highest level of specificity—the more digits, the more specific. Do not code probable, rule out, suspected, or questionable conditions. Assign the correct code(s), entering it (them) on the blank line.

1. A patient, Mrs. Jennifer Hanson, calls Dr. Input's office stating she has blood in her stool. Dr. Input suspects a GI bleed and tells Mrs. Hanson to come in immediately. It is discovered that the reason for the blood in the stool is a bleeding duodenal ulcer. Code the diagnosis to be listed on the insurance claim for the office visit. 532.40

2. a. Jason Belmen comes in with a fractured humerus. He also has chronic obstructive pulmonary disease (COPD), which is not treated. Code the diagnosis. a. 496 812.20

   b. Assume Mr. Belmen needs general anesthesia for open reduction of the fractured humerus. The COPD could now be considered a risk factor. List the diagnostic code in the second part of this scenario. b. V64.1

3. Margarita Sanchez came into the office for removal of sutures. Code the diagnosis. 97.89

4. A patient, George Martin, has benign prostatic hyperplasia (BPH). He is seen for catheterization because of urinary retention. Code the primary and secondary diagnoses for the office visit. (Note: BPH is an enlargement of the prostate gland, due to overgrowth of androgen-sensitive glandular elements, which occurs naturally with aging.) a. 600.2 b. 788.2 57.94

5. Mia Bartholomew is seen in the office complaining of a sore throat. A throat culture is done and the specimen is sent to an outside laboratory for a culture and sensitivity study to determine streptococcus. List the diagnostic code the physician would use if the insurance claim is submitted before the results are known. a. 90.33

   List the diagnostic code if the physician submits the insurance claim after the laboratory report is received that indicates streptococcus is present. b. 90.33 041.00

ASSIGNMENT 4–7 ► CODE DIAGNOSES USING V CODES

Performance Objective

Task: Locate the correct diagnostic code for each case scenario.

Conditions: Use pen or pencil and *ICD-9-CM* diagnostic code book.

Standards: Time: ______________ minutes

Accuracy: ______________

(Note: The time element and accuracy criteria may be given by your instructor.)

Directions: In this exercise you will be reviewing V codes in the *ICD-9-CM* code book. Assign the correct code, entering it on the blank line. These are some key words under which V codes may be located in Volume 2.

admission
aftercare
attention to
border
care of
carrier
checking/checkup
conflict
contact
contraception
counseling
dialysis
donor
evaluation
examination
fitting of
follow-up
history of
insertion of
maintenance
observation
person with
problem with
screening
status post
vaccination

1. Kathy Osborn, a patient, is seen in the office for an annual checkup V70.0

2. Daniel Matsui is seen in the office for adjustment of a lumbosacral corset. V53

3. Philip O'Brien comes into the office to receive a prophylactic flu shot. V04.8

4. Bernadette Murphy is seen in the office for a pregnancy test. V72.4

5. Michiko Fujita is seen in the office for a fractured rib. No x-rays are taken because Mrs. Fujita thinks she is pregnant.
   a. 807.00
   b. V64.1

6. Dr. Perry Cardi sees Kenneth Pickford in the office for cardiac pacemaker adjustment. The pacemaker was implanted due to sick sinus syndrome. V53.31

7. Frank Meadows returns for follow-up, postoperative transurethral prostatic resection (TURP) for prostate cancer after treatment has been completed.
   a. V670
   b. V107.29

ASSIGNMENT 4–8 ► CODE NEOPLASTIC DIAGNOSES

Performance Objective

Task: Locate the correct diagnostic code for each diagnosis listed.

Conditions: Use pen or pencil and *ICD-9-CM* diagnostic code book.

Standards: Time: ________ minutes V10.3

Accuracy: ________

(Note: The time element and accuracy criteria may be given by your instructor.)

Directions: In this exercise, you will be reviewing diagnostic codes in the *ICD-9-CM* code book involving neoplasms. The morphology of neoplasm is found in Appendix A of Volume 1. Neoplasms are classified according to their histology. Morphology (M) codes are sometimes used to supplement a diagnostic code. M codes are *not* used on insurance forms when submitting claims by physicians; therefore, they will not be used in this assignment. M codes are *never* used as a primary diagnostic code. Assign the correct code, entering it on the blank line.

1. Leiomyoma, uterus 218.9
2. Ewing's sarcoma, forearm 170.4
3. Adenocarcinoma, right breast, central portion 174.1
4. Dyspnea due to carcinoma of the breast with metastasis to the lung
   a. 197.0
   b. 786.09
5. Patient is seen for a yearly examination one year after a mastectomy for breast cancer; she is disease free at this time.
   a. V10.3
   b. V67.0
6. Patient comes in for chemotherapy because of lymphosarcoma of the intrathoracic lymph nodes.
   a. 202.92
   b. V58.1

ASSIGNMENT 4–9 ► CODE DIAGNOSES FOR DIABETIC CASES

Performance Objective

Task: Locate the correct diagnostic code for each diagnosis listed.

Conditions: Use pen or pencil and *ICD-9-CM* diagnostic code book.

Standards: Time: ________________ minutes

Accuracy: ________________

(Note: The time element and accuracy criteria may be given by your instructor.)

Directions: In this exercise, you will review diagnostic codes in the *ICD-9-CM* code book involving diabetic cases. When coding diabetes, first find out the type of diabetes being treated, type I or type II. Then look to see whether the diabetes is under control. These two answers determine the assignment of the fifth digit.

For diabetic complications, determine whether the complication is due to the diabetes and whether the diabetes is out of control. These points need to be regarded as two distinctly different issues. A patient can have controlled diabetes but still have a complication caused by diabetes. Complications arising from diabetes must be coded. The code for the complication is listed after the subterm in brackets.

Example: If a type II uncontrolled diabetic is treated for a skin ulcer on the lower extremity, look up "diabetes" in Volume 2 and find the subterm "ulcer." The diabetes code listed is 250.8 and under the subterm "ulcer" is a sub-subterm of "lower extremity" with the code 707.1 in brackets. Go to Volume 1 and verify the diabetes code and assign a fifth digit. The correct code is 250.82 (2 for type II, uncontrolled). Now verify the *ulcer* code in Volume 1. You will see that code 707.1 does not mention diabetes. If diabetes is the cause of the ulcer, code the diabetes first and the ulcer second. If the patient's diabetes is under control and is not being treated at the visit, code the ulcer first and diabetes second as an underlying disease. Other complications, such as bone changes (731.8) may tell you to code the *underlying disease first*. Therefore, always verify all codes in Volume 1 before assigning them.

Assign the correct code(s) for each diabetic case, entering it (them) on the blank line.

1. Diabetes mellitus
2. Uncontrolled noninsulin-dependent diabetes mellitus with ketoacidosis
3. Diabetic gangrene (type I diabetes, out of control)
4. Controlled type II diabetes with cataract
5. Type I diabetes with diabetic polyneuropathy and retinopathy

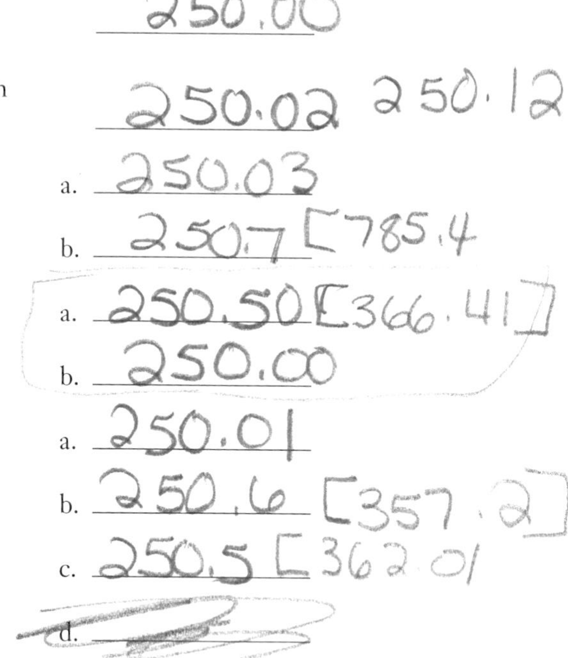

ASSIGNMENT 4–10 ► CODE DIAGNOSES FOR HYPERTENSION CASES

Performance Objective

Task: Locate the correct diagnostic code for each diagnosis listed.

Conditions: Use pen or pencil and *ICD-9-CM* diagnostic code book.

Standards: Time: ____________ minutes

Accuracy: ____________

(Note: The time element and accuracy criteria may be given by your instructor.)

Directions: In this exercise, you will review diagnostic codes in the *ICD-9-CM* code book involving patients that have hypertension. To begin coding, look in Volume 2 under "hypertension" and find the Hypertension Table. This is designed to simplify coding conditions due to, or associated with, hypertension or hypertensive disease. At the beginning of the table there are many terms listed in parentheses. These terms are nonessential modifiers, which means that the absence or presence of one of these terms does not change the meaning of the code. From the table the hypertensive codes begin with 401. Go to this number in Volume 1 and look through this section to become familiar with it.

Assign the correct code(s) for each case, entering it (them) on the blank line.

1. High blood pressure 401.9
2. Malignant hypertension 401.0
3. Antepartum hypertension complicating pregnancy 642.9
4. Hypertension with kidney disease 403.90
5. Hypertension due to arteriosclerotic cardiovascular disease (ASCVD) and congestive heart failure (CHF) 402.91
6. Myocarditis and CHF due to malignant hypertension a. 401.0
   b. 402.01

ASSIGNMENT 4–11 ▶ CODE DIAGNOSES FOR INJURIES, FRACTURES, BURNS, LATE EFFECTS, AND COMPLICATIONS

Performance Objective

Task: Locate the correct diagnostic code for each diagnosis listed.

Conditions: Use pen or pencil and *ICD-9-CM* diagnostic code book.

Standards: Time: ____________ minutes

Accuracy: ____________

(Note: The time element and accuracy criteria may be given by your instructor.)

Directions: In this exercise, you will review diagnostic codes from the *ICD-9-CM* code book involving patients who have suffered injuries, burns, fractures, and late effects. Some guidelines for coding *injuries, fractures, burns, late effects, and complications* are:

Injuries

- ✔ Code injuries separately according to their general type and then by anatomic site. Fifth digits are commonly used in the injury section to specify anatomic sites and severity.
- ✔ Code injuries separately if they are classifiable to more than one subcategory unless the diagnosis does not support separate injuries or the Alphabetic Index provides instructions to use a combination code.

Fractures

- ✔ Fractures are presumed to be closed unless otherwise specified.
- ✔ Fracture/dislocations are coded as fractures.
- ✔ Pathologic fractures are coded first and the cause (disease process) coded second.

Burns

- ✔ Multiple burns at the same site, but of different degrees, are coded to the most severe degree.
- ✔ Code the extent of body surface involved (percentage of body surface), when specified, as an additional code.

Late Effects

- ✔ A residual, late effect is defined as the current condition resulting from a previous acute illness or injury that is no longer the current problem. Late effects are coded using the residual or late effect as the primary diagnosis. The *cause* of the residual or late effect is coded second.

Complications

- ✔ For conditions resulting from the malfunction of internal devices, use the subterm "mechanical" found under the main term "complication."
- ✔ Postoperative complications are sometimes found under the subterm "postoperative," which appears under the main term identifying the condition. If not found there, look for a subterm identifying the type of procedure, type of complication, or surgical procedure under the main term "complication."

Assign the correct code(s) for each case, entering it (them) on the blank line.

1. Supracondylar fracture of right femur
2. Fracture of left humerus and left foot
3. Comminuted fracture of left radius and ulna
4. Pathologic fracture of right hip due to drug-induced osteoporosis
5. Lacerations of arm, with embedded glass
6. Burns on the face and neck
7. Second- and third-degree burns on chest wall; 20% of body involved, 10% third-degree
8. Bursitis of the knee due to crushing injury to the knee one year ago

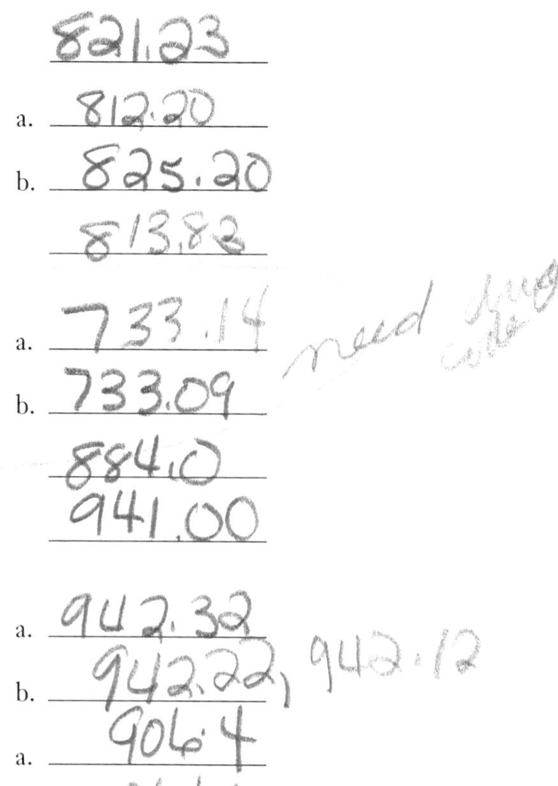

ASSIGNMENT 4–12 ► CODE DIAGNOSES FOR PREGNANCY, DELIVERY, AND NEWBORN CARE

Performance Objective

Task: Locate the correct diagnostic code for each case scenario.

Conditions: Use pen or pencil and *ICD-9-CM* diagnostic code book.

Standards: Time: ______________ minutes

Accuracy: ______________

(Note: The time element and accuracy criteria may be given by your instructor.)

Directions: In this exercise, you will review diagnostic codes from the *ICD-9-CM* code book involving patients who have conditions involving pregnancy and delivery, and newborn infants.

For the *supervision* of a *normal pregnancy*, turn to Volume 2 and look up "pregnancy." This is a long category. Look up the subterm "supervision" and find the sub-subterm "normal" (NEC V22.1) and "first" (V22.0). Check Volume 1 to verify these codes. Also see code V22.2 "pregnancy state, incidental." This code is used in the second position to tell the insurance carrier that the patient is pregnant in addition to any other diagnosis.

If a patient develops *complications*, turn to Volume 2 and look under the main term "pregnancy." Find the subterm "complicated by," and find the sub-subterm stating the complication. These are codes from *ICD-9-CM* Chapter 11: "Complications of Pregnancy, Childbirth, and Puerperium" (630-677).

Delivery in a completely normal case is coded 650 and is listed under the main term "delivery, uncomplicated." Normal is described as "delivery without abnormality or complication and with spontaneous cephalic delivery, without mention of fetal manipulation or instrumentation." A different code must be used to describe any complication or deviation from this description of normal.

When coding deliveries, always include a code for the status of the infant. Look up "outcome of delivery" in Volume 2 and you will find various V27 codes listing possible outcomes. These codes would be listed as secondary codes on the insurance claim form for the delivery.

On the insurance claim form for the *newborn*, turn to "newborn" in Volume 2. You will find V codes from V30.X to V39.X describing the birth of the newborn. Use these codes in the *first position* when billing for services for the newborn infant.

Assign the correct code(s) for each case entering it (them) on the blank line.

1. A pregnant patient who is due to deliver in 6 weeks presents in the office with preeclampsia. 642.40

2. A patient presents with a chief complaint of severe episodes of pain and vaginal hemorrhage. The physician determines that the patient has an incomplete spontaneous abortion complicated by excessive hemorrhage; she was 6 weeks pregnant. 637.11

3. A patient comes in who is diagnosed with a kidney stone; the patient is also pregnant.
   a. 592.0
   b. V22.2

4. A patient delivers twins by cesarean section because of cephalopelvic disproportion, which caused an obstruction.
   a. 660.1
   b. 653.9
   c. V31.1

ASSIGNMENT 4–13 ▸ CODE DIAGNOSES USING E CODES

Performance Objective

Task: Locate the correct diagnostic code for each diagnosis listed.

Conditions: Use pen or pencil and the *ICD-9-CM* diagnostic code book.

Standards: Time: ____________________ minutes

Accuracy: ____________________

(Note: The time element and accuracy criteria may be given by your instructor.)

Directions: In this exercise you will be reviewing diagnostic codes from the *ICD-9-CM* code book involving patients who may have been in an accident, had an adverse effect from ingesting a toxic substance, or suffered an injury. Read the definitions for poisoning and drug intoxication in the *Handbook*.

✔ E codes are not used to describe the primary reason for a patient's visit but identify external environmental events, circumstances, and conditions as the cause of injury, poisoning, and other adverse effects (unfavorable results).

✔ E codes that identify external environmental events, such as an injury, are used only as supplemental codes to describe how an injury occurred. These codes are listed in the back of Volume 2 and provide a more descriptive clinical picture for the insurance carrier. They may or may not be required and in some cases may speed up the payment of the claim.

✔ E codes are used for coding adverse effects of drugs and chemicals but are not required when coding a poisoning. Use the Table of Drugs and Chemicals at the back of Volume 2 and go to the column titled "Therapeutic Use." In addition, it is necessary to use a code to describe the adverse effect of using a particular drug or medicine. Find this in Volume 2 and verify it in Volume 1.

Assign the correct code(s) for each case and enter it (them) on the blank line.

1. Light-headedness due to digitalis intoxication
2. Treatment of a rash after an initial dose of penicillin is given
3. Accidental overdose of meperidine (Demerol)
4. A 20-month-old baby accidentally ingests approximately 15 aspirin and is severely nauseated

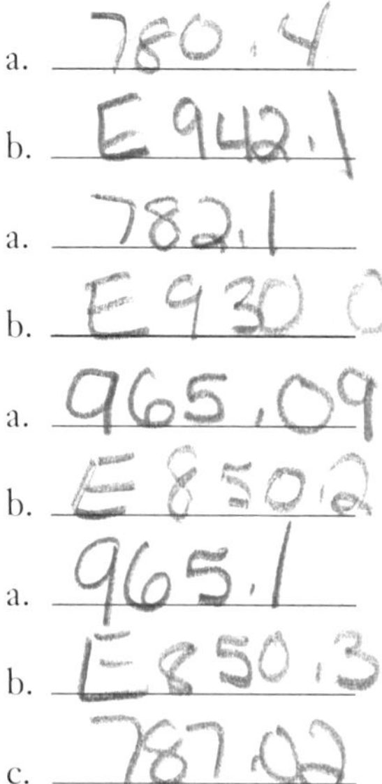

5. A patient presents in the physician's office with a vague complaint of not feeling well. The physician notices that the patient has ataxia (a staggering gait). After reviewing the patient's history, the physician determines the ataxia is due to the meprobamate the patient is taking.

a. 781.3

b. E939.5

6. Internal bleeding: abnormal reaction to a combination of chloramphenicol and warfarin (Coumadin)

a. 459.0

b. E930.2

c. E934.2

5

Procedural Coding

KEY TERMS

Your instructor may wish to select some words pertinent to this chapter for a test. For definitions of the terms, further study, and/or reference, the words, phrases, and abbreviations may be found in the Glossary at the end of the Handbook. *Key terms for this chapter follow.*

actual charge
bilateral
bundled codes
comprehensive code
conversion factor
customary fee
downcoding
fee schedule
global surgery policy
Health Care Financing Administration Common Procedure Coding System (HCPCS)
modifier
Current Procedural Terminology (CPT)
prevailing charge
procedure code numbers
professional component (PC)
reasonable fee
relative value studies (RVS)
star symbol
surgical package
technical component (TC)
unbundling
upcoding
usual, customary, and reasonable (UCR)

PERFORMANCE OBJECTIVES

The student will be able to

- Define and spell the key terms for this chapter, given the information from the *Handbook* Glossary, within a reasonable period of time and with enough accuracy to obtain satisfactory evaluation.
- Answer the self-study review questions after reading the chapter with enough accuracy to obtain a satisfactory evaluation.
- Select the five-digit procedure code numbers, modifiers, and/or descriptors of each service, given a series of problems relating to various medical procedures and services and using the *Current Procedural Terminology* (CPT) code book or the Mock Fee Schedule in Appendix A of the *Workbook* with enough accuracy to obtain a satisfactory evaluation.
- Fill in the correct meaning of each abbreviation given in a list of common medical abbreviations and symbols that appear in chart notes, and with enough accuracy to obtain a satisfactory evaluation.

STUDY OUTLINE

Understanding the Importance of Procedural Coding Skills
- Current Procedural Terminology (CPT)

Methods of Payment
- Fee Schedule
- Usual, Customary, and Reasonable (UCR)
- Relative Value Studies (RVS)

Procedure: Determining Relative Value Studies Conversion Factors

How to Use the *CPT* Code Book
- Code Book Symbols
- Evaluation and Management Section
  - Consultation
  - Critical Care
  - Emergency Care
  - Counseling
  - Categories and Subcategories
- Surgery Section
  - Surgical Package
  - Medicare Global Package
  - Follow-up Days
  - Repair of Lacerations
  - Multiple Lesions
  - Supplies
  - Prolonged Services, Detention, or Standby

Procedure: How to Code Effectively
- Unlisted Procedures
- Coding Guidelines for Code Edits
  - Comprehensive/Component Edits
  - Mutually Exclusive Code Denials
  - Bundled Codes
  - Unbundling
  - Downcoding
  - Upcoding
- Code Monitoring

Helpful Hints in Coding
- Office Visits
- Drugs and Injections
- Adjunct Codes
- Basic Life and/or Disability Evaluation Services

Code Modifiers
- Correct Use of Common Modifiers
  - -21 Prolonged Evaluation and Management Services
  - -22 Unusual Procedural Services
  - -26 Professional Component
  - -51 Multiple Procedures
  - -52 Reduced Services
  - -57 Decision for Surgery
  - -25 Significant, Separately Identifiable E/M Service
  - -58 Staged or Related Procedure
  - -62, -66, -80, -81, -82 More Than One Surgeon
  - -99 Multiple Modifiers
  - HCPCS Modifiers
- Comprehensive List of Modifier Codes

SELF-STUDY 5–1 ► REVIEW QUESTIONS

Review the objectives, key terms, and chapter information before completing the following review questions.

1. The coding system used for billing professional medical services and procedures is found in a book entitled ______________________

2. The Medicare program uses a system of coding composed of three levels, and this is called ______________________

3. Complications or special circumstances about a medical service or procedure may be shown by using a CPT code with a/an ______________________

4. A relative value scale or schedule is a listing of procedure codes indicating the relative value of services performed, which is shown by ______________________________

5. Name three methods for basing payments adopted by insurance companies and state and federal programs.

   a. ______________________________

   b. ______________________________

   c. ______________________________

6. List four programs or plans when a medical practice may elect to use more than one fee schedule.

   a. ______________________________

   b. ______________________________

   c. ______________________________

   d. ______________________________

7. Name the six main sections of *CPT*.

   a. ______________________________

   b. ______________________________

   c. ______________________________

   d. ______________________________

   e. ______________________________

   f. ______________________________

8. Match the symbol in the first column with the definitions in the second column. Write the correct letters on the blanks.

▶◀ ______ a. New code

● ______ b. Modifier −51 exempt

* ______ c. Add-on code

⃠ ______ d. New or revised text

+ ______ e. Revised code

▲ ______ f. Service includes surgical procedure only

9. Name four hospital departments where critical care of a patient may take place.

a. ______________________________

b. ______________________________

c. ______________________________

d. ______________________________

10. A surgical package includes

a. ______________________________

b. ______________________________

c. ______________________________

11. Medicare global surgery policy includes

a. ______________________________

b. ______________________________

c. ______________________________

d. ______________________________

12. A function of computer software that performs online checking of codes on an insurance claim to detect improper code submission is called a/an ______________________________

13. A single code that describes two or more component codes bundled together as one unit is known as a/an ______________________________

14. Codes grouped together that are related to a procedure are referred to as ______________________________

15. Use of many procedural codes to identify procedures that may be described by one code is termed ______________________________

16. A code used on a claim that does not match the code system used by the insurance carrier and is converted to the closest code rendering less payment is termed ______________________________

17. Intentional manipulation of procedural codes to generate increased reimbursement is called ______________________________

18. Give eight reasons for using modifiers on insurance claims.

    a. ______________________________

    b. ______________________________

    c. ______________________________

    d. ______________________________

    e. ______________________________

    f. ______________________________

    g. ______________________________

    h. ______________________________

19. Match the symbol in the first column with the definitions in the second column. Write the correct letters on the blanks.

-21	________	a. Unusual procedural services
-22	________	b. Multiple procedures
-25	________	c. Staged or related procedure
-26	________	d. Decision for surgery
-51	________	e. Significant, separately identifiable E/M service by the same physician on the same day of the procedure or other service
-52	________	f. Prolonged evaluation and management services
-57	________	g. Reduced services
-58	________	h. Professional component

20. What modifier is usually used when billing for an assistant surgeon? ______________________________

21. Explain when to use the -99 or 09999 modifier code. ______________________________

    ____

    ____

To check your answers to this self-study assignment, see Appendix D.

SELF-STUDY ASSIGNMENT 5–2 ▸ DEFINE MEDICAL ABBREVIATIONS

To reinforce abbreviations you have learned, let's review some of those encountered during the *Workbook* assignments presented in this chapter. You should be able to decode these abbreviations without a reference. However, if you have difficulty with one or two, simply refer to Appendix A of this *Workbook*.

I & D	____________	UA	____________
IM	____________	est pt	____________
Pap	____________	ASHD	____________
ER	____________	tet. tox.	____________
EEG	____________	CBC	____________
DPT	____________	E/M	____________
ECG	____________	*CPT*	____________
IUD	____________	Ob-Gyn	____________
OB	____________	TURP	____________
D & C	____________	cm	____________
OV	____________	T & A	____________
KUB	____________	mL	____________
GI	____________	inj	____________
Hgb	____________	hx	____________
new pt	____________	NC	____________
rt	____________		

To check your answers to this self-study assignment, see Appendix D.

ASSIGNMENT 5–3 ▸ INTRODUCTION TO *CPT* AND CODING EVALUATION AND MANAGEMENT SERVICES

Performance Objective

Task: Locate the correct information and/or procedure code for each question and/or case scenario.

Conditions: Use pen or pencil and the *Current Procedural Terminology* code book.

Standards: Time: _______________ minutes

Accuracy: ________________

(Note: The time element and accuracy criteria may be given by your instructor.)

1. To become acquainted with the sections of the *Current Procedure Terminology* code book, match the code number in the left column with the appropriate description in the right column by writing the letters in the blanks. Locate each code number in the *Current Procedural Terminology* code book. As you work though the assignment, the problems are easy at the beginning and get more difficult and complex as you progress.

   99231 _______ a. Chest x-ray

   59400 _______ b. Anesthesia for procedures on cervical spine and cord

   71010 _______ c. Subsequent hospital care

   00600 _______ d. Supplies and materials

   85031 _______ e. Routine OB care, ante- and postpartum

   99070 _______ f. CBC

2. Name the section of *CPT* where each of the following codes is located.

   a. 65091 ________________________________

   b. 86038 ________________________________

   c. 92596 ________________________________

   d. 75982 ________________________________

   e. 00600 ________________________________

   f. 99321 ________________________________

3. Evaluation and Management (E/M) codes are used by physicians to report a significant portion of their services. Remember, it is the physician's responsibility to assign E/M codes, and the exercises presented are only for familiarization. The problems will acquaint you with terminology for this section of the *CPT* code book. Select the appropriate **new patient** office visit codes using the key components:

   a. This is a Level 3 case: Detailed history ________________
      Detailed examination
      Low-complexity decision making

   b. This is a Level 1 case: Problem-focused history ________________
      Problem-focused examination
      Straightforward decision making

---

c. This is a Level 5 case: Comprehensive history ________________
Comprehensive examination
High-complexity decision making

4. Select the appropriate **established patient** office visit codes using the key components. Coding these cases illustrates consideration of two of three components.

a. This is a Level 4 case: Detailed history ________________
Detailed examination
Low-complexity decision making

b. This is a Level 5 case: Comprehensive history ________________
Comprehensive examination
Moderate-complexity decision making

c. This is a Level 5 case: Detailed history ________________
Comprehensive examination
High-complexity decision making

5. Evaluation and Management (E/M) codes **99201** to **99239** are used for services provided in the physician's office or in an outpatient or hospital facility. Read the brief statement and then locate the code number in the *Current Procedural Terminology* code book.

a. Office visit of a 20-year-old seen within the last 3 years for instruction in diabetes injection sites by RN (minimal problem). Patient not seen by physician at this brief visit. ________________

b. Office visit of a 30-year-old new patient with allergic rhinitis. This case had an expanded problem-focused hx & exam and straightforward decision making. ________________

c. Discussion of medication with the son of an 80-year-old patient with dementia on discharge from the *observation* unit. ________________

d. Admission to hospital of 60-year-old established patient in acute respiratory distress with bronchitis. Comprehensive hx & exam and medical decision making of moderate complexity. ________________

e. Hospital visit of a 4-year-old boy, now stable, who will be discharged the next day. This is a problem-focused interval hx & exam and medical decision making of low complexity. ________________

f. New patient seen in the office for chest pain, congestive heart failure, and hypertension. Comprehensive hx & exam and highly complex decision making. ________________

---

6. Evaluation and Management codes **99241** to **99275** are used for consultations provided in the physician's office or in an outpatient or inpatient hospital facility. A consultation is a service provided by a physician whose *opinion* about a case is requested by another physician. Read the brief statement and then locate the code number in the *Current Procedural Terminology* code book.

   a. Office consultation for a 30-year-old woman complaining of palpitations and chest pains. Her family physician described a mild systolic click. This is an expanded problem-focused hx & exam and straightforward decision making. ________________

   b. Follow-up inpatient consultation for a 64-year-old woman, who is now stable, admitted 2 days ago for a bleeding ulcer. This case is a problem-focused hx & exam and low-complexity decision making. ________________

   c. Office consultation for a 14-year-old boy with poor grades in school and suspected alcohol abuse. Comprehensive hx & exam and medical decision making of moderate complexity. ________________

   d. Follow-up inpatient consultation for a 70-year-old man who is diabetic and is suffering with fever, chills, gangrenous heel ulcer, rhonchi, and dyspnea (difficulty breathing), an unstable condition. The patient appears lethargic and tachypneic (rapid breathing). Took detailed hx & exam and made highly complex medical decision. ________________

   e. Initial emergency department consultation for a senior who presents with thyrotoxicosis, exophthalmos, cardiac arrhythmia, and congestive heart failure. Comprehensive hx & exam and highly complex medical decision making. ________________

   f. Initial hospital consultation for a 30-year-old woman, postabdominal surgery, who is exhibiting a fever. Took expanded problem-focused hx & exam and made straightforward medical decision. ________________

7. Evaluation and Management codes **99281** to **99499** are used for emergency department, critical care, nursing facility, rest home, custodial care, home, prolonged, physician standby, and preventive medicine services. Read the brief statement and then locate the code number in the *Current Procedural Terminology* code book.

   a. First hour of critical care of a senior who, following major surgery, suffers a cardiac arrest from a pulmonary embolus. ________________

   b. A 40-year-old woman is admitted to the OB unit, and the primary care physician has requested the neonatologist to *stand by* for possible cesarean section and neonatal resuscitation. Code for a 1-hour standby. ________________

c. A child is seen in the emergency department with a fever, diarrhea, abdominal cramps, and vomiting. This case had an expanded problem-focused hx & exam, and a moderately complex medical decision was made. ________________

d. A patient is seen for an annual visit at a nursing facility for detailed hx & comprehensive exam and straightforward medical decision making. ________________

e. Initial visit to a domiciliary care facility for a developmentally disabled individual with a mild rash on hands and face. This case had a problem-focused hx & exam and low-complexity medical decision making. ________________

f. A 50-year-old man with a history of asthma comes into the office with acute bronchospasm and moderate respiratory distress. Office treatment is initiated. The case requires intermittent physician face-to-face time with the patient for 2 hours, prolonged services. Assume the appropriate E & M code has been assigned for this case. ________________ ________________

ASSIGNMENT 5–4 ▶ CODE ANESTHESIA PROBLEMS

Performance Objective

Task: Locate the correct procedure code and modifier, if necessary, for each question and/or case scenario.

Conditions: Use pen or pencil and *Current Procedural Terminology* code book.

Standards: Time: ________________ minutes

Accuracy: ________________

(Note: The time element and accuracy criteria may be given by your instructor.)

Directions: Anesthesia codes **00100** to **01999** may be used by anesthesiologists as well as physicians. Some plastic surgeons, other medical specialists, and large clinics may have a room set aside to perform surgical procedures that might be performed in a hospital outpatient surgical department. For Medicare claims, some regions do not use the Anesthesia Section of *CPT* for billing but use a surgical code with a HCPCS modifier appended. Read the brief statement and then locate the code number in the *Current Procedural Terminology* code book. Special modifiers **P1** through **P6** may be needed when coding for this section, as well as code numbers for cases that have difficult circumstances. Definitions for abbreviations may be found in Appendix A.

A. Labor and cesarean section with epidural anesthesia, normal, healthy patient ________________

B. Reduction mammoplasty of a woman with mild systemic disease ________________

C. Total right hip replacement, 71-year-old patient, normal, healthy patient ________________

D. Repair of cleft palate, newborn infant, normal, healthy patient ________________

E. TURP, normal healthy male ________________

ASSIGNMENT 5–5 ▶ CODE SURGICAL PROBLEMS

Performance Objective

Task: Locate the correct procedure code and modifier, if necessary, for each question and/or case scenario.

Conditions: Use pen or pencil and *Current Procedural Terminology* code book.

Standards: Time: ________________ minutes

Accuracy: ________________

(Note: The time element and accuracy criteria may be given by your instructor.)

Directions: Surgery codes **10040** to **69979** are used for each anatomic part of the body. Read over each case carefully. It is preferable to use the *Current Procedural Terminology* code book, but if you do not have one then refer to the Mock Fee Schedule found in Appendix A of this *Workbook* to obtain the correct code number for each descriptor given. Full descriptors for services rendered have been omitted in some instances to give you practice in abstracting the correct descriptor from the available information. Indicate the correct two-digit modifier if necessary. The skill of critical thinking enters this section of the assignment, since you may have to use your own judgment to code as the cases do not contain full details, Definitions for abbreviations may be found in Appendix A. Remember to use the index at the back of the *CPT* code book.

a. Suppose you work in an office that has an encounter form listing either code 36240 or 36250. Check your edition of *CPT* and see whether you can locate either one or both of them. If the code(s) does(do) not appear, what code number are you directed to use? ________________

Integumentary System 10040–19499

b. Removal of benign lesion from the back (1.0 cm) and left foot (0.5 cm) ________________

____

c. Drainage of deep breast abscess ________________

d. Laser destruction of two benign facial lesions ________________

____

Musculoskeletal System 20000–29909

e. Aspiration of fluid (arthrocentesis) from right knee joint; not infectious ________

f. Deep tissue biopsy of left upper arm ________

g. Fracture of the left tibia, closed treatment ________

Does the procedural code include the application and removal of the first cast?

________ If done as an office procedure, may supplies be coded?

____

If so, what is the code number from the Medicine section? ________
Does the procedural code include subsequent replacement of a cast for follow-up care? ________

If not, list the code number for application of a walking short

leg cast ________

Respiratory System 30000–32999

h. Parietal pleurectomy ________

i. Removal of two nasal polyps, simple ________

j. Diagnostic bronchoscopy with biopsy ________

Cardiovascular System 33010–37799

k. Pacemaker insertion with transvenous electrode, atrial ________

l. Thromboendarterectomy with patch graft ________

m. Introduction of intracatheter and injection procedure for contrast venography ________

Hemic/Lymphatic/Diaphragm 38100–39599

n. Repair, esophageal/diaphragmatic hernia ________

o. Partial splenectomy ________

p. Excision, two deep cervical nodes ________

Digestive System 40490–49999

q. T & A, 12-year-old boy ________

r. Balloon dilation of esophagus ________

Urinary System/Male and Female Genital 50010–55980

s. Removal of urethral diverticulum from female patient ________

t. Anastomosis of single ureter to bladder ________

Laparoscopy/Peritoneoscopy/Hysteroscopy/Female Genital/Maternity 56300–59899

u. Routine OB care, ante- and postpartum care ________________

v. Therapeutic D & C, nonobstetric ________________

ASSIGNMENT 5–6 ▶ CODE PROBLEMS FOR RADIOLOGY AND PATHOLOGY

Performance Objective

Task: Locate the correct procedure code and modifier, if necessary, for each question and/or case scenario.

Conditions: Use pen or pencil and *Current Procedural Terminology* code book.

Standards: Time: ________________ minutes

Accuracy: ________________

(Note: The time element and accuracy criteria may be given by your instructor.)

Radiologists as well as other physicians in many specialties perform these studies. A physician who interprets, dictates, and signs a report may not bill for the report separately as it is considered part of the radiology procedure.

Some medical practices perform basic laboratory tests under a waived test certificate that complies with the rules of the Clinical Laboratory Improvement Amendments (CLIA) of 1988, implemented in September, 1992.

a. Upper GI x-ray study with films and KUB ________________

b. Ultrasound, pregnant uterus after first trimester, multiple gestation ________________

c. Routine urinalysis with microscopy, nonautomated ________________

d. Hemoglobin (Hgb), electrophoretic method ________________

ASSIGNMENT 5–7 ▶ PROCEDURE CODE AND MODIFIER PROBLEMS

Performance Objective

Task: Locate the correct procedure codes and modifiers, if necessary, for each case scenario.

Conditions: Use pen or pencil and *Current Procedural Terminology* code book.

Standards: Time: ________________ minutes

Accuracy: ________________

(Note: The time element and accuracy criteria may be given by your instructor.)

Directions: Find the correct procedure codes and modifiers, if necessary. This assignment will reinforce what you have already learned about procedural coding, since code numbers for the case scenarios presented are located in all the sections of the *CPT* code book. Also search for codes in the Medicine Section, if necessary. The *CPT* list of modifiers may be found in the *Handbook*.

1. A new patient had five benign skin lesions on the right arm destroyed with surgical curettement. Complete the coding for the surgery.

Code Number *Description*

a. ________________ Initial new pt office visit

b. ________________ Destruction of benign skin lesion rt arm

c. ________________ Destruction of second, third, fourth, and fifth lesions

2. Mrs. Stayman had four moles on her back. Dr. Davis excised the multiple nevi in one office visit. The information on the pathology report stated nonmalignant lesions measuring 2.2 cm, 1.5 cm, 1 cm, and 0.75 cm.

Code Number *Description*

a. ________________ _____ Initial OV

b. ________________ Excision, benign lesion 2.2 cm

c. ________________ _____ Excision, benign lesion 1.5 cm

d. ________________ _____ Excision, benign lesion 1 cm

e. ________________ _____ Excision, benign lesion 0.75 cm

In another case, if a patient required removal of a 1.0-cm lesion on the back and a 0.5-cm lesion on the neck, the procedural codes would be ________________ for the back lesion and ________________ for the neck lesion.

3. Dr. Davis stated on his operative report that Mr. Allen was suffering from a complex, complicated nasal fracture. Dr. Davis debrided the wound, since it was contaminated, and performed an open reduction with internal fixation in a complex and complicated procedure.

Code Number *Description*

_______ ____________ Initial OV, complex hx & exam, moderate-complexity decision making

_______ Open tx nasal fracture complicated

_______ ____________ Debridement, skin, subcutaneous tissue, muscle, and bone

4. An RN, an established patient (est pt), age 40 years, sees the doctor for an annual physical. A Pap (Papanicolaou) smear is taken and sent to an outside laboratory. The patient also has a furuncle on the right axilla at the time of the visit, which the doctor incises and drains (I & D).

Code Number	*Description*
________________	Periodic physical examination
________________	Handling of specimen
________________	I & D, furuncle, right axilla
________________	5-mL penicillin inj IM

5. While making his rounds in the hospital during the noon hour, Dr. James sees a new patient in the ED (emergency department) for a laceration of the forehead, 5.0 cm long. The doctor does a work-up for a possible concussion.

Code Number	*Description*
________________	ED care, expanded problem-focused history, expanded problem-focused examination, low-complexity decision making
________________	Repair of laceration, simple, face

6. The doctor sees a new patient in the office with the same condition as the patient in Problem 5; however, an infection has developed and the patient is seen for daily dressing changes. On day 11, the sutures are removed, and on day 12 a final dressing change is made, and the patient is discharged.

Code Number	*Description*
________________	Initial new patient office visit
________________	Repair of laceration
________________	Tet tox (tetanus toxoid) 0.5 cc
________________	Minimal service, OV, dressing change (2 days)
________________	OV, suture removal (4 days)

Note: Some fee schedules allow no follow-up days; Medicare fee schedule allows 10 follow-up days for the procedural code number for repair of laceration.

7. The doctor is seeing 13-year-old Bobby Jones (est pt) for a Scout physical. Bobby is in good health and well groomed. His troop is going for a 1-week camping trip in 12 days. Doctor reviewed safety issues with him and talked to him about school and not getting into drugs or alcohol. He denied any problems with that or being sexually active. He said he plays baseball. He has no allergies. A detailed examination was performed. Doctor completed information for Scouting papers and cleared him for camping activity.

Code Number *Description*

________________ ____________ Periodic preventive evaluation and management

8. A new patient, David Ramsey, age 15 years, was seen by Dr. Menter for lapses of memory and frequent headaches. The doctor performed an EEG (electroencephalogram) and some psychologic tests (including psychodiagnostic assessment of personality and psychopathology tests [Rorschach and MMPI]). Dr. Astro Parkinson was called in as a consultant. All the tests were negative, and the patient was advised to come in for weekly psychotherapy.

Code Number *Description*

Dr. Menter's bill:

________________ OV, comp hx & exam, moderate-complexity decision making

________________ EEG, extended monitoring (1 hr)

________________ Psychologic tests (Rorschach and MMPI)

________________ Psychotherapy (50 min)

Dr. Parkinson's bill:

________________ Consultation, expanded problem-focused hx and exam, straightforward decision making

9. An est pt, age 70 years, requires repair of a bilateral initial inguinal hernia. The

   code for this initial procedure is ______________ _________

ASSIGNMENT 5–8 ▶ HCPCS/MODIFIER CODE MATCH

Performance Objective

Task: Locate the correct HCPCS code and modifier, if necessary, for each medical drug, supply item, or service presented.

Conditions: Use pen or pencil and HCPCS code reference list in Appendix B of this workbook.

Standards: Time: ________________ minutes

Accuracy: ________________

(Note: The time element and accuracy criteria may be given by your instructor.)

Directions: Match the HCPCS code in the first or second column with the description of the drug, supply item, or service presented in the third or fourth column. Write the correct letters on the blanks.

E1069	______	J0760	______	a. Vitamin B_{12}, to 1000 μg	k. Gamma globulin, 1 mL-inj

Current Procedural Terminology codes, descriptions, and two-digit numeric modifiers only are from *CPT 2001*, copyright 2000, American Medical Association. All rights reserved.

E0141	_______	A9150	_______	b. Recombinant DNA insulin	l. Wheelchair batteries
J0290	_______	J2000	_______	c. Rigid walker, wheeled, without seat	m. Ampicillin inj, up to 500 mg
J3420	_______	L0160	_______	d. Waiver of liability statement on file	n. Dimethyl sulfoxide, DMSO inj
J1820	_______	L3100-RT	_______	e. Nonemergency transportation, taxi	o. Urine strips
P9014	_______	A4253	_______	f. Inj of colchicine	p. Vancomycin (Vancocin) inj
J1212	_______	J2590	_______	g. Cervical occipital/ mandibular support	q. Oxytocin (Pitocin) inj
J3370	_______	A4900	_______	h. Inj of lidocaine (Xylocaine)	r. Standard youth wheelchair, new equipment
E1091-NU	_______	A0100	_______	i. CAPD supply kit	s. Rt hallux valgus night splint
A2000	_______	-GA	_______	j. Manipulation of spine by chiropractor	t. Aspirin, nonprescription drug

ASSIGNMENT 5–9 ► PROCEDURAL CODING CASE SCENARIOS

Performance Objective

Task: Locate the correct procedure code and modifier, if necessary, for each case scenario.

Conditions: Use pen or pencil and *Current Procedural Terminology* code book.

Standards: Time: ________________ minutes

Accuracy: ________________

(Note: The time element and accuracy criteria may be given by your instructor.)

Directions: Find the correct procedure codes and modifiers, if necessary, for each case secnario.

1. The doctor sees Horace Hart, a 60-year-old new patient, in the office for bronchial asthma, ASHD (arteriosclerotic heart disease), and hypertension. He performs an ECG (electrocardiogram) and UA (urinalysis) without microscopy, and takes x-rays. Comprehensive metabolic and lipid panels and a CBC (complete blood count) are done by an outside laboratory.

Code Number	*Description*
Physician's bill:	
________________	Initial OV, comp hx & exam, high-complexity decision making
________________	ECG with interpret and report
________________	UA, routine, nonautomated
________________	Chest x-ray, 2 views
________________	Routine venipuncture for handling of specimen
Laboratory's bill:	
________________	Comprehensive metabolic panel: albumin, bilirubin, calcium, carbon dioxide, chloride, creatinine, glucose, phosphatase (alkaline), potassium, protein, sodium, ALT, AST, and urea nitrogen
________________	Lipid panel
________________	CBC, completely automated with complete differential

If the doctor decides to have the chest x-rays interpreted by a radiologist, the procedural code billed by the radiologist would be ____________ ______.

2. Mr. Hart is seen again in the office on May 12. On May 25 he is seen at home at 2 AM with asthma exacerbation, possible myocardial infarct, and congestive heart failure. The doctor consulted with a thoracic cardiovascular surgeon by telephone. He also called to make arrangements for hospitalization. These services required 2 hours and 40 minutes to complete the patient care.

Code Number	*Description*
_________	OV, problem-focused hx & exam, straightforward decision making
_________	Home visit, detailed interval hx & exam, high-complexity decision making
_________	Detention time, prolonged (list time required)
_________	

3. On June 9, Horace Hart is seen again in the hospital. The thoracic cardiovascular surgeon who was called in for consultation examines him and says that surgery is necessary, which is scheduled that afternoon. The patient's doctor acts as assistant surgeon and visits the patient for his asthmatic condition. The surgeon does the follow-up care and assumes care in the case.

Code Number	*Description*
Assistant surgeon's bill:	
________________	Hospital visit, problem-focused hx & exam, low-complexity decision making
________________ _______	Pericardiotomy
Thoracic cardiovascular surgeon's bill:	
________________ _______	Consultation, comp hx & exam, moderate-complexity decision making
________________	Pericardiotomy

ASSIGNMENT 5–10 ▶ CASE SCENARIO FOR CRITICAL THINKING

Performance Objective

Task: Locate the correct procedure codes and modifiers, if necessary, for a case scenario.

Conditions: Use pen or pencil and *Current Procedural terminology* code book.

Standards: Time: ________________ minutes

Accuracy: ________________

(Note: The time element and accuracy criteria may be given by your instructor.)

Directions: Read through this progress note on Roy A. Takashima. Abstract information from the note about the subjective symptoms, objective findings, and diagnoses. List the diagnostic and procedure codes you think this case would warrant.

Takashima, Roy A.
October 5, 20XX

Pt. has many things going on. First, he's had no difficulties following the feral cat bite, and the cat was normal on quarantine.

He seemed to be recovering from the flu but is plagued with a very persisting cough and pain down the center of his chest without fever or grossly discolored phlegm.

Physical exam shows expiratory rhonchi and gross exacerbation of his cough on forced expiration. Spirometry before and after bronchodilator was remarkably good; nonetheless, it is improved and he is symptomatically improved with a Proventil inhaler, which he is given as a sample. I don't think other antibiotics would help.

His reflux is under good control with proprietary antacids with a clear exam.

He has several areas of seborrheic keratoses on his face and head that need attention.

Finally, in follow-up of all the above, he needs a complete physical exam.

Diagnosis: Influenza and acute bronchitis.

mtf Ting Cho, MD

Subjective symptoms ______________________________

____

Objective findings ______________________________

______________________________ __________

______________________________ __________

Diagnosis and Dx code ______________________________ __________

______________________________ __________

______________________________ __________

______________________________ __________

E/M code ____________________

Spirometry code ____________________

6

The Health Insurance Claim Form

KEY TERMS

Your instructor may wish to select some specific words pertinent to this chapter for a test. For definitions of the terms, further study, and/or reference, words, phrases, and abbreviations may be found in the Glossary at the end of the Handbook. *Key terms for this chapter follow.*

clean claim
digital fax claim
dingy claim
dirty claim
durable medical equipment (DME) number
electronic claim
employer identification number (EIN)
facility provider number
group provider number
Health Insurance Claim Form (HCFA-1500)
incomplete claim
intelligent character recognition (ICR)
invalid claim
national provider identifier (NPI)
optical character recognition (OCR)
"other" claims
paper claim
pending claim
physically clean claim
provider identification number (PIN)
rejected claim
Social Security number (SSN)
state license number
unique provider identification number (UPIN)

PERFORMANCE OBJECTIVES

The student will be able to

- Define and spell the key terms for this chapter, given the information from the *Handbook* Glossary, within a reasonable period of time and with enough accuracy to obtain a satisfactory evaluation.
- Answer the self-study review questions after reading the chapter, with enough accuracy to obtain a satisfactory evaluation.
- Type a HCFA-1500 Health Insurance Claim Form and list the reasons why the claim was either rejected or delayed, given a handwritten HCFA-1500 form, within a reasonable period of time and with enough accuracy to obtain a satisfactory evaluation.
- Complete each HCFA-1500 Health Insurance Claim Form for billing, given the patients' medical chart notes, ledger cards, encounter forms, and blank insurance claim forms, within a reasonable period of time and with enough accuracy to obtain a satisfactory evaluation.
- Correctly post payments, adjustments, and balances to the patients' ledger cards, using the Mock Fee Schedule in Appendix A, within a

reasonable period of time and with enough accuracy to obtain a satisfactory evaluation.

- Fill in the correct meaning of each abbreviation, given a list of common medical abbreviations and symbols that appear in chart notes, within a reasonable period of time and with enough accuracy to obtain a satisfactory evaluation.

STUDY OUTLINE

History
- Types of Claims
- Claim Status
  - Medicare Claim Status

Abstracting from Medical Records
- Cover Letter Accompanying Insurance Claims
- Life or Health Insurance Applications

Health Insurance Claim Form (HCFA-1500)
- Basic Guidelines for Submitting a Claim
  - Individual Insurance
  - Group Insurance
  - Secondary Insurance
- Completion of Insurance Claim Forms
  - Diagnosis
  - Service Dates
  - Consecutive Dates
  - No Charge
  - Physicians' Identification Numbers
  - Physician's Signature
  - Insurance Biller's Initials
  - Proofread
  - Supporting Documentation
  - Office Pending File

Common Reasons Why Claim Forms Are Delayed or Rejected
- Additional Reasons Why Claim Forms Are Delayed

Optical Scanning Format Guidelines
- Optical Character Recognition
- Do's and Don'ts for Optical Character Recognition

Instructions for the Health Insurance Claim Form (HCFA-1500)
- Insurance Program Templates

SELF-STUDY 6–1 ▶ REVIEW QUESTIONS

Review the objectives, key terms, chapter information, glossary definitions to key terms, and figures before completing the following review questions.

1. Who developed the Standard Form? The Health Insurance association of America and the American medical association

2. State the name of the insurance form approved by the American Medical Association. Health Insurance Claim Form (HCFA 1500)

3. Does Medicare accept the HCFA-1500 claim form? yes

4. What important document must you have before an insurance company can photocopy a patient's chart? Release of Information form signed by patient

5. What is dual coverage? when the patient has two insurance policies and one is considered primary and the other secondary

6. The insurance company with the first responsibility for payment of a bill for medical services is known as primary payer

7. Match the word from the left column with its definition from the right column. Write the correct letters in the blanks.

clean claim	g	a. Insurance carrier is unable to process a claim for a certain service, and claim is held until system changes are made.
paper claim	c	b. A phrase used when a claim is held back from payment.
invalid claim	h	c. Claim submitted and then optically scanned by the insurance carrier and converted to electronic form.
dirty claim	d	d. Claim that needs manual processing because of errors or to solve a problem.
electronic claim	F	e. Claim needing clarification and answers to questions.
suspense claim	b	f. Claim submitted via telephone, fax, or computer modem.
rejected claim	e	g. Claim submitted within the time limit and correctly completed.
dingy claim	a	h. Medicare claim that contains complete, necessary information but is illogical or incorrect.

8. If the patient brings in a private insurance form that is not group insurance, where do you send the form after completion? It must be sent to that particular insurance company

9. Match the phrase in the first column with the definitions in the second column. Write the correct letters on the blanks.

State license number	F	a. A number issued by the federal government to each individual for personal use.
Employer identification number	I	b. A number issued by the Medicare program to each member of a group at each specific site of medical practice.
Social Security number	A	c. A Medicare lifetime provider number.
Provider identification number	J	d. A number listed on a claim when submitting insurance claims to insurance companies under a group name.
Unique provider identification number	E	e. A number issued by the Medicare program to each physician who treats and submits claims to this program.
Performing provider identification number	B	f. A number a physician must obtain to practice in a state.
Group provider number	D	g. A number used when billing for supplies and equipment.

National Provider Identifier	C	h. A number issued to a hospital.
Durable Medical Equipment number	G	i. An individual physician's federal tax identification number issued by the Internal Revenue Service.
Facility provider number	H	j. A number issued by the insurance carrier to every physician who renders services to patients.

10. An insurance claim is returned for the reason "diagnosis incomplete." State solution(s) to this problem on how you would try to obtain reimbursement.

Verify and submit correct diagnostic codes by referring to an updated code book and reviewing the patient record. Check with the physician if the dx code listed does not go with the procedure code shown

11. Indicate whether the following statements are True (T) or False (F).

a. A photocopy of a claim form may be optically scanned. F

b. Handwriting is permitted on optically scanned insurance claims. F

c. Do not fold or crease an insurance form that will be optically scanned. T

d. Never strike over errors when making a correction on a claim form that is to be optically scanned. T

12. When preparing a claim that is to be optically scanned, birth dates are keyed in using 8 digits

13. Define this abbreviation. MG/MCD Medigap and Medicaid coverage

14. A HCFA-assigned National Provider Identifier (NPI) Number consists of 10 characters.

To check your answers to this self-study assignment, see Appendix D.

ASSIGNMENT 6–2 ► LOCATE ERRORS ON A COMPLETED HEALTH INSURANCE CLAIM FORM

Performance Objective

Task: Complete a health insurance claim form and post the information to the patient's ledger card.

Conditions: Use Tom N. Parkinson's completed insurance claim (Figure 6–1), one health insurance claim form (Figure 6–2), typewriter and/or computer, or pen.

PLEASE DO NOT STAPLE IN THIS AREA

APPROVED OMB 0936-006

ABC INSURANCE COMPANY
111 MAIN STREET
DENVER CO 80210

CARRIER

HEALTH INSURANCE CLAIM FORM

PICA

1. MEDICARE (Medicare #) / MEDICAID (Medicaid #) / CHAMPUS (Sponsor's SSN) / CHAMPVA (VA File #) / GROUP HEALTH PLAN (SSN or ID) [X] / FECA BLK LUNG (SSN) / OTHER (ID)

1a. INSURED'S I.D. NUMBER (FOR PROGRAM IN ITEM 1): PX4278A

2. PATIENT'S NAME (Last Name, First Name, Middle Initial): PARKINSON TOM N

3. PATIENT'S BIRTH DATE MM DD YYYY: 04 06 1993 SEX M [X] F [ ]

4. INSURED'S NAME (Last Name, First Name, Middle Initial): PARKINSON, JAMIE B

5. PATIENT'S ADDRESS (No., Street): 4510 SOUTH A STREET

6. PATIENT RELATIONSHIP TO INSURED: Self [ ] Spouse [ ] Child [X] Other [ ]

7. INSURED'S ADDRESS (No., Street): 4510 SOUTH A STREET

CITY: WOODLAND HILLS STATE: XY

8. PATIENT STATUS: Single [X] Married [ ] Other [ ]; Employed [ ] Full-Time Student [X] Part-Time Student [ ]

CITY: WOODLAND HILLS STATE: XY

ZIP CODE: 12345 TELEPHONE (Include Area Code): (013) 742-1560

ZIP CODE: 12345 TELEPHONE (Include Area Code): (013) 742 1560

9. OTHER INSURED'S NAME (Last Name, First Name, Middle Initial)

a. OTHER INSURED'S POLICY OR GROUP NUMBER

b. OTHER INSURED'S DATE OF BIRTH MM DD YY SEX M [ ] F [ ]

c. EMPLOYER'S NAME OR SCHOOL NAME

d. INSURANCE PLAN NAME OR PROGRAM NAME

10. IS PATIENT'S CONDITION RELATED TO:

a. EMPLOYMENT? (CURRENT OR PREVIOUS) YES [ ] NO [X]

b. AUTO ACCIDENT? YES [ ] NO [X] PLACE (State)

c. OTHER ACCIDENT? YES [ ] NO [X]

10d. RESERVED FOR LOCAL USE

11. INSURED'S POLICY GROUP OR FECA NUMBER

a. INSURED'S DATE OF BIRTH MM DD YY SEX M [ ] F [ ]

b. EMPLOYER'S NAME OR SCHOOL NAME

c. INSURANCE PLAN NAME OR PROGRAM NAME

d. IS THERE ANOTHER HEALTH BENEFIT PLAN? YES [ ] NO [X] *If yes, return to and complete item 9 a-d.*

READ BACK OF FORM BEFORE COMPLETING AND SIGNING THIS FORM.

12. PATIENT'S OR AUTHORIZED PERSON'S SIGNATURE I authorize the release of any medical or other information necessary to process this claim. I also request payment of government benefits either to myself or to the party who accepts assignment below.

SIGNED ______ DATE ______

13. INSURED'S OR AUTHORIZED PERSON'S SIGNATURE I authorize payment of medical benefits to the undersigned physician or supplier for services described below.

SIGNED ______

PATIENT AND INSURED INFORMATION

14. DATE OF CURRENT: MM DD YY ◄ ILLNESS (First symptom) OR INJURY (Accident) OR PREGNANCY (LMP)

15. IF PATIENT HAS HAD SAME OR SIMILAR ILLNESS, GIVE FIRST DATE MM DD YY

16. DATES PATIENT UNABLE TO WORK IN CURRENT OCCUPATION FROM MM DD YY TO MM DD YY

17. NAME OF REFERRING PHYSICIAN OR OTHER SOURCE

17a. I.D. NUMBER OF REFERRING PHYSICIAN

18. HOSPITALIZATION DATES RELATED TO CURRENT SERVICES FROM MM DD YY TO MM DD YY

19. RESERVED FOR LOCAL USE

20. OUTSIDE LAB? YES [ ] NO [X] $ CHARGES

21. DIAGNOSIS OR NATURE OF ILLNESS OR INJURY. (RELATE ITEMS 1,2,3 OR 4 TO ITEM 24E BY LINE)

1. ______ 3. ______

2. ______ 4. ______

22. MEDICAID RESUBMISSION CODE ORIGINAL REF. NO.

23. PRIOR AUTHORIZATION NUMBER

24. A DATE(S) OF SERVICE From MM DD YY	To MM DD YY	B Place of Service	C Type of Service	D PROCEDURES, SERVICES, OR SUPPLIES (Explain Unusual Circumstances) CPT/HCPCS MODIFIER	E DIAGNOSIS CODE	F $ CHARGES	G DAYS OR UNITS	H EPSDT Family Plan	I EMG	J COB	K RESERVED FOR LOCAL USE
07 14 20XX				99242		80 24	1				
07 14 20XX				71020	1	38 96	1			46	27889700

25. FEDERAL TAX I.D. NUMBER: 70 3459766 SSN [ ] EIN [ ]

26. PATIENT'S ACCOUNT NO.

27. ACCEPT ASSIGNMENT? (For govt. claims, see back) YES [X] NO [ ]

28. TOTAL CHARGE: $ 119 20

29. AMOUNT PAID: $

30. BALANCE DUE: $

31. SIGNATURE OF PHYSICIAN OR SUPPLIER INCLUDING DEGREES OR CREDENTIALS (I certify that the statements on the reverse apply to this bill and are made a part thereof.)

GERALD PRACTON MD

SIGNED 07 14 20XX DATE

32. NAME AND ADDRESS OF FACILITY WHERE SERVICES WERE RENDERED (If other than home or office): SAME

33. PHYSICIAN'S, SUPPLIER'S BILLING NAME, ADDRESS, ZIP CODE AND PHONE #

COLLEGE CLINIC 013 486 9002
4567 BROAD AVENUE
WOODLAND HILLS XY 12345

PIN# GRP# 3664021CC

PHYSICIAN OR SUPPLIER INFORMATION

(APPROVED BY AMA COUNCIL ON MEDICAL SERVICE 8/88) *PLEASE PRINT OR TYPE* FORM HCFA (12 90) FORM OCWP 1500 FORM RRB 1500

REORDER FROM STANDARD REGISTERFORM NO HC0901B-2

Figure 6–1

APPROVED OMB 0938-0008

PLEASE DO NOT STAPLE IN THIS AREA

ABC Insurance Company
111 Main Street
Denver CO 80210

CARRIER

HEALTH INSURANCE CLAIM FORM

PICA

1. MEDICARE (Medicare #) | MEDICAID (Medicaid #) | CHAMPUS (Sponsor's SSN) | CHAMPVA (VA File #) | GROUP HEALTH PLAN (SSN or ID) [X] | FECA BLK LUNG (SSN) | OTHER (ID)

1a. INSURED'S I.D. NUMBER (FOR PROGRAM IN ITEM 1): Px 4278A

2. PATIENT'S NAME (Last Name, First Name, Middle Initial): Parkinson Tom N

3. PATIENT'S BIRTH DATE MM DD YYYY: 04 06 1993 SEX M [X] F

4. INSURED'S NAME (Last Name, First Name, Middle Initial): Parkinson Jamie B

5. PATIENT'S ADDRESS (No., Street): 4510 South A Street

6. PATIENT RELATIONSHIP TO INSURED: Self Spouse Child [X] Other

7. INSURED'S ADDRESS (No., Street): Same

CITY: Woodland Hills STATE: XY

8. PATIENT STATUS: Single [X] Married Other; Employed Full-Time Student [X] Part-Time Student

CITY STATE

ZIP CODE: 12345 TELEPHONE (Include Area Code): (013) 742-1560

ZIP CODE TELEPHONE (Include Area Code) ( )

9. OTHER INSURED'S NAME (Last Name, First Name, Middle Initial)

10. IS PATIENT'S CONDITION RELATED TO:

11. INSURED'S POLICY GROUP OR FECA NUMBER

a. OTHER INSURED'S POLICY OR GROUP NUMBER

a. EMPLOYMENT? (CURRENT OR PREVIOUS) YES NO [X]

a. INSURED'S DATE OF BIRTH MM DD YY: Need SEX M F Need

b. OTHER INSURED'S DATE OF BIRTH MM DD YY SEX M F

b. AUTO ACCIDENT? YES NO [X] PLACE (State)

b. EMPLOYER'S NAME OR SCHOOL NAME: Need

c. EMPLOYER'S NAME OR SCHOOL NAME

c. OTHER ACCIDENT? YES NO [X]

c. INSURANCE PLAN NAME OR PROGRAM NAME

d. INSURANCE PLAN NAME OR PROGRAM NAME

10d. RESERVED FOR LOCAL USE

d. IS THERE ANOTHER HEALTH BENEFIT PLAN? YES NO [X] *If yes, return to and complete item 9 a-d.*

READ BACK OF FORM BEFORE COMPLETING AND SIGNING THIS FORM

12. PATIENT'S OR AUTHORIZED PERSON'S SIGNATURE I authorize the release of any medical or other information necessary to process this claim. I also request payment of government benefits either to myself or to the party who accepts assignment below.

SIGNED Sig on File DATE

13. INSURED'S OR AUTHORIZED PERSON'S SIGNATURE I authorize payment of medical benefits to the undersigned physician or supplier for services described below.

SIGNED

PATIENT AND INSURED INFORMATION

14. DATE OF CURRENT: MM DD YY ILLNESS (First symptom) OR INJURY (Accident) OR PREGNANCY (LMP)

15. IF PATIENT HAS HAD SAME OR SIMILAR ILLNESS GIVE FIRST DATE MM DD YY

16. DATES PATIENT UNABLE TO WORK IN CURRENT OCCUPATION FROM MM DD YY TO MM DD YY

17. NAME OF REFERRING PHYSICIAN OR OTHER SOURCE

17a. I.D. NUMBER OF REFERRING PHYSICIAN

18. HOSPITALIZATION DATES RELATED TO CURRENT SERVICES FROM MM DD YY TO MM DD YY

19. RESERVED FOR LOCAL USE

20. OUTSIDE LAB? YES NO [X] $ CHARGES

21. DIAGNOSIS OR NATURE OF ILLNESS OR INJURY (RELATE ITEMS 1,2,3 OR 4 TO ITEM 24E BY LINE)

1. ← Need
2.
3.
4.

22. MEDICAID RESUBMISSION CODE ORIGINAL REF. NO.

23. PRIOR AUTHORIZATION NUMBER

24. A DATE(S) OF SERVICE From MM DD YY	To MM DD YY	B Place of Service	C Type of Service	D PROCEDURES, SERVICES, OR SUPPLIES (Explain Unusual Circumstances) CPT/HCPCS	MODIFIER	E DIAGNOSIS CODE	F $ CHARGES	G DAYS OR UNITS	H EPSDT Family Plan	I EMG	J COB	K RESERVED FOR LOCAL USE
07 14 20XX				99242		1	80 24	1			46	27889700
07 14 20XX				71020		1	38 96	1			46	27889700

PHYSICIAN OR SUPPLIER INFORMATION

25. FEDERAL TAX I.D. NUMBER SSN EIN: 70 3459766

26. PATIENT'S ACCOUNT NO.: Need

27. ACCEPT ASSIGNMENT? (For govt. claims, see back) YES [X] NO

28. TOTAL CHARGE $ 119 20

29. AMOUNT PAID $

30. BALANCE DUE $

31. SIGNATURE OF PHYSICIAN OR SUPPLIER INCLUDING DEGREES OR CREDENTIALS (I certify that the statements on the reverse apply to this bill and are made a part thereof.)

Gerald Practon MD 07 14 20XX

SIGNED Need DATE

32. NAME AND ADDRESS OF FACILITY WHERE SERVICES WERE RENDERED (If other than home or office): Same

33. PHYSICIAN'S, SUPPLIER'S BILLING NAME, ADDRESS, ZIP CODE AND PHONE #

College Clinic 0134864002
4567 Broad Avenue
Woodland Hills XY 12345

PIN# GRP# 3664021CC

(APPROVED BY AMA COUNCIL ON MEDICAL SERVICE 8/88) PLEASE PRINT OR TYPE FORM HCFA-1500 (12-90) FORM OCWP-1500 FORM RRB-1500

REORDER FROM STANDARD REGISTER FORM NO HC0901B-2

Figure 6–2

Standards: Time: ________________ minutes

Accuracy: ________________

(Note: The time element and accuracy criteria may be given by your instructor.)

Guidance: To alleviate frustration and ease the process of completing a claim form for the first time, you will be editing a claim and then taking the correct information and inserting it on a blank HCFA-1500 form (Figure 6–2). Refer to Chapter 6 of the *Handbook* for block-by-block private payer instructions for completing the HCFA-1500 insurance claim form. Refer to *Handbook* Figure 6–6 for visual placement of data. Refer to *Workbook* Appendix A for the physician/clinic information and the clinic's mock fee schedule. The billing physician is Gerald Practon. The name of the insurance carrier is ABC Insurance Company at 111 Main Street in Denver, Colorado 80210.

Directions: Study the completed claim form (Figure 6–1) and search for missing or incorrect information. If possible, verify all information. Highlight or circle in red all incorrect or missing information. Insert the correct information on the claim form. Now transfer all the data to a blank HCFA-1500 claim form (Figure 6–2). If mandatory information is missing, insert the word "NEED" in the corresponding block of the claim form.

A Performance Evaluation Checklist may be reproduced from the Instruction Guide to the *Workbook* chapter if your instructor wishes you to submit it to assist with scoring and comments.

Optional: List, in block-by-block order, the reasons why the claim may be either rejected or delayed according to the errors found.

ASSIGNMENT 6–3 ▶ COMPLETE A HEALTH INSURANCE CLAIM FORM

Performance Objective

Task: Complete a health insurance claim form and post the information to the patient's ledger card.

Conditions: Use Merry M. Mclean's E/M code slip (Figure 6–3), patient record (Figure 6–4) and ledger card (Figure 6–5); one health insurance claim form (Figure 6–6); typewriter, computer, or pen; procedural and diagnostic code books; and *Workbook* Appendices A and B.

Standards: Claim Productivity Measurement

Time: ________________ minutes

Accuracy: ________________

(Note: The time element and accuracy criteria may be given by your instructor.)

Directions:

1. Assume the *Health Insurance Claim Form** HCFA-1500 claim form is printed in red ink for processing by OCR or ICR. Complete the form using OCR or ICR guidelines and send the form to the Prudential Insurance Company for Mrs. Merry M. Mclean by referring to her E/M Code Slip, patient record, and ledger card. Date the claim June 15. Refer to Appendix A to fill in the fees on the ledger card. Many physicians complete an E/M Code Slip for each patient encounter. This chapter's assignments feature examples of this form as a

*See Chapter six for help in completing this form.

reference for part of each exercise to give you experience and to assist you with E/M *CPT* code selection. Be sure to type your initials at the lower left corner of the claim form.

2. Use your *Current Procedural Terminology (CPT)* code book or Appendix A to determine the correct five-digit code number for each professional service rendered. Remember to include modifiers if necessary. Check the Mock Fee Schedule in Appendix A to see how many follow-up days are included for the surgical fee that would be listed as in-office documentation and would not receive a charge. Refer to the *Handbook* for detailed discussion about follow-up days. Do not type *no charge* entries on the insurance claim, which may appear on the ledger card for documentation purposes.
3. Record on the ledger card when you have billed the insurance company.
4. A Performance Evaluation Checklist may be reproduced from the Instruction Guide to the *Workbook* chapter if your instructor wishes you to submit it to assist with scoring and comments.
5. After the instructor has returned your work to you, either make the necessary corrections and place in a 3-ring notebook for future reference, or, if you received a high score, place it in your portfolio for reference when applying for a job.

Abbreviations pertinent to this record:

adm admission

c̄ with

CC Chief Complaint

Cont Continue

Cysto cystoscopy

Disch Discharge

Dx Diagnosis

hosp hospital

HV Hospital Visit

init initial

intermed Intermediate (office visit)

IVP Intravenous Pyelogram

mo month

NC no charge

OC office call

Op operation

PC present complaint

E/M Code Slip

Patient *Mclean, Merry M.*

Date *5-6-XX*
CPT Code ______
Dx Code ______

HISTORY

- ☐ Problem Focused
  Chief complaint; Brief history of present illness
- ☐ Expanded Problem Focused
  Chief complaint; Brief history of present illness;
  Problem pertinent system review
- ☑ Detailed
  Chief complaint: Extended history of present illness;
  Extended system review; Pertinent past family, social history
- ☐ Comprehensive
  Chief complaint; Extended history of present illness;
  Complete system review; Complete past family, social history

EXAMINATION

- ☐ Problem Focused
  Exam limited to affected body area or organ system
- ☐ Expanded Problem Focused
  Exam extended to other symptomatic or related organ systems
- ☑ Detailed
  Extended exam of affected area(s) and other symptomatic or related systems
- ☐ Comprehensive
  Complete single system specialty exam or complete multi-system exam

MEDICAL DECISION MAKING

	Medical Decision	Number of Dx Options	Amount of Data	Risk M and M
☐	Straightforward	minimal 1 dx	minimal	minimal
☑	Low Complexity	limited 1-2 dx	limited	low
☐	Moderate Complexity	multiple 1-2 dx	moderate	moderate
☐	High Complexity	extensive 2-3 dx	extensive	high

☐ Counseling ☐ Time ______
☐ Consult ☐ Referring Dr. ______
Diagnosis *See Pt record*

NP ✓ Est pt ______

Figure 6–3

PATIENT RECORD NO. 6001

LAST NAME	FIRST NAME	MIDDLE NAME	BIRTH DATE	SEX	HOME PHONE
McLean,	Merry	M.	02-02-48	F	013-486-1859

ADDRESS	CITY	STATE	ZIP CODE
4919 Dolphin Way,	Woodland Hills,	XY	12345

PATIENT'S OCCUPATION: secretary
NAME OF COMPANY: Porter Company

ADDRESS OF EMPLOYER: 5490 Wilshire Blvd., Merck, XY 12346
PHONE: 013-446-7781

SPOUSE OR PARENT: Harry L. McLean
OCCUPATION: computer programmer

EMPLOYER: IBM Corporation, ADDRESS: 5616 Wilshire Blvd., Merck, XY 12346
PHONE: 013-664-9023

NAME OF INSURANCE: Prudential Insurance Co., 5621 Wilshire Blvd., Merck, XY 12346
INSURED OR SUBSCRIBER: Harry L. McLean

POLICY NO.	GROUP NO.	EFFECTIVE DATE
459-62-9989	8832	6-2-80

MEDICARE NO.	MEDICAID NO.	EFFECTIVE DATE	SOC. SEC. NO.
			459-62-9989

REFERRED BY: Emdee Fine, MD, 5000 Wilshire Blvd., Merck, XY 12346 NPI#7302717540

DATE	PROGRESS
5-6-xx	Began in March, 20xx cc constant dribbling, wetting at night, use 15 pads/day.
	UA Sp Gr 1.0. Few bacteria, few urates. Dx: urinary incontinence. ptr 4 days
	for cystourethroscopy. Gene Ulibarri, MD
5-10-xx	Cystro revealed multiple fistula of bladder with 2 openings into urinary bladder
	and copious leakage into vagina. Schedule surgery to repair fistulae. Cont to
	work. Gene Ulibarri, MD
5-16-xx	Adm to hosp. Dx: multiple vesicovaginal fistulae. Gene Ulibarri, MD
5-17-xx	Op: Repair of vesicovaginal fistulae. Gene Ulibarri, MD
5-18-xx	through 5-30-xx HV brief. Disch 5-31. To be seen in 1 mo. Gene Ulibarri, MD
6-10-xx	Pt presents complaining of pain near operative site. Pt reports she has been
	walking daily and lifting more than 5 lb objects. Pt adv no excessive walking, no lifting,
	stooping, or bending until surgical site is healed. Retn to clinic in 1 wk.
	Est return to work 7-1-xx. Gene Ulibarri, MD
6-17-xx	No show.

Figure 6–4

STATEMENT

College Clinic
4567 Broad Avenue
Woodland Hills, XY 12345-0001
Telephone: 013-486-9002
Fax: 013-487-8976

Mrs. Merry M. McLean
4919 Dolphin Way
Woodland Hills, XY 12345-0001

DATE	PROFESSIONAL SERVICE DESCRIPTION	CHARGE	CREDITS		CURRENT BALANCE
			PAYMENTS	ADJUSTMENTS	
5-6-xx	OV	70 92			
5-6-xx	Lab, UA dipstick, nonautomated, complete microscopic				
5-10-xx	Cystourethroscopy				
5-16-xx	Initial hospital care, C hx/exam LC decision making				
5-17-xx	Closure of vesicovaginal fistula abdominal approach				
5-18-xx	thru 5-30-xx HV, brief				
5-31-xx	Discharge				
6-10-xx	OV, PF hx/exam, SF decision making				

Due and payable within 10 days.

Pay last amount in balance column 

Key:							
PF:	Problem-focused	SF:	Straightforward	CON:	Consultation	HCD:	House call (day)
EPF:	Expanded problem-focused	LC:	Low complexity	CPX:	Complete phys exam	HCN:	House call (night)
D:	Detailed	MC:	Moderate complexity	E:	Emergency	HV:	Hospital visit
C:	Comprehensive	HC:	High complexity	ER:	Emergency dept.	OV:	Office visit

Figure 6–5

APPROVED OMB 0938-0008

PLEASE DO NOT STAPLE IN THIS AREA

CARRIER

PICA

HEALTH INSURANCE CLAIM FORM

PICA

1. MEDICARE (Medicare #) MEDICAID (Medicaid #) CHAMPUS (Sponsor's SSN) CHAMPVA (VA File #) GROUP HEALTH PLAN (SSN or ID) FECA BLK LUNG (SSN) OTHER (ID)

1a. INSURED'S I.D. NUMBER (FOR PROGRAM IN ITEM 1)

2. PATIENT'S NAME (Last Name, First Name, Middle Initial)

3. PATIENT'S BIRTH DATE MM | DD | YYYY SEX M F

4. INSURED'S NAME (Last Name, First Name, Middle Initial)

5. PATIENT'S ADDRESS (No., Street)

6. PATIENT RELATIONSHIP TO INSURED Self Spouse Child Other

7. INSURED'S ADDRESS (No., Street)

CITY STATE

8. PATIENT STATUS Single Married Other

CITY STATE

ZIP CODE TELEPHONE (Include Area Code)

Employed Full-Time Student Part-Time Student

ZIP CODE TELEPHONE (Include Area Code) ( )

9. OTHER INSURED'S NAME (Last Name, First Name, Middle Initial)

10. IS PATIENT'S CONDITION RELATED TO:

11. INSURED'S POLICY GROUP OR FECA NUMBER

a. OTHER INSURED'S POLICY OR GROUP NUMBER

a. EMPLOYMENT? (CURRENT OR PREVIOUS) YES NO

a. INSURED'S DATE OF BIRTH MM | DD | YY SEX M F

b. OTHER INSURED'S DATE OF BIRTH MM | DD | YY SEX M F

b. AUTO ACCIDENT? YES NO PLACE (State)

b. EMPLOYER'S NAME OR SCHOOL NAME

c. EMPLOYER'S NAME OR SCHOOL NAME

c. OTHER ACCIDENT? YES NO

c. INSURANCE PLAN NAME OR PROGRAM NAME

d. INSURANCE PLAN NAME OR PROGRAM NAME

10d. RESERVED FOR LOCAL USE

d. IS THERE ANOTHER HEALTH BENEFIT PLAN? YES NO *If yes, return to and complete item 9 a-d.*

READ BACK OF FORM BEFORE COMPLETING AND SIGNING THIS FORM.

12. PATIENT'S OR AUTHORIZED PERSON'S SIGNATURE I authorize the release of any medical or other information necessary to process this claim. I also request payment of government benefits either to myself or to the party who accepts assignment below.

SIGNED ______ DATE ______

13. INSURED'S OR AUTHORIZED PERSON'S SIGNATURE I authorize payment of medical benefits to the undersigned physician or supplier for services described below.

SIGNED ______

PATIENT AND INSURED INFORMATION

14. DATE OF CURRENT: MM | DD | YY ILLNESS (First symptom) OR INJURY (Accident) OR PREGNANCY (LMP)

15. IF PATIENT HAS HAD SAME OR SIMILAR ILLNESS GIVE FIRST DATE MM | DD | YY

16. DATES PATIENT UNABLE TO WORK IN CURRENT OCCUPATION FROM MM | DD | YY TO MM | DD | YY

17. NAME OF REFERRING PHYSICIAN OR OTHER SOURCE

17a. I.D. NUMBER OF REFERRING PHYSICIAN

18. HOSPITALIZATION DATES RELATED TO CURRENT SERVICES FROM MM | DD | YY TO MM | DD | YY

19. RESERVED FOR LOCAL USE

20. OUTSIDE LAB? YES NO $ CHARGES

21. DIAGNOSIS OR NATURE OF ILLNESS OR INJURY. (RELATE ITEMS 1,2,3 OR 4 TO ITEM 24E BY LINE)

1. ______ 3. ______

2. ______ 4. ______

22. MEDICAID RESUBMISSION CODE ORIGINAL REF. NO.

23. PRIOR AUTHORIZATION NUMBER

24. A DATE(S) OF SERVICE From MM DD YY To MM DD YY	B Place of Service	C Type of Service	D PROCEDURES, SERVICES, OR SUPPLIES (Explain Unusual Circumstances) CPT/HCPCS | MODIFIER	E DIAGNOSIS CODE	F $ CHARGES	G DAYS OR UNITS	H EPSDT Family Plan	I EMG	J COB	K RESERVED FOR LOCAL USE

25. FEDERAL TAX I.D. NUMBER SSN EIN

26. PATIENT'S ACCOUNT NO.

27. ACCEPT ASSIGNMENT? (For govt. claims, see back) YES NO

28. TOTAL CHARGE $

29. AMOUNT PAID $

30. BALANCE DUE $

31. SIGNATURE OF PHYSICIAN OR SUPPLIER INCLUDING DEGREES OR CREDENTIALS (I certify that the statements on the reverse apply to this bill and are made a part thereof.)

SIGNED DATE

32. NAME AND ADDRESS OF FACILITY WHERE SERVICES WERE RENDERED (if other than home or office)

33. PHYSICIAN'S, SUPPLIER'S BILLING NAME, ADDRESS, ZIP CODE AND PHONE #

PIN# GRP#

PHYSICIAN OR SUPPLIER INFORMATION

(APPROVED BY AMA COUNCIL ON MEDICAL SERVICE8/88) *PLEASE PRINT OR TYPE* FORM HCFA-1500 (U2) (12-90) FORM OCWP-1500 FORM RRB-1500

Figure 6–6

ASSIGNMENT 6-4 ► COMPLETE A HEALTH INSURANCE CLAIM FORM

Performance Objective

Task: Complete a health insurance claim form and post the information to the patient's ledger card.

Conditions: Use Billy S. Rubin's E/M code slip (Figure 6–7), patient record (Figure 6–8), and ledger card (Figure 6–9), one health insurance claim form (Figure 6–10), typewriter, computer or pen, procedural and diagnostic code books, and *Workbook* Appendices A and B.

Standards: Claim Productivity Measurement

Time: ________________ minutes

Accuracy: ________________

(Note: The time element and accuracy criteria may be given by your instructor.)

Directions:

1. Complete the *Health Insurance Claim Form** to Aetna Life and Casualty Company on Mr. Billy S. Rubin by referring to his E/M Code Slip, patient slip, and ledger card. Date the Claim August 30. Refer to Appendix A to fill in the fees on the ledger card. Use OCR guidelines.
2. Use your *CPT* code book or Appendix A to determine the correct five-digit code number and modifiers for each professional service rendered. Do not type *no charge* entries on the claim form.
3. Record when you have billed the insurance company on the ledger card.

Text continued on page 111

E/M Code Slip

Patient Rubin, Billy S.

Date * ________
CPT Code ________
Dx code ________

HISTORY

- [x] Problem Focused
  Chief complaint; Brief history of present illness
- [ ] Expanded Problem Focused
  Chief complaint; Brief history of present illness; Problem pertinent system review
- [ ] Detailed
  Chief complaint: Extended history of present illness; Extended system review; Pertinent past family, social history
- [ ] Comprehensive
  Chief complaint; Extended history of present illness; Complete system review; Complete past family, social history

EXAMINATION

- [x] Problem Focused
  Exam limited to affected body area or organ system
- [ ] Expanded Problem Focused
  Exam extended to other symptomatic or related organ systems
- [ ] Detailed
  Extended exam of affected area(s) and other symptomatic or related symptoms
- [ ] Comprehensive
  Complete single system specialty exam or complete multi-system exam

MEDICAL DECISION MAKING

	Medical Decision	Number of Dx Options	Amount of Data	Risk M and M
[ ]	Straightforward	minimal 1 dx	minimal	minimal
[x]	Low Complexity	limited 1-2 dx	limited	low
[ ]	Moderate Complexity	multiple 1-2 dx	moderate	moderate
[ ]	High Complexity	extensive 2-3 dx	extensive	high

[ ] Counseling [ ] Time ________
[ ] Consult [ ] Referring Dr. ________
Diagnosis ________

NP ____ Est pt ✓

* For space constraints, this E/M code slip is being used for 8-7-00 and 8-14-00.

Figure 6–7

*See Chapter six of the *Handbook* for help in completing this form.

PATIENT RECORD NO. 6002

LAST NAME	FIRST NAME	MIDDLE NAME	BIRTH DATE	SEX	HOME PHONE
Rubin,	Billy	S.	11-09-53	M	013-893-5770

ADDRESS	CITY	STATE	ZIP CODE
547 North Oliver Rd.,	Woodland Hills,	XY	12345

PATIENT'S OCCUPATION: salesman
NAME OF COMPANY: Nate's Clothier's

ADDRESS OF EMPLOYER: 7786 East Chabner Boulevard, Dorland, XY 12347
PHONE: 013-449-6605

SPOUSE OR PARENT: Lydia B. Rubin (wife)
OCCUPATION:

EMPLOYER: ADDRESS: PHONE:

NAME OF INSURANCE: Aetna Life and Casualty Insurance Co., 3055 Wilshire Blvd., Merck, XY 12345
INSURED OR SUBSCRIBER: Billy S. Rubin

POLICY NO.	GROUP NO.	EFFECTIVE DATE
Policy No. 42107	2641	3-5-80

MEDICARE NO.	MEDICAID NO.	EFFECTIVE DATE	SOC. SEC. NO.
			505-12-1159

REFERRED BY: U. R. Wright, MD, 5010 Wrong Road, Torres, XY 12349 013-907-5440 NPI#2738555400

DATE	PROGRESS
8-7-XX	Office exam est. pt. CC: urinary hesitancy, frequency and posturinary dribbling since
	July 15 of this year. Exam revealed hard nodule in prostate. Silverman needle biopsy
	of prostate performed in office. Gene Ulibarri, MD
8-14-XX	Office exam. Biopsy report positive for Ca of prostate in situ. Advised patient that an
	operation was necessary and explained surgery to pt. Arranged for adm to
	hosp. Gene Ulibarri, MD
8-22-XX	Adm to hosp. Pt last worked 8-21-XX. Gene Ulibarri, MD
8-23-XX	Surg: Bilateral orchiectomy (scrotal), TURP. Est disability 6 wks. Pt to be kept under
	observation for 2 mo and will return to wk 12-3-XX. Gene Ulibarri, MD
8-28-XX	Disch from hosp. Confined at home for 1 wk at which time patient will be seen
	in office. Gene Ulibarri, MD

Figure 6–8

STATEMENT

College Clinic
4567 Broad Avenue
Woodland Hills, XY 12345-0001
Telephone: 013-486-9002
Fax: 013-487-8976

Mr. Billy S. Rubin
547 North Oliver Road
Woodland Hills, XY 12345-0001

DATE	PROFESSIONAL SERVICE DESCRIPTION	CHARGE	CREDITS		CURRENT BALANCE
			PAYMENTS	ADJUSTMENTS	
8-7-xx	Balance forward OV				10 –
8-7-xx	Biopsy, prostate				
8-14-xx	OV				
8-22-xx	Adm hosp, comp hx/exam, HC decision making				
8-23-xx	Bilateral orchiectomy, simple (scrotal)				
8-23-xx	TURP, complete				
8-24-xx	to 8-28-xx HV, PF hx/exam LC decision making				

Due and payable within 10 days. **Pay last amount in balance column** 

Key:
PF: Problem-focused
EPF: Expanded problem-focused
D: Detailed
C: Comprehensive
SF: Straightforward
LC: Low complexity
MC: Moderate complexity
HC: High complexity
CON: Consultation
CPX: Complete phys exam
E: Emergency
ER: Emergency dept.
HCD: House call (day)
HCN: House call (night)
HV: Hospital visit
OV: Office visit

Figure 6–9

APPROVED OMB 0938-0008

PLEASE DO NOT STAPLE IN THIS AREA

CARRIER

PICA

HEALTH INSURANCE CLAIM FORM

PICA

1. MEDICARE (Medicare #) MEDICAID (Medicaid #) CHAMPUS (Sponsor's SSN) CHAMPVA (VA File #) GROUP HEALTH PLAN (SSN or ID) FECA BLK LUNG (SSN) OTHER (ID)

1a. INSURED'S I.D. NUMBER (FOR PROGRAM IN ITEM 1)

2. PATIENT'S NAME (Last Name, First Name, Middle Initial)

3. PATIENT'S BIRTH DATE MM | DD | YYYY SEX M F

4. INSURED'S NAME (Last Name, First Name, Middle Initial)

5. PATIENT'S ADDRESS (No., Street)

6. PATIENT RELATIONSHIP TO INSURED Self Spouse Child Other

7. INSURED'S ADDRESS (No., Street)

CITY STATE

8. PATIENT STATUS Single Married Other

CITY STATE

ZIP CODE TELEPHONE (Include Area Code)

Employed Full-Time Student Part-Time Student

ZIP CODE TELEPHONE (Include Area Code) ( )

9. OTHER INSURED'S NAME (Last Name, First Name, Middle Initial)

10. IS PATIENT'S CONDITION RELATED TO:

11. INSURED'S POLICY GROUP OR FECA NUMBER

a. OTHER INSURED'S POLICY OR GROUP NUMBER

a. EMPLOYMENT? (CURRENT OR PREVIOUS) YES NO

a. INSURED'S DATE OF BIRTH MM | DD | YY SEX M F

b. OTHER INSURED'S DATE OF BIRTH MM | DD | YY SEX M F

b. AUTO ACCIDENT? YES NO PLACE (State)

b. EMPLOYER'S NAME OR SCHOOL NAME

c. EMPLOYER'S NAME OR SCHOOL NAME

c. OTHER ACCIDENT? YES NO

c. INSURANCE PLAN NAME OR PROGRAM NAME

d. INSURANCE PLAN NAME OR PROGRAM NAME

10d. RESERVED FOR LOCAL USE

d. IS THERE ANOTHER HEALTH BENEFIT PLAN? YES NO *If yes, return to and complete item 9 a-d.*

READ BACK OF FORM BEFORE COMPLETING AND SIGNING THIS FORM.

12. PATIENT'S OR AUTHORIZED PERSON'S SIGNATURE I authorize the release of any medical or other information necessary to process this claim. I also request payment of government benefits either to myself or to the party who accepts assignment below.

SIGNED ______ DATE ______

13. INSURED'S OR AUTHORIZED PERSON'S SIGNATURE I authorize payment of medical benefits to the undersigned physician or supplier for services described below.

SIGNED ______

PATIENT AND INSURED INFORMATION

14. DATE OF CURRENT: MM | DD | YY ILLNESS (First symptom) OR INJURY (Accident) OR PREGNANCY (LMP)

15. IF PATIENT HAS HAD SAME OR SIMILAR ILLNESS GIVE FIRST DATE MM | DD | YY

16. DATES PATIENT UNABLE TO WORK IN CURRENT OCCUPATION FROM MM | DD | YY TO MM | DD | YY

17. NAME OF REFERRING PHYSICIAN OR OTHER SOURCE

17a. I.D. NUMBER OF REFERRING PHYSICIAN

18. HOSPITALIZATION DATES RELATED TO CURRENT SERVICES FROM MM | DD | YY TO MM | DD | YY

19. RESERVED FOR LOCAL USE

20. OUTSIDE LAB? YES NO $ CHARGES

21. DIAGNOSIS OR NATURE OF ILLNESS OR INJURY. (RELATE ITEMS 1,2,3 OR 4 TO ITEM 24E BY LINE)

1. ______ 3. ______

2. ______ 4. ______

22. MEDICAID RESUBMISSION CODE ORIGINAL REF. NO.

23. PRIOR AUTHORIZATION NUMBER

24. A DATE(S) OF SERVICE From MM DD YY To MM DD YY	B Place of Service	C Type of Service	D PROCEDURES, SERVICES, OR SUPPLIES (Explain Unusual Circumstances) CPT/HCPCS | MODIFIER	E DIAGNOSIS CODE	F $ CHARGES	G DAYS OR UNITS	H EPSDT Family Plan	I EMG	J COB	K RESERVED FOR LOCAL USE

25. FEDERAL TAX I.D. NUMBER SSN EIN

26. PATIENT'S ACCOUNT NO.

27. ACCEPT ASSIGNMENT? (For govt. claims, see back) YES NO

28. TOTAL CHARGE $

29. AMOUNT PAID $

30. BALANCE DUE $

31. SIGNATURE OF PHYSICIAN OR SUPPLIER INCLUDING DEGREES OR CREDENTIALS (I certify that the statements on the reverse apply to this bill and are made a part thereof.)

SIGNED DATE

32. NAME AND ADDRESS OF FACILITY WHERE SERVICES WERE RENDERED (if other than home or office)

33. PHYSICIAN'S, SUPPLIER'S BILLING NAME, ADDRESS, ZIP CODE AND PHONE #

PIN# GRP#

PHYSICIAN OR SUPPLIER INFORMATION

(APPROVED BY AMA COUNCIL ON MEDICAL SERVICE 8/88) *PLEASE PRINT OR TYPE* FORM HCFA-1500 (U2) (12-90) FORM OCWP-1500 FORM RRB-1500

Figure 6–10

4. On September 1, Mr. Rubin sends you check No. 421 in the amount of $200 to apply to his account. Post this entry and show the balance due.
5. A Performance Evaluation Checklist may be reproduced from the Instruction Guide to the *Workbook* chapter if your instructor wishes you to submit it to assist with scoring and comments.
6. After the instructor has returned your work to you, either make the necessary corrections and place in a 3-ring notebook for future reference, or, if you received a high score, place it in your portfolio for reference when applying for a job.

Abbreviations pertinent to this record:

adm admission
CA cancer, carcinoma
CC cheif complaint
Comp complete/comprehensive
Disch Discharge
est established
exam examination
hist history
hosp hospital
HV Hospital visit
hx history

mo month
NC no charge
OC office call
phys physical
Pt pt
retn return
surg surgery
TURP Transurethral resection of prostate
wk week
wks weeks

ASSIGNMENT 6–5 ▶ COMPLETE A HEALTH INSURANCE CLAIM FORM

Performance Objective

Task: Complete a health insurance claim form and post the information to the patient's ledger card.

Conditions: Use Walter J. Stone's E/M code slip (Figure 6–11), patient record (Figure 6–12), and ledger card (Figure 6–13), one health insurance claim form (Figure 6–14), typewriter, computer or pen, procedural and diagnostic code books, and *Workbook* Appendices A and B.

Standards: Claim Productivity Measurement

Time: ______________ minutes

Accuracy: ______________

(Note: The time element and accuracy criteria may be given by your instructor.)

Directions:

1. Complete two Health Insurance Claim Forms* to Travelers Insurance Company on Mr. Walter J. Stone by referring to his E/M Code Slip, patient record, and ledger card. Date the claims June 1 and make a photocopy of this form to use as the second claim form. Refer to Appendix A to fill in the fees on the ledger card. Use OCR guidelines.

*See Chapter six of the *Handbook* for help in completing this form.

E/M Code Slip

Patient Stone, Walter J. Date 5/21/XX

CPT Code ______ Dx Code ______

HISTORY

- [x] Problem Focused
  Chief complaint; Brief history of present illness
- [ ] Expanded Problem Focused
  Chief complaint; Brief history of present illness; Problem pertinent system review
- [ ] Detailed
  Chief complaint: Extended history of present illness; Extended system review; Pertinent past family, social history
- [ ] Comprehensive
  Chief complaint; Extended history of present illness; Complete system review; Complete past family, social history

EXAMINATION

- [x] Problem Focused
  Exam limited to affected body area or organ system
- [ ] Expanded Problem Focused
  Exam extended to other symptomatic or related organ systems
- [ ] Detailed
  Extended exam of affected area(s) and other symptomatic or related systems
- [ ] Comprehensive
  Complete single system specialty exam or complete multi-system exam

MEDICAL DECISION MAKING

	Medical Decision	Number of Dx Options	Amount of Data	Risk M and M
[ ]	Straightforward	minimal 1 dx	minimal	minimal
[x]	Low Complexity	limited 1-2 dx	limited	low
[ ]	Moderate Complexity	multiple 1-2 dx	moderate	moderate
[ ]	High Complexity	extensive 2-3 dx	extensive	high

- [ ] Counseling [ ] Time ______
- [ ] Consult [ ] Referring Dr. ______

Diagnosis ______

NP ______ Est pt ✓

Figure 6–11

2. Use your *CPT* code book or Appendix A to determine the correct five-digit code number and modifiers for each professional service rendered. The surgeon, Dr. Cutler, is charging $937.74 for the cholecystectomy. You are submitting a claim for the assistant surgeon, Dr. Input, and using a standard 20% of the surgeon's fee.
3. On May 14, the insurance company sends the physician check number 48572 for $25. Post this entry.
4. Record on the ledger when you have billed the insurance company.
5. A Performance Evaluation Checklist may be reproduced from the Instruction Guide to the *Workbook* chapter if your instructor wishes you to submit it to assist with scoring and comments.
6. After the instructor has returned your work to you, either make the necessary corrections and place in a 3-ring notebook for future reference, or, if you received a high score, place it in your portfolio for reference when applying for a job.

Abbreviations pertinent to this record:

abt	about	GB	gall bladder
adm	admission	hosp	hospital
asst	assistant	inflam	inflammation
BP	Blood Pressure	intermed	intermediate (office visit)
DX	Diagnosis	OC	office call
E	emergency	ofc	office
ER	emergency room	pt	patient
est	established	wk	week

PATIENT RECORD NO. 6003

LAST NAME	FIRST NAME	MIDDLE NAME	BIRTH DATE	SEX	HOME PHONE
Stone,	Walter	J.	03-14-49	M	013-345-0776

ADDRESS	CITY	STATE	ZIP CODE
2008 Converse Street,	Woodland Hills,	XY	12345

PATIENT'S OCCUPATION: advertising agent
NAME OF COMPANY: R.V. Black and Associates

ADDRESS OF EMPLOYER: 1267 Broad Street, Woodland Hills, XY 12345
PHONE: 013-345-6012

SPOUSE OR PARENT: widow
OCCUPATION:

EMPLOYER: ADDRESS: PHONE:

NAME OF INSURANCE: Travelers Insurance Co. 5460 Olympic Blvd., Woodland Hills, XY 12345
INSURED OR SUBSCRIBER: Walter J. Stone

POLICY NO.: GROUP NO.: 6754 EFFECTIVE DATE: 6-1-81

MEDICARE NO.: MEDICAID NO.: EFFECTIVE DATE: SOC. SEC. NO.: 456-65-9989

REFERRED BY: brother: John B. Stone (former patient of Dr. Input)

DATE	PROGRESS
5-3-XX	Est pt presented in ER after experiencing sudden onset of profuse rectal bleeding with
	nausea and severe abdominal pains; Dr. Input called to ER. Consulted with Dr. Cutler
	who recommended pt be admitted for further evaluation and diagnostic treatment.
	Diagnosis: Unspecified GI hemorrhage. Disabled from wk. BP 180/100.
	Pt admitted to hosp. Gaston Input, MD
5-4-XX	Pt symptoms have subsided somewhat. GB series showed prepyloric gastric ulcer, inflam
	of gb and gallstones present. Gaston Input, MD
5-5-XX	Discharged to home. To be seen in ofc in 1 wk. Gaston Input, MD
5-21-XX	Pt complains of GI distress. BP 180/100 shows a concern for hypertension. Adv to see
	Dr. Cutler for further evaluation and possible surgery. Dx: Acute prepyloric gastric
	ulcer with hemorrhage, cholecystitis with cholelithiasis,
	benign hypertension. Gaston Input, MD
5-26-XX	Adm to hosp by Dr. Input. Gaston Input, MD
5-27-XX	Cholecystectomy, acted as asst surgeon to Dr. Cutler. Pt will resume wk 6-22-XX. Gaston Input, MD

Figure 6–12

SELF-STUDY 6–6 ▶ REVIEW PATIENT RECORD ABBREVIATIONS

Performance Objective

Task: Insert meanings of abbreviations.

Conditions: Use pencil or pen.

Standards: Time: ________________ minutes

Accuracy: ________________

(Note: The time element and accuracy criteria may be given by your instructor.)

Directions: After completing all the patient records in the *Workbook* pertinent to this chapter, you will be able to answer the next two questions.

1. What do these abbreviations mean?

a. PTR patient to return
b. TURP Transurethral resection of prostate
c. HX History
d. IVP Intravenous pyelogram
e. c̄ with
f. Dx diagnosis
g. BP Blood pressure
h. CC Chief complaint
i. UA Urinalysis
j. PE Physical Examination

2. Give the abbreviations for the following terms.

a. return RTN or rtn
b. cancer, carcinoma CA or CA
c. patient Pt
d. established est
e. discharged DC or disch
f. gallbladder gb or GB
g. initial init

To check your answers to this self-study assignment, see Appendix D.

Computer Disk Do the exercises for cases 1 through 5 on the computer disk to review concepts you have learned for this chapter. In regard to case 6 (Blue Plan), a large number of Blue Plans across the nation have been bought by private insurance companies. Since each company has different requirements for completion of the HCFA-1500 claim form, written instructions have been omitted from this edition of the *Handbook*. However, basic Blue Plan instructions are incorporated into the computer disk software. For case 6, most block instructions are the same as those for private carriers except blocks 1a, 11, 11a, 11b, 11c, 24E, and 24G. Check Block Help for Private/Blue Plan instructions for these blocks and leave Blocks 13 and 27 blank.

STATEMENT

College Clinic
4567 Broad Avenue
Woodland Hills, XY 12345-0001
Telephone: 013-486-9002
Fax: 013-487-8976

Mr. Walter J. Stone
2008 Converse Street
Woodland Hills, XY 12345-0001

DATE	PROFESSIONAL SERVICE DESCRIPTION	CHARGE	CREDITS PAYMENTS	CREDITS ADJUSTMENTS	CURRENT BALANCE
1-3-xx	OV	75 --			75 --
1-15-xx	Billed Travelers Insurance Co. (1-3-xx)				75 --
3-2-xx	ROA ins ck#95268		60 --		15 --
3-3-xx	OV	50 --			65 --
4-3-xx	Billed Travelers Insurance Co. (3-3-xx)				
5-3-xx	Init hosp care, comp hx/exam, mod decision making				
5-4-xx	HV, PF hx./exam, LC decision making				
5-5-xx	Hosp. discharge				
5-21-xx	OV, EPF, hx/exam, LC decision making				
5-26-xx	Hosp. admit				
5-27-xx	Cholecystectomy asst.				

Due and payable within 10 days. **Pay last amount in balance column** 

Key: PF: Problem-focused; EPF: Expanded problem-focused; D: Detailed; C: Comprehensive; SF: Straightforward; LC: Low complexity; MC: Moderate complexity; HC: High complexity; CON: Consultation; CPX: Complete phys exam; E: Emergency; ER: Emergency dept.; HCD: House call (day); HCN: House call (night); HV: Hospital visit; OV: Office visit

Figure 6–13

APPROVED OMB 0938-0008

PLEASE DO NOT STAPLE IN THIS AREA

CARRIER

PICA

HEALTH INSURANCE CLAIM FORM

PICA

1. MEDICARE (Medicare #) | MEDICAID (Medicaid #) | CHAMPUS (Sponsor's SSN) | CHAMPVA (VA File #) | GROUP HEALTH PLAN (SSN or ID) | FECA BLK LUNG (SSN) | OTHER (ID)

1a. INSURED'S I.D. NUMBER (FOR PROGRAM IN ITEM 1)

2. PATIENT'S NAME (Last Name, First Name, Middle Initial)

3. PATIENT'S BIRTH DATE MM | DD | YYYY SEX M F

4. INSURED'S NAME (Last Name, First Name, Middle Initial)

5. PATIENT'S ADDRESS (No., Street)

6. PATIENT RELATIONSHIP TO INSURED Self Spouse Child Other

7. INSURED'S ADDRESS (No., Street)

CITY STATE

8. PATIENT STATUS Single Married Other

CITY STATE

ZIP CODE TELEPHONE (Include Area Code)

Employed Full-Time Student Part-Time Student

ZIP CODE TELEPHONE (include Area Code) ( )

9. OTHER INSURED'S NAME (Last Name, First Name, Middle Initial)

10. IS PATIENT'S CONDITION RELATED TO:

11. INSURED'S POLICY GROUP OR FECA NUMBER

a. OTHER INSURED'S POLICY OR GROUP NUMBER

a. EMPLOYMENT? (CURRENT OR PREVIOUS) YES NO

a. INSURED'S DATE OF BIRTH MM | DD | YY SEX M F

b. OTHER INSURED'S DATE OF BIRTH MM | DD | YY SEX M F

b. AUTO ACCIDENT? PLACE (State) YES NO

b. EMPLOYER'S NAME OR SCHOOL NAME

c. EMPLOYER'S NAME OR SCHOOL NAME

c. OTHER ACCIDENT? YES NO

c. INSURANCE PLAN NAME OR PROGRAM NAME

d. INSURANCE PLAN NAME OR PROGRAM NAME

10d. RESERVED FOR LOCAL USE

d. IS THERE ANOTHER HEALTH BENEFIT PLAN? YES NO *If yes*, return to and complete item 9 a-d.

READ BACK OF FORM BEFORE COMPLETING AND SIGNING THIS FORM.

12. PATIENT'S OR AUTHORIZED PERSON'S SIGNATURE I authorize the release of any medical or other information necessary to process this claim. I also request payment of government benefits either to myself or to the party who accepts assignment below.

SIGNED ______ DATE ______

13. INSURED'S OR AUTHORIZED PERSON'S SIGNATURE I authorize payment of medical benefits to the undersigned physician or supplier for services described below.

SIGNED ______

PATIENT AND INSURED INFORMATION

14. DATE OF CURRENT: MM | DD | YY ◀ ILLNESS (First symptom) OR INJURY (Accident) OR PREGNANCY (LMP)

15. IF PATIENT HAS HAD SAME OR SIMILAR ILLNESS GIVE FIRST DATE MM | DD | YY

16. DATES PATIENT UNABLE TO WORK IN CURRENT OCCUPATION FROM MM | DD | YY TO MM | DD | YY

17. NAME OF REFERRING PHYSICIAN OR OTHER SOURCE

17a. I.D. NUMBER OF REFERRING PHYSICIAN

18. HOSPITALIZATION DATES RELATED TO CURRENT SERVICES FROM MM | DD | YY TO MM | DD | YY

19. RESERVED FOR LOCAL USE

20. OUTSIDE LAB? YES NO $ CHARGES

21. DIAGNOSIS OR NATURE OF ILLNESS OR INJURY. (RELATE ITEMS 1,2,3 OR 4 TO ITEM 24E BY LINE)

1. ______ 3. ______

2. ______ 4. ______

22. MEDICAID RESUBMISSION CODE ORIGINAL REF. NO.

23. PRIOR AUTHORIZATION NUMBER

24. A DATE(S) OF SERVICE From MM DD YY To MM DD YY	B Place of Service	C Type of Service	D PROCEDURES, SERVICES, OR SUPPLIES (Explain Unusual Circumstances) CPT/HCPCS | MODIFIER	E DIAGNOSIS CODE	F $ CHARGES	G DAYS OR UNITS	H EPSDT Family Plan	I EMG	J COB	K RESERVED FOR LOCAL USE

25. FEDERAL TAX I.D. NUMBER SSN EIN

26. PATIENT'S ACCOUNT NO.

27. ACCEPT ASSIGNMENT? (For govt. claims, see back) YES NO

28. TOTAL CHARGE $

29. AMOUNT PAID $

30. BALANCE DUE $

31. SIGNATURE OF PHYSICIAN OR SUPPLIER INCLUDING DEGREES OR CREDENTIALS (I certify that the statements on the reverse apply to this bill and are made a part thereof.)

SIGNED DATE

32. NAME AND ADDRESS OF FACILITY WHERE SERVICES WERE RENDERED (If other than home or office)

33. PHYSICIAN'S, SUPPLIER'S BILLING NAME, ADDRESS, ZIP CODE AND PHONE #

PIN# GRP#

PHYSICIAN OR SUPPLIER INFORMATION

(APPROVED BY AMA COUNCIL ON MEDICAL SERVICE 8/88) *PLEASE PRINT OR TYPE* FORM HCFA 1500 (U2)(12 90) FORM OCWP 1500 FORM RRB 1500

Figure 6–14

7

Electronic Data Interchange (EDI)

KEY TERMS

Your instructor may wish to select some specific words pertinent to this chapter for a test. For definitions of the terms, further study, and/or reference, the words, phrases, and abbreviations may be found in the Glossary at the end of the Handbook. *Key terms for this chapter follow.*

audit trail
back up
batch
bit
bug
byte
carrier-direct system
central processing unit (CPU)
clearinghouse
debug
down time
electronic claims processor (ECP)
electronic claim submission (ECS)
electronic data interchange (EDI)
electronic mail (e-mail)
encryption
file
format
gigabyte
hard copy
hardware
input
interactive transaction
interface
Internet
keypad
kilobyte (K)
local area network (LAN)
megabyte
memory
modem
mouse
multipurpose billing form
output
password
program
prompt
random access memory (RAM)
read-only memory (ROM)
soft copy
software
video display terminal (VDT)
virus

PERFORMANCE OBJECTIVES

The student will be able to

- Define and spell the key terms for this chapter, given the information from the *Handbook* Glossary, within a reasonable period of time and with enough accuracy to obtain a satisfactory evaluation.
- Answer the self-study review questions after reading the chapter, with enough accuracy to obtain a satisfactory evaluation.
- Locate errors, given computer-generated insurance forms, within a reasonable period of time and with enough accuracy to obtain a satisfactory evaluation.
- Fill in the correct meaning of each abbreviation, given a list of common medical abbreviations and symbols that appear in chart notes, with enough accuracy to obtain a satisfactory evaluation.

STUDY OUTLINE

History of an Electronic Claim
- Advantages of Electronic Claim Submission

Computer Components
- Hardware
- Software
- Memory

Networks
- Local Area Network
- Wide Area Network
- Internet/World Wide Web
  - Electronic Mail
  - Web Search Engine

Computer Confidentiality
- Confidentiality Statement
- Prevention Measures

Records Management
- Data Storage
- Electronic Power Protection

Selection of an Office Computer System

Computer Claims Systems
- Carrier-Direct
- Clearinghouse

Electronic Claim Processor

Electronic Data Interchange
- Carrier Agreements
- Signature Requirements
  - Physician
  - Patient
- Multipurpose Billing Forms
  - Crib Sheet Encounter Form
  - Scannable Encounter Form
- Keying Insurance Data for Claim Transmission
- Electronically Completing the Claim
  - Coding Requirements
- Electronic Processing Problems
  - Bug
  - Virus
- Facsimile Communication Transmission

Electronic Inquiry or Claims Status Review
- Eligibility Verification
  - Smart Card
  - Swipe Card
  - Computer Verification
  - Interactive Transaction
- Remittance Advice Statements

SELF-STUDY 7–1 ▸ REVIEW QUESTIONS

Review the objectives, key terms, glossary definitions to key terms, chapter information, and figures before completing the following review questions.

1. Insurance claims prepared on a computer and submitted via modem (telephone lines) to the insurance carrier's computer system are known as Elctronic Claim submission.

2. The process by which understandable data items are sent back and forth via computer linkages between two or more entities functioning as sender and receiver is known as Electronic Data Interchange.

3. Match the terms below with the definitions that follow (write the correct letters in the blanks):

a. batch
b. software
c. clearinghouse
d. hardware
e. RAM
f. ROM
g. CPU
h. smart card
i. swipe card
j. back up
k. local area network (LAN)
l. keypad
m. soft copy
n. input
o. file
p. hard copy
q. modem
r. memory
s. disk

1. E Memory into which the user can enter information and instructions and from which the user can call up data.
2. L A device that contains keys to control mathematical functions.
3. P A printout.
4. K Two or more interconnected computers.
5. G The brains of a computer device controlling the internal memory, which directs the flow and processing of information.
6. J A duplicate data file.
7. N Data that go into a computer memory bank.
8. O A single, stored unit of information assigned a file name.
9. Q A device that converts data into signals for telephone transmission.
10. M That which is displayed on a CRT screen.
11. S A magnetic storage device.
12. R Storage in a computer.
13. B Instructions required to make hardware perform a certain task.
14. D Physical components of a computer system.
15. A Group of claims for many patients submitted in one computer transmission from one office.
16. F Computer memory permanently programmed with a group of frequently used instructions.
17. H Card containing a computer chip allowing storage of a variety of information.

18. C Third-party administrator who receives transmission of claims, separates them, and sends each one to the correct insurance payer.

19. I Card with a magnetic stripe containing a small-capacity microchip that holds small amounts of information.

4. When electronically transmitting a claim directly to an insurance carrier, insurance billing specialists may be made aware of errors immediately and can make corrections using a process called Error-edit process.

5. To maintain confidentiality and enhance security, passwords or access codes should be developed and changed at regular intervals.

6. To prevent computer and data file damage caused by electric power spikes, computer equipment may be plugged into a/an surge suppressor.

7. Two types of computer claim systems that may be used when transmitting insurance claims via modem to insurance carriers are carrier direct and clearing-house.

8. An individual who converts insurance claims to standardized electronic formats and transmits them to the insurance carrier is known as a/an Electronic claims processor or professional (ECP).

9. For electronic insurance claims, an assignment of benefits agreement requires that each patient's signature be obtained either Once a month Once a year, or on a one-time basis.

10. Forms used for verifying data regarding services rendered to each patient during a visit are called Encounter form.

11. Mrs. James comes in for an office visit to see Dr. Doe on March 12. She returns again on March 14, 15, and 16. Abbreviated routing slips for E & M procedural codes used by Dr. Doe's office are called Cribsheets or charge slips.

12. Codes required when electronically transmitting claims are:

a. Medicare HCPCS national and regional codes for services, supplies and procedures

b. CPT codes with Modifiers

c. ICD9 CM diagnostic codes

13. After receiving a faxed insurance claim, some insurance carriers send a faxback report.

14. State the definition of an electronic remittance notice.

an on-line transaction about the status of a claim

15. Various limiting conditions and guidelines that tell the computer to deny, review, or pay transmitted insurance claims are known as screens or paramaters.

To check your answers to this self-study assignment, see Appendix D.

ASSIGNMENT 7–2 ▶ COMPOSE ELECTRONIC MAIL MESSAGES

Performance Objective

Task: Compose brief messages for electronic mail transmission after reading each scenario.

Conditions: List of scenarios and one sheet of 8 1/2" × 11" plain typing paper, typewriter and/or computer, or pen.

Standards: Time: ______________ minutes

Accuracy: ______________

(Note: The time element and accuracy criteria may be given by your instructor.)

Directions: Read each scenario. Compose polite, effective, and brief messages that when on the job would be transmitted via electronic mail (e-mail). Use the guidelines presented in the textbook. Be sure to list a descriptive subject line as the first item in each composition. Single-space the message. Insert a short signature at the end of the message to include your name and affiliation, and create your e-mail address if you do not have one.

Scenario 1: Ask insurance biller, Mary Davis, in a satellite office to locate and fax you a copy of the billing done on Account number 43500 for services rendered to Margarita Sylva on March 2, 20XX. Explain that you must telephone the patient about her account. Mary Davis' e-mail address is: mdavis@aol.com

Scenario 2: Patient Ellen Worth was recently hospitalized, her hospital number is 20-9870-11. Compose a message to the medical record department at College Hospital (collegehospmedrecords@rrv.net) for her final diagnosis and the assigned diagnostic code needed to complete the insurance claim form.

Scenario 3: You are working for a billing service and receive an encounter form that is missing the information about the patient's professional service received on August 2, 20XX. The patient's account number is 45098. You have the diagnosis data. Compose an e-mail message to Dr. Mason (pmason@email.mc.com) explaining what you must obtain to complete the billing portion of the insurance claim form.

Scenario 4: A new patient, John Phillips, has e-mailed your office to ask what the outstanding balance is on his account. The account number is 42990. You look up the financial record and note the service was for an office visit on June 14, 20XX. The charge was $106.11. Compose an e-mail response to Mr. Phillips whose e-mail address is: bphillips@hotmail.com.

Scenario 5: You are having difficulty deciding whether the codes 13101, 13102, and 13132 with modifier -51 selected for a case are appropriate. Compose an e-mail message that will be posted on the Part B News Internet listserv (PartB-L@usa.net) asking for comments. The case involves a 12-year-old boy who fell against a bicycle, lacerating his left chest to the pectoralis muscle through a 12-cm gaping wound. He also sustained a 5-cm laceration to his left cheek. Complex repairs were required for these two wounds that totaled 17 cm. Find out whether modifier -15 should be appended to the second code or to the third code.

After the instructor has returned your work to you, either make the necessary corrections and place it in a 3-ring notebook for future reference, or, if you receive a high score, place it in your portfolio for use when applying for a job.

ASSIGNMENT 7–3 ▶ LOCATE MISSING DATA ON A COMPUTER GENERATED HEALTH INSURANCE CLAIM FORM

Performance Objective

Task: Locate the blocks on the computer-generated insurance claim form that need completion of missing information or data that need to be added before submission to the insurance company.

Conditions: Use Brad E. Diehl's patient record (Figure 7–1), completed insurance claim (Figure 7–2), and a red ink pen.

Standards: Time: ________________ minutes

Accuracy: ________________

(Note: The time element and accuracy criteria may be given by your instructor.)

Directions: Refer to the patient's record (Figure 7–1) if you need any pertinent information for the insurance claim. Locate the blocks on the insurance claim form (Figure 7–2) that need completion of missing information or that need data to be added before submission to the insurance company. Highlight all errors you discover. Insert all corrections and missing information in red. If you cannot locate the necessary information but know it is mandatory, write "NEED" in the corresponding block.

Optional: Retype a blank HCFA-1500 claim form with your corrections and changes.

ASSIGNMENT 7–4 ▶ LOCATE MISSING DATA ON A COMPUTER-GENERATED HEALTH INSURANCE CLAIM FORM

Performance Objective

Task: Locate the blocks on the computer-generated insurance claim form that need completion of missing information or data that need to be added before submission to the insurance company.

PATIENT RECORD

Account No. 378210

Diehl,	Brad	E.	09-21-46	M	013-222-0123
LAST NAME	FIRST NAME	MIDDLE NAME	BIRTH DATE	SEX	HOME PHONE

3975 Hills Road,	Woodland Hills,	XY	12345
ADDRESS	CITY	STATE	ZIP CODE

radio advertising salesman	KACY Radio
PATIENT'S OCCUPATION	NAME OF COMPANY

4071 Mills Road, Woodland Hills, XY 12345	013-201-6666
ADDRESS OF EMPLOYER	PHONE

Tak E. Diehl (birthdate 4-7-45)	legal secretary
SPOUSE OR PARENT	OCCUPATION

Attys. Dilman, Foreswise, & Gilson,	12 West Dix Street, Woodland Hills, XY 12345	013-222-6432
EMPLOYER	ADDRESS	PHONE

Aetnal Insurance Co., 2412 Main Street, Woodland Hills, XY 12345	Brad E Diehl
NAME OF INSURANCE	INSURED OR SUBSCRIBER

403119		3-2-80
POLICY NO.	GROUP NO.	EFFECTIVE DATE

			561-02-1501
MEDICARE NO.	MEDICAID NO.	EFFECTIVE DATE	SOC. SEC. NO.

REFERRED BY: Raymond Skeleton, MD

DATE	PROGRESS
1-5-20xx	Pt comes in complaining of coughing and sneezing. Some difficulty in breathing.
	Dizziness occasionally and stomach pain with cramping of 6 mo duration. AP & lat
	chest x-rays neg. Pt. brought in bone marrow aspiration report done by Dr. Skelton.
	BP 180/100. Pt. to have oral cholecystography at ABC Radiology. CBC at next visit.
	Dx: irritable colon (ICD-9-CM diagnosis code no. 564.1), hypertension (ICD-9-CM
	diagnosis code no. 401.1), and respiratory distress (ICD-9-CM diagnosis code no.
	786.09). No disability at this time. Gaston Input, MD
1-20-20xx	Oral cholecystography reveals a single 1.5 cm in maximal diameter radiolucent
	calculus within the cholecyst. CBC performed in office indicates WBC 10,000.
	DX: cholecystitis with cholelithiasis (ICD-9-CM diagnosis code no. 574.10). Adv.
	cholecystectomy as soon as possible. Gaston Input, MD

Figure 7–1

Conditions: Use Evert I. Strain's patient record (Figure 7–3), completed insurance claim (Figure 7–4), and a red ink pen.

Standards: Time: ________________ minutes

Accuracy: ________________

(Note: The time element and accuracy criteria may be given by your instructor.)

Directions: Refer to the patient's record (Figure 7–3) if you need any pertinent information for the insurance claim. Locate the blocks on the insurance claim form (Figure 7–4) that need completion of missing information or that need data to be added before submission to the insurance company. Mr. Strain did not pay anything on his account. Highlight all errors you discover. Insert all corrections and missing information in red. If you cannot locate the necessary information but know it is mandatory, write "NEED" in the corresponding block.

Optional: Retype a blank HCFA-1500 claim form with your corrections and changes.

SELF-STUDY 7–5 ▶ DEFINE PATIENT RECORD ABBREVIATIONS

Performance Objective

Task: Insert definitions of abbreviations.

Conditions: Use pencil or pen.

Standards: Time: ________________ minutes

Accuracy: ________________

(Note: The time element and accuracy criteria may be given by your instructor.)

Directions: After completing the assignments in this chapter, you will be able to define the abbreviations shown here.

Abbreviations pertinent to the record of Brad E. Diehl:

abt	about	AP	anteroposterior
adv	advise	BP	Blood Pressure
CBC	complete blood count	neg	negative
cm	centimeter	Pt	patient
Dx	diagnosis	WBC	white blood cell count
ECG	electrocardiogram	WNL	within normal limits
hr	hour	wk	week
lat	lateral	c̄	with
mo	month		

Text continued on page 130

ASSIGNMENT 7-3

1. MEDICARE (Medicare #) [ ] MEDICAID (Medicaid #) [ ] CHAMPUS (Sponsor's SSN) [ ] CHAMPVA (VA File #) [ ] GROUP HEALTH PLAN (SSN or ID) [X] FECA BLK LUNG (SSN) [ ] OTHER (ID) [ ]

1a. INSURED'S I.D. NUMBER (FOR PROGRAM IN ITEM 1): 403119

2. PATIENT'S NAME (Last Name, First Name, Middle Initial): DIEHL BRAD E

3. PATIENT'S BIRTH DATE MM DD YYYY: 09 21 1946 SEX M [ ] F [ ]

4. INSURED'S NAME (Last Name, First Name, Middle Initial): SAME

5. PATIENT'S ADDRESS (No., Street): 3975 HILLS ROAD

6. PATIENT RELATIONSHIP TO INSURED: Self [ ] Spouse [ ] Child [ ] Other [ ]

7. INSURED'S ADDRESS (No., Street)

CITY: WOODLAND HILLS STATE: XY

8. PATIENT STATUS: Single [ ] Married [X] Other [ ]

CITY STATE

ZIP CODE: 12345 TELEPHONE (Include Area Code): (013) 222 0123

Employed [X] Full-Time Student [ ] Part-Time Student [ ]

ZIP CODE TELEPHONE (include Area Code) ( )

9. OTHER INSURED'S NAME (Last Name, First Name, Middle Initial)

10. IS PATIENT'S CONDITION RELATED TO:

11. INSURED'S POLICY GROUP OR FECA NUMBER

a. OTHER INSURED'S POLICY OR GROUP NUMBER

a. EMPLOYMENT? (CURRENT OR PREVIOUS) [ ] YES [X] NO

a. INSURED'S DATE OF BIRTH MM DD YY SEX M [ ] F [ ]

b. OTHER INSURED'S DATE OF BIRTH MM DD YY SEX M [ ] F [ ]

b. AUTO ACCIDENT? PLACE (State) [ ] YES [X] NO

b. EMPLOYER'S NAME OR SCHOOL NAME

c. EMPLOYER'S NAME OR SCHOOL NAME

c. OTHER ACCIDENT? [ ] YES [X] NO

c. INSURANCE PLAN NAME OR PROGRAM NAME

d. INSURANCE PLAN NAME OR PROGRAM NAME

10d. RESERVED FOR LOCAL USE

d. IS THERE ANOTHER HEALTH BENEFIT PLAN? [ ] YES [X] NO *If yes*, return to and complete item 9 a-d.

READ BACK OF FORM BEFORE COMPLETING AND SIGNING THIS FORM.

12. PATIENT'S OR AUTHORIZED PERSON'S SIGNATURE I authorize the release of any medical or other information necessary to process this claim. I also request payment of government benefits either to myself or to the party who accepts assignment below.

SIGNED ______ DATE ______

13. INSURED'S OR AUTHORIZED PERSON'S SIGNATURE I authorize payment of medical benefits to the undersigned physician or supplier for services described below.

SIGNED ______

14. DATE OF CURRENT: MM DD YY ILLNESS (First symptom) OR INJURY (Accident) OR PREGNANCY (LMP)

15. IF PATIENT HAS HAD SAME OR SIMILAR ILLNESS GIVE FIRST DATE MM DD YY

16. DATES PATIENT UNABLE TO WORK IN CURRENT OCCUPATION FROM MM DD YY TO MM DD YY

17. NAME OF REFERRING PHYSICIAN OR OTHER SOURCE: RAYMOND SKELETON MD

17a. I.D. NUMBER OF REFERRING PHYSICIAN

18. HOSPITALIZATION DATES RELATED TO CURRENT SERVICES FROM MM DD YY TO MM DD YY

19. RESERVED FOR LOCAL USE

20. OUTSIDE LAB? [ ] YES [ ] NO $ CHARGES

21. DIAGNOSIS OR NATURE OF ILLNESS OR INJURY. (RELATE ITEMS 1,2,3 OR 4 TO ITEM 24E BY LINE)

1. 564 1
2.
3. 78609
4.

22. MEDICAID RESUBMISSION CODE ORIGINAL REF. NO.

23. PRIOR AUTHORIZATION NUMBER

24. A DATE(S) OF SERVICE From MM DD YY	To MM DD YY	B Place of Service	C Type of Service	D PROCEDURES, SERVICES, OR SUPPLIES (Explain Unusual Circumstances) CPT/HCPCS	MODIFIER	E DIAGNOSIS CODE	F $ CHARGES	G DAYS OR UNITS	H EPSDT Family Plan	I EMG	J COB	K RESERVED FOR LOCAL USE
010520XX		11		99203		123	70 92	1			32	78312700
010520XX		11		71020			80 00	1			32	78312700
012020XX		11		99213			40 20	1			32	78312700
012020XX		11		85025		4	25 00	1			32	78312700
012020XX		11				4	175 00	1			32	78312700

25. FEDERAL TAX I.D. NUMBER SSN [ ] EIN [ ]

26. PATIENT'S ACCOUNT NO.: 378210

27. ACCEPT ASSIGNMENT? (For govt. claims, see back) [ ] YES [ ] NO

28. TOTAL CHARGE $

29. AMOUNT PAID $

30. BALANCE DUE $

31. SIGNATURE OF PHYSICIAN OR SUPPLIER INCLUDING DEGREES OR CREDENTIALS (I certify that the statements on the reverse apply to this bill and are made a part thereof.)

SIGNED ______ DATE 01 25 20XX

32. NAME AND ADDRESS OF FACILITY WHERE SERVICES WERE RENDERED (if other than home or office): SAME

33. PHYSICIAN'S, SUPPLIER'S BILLING NAME, ADDRESS, ZIP CODE AND PHONE #

COLLEGE CLINIC
4567 BROAD AVENUE
WOODLAND HILLS XY 12345
013 486 9002

PIN# GRP# 3664021CC

reference initials

Figure 7–2

PATIENT RECORD

Account No. 273458

Strain,	Evert	I.	09-11-46	M	013-678-0211
LAST NAME	FIRST NAME	MIDDLE NAME	BIRTH DATE	SEX	HOME PHONE

7650 None Such Road,	Woodland Hills,	XY	12345
ADDRESS	CITY	STATE	ZIP CODE

mechanical engineer	R & R Company
PATIENT'S OCCUPATION	NAME OF COMPANY

2400 Davon Road, Woodland Hills, XY 12345	013-520-8977
ADDRESS OF EMPLOYER	PHONE

Ester I. Strain (wife)	administrative assistant
SPOUSE OR PARENT	OCCUPATION

University College,	4021 Book Road, Woodland Hills, XY 12345	013-450-9908
EMPLOYER	ADDRESS	PHONE

ABC Insurance Co., P.O. Box 130, Woodland Hills, XY 12345	Evert I. Strain
NAME OF INSURANCE	INSURED OR SUBSCRIBER

453-32-4739	96476A	1-1-80
POLICY NO.	GROUP NO.	EFFECTIVE DATE

			453-32-4739
MEDICARE NO.	MEDICAID NO.	EFFECTIVE DATE	SOC. SEC. NO.

REFERRED BY: Gerald C. Jones, MD, 1403 Haven Street, Woodland Hills, XY, 12345 NPI #5475496608

DATE	PROGRESS
1-8-20xx	Est pt comes in complaining of frequency in urination, headaches, polyphagia, unable
	to remember current events. These problems have been present for almost a year.
	PE: BP 160/110. Lab work done at an urgent care center showed SGOT, cholesterol
	elevated. Blood sugar glucose extremely high range. DX: diabetes mellitus (Diagnostic
	code No. 250.00), ASHD (Diagnostic code No. 414.00), hypertension (Diagnostic
	code No. 401.1). Adv. hospitalization at College Hospital on 1-9. Disability 1-9
	through 1-31. Gerald Practon, MD
1-9-20xx	Adm to hosp. H & P. Gerald Practon, MD
1-10-20xx	Hosp visit. Pt doing well on special diet. Pt to remain in hosp for one more day.
	BP 130/85. Gerald Practon, MD
1-11-20xx	DC from hosp. Pt to be seen in one month. Gerald Practon, MD

Figure 7–3

Abbreviations pertinent to the record of Evert I. Strain:

adv advise

ASHD arteriosclerotic heart Disease

BP Blood Pressure

DC discharge

Dx Diagnosis

est established

hosp hospital

ltd limited

PE Physical examination

pt patient

SGOT* serum glutamic oxaloacetic transminase

To check your answers to this self-study assignment, see Appendix D.

*See laboratory abbreviations in Appendix A of this *Workbook*.

ASSIGNMENT 7-4

1. MEDICARE (Medicare #) [ ] MEDICAID (Medicaid #) [ ] CHAMPUS (Sponsor's SSN) [ ] CHAMPVA (VA File #) [ ] GROUP HEALTH PLAN (SSN or ID) [X] FECA BLK LUNG (SSN) [ ] OTHER (ID) [ ]

1a. INSURED'S I.D. NUMBER (FOR PROGRAM IN ITEM 1): 45332 4739 96476A

2. PATIENT'S NAME (Last Name, First Name, Middle Initial): STRAIN EVERT I

3. PATIENT'S BIRTH DATE MM | DD | YYYY — SEX M [X] F [ ]

4. INSURED'S NAME (Last Name, First Name, Middle Initial): SAME

5. PATIENT'S ADDRESS (No., Street): 7650 NONE SUCH ROAD

6. PATIENT RELATIONSHIP TO INSURED: Self [ ] Spouse [X] Child [ ] Other [ ]

7. INSURED'S ADDRESS (No., Street)

CITY: WOODLAND HILLS STATE: XY

8. PATIENT STATUS: Single [ ] Married [X] Other [ ]

CITY STATE

ZIP CODE TELEPHONE (Include Area Code) ( )

Employed [X] Full-Time Student [ ] Part-Time Student [ ]

ZIP CODE TELEPHONE (include Area Code) ( )

9. OTHER INSURED'S NAME (Last Name, First Name, Middle Initial)

10. IS PATIENT'S CONDITION RELATED TO:

11. INSURED'S POLICY GROUP OR FECA NUMBER

a. OTHER INSURED'S POLICY OR GROUP NUMBER

a. EMPLOYMENT? (CURRENT OR PREVIOUS) [ ] YES [X] NO

a. INSURED'S DATE OF BIRTH MM | DD | YY SEX M [ ] F [ ]

b. OTHER INSURED'S DATE OF BIRTH MM | DD | YY SEX M [ ] F [ ]

b. AUTO ACCIDENT? PLACE (State) [ ] YES [X] NO

b. EMPLOYER'S NAME OR SCHOOL NAME

c. EMPLOYER'S NAME OR SCHOOL NAME

c. OTHER ACCIDENT? [ ] YES [X] NO

c. INSURANCE PLAN NAME OR PROGRAM NAME

d. INSURANCE PLAN NAME OR PROGRAM NAME

10d. RESERVED FOR LOCAL USE

d. IS THERE ANOTHER HEALTH BENEFIT PLAN? [ ] YES [ ] NO *If yes, return to and complete item 9 a-d.*

READ BACK OF FORM BEFORE COMPLETING AND SIGNING THIS FORM.

12. PATIENT'S OR AUTHORIZED PERSON'S SIGNATURE I authorize the release of any medical or other information necessary to process this claim. I also request payment of government benefits either to myself or to the party who accepts assignment below.

SIGNED ______ DATE ______

13. INSURED'S OR AUTHORIZED PERSON'S SIGNATURE I authorize payment of medical benefits to the undersigned physician or supplier for services described below.

SIGNED ______

14. DATE OF CURRENT: MM | DD | YY ◀ ILLNESS (First symptom) OR INJURY (Accident) OR PREGNANCY (LMP)

15. IF PATIENT HAS HAD SAME OR SIMILAR ILLNESS GIVE FIRST DATE MM | DD | YY

16. DATES PATIENT UNABLE TO WORK IN CURRENT OCCUPATION FROM MM | DD | YY TO MM | DD | YY

17. NAME OF REFERRING PHYSICIAN OR OTHER SOURCE: GERALD C JONES MD

17a. I.D. NUMBER OF REFERRING PHYSICIAN: 690235

18. HOSPITALIZATION DATES RELATED TO CURRENT SERVICES FROM 01 09 20XX TO 01 11 20XX

19. RESERVED FOR LOCAL USE

20. OUTSIDE LAB? [ ] YES [ ] NO $ CHARGES

21. DIAGNOSIS OR NATURE OF ILLNESS OR INJURY. (RELATE ITEMS 1,2,3 OR 4 TO ITEM 24E BY LINE)

1. 25000
2. 414 0
3. 401 0
4.

22. MEDICAID RESUBMISSION CODE ORIGINAL REF. NO.

23. PRIOR AUTHORIZATION NUMBER

24. A DATE(S) OF SERVICE From MM DD YY	To MM DD YY	B Place of Service	C Type of Service	D PROCEDURES, SERVICES, OR SUPPLIES (Explain Unusual Circumstances) CPT/HCPCS MODIFIER	E DIAGNOSIS CODE	F $ CHARGES	G DAYS OR UNITS	H EPSDT Family Plan	I EMG	J COB	K RESERVED FOR LOCAL USE
010820XX		11		99215		75 00	1			46	27889700
010920XX		21		99222		100 00	1			46	27889700
011020XX		21		99231		37 74	1			46	27889700
011120XX		21		99231		37 74	1				

25. FEDERAL TAX I.D. NUMBER: 70 3459766 SSN [ ] EIN [X]

26. PATIENT'S ACCOUNT NO.

27. ACCEPT ASSIGNMENT? (For govt. claims, see back) [ ] YES [ ] NO

28. TOTAL CHARGE $ 250 48

29. AMOUNT PAID $

30. BALANCE DUE $ 250 48

31. SIGNATURE OF PHYSICIAN OR SUPPLIER INCLUDING DEGREES OR CREDENTIALS (I certify that the statements on the reverse apply to this bill and are made a part thereof.)

SIGNED DATE 01 25 20XX

reference initials

32. NAME AND ADDRESS OF FACILITY WHERE SERVICES WERE RENDERED (if other than home or office)

33. PHYSICIAN'S, SUPPLIER'S BILLING NAME, ADDRESS, ZIP CODE AND PHONE #

COLLEGE CLINIC
4567 BROAD AVENUE
WOODLAND HILLS XY 12345
013 486 9002

PIN# GRP# 3664021CC

Figure 7–4

8

Receiving Payments and Insurance Problem Solving

KEY TERMS

Your instructor may wish to select some specific words pertinent to this chapter for a test. For definitions of the terms, further study, and/or reference, the words, phrases, and abbreviations may be found in the Glossary at the end of the Handbook. *Key terms for this chapter follow.*

appeal
delinquent claim
denied claim
explanation of benefits (EOB)
inquiry
lost claim
overpayment
peer review
rebill
rejected claim
remittance advice (RA)
review
suspense
tracer
two-party check

PERFORMANCE OBJECTIVES

The student will be able to

- Define and spell the key terms for this chapter, given the information from the *Handbook* Glossary, within a reasonable period of time and with enough accuracy to obtain a satisfactory evaluation.
- Answer the self-study review questions after reading the chapter, with enough accuracy to obtain a satisfactory evaluation.
- Complete the insurance claim tracer form, given a request for an insurance claim trace and the patient's insurance claim, within a reasonable period of time and with enough accuracy to obtain a satisfactory evaluation.
- Locate the errors on each claim, given three returned insurance claims, within a reasonable period of time and with enough accuracy to obtain a satisfactory evaluation.
- Complete a form, given form HCFA-1965, Request for Hearing, Part B, Medicare Claim, within a reasonable period of time and with enough accuracy to obtain a satisfactory evaluation.

STUDY OUTLINE

Follow-up After Claim Submission
Claim Policy Provisions
- Insured
- Payment Time Limits

Explanation of Benefits
- Components of an EOB
- Interpretation of an EOB
- Posting an EOB

State Insurance Commissioner
- Commission Objectives
- Types of Problems
- Commission Inquiries

Claim Management Techniques
- Insurance Claims Register
- Tickler File
- Insurance Company Payment History

Claim Inquiries
Problem Claims
- Types of Problems
  - Delinquent, Pending, or Suspense
  - Lost Claims
  - Rejected Claims
  - Denied Claims
  - Downcoding
  - Payment Paid to the Patient
  - Two-Party Check
  - Overpayment

Rebilling
Review and Appeal Process
Procedure: Filing an Official Appeal
- Medicare Review and Appeal Process
  - Inquiry (Level 1)
  - Review (Level 2)
  - Fair Hearing (Level 3)
  - Administrative Law Judge Hearing (Level 4)
  - Appeals Council Review (Level 5)
  - Federal District Court Hearing (Level 6)
  - HCFA Regional Offices
  - Medigap

TRICARE Review and Appeal Process
- Reconsideration
- Formal Review
- Hearing

SELF-STUDY 8–1 ▶ REVIEW QUESTIONS

Review the objectives, key terms, and chapter information before completing the following review questions.

1. Name provisions seen in health insurance policies.

   a. The claimant is obligated to notify the insurance company of a loss within a certain period of time or the insurance company can deny benefits

   b. If the insured is in disagreement with the insurer for settlement of a claim, a suit must begin within 3 years after the claim was submitted

   c. an insured person cannot bring legal action against an insurance company until 60 days after a claim is submitted to the insurance company

d. The insurance company is obligated to pay benefits promptly when a claim is submitted

2. After an insurance claim is processed by the insurance carrier (paid, suspended, rejected, or denied), a document known as a/an explanation of benefits is sent to the patient and to the provider of professional medical services.

3. Name other items that indicate the patient's responsibility to pay that may appear on the document explaining the payment and check issued by the insurance carrier.
   a. amount not covered
   b. copayment amount
   c. deductible
   d. coinsurance
   e. other insurance payment
   f. patient's total responsibility

4. After receiving an explanation of benefits document and posting insurance payment, the copy of the insurance claim form is put into a file marked closed claims.

5. A state department or agency that helps resolve insurance conflicts and verifies that insurance contracts are carried out in good faith is known as a/an insurance commission of the state.

6. When an insurance company continually pays slow on insurance claims, it may help speed up payments if a formal written complaint is made to the insurance commissioner.

7. To locate delinquent insurance claims on an insurance claims register quickly, which column should be looked at first? Data claim paid column

   Would it appear blank or completed? Blank

8. When no payment has been received from an insurance company, what follow-up should take place? a tracer

9. Name some of the principal procedures that should be followed in good bookkeeping and record-keeping practice when a payment has been received from an insurance company.

pull out copies of the insurance claims that correspond with the payments and dispose of them, post payment to the patient's ledger and to the day sheet, and deposit the payment check in the bank

10. In good office management, to track submitted pending or resubmitted insurance claims, a/an tickler, suspense or follow up file is used.

11. Two routine procedures to include in a reminder system to track pending claims are

a. Divide active claims by month

b. File active claims in chronologic order by date of service

12. It is reasonable to assume that a private insurance claim would become delinquent after 4 to 6 weeks and a TRICARE claim after 8 to 12 weeks.

13. When making an inquiry about a claim by telephone, efficient secretarial procedure would be to document the date, time of the call, name of the person spoken to and their telephone extension, and outline or briefly note the conversation.

14. Two categories of claim denials are technical errors and medical coverage policy issues.

15. State the solution if a claim has been denied because the professional service rendered was for an injury that is being considered as compensable under workers' compensation.

Locate the insurance carrier for the industrial injury and send them a report of the case with a bill. Notify the patient's health insurance carrier monthly to let them know the status of the case

16. The best solution to prevent down coding is to monitor reimbursements and monitor downcodes to discover which codes are affected. Ask the insurance carrier which code system is in use and obtain the code book.

17. This question is presented to enhance your skill in critical thinking. Using your diagnostic code book, look up the *ICD-9-CM* diagnostic code for a patient being treated for a perforated and hemorrhaging gastric ulcer, with no mention of whether it was acute or chronic. To code such a case, what would you do and why? Use code 531.5 or ask the physician if the condition was acute 531.2 or Chronic 531.6 Since there are fourth and fifth digits with this code category try not to list the dx as unspecified 531.9 because use of many unspecified codes may result in downcoding or denial of the claim

18. At the time of his first office visit, Mr. Doi signed an Assignment of Benefits, and Dr. James' office submitted a claim to ABC Insurance Company. Mr. Doi received, in error, a check from the insurance company and cashed it. What step(s) should be taken by Dr. James' office after this error is discovered?

a. call the insurance company

b. call the patient or send a letter by certified mail

c. File a complaint with the state insurance commissioner

19. If an appeal of an insurance claim is not successful, the next step to proceed with is a/an peer review.

20. Name the six levels for appealing a Medicare claim.

a. inquiry

b. review

c. fair hearing

d. administrative law judge hearing

e. appeals council review

f. federal district court hearing

21. Medicare reviews by the insurance carrier are usually completed within 30 to 45 days.

22. A Medicare patient has insurance with United American (a Medigap policy), and payment has not been received from the Medigap insurer within a reasonable length of time. State the action to take in this case contact the insurance company and state that if you do not receive payment you will contact the state insurance commissioner.

23. A TRICARE explanation of benefits is received stating that the allowable charge for Mrs. Dayton's office visit is $30. Is it possible to appeal this for additional payment? Generally, when the Tricare contractor determines the allowable charge for a certain medical service, it is nonappealable

To check your answers to this self-study assignment, see Appendix D.

ASSIGNMENT 8–2 ► POST TO A LEDGER CARD FROM AN EXPLANATION OF BENEFITS DOCUMENT

Performance Objective

Task: Post data from an explanation of benefits document to a patient's ledger card.

Conditions: Use explanation of benefits document (Figure 8–1), blank ledger card (Figure 8–2), and pen or typewriter.

Standards: Time: ________________ minutes

Accuracy: ________________

(Note: The time element and accuracy criteria may be given by your instructor.)

Directions: Post in ink the payment received and PPO discount to a patient's ledger card (Figure 8–1) by referring to an explanation of benefits document (Figure 8–2). An example of ledger card entries is shown in Chapter 2, Figure 2–17. An explanation of benefits document is defined in Chapter 8, Figure 8–1.

After the instructor has returned your work to you, either make the necessary corrections and place it in a 3-ring notebook for future reference, or, if you received a high score, place it in your portfolio for reference when applying for a job.

ASSIGNMENT 8–3 ► TRACE AN UNPAID INSURANCE CLAIM

Performance Objective

Task: Complete an insurance claim tracer form and attach to this document a photocopy of the claim submitted.

Conditions: Use Insurance Claim Tracer form (Figure 8–3), insurance claim form from Chapter 6 (Figure 6–9), and computer or typewriter.

Standards: Time: ________________ minutes

Accuracy: ________________

(Note: The time element and accuracy criteria may be given by your instructor.)

Directions: You discover that the Medicare claim you submitted to Medicare Blue Shield, 146 Main Street, Woodland Hills, XY 12345 on Bill Hutch 3 months ago was never paid. Complete an insurance claim tracer form (Figure 8–3). Make a photocopy of Bill Hutch's insurance claim form from the *Handbook* in Chapter 6 to attach to the tracer form. Mr. Hutch is retired. Place your name on the tracer form as the person to contact at Dr. Coccidioides' office.

After the instructor has returned your work to you, either make the necessary corrections and place it in a 3-ring notebook for future reference, or, if you received a high score, place it in your portfolio for reference when applying for a job.

STATEMENT

College Clinic
4567 Broad Avenue
Woodland Hills, XY 12345-0001
Telephone: 013-486-9002
Fax: 013-487-8976

Mr. Jabe V. Bortolussi
989 Moorpark Road
Woodland Hills, XY 12345

DATE	REFERENCE	DESCRIPTION	CHARGE		CREDITS				CURRENT BALANCE	
					PAYMENTS		ADJUSTMENTS			
6-3-xx	99204	E/M NP Level 4	250	00					250	00
6-3-xx	94375	Respiratory flow voL loop	40	00					290	00
6-3-xx	94060	Spirometry	75	00					365	00
6-3-xx	94664	Aerosol inhalation	50	00					415	00
6-3-xx	94760	Pulse Oximetry	50	00					465	00

Due and payable within 10 days. **Pay last amount in balance column** 

Key: PF: Problem-focused
EPF: Expanded problem-focused
D: Detailed
C: Comprehensive
SF: Straightforward
LC: Low complexity
MC: Moderate complexity
HC: High complexity
CON: Consultation
CPX: Complete phys exam
E: Emergency
ER: Emergency dept.
HCD: House call (day)
HCN: House call (night)
HV: Hospital visit
OV: Office visit

Figure 8–1

ABC Insurance Company
P.O. Box 4300
Woodland Hills, XY 12345-0001

Claim No.:	1-00-16987087-00-zmm
Group Name:	COLLEGE CLINIC
Group No.:	010
Employee:	JABE V. BORTOLUSSI
Patient:	JABE V. BORTOLUSSI
SSN:	554-98-8876
Plan No.:	4206
Prepared by:	M. SMITH
Prepared on:	07/04/20XX

GERALD PRACTON MD
4567 BROAD AVENUE
WOODLAND HILLS XY 12345

Patient Responsibility	
Amount not covered:	00
Co-pay amount:	00
Deductible:	00
Co-insurance:	64.61
Patient's total responsibility:	64.61
Other insurance payment:	00

EXPLANATION OF BENEFITS

Treatment Dates	Service Code	CPT Code	Charge Amount	Not Covered	Reason Code	PPO Discount	Covered Amount	Deductible Amount	Co-pay Amount	Paid At	Payment Amount
06/03/00	200	99204	250.00	00	48	136.00	114.00	00	00	80%	91.20
06/03/00	540	94375	40.00	00	48	00	40.00	00	00	80%	32.00
06/03/00	540	94060	75.00	00	48	00	75.00	00	00	80%	60.00
06/03/00	200	94664	50.00	00	48	1.55	48.45	00	00	80%	38.76
06/03/00	540	94760	50.00	00	48	4.40	45.60	00	00	80%	36.48
		TOTAL	465.00	00		141.95	123.05	00	00		258.44

Other Insurance Credits or Adjustments 00

Total Payment Amount 258.44

CPT Code
99204 OFFICE/OUTPT VISIT E&M NEW MOD-HI SEVERIT
94375 RESPIRATORY FLOW VOLUM LOOP
94060 BRONCHOSPSM EVAL SPIROM PRE & POST BRON
94664 AEROSOL/VAPOR INHALA; INIT DEMO & EVAL
94760 NONINVASIVE EAR/PULSE OXIMETRY-02 SAT

Reason Code
48 CON DISCOUNT/PT NOT RESPONSIBLE

Participant		Date
GERALD PRACTON MD		07-04-xx
Patient		ID Number
JABE V. BORTOLUSSI		554-98-8876
Plan Number	Patient Number	Office No.
4206		010

GC 1234567890

258.44

PAY TO THE ORDER OF

COLLEGE CLINIC
4567 BROAD AVENUE
WOODLAND HILLS XY 12345

J M Smith
ABC Insurance Company

Figure 8–2

INSURANCE CLAIM TRACER

INSURANCE COMPANY NAME:____________________ DATE:____________________

ADDRESS____________________

PATIENT NAME:____________________ INSURED:____________________

POLICY/CERTIFICATE NUMBER:____________________ GROUP NAME/NUMBER:____________________

EMPLOYER NAME AND ADDRESS:____________________

DATE OF INITIAL CLAIM SUBMISSION:____________ AMOUNT:____________________

An inordinate amount of time has passed since submission of our original claim as described above. We have not received a request for additional information and still await payment of this assigned claim. Please review the attached duplicate and process for payment within seven (7) days.

If there is any difficulty with this claim, please check one of these below and return this letter to our office.

Claim pending because:____________________

Payment of claim in process:____________________

Payment made on claim:________ Date:____________ To Whom:____________________

Claim denied: (Reason)____________________

Patient notified: Yes__________ No__________

Remarks:____________________

____

Thank you for your assistance in this important matter. Please contact ____________________ in our office if you have any questions regarding this claim.

Office of:____________________ M.D.

Address:____________________

____________________ TELEPHONE NUMBER:____________________

Figure 8–3

ASSIGNMENT 8–4 ▶ LOCATE ERRORS ON A RETURNED INSURANCE CLAIM

Performance Objective

Task: Highlight the blocks on the insurance claim form where errors are discovered.

Conditions: Use insurance claim form (Figure 8–4) and highlighter or red pen.

Standards: Time: ________________ minutes

Accuracy: ________________

(Note: The time element and accuracy criteria may be given by your instructor.)

Directions: An insurance claim (Figure 8–4) was returned by the Prudential Insurance Company. Highlight or circle in red all blocks on the claim form where errors are discovered.

Option 1: Retype the claim and either insert the correction if data are available to fix the error or insert the word "NEED" in the block of the claim form.

Option 2: On a separate sheet of paper, list the blocks from 1 to 33 and state where errors occur.

A Performance Evaluation Checklist may be reproduced from the Instruction Guide to the *Workbook* chapter if your instructor wishes you to submit it to assist with scoring and comments.

After the instructor has returned your work to you, either make the necessary corrections and place it in a 3-ring notebook for future reference, or, if you received a high score, place it in your portfolio for reference when applying for a job.

ASSIGNMENT 8–5 ▶ LOCATE ERRORS ON A RETURNED INSURANCE CLAIM

Performance Objective

Task: Highlight the blocks on the insurance claim form where errors are discovered.

Conditions: Use insurance claim form (Figure 8–5) and highlighter or red pen.

Standards: Time: ________________ minutes

Accuracy: ________________

(Note: The time element and accuracy criteria may be given by your instructor.)

Directions: An insurance claim was returned by the Healthtech Insurance Company. Highlight or circle in red all blocks on the claim form where errors are discovered.

Option 1: Retype the claim and either insert the correction if data are available to fix the error or insert the word "NEED" in the block of the claim form.

Option 2: On a separate sheet of paper, list the blocks from 1 to 33 and state where errors occur.

Text continued on page 145

APPROVED OMB-0938-0008

PLEASE DO NOT STAPLE IN THIS AREA

PRUDENTIAL INSURANCE COMPANY
500 SOUTH BEND STREET
WOODLAND HILLS XY 12345

CARRIER

HEALTH INSURANCE CLAIM FORM

PICA

1. MEDICARE (Medicare #) MEDICAID (Medicaid #) CHAMPUS (Sponsor's SSN) CHAMPVA (VA File #) GROUP HEALTH PLAN (SSN or ID) FECA BLK LUNG (SSN) OTHER [X] (ID)

1a. INSURED'S I.D. NUMBER (FOR PROGRAM IN ITEM 1)

2. PATIENT'S NAME (Last Name, First Name, Middle Initial): JOHNSON EMILY B.

3. PATIENT'S BIRTH DATE MM DD YYYY: 02 12 1963 SEX M F

4. INSURED'S NAME (Last Name, First Name, Middle Initial): JOHNSON ERRON T.

5. PATIENT'S ADDRESS (No., Street): 4391 EVERETT STREET

6. PATIENT RELATIONSHIP TO INSURED: Self Spouse [X] Child Other

7. INSURED'S ADDRESS (No., Street): SAME

CITY: WOODLAND HILLS STATE: XY

8. PATIENT STATUS: Single Married [X] Other; Employed Full-Time Student Part-Time Student

CITY STATE

ZIP CODE: 12345 TELEPHONE (Include Area Code)

ZIP CODE TELEPHONE (Include Area Code) ( )

9. OTHER INSURED'S NAME (Last Name, First Name, Middle Initial)

10. IS PATIENT'S CONDITION RELATED TO:

11. INSURED'S POLICY GROUP OR FECA NUMBER

a. OTHER INSURED'S POLICY OR GROUP NUMBER

a. EMPLOYMENT? (CURRENT OR PREVIOUS) YES NO

a. INSURED'S DATE OF BIRTH MM DD YY SEX M F

b. OTHER INSURED'S DATE OF BIRTH MM DD YY SEX M F

b. AUTO ACCIDENT? YES NO PLACE (State)

b. EMPLOYER'S NAME OR SCHOOL NAME

c. EMPLOYER'S NAME OR SCHOOL NAME

c. OTHER ACCIDENT? YES NO

c. INSURANCE PLAN NAME OR PROGRAM NAME

d. INSURANCE PLAN NAME OR PROGRAM NAME

10d. RESERVED FOR LOCAL USE

d. IS THERE ANOTHER HEALTH BENEFIT PLAN? YES [X] NO If yes, return to and complete item 9 a-d.

READ BACK OF FORM BEFORE COMPLETING AND SIGNING THIS FORM.

12. PATIENT'S OR AUTHORIZED PERSON'S SIGNATURE I authorize the release of any medical or other information necessary to process this claim. I also request payment of government benefits either to myself or to the party who accepts assignment below.

SIGNED *Emily B. Johnson* DATE 01 04 20XX

13. INSURED'S OR AUTHORIZED PERSON'S SIGNATURE I authorize payment of medical benefits to the undersigned physician or supplier for services described below.

SIGNED *Emily B. Johnson*

PATIENT AND INSURED INFORMATION

14. DATE OF CURRENT: MM DD YY ILLNESS (First symptom) OR INJURY (Accident) OR PREGNANCY (LMP)

15. IF PATIENT HAS HAD SAME OR SIMILAR ILLNESS GIVE FIRST DATE MM DD YY

16. DATES PATIENT UNABLE TO WORK IN CURRENT OCCUPATION FROM MM DD YY TO MM DD YY

17. NAME OF REFERRING PHYSICIAN OR OTHER SOURCE

17a. I.D. NUMBER OF REFERRING PHYSICIAN

18. HOSPITALIZATION DATES RELATED TO CURRENT SERVICES FROM MM DD YY TO MM DD YY

19. RESERVED FOR LOCAL USE

20. OUTSIDE LAB? YES [X] NO $ CHARGES

21. DIAGNOSIS OR NATURE OF ILLNESS OR INJURY. (RELATE ITEMS 1,2,3 OR 4 TO ITEM 24E BY LINE)

1. 3.

2. 4.

22. MEDICAID RESUBMISSION CODE ORIGINAL REF. NO.

23. PRIOR AUTHORIZATION NUMBER

24. A DATE(S) OF SERVICE From MM DD YY	To MM DD YY	B Place of Service	C Type of Service	D PROCEDURES, SERVICES, OR SUPPLIES (Explain Unusual Circumstances) CPT/HCPCS MODIFIER	E DIAGNOSIS CODE	F $ CHARGES	G DAYS OR UNITS	H EPSDT Family Plan	I EMG	J COB	K RESERVED FOR LOCAL USE
01 04 20XX		11		99213	1	25 00					70 56871700
01 04 20XX		11		99213	1	25 00					

25. FEDERAL TAX I.D. NUMBER SSN EIN: 71 8056112

26. PATIENT'S ACCOUNT NO.

27. ACCEPT ASSIGNMENT? (For govt. claims, see back) [X] YES NO

28. TOTAL CHARGE $ 60 00

29. AMOUNT PAID $

30. BALANCE DUE $ 60 00

31. SIGNATURE OF PHYSICIAN OR SUPPLIER INCLUDING DEGREES OR CREDENTIALS (I certify that the statements on the reverse apply to this bill and are made a part thereof.)

VERA CUTIS MD

SIGNED *Vera Cutis MD* DATE 01 06 20XX

32. NAME AND ADDRESS OF FACILITY WHERE SERVICES WERE RENDERED (If other than home or office)

33. PHYSICIAN'S, SUPPLIER'S BILLING NAME, ADDRESS, ZIP CODE AND PHONE #

COLLEGE CLINIC
4567 BROAD AVENUE
WOODLAND HILLS XY 12345
PIN# 013 486 9002 GRP# 3664021CC

PHYSICIAN OR SUPPLIER INFORMATION

(APPROVED BY AMA COUNCIL ON MEDICAL SERVICE 8/88) PLEASE PRINT OR TYPE FORM HCFA-1500 (U2) (12-90) FORM OCWP-1500 FORM RRB-1500

Figure 8–4

ASSIGNMENT 8-5

HEALTHTECH INSURANCE COMPANY
4821 WESTLAKE AVENUE
WOODLAND HILLS XY 12345

1. MEDICARE (Medicare #) [ ] MEDICAID (Medicaid #) [ ] CHAMPUS (Sponsor's SSN) [X] CHAMPVA (VA File #) [ ] GROUP HEALTH PLAN (SSN or ID) [ ] FECA BLK LUNG (SSN) [ ] OTHER (ID) [X]

1a. INSURED'S I.D. NUMBER (FOR PROGRAM IN ITEM 1): 433 12 9870ANC

2. PATIENT'S NAME (Last Name, First Name, Middle Initial): DUGAN CHARLES C

3. PATIENT'S BIRTH DATE MM DD YYYY: 12 24 1968 SEX M [X] F [ ]

4. INSURED'S NAME (Last Name, First Name, Middle Initial): SAME

5. PATIENT'S ADDRESS (No., Street): 5900 ELM STREET

6. PATIENT RELATIONSHIP TO INSURED: Self [X] Spouse [ ] Child [ ] Other [ ]

7. INSURED'S ADDRESS (No., Street): SAME

CITY: WOODLAND HILLS STATE: XY

8. PATIENT STATUS: Single [ ] Married [X] Other [ ]

CITY STATE

ZIP CODE: 12345 TELEPHONE (Include Area Code): (013) 559 3300

Employed [ ] Full-Time Student [ ] Part-Time Student [ ]

ZIP CODE TELEPHONE (Include Area Code) ( )

9. OTHER INSURED'S NAME (Last Name, First Name, Middle Initial)

10. IS PATIENT'S CONDITION RELATED TO:

11. INSURED'S POLICY GROUP OR FECA NUMBER

a. OTHER INSURED'S POLICY OR GROUP NUMBER

a. EMPLOYMENT? (CURRENT OR PREVIOUS) [ ] YES [X] NO

a. INSURED'S DATE OF BIRTH MM DD YY SEX M [ ] F [ ]

b. OTHER INSURED'S DATE OF BIRTH MM DD YY SEX M [ ] F [ ]

b. AUTO ACCIDENT? [ ] YES [X] NO PLACE (State)

b. EMPLOYER'S NAME OR SCHOOL NAME

c. EMPLOYER'S NAME OR SCHOOL NAME

c. OTHER ACCIDENT? [ ] YES [X] NO

c. INSURANCE PLAN NAME OR PROGRAM NAME

d. INSURANCE PLAN NAME OR PROGRAM NAME

10d. RESERVED FOR LOCAL USE

d. IS THERE ANOTHER HEALTH BENEFIT PLAN? [ ] YES [ ] NO *If yes, return to and complete item 9 a-d.*

READ BACK OF FORM BEFORE COMPLETING AND SIGNING THIS FORM.

12. PATIENT'S OR AUTHORIZED PERSON'S SIGNATURE I authorize the release of any medical or other information necessary to process this claim. I also request payment of government benefits either to myself or to the party who accepts assignment below.

SIGNED ______ DATE ______

13. INSURED'S OR AUTHORIZED PERSON'S SIGNATURE I authorize payment of medical benefits to the undersigned physician or supplier for services described below.

SIGNED ______

14. DATE OF CURRENT MM DD YY ILLNESS (First symptom) OR INJURY (Accident) OR PREGNANCY (LMP)

15. IF PATIENT HAS HAD SAME OR SIMILAR ILLNESS GIVE FIRST DATE MM DD YY

16. DATES PATIENT UNABLE TO WORK IN CURRENT OCCUPATION FROM MM DD YY TO MM DD YY

17. NAME OF REFERRING PHYSICIAN OR OTHER SOURCE

17a. I.D. NUMBER OF REFERRING PHYSICIAN: 6780502700

18. HOSPITALIZATION DATES RELATED TO CURRENT SERVICES FROM MM DD YY TO MM DD YY

19. RESERVED FOR LOCAL USE

20. OUTSIDE LAB? [ ] YES [X] NO $ CHARGES

21. DIAGNOSIS OR NATURE OF ILLNESS OR INJURY (RELATE ITEMS 1,2,3 OR 4 TO ITEM 24E BY LINE)

1. 239 9
2.
3.
4.

22. MEDICAID RESUBMISSION CODE ORIGINAL REF. NO.

23. PRIOR AUTHORIZATION NUMBER

24. A DATE(S) OF SERVICE From MM DD YY	To MM DD YY	B Place of Service	C Type of Service	D PROCEDURES, SERVICES, OR SUPPLIES (Explain Unusual Circumstances) CPT/HCPCS MODIFIER	E DIAGNOSIS CODE	F $ CHARGES	G DAYS OR UNITS	H EPSDT Family Plan	I EMG	J COB	K RESERVED FOR LOCAL USE
09 15 20XX		11		99203	1	70 92	1			46	27889700
09 25 20XX		11		12001	1					46	27889700

25. FEDERAL TAX I.D. NUMBER SSN [ ] EIN [X]

26. PATIENT'S ACCOUNT NO.

27. ACCEPT ASSIGNMENT? (For govt. claims, see back) [X] YES [ ] NO

28. TOTAL CHARGE $

29. AMOUNT PAID $

30. BALANCE DUE $

31. SIGNATURE OF PHYSICIAN OR SUPPLIER INCLUDING DEGREES OR CREDENTIALS (I certify that the statements on the reverse apply to this bill and are made a part thereof.)

GERALD PRACTON MD 09 30 20XX

SIGNED *Gerald Practon MD* DATE

32. NAME AND ADDRESS OF FACILITY WHERE SERVICES WERE RENDERED (if other than home or office)

COLLEGE HOSPITAL
4500 BROAD AVENUE
WOODLAND HILLS XY 12345
93 731067

33. PHYSICIAN'S, SUPPLIER'S BILLING NAME, ADDRESS, ZIP CODE AND PHONE #

COLLEGE CLINIC
4567 BROAD AVENUE
WOODLAND HILLS XY 12345
013 486 9002

PIN# GRP# 3664021CC

Figure 8–5

A Performance Evaluation Checklist may be reproduced from the Instruction Guide to the *Workbook* chapter if your instructor wishes you to submit it to assist with scoring and comments.
After the instructor has returned your work to you, either make the necessary corrections and place it in a 3-ring notebook for future reference, or, if you received a high score, place it in your portfolio for reference when applying for a job.

ASSIGNMENT 8–6 ▶ LOCATE ERRORS ON A RETURNED INSURANCE CLAIM

Performance Objective

Task: Highlight the blocks on the insurance claim form where errors are discovered.

Conditions: Use insurance claim form (Figure 8–6) and highlighter or red pen.

Standards: Time: ______________ minutes

Accuracy: ______________

(Note: The time element and accuracy criteria may be given by your instructor.)

Directions: An insurance claim (Figure 8–6) was returned by an insurance plan. Highlight or circle in red all blocks on the claim form where errors are discovered.

Option 1: Retype the claim and either insert the correction if data are available to fix the error or insert the word “NEED” in the block of the claim form.

Option 2: On a separate sheet of paper, list the blocks from 1 to 33 and state where errors occur.

A Performance Evaluation Checklist may be reproduced from the Instruction Guide to the *Workbook* chapter if your instructor wishes you to submit it to assist with scoring and comments.
After the instructor has returned your work to you, either make the necessary corrections and place it in a 3-ring notebook for future reference, or, if you received a high score, place it in your portfolio for reference when applying for a job.

ASSIGNMENT 8–7 ▶ REQUEST A HEARING ON A PREVIOUSLY APPEALED CLAIM

Performance Objective

Task: Insert information on a HCFA-1965 Request for Hearing, Part B, Medicare Claim form.

Conditions: Use Request for Hearing, Part B, Medicare Claim form (Figure 8–7) and typewriter.

Standards: Time: ______________ minutes

Accuracy: ______________

(Note: The time element and accuracy criteria may be given by your instructor.)

Text continued on page 148

ASSIGNMENT 8-6

AMERICAN INSURANCE COMPANY
509 MAIN STREET
WOODLAND HILLS XY 12345

1. MEDICARE (Medicare #) ☐ MEDICAID (Medicaid #) ☐ CHAMPUS (Sponsor's SSN) ☐ CHAMPVA (VA File #) ☐ GROUP HEALTH PLAN (SSN or ID) ☐ FECA BLK LUNG (SSN) ☐ OTHER (ID) ☒

1a. INSURED'S I.D. NUMBER (FOR PROGRAM IN ITEM 1)

2. PATIENT'S NAME (Last Name, First Name, Middle Initial): MARY T AVERY

3. PATIENT'S BIRTH DATE MM DD YYYY: 05 07 1980 SEX M ☐ F ☐

4. INSURED'S NAME (Last Name, First Name, Middle Initial): SAME

5. PATIENT'S ADDRESS (No., Street): 4309 MAIN STREET

6. PATIENT RELATIONSHIP TO INSURED: Self ☒ Spouse ☐ Child ☐ Other ☐

7. INSURED'S ADDRESS (No., Street)

CITY: WOODLAND HILLS STATE: XY

8. PATIENT STATUS: Single ☐ Married ☐ Other ☐

CITY STATE

ZIP CODE: 12345 TELEPHONE (Include Area Code): (013) 450-9899

Employed ☐ Full-Time Student ☐ Part-Time Student ☐

ZIP CODE TELEPHONE (Include Area Code) ( )

9. OTHER INSURED'S NAME (Last Name, First Name, Middle Initial)

10. IS PATIENT'S CONDITION RELATED TO:

11. INSURED'S POLICY GROUP OR FECA NUMBER

a. OTHER INSURED'S POLICY OR GROUP NUMBER

a. EMPLOYMENT? (CURRENT OR PREVIOUS) ☐ YES ☒ NO

a. INSURED'S DATE OF BIRTH MM DD YY SEX M ☐ F ☐

b. OTHER INSURED'S DATE OF BIRTH MM DD YY SEX M ☐ F ☐

b. AUTO ACCIDENT? ☐ YES ☒ NO PLACE (State)

b. EMPLOYER'S NAME OR SCHOOL NAME

c. EMPLOYER'S NAME OR SCHOOL NAME

c. OTHER ACCIDENT? ☐ YES ☒ NO

c. INSURANCE PLAN NAME OR PROGRAM NAME

d. INSURANCE PLAN NAME OR PROGRAM NAME

10d. RESERVED FOR LOCAL USE

d. IS THERE ANOTHER HEALTH BENEFIT PLAN? ☐ YES ☐ NO *If yes, return to and complete item 9 a-d.*

READ BACK OF FORM BEFORE COMPLETING AND SIGNING THIS FORM.

12. PATIENT'S OR AUTHORIZED PERSON'S SIGNATURE I authorize the release of any medical or other information necessary to process this claim. I also request payment of government benefits either to myself or to the party who accepts assignment below.

SIGNED *Mary T. Avery* DATE 11 10 20XX

13. INSURED'S OR AUTHORIZED PERSON'S SIGNATURE I authorize payment of medical benefits to the undersigned physician or supplier for services described below.

SIGNED *Mary T. Avery*

14. DATE OF CURRENT: MM DD YY ◀ ILLNESS (First symptom) OR INJURY (Accident) OR PREGNANCY (LMP)

15. IF PATIENT HAS HAD SAME OR SIMILAR ILLNESS GIVE FIRST DATE MM DD YY

16. DATES PATIENT UNABLE TO WORK IN CURRENT OCCUPATION FROM MM DD YY TO MM DD YY

17. NAME OF REFERRING PHYSICIAN OR OTHER SOURCE: GERALD PRACTON MD

17a. I.D. NUMBER OF REFERRING PHYSICIAN

18. HOSPITALIZATION DATES RELATED TO CURRENT SERVICES FROM 11 11 20XX TO 11 12 20XX

19. RESERVED FOR LOCAL USE

20. OUTSIDE LAB? ☐ YES ☒ NO $ CHARGES

21. DIAGNOSIS OR NATURE OF ILLNESS OR INJURY. (RELATE ITEMS 1,2,3 OR 4 TO ITEM 24E BY LINE)

1. 463
2.
3.
4.

22. MEDICAID RESUBMISSION CODE ORIGINAL REF. NO.

23. PRIOR AUTHORIZATION NUMBER

24.

A DATE(S) OF SERVICE From MM DD YY	To MM DD YY	B Place of Service	C Type of Service	D PROCEDURES, SERVICES, OR SUPPLIES (Explain Unusual Circumstances) CPT/HCPCS	MODIFIER	E DIAGNOSIS CODE	F $ CHARGES	G DAYS OR UNITS	H EPSDT Family Plan	I EMG	J COB	K RESERVED FOR LOCAL USE
11 10 20XX		11		99203		1	50 00	1			43	05004700
11 11 20XX		21		99222		1	120 00	1			43	05004700
11 11 20XX		21		42821		1	410 73				43	05004700
11 12 20XX		21		99231		1	20 00					

25. FEDERAL TAX I.D. NUMBER: 71 5737291 SSN ☐ EIN ☒

26. PATIENT'S ACCOUNT NO.

27. ACCEPT ASSIGNMENT? (For govt. claims, see back) ☐ YES ☐ NO

28. TOTAL CHARGE $

29. AMOUNT PAID $

30. BALANCE DUE $

31. SIGNATURE OF PHYSICIAN OR SUPPLIER INCLUDING DEGREES OR CREDENTIALS (I certify that the statements on the reverse apply to this bill and are made a part thereof.)

SIGNED DATE 11 15 20XX

32. NAME AND ADDRESS OF FACILITY WHERE SERVICES WERE RENDERED (If other than home or office)
COLLEGE HOSPITAL
4500 BROAD AVENUE
WOODLAND HILLS XY 12345
95 0731067

33. PHYSICIAN'S, SUPPLIER'S BILLING NAME, ADDRESS, ZIP CODE AND PHONE #
COLLEGE CLINIC
4567 BROAD AVENUE
WOODLAND HILLS XY 12345
013 486 9002

PIN# GRP# 3664021CC

Figure 8–6

DEPARTMENT OF HEALTH AND HUMAN SERVICES
HEALTH CARE FINANCING ADMINISTRATION

Form Approved
OMB No. 0938-0034

REQUEST FOR HEARING — PART B MEDICARE CLAIM

Medical Insurance Benefits – Social Security Act

NOTICE—Anyone who misrepresents or falsifies essential information requested by this form may upon conviction be subject to fine and imprisonment under Federal Law.

Carrier's Name and Address

1 Name of Patient

2 Health Insurance Claim Number

3 I disagree with the review determination on my claim, and request a hearing before a hearing officer of the insurance carrier named above.
MY REASONS ARE: *(Attach a copy of the Review Notice. NOTE—If the review decision was made more than 6 months ago include your reason for not making this request earlier.)*

4 Check one of the following:

☐ I have additional evidence to submit. *(Attach such evidence to this form or forward it to the carrier within 10 days.)*

☐ I do not have additional evidence.

Check <u>Only One</u> of the Statements Below:

☐ I wish to appear in person before the Hearing Officer.

☐ I do not wish to appear and hereby request a decision on the evidence before the Hearing Officer.

5 EITHER THE CLAIMANT OR REPRESENTATIVE SHOULD SIGN IN THE APPROPRIATE SPACE BELOW:

Signature or Name of Claimant's Representative ➔		Claimant's Signature ➔	
Address		Address	
City, State, and ZIP Code		City, State, and ZIP Code	
Telephone Number	Date	Telephone Number	Date

(Claimant should not write below this line)

Your request for a hearing was received on ______________________. You will be notified of the time and place of the hearing at least 10 days before the date of the hearing.

Signed	Date

Form HCFA-1965 (8-79)

CARRIER COPY

Figure 8–7

Directions: After Medicare processes the insurance claim tracer on Bill Hutch, you receive a Medicare EOB and payment check but the amount is incorrect due to an excessive reduction in the allowed payment. An appeal was made in September and denied; Dr. John Doe feels a mistake has been made and wishes to request a hearing.

Complete the HCFA-1965 Request for Hearing, Part B, Medicare Claim form for this case (Figure 8–7) by referring to the tracer form completed for Assignment 8–2 (Figure 8–3) and *Handbook* Figure 6–10 in Chapter 6. As you will learn in the chapter on Medicare, the Health Insurance Claim Number is the patient's Medicare identification number as shown in Figure 6–10, Block 1a. No additional evidence is to be presented and the doctor does not wish to appear for the hearing. Date the form December 5, 20XX.

After the instructor has returned your work to you, either make the necessary corrections and place it in a 3-ring notebook for future reference, or, if you received a high score, place it in your portfolio for reference when applying for a job.

ASSIGNMENT 8–8 ▶ OBSERVATIONS OF INSURANCE VIDEO

Performance Objective

Task: View the video "The HCFA Files: A Case for Medical Billing Accuracy." Take notes and answer questions regarding the remarks of the three insurance billing specialists who lend their comments about the scenarios presented.

Conditions: VHS video equipment, paper, and pencil or pen.

Standards: Time: ________________ minutes

Accuracy: ________________

(Note: The time element and accuracy criteria may be given by your instructor.)

Directions: After viewing the video, use your notes to answer the following questions.

1. The two penalties possible if someone is convicted of Medicare fraud are:

   a. ____

   b. ____

2. In the first part of the video, it mentions the format for the birth date must appear on the HCFA-1500 claim form as ______________________________.

3. As mentioned in the video, when plastic surgery is performed on an individual with a deviated septum, what may be a medical justification for payment since this may be considered cosmetic in the eyes of the insurance company? ______________________________

4. List some items that must agree or match during the editing process to eliminate the claim being denied or rejected.

   a. ____

b. ______

c. ______

d. ______

5. State when these modifiers are used.

   -78 ______

   -79 ______

6. If a patient receives a laparoscopic cholecystectomy with a cholangiograph, how should these services be submitted when completing an insurance claim?

   ______

7. When a cholecystectomy is performed and the patient's gallbladder is listed as obstructed or not obstructed, the diagnosis code must ______.

8. If a service is down- or undercoded, it means the reimbursement by the insurance carrier for the procedure is ______.

9. List two items you learned from the video in regard to billing for a patient who has had a hernia repair.

   a. ______

   b. ______

10. List types of problems why a claim may be either denied or rejected after receipt by the insurance company. See how many you noted after viewing this video.

    a. ______

    b. ______

    c. ______

    d. ______

    e. ______

    f. ______

    g. ______

    h. ______

    i. ______

    j. ______

k. ______________________________

l. ______________________________

m. ______________________________

n. ______________________________

11. On average, what percentage of submitted insurance claims is rejected?

____

9

Office and Insurance Collection Strategies

KEY TERMS

Your instructor may wish to select some specific words pertinent to this chapter for a test. For definitions of the terms, further study, and/or reference, the words, phrases, and abbreviations may be found in the Glossary at the end of the Handbook. *Key terms for this chapter follow.*

accounts receivable
age analysis
automatic stay
balance
bankruptcy
cash flow
collateral
collection ratio
computer billing
credit
credit card
creditor
cycle billing
debit card
debit
debtor
discount
dun message
estate administrator
estate executor
fee schedule
garnishment
insurance balance billing
itemized statement
ledger card
lien
manual billing
netback
no charge (NC)
nonexempt assets
professional courtesy
reimbursement
secured debt
skip
statute of limitations
unsecured debt
write-off

PERFORMANCE OBJECTIVES

The student will be able to

- Define and spell the key terms for this chapter, given the Information from the *Handbook* Glossary, within a reasonable period of time and with enough accuracy to obtain a satisfactory evaluation.
- Answer the self-study review questions after reading the chapter, with enough accuracy to obtain a satisfactory evaluation.
- Choose an appropriate dun message for a patient's bill, given a patient's ledger/statement, within a reasonable period of time and with enough accuracy to obtain a satisfactory evaluation.
- Post a courtesy adjustment, given a patient's ledger/statement, within a reasonable period of time and with enough accuracy to obtain a satisfactory evaluation.
- Post a patient's payment to the ledger/statement, using the Mock Fee Schedule in Appendix A, within a reasonable period of time and with enough accuracy to obtain a satisfactory evaluation.
- Compose a collection letter for a delinquent account, given letterhead stationery, within a reasonable period of time and with enough accuracy to obtain a satisfactory evaluation.
- Complete a credit card voucher, given a patient's ledger/statement, within a reasonable period of time and with enough accuracy to obtain a satisfactory evaluation.
- Complete a financial agreement, given a patient's ledger/statement, within a reasonable period of time and with enough accuracy to obtain a satisfactory evaluation.

STUDY OUTLINE

Cash Flow Cycle
- Accounts Receivable
- Patient Education
- Patient Registration Form

Fees
- Fee Schedule
- Fee Adjustments
  - Discounting Fees
    - Cash Discounts
    - Financial Hardship
  - Write-off or Courtesy Adjustment
  - Professional Courtesy
  - Copayment Waiver
  - No Charge
  - Reduced Fee
- Communicating Fees
- Collecting Fees
  - Payment at the Time of Service
    - Encounter Forms
    - Patient Excuses
  - Payment by Check
    - Check Verification
    - Check Forgery
    - Payment Disputes
    - Unsigned Checks
    - Returned Checks
  - Itemized Statements
    - Age Analysis
    - Dun Messages
    - Manual Billing
    - Computer Billing
    - Billing Services
    - Billing Guidelines

Procedure: Seven-step Billing and Collection Guideline

Credit Arrangements
- Payment Options
  - Credit Card Billing
    - Verifying Credit Cards
    - Verifying Credit Cardholders
    - Credit Card Fees
    - Credit Card Options
  - Debit Cards
  - Payment Plans

Credit and Collection Laws
- Statute of Limitations
- Equal Credit Opportunity Act
- Fair Credit Reporting Act
- Fair Credit Billing Act
- Truth in Lending Act
  - Late Payment Charges
- Truth in Lending Consumer Credit Cost Disclosure
- Fair Debt Collecting Practices Act

The Collection Process

Office Collection Techniques

- Telephone Debt Collection

Procedure: Telephone Collection Plan

- Telephone "Do Nots"
- Telephone Collection Scenarios
- Collection Letters
- Types of Collection Letters
- Collection Abbreviations
- Insurance Collections
- History of Accounts
- Coinsurance Payments
- Insurance Checks Sent to Patients
- Managed Care Organizations
- Medicare
- Medigap Insurance
- Workers' Compensation
- Suing an Insurance Carrier
- Collection Agencies
  - Choosing an Agency
  - Types of Agencies
  - Agency Operating Techniques
  - Agency Charges
  - Agency-Assigned Accounts
- Credit Bureaus
- Credit Counseling
- Small Claims Court

Procedure: Basic Steps to Filing a Claim

- Claim Resolution
- Trial Preparation
  - Federal Wage Garnishment Laws
- Tracing a Skip
  - Skip Tracing Techniques
  - Skip Tracing Services
  - Search Via Computer
- Special Collection Issues
  - Bankruptcy
  - Bankruptcy Rules
  - Terminally Ill Patients
  - Estate Claims

Procedure: Filing an Estate Claim

- Litigation
  - Liens
- Patient Complaints
- Collection Controls

SELF-STUDY 9–1 ▶ REVIEW QUESTIONS

Review the objectives, key terms, chapter information, glossary definitions to key terms, and figures before completing the following review questions.

1. Third-party payers are composed of

   a. private insurance

   b. government plans

   c. managed care contracts

   d. workers compensation

2. The unpaid balance due from patients for professional services rendered is known as

   a/an accounts receivable.

3. Write the formula for calculating the office A/R ratio Divide the month-end accounts receivable balance by the monthly average of the medical practice charge for the prior 12 month period

4. What is the collection rate if a total of $40,300 was collected for the month and the total of the accounts receivable is $50,670? 80% %

5. An important document that provides identifying data for each patient and assists in billing and collection is called a/an Patient registration form or patient information sheet.

6. A preferable term for "write-off" when used in a medical practice is courtesy adjustment.

7. To verify a check, ask the patient for a/an drivers license and one other form of identificaton

8. The procedure of systematically arranging the accounts receivable, by age, from the date of service is called age analysis.

9. A system of billing accounts at spaced intervals during the month based on breakdown of accounts by alphabet, account number, insurance type, or date of service is known as cycle billing.

10. Are physicians' patient accounts single-entry accounts, open book accounts, or written contract accounts? open book accounts

11. Match the terms with the definitions. Write the correct letters in the blanks.

1.	D	Reductions of the normal fee based on a specific amount of money or a percentage of the charge	a. debtor
2.	G	Phrase to remind a patient about a delinquent account	b. itemized statement
3.	H	Item that permits bank customers to withdraw cash at any hour from an automated teller machine	c. fee schedule
4.	A	Individual owing money	d. discounts
5.	I	Claim on the property of another as security for a debt	e. ledger card
6.	E	Individual record indicating charges, payments, adjustments, and balances owed for services rendered	f. creditor
7.	B	Detailed summary of all transactions of a creditor's account	g. dun message
8.	F	Person to whom money is owed	h. debit card
9.	C	Listing of accepted charges or established allowances for specific medical procedures	i. lien

12. A court order attaching a debtor's property or wages to pay off a debt is known as garnishment

13. Match the terms with the definitions. Write the correct letters in the blanks.

1. C Law stating that a person has 60 days to complain about an error from the date that a statement is mailed
2. D Consumer protection act that applies to anyone who charges interest or agrees on payment of a bill in more than four installments, excluding a down payment
3. E Regulates collection practices of third-party debt collectors and attorneys who collect debts for others
4. A Federal law prohibiting discrimination in all areas of granting credit
5. B Regulates agencies who issue or use credit reports on consumers

a. Equal Credit Opportunity Act
b. Fair Credit Reporting Act
c. Fair Credit Billing Act
d. Truth in Lending Act
e. Fair Debt Collection Practices Act

14. An individual who owes on an account and moves, leaving no forwarding address, is called a/an skip.

15. A straight petition in bankruptcy or absolute bankruptcy is also known as a/an chapter 7.

16. A wage earner's bankruptcy is sometimes referred to as a/an Chapter 13.

17. Translate these credit and collection abbreviations.

NSF not sufficient funds T Telephoned
WCO will call office SK skip or skipped
PIF Payment in Full FN Final notice
NLE no longer emploked UE unemployed

To check your answers to this self-study assignment, see Appendix D.

ASSIGNMENT **9–2 ▶ SELECT A DUN MESSAGE**

Performance Objective

Task: Select an appropriate dun message and insert it on a patient's ledger card.

Conditions: Use the patient's ledger card (Figure 9–1) and typewriter.

Standards: Time: ____________ minutes

Accuracy: ______________

(Note: The time element and accuracy criteria may be given by your instructor.)

Directions: Read the scenario and refer to the patient`s ledger/statement (Figure 9–1). Select appropriate dun messages for each month the patient has been billed. You may wish to refer to *Handbook* Figure 9–2.

Scenario: Carrie Jones was on vacation in June and July and did not pay on her account. It is August (current year).

After the instructor has returned your work to you, either make the necessary corrections and place it in a 3-ring notebook for future reference, or, if you received a high score, place it in your portfolio for reference when applying for a job.

ASSIGNMENT 9–3 ► POST A COURTESY ADJUSTMENT

Performance Objective

Task: Post a courtesy adjustment to a patient's ledger card.

Conditions: Use the patient's ledger card (Figure 9–2) and a pen.

Standards: Time: ___________ minutes

Accuracy: _______________

(Note: The time element and accuracy criteria may be given by your instructor.)

Directions: Read the case scenario and refer to the patient's ledger/statement (Figure 9–2). You may wish to refer to *Handbook* Figure 9–2. Post a courtesy adjustment to her ledger/statement.

Scenario: Maria Smith recently lost her job and is raising two children as a single parent. It is September 1 (current year). A discussion with Dr. Gerald Practon leads to a decision to write off the balance on the account.

After the instructor has returned your work to you, either make the necessary corrections and place it in a 3-ring notebook for future reference, or, if you received a high score, place it in your portfolio for reference when applying for a job.

ASSIGNMENT 9–4 ► POST A PATIENT'S PAYMENT

Performance Objective

Task: Post a payment to a patient's ledger card.

Conditions: Use the patient's ledger card (Figure 9–3), Mock Fee Schedule in Appendix A, and a pen.

Standards: Time: ________________ minutes

Accuracy: _________________

(Note: The time element and accuracy criteria may be given by your instructor.)

Directions: Read the case scenario, refer to the patient`s ledger/statement (Figure 9–3), and refer to the Mock Fee Schedule in Appendix A. You may wish to refer to *Handbook* Figure 9–2. Post the charges for the services rendered and payment to his ledger/statement.

Text continued on page 163

STATEMENT

College Clinic
4567 Broad Avenue
Woodland Hills, XY 12345-0001
Telephone: 013-486-9002
Fax: 013-487-8976

Account No. 34455
Carrie Jones
15543 Dean Street
Woodland Hills, XY 12345

DATE	PROFESSIONAL SERVICE DESCRIPTION	CHARGE		CREDITS PAYMENTS		CREDITS ADJUSTMENTS		CURRENT BALANCE	
	Balance forward							20	00
4-16-xx	C hx/exam HC DM DX 582	134	99					154	99
4-17-xx	Prudential billed (4-16-xx)							154	99
5-27-xx	Rec'd insurance ck # 435			30	00			124	99
6-1-xx	Billed pt							124	99
7-1-xx	Billed pt							124	99
8-1-xx	Billed pt							124	99

Due and payable within 10 days. **Pay last amount in balance column** 

Key: PF: Problem-focused
EPF: Expanded problem-focused
D: Detailed
C: Comprehensive
SF: Straightforward
LC: Low complexity
MC: Moderate complexity
HC: High complexity
CON: Consultation
CPX: Complete phys exam
E: Emergency
ER: Emergency dept.
HCD: House call (day)
HCN: House call (night)
HV: Hospital visit
OV: Office visit

Figure 9–1

STATEMENT

College Clinic
4567 Broad Avenue
Woodland Hills, XY 12345-0001
Telephone: 013-486-9002
Fax: 013-487-8976

Account No. 34211
Maria Smith
3737 Unser Road
Woodland Hills, XY 12345

DATE	PROFESSIONAL SERVICE DESCRIPTION	CHARGE		CREDITS PAYMENTS		CREDITS ADJUSTMENTS		CURRENT BALANCE	
	Balance forward							20	00
5-19-xx	OV DX 582	61	51					81	51
5-20-xx	Metropolitan billed (5-19-xx)							81	51
6-20-xx	Rec'd ins ck # 6778			25	00			56	51
7-1-xx	Pt billed							56	51
8-1-xx	Pt billed							56	51

Due and payable within 10 days. **Pay last amount in balance column** 

Key: PF: Problem-focused
EPF: Expanded problem-focused
D: Detailed
C: Comprehensive
SF: Straightforward
LC: Low complexity
MC: Moderate complexity
HC: High complexity
CON: Consultation
CPX: Complete phys exam
E: Emergency
ER: Emergency dept.
HCD: House call (day)
HCN: House call (night)
HV: Hospital visit
OV: Office visit

Figure 9–2

STATEMENT

College Clinic
4567 Broad Avenue
Woodland Hills, XY 12345-0001
Telephone: 013-486-9002
Fax: 013-487-8976

Account No. 78650
Kenneth Brown
8896 Aster Drive
Woodland Hills, XY 12345

DATE	PROFESSIONAL SERVICE DESCRIPTION	CHARGE	CREDITS		CURRENT BALANCE
			PAYMENTS	ADJUSTMENTS	

Due and payable within 10 days. **Pay last amount in balance column** 

Key: PF: Problem-focused
EPF: Expanded problem-focused
D: Detailed
C: Comprehensive
SF: Straightforward
LC: Low complexity
MC: Moderate complexity
HC: High complexity
CON: Consultation
CPX: Complete phys exam
E: Emergency
ER: Emergency dept.
HCD: House call (day)
HCN: House call (night)
HV: Hospital visit
OV: Office visit

Figure 9–3

Scenario: On October 12 (current year) new patient Kenneth Brown came in for a Level III office visit and ECG. He has no insurance and paid $50 on his account with check number 3421.

After the instructor has returned your work to you, either make the necessary corrections and place it in a 3-ring notebook for future reference, or, if you received a high score, place it in your portfolio for reference when applying for a job.

ASSIGNMENT 9–5 ▶ COMPOSE A COLLECTION LETTER

Performance Objective

Task: Key letter for the physician's signature and post entry on patient's ledger card.

Conditions: Use the patient's ledger card (Figure 9–4), one sheet of letterhead (Figure 9–5), a number 10 envelope, and a pen.

Standards: Time: ________________ minutes

Accuracy: ________________

(Note: The time element and accuracy criteria may be given by your instructor.)

Directions: Read the case scenario, refer to the patient's ledger/statement (Figure 9–4), and compose a collection letter using your signature and request payment. Type this letter on letterhead stationery in full block format (paragraphs to left margin). Include a paragraph stating that a copy of the delinquent statement is enclosed. You may wish to refer to the *Handbook* Figure 9–16. Post an entry on the patient's statement.

Scenario: It is December 1 (current year) and you have sent Mr. Ron Kelsey two statements with no response. You tried to reach him by telephone without success and have decided to send him a collection letter (Figure 9–5).

After the instructor has returned your work to you, either make the necessary corrections and place it in a 3-ring notebook for future reference, or, if you received a high score, place it in your portfolio for reference when applying for a job.

ASSIGNMENT 9–6 ▶ COMPLETE A CREDIT CARD VOUCHER

Performance Objective

Task: Complete a credit card voucher and post an entry on the patient's ledger.

Conditions: Use the patient's ledger card (Figure 9–6), a credit card voucher (Figure 9–7), and a pen.

Standards: Time: ________________ minutes

Accuracy: ________________

(Note: The time element and accuracy criteria may be given by your instructor.)

Directions: Read the case scenario and refer to the patient's ledger/statement (Figure 9–6). Fill in the credit card voucher (Figure 9–7) and post an appropriate entry on the ledger/statement. You may wish to refer to the *Handbook* Figure 9–11.

Scenario: It is November 6 (current year) and you receive a telephone call at the College Clinic. It is Kevin Long, who has an unpaid balance, and it is up to you to discuss this delinquency with Mr. Long and come to an agreement on how the account can be paid. After discussion, Mr. Long decides to pay the total balance due by MasterCard credit card, giving you his authorization and account number: 5676 1342 5437 3455 (expiration date 12-31-xx). His name is listed on the card as Kevin O. Long. You call the bank, and the authorization number given is 534889.

After the instructor has returned your work to you, either make the necessary corrections and place it in a 3-ring notebook for future reference, or, if you received a high score, place it in your portfolio for reference when applying for a job.

ASSIGNMENT 9–7 ▶ COMPLETE A FINANCIAL AGREEMENT

Performance Objective

Task: Complete a financial agreement and post an entry on the patient's ledger.

Conditions: Use the patient's ledger card (Figure 9–8), a financial statement form (Figure 9–9), and a pen.

Standards: Time: ___________ minutes

Accuracy: ________________

(Note: The time element and accuracy criteria may be given by your instructor.)

Directions: Read the case scenario and refer to the patient's ledger/statement (Figure 9–8). Complete a financial agreement (Figure 9–9) and post an appropriate entry to the ledger/statement using a pen. You may wish to refer to the *Handbook* Figure 9–5.

Scenario: Mr. Joseph Small has a large balance due. Create a payment plan for this case. On June 1 (current year), Mr. Small is paying $500 cash as a down payment and the balance is to be divided into five equal payments due on the first of each month. There will be no monthly finance charge. Mr. Small's daytime telephone number is 013-655-0988. He is a patient of Dr. Brady Coccidioides.

After the instructor has returned your work to you, either make the necessary corrections and place it in a 3-ring notebook for future reference, or, if you received a high score, place it in your portfolio for reference when applying for a job.

STATEMENT

College Clinic
4567 Broad Avenue
Woodland Hills, XY 12345-0001
Telephone: 013-486-9002
Fax: 013-487-8976

Account No. 16549
Ron Kelsey
6321 Ocean Street
Woodland Hills, XY 12345

DATE	PROFESSIONAL SERVICE DESCRIPTION	CHARGE		CREDITS				CURRENT BALANCE	
				PAYMENTS		ADJUSTMENTS			
7-9-xx	ER new pt EPF hx/exam MC DM	66	23					66	23
7-10-xx	XYZ Insurance billed (3-9-xx)							66	23
9-20-xx	EOB rec'd pt has not met deductible							66	23
10-1-xx	Billed pt							66	23
11-1-xx	Billed pt							66	23

Due and payable within 10 days. **Pay last amount in balance column** 

Key: PF: Problem-focused
EPF: Expanded problem-focused
D: Detailed
C: Comprehensive
SF: Straightforward
LC: Low complexity
MC: Moderate complexity
HC: High complexity
CON: Consultation
CPX: Complete phys exam
E: Emergency
ER: Emergency dept.
HCD: House call (day)
HCN: House call (night)
HV: Hospital visit
OV: Office visit

Figure 9–4

COLLEGE CLINIC
4567 Broad Avenue
Woodland Hills, XY 12345-0001
Tel. (013) 486-9002
FAX (013) 487-8976

Figure 9–5

STATEMENT

College Clinic
4567 Broad Avenue
Woodland Hills, XY 12345-0001
Telephone: 013-486-9002
Fax: 013-487-8976

Account No. 1098
Kevin O. Long
2443 Davis Street
Woodland Hills, XY 12345

DATE	PROFESSIONAL SERVICE DESCRIPTION	CHARGE		CREDITS PAYMENTS		CREDITS ADJUSTMENTS		CURRENT BALANCE	
9-8-xx	OV Level V DX 582	132	28					132	28
9-9-xx	Blue Cross billed (9-8-xx)							132	28
10-12-xx	BC EOB rec'd pt has not met deductible							132	28
10-23-xx	Not covered by insurance. Balance due							132	28

Due and payable within 10 days. **Pay last amount in balance column** 

Key: PF: Problem-focused
EPF: Expanded problem-focused
D: Detailed
C: Comprehensive
SF: Straightforward
LC: Low complexity
MC: Moderate complexity
HC: High complexity
CON: Consultation
CPX: Complete phys exam
E: Emergency
ER: Emergency dept.
HCD: House call (day)
HCN: House call (night)
HV: Hospital visit
OV: Office visit

Figure 9–6

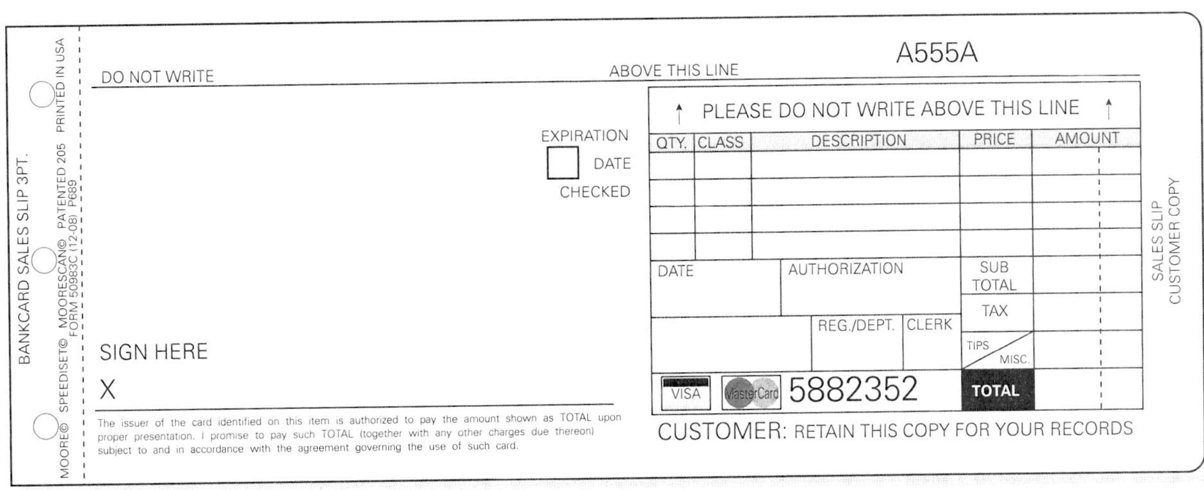
BANKCARD SALES SLIP 3PT.
MOORE© SPEEDISET© MOORESCAN© PATENTED 205 PRINTED IN USA
FORM 50983C (12-08) F689

DO NOT WRITE ABOVE THIS LINE

A555A

↑ PLEASE DO NOT WRITE ABOVE THIS LINE ↑

EXPIRATION DATE CHECKED

QTY.	CLASS	DESCRIPTION	PRICE	AMOUNT

DATE	AUTHORIZATION		SUB TOTAL	
	REG./DEPT.	CLERK	TAX	
			TIPS / MISC.	
VISA MasterCard 5882352			TOTAL	

SIGN HERE

X

The issuer of the card identified on this item is authorized to pay the amount shown as TOTAL upon proper presentation. I promise to pay such TOTAL (together with any other charges due thereon) subject to and in accordance with the agreement governing the use of such card.

CUSTOMER: RETAIN THIS COPY FOR YOUR RECORDS

SALES SLIP
CUSTOMER COPY

Figure 9–7

STATEMENT

College Clinic
4567 Broad Avenue
Woodland Hills, XY 12345-0001
Telephone: 013-486-9002
Fax: 013-487-8976

Account No. 34322
Joseph Small
655 Sherry Street
Woodland Hills, XY 12345

DATE	PROFESSIONAL SERVICE DESCRIPTION	CHARGE		CREDITS PAYMENTS		CREDITS ADJUSTMENTS		CURRENT BALANCE	
	Balance forward							20	00
4-19-xx	OV Level V	96	97					116	97
4-30-xx	Adm hosp	74	22					191	19
4-30-xx	Pneumonectomy, total	1972	10					2113	29
5-20-xx	Blue Shield billed (1-19 to 30-xx)							2113	29
5-15-xx	BS EOB Pt deductible $2000 rec'd ck# 544			113	29			2000	00

Due and payable within 10 days. **Pay last amount in balance column** 

Key:
PF: Problem-focused
EPF: Expanded problem-focused
D: Detailed
C: Comprehensive
SF: Straightforward
LC: Low complexity
MC: Moderate complexity
HC: High complexity
CON: Consultation
CPX: Complete phys exam
E: Emergency
ER: Emergency dept.
HCD: House call (day)
HCN: House call (night)
HV: Hospital visit
OV: Office visit

Figure 9–8

FINANCIAL AGREEMENT

For PROFESSIONAL SERVICES rendered or to be rendered to:

Patient ______________ Daytime Phone ______________

Parent if patient is a minor ______________

1. Cash price for services . . . . . . $ ______
2. Cash down payment . . . . . . $ ______
3. Charges covered by insurance service plan . . . . . . $ ______
4. Unpaid balance of cash price. . . . . . $ ______
5. Amount financed (the amount of credit provided to you) . . . . . . $ ______
6. FINANCE CHARGE (the dollar amount the credit will cost you) . . . . . $ ______
7. ANNUAL PERCENTAGE RATE (the cost of credit as a yearly rate) . . . . . . ______ %
8. Total of payments (5 + 6 above-the amount you will have paid when you have made all scheduled payments). . . . . . $ ______
9. Total sales price (1 + 6 above-sum of cash price, financing charge and any other amounts financed by the creditor, not part of the finance charge) . . . . . . $ ______

You have the right at any time to pay the unpaid balance due under this agreement without penalty.
You have the right at this time to receive an itemization of the amount financed.

☐ I want an itemization ☐ I do not want an itemization

Total of payments (#8 above) is payable to Dr. ______________
in ______ monthly installments of $ ______ each and ______ installments of $ ______ each. The first installment being payable on ______ 20 ______ and subsequent installments on the same day of each consecutive month until paid in full.

NOTICE TO PATIENT

Do not sign this agreement if it contains any blank spaces. You are entitled to an exact copy of any agreement you sign. You have the right at any time to pay the unpaid balance due under this agreement.

The patient (parent or guardian) agrees to be and is fully responsible for total payment of services performed in this office including any amounts not covered by health insurance or prepayment program the responsible party may have. See your contract documents for any additional information about nonpayment, default, any required prepayment in full before the scheduled date and prepayment refunds and penalties.

Signature of patient or one parent if patient is a minor:

X ______________

Doctor's Signature ______________

Form 1826 • 1982

SCHEDULE OF PAYMENT

No.	Date Due	Amount of Installment	Date Paid	Amount Paid	Balance Owed
	Total Amount				
D.P.					
1					
2					
3					
4					
5					
6					
7					
8					
9					
10					
11					
12					
13					
14					
15					
16					
17					
18					
19					
20					
21					
22					
23					

Figure 9–9

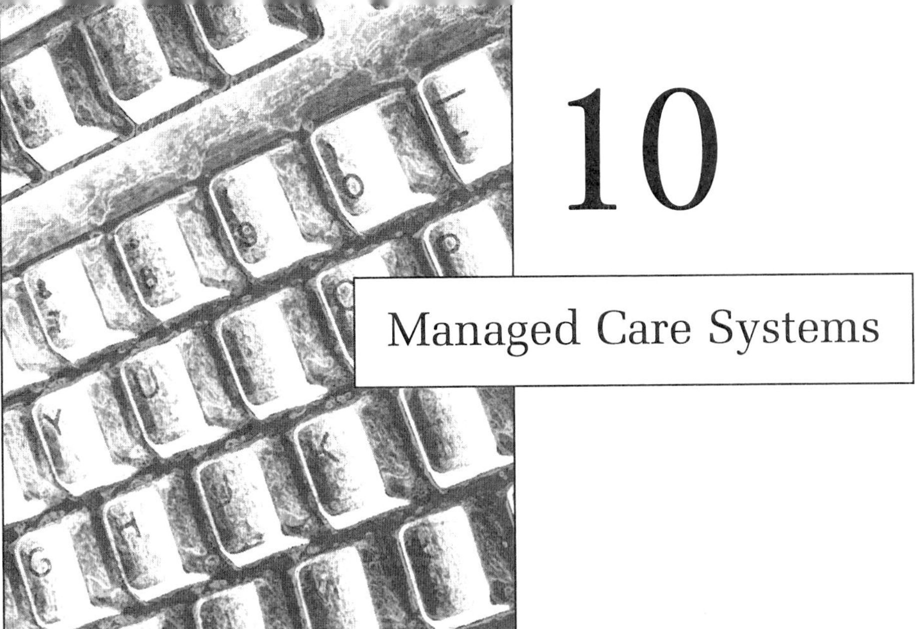

10

Managed Care Systems

KEY TERMS

Your instructor may wish to select some specific words pertinent to this chapter for a test. For definitions of the terms, further study, and/or reference, the words, phrases, and abbreviations may be found in the Glossary at the end of the Handbook. *Key terms for this chapter follow.*

ancillary services
buffing
capitation
carve outs
churning
claims-review type of foundation
closed panel program
comprehensive type of foundation
copayment (copay)
deductible
direct referral
disenrollment
exclusive provider organization (EPO)
fee for service
formal referral
foundation for medical care (FMC)
gatekeeper
health maintenance organization (HMO)
in-area
Independent (or Individual) Practice Association (IPA)
managed care organizations (MCOs)
participating physician
per capita
physician provider group (PPG)
point-of-service (POS) plan
preferred provider organization (PPO)
prepaid group practice model
primary care physician (PCP)
self-referral
service area
staff model
stop loss
tertiary care
turfing
utilization review (UR)
verbal referral
withhold

PERFORMANCE OBJECTIVES

The student will be able to

- Define and spell the key terms for this chapter, given the information from the *Handbook* Glossary, within a reasonable period of time and with enough accuracy to obtain a satisfactory evaluation.
- Answer the self-study review questions after reading the chapter, with enough accuracy to obtain a satisfactory evaluation.
- Complete treatment authorization forms of managed care plans, given completed new patient information forms, within a reasonable period of time and with enough accuracy to obtain a satisfactory evaluation.

STUDY OUTLINE

History
- Prepaid Group Practice Health Plans
  - Health Maintenance Organization Act of 1973
  - Eligibility
  - Benefits
- Health Care Reform

Managed Care Systems
- Health Maintenance Organizations
  - Prepaid Group Practice Model
  - Staff Model
  - Network HMO
- Exclusive Provider Organizations
- Foundations for Medical Care
- Independent Practice Association
- Preferred Provider Organizations
- Physician Provider Groups
- Point of Service Plans
- Triple Option Health Plan

Medical Review
- Professional Review Organizations
- Utilization Review or Management

Management of Plans
- Contracts
  - Carve Outs
- Preauthorization or Prior Approval
- Diagnostic Tests
- Managed Care Guide
- Plan Administration
  - Patient Information Letter
  - Medical Records
  - Scheduling Appointments
  - Encounter Form

Financial Management
- Payment
  - Deductibles
  - Copayments
  - Contact Capitation
  - Case Rate Pricing
  - Stop-Loss Limit
  - Contract Payment Time Limits
  - Monitoring Payment
- Statement of Remittance
- Accounting
- Fee for Service
- Year-End Evaluation
  - Capitation Versus Fee for Service
  - Withholds
- Bankruptcy

SELF-STUDY 10–1 ► REVIEW QUESTIONS

Review the objectives, key terms, glossary definitions to key terms, figures, and chapter information before completing the following review questions.

1. If a physician or hospital in a managed care plan is paid a fixed, per capita amount for each patient enrolled regardless of the type and number of services rendered,

   this is a payment system known as 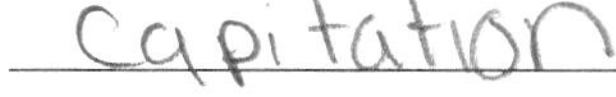 capitation.

2. When a prepaid group practice plan limits the patient's choice of personal physicians, this is termed a/an Closed panel program.

3. In a managed care setting, a physician who controls patient access to specialists and diagnostic testing services is known as a/an Gate Keeper.

4. Systems that allow for better negotiations for contracts with large employers are

a. managed care organizations

b. physician-hospital organizations

c. Group practices accepting a variety of MCO's and fee for service patients

5. The oldest of the prepaid health plans is Health maintenance organizations.

6. Name three types of HMOs.

a. prepaid group practice model

b. staff model

c. Network HMO

7. What is a foundation for medical care? an organization of physician sponsored by a state or local medical association concerned with the development and delivery of medical services and the cost of health care.

8. Name two types of operations used by foundations for medical care and explain the main feature of each.

a. comprehensive Type: Designs and sponsors prepaid health programs or sets minimum benefits of coverage

b. Claims-review Type: Provides evaluation of the quality and efficiency of services by a panel of physicians to the numerous fiscal agents involved in its area

9. A health benefit program in which enrollees may choose any physician or hospital for services but obtain a higher level of benefits if preferred providers are used is known as a/an preferred provider organization.

10. HMOs and PPOs consisting of a network of physicians and hospitals that provide an insurance company or employer with discounts on their services are referred to as a/an Point of Service (POS) plan

11. Professional review organizations are established to determine and assure quality and operation of health care and through a process called peer review.

12. Name the three responsibilities and/or tasks of the PROs.

a. one or more physicians working with the federal government under federal guide lines

b. examines evidence for admission and discharge of a patient from the hospital

c. Settles disputes on fees

13. To control health care costs, the process of reviewing and establishing medical necessity for services and providers' use of medical care resources is termed Utilization review.

14. Explain the meaning of a "stop-loss" provision that might appear in a managed care contract If the patients services go over a certain amount, then the physician may ask the patient to pay.

15. When a certain percentage of the premium fund is set aside to operate an individual practice association, this is known as a/an withhold.

16. Mark the following statements as true or false.

a. An HMO can be sponsored and operated by a foundation. (T) F

b. Peer review determines the quality and operation of health care. (T) F

c. An employer may offer the services of an HMO clinic if he or she has five or more employees. T (F)

d. Medicare and Medicaid beneficiaries may not join an HMO. T (F)

e. Managed care withheld amounts that are not yet received from the managed care plan by the medical practice should be shown as a write-off in an accounts journal. T (F)

To check your answers to this self-study assignment, see Appendix D.

ASSIGNMENT 10–2 ► OBTAIN AUTHORIZATION FOR A CONSULTATION FROM A MANAGED CARE PLAN

Performance Objective

Task: Complete a treatment authorization form to obtain permission for an office consultation for a patient from a managed care plan.

Conditions: Treatment authorization form (Figure 10–1), new patient information form (Figure 10–2), and typewriter.

Standards: Time: ________________ minutes

Accuracy : ________________

(Note: The time element and accuracy criteria may be given by your instructor.)

Directions: Complete a treatment authorization form (Figure 10–1) for Mrs. Cohn's managed care plan to obtain permission for the office consultation and date it August 2 of the current year. To obtain information, refer to the New Patient Information form completed by Mrs. Cohn when she came into the office for her visit with Dr. Practon (Figure 10–2). Dr. Practon's FHP provider number is FHP C14021.

Scenario: Meriweather B. Cohn's primary care physician, Gerald Practon, MD, took her clinical history. Physical examination revealed a normal blood pressure (120/80); however, abnormal heart sounds were heard and a diagnosis of a heart murmur was made. Dr. Practon decided to make a semiurgent request to refer Mrs. Cohn for a cardiac consultation (other service) to Victor M. Salazar, MD. His office is located at 20 Excalibur Street, Woodland Hills, XY 12345, telephone 013-625-7344. Dr. Salazar will take a detailed history, perform a detailed examination, and medical decision making will be of low complexity to evaluate Mrs. Cohn's heart murmur.

After the instructor has returned your work to you, either make the necessary corrections and place it in a 3-ring notebook for future reference, or, if you receive a high score, place it in your portfolio for reference when applying for a job.

ASSIGNMENT 10–3 ► OBTAIN AUTHORIZATION FOR PHYSICAL THERAPY FROM A MANAGED CARE PLAN

Performance Objective

Task: Complete a treatment authorization form to obtain permission for physical therapy for a patient from a managed care plan.

Conditions: Treatment authorization form (Figure 10–3) and typewriter.

Standards: Time: ________________ minutes

Accuracy: ________________

(Note: The time element and accuracy criteria may be given by your instructor.)

Directions: Complete the managed care authorization form for this patient (Figure 10–3), date it July 7 of the current year, and submit it to the managed care plan. Refer to *Handbook* Figure 10–1 for visual guidance.

Scenario: Mrs. Rosario Jimenez comes into Dr. Gerald Practon's office complaining of neck pain. He is the primary care physician for the managed care program, Healthnet, of which Mrs. Jimenez is a member. Mrs. Jimenez lives at 350 South Carib Street, Woodland Hills, XY 12340-0329, telephone number 013-450-9987, and she was born April 6, 1960. Her plan identification number is JIM40896, and the effective date is 1-1-20XX. After taking a history, completing a physical examination, and taking x-rays and reviewing them, Dr. Practon makes a diagnosis of cervical radiculitis. He gives her a prescription for some medication and says it is necessary to order outpatient physical therapy (one area 15 minutes; therapeutic exercises to develop strength, motion, and flexibility) 2 × a week for 6 weeks at College Hospital. Authorization must be obtained for this treatment. Dr. Practon's Healthnet provider number is HN C14021.

After the instructor has returned your work to you, either make the necessary corrections and place it in a 3-ring notebook for future reference, or, if you receive a high score, place it in your portfolio for reference when applying for a job.

ASSIGNMENT 10–4 ▶ OBTAIN AUTHORIZATION FOR DIAGNOSTIC ARTHROSCOPY FROM A MANAGED CARE PLAN

Performance Objective

Task: Complete a treatment authorization form to obtain permission for diagnostic arthroscopy with debridement for a patient from a managed care plan.

Conditions: Treatment authorization form (Figure 10–4) and typewriter.

Standards: Time: ______________ minutes

Accuracy: ______________

(Note: The time element and accuracy criteria may be given by your instructor.)

Directions: Complete the managed care authorization form for this patient (Figure 10–4), date it August 12 of the current year, and submit it to the managed care plan. Refer to *Handbook* Figure 10–1 for visual guidance.

Scenario: Daniel Chan is referred by his primary care physician, Dr. Gerald Practon, to an orthopedic surgeon, Dr. Raymond Skeleton. Both physicians are members of his managed care plan, Met Life. The patient comes into Dr. Skeleton's office complaining of pain, swelling, and crepitus of the right knee. The patient is having difficulty walking but indicates no recent injury to the knee.

Mr. Chan lives at 226 West Olive Avenue, Woodland Hills, XY 12340-0329, and his telephone number is 013-540-6700. His plan identification number is FTW90876, effective 2-1-20XX, and he was born February 23, 1971.

After taking a history, completing a physical examination, and taking x-rays and reviewing them, Dr. Skeleton decides to send Mr. Chan for diagnostic arthroscopy to determine the cause of the symptoms. He suspects the patient has a tear of the medial meniscus and may require debridement of articular cartilage. This procedure will be done as an outpatient at College Hospital. Authorization must be obtained for the diagnostic arthroscopy with debridement of articular cartilage. Dr. Practon's Met Life provider number is ML C14021 and Dr. Skeleton's Met Life provider number is ML C45612.

After the instructor has returned your work to you, either make the necessary corrections and place it in a 3-ring notebook for future reference, or, if you received a high score, place it in your portfolio for reference when applying for a job.

FHP® HEALTH CARE

IPA TREATMENT AUTHORIZATION FORM

____ Referral
____ Participating
____ Non-Participating
____ Commercial
____ Senior

For Billing Instructions, Patient and Non-Affiliated Providers, and Consultants please see reverse side for instructions

THIS PORTION COMPLETED BY PHYSICIAN

Patient Name ______________________ Date ____/____/____

M _____ F _____ Age _____ FHP # ____________ Home Phone ____________

Address ______________________

Primary Care MD ____________ Primary Care MD's FHP # ____________

Referring MD ____________ Referring MD's FHP # ____________

Referred To ____________ Address ____________

____________ Office Phone ____________

Type of service: ☐ In-Patient ☐ Out-Patient Services ☐ Initial Visit ☐ Return Visit ☐ Other

Clinical History and Findings ______________________

____

____

Diagnosis ______________________

______________________ **ICD-9-CM CODE**

Evaluation and Treatment to Date ______________________

____

____

Procedure ______________________

______________________ **RVS CPT-4 CODE**

____

Reason for Referral/Consultation/Procedure ______________________

____

____

Accident: ☐ Yes ☐ No Where Occurred: ☐ Home ☐ Work ☐ Auto ☐ Other

☐ Urgent ☐ Semi-Urgent ☐ Elective

Facility To Be Used: ____________ Estimated Length of Stay ____________

☐ Office ☐ Out-Patient ☐ In-Patient

THIS PORTION COMPLETED BY FHP UR

THIS AUTHORIZATION GOOD FOR 60 DAYS ONLY

Type of Contract: ☐ Capitation ☐ Fee For Service ☐ Per Diem

Projected Cost of Procedure ____________ Projected Cost of Facility ____________

HMO Verification: Effective ____________ Group # ____________

Benefits: Co-Pay Per Visit ____________ Hospital ____________

Limitations: ______________________

_____ Authorized Date _____ Initials _____ Reason ____________ Authorization # ____________

_____ Deferred Date _____ Initials _____ Reason ____________

_____ Denied Date _____ Initials _____ Reason ____________

_____ Modified Date _____ Initials _____ Reason ____________

WHITE – UR Copy CANARY – Hospital Copy PINK – Physician Copy GOLDENROD – Claims Copy

Figure 10–1

Welcome To Our Office

NEW PATIENT INFORMATION

DATE 8-2-20xx

PATIENT'S NAME (PLEASE PRINT)	S.S. #	MARITAL STATUS	SEX	BIRTH DATE	AGE	RELIGION (optional)
Meriweather B. Cohn	430-17-0261	S [X] M W D SEP	M [X] F	11-14-65		

STREET ADDRESS PERMANENT TEMPORARY	CITY AND STATE	ZIP CODE	HOME PHONE #
267 Blake Street	Woodland Hills XY	12345	013-263-0911

PATIENT'S OR PARENT'S EMPLOYER	OCCUPATION (INDICATE IF STUDENT)	HOW LONG EMPLOYED	BUS. PHONE # EXT #
Sun Corporation	sales representative	5 yrs	013-263-0099

EMPLOYER'S STREET ADDRESS	CITY AND STATE	ZIP CODE
74 Rain Street	Woodland Hills XY	12345

DRUG ALLERGIES, IF ANY
Penicillin

SPOUSE OR PARENT'S NAME	S.S. #	BIRTH DATE
Starkweather L. Cohn	273-05-9961	7-9-63

SPOUSE OR PARENT'S EMPLOYER	OCCUPATION (INDICATE IF STUDENT)	HOW LONG EMPLOYED	BUS. PHONE #
B & L Stormdrain Co.	accountant	10 yrs	013-421-0091

EMPLOYER'S STREET ADDRESS	CITY AND STATE	ZIP CODE
20 South Wind Road	Woodland Hills XY	12345

*SPOUSE'S STREET ADDRESS, IF DIVORCED OR SEPARATED	CITY AND STATE	ZIP CODE	HOME PHONE #

PLEASE READ: ALL CHARGES ARE DUE AT THE TIME OF SERVICES. IF HOSPITALIZATION IS INDICATED, THE PATIENT IS RESPONSIBLE FOR FURNISHING INSURANCE CLAIM FORMS TO THE OFFICE PRIOR TO HOSPITALIZATION.

PERSON RESPONSIBLE FOR PAYMENT, IF NOT ABOVE	STREET ADDRESS, CITY, STATE	ZIP CODE	HOME PHONE #

BLUE SHIELD (GIVE NAME OF POLICYHOLDER)	EFFECTIVE DATE	CERTIFICATE #	GROUP #	COVERAGE CODE
☐				

OTHER (WRITE IN NAME OF INSURANCE COMPANY)	EFFECTIVE DATE	POLICY #
☐ FHP Healthcare	1-1-8X	FHP # A4932
OTHER (WRITE IN NAME OF INSURANCE COMPANY) ☐	EFFECTIVE DATE	POLICY #

MEDICARE (PLEASE GIVE NUMBER)	RAILROAD RETIREMENT (PLEASE GIVE NUMBER)
☐	☐

MEDICAID	EFFECTIVE DATE	PROGRAM #	COUNTY #	CASE #	ACCOUNT #
☐					

INDUSTRIAL	WERE YOU INJURED ON THE JOB?	DATE OF INJURY	INDUSTRIAL CLAIM #
☐	☐ YES [X] NO		

ACCIDENT	WAS AN AUTOMOBILE INVOLVED?	DATE OF ACCIDENT	NAME OF ATTORNEY
☐	☐ YES [X] NO		

WERE X-RAYS TAKEN OF THIS INJURY OR PROBLEM?	IF YES, WHERE WERE X-RAYS TAKEN? (HOSPITAL, ETC)	DATE X-RAYS TAKEN
☐ YES [X] NO		

HAS ANY MEMBER OF YOUR IMMEDIATE FAMILY BEEN TREATED BY OUR PHYSICIAN(S) BEFORE? INCLUDE NAME OF PHYSICIAN AND FAMILY MEMBER
No

REFERRED BY	STREET ADDRESS, CITY, STATE	ZIP CODE	PHONE #
BREEZIE N. CLOUD	521 N. Wind Rd., Woodland Hills XY	12345	013-721-9641

ALL PROFESSIONAL SERVICES RENDERED ARE CHARGED TO THE PATIENT, NECESSARY FORMS WILL BE COMPLETED TO HELP EXPEDITE INSURANCE CARRIER PAYMENTS. HOWEVER, THE PATIENT IS RESPONSIBLE FOR ALL FEES, REGARDLESS OF INSURANCE COVERAGE. IT IS ALSO CUSTOMARY TO PAY FOR SERVICES WHEN RENDERED UNLESS OTHER ARRANGEMENTS HAVE BEEN MADE IN ADVANCE WITH OUR OFFICE BOOKKEEPER.

INSURANCE AUTHORIZATION AND ASSIGNMENT

Name of Policy Holder Meriweather B. Cohn HC Number

I request that payment of authorized Medicare/Other Insurance company benefits be made either to me or on my behalf to College Clinic for any services furnished me by that party who accepts assignment/physcian. Regulations pertaining to Medicare assignment of benefits apply.

I authorize any holder of medical or other information about me to release to the Social Security Administration and Health Care Financing Administration or its intermediaries or carrier or any other insurance company any information needed for this or a related Medicare/Other Insurance company claim.

I understand my signature requests that payment be made and authorizes release of medical information necessary to pay the claim. If item 9 of the HCFA-1500 claim form is completed, my signature authorizes releasing of the information to the insurer or agency shown. In Medicare/Other Insurance company assigned cases, the physician or supplier agrees to accept the charge determination of the Medicare/Other Insurance company as the full charge, and the patient is responsible only for the deductible, coinsurance, and noncovered services. Coinsurance and the deductible are based upon the charge determination of the Medicare/Other Insurance company.

Signature Meriweather B. Cohn Date 8-2-20XX

NEW PATIENT INFORMATION

Figure 10–2

MANAGED CARE PLAN
AUTHORIZATION REQUEST

Health Net	☐	Met Life	☐
Pacificare	☐	Travelers	☐
Secure Horizons	☐	Pru Care	☐

Member No. ______________

TO BE COMPLETED BY PRIMARY CARE PHYSICIAN OR OUTSIDE PROVIDER

Patient Name: ______________________________ Date: ______________

M ______ F ______ Birthdate ______________ Home telephone number ______________

Address ______________________________

Primary Care Physician ______________________________ Provider ID# ______________

Referring Physician ______________________________ Provider ID# ______________

Referred To ______________________________ Address ______________________________

______________________________ Office telephone number ______________

Diagnosis Code ______________ Diagnosis ______________________________

Diagnosis Code ______________ Diagnosis ______________________________

Treatment Plan: ______________________________

Authorization requested for procedures/tests/visits:

Procedure Code ______________ Description ______________________________

Procedure Code ______________ Description ______________________________

Facility to be used: ______________________________ Estimated length of stay ______________

Office ☐ Outpatient ☐ Inpatient ☐ Other ☐

List of potential consultants (i.e., anesthetists, assistants, or medical/surgical):

____

Physician's signature ______________________________

TO BE COMPLETED BY PRIMARY CARE PHYSICIAN

PCP Recommendations: ______________________________ PCP Initials ______________

Date eligibility checked ______________________________ Effective date ______________

TO BE COMPLETED BY UTILIZATION MANAGEMENT

Authorized ______________________________ Not authorized ______________________________

Deferred ______________________________ Modified ______________________________

Authorization Request # ______________________________

Comments: ______________________________

Figure 10–3

MANAGED CARE PLAN AUTHORIZATION REQUEST

Health Net	☐	Met Life	☐
Pacificare	☐	Travelers	☐
Secure Horizons	☐	Pru Care	☐

Member No. ______________

TO BE COMPLETED BY PRIMARY CARE PHYSICIAN OR OUTSIDE PROVIDER

Patient Name: ______________________________ Date: ______________

M ______ F ______ Birthdate ______________ Home telephone number ______________

Address ____

Primary Care Physician ______________________________ Provider ID# ______________

Referring Physician ______________________________ Provider ID# ______________

Referred To ______________________________ Address ______________________________

______________________________ Office telephone number ______________

Diagnosis Code ______________ Diagnosis ______________________________

Diagnosis Code ______________ Diagnosis ______________________________

Treatment Plan: ____

Authorization requested for procedures/tests/visits:

Procedure Code ______________ Description ______________________________

Procedure Code ______________ Description ______________________________

Facility to be used: ______________________________ Estimated length of stay ______________

Office ☐ Outpatient ☐ Inpatient ☐ Other ☐

List of potential consultants (i.e., anesthetists, assistants, or medical/surgical):

____

Physician's signature ____

TO BE COMPLETED BY PRIMARY CARE PHYSICIAN

PCP Recommendations: ______________________________ PCP Initials ______________

Date eligibility checked ______________________________ Effective date ______________

TO BE COMPLETED BY UTILIZATION MANAGEMENT

Authorized ______________________________ Not authorized ______________________________

Deferred ______________________________ Modified ______________________________

Authorization Request # ____

Comments: ____

Figure 10–4

ASSIGNMENT 10–5 ▸ OBTAIN AUTHORIZATION FOR CONSULTATION FROM A MANAGED CARE PLAN

Performance Objective

Task: Complete a treatment authorization form to obtain permission for consultation for a patient from a managed care plan.

Conditions: Treatment authorization form (Figure 10–5) and typewriter.

Standards: Time: ______________ minutes

Accuracy: ______________

(Note: The time element and accuracy criteria may be given by your instructor.)

Directions: Complete the managed care authorization form for this patient (Figure 10–5), date it September 3 of the current year, and submit it to the managed care plan. Refer to *Handbook* Figure 10–1 for visual guidance.

Scenario: Frederico Fellini was seen by his primary care physician, Dr. Gerald Practon, with a history of getting up four times during the night with a slow urinary stream. An intravenous pyelogram was negative except for a distended urinary bladder. Physical examination of the prostate showed an enlargement. The preliminary diagnosis is benign prostatic hypertrophy (BPH).

The patient will be referred to Dr. Douglas Lee, a urologist, for consultation (Level 4) and cystoscopy. Possible transurethral resection of the prostate at a future date. Dr. Lee's address is 4300 Cyber Street, Woodland Hills, XY 12345, and his office telephone number is 013-675-3322.

Dr. Practon's managed care contract is with Pru Care, ID# PC C14021, of which this patient is a member.

Mr. Fellini lives at 476 Miner Street, Woodland Hills, XY 12345, and his telephone number is 013-679-0098. His Pru Care plan identification number is VRG87655, effective 1-1-20XX. His birthdate is May 24, 1944.

After the instructor has returned your work to you, either make the necessary corrections and place it in a 3-ring notebook for future reference, or, if you received a high score, place it in your portfolio for reference when applying for a job.

ASSIGNMENT 10–6 ▸ OBTAIN AUTHORIZATION FOR DIAGNOSTIC BODY SCAN FROM A MANAGED CARE PLAN

Performance Objective

Task: Complete a treatment authorization form to obtain permission for diagnostic complete body bone scan for a patient from a managed care plan.

Conditions: Treatment authorization form (Figure 10–6) and typewriter.

Standards: Time: ______________ minutes

Accuracy: ______________

(Note: The time element and accuracy criteria may be given by your instructor.)

Directions: Complete the managed care authorization form for this patient (Figure 10–6), date it October 23 of the current year, and submit it to the managed care plan. Refer to *Handbook* Figure 10–1 for visual guidance.

Scenario: A patient, Debbie Dye, sees her primary care physician, Dr. Gerald Practon, for complaint of midback pain. She had a lumpectomy 2 years ago for a malignant neoplasm of the lower left breast; history of breast cancer. She has been referred by Dr. Practon (Pacificare identification number PC C14021) to Dr. Donald Patos, an oncologist, for a complete work up. He finds that her complaint of midback pain warrants the need to refer her to XYZ Radiology for a diagnostic mammogram and complete body bone scan.

Dr. Patos' address is 4466 East Canter Drive, Woodland Hills, XY 12345, and his office telephone number is 013-980-5566. Dr. Patos' Pacificare identification number is PC 56734.

Ms. Dye lives at 6700 Flora Road, Woodland Hills, XY 12345, and her telephone number is 013-433-6755. Her Pacificare plan identification number is SR45380, effective 1-1-20XX. Her birthdate is August 6, 1952.

XYZ Radiology's address is 4767 Broad Avenue, Woodland Hills, XY 12345-0001, and their telephone number is 013-486-9162.

After the instructor has returned your work to you, either make the necessary corrections and place it in a 3-ring notebook for future reference, or, if you received a high score, place it in your portfolio for reference when applying for a job.

MANAGED CARE PLAN AUTHORIZATION REQUEST

Health Net	☐	Met Life	☐
Pacificare	☐	Travelers	☐
Secure Horizons	☐	Pru Care	☐

Member No. ______________

TO BE COMPLETED BY PRIMARY CARE PHYSICIAN OR OUTSIDE PROVIDER

Patient Name: ______________________________ Date: ______________

M ______ F ______ Birthdate ______________ Home telephone number ______________

Address ______________________________

Primary Care Physician ______________________ Provider ID# ______________

Referring Physician ______________________ Provider ID# ______________

Referred To ______________________ Address ______________________

______________________ Office telephone number ______________

Diagnosis Code ______________ Diagnosis ______________________

Diagnosis Code ______________ Diagnosis ______________________

Treatment Plan: ______________________________

Authorization requested for procedures/tests/visits:

Procedure Code ______________ Description ______________________

Procedure Code ______________ Description ______________________

Facility to be used: ______________________ Estimated length of stay ______________

Office ☐ Outpatient ☐ Inpatient ☐ Other ☐

List of potential consultants (i.e., anesthetists, assistants, or medical/surgical):

____

Physician's signature ______________________________

TO BE COMPLETED BY PRIMARY CARE PHYSICIAN

PCP Recommendations: ______________________ PCP Initials ______________

Date eligibility checked ______________________ Effective date ______________

TO BE COMPLETED BY UTILIZATION MANAGEMENT

Authorized ______________________ Not authorized ______________________

Deferred ______________________ Modified ______________________

Authorization Request # ______________________________

Comments: ______________________________

Figure 10–5

MANAGED CARE PLAN AUTHORIZATION REQUEST

Health Net ☐ Met Life ☐
Pacificare ☐ Travelers ☐
Secure Horizons ☐ Pru Care ☐

Member No. ______________

TO BE COMPLETED BY PRIMARY CARE PHYSICIAN OR OUTSIDE PROVIDER

Patient Name: ______________________ Date: ______________

M ______ F ______ Birthdate ______________ Home telephone number ______________

Address ____

Primary Care Physician ______________________ Provider ID# ______________

Referring Physician ______________________ Provider ID# ______________

Referred To ______________________ Address ______________________

______________________ Office telephone number ______________

Diagnosis Code ______________ Diagnosis ______________________

Diagnosis Code ______________ Diagnosis ______________________

Treatment Plan: ____

Authorization requested for procedures/tests/visits:

Procedure Code ______________ Description ______________________

Procedure Code ______________ Description ______________________

Facility to be used: ______________________ Estimated length of stay ______________

Office ☐ Outpatient ☐ Inpatient ☐ Other ☐

List of potential consultants (i.e., anesthetists, assistants, or medical/surgical):

____

Physician's signature ____

TO BE COMPLETED BY PRIMARY CARE PHYSICIAN

PCP Recommendations: ______________________ PCP Initials ______________

Date eligibility checked ______________________ Effective date ______________

TO BE COMPLETED BY UTILIZATION MANAGEMENT

Authorized ______________________ Not authorized ______________________

Deferred ______________________ Modified ______________________

Authorization Request # ____

Comments: ____

Figure 10–6

11

Medicare

KEY TERMS

Your instructor may wish to select some specific words pertinent to this chapter for a test. For definitions of the terms, further study, and/or reference, the words, phrases, and abbreviations may be found in the Glossary at the end of the Handbook. *Key terms for this chapter follow.*

approved charges
assignment
benefit period
crossover claim
diagnostic cost groups (DCGs)
disabled
end-stage renal disease (ESRD)
fiscal intermediary
Health Care Financing Administration (HCFA)
hospice
hospital insurance
intermediate care facilities (ICFs)
limiting charge
medical necessity
Medicare
Medicare/Medicaid (Medi-Medi)
Medicare Secondary Payer (MSP)
Medicare Summary Notice (MSN)
Medigap (MG)
national alphanumeric codes
nonparticipating physician (nonpar)
nursing facility (NF)
participating physician (par)
peer review organization (PRO)
premium
prospective payment system (PPS)
qui tam action
reasonable fee
relative value unit (RVU)
remittance advice (RA)
resource-based relative value scale (RBRVS)
respite care
Supplemental Security Income (SSI)
supplementary medical insurance (SMI)
volume performance standard (VPS)

PERFORMANCE OBJECTIVES

The student will be able to

- Define and spell the key terms for this chapter, given the information from the textbook Glossary, within a reasonable period of time and with enough accuracy to obtain a satisfactory evaluation.
- Answer the self-study review questions after reading the chapter, with enough accuracy to obtain a satisfactory evaluation.
- Fill in the correct meaning of each abbreviation, given a list of common medical abbreviations

and symbols that appear in chart notes, within a reasonable period of time and with enough accuracy to obtain a satisfactory evaluation.

- Complete each HCFA-1500 Health Insurance Claim Form for billing, given the patients' medical chart notes, ledger cards, and blank insurance claim forms, within a reasonable period of time and with enough accuracy to obtain a satisfactory evaluation.
- Post payments, adjustments, and balances on the patients' ledger cards, using the Medicare Mock Fee Schedule in Appendix A, within a reasonable period of time and with enough accuracy to obtain a satisfactory evaluation.
- Compute mathematical calculations, given Medicare problem situations, within a reasonable period of time and with enough accuracy to obtain a satisfactory evaluation.
- Select the HCPCS and/or procedural code numbers, given a series of medical services, procedures, or supplies, using the *Current Procedural Terminology (CPT)* code book or the Mock Fee Schedule in Appendix A and the HCPCS list of codes in Appendix B, within a reasonable period of time and with enough accuracy to obtain a satisfactory evaluation.

STUDY OUTLINE

Chartrand's Medicare Laws

Policies and Regulations

- Eligibility Requirements
  - Aliens
- Health Insurance Card
- Enrollment Status
- Benefits and Nonbenefits
  - Medicare Part A—Hospital Benefits
  - Medicare Part B—Medical Benefits
  - Medicare Part C—Medicare Plus(+) Choice
  - Railroad Retirement Benefits
  - Employed Elderly Benefits
  - Omnibus Budget Reconciliation Act
  - Tax Equity and Fiscal Responsibility Act
  - Deficit Reduction Act
  - Consolidated Omnibus Budget Reconciliation Act
  - Tax Reform Act

Additional Insurance Programs

- Medicare/Medicaid
- Medicare/Medigap
- Medicare Supplemental Insurance
- Medicare Secondary Payer

Procedure: Determining if Medicare Is Primary or Secondary/Determining Additional Benefits

- Managed Care and Medicare
- Automobile or Liability Insurance Coverage

Medicare Managed Care Plans

- Health Maintenance Organizations
  - Risk Plan
  - Cost Plan
  - Noncontract Physician
- Carrier Dealing Prepayment Organization

Utilization and Quality Control

- Peer Review Organization
- Federal False Claims Amendment Act
- Health Insurance Portability and Accountability Act
- Civil Monetary Penalties Law
- Stark I and II Regulations—Physicians' Self-Referrals
- Clinical Laboratory Improvement Amendment

Payment Fundamentals

- Provider
  - Participating Physician
  - Nonparticipating Physician
- Prior Authorization
- Waiver of Liability Provision
  - Limited Liability
  - Noncovered Services
- Elective Surgery Estimate
- Prepayment Screens

Medicare Reimbursement

- Chronology of Payment
- Reasonable Fee
- Resource-based Relative Value Scale
- Medicare Fee Schedule
- Health Care Financing Administration Common Procedure Coding System (HCPCS)

Claim Submission

- Fiscal Intermediaries and Fiscal Agents
- Provider Identification Numbers
- Patient's Signature Authorization
- Time Limit
- Manual Claims
- Electronic Claims
- Medicare/Medicaid Claims

Medicare/Medigap Claims
Medicare/Supplemental and MSP Claims
Deceased Patients' Claims
Physician Substitute Coverage

After Claim Submission

Remittance Advice
Medicare Summary Notice
Beneficiary Representative/Representative Payee
Posting Payments
Review and Appeal Process

SELF-STUDY 11–1 ▶ REVIEW QUESTIONS

Review the objectives, key terms, and glossary definitions to key terms, chapter information, and figures before completing the following review questions.

1. An individual becomes eligible for Medicare Parts A and B at age 65.

2. Medicare Part A is Hospital coverage and Medicare Part B is outpatient coverage.

3. An eligibility requirement for aliens to receive Medicare benefits is that a/an must haved lived in the united states as a permanent resident for 5 consecutive years.

4. Funding for the Medicare Part A program is obtained from special contributions from employees and self employed persons, with employers matching contributions, and for the Medicare Part B program is obtained equally from those who sign up for Medicare and from the federal government.

5. Define a Medicare Part A hospital benefit period.

   Begins the day a patient enters a hospital and ends when the patient has not been a bed patient in any hospital or skilled nursing facility for 60 consecutive days. It also ends if a patient has been in a nursing facility but has not received skilled nursing care there for 60 consecutive days.

6. A program designed to provide pain relief, symptom management, and supportive services to terminally ill individuals and their families is known as hospice.

7. Short-term inpatient medical care for terminally ill individuals to give temporary relief to the caregiver is known as respite care.

8. The frequency of Pap tests for Medicare patients is once every 3 years and for mammograms, annual for women aged 40 years and older plus a one-time baseline mammogram for women aged 35 to 39.

9. Policies offered by third-party payers that fall under guidelines issued by the federal government and cover prescription costs, Medicare deductibles, and copayments are known as Medigap or Medifill insurance policies.

10. Name two types of policies for Medicare supplemental insurance.

a. Service benefit or incurred type

b. indemnity benefit type

11. If an individual is 65 years of age and a Medicare beneficiary but is working and has a group insurance policy, where is the insurance claim form sent initially? To the employer's sponsored plan

12. If a person on Medicare is injured in an automobile accident, the physician submits the claim form to the automobile or liability insurance company.

13. Name two types of HMO plans that may have Medicare Part B contracts.

a. HMO risk plans

b. HMO cost plans

14. The federal laws that prohibit a physician from referring a patient to a laboratory in which he or she has a financial interest are known as stark I and II regulations.

15. The federal laws establishing standards of quality control and safety measures in clinical laboratories are known as Clinical Laboratory Improvement Amendment of 1988.

16. A participating physician who accepts assignment means he or she agrees to accept payment from medicare (80% of the approved charges) plus payment from the patient (20% of the approved charges. after the $ 100 deductible has been met.

17. Philip Lenz is seen by Dr. Doe, who schedules an operative procedure in 1 month. This type of surgery is known as elective, since it does not have to be performed immediately.

18. A Medicare insurance claim form showed a number, J0540, for an injection of 600,000 units of penicillin G. This number is referred to as a/an Hcfa common Procedure coding system (Hcpcs) Level 2 code number.

19. Organizations or claims processors under contract to the federal government that handle insurance claims and payments for hospitals under Medicare Part A are known as fiscal intermediaries, and those that process claims

for physicians and other suppliers of services under Medicare Part B are called Carriers or fiscal agents.

20. An HCFA-assigned provider identification number is known as a/an Pin, Upin, PPin, or National Provider identifier. Physicians who supply durable medical equipment must have a/an DME supplier number.

21. If circumstances make it impossible to obtain a signature on an insurance claim from a Medicare patient, physicians may obtain a/an Beneficiary claim authorization and information release form,

22. The time limit for sending in a Medicare insurance claim is the end of the calendar year following the fiscal year in which services were used. Ex Oct 1, 2001 to Sept 30 2002 bill by december 31, 2002

23. Mrs. Davis, a Medi-Medi patient, has a cholecystectomy. In completing the insurance claim form, the assignment portion is left blank in error. What will happen in this case?

only Medicare processing will occur and the payment check will go directly to the patient. Medicaid will not pay

To check your answers to this self-study assignment, see Appendix D.

ASSIGNMENT 11–2 ▶ CALCULATE MATHEMATIC PROBLEMS

Task: Calculate and insert the correct amounts for seven Medicare scenarios.

Conditions: Use pen or pencil, description of problem, and *Workbook* Figures 11–1 and 11–2 for Problem 7.

Standards: Time: ______________ minutes

Accuracy: ______________

(Note: The time element and accuracy criteria may be given by your instructor.)

Directions: Submitting insurance claims, particularly Medicare claims, involves a bit of arithmetic. Several problems will be given here so you will gain experience with situations encountered daily in your work. The Medicare deductible is always subtracted from the allowed amount first before continuing mathematic computations.

Problem 1: Mr. Doolittle has Medicare Part B coverage. He was well during the entire past year. It is now January 1 and Mr. Doolittle is rushed to the hospital, where Dr. Input performs an emergency gastric resection. Medicare is billed for $450, and the doctor agrees to accept assignment. The patient has not paid any deductible. Complete the following statements by putting in the correct amounts.

Original Bill ____________________

A. Medicare allows $400. Medicare payment ____________________

B. Patient owes Dr. Input ____________________

C. Dr. Input's courtesy adjustment ____________________

Mathematical computations:

Problem 2: Mrs. James has Medicare Part B coverage. She met her deductible when she was ill in March of this year. It is now November 1 and Dr. Caesar performs a bilateral salpingo-oophorectomy, for which he bills her $300 and agrees to accept a Medicare assignment.

Original Bill ____________________

A. Medicare allows $275. Medicare payment ____________________

B. Patient owes Dr. Caesar ____________________

C. Dr. Caesar's courtesy adjustment ____________________

Mathematical computations for surgeon:

The assistant surgeon charged Mrs. James $60 and does not accept an assignment. After receiving her check from Medicare, Mrs. James sends the surgeon his $60. Medicare has allowed $55 for the fee, which is the physician's limiting charge. How much of the money was from Mrs. James' private funds? $________________. How much did Medicare pay? $________________.

Mathematical computations for assistant surgeon:

Problem 3: You work for Dr. Coccidioides. He does not accept assignment. He is treating Mr. Robinson for allergies. Mr. Robinson has Medicare Part A. You send in a bill to Medicare for the $135 that Mr. Robinson owes you. What portion of the bill will Medicare pay?

____

Problem 4: In June, Mr. Fay has an illness that incurs $89 in medical bills. He asks you to bill Medicare, and the physician does not accept assignment. He has paid the deductible at another physician's office. Assuming that Medicare allows the entire amount of your fees, the Medicare check to the patient is

$______________ (which comes to you). The patient's part of the bill to you is $______________.

Mathematical computations:

Problem 5: Mr. Iba, a Medicare patient with a Medigap insurance policy, is seen for an office visit and the fee is $80. The Medicare approved amount is $54.44. The patient has met his deductible for the year. The Medicare payment check is

$______________. After submitting the claim to the Medigap insurance, the Medigap payment check is $______________.

(Note: Chapter 11 in the *Handbook* gives details on Medigap coverage guidelines. To zero out the balance, the Medicare courtesy adjustment is $ ______________.

Mathematical computations:

Problem 6: Mrs. Smith, a Medicare patient, had surgery, and the participating physician's fee is $1,250. This patient is working part-time, and the patient's employer group health plan (primary insurance) allowed $1,100, applied $500 to the deductible, and paid 80% of $600.

Amount paid by this plan: $______________.

The spouse's employer group health plan (secondary insurance) is billed for the balance,

which is $______________, and this program also has a $500 deductible. This plan pays 100% of the fee billed, less the deductible. The spouse's employer group plan

makes a payment of $______________. You send copies of RAs from the two group health plans and submit a claim to Medicare (the third insurance) for $1,250. The balance at this point is $______________.

Mathematical computations:

Problem 7: In the late 1980s, Medicare's Resource-Based Relative Value System (RBRVS) became the way payment was determined each year. However, since the early 1990s, annual fee schedules are supplied by local fiscal intermediaries, so the RBRVS has become more useful in determining practice cost to convert patients to capitation when negotiating managed care contracts. Because physicians may request determination of fees for certain procedures to discover actual cost and what compensation ratios should be, it is important to know how Medicare fees are determined. Each year the

Federal Register publishes geographic practice cost indices by Medicare carrier and locality as well as relative value units and related information. This assignment will give you some mathematical practice using figures for annual conversion factors to determine fees for given procedures in various regions of the United States. Refer to *Workbook* Figures 11–1, and 11–2, which are pages of the *Federal Register*.

a. HCPCS Code 47600: Removal of gallbladder. The medical practice is located in Phoenix, Arizona.

	Work	*Overhead*	*Malpractice*
RVUs	________	________	________
GPCI	× ________	× ________	× ________

________ + ________ + ________ = Total adj. RVUs ________

2001 Conversion factor $38.2581 × Total adj. RVUs ________= allowed amount

$________

b. HCPCS Code 47715: Excision of bile duct cyst. The medical practice is located in Arkansas.

	Work	*Overhead*	*Malpractice*
RVUs	________	________	________
GPCI	× ________	× ________	× ________

________ + ________ + ________ = Total adj. RVUs ________

2001 Conversion factor $38.2581 × Total adj. RVUs ________ = allowed

amount $ ________

ADDENDUM D.---GEOGRAPHIC PRACTICE COST INDICES BY MEDICARE CARRIER AND LOCALITY

Carrier number	Locality number	Locality name	Work	Practice expense	Mal-practice
510	5	Birmingham, AL	0.981	0.913	0.824
510	4	Mobile, AL	0.964	0.911	0.824
510	2	North Central AL	0.970	0.867	0.824
510	1	Northwest AL	0.985	0.869	0.824
510	6	Rest of AL	0.975	0.851	0.824
510	3	Southeast AL	0.972	0.869	0.824
1020	1	Alaska	1.106	1.255	1.042
1030	5	Flagstaff (city), AZ	0.983	0.911	1.255
1030	1	Phoenix, AZ	1.003	1.016	1.255
1030	7	Prescott (city), AZ	0.983	0.911	1.255
1030	99	Rest of Arizona	0.987	0.943	1.255
1030	2	Tucson (city), AZ	0.987	0.989	1.255
1030	8	Yuma (city), AZ	0.983	0.911	1.255
520	13	Arkansas	0.960	0.856	0.302
2050	26	Anaheim-Santa Ana, CA	1.046	1.220	1.370
542	14	Bakersfield, CA	1.028	1.050	1.370
542	11	Fresno/Madera, CA	1.006	1.009	1.370
542	13	Kings/Tulare, CA	0.999	1.001	1.370
2050	18	Los Angeles, CA (1st of 8)	1.060	1.196	1.370
2050	19	Los Angeles, CA (2nd of 8)	1.060	1.196	1.370

Figure 11–1

ADDENDUM B.—RELATIVE VALUE UNITS (RVUs) AND RELATED INFORMATION										
HCPCS[1]	MOD	Status	Description	Work RVUs	Practice expense RVUs[2]	Malpractice RVUs	Total	Global period	Update
47399	....	C	Liver surgery procedure	0.00	0.00	0.00	0.00	YYY	S
47400	....	A	Incision of liver duct	19.11	8.62	1.38	29.11	090	S
47420	....	A	Incision of bile duct	15.48	9.59	2.01	27.08	090	S
47425	....	A	Incision of bile duct	14.95	11.84	2.48	29.27	090	S
47440	....	A	Incision of bile duct	18.51	10.61	2.23	31.35	090	S
47460	....	A	Incision of bile duct sphincter	14.57	15.71	1.84	32.12	090	N
47480	....	A	Incision of gallbladder	8.14	7.68	1.61	17.43	090	S
47490	....	A	Incision of gallbladder	6.11	3.61	0.38	10.10	090	N
47500	....	A	Injection for liver x-rays	1.98	1.53	0.14	3.65	000	N
47505	....	A	Injection for liver x-rays	0.77	1.34	0.14	2.25	000	N
47510	....	A	Insert catheter, bile duct	7.47	2.90	0.25	10.62	090	N
47511	....	A	Insert bile duct drain	10.02	2.90	0.25	13.17	090	N
47525	....	A	Change bile duct catheter	5.47	1.61	0.16	7.24	010	N
47530	....	A	Revise, reinsert bile tube	5.47	1.53	0.19	7.19	090	N
47550	....	A	Bile duct endoscopy	3.05	1.58	0.35	4.98	000	S
47552	....	A	Biliary endoscopy, thru skin	6.11	1.38	0.21	7.70	000	S
47553	....	A	Biliary endoscopy, thru skin	6.42	3.84	0.63	10.89	000	N
47554	....	A	Biliary endoscopy, thru skin	9.16	3.97	0.68	13.81	000	S
47555	....	A	Biliary endoscopy, thru skin	7.64	2.66	0.30	10.60	000	N
47556	....	A	Biliary endoscopy, thru skin	8.66	2.66	0.30	11.62	000	N
47600	....	A	Removal of gallbladder	10.80	7.61	1.60	20.01	090	S
47605	....	A	Removal of gallbladder	11.66	8.23	1.77	21.66	090	S
47610	....	A	Removal of gallbladder	14.01	9.47	2.02	25.50	090	S
47612	....	A	Removal of gallbladder	14.91	14.39	3.08	32.38	090	S
47620	....	A	Removal of gallbladder	15.97	11.35	2.39	29.71	090	S
47630	....	A	Removal of bile duct stone	8.40	3.79	0.40	12.59	090	N
47700	....	A	Exploration of bile ducts	13.90	7.71	1.60	23.21	090	S
47701	....	A	Bile duct revision	26.87	8.30	1.92	37.09	090	S
47710	....	A	Excision of bile duct tumor	18.64	12.19	2.49	33.32	090	S
47715	....	A	Excision of bile duct cyst	14.66	8.31	1.73	24.70	090	S
47716	....	A	Fusion of bile duct cyst	12.67	6.63	1.55	20.85	090	S
47720	....	A	Fuse gallbladder and bowel	12.03	9.26	1.95	23.34	090	S
47721	....	A	Fuse upper gi structures	14.57	11.55	2.50	28.62	090	S
47740	....	A	Fuse gallbladder and bowel	14.08	10.32	2.16	26.56	090	S
47760	....	A	Fuse bile ducts and bowel	20.15	11.74	2.56	34.45	090	S
47765	....	A	Fuse liver ducts and bowel	19.25	14.77	3.00	37.02	090	S
47780	....	A	Fuse bile ducts and bowel	20.63	13.22	2.76	36.61	090	S
47800	....	A	Reconstruction of bile ducts	17.91	13.37	2.46	33.74	090	S
47801	....	A	Placement, bile duct support	11.41	5.54	0.82	17.77	090	S
47802	....	A	Fuse liver duct and intestine	16.19	10.38	1.77	28.34	090	S
47999	....	C	Bile tract surgery procedure	0.00	0.00	0.00	0.00	YYY	S
48000	....	A	Drainage of abdomen	13.25	7.13	1.42	21.80	090	S
48001	....	A	Placement of drain, pancreas	15.71	8.22	1.91	25.84	090	S
48005	....	A	Resect/debride pancreas	17.77	9.29	2.16	29.22	090	S
48020	....	A	Removal of pancreatic stone	13.12	6.86	1.59	21.57	090	S
48100	....	A	Biopsy of pancreas	10.30	4.26	0.80	15.36	090	S
48102	....	A	Needle biopsy, pancreas	4.48	2.44	0.25	7.17	010	N
48120	....	A	Removal of pancreas lesion	12.93	9.83	2.09	24.85	090	S
48140	....	A	Partial removal of pancreas	18.47	13.44	2.86	34.77	090	S
48145	....	A	Partial removal of pancreas	19.30	15.88	3.20	38.38	090	S
48146	....	A	Pancreatectomy	21.97	16.67	1.94	40.58	090	S
48148	....	A	Removal of pancrearic duct	14.57	8.32	1.70	24.59	090	S
48150	....	A	Partial removal of pancreas	34.55	22.79	4.80	62.14	090	S
48151	....	D	Partial removal of pancreas	0.00	0.00	0.00	0.00	090	0
48152	....	A	Pancreatectomy	31.33	22.79	4.80	58.92	090	S
48153	....	A	Pancreatectomy	34.55	22.79	4.80	62.14	090	S
48154	....	A	Pancreatectomy	31.33	22.79	4.80	58.92	090	S
48155	....	A	Removal of pancreas	19.65	20.63	4.31	44.59	090	S
48160	....	N	Pancreas removal, transplant	0.00	0.00	0.00	0.00	XXX	0
48180	....	A	Fuse pancreas and bowel	21.11	12.74	2.66	36.51	090	S
48400	....	A	Injection, intraoperative	1.97	1.04	0.24	3.25	ZZZ	S
48500	....	A	Surgery of pancreas cyst	12.17	8.62	1.68	22.47	090	S
48510	....	A	Drain pancreatic pseudocyst	11.34	7.62	1.46	20.42	090	S
48520	....	A	Fuse pancreas cyst and bowel	13.11	11.43	2.46	27.00	090	S
48540	....	A	Fuse pancreas cyst and bowel	15.95	12.80	2.68	31.43	090	S
48545	....	A	Pancreatorrhaphy	14.81	7.75	1.81	24.37	090	S
48547	....	A	Duodenal exclusion	21.42	11.20	2.61	35.23	090	S

[1] All numeric CPT HCPCS Copyright 1993 American Medical Association.
[2] *Indicates reduction of Practice Expense RVUs as a result of OBRA 1993.

Figure 11–2

c. HCPCS Code 48146: Pancreatectomy. The medical practice is located in Fresno, California.

	Work	*Overhead*	*Malpractice*
RVUs	________	________	________
GPCI	× ________	× ________	× ________

________ + ________ + ________ = Total adj. RVUs ________

2001 Conversion factor \$38.2581 × Total adj. RVUs ____________ = allowed amount \$ ____________

ASSIGNMENT 11–3 ▸ LOCATE HCPCS ALPHA/NUMERIC CODES

Task: Insert the correct HCPCS codes for problems presented.

Conditions: Use pen or pencil, *CPT* code book, and *Workbook* Appendix B.

Standards: Time: ____________ minutes

Accuracy: ____________

(Note: The time element and accuracy criteria may be given by your instructor.)

Directions: As you have learned from the *Handbook*, it is necessary to use three levels of codes (*CPT*, HCPCS, and regional codes) when submitting Medicare claims. Refer to Appendix B to complete this HCPCS coding exercise for Medicare claims.

1. Cellular therapy ____________
2. Injection amygdalin ____________
3. Xylocaine (lidocaine) injection for local anesthestic ____________
4. Splint, wrist ____________
5. Crutches ____________
6. Cervical head harness ____________
7. 1 mL gamma globulin ____________
8. Coumadin (warfarin sodium) injection ____________
9. Contraceptives (unclassified drugs) ____________
10. Surgical tray ____________
11. Penicillin, procaine, aqueous, injection ____________

Now let's get some practice in selecting HCPCS modifiers. For this part of the assignment, in addition to referring to Appendix B, you will need to refer to your *CPT* code book or Appendix A to complete these Medicare problems.

12. Second surgical opinion by a professional review organization, detailed hx/exam, low-complexity decision making ________________

13. Chiropractic manipulation of spine, acute treatment ________________

14. Office visit by a locum tenens physician of established patient, problem-focused history and exam with straightforward decision making ________________

15. Strapping of thumb of left hand ________________

Insurance Claim Assignments

Assignments presented in this section are to give you hands-on experience in completing a variety of Medicare insurance cases using the HCFA-1500 claim form. Periodically, bulletins are issued by Medicare fiscal carriers relaying new federal policies and guidelines. This may mean lower reimbursement or denial of reimbursement for a particular code number. Cases shown do not necessarily indicate that the provider may get paid for the service, as this depends on federal guidelines at the time of submission of the claim. The cases presented in this section are

Assignment 11–4	Medicare
Assignment 11–5	Medicare/Medicaid (Medi-Medi)
Assignment 11–6	Third-party payer—liability insurance/Medicare
Assignment 11–7	Medicare/Medigap
Assignment 11–8	Medicare railroad, retiree
Assignment 11–9	Medicare/Medicaid (Medi-Medi)

ASSIGNMENT **11–4** ▶ **COMPLETE A MEDICARE CLAIM FORM**

Task: Complete a Medicare HCFA-1500 claim form, post transactions to the ledger card, and define patient record abbreviations.

Conditions: Use the patient's record (Figure 11–3) and ledger card (Figure 11–4), one health insurance claim form (Figure 11–5), typewriter or computer, procedural and diagnostic code books, and *Workbook* Appendices A and B.

Standards: Claim Productivity Measurement

Time: ________________ minutes

Accuracy: ________________

(Note: The time element and accuracy criteria may be given by your instructor.)

PATIENT RECORD NO. 1101

LAST NAME	FIRST NAME	MIDDLE NAME	BIRTH DATE	SEX	HOME PHONE
Mooney,	Elsa	M.	02-06-10	F	013-452-4968

ADDRESS	CITY	STATE	ZIP CODE
5750 Canyon Road ,	Woodland Hills,	XY	12345

PATIENT'S OCCUPATION: retired secretary
NAME OF COMPANY:

ADDRESS OF EMPLOYER:
PHONE:

SPOUSE OR PARENT: husband deceased
OCCUPATION:

EMPLOYER:
ADDRESS:
PHONE:

NAME OF INSURANCE: Medicare
INSURED OR SUBSCRIBER:

POLICY NO.:
GROUP NO.:
EFFECTIVE DATE:

MEDICARE NO.	MEDICAID NO.	EFFECTIVE DATE	SOC. SEC. NO.
321-10-2653A			321-10-2653

REFERRED BY: George Gentle, MD, 1000 N, Main Street, Woodland Hills, XY 12345 NPI# 4021310213

DATE	PROGRESS
12-15-XX	New pt referred by Dr. Gentle comes in complaining of chest pain and shortness of breath. Exam essentially
	N. EKG done to rule out myocardial infarction. Imp: ASCVD- angina pectoris.
	Given Rx and advised to retn in 1 mo. Perry Cardi, MD

Figure 11–3

Directions:

1. Complete the Medicare Form* using OCR guidelines, directing it to your local fiscal intermediary. Refer to Elsa M. Mooney's patient record and ledger card for information. Refer to Appendix A to fill in the fees on the ledger card. Date the claim December 21. Dr. Cardi is accepting assignment in this particular case. Mrs. Mooney has already met her deductible for the year, owing to previous medical expenses with another physician.

2. Use your *CPT* code book or Appendix A to determine the correct five-digit code number and modifiers for each professional service rendered. Refer to Appendix B for HCPCS procedure codes and modifiers.

3. Record all transactions on the ledger card and indicate when you have billed Medicare.

4. On February 12, Medicare allowed $75 on this claim. Post 80% of this payment from Medicare check No. 115620 to the patient's ledger card. Post the courtesy adjustment and show the balance due from the patient.

5. A Performance Evaluation Checklist may be reproduced from the Instruction Guide to the *Workbook* chapter if your instructor wishes you to submit it to assist with scoring and comments.

6. After the instructor has returned your work to you, either make the necessary corrections and place in a 3-ring notebook for future reference or if you received a high score, place it in your portfolio for reference when applying for a job.

Here are three questions suggested for critical thinking and class discussion after completion of the Medicare health insurance claim form. Refer to the Mock Fee Schedule shown in Appendix A.

1. If Dr. Cardi is **participating**, how much will he receive from Medicare for the **office** visit and

   ECG? $ ______________

2. If Dr. Cardi is **not participating**, how much will

   he receive for the ECG? $ ______________

3. If Dr. Cardi is a **nonparticipating** physician in the Medicare program, what is the maximum (limiting charge) he can bill for the **office visit**?

   $ ______________

Abbreviations pertinent to this record:

ASCVD ______________ N ______________

ECG ______________ OV ______________

exam ______________ Pt ______________

interpret ______________ ret ______________

init ______________ Rx ______________

mo ______________ c̄ ______________

*See Chapter 6 of the *Handbook* for help in completing this form and refer to Figure 6–9.

ASSIGNMENT 11–5 ▶ COMPLETE A MEDICARE/MEDICAID CLAIM FORM

Task: Complete a Medicare HCFA-1500 claim form, post transactions to the ledger card, and define patient record abbreviations.

Conditions: Use the patient's record (Figure 11–6) and ledger card (Figure 11–7), one health insurance claim form (Figure 11–8), typewriter or computer, procedural and diagnostic code books, and *Workbook* Appendixes A and B.

Standards: Claim Productivity Measurement

Time: ______________ minutes

Accuracy: ______________

(Note: The time element and accuracy criteria may be given by your instructor.)

Directions:

1. Complete the Medicare Form using OCR guidelines, directing it to your local Medicare fiscal intermediary and on to Medicaid. Refer to Chapter 6 and Figure 6–10 for instructions on how to complete the HCFA-1500 claim form. Refer to Mrs. Helen P. Nolan's patient record and ledger card for information. Refer to Appendix A to fill in the fees on the ledger card. Date the claim May 31.

2. Use your *CPT* code book or Appendix A to determine the correct five-digit code number and modifiers for each professional service rendered. Refer to Appendix B for HCPCS procedure codes and modifiers.

3. Record all transactions on the ledger card and indicate the proper information when you have billed Medicare/Medicaid. On July 1 you receive a check (No. 107621) from Medicare for $400, and on July 15 you receive a voucher #3571 from Medicaid for $150. Record these payments on the ledger and show the courtesy adjustment.

4. A Performance Evaluation Checklist may be reproduced from the Instruction Guide to the *Workbook* chapter if your instructor wishes you to submit it to assist with scoring and comments.

5. After the instructor has returned your work to you, either make the necessary corrections and place it in a 3-ring notebook for future reference, or, if you received a high score, place it in your portfolio for reference when applying for a job.

Abbreviations pertinent to this record:

adm ______________	OC ______________
adv ______________	phys ______________
BP ______________	prep ______________
Dx ______________	PRN ______________
exam ______________	Pt ______________
ext ______________	Rx ______________
hosp ______________	slt ______________
int ______________	wk ______________
NC ______________	c̄ ______________

STATEMENT

College Clinic
4567 Broad Avenue
Woodland Hills, XY 12345-0001
Telephone: 013-486-9002
Fax: 013-487-8976

Mrs. Elsa M. Mooney
5750 Canyon Road
Woodland Hills, XY 12345-0001

DATE	PROFESSIONAL SERVICE DESCRIPTION	CHARGE		CREDITS				CURRENT BALANCE	
				PAYMENTS		ADJUSTMENTS			
12-15-xx	Init OV, D hx/exam, LC decision making.								
12-15-xx	EKG c̄ interpret & report.								

Due and payable within 10 days. **Pay last amount in balance column** 

Key: PF:	Problem-focused	SF:	Straightforward	CON:	Consultation	HCD:	House call (day)
EPF:	Expanded problem-focused	LC:	Low complexity	CPX:	Complete phys exam	HCN:	House call (night)
D:	Detailed	MC:	Moderate complexity	E:	Emergency	HV:	Hospital visit
C:	Comprehensive	HC:	High complexity	ER:	Emergency dept.	OV:	Office visit

Figure 11–4

APPROVED OMB-0938-0008

PLEASE DO NOT STAPLE IN THIS AREA

CARRIER

PICA

HEALTH INSURANCE CLAIM FORM

PICA

1. MEDICARE (Medicare #) MEDICAID (Medicaid #) CHAMPUS (Sponsor's SSN) CHAMPVA (VA File #) GROUP HEALTH PLAN (SSN or ID) FECA BLK LUNG (SSN) OTHER (ID)

1a. INSURED'S I.D. NUMBER (FOR PROGRAM IN ITEM 1)

2. PATIENT'S NAME (Last Name, First Name, Middle Initial)

3. PATIENT'S BIRTH DATE MM | DD | YYYY SEX M F

4. INSURED'S NAME (Last Name, First Name, Middle Initial)

5. PATIENT'S ADDRESS (No., Street)

6. PATIENT RELATIONSHIP TO INSURED Self Spouse Child Other

7. INSURED'S ADDRESS (No., Street)

CITY STATE

8. PATIENT STATUS Single Married Other

CITY STATE

ZIP CODE TELEPHONE (Include Area Code)

Employed Full-Time Student Part-Time Student

ZIP CODE TELEPHONE (include Area Code) ( )

9. OTHER INSURED'S NAME (Last Name, First Name, Middle Initial)

10. IS PATIENT'S CONDITION RELATED TO:

11. INSURED'S POLICY GROUP OR FECA NUMBER

a. OTHER INSURED'S POLICY OR GROUP NUMBER

a. EMPLOYMENT? (CURRENT OR PREVIOUS) YES NO

a. INSURED'S DATE OF BIRTH MM | DD | YY SEX M F

b. OTHER INSURED'S DATE OF BIRTH MM | DD | YY SEX M F

b. AUTO ACCIDENT? PLACE (State) YES NO

b. EMPLOYER'S NAME OR SCHOOL NAME

c. EMPLOYER'S NAME OR SCHOOL NAME

c. OTHER ACCIDENT? YES NO

c. INSURANCE PLAN NAME OR PROGRAM NAME

d. INSURANCE PLAN NAME OR PROGRAM NAME

10d. RESERVED FOR LOCAL USE

d. IS THERE ANOTHER HEALTH BENEFIT PLAN? YES NO *If yes, return to and complete item 9 a-d.*

READ BACK OF FORM BEFORE COMPLETING AND SIGNING THIS FORM.

12. PATIENT'S OR AUTHORIZED PERSON'S SIGNATURE I authorize the release of any medical or other information necessary to process this claim. I also request payment of government benefits either to myself or to the party who accepts assignment below.

SIGNED ____ DATE ____

13. INSURED'S OR AUTHORIZED PERSON'S SIGNATURE I authorize payment of medical benefits to the undersigned physician or supplier for services described below.

SIGNED ____

PATIENT AND INSURED INFORMATION

14. DATE OF CURRENT: MM | DD | YY ILLNESS (First symptom) OR INJURY (Accident) OR PREGNANCY (LMP)

15. IF PATIENT HAS HAD SAME OR SIMILAR ILLNESS GIVE FIRST DATE MM | DD | YY

16. DATES PATIENT UNABLE TO WORK IN CURRENT OCCUPATION FROM MM | DD | YY TO MM | DD | YY

17. NAME OF REFERRING PHYSICIAN OR OTHER SOURCE

17a. I.D. NUMBER OF REFERRING PHYSICIAN

18. HOSPITALIZATION DATES RELATED TO CURRENT SERVICES FROM MM | DD | YY TO MM | DD | YY

19. RESERVED FOR LOCAL USE

20. OUTSIDE LAB? YES NO $ CHARGES

21. DIAGNOSIS OR NATURE OF ILLNESS OR INJURY. (RELATE ITEMS 1,2,3 OR 4 TO ITEM 24E BY LINE)

1. ____ 3. ____

2. ____ 4. ____

22. MEDICAID RESUBMISSION CODE ORIGINAL REF. NO.

23. PRIOR AUTHORIZATION NUMBER

24. A DATE(S) OF SERVICE From MM DD YY To MM DD YY	B Place of Service	C Type of Service	D PROCEDURES, SERVICES, OR SUPPLIES (Explain Unusual Circumstances) CPT/HCPCS | MODIFIER	E DIAGNOSIS CODE	F $ CHARGES	G DAYS OR UNITS	H EPSDT Family Plan	I EMG	J COB	K RESERVED FOR LOCAL USE

25. FEDERAL TAX I.D. NUMBER SSN EIN

26. PATIENT'S ACCOUNT NO.

27. ACCEPT ASSIGNMENT? (For govt. claims, see back) YES NO

28. TOTAL CHARGE $

29. AMOUNT PAID $

30. BALANCE DUE $

31. SIGNATURE OF PHYSICIAN OR SUPPLIER INCLUDING DEGREES OR CREDENTIALS (I certify that the statements on the reverse apply to this bill and are made a part thereof.)

SIGNED DATE

32. NAME AND ADDRESS OF FACILITY WHERE SERVICES WERE RENDERED (if other than home or office)

33. PHYSICIAN'S, SUPPLIER'S BILLING NAME, ADDRESS, ZIP CODE AND PHONE #

PIN# GRP#

PHYSICIAN OR SUPPLIER INFORMATION

(APPROVED BY AMA COUNCIL ON MEDICAL SERVICE8/88) *PLEASE PRINT OR TYPE* FORM HCFA-1500 (U2) (12-90) FORM OCWP-1500 FORM RRB-1500

Figure 11–5

PATIENT RECORD NO. 1102

LAST NAME	FIRST NAME	MIDDLE NAME	BIRTH DATE	SEX	HOME PHONE
Nolan,	Helen	P.	05-10-07	F	013-660-9878

ADDRESS	CITY	STATE	ZIP CODE
2588 Ceder Street,	Woodland Hills,	XY	12345

PATIENT'S OCCUPATION	NAME OF COMPANY
homemaker	

ADDRESS OF EMPLOYER	PHONE

SPOUSE OR PARENT	OCCUPATION
James J. Nolan	retired journalist

EMPLOYER	ADDRESS	PHONE

NAME OF INSURANCE	INSURED OR SUBSCRIBER
Medicare/Medicaid	

POLICY NO.	GROUP NO.	EFFECTIVE DATE

MEDICARE NO.	MEDICAID NO.	EFFECTIVE DATE	SOC. SEC. NO.
732-32-1573B	19-60-2358490-1-01		732-32-1573

REFERRED BY: James B. Jeffers, MD, 100 S. Broadway, Woodland Hills, XY 12345 NPI# 1234506972

DATE	PROGRESS
5-1-XX	This new pt comes in complaining of constipation & some rectal bleeding & pain. Exam reveals int &
	ext hemorrhoids. BP 120/80. Dx: Hemorrhoids; int & ext bleeding anal fistula. Rx: Adv hospitalization
	for removal of hemorrhoids and fistula repair . Rex Rumsey, MD
5-8-XX	Adm to hosp-phys exam & prep hosp records. Hemorrhoidectomy with fistulectomy. Rex Rumsey, MD
5-9-X	Hosp visit, brief. Pt comfortable, slt pain. Rex Rumsey, MD
5-10-XX	Hosp visit, no pain. Rex Rumsey, MD
5-11-XX	Hosp visit. Discharged. To be seen in office in 1 wk. Rex Rumsey, MD
5-17-XX	Well healed, no pain. Return prn. Rex Rumsey, MD

Figure 11–6

ASSIGNMENT 11–6 ▶ COMPLETE ANOTHER INSURANCE/MEDICARE CLAIM-MSP FORM

Task: Complete a Medicare HCFA-1500 claim form, post transactions to the ledger card, and define patient record abbreviations.

Conditions: Use the patient's record (Figure 11–9) and ledger card (Figure 11–10), one health insurance claim form (Figure 11–11), typewriter or computer, procedural and diagnostic code books, and *Workbook* Appendixes A and B.

Standards: Claim Productivity Measurement

Time: ______________ minutes

Accuracy: ______________

(Note: The time element and accuracy criteria may be given by your instructor.)

Directions:

1. Complete the HCFA-1500 Form using OCR guidelines, directing it to the primary insurance carrier. This assignment requires two claim forms, so make a photocopy of the HCFA-1500 claim form. See Chapter 6 of the *Handbook* (Figure 6–12) for help in completing these forms. Refer to Peter F. Donlon's patient record and ledger card for information. Refer to Appendix A to fill in the fees on the ledger card. Date the claim May 14. Dr. Antrum is not accepting assignment in this case. For a nonparticipating physician, use the limiting charge column of the mock fee schedule.
2. Use your *CPT* code book or Appendix A to determine the correct five-digit code number and modifiers for each professional service rendered. Refer to Appendix B for HCPCS procedure codes and modifiers.
3. Record all transactions on the ledger card and indicate when you have billed the primary insurance carrier.
4. On July 3, the insurance carrier paid $400 (check No. 45632) on this claim. Post this payment to the patient's ledger card. *Note*: The EOB from the insurance carrier would be sent with a completed HCFA-1500 claim form to Medicare.
5. A Performance Evaluation Checklist may be reproduced from the Instruction Guide to the *Workbook* chapter if your instructor wishes you to submit it to assist with scoring and comments.
6. After the instructor has returned your work to you, either make the necessary corrections and place it in a 3-ring notebook for future reference, or, if you received a high score, place it in your portfolio for reference when applying for a job.

Abbreviations pertinent to this record:

adm ______________

a.m. ______________

auto ______________

ER ______________

est ______________

hosp ______________

hrs ______________

imp ______________

NC ______________

OC ______________

PO ______________

postop ______________

Pt ______________

surg ______________

c̄ ______________

STATEMENT

College Clinic
4567 Broad Avenue
Woodland Hills, XY 12345-0001
Telephone: 013-486-9002
Fax: 013-487-8976

Mrs. Helen P. Nolan
2588 Cedar Street
Woodland Hills, XY 12345-0001

DATE	PROFESSIONAL SERVICE DESCRIPTION	CHARGE	CREDITS		CURRENT BALANCE
			PAYMENTS	ADJUSTMENTS	
5-1-xx	OV, hx/exam, LC decision making				
5-8-xx	Hemorrhoidectomy with fistulectomy				
5-9-xx	HV				
5-10-xx	HV				
5-11-xx	HV/Discharge				
5-17-xx	OV				

Due and payable within 10 days. **Pay last amount in balance column** 

Key: PF: Problem-focused
EPF: Expanded problem-focused
D: Detailed
C: Comprehensive
SF: Straightforward
LC: Low complexity
MC: Moderate complexity
HC: High complexity
CON: Consultation
CPX: Complete phys exam
E: Emergency
ER: Emergency dept.
HCD: House call (day)
HCN: House call (night)
HV: Hospital visit
OV: Office visit

Figure 11–7

APPROVED OMB-0938-0008

PLEASE DO NOT STAPLE IN THIS AREA

CARRIER

PICA

HEALTH INSURANCE CLAIM FORM

PICA

1. MEDICARE MEDICAID CHAMPUS CHAMPVA GROUP HEALTH PLAN FECA BLK LUNG OTHER
(Medicare #) (Medicaid #) (Sponsor's SSN) (VA File #) (SSN or ID) (SSN) (ID)

1a. INSURED'S I.D. NUMBER (FOR PROGRAM IN ITEM 1)

2. PATIENT'S NAME (Last Name, First Name, Middle Initial)

3. PATIENT'S BIRTH DATE MM | DD | YYYY SEX M F

4. INSURED'S NAME (Last Name, First Name, Middle Initial)

5. PATIENT'S ADDRESS (No., Street)

6. PATIENT RELATIONSHIP TO INSURED Self Spouse Child Other

7. INSURED'S ADDRESS (No., Street)

CITY STATE

8. PATIENT STATUS Single Married Other

CITY STATE

ZIP CODE TELEPHONE (Include Area Code)

Employed Full-Time Student Part-Time Student

ZIP CODE TELEPHONE (include Area Code) ( )

9. OTHER INSURED'S NAME (Last Name, First Name, Middle Initial)

10. IS PATIENT'S CONDITION RELATED TO:

11. INSURED'S POLICY GROUP OR FECA NUMBER

a. OTHER INSURED'S POLICY OR GROUP NUMBER

a. EMPLOYMENT? (CURRENT OR PREVIOUS) YES NO

a. INSURED'S DATE OF BIRTH MM | DD | YY SEX M F

b. OTHER INSURED'S DATE OF BIRTH MM | DD | YY SEX M F

b. AUTO ACCIDENT? PLACE (State) YES NO

b. EMPLOYER'S NAME OR SCHOOL NAME

c. EMPLOYER'S NAME OR SCHOOL NAME

c. OTHER ACCIDENT? YES NO

c. INSURANCE PLAN NAME OR PROGRAM NAME

d. INSURANCE PLAN NAME OR PROGRAM NAME

10d. RESERVED FOR LOCAL USE

d. IS THERE ANOTHER HEALTH BENEFIT PLAN? YES NO *If yes, return to and complete item 9 a-d.*

READ BACK OF FORM BEFORE COMPLETING AND SIGNING THIS FORM.

12. PATIENT'S OR AUTHORIZED PERSON'S SIGNATURE I authorize the release of any medical or other information necessary to process this claim. I also request payment of government benefits either to myself or to the party who accepts assignment below.

SIGNED DATE

13. INSURED'S OR AUTHORIZED PERSON'S SIGNATURE I authorize payment of medical benefits to the undersigned physician or supplier for services described below.

SIGNED

PATIENT AND INSURED INFORMATION

14. DATE OF CURRENT: MM | DD | YY ILLNESS (First symptom) OR INJURY (Accident) OR PREGNANCY (LMP)

15. IF PATIENT HAS HAD SAME OR SIMILAR ILLNESS GIVE FIRST DATE MM | DD | YY

16. DATES PATIENT UNABLE TO WORK IN CURRENT OCCUPATION FROM MM | DD | YY TO MM | DD | YY

17. NAME OF REFERRING PHYSICIAN OR OTHER SOURCE

17a. I.D. NUMBER OF REFERRING PHYSICIAN

18. HOSPITALIZATION DATES RELATED TO CURRENT SERVICES FROM MM | DD | YY TO MM | DD | YY

19. RESERVED FOR LOCAL USE

20. OUTSIDE LAB? YES NO $ CHARGES

21. DIAGNOSIS OR NATURE OF ILLNESS OR INJURY. (RELATE ITEMS 1,2,3 OR 4 TO ITEM 24E BY LINE)

1. 3.

2. 4.

22. MEDICAID RESUBMISSION CODE ORIGINAL REF. NO.

23. PRIOR AUTHORIZATION NUMBER

24. A DATE(S) OF SERVICE From MM DD YY To MM DD YY	B Place of Service	C Type of Service	D PROCEDURES, SERVICES, OR SUPPLIES (Explain Unusual Circumstances) CPT/HCPCS | MODIFIER	E DIAGNOSIS CODE	F $ CHARGES	G DAYS OR UNITS	H EPSDT Family Plan	I EMG	J COB	K RESERVED FOR LOCAL USE

25. FEDERAL TAX I.D. NUMBER SSN EIN

26. PATIENT'S ACCOUNT NO.

27. ACCEPT ASSIGNMENT? (For govt. claims, see back) YES NO

28. TOTAL CHARGE $

29. AMOUNT PAID $

30. BALANCE DUE $

31. SIGNATURE OF PHYSICIAN OR SUPPLIER INCLUDING DEGREES OR CREDENTIALS (I certify that the statements on the reverse apply to this bill and are made a part thereof.)

SIGNED DATE

32. NAME AND ADDRESS OF FACILITY WHERE SERVICES WERE RENDERED (if other than home or office)

33. PHYSICIAN'S, SUPPLIER'S BILLING NAME, ADDRESS, ZIP CODE AND PHONE #

PIN# GRP#

PHYSICIAN OR SUPPLIER INFORMATION

(APPROVED BY AMA COUNCIL ON MEDICAL SERVICE 8/88) *PLEASE PRINT OR TYPE* FORM HCFA-1500 (U2) (12-90) FORM OCWP-1500 FORM RRB-1500

Figure 11–8

PATIENT RECORD NO. 1103

Donlon,	Peter	F	08-09-24	M	013-762-3580
LAST NAME	FIRST NAME	MIDDLE NAME	BIRTH DATE	SEX	HOME PHONE

1840 East Chevy Chase Drive ,	Woodland Hills,	XY	12345
ADDRESS	CITY	STATE	ZIP CODE

retired chef
PATIENT'S OCCUPATION NAME OF COMPANY

ADDRESS OF EMPLOYER PHONE

wife deceased
SPOUSE OR PARENT OCCUPATION

EMPLOYER ADDRESS PHONE

Medicare
NAME OF HEALTH INSURANCE INSURED OR SUBSCRIBER

Farmers Insurance Co. (auto ins) 10 N. Main St., Woodland Hills, XY 12345 Policy#34276
LIABILITY INSURANCE

987-65-4321A			987-65-4321
MEDICARE NO.	MEDICAID NO.	EFFECTIVE DATE	SOC. SEC. NO.

REFERRED BY: Martha Frederick, MD, 1000 N. Main Street, Woodland Hills, XY 12345 NPI# 2710662710

DATE	PROGRESS
5-1-9X	Est pt injured in auto accident. The policyholder of the auto insurance is the individual who caused the
	accident and not Mr. Donlon. Called to ER on Sunday from outside hosp at 3 a.m. Pt complains
	of acute headache and 2.0 cm laceration of nose. Request ER consult c̄ neurologist, Dr. Parkinson, who
	rec pt be adm to hosp. Sutured 2.0 cm laceration of nose. Pt adm.
	Imp: Acute cephalgia, nasal laceration, deviated septum. Concha Antrum, MD
5-2-xx	Hosp visit Concha Antrum, MD
5-3-xx	Hosp visit Concha Antrum, MD
5-4-xx	Discharged from hosp. See hosp records for daily notes. Concha Antrum, MD
5-7-xx	Sutures removed. Recommended to have septoplasty surg. Concha Antrum, MD
5-9-xx	Adm to hosp Concha Antrum, MD
5-10-xx	Septoplasty, Pt. doing well after surg. Concha Antrum, MD
5-11-xx	Hosp visit. Pt seems to be improving. No hemorrhaging. Discharge. Concha Antrum, MD
5-12-xx	Postop anterior nasal hemorrhage & cauterization of rt side. Concha Antrum, MD

Figure 11–9

ASSIGNMENT 11–7 ► COMPLETE A MEDICARE/MEDIGAP CLAIM FORM

Task: Complete a Medicare HCFA-1500 claim form, post transactions to the ledger card, and define patient record abbreviations.

Conditions: Use the patient's record (Figure 11–12) and ledger card (Figure 11–13), one health insurance claim form (Figure 11–14), typewriter or computer, procedural and diagnostic code books, and *Workbook* Appendixes A and B.

Standards: Claim Productivity Measurement

Time: ______________ minutes

Accuracy: ______________

(Note: The time element and accuracy criteria may be given by your instructor.)

Directions:

1. Complete the Medicare Form using OCR guidelines. This case involves a patient who has a Medigap supplemental policy that is secondary payer. Refer to Chapter 6 and Figure 6–11 for instructions on how to complete the HCFA-1500 claim form. Refer to Jeremiah W. Diffenderffer's patient record and ledger card for information. See Appendix A to fill in the fees on the ledger card. Date the claim June 13. Dr. Coccidioides is accepting assignment in this case. Mr. Diffenderffer has met his deductible for the year, owing to previous care by Dr. Coccidioides in March. (This part of the case has been omitted from the patient record for the sake of brevity.)

2. Use your *CPT* code book or Appendix A to determine the correct five-digit code number and modifiers for each professional service rendered. In this case the doctor is billing for the x-rays and bronchogram. Refer to Appendix B for HCPCS procedure codes and modifiers.

3. Record all transactions on the ledger card and indicate the proper information when you have billed Medicare.

4. On August 3, Medicare paid $240 (check No. 654821) on this claim. Post this payment to the patient's ledger card. Medicare allowed $300 on this claim. Calculate and post the adjustment and post the balance due from the patient.

5. A Performance Evaluation Checklist may be reproduced from the Instruction Guide to the *Workbook* chapter if your instructor wishes to submit it to assist with scoring and comments.

6. After the instructor has returned your work to you, either make the necessary corrections and place it in a 3-ring notebook for future reference, or, if you received a high score, place it in your portfolio for reference when applying for a job.

Abbreviations pertinent to this record:

adv ______________

AP ______________

CPX ______________

est ______________

exam ______________

HCN ______________

imp ______________

lat ______________

phys ______________

pt ______________

re-exam ______________

t.i.d. ______________

wk ______________

STATEMENT

College Clinic
4567 Broad Avenue
Woodland Hills, XY 12345-0001
Telephone: 013-486-9002
Fax: 013-487-8976

Mr. Peter F. Donlon
1840 East Chevy Chase Drive
Woodland Hills, XY 12345-0001

DATE	PROFESSIONAL SERVICE DESCRIPTION	CHARGE		CREDITS PAYMENTS		CREDITS ADJUSTMENTS		CURRENT BALANCE	
5-1-xx	ER visit & hosp admit, D hx/exam, MC decision making								
5-1-xx	Suture 2.0 cm laceration of nose								
5-2-xx	HV, PF hx/exam, LC decision making								
5-3-xx	HV, PF hx/exam, LC decision making								
5-4-xx	Hospital discharge								
5-7-xx	OV, D hx/exam, MC decision making								
5-9-xx	Hosp. adm, D hx/exam, LC decision making								
5-10-xx	Septoplasty								
5-11-xx	Hospital discharge								
5-12-xx	OV, PO nasal hemorrhage								

Due and payable within 10 days. **Pay last amount in balance column** 

Key:							
PF:	Problem-focused	SF:	Straightforward	CON:	Consultation	HCD:	House call (day)
EPF:	Expanded problem-focused	LC:	Low complexity	CPX:	Complete phys exam	HCN:	House call (night)
D:	Detailed	MC:	Moderate complexity	E:	Emergency	HV:	Hospital visit
C:	Comprehensive	HC:	High complexity	ER:	Emergency dept.	OV:	Office visit

Figure 11–10

APPROVED OMB 0938-0008

PLEASE DO NOT STAPLE IN THIS AREA

CARRIER

PICA

HEALTH INSURANCE CLAIM FORM

PICA

1. MEDICARE (Medicare #) MEDICAID (Medicaid #) CHAMPUS (Sponsor's SSN) CHAMPVA (VA File #) GROUP HEALTH PLAN (SSN or ID) FECA BLK LUNG (SSN) OTHER (ID)

1a. INSURED'S I.D. NUMBER (FOR PROGRAM IN ITEM 1)

2. PATIENT'S NAME (Last Name, First Name, Middle Initial)

3. PATIENT'S BIRTH DATE MM DD YYYY SEX M F

4. INSURED'S NAME (Last Name, First Name, Middle Initial)

5. PATIENT'S ADDRESS (No., Street)

6. PATIENT RELATIONSHIP TO INSURED Self Spouse Child Other

7. INSURED'S ADDRESS (No., Street)

CITY STATE

8. PATIENT STATUS Single Married Other

CITY STATE

ZIP CODE TELEPHONE (Include Area Code) ( )

Employed Full-Time Student Part-Time Student

ZIP CODE TELEPHONE (Include Area Code) ( )

9. OTHER INSURED'S NAME (Last Name, First Name, Middle Initial)

10. IS PATIENT'S CONDITION RELATED TO:

11. INSURED'S POLICY GROUP OR FECA NUMBER

a. OTHER INSURED'S POLICY OR GROUP NUMBER

a. EMPLOYMENT? (CURRENT OR PREVIOUS) YES NO

a. INSURED'S DATE OF BIRTH MM DD YY SEX M F

b. OTHER INSURED'S DATE OF BIRTH MM DD YY SEX M F

b. AUTO ACCIDENT? YES NO PLACE (State)

b. EMPLOYER'S NAME OR SCHOOL NAME

c. EMPLOYER'S NAME OR SCHOOL NAME

c. OTHER ACCIDENT? YES NO

c. INSURANCE PLAN NAME OR PROGRAM NAME

d. INSURANCE PLAN NAME OR PROGRAM NAME

10d. RESERVED FOR LOCAL USE

d. IS THERE ANOTHER HEALTH BENEFIT PLAN? YES NO *If yes,* return to and complete item 9 a-d.

READ BACK OF FORM BEFORE COMPLETING AND SIGNING THIS FORM.

12. PATIENT'S OR AUTHORIZED PERSON'S SIGNATURE I authorize the release of any medical or other information necessary to process this claim. I also request payment of government benefits either to myself or to the party who accepts assignment below.

SIGNED ______ DATE ______

13. INSURED'S OR AUTHORIZED PERSON'S SIGNATURE I authorize payment of medical benefits to the undersigned physician or supplier for services described below.

SIGNED ______

PATIENT AND INSURED INFORMATION

14. DATE OF CURRENT: MM DD YY ILLNESS (First symptom) OR INJURY (Accident) OR PREGNANCY (LMP)

15. IF PATIENT HAS HAD SAME OR SIMILAR ILLNESS GIVE FIRST DATE MM DD YY

16. DATES PATIENT UNABLE TO WORK IN CURRENT OCCUPATION FROM MM DD YY TO MM DD YY

17. NAME OF REFERRING PHYSICIAN OR OTHER SOURCE

17a. I.D. NUMBER OF REFERRING PHYSICIAN

18. HOSPITALIZATION DATES RELATED TO CURRENT SERVICES FROM MM DD YY TO MM DD YY

19. RESERVED FOR LOCAL USE

20. OUTSIDE LAB? YES NO $ CHARGES

21. DIAGNOSIS OR NATURE OF ILLNESS OR INJURY. (RELATE ITEMS 1,2,3 OR 4 TO ITEM 24E BY LINE)

1. ______ 3. ______

2. ______ 4. ______

22. MEDICAID RESUBMISSION CODE ORIGINAL REF. NO.

23. PRIOR AUTHORIZATION NUMBER

24. A DATE(S) OF SERVICE From MM DD YY To MM DD YY	B Place of Service	C Type of Service	D PROCEDURES, SERVICES, OR SUPPLIES (Explain Unusual Circumstances) CPT/HCPCS MODIFIER	E DIAGNOSIS CODE	F $ CHARGES	G DAYS OR UNITS	H EPSDT Family Plan	I EMG	J COB	K RESERVED FOR LOCAL USE

25. FEDERAL TAX I.D. NUMBER SSN EIN

26. PATIENT'S ACCOUNT NO.

27. ACCEPT ASSIGNMENT? (For govt. claims, see back) YES NO

28. TOTAL CHARGE $

29. AMOUNT PAID $

30. BALANCE DUE $

31. SIGNATURE OF PHYSICIAN OR SUPPLIER INCLUDING DEGREES OR CREDENTIALS (I certify that the statements on the reverse apply to this bill and are made a part thereof.)

SIGNED DATE

32. NAME AND ADDRESS OF FACILITY WHERE SERVICES WERE RENDERED (If other than home or office)

33. PHYSICIAN'S, SUPPLIER'S BILLING NAME, ADDRESS, ZIP CODE AND PHONE #

PIN# GRP#

PHYSICIAN OR SUPPLIER INFORMATION

(APPROVED BY AMA COUNCIL ON MEDICAL SERVICE8/88) *PLEASE PRINT OR TYPE* FORM HCFA -1500 (U2) (12-90) FORM OCWP-1500 FORM RRB-1500

Figure 11–11

PATIENT RECORD NO. 1104

LAST NAME	FIRST NAME	MIDDLE NAME	BIRTH DATE	SEX	HOME PHONE
Diffenderffer,	Jeremiah	W.	08-24-31	M	013-471-9930

ADDRESS	CITY	STATE	ZIP CODE
120 Elm Street,	Woodland Hills,	XY	12345

PATIENT'S OCCUPATION	NAME OF COMPANY
retired painter	

ADDRESS OF EMPLOYER	PHONE

SPOUSE OR PARENT	OCCUPATION
deceased	

EMPLOYER	ADDRESS	PHONE

NAME OF INSURANCE	INSURED OR SUBSCRIBER
Medicare	

OTHER INSURANCE: United American Insurance Co., P.O. Box 810, Dallas, TX 75221 214-328-2841

MEDICARE NO.	MEDICAID NO.	EFFECTIVE DATE	SOC. SEC. NO.
731-32-7401T	Other insurance policy #007559715		731-32-7401

REFERRED BY: John M. Diffenderffer (brother)

DATE	PROGRESS
6-1-XX	Est pt phoned stating he breathed paint fumes and is having SOB & coughing. Dr. ordered chest x-rays to be taken in office this p.m. as well as bilateral bronchogram. *Brady Coccidioides, MD*
6-2-XX	Ap & lat chest x-rays showed pulmonary emphysema. Bilateral bronchogram showed pulmonary emphysema. Adv pt by telephone to come in for PE. *Brady Cocciadioides, MD*
6-5-XX	Pt given comprehensive physical re-exam. Imp: bronchitis and pneumonitis due to inhalation of fumes and vapors at home. Adv bed rest. *Brady Cocciadioides, MD*
6-12-XX	HCN PF, hx/exam, SF decision making. Administered medication (Coramine 1.5 ml two ampules IV). Imp: recurrent bronchitis and pneumonitis, exertional dyspnea. Adv bed rest. To be seen in 1 wk. *Brady Cocciadioides, MD*

Figure 11–12

ASSIGNMENT 11–8 ▶ COMPLETE A MEDICARE CLAIM FORM

Task: Complete a Medicare HCFA-1500 claim form and a waiver of liability agreement form, post transactions to the ledger card, and define patient record abbreviations.

Conditions: Use the patient's record (Figure 11–15) and ledger card (Figure 11–16), waiver of liability agreement form (Figure 11–17), one health insurance claim form (Figure 11–18), typewriter or computer, procedural and diagnostic code books, and *Workbook* Appendixes A and B.

Standards: Claim Productivity Measurement

Time: ____________ minutes

Accuracy: ______________

(Note: The time element and accuracy criteria may be given by your instructor.)

Directions:

1. Complete the Medicare Form using OCR guidelines, directing it to your local fiscal intermediary. This assignment requires two claim forms, so make a photocopy of the HCFA-1500 claim form. Refer to the *Handboook*, Chapter 6, Figure 6–11, for instructions on how to complete the HCFA-1500 form. Refer to Raymond D. Fay's patient record and ledger card for information. Refer to Appendix A to fill in the fees on the ledger card. Date the claim December 31. Dr. Antrum is accepting assignment in this case. Mr. Fay has met his deductible for the year, owing to previous care by another physician.

2. The nystagmus service is disallowed by Medicare. For this reason, complete the waiver of liability agreement form. Refer to the *Handbook*, Chapter 11, Figure 11–10, for a completed example of this form.

3. Use your *CPT* code book or Appendix A to determine the correct five-digit code number and modifiers for each professional service rendered. Refer to Appendix B for HCPCS procedure codes and modifiers.

4. Record all transactions on the ledger card and indicate the proper information when you have billed Medicare.

5. On February 4, Medicare paid $680 (check No. 438911) on this claim. Post this payment to the patient's ledger card. Medicare allowed $850 on this claim. Post the courtesy adjustment. Post the balance due from the patient.

6. A Performance Evaluation Checklist may be reproduced from the Instruction Guide to the *Workbook* chapter if your instructor wishes you to submit it to assist with scoring and comments.

7. After the instructor has returned your work to you, either make the necessary corrections and place it in a 3-ring notebook for future reference, or, if you received a high score, place it in your portfolio for reference when applying for a job.

Abbreviations pertinent to this record:

exam ______________ OV ______________

imp ______________ Pt ______________

inj ______________ retn ______________

N ______________ R/O ______________

OC ______________ X ______________

STATEMENT

College Clinic
4567 Broad Avenue
Woodland Hills, XY 12345-0001
Telephone: 013-486-9002
Fax: 013-487-8976

Mr. Jeremiah W. Diffenderffer
120 Elm Street
Woodland Hills, XY 12345-0001

DATE	PROFESSIONAL SERVICE DESCRIPTION	CHARGE	CREDITS PAYMENTS	CREDITS ADJUSTMENTS	CURRENT BALANCE
	Balance forward				20 00
6-1-xx	Chest x-rays				
6-1-xx	Bilateral bronchogram				
6-5-xx	C hx/exam, HC decision making				
6-12-xx	HCN, PF hx/exam, SF decision making				
6-12-xx	Coramine IV (nikethamide)	25 00			

Due and payable within 10 days.

Pay last amount in balance column 

Key: PF: Problem-focused
EPF: Expanded problem-focused
D: Detailed
C: Comprehensive
SF: Straightforward
LC: Low complexity
MC: Moderate complexity
HC: High complexity
CON: Consultation
CPX: Complete phys exam
E: Emergency
ER: Emergency dept.
HCD: House call (day)
HCN: House call (night)
HV: Hospital visit
OV: Office visit

Figure 11–13

APPROVED OMB-0938-0008

PLEASE DO NOT STAPLE IN THIS AREA

CARRIER

PICA

HEALTH INSURANCE CLAIM FORM

PICA

1. MEDICARE (Medicare #) MEDICAID (Medicaid #) CHAMPUS (Sponsor's SSN) CHAMPVA (VA File #) GROUP HEALTH PLAN (SSN or ID) FECA BLK LUNG (SSN) OTHER (ID)

1a. INSURED'S I.D. NUMBER (FOR PROGRAM IN ITEM 1)

2. PATIENT'S NAME (Last Name, First Name, Middle Initial)

3. PATIENT'S BIRTH DATE MM | DD | YYYY SEX M F

4. INSURED'S NAME (Last Name, First Name, Middle Initial)

5. PATIENT'S ADDRESS (No., Street)

6. PATIENT RELATIONSHIP TO INSURED Self Spouse Child Other

7. INSURED'S ADDRESS (No., Street)

CITY STATE

8. PATIENT STATUS Single Married Other

CITY STATE

ZIP CODE TELEPHONE (Include Area Code)

Employed Full-Time Student Part-Time Student

ZIP CODE TELEPHONE (Include Area Code) ( )

9. OTHER INSURED'S NAME (Last Name, First Name, Middle Initial)

10. IS PATIENT'S CONDITION RELATED TO:

11. INSURED'S POLICY GROUP OR FECA NUMBER

a. OTHER INSURED'S POLICY OR GROUP NUMBER

a. EMPLOYMENT? (CURRENT OR PREVIOUS) YES NO

a. INSURED'S DATE OF BIRTH MM | DD | YY SEX M F

b. OTHER INSURED'S DATE OF BIRTH MM | DD | YY SEX M F

b. AUTO ACCIDENT? PLACE (State) YES NO

b. EMPLOYER'S NAME OR SCHOOL NAME

c. EMPLOYER'S NAME OR SCHOOL NAME

c. OTHER ACCIDENT? YES NO

c. INSURANCE PLAN NAME OR PROGRAM NAME

d. INSURANCE PLAN NAME OR PROGRAM NAME

10d. RESERVED FOR LOCAL USE

d. IS THERE ANOTHER HEALTH BENEFIT PLAN? YES NO *If yes, return to and complete item 9 a-d.*

READ BACK OF FORM BEFORE COMPLETING AND SIGNING THIS FORM.

12. PATIENT'S OR AUTHORIZED PERSON'S SIGNATURE I authorize the release of any medical or other information necessary to process this claim. I also request payment of government benefits either to myself or to the party who accepts assignment below.

SIGNED ______ DATE ______

13. INSURED'S OR AUTHORIZED PERSON'S SIGNATURE I authorize payment of medical benefits to the undersigned physician or supplier for services described below.

SIGNED ______

PATIENT AND INSURED INFORMATION

14. DATE OF CURRENT: MM | DD | YY ILLNESS (First symptom) OR INJURY (Accident) OR PREGNANCY (LMP)

15. IF PATIENT HAS HAD SAME OR SIMILAR ILLNESS GIVE FIRST DATE MM | DD | YY

16. DATES PATIENT UNABLE TO WORK IN CURRENT OCCUPATION FROM MM | DD | YY TO MM | DD | YY

17. NAME OF REFERRING PHYSICIAN OR OTHER SOURCE

17a. I.D. NUMBER OF REFERRING PHYSICIAN

18. HOSPITALIZATION DATES RELATED TO CURRENT SERVICES FROM MM | DD | YY TO MM | DD | YY

19. RESERVED FOR LOCAL USE

20. OUTSIDE LAB? YES NO $ CHARGES

21. DIAGNOSIS OR NATURE OF ILLNESS OR INJURY. (RELATE ITEMS 1,2,3 OR 4 TO ITEM 24E BY LINE)

1. ______ 3. ______

2. ______ 4. ______

22. MEDICAID RESUBMISSION CODE ORIGINAL REF. NO.

23. PRIOR AUTHORIZATION NUMBER

24. A DATE(S) OF SERVICE From MM DD YY To MM DD YY	B Place of Service	C Type of Service	D PROCEDURES, SERVICES, OR SUPPLIES (Explain Unusual Circumstances) CPT/HCPCS | MODIFIER	E DIAGNOSIS CODE	F $ CHARGES	G DAYS OR UNITS	H EPSDT Family Plan	I EMG	J COB	K RESERVED FOR LOCAL USE

25. FEDERAL TAX I.D. NUMBER SSN EIN

26. PATIENT'S ACCOUNT NO.

27. ACCEPT ASSIGNMENT? (For govt. claims, see back) YES NO

28. TOTAL CHARGE $

29. AMOUNT PAID $

30. BALANCE DUE $

31. SIGNATURE OF PHYSICIAN OR SUPPLIER INCLUDING DEGREES OR CREDENTIALS (I certify that the statements on the reverse apply to this bill and are made a part thereof.)

SIGNED DATE

32. NAME AND ADDRESS OF FACILITY WHERE SERVICES WERE RENDERED (if other than home or office)

33. PHYSICIAN'S, SUPPLIER'S BILLING NAME, ADDRESS, ZIP CODE AND PHONE #

PIN# GRP#

PHYSICIAN OR SUPPLIER INFORMATION

(APPROVED BY AMA COUNCIL ON MEDICAL SERVICE8/88) *PLEASE PRINT OR TYPE* FORM HCFA-1500 (U2) (12-90) FORM OCWP-1500 FORM RRB-1500

Figure 11–14

PATIENT RECORD NO. 1105

LAST NAME	FIRST NAME	MIDDLE NAME	BIRTH DATE	SEX	HOME PHONE
Fay,	Raymond	-	02-03-02	M	013-788-9090

ADDRESS	CITY	STATE	ZIP CODE
33 North Pencil Avenue,	Woodland Hills,	XY	12345

PATIENT'S OCCUPATION	NAME OF COMPANY
retired railroad engineer	Santa Fe Railroad

ADDRESS OF EMPLOYER	PHONE

SPOUSE OR PARENT	OCCUPATION
Marilyn B. Fay	homemaker

EMPLOYER	ADDRESS	PHONE

NAME OF INSURANCE	INSURED OR SUBSCRIBER
Medicare	

POLICY NO.	GROUP NO.	EFFECTIVE DATE

MEDICARE NO.	MEDICAID NO.	EFFECTIVE DATE	SOC. SEC. NO.
A 887-66-1235A			887-66-1235

REFERRED BY: George Gentle, MD, 1000 N. Main St., Woodland Hills, XY 12345 NPI# 4021310213

DATE	PROGRESS
10-31-XX	New pt complains of skin rash and dizziness for 3 days. Exam reveals rash on chest and arms.
	R/O food allergy . Retn in 4 days for tests. Concha Antrum, MD
11-4-XX	Audiometric hearing tests (air, bone, and speech)- N. 10 intradermal allergy tests. Bilateral
	mastoid X-N. Nystagmus test, spontaneous incl. gaze. Concha Antrum, MD
11-10-XX	OV ltd. Pt to purchase allergen extract and retn daily for immunotherapy inj. for food allergies.
11-11-XX	Immunotherapy inj. Concha Antrum, MD
through	" " Concha Antrum, MD
12-11-XX	OV, PF hx/exam, SF decision making. Pt improved. Received final inj. (#31) & evaluated for
	discharge. Concha Antrum, MD

Figure 11–15

STATEMENT

College Clinic
4567 Broad Avenue
Woodland Hills, XY 12345-0001
Telephone: 013-486-9002
Fax: 013-487-8976

Mr. Raymond D. Fay
333 North Pencil Avenue
Woodland Hills, XY 12345-0001

DATE	PROFESSIONAL SERVICE DESCRIPTION	CHARGE		CREDITS				CURRENT BALANCE	
				PAYMENTS		ADJUSTMENTS			
10-31-xx	OV, D hx/exam, LC decision making								
11-4-xx	Audiometric comp. hearing test (air, bone, and speech)								
11-4-xx	Nystagmus spontaneous test								
11-4-xx	Intradermal allergy tests allergenic extracts								
11-4-xx	Mastoid x-rays (3 views/side) Rt/Lt								
11-11-xx to 12-11-xx	Immunotherapy injections (31)								
12-11-xx	Discharged OV, PF Hx/exam, SF decision making								

Due and payable within 10 days. **Pay last amount in balance column** 

Key: PF:	Problem-focused	SF:	Straightforward	CON:	Consultation	HCD:	House call (day)
EPF:	Expanded problem-focused	LC:	Low complexity	CPX:	Complete phys exam	HCN:	House call (night)
D:	Detailed	MC:	Moderate complexity	E:	Emergency	HV:	Hospital visit
C:	Comprehensive	HC:	High complexity	ER:	Emergency dept.	OV:	Office visit

Figure 11–16

College Clinic
4567 Broad Avenue
Woodland Hills, XY 12345-0001

ADVANCE NOTICE MEDICARE BENEFICIARY AGREEMENT

If Medicare determines that a particular service, although it would be otherwise covered, is not reasonable and necessary under Medicare program standards, Medicare will deny payment for that service. In your case, Medicare might deny payment for:

1. ____

2. ____

for the following reasons:

Medicare does usually not pay for this:

_________ many visits or treatments
_________ service (or this many services within this period of time)
_________ injection (or this many injections)
_________ because it is a treatment that is yet to be proved effective
_________ office visit unless it was needed because of an emergency
_________ same services by more than one doctor during the same period
_________ equipment
_________ laboratory test
_________ visit since it is more than one visit per day
_________ extensive procedure
_________ same service by more than one doctor of the same specialty
_________ nursing home visit since only one is allowed per month

Beneficiary Agreement

I have been notified by my physician that, in my case, Medicare might deny payment for the service(s) checked above. If Medicare denies payment, I agree to be personally and fully responsible for payment.

______________________ November 4, 20XX

Beneficiary's Signature Date Signed

Figure 11–17

ASSIGNMENT 11–9 ▶ COMPLETE A MEDICARE/MEDICAID CLAIM FORM

Task: Complete a Medicare HCFA-1500 claim form, post transactions to the ledger card, and define patient record abbreviations.

Conditions: Use the patient's record (Figure 11–19) and ledger card (Figure 11–20), one health insurance claim form (Figure 11–21), typewriter or computer, procedural and diagnostic code books, and *Workbook* Appendixes A and B.

Standards: Claim Productivity Measurement

Time: ________________ minutes

Accuracy: ________________

(Note: The time element and accuracy criteria may be given by your instructor.)

Directions:

1. Complete the Medicare Form using OCR guidelines, directing it to both your local Medicare fiscal intermediary and Medicaid. Refer to Chapter 6 and Figure 6–10 for instructions on how to complete the HCFA-1500 claim form. Refer to Mr. Harris Fremont's patient record and ledger card for information. Refer to Appendix A to fill in the fees on the ledger card. Date the claim October 31.

2. Use your *CPT* code book or Appendix A to determine the correct five-digit code number and modifiers for each professional service rendered. Refer to Appendix B for HCPCS procedure codes and modifiers.

3. Record all transactions on the ledger card and indicate the proper information when you have billed Medicare/Medicaid.

4. On December 12, Medicare paid $125 (check No. 281362) on this claim. Post this payment to the patient's ledger card. On December 29 you receive a voucher #7234 from Medicaid for $45. Post this payment to the patient's ledger card and show the courtesy adjustment.

5. A Performance Evaluation Checklist may be reproduced from the Instruction Guide to the *Workbook* chapter if your instructor wishes you to submit it to assist with scoring and comments.

6. After the instructor has returned your work to you, either make the necessary corrections and place it in a 3-ring notebook for future reference, or, if you received a high score, place it in your portfolio for reference when applying for a job.

Abbreviations pertinent to this record:

adv ________________ N ________________

c/o ________________ NP ________________

D.P.M. ________________ prn ________________

exam ________________ Pt ________________

hx ________________ rtn ________________

imp ________________ Rx ________________

L ________________

APPROVED OMB-0938-0008

CARRIER

PLEASE
DO NOT
STAPLE
IN THIS
AREA

PICA

HEALTH INSURANCE CLAIM FORM

PICA

1. MEDICARE (Medicare #) MEDICAID (Medicaid #) CHAMPUS (Sponsor's SSN) CHAMPVA (VA File #) GROUP HEALTH PLAN (SSN or ID) FECA BLK LUNG (SSN) OTHER (ID)

1a. INSURED'S I.D. NUMBER (FOR PROGRAM IN ITEM 1)

2. PATIENT'S NAME (Last Name, First Name, Middle Initial)

3. PATIENT'S BIRTH DATE MM | DD | YYYY SEX M F

4. INSURED'S NAME (Last Name, First Name, Middle Initial)

5. PATIENT'S ADDRESS (No., Street)

6. PATIENT RELATIONSHIP TO INSURED Self Spouse Child Other

7. INSURED'S ADDRESS (No., Street)

CITY STATE

8. PATIENT STATUS Single Married Other

CITY STATE

ZIP CODE TELEPHONE (Include Area Code)

Employed Full-Time Student Part-Time Student

ZIP CODE TELEPHONE (include Area Code) ( )

9. OTHER INSURED'S NAME (Last Name, First Name, Middle Initial)

10. IS PATIENT'S CONDITION RELATED TO:

11. INSURED'S POLICY GROUP OR FECA NUMBER

a. OTHER INSURED'S POLICY OR GROUP NUMBER

a. EMPLOYMENT? (CURRENT OR PREVIOUS) YES NO

a. INSURED'S DATE OF BIRTH MM | DD | YY SEX M F

b. OTHER INSURED'S DATE OF BIRTH MM | DD | YY SEX M F

b. AUTO ACCIDENT? YES NO PLACE (State)

b. EMPLOYER'S NAME OR SCHOOL NAME

c. EMPLOYER'S NAME OR SCHOOL NAME

c. OTHER ACCIDENT? YES NO

c. INSURANCE PLAN NAME OR PROGRAM NAME

d. INSURANCE PLAN NAME OR PROGRAM NAME

10d. RESERVED FOR LOCAL USE

d. IS THERE ANOTHER HEALTH BENEFIT PLAN? YES NO *If yes, return to and complete item 9 a-d.*

READ BACK OF FORM BEFORE COMPLETING AND SIGNING THIS FORM.

12. PATIENT'S OR AUTHORIZED PERSON'S SIGNATURE I authorize the release of any medical or other information necessary to process this claim. I also request payment of government benefits either to myself or to the party who accepts assignment below.

SIGNED ______ DATE ______

13. INSURED'S OR AUTHORIZED PERSON'S SIGNATURE I authorize payment of medical benefits to the undersigned physician or supplier for services described below.

SIGNED ______

PATIENT AND INSURED INFORMATION

14. DATE OF CURRENT: MM | DD | YY ◀ ILLNESS (First symptom) OR INJURY (Accident) OR PREGNANCY (LMP)

15. IF PATIENT HAS HAD SAME OR SIMILAR ILLNESS GIVE FIRST DATE MM | DD | YY

16. DATES PATIENT UNABLE TO WORK IN CURRENT OCCUPATION FROM MM | DD | YY TO MM | DD | YY

17. NAME OF REFERRING PHYSICIAN OR OTHER SOURCE

17a. I.D. NUMBER OF REFERRING PHYSICIAN

18. HOSPITALIZATION DATES RELATED TO CURRENT SERVICES FROM MM | DD | YY TO MM | DD | YY

19. RESERVED FOR LOCAL USE

20. OUTSIDE LAB? YES NO $ CHARGES

21. DIAGNOSIS OR NATURE OF ILLNESS OR INJURY. (RELATE ITEMS 1,2,3 OR 4 TO ITEM 24E BY LINE)

1. ______ 3. ______

2. ______ 4. ______

22. MEDICAID RESUBMISSION CODE ORIGINAL REF. NO.

23. PRIOR AUTHORIZATION NUMBER

24. A DATE(S) OF SERVICE From MM DD YY To MM DD YY	B Place of Service	C Type of Service	D PROCEDURES, SERVICES, OR SUPPLIES (Explain Unusual Circumstances) CPT/HCPCS | MODIFIER	E DIAGNOSIS CODE	F $ CHARGES	G DAYS OR UNITS	H EPSDT Family Plan	I EMG	J COB	K RESERVED FOR LOCAL USE

25. FEDERAL TAX I.D. NUMBER SSN EIN

26. PATIENT'S ACCOUNT NO.

27. ACCEPT ASSIGNMENT? (For govt. claims, see back) YES NO

28. TOTAL CHARGE $

29. AMOUNT PAID $

30. BALANCE DUE $

31. SIGNATURE OF PHYSICIAN OR SUPPLIER INCLUDING DEGREES OR CREDENTIALS (I certify that the statements on the reverse apply to this bill and are made a part thereof.)

SIGNED DATE

32. NAME AND ADDRESS OF FACILITY WHERE SERVICES WERE RENDERED (if other than home or office)

33. PHYSICIAN'S, SUPPLIER'S BILLING NAME, ADDRESS, ZIP CODE AND PHONE #

PIN# GRP#

PHYSICIAN OR SUPPLIER INFORMATION

(APPROVED BY AMA COUNCIL ON MEDICAL SERVICE8/88) *PLEASE PRINT OR TYPE* FORM HCFA-1500 (U2) (12-90) FORM OCWP-1500 FORM RRB-1500

Figure 11–18

PATIENT RECORD NO. 1106

Fremont,	Harris	-	07-10-23	M	013-899-0109
LAST NAME	FIRST NAME	MIDDLE NAME	BIRTH DATE	SEX	HOME PHONE

735 North Center Street,	Woodland Hills,	XY	12345
ADDRESS	CITY	STATE	ZIP CODE

retired baseball coach
PATIENT'S OCCUPATION — NAME OF COMPANY

ADDRESS OF EMPLOYER — PHONE

Emily B. Fremont — homemaker
SPOUSE OR PARENT — OCCUPATION

EMPLOYER — ADDRESS — PHONE

Medicare/Medicaid
NAME OF INSURANCE — INSURED OR SUBSCRIBER

POLICY NO. — GROUP NO. — EFFECTIVE DATE

454-01-9569A	56-10-0020205-0-00		454-01-9569
MEDICARE NO.	MEDICAID NO.	EFFECTIVE DATE	SOC. SEC. NO.

REFERRED BY: Raymond Skeleton, MD

DATE	PROGRESS
10-2-XX	NP referred by Dr. Skeleton with hx of gout and mycotic nails. He comes in c/o discomfort around toes
	of both feet and has difficulty walking. Pt states he dropped shelf on both feet about a month ago.
	X-ray R and L feet N. Exam shows bilateral mycotic nails ingrown on great R toe. Rx: Debridement--
	electrically trimmed overgrowth and adv to rtn if pain continues in great R toe. Imp: Mycotic nails;
	difficulty in walking Nick Pedro, DPM
10-18-XX	Pt returns c/o ingrown nail. Performed wedge excision of skin fold on R great toe. Rtn prn.
	Imp: Ingrown nail-- great R toe; toe pain-- great R toe Nick Pedro ,DPM

Figure 11–19

COMPUTER EXERCISE

Medicare

Before proceeding, you may want to do additional exercises based on the concepts you have learned. Practice material is on your CD-ROM.

Directions: Insert the CD-ROM into the computer and follow the instructions on the screen for Cases 8, 9, and 10.

STATEMENT

College Clinic
4567 Broad Avenue
Woodland Hills, XY 12345-0001
Telephone: 013-486-9002
Fax: 013-487-8976

Mr. Harris Fremont
735 North Center Street
Woodland Hills, XY 12345-0001

DATE	PROFESSIONAL SERVICE DESCRIPTION	CHARGE	CREDITS		CURRENT BALANCE
			PAYMENTS	ADJUSTMENTS	
10-2-xx	OV, D hx/exam, MC decision making				
10-2-xx	AP & lat x-rays R/L feet				
10-2-xx	Debridement nails , elect.				
10-5-xx	OV, PF hx/exam, LC decision making				
10-5-xx	Wedge excision R. great toe				

Due and payable within 10 days. **Pay last amount in balance column** 

Key: PF: Problem-focused
EPF: Expanded problem-focused
D: Detailed
C: Comprehensive
SF: Straightforward
LC: Low complexity
MC: Moderate complexity
HC: High complexity
CON: Consultation
CPX: Complete phys exam
E: Emergency
ER: Emergency dept.
HCD: House call (day)
HCN: House call (night)
HV: Hospital visit
OV: Office visit

Figure 11–20

APPROVED OMB-0938-0008

PLEASE DO NOT STAPLE IN THIS AREA

CARRIER

PICA

HEALTH INSURANCE CLAIM FORM

PICA

1. MEDICARE (Medicare #) | MEDICAID (Medicaid #) | CHAMPUS (Sponsor's SSN) | CHAMPVA (VA File #) | GROUP HEALTH PLAN (SSN or ID) | FECA BLK LUNG (SSN) | OTHER (ID)

1a. INSURED'S I.D. NUMBER (FOR PROGRAM IN ITEM 1)

2. PATIENT'S NAME (Last Name, First Name, Middle Initial)

3. PATIENT'S BIRTH DATE MM | DD | YYYY SEX M F

4. INSURED'S NAME (Last Name, First Name, Middle Initial)

5. PATIENT'S ADDRESS (No., Street)

6. PATIENT RELATIONSHIP TO INSURED Self Spouse Child Other

7. INSURED'S ADDRESS (No., Street)

CITY STATE

8. PATIENT STATUS Single Married Other

CITY STATE

ZIP CODE TELEPHONE (Include Area Code)

Employed Full-Time Student Part-Time Student

ZIP CODE TELEPHONE (include Area Code) ( )

9. OTHER INSURED'S NAME (Last Name, First Name, Middle Initial)

10. IS PATIENT'S CONDITION RELATED TO:

11. INSURED'S POLICY GROUP OR FECA NUMBER

a. OTHER INSURED'S POLICY OR GROUP NUMBER

a. EMPLOYMENT? (CURRENT OR PREVIOUS) YES NO

a. INSURED'S DATE OF BIRTH MM | DD | YY SEX M F

b. OTHER INSURED'S DATE OF BIRTH MM | DD | YY SEX M F

b. AUTO ACCIDENT? YES NO PLACE (State)

b. EMPLOYER'S NAME OR SCHOOL NAME

c. EMPLOYER'S NAME OR SCHOOL NAME

c. OTHER ACCIDENT? YES NO

c. INSURANCE PLAN NAME OR PROGRAM NAME

d. INSURANCE PLAN NAME OR PROGRAM NAME

10d. RESERVED FOR LOCAL USE

d. IS THERE ANOTHER HEALTH BENEFIT PLAN? YES NO *If yes, return to and complete item 9 a-d.*

READ BACK OF FORM BEFORE COMPLETING AND SIGNING THIS FORM.

12. PATIENT'S OR AUTHORIZED PERSON'S SIGNATURE I authorize the release of any medical or other information necessary to process this claim. I also request payment of government benefits either to myself or to the party who accepts assignment below.

SIGNED ____ DATE ____

13. INSURED'S OR AUTHORIZED PERSON'S SIGNATURE I authorize payment of medical benefits to the undersigned physician or supplier for services described below.

SIGNED ____

PATIENT AND INSURED INFORMATION

14. DATE OF CURRENT: MM | DD | YY ILLNESS (First symptom) OR INJURY (Accident) OR PREGNANCY (LMP)

15. IF PATIENT HAS HAD SAME OR SIMILAR ILLNESS GIVE FIRST DATE MM | DD | YY

16. DATES PATIENT UNABLE TO WORK IN CURRENT OCCUPATION FROM MM | DD | YY TO MM | DD | YY

17. NAME OF REFERRING PHYSICIAN OR OTHER SOURCE

17a. I.D. NUMBER OF REFERRING PHYSICIAN

18. HOSPITALIZATION DATES RELATED TO CURRENT SERVICES FROM MM | DD | YY TO MM | DD | YY

19. RESERVED FOR LOCAL USE

20. OUTSIDE LAB? YES NO $ CHARGES

21. DIAGNOSIS OR NATURE OF ILLNESS OR INJURY. (RELATE ITEMS 1,2,3 OR 4 TO ITEM 24E BY LINE)

1. ____ 3. ____

2. ____ 4. ____

22. MEDICAID RESUBMISSION CODE ORIGINAL REF. NO.

23. PRIOR AUTHORIZATION NUMBER

24. A DATE(S) OF SERVICE From MM DD YY To MM DD YY	B Place of Service	C Type of Service	D PROCEDURES, SERVICES, OR SUPPLIES (Explain Unusual Circumstances) CPT/HCPCS | MODIFIER	E DIAGNOSIS CODE	F $ CHARGES	G DAYS OR UNITS	H EPSDT Family Plan	I EMG	J COB	K RESERVED FOR LOCAL USE

25. FEDERAL TAX I.D. NUMBER SSN EIN

26. PATIENT'S ACCOUNT NO.

27. ACCEPT ASSIGNMENT? (For govt. claims, see back) YES NO

28. TOTAL CHARGE $

29. AMOUNT PAID $

30. BALANCE DUE $

31. SIGNATURE OF PHYSICIAN OR SUPPLIER INCLUDING DEGREES OR CREDENTIALS (I certify that the statements on the reverse apply to this bill and are made a part thereof.)

SIGNED DATE

32. NAME AND ADDRESS OF FACILITY WHERE SERVICES WERE RENDERED (if other than home or office)

33. PHYSICIAN'S, SUPPLIER'S BILLING NAME, ADDRESS, ZIP CODE AND PHONE #

PIN# GRP#

PHYSICIAN OR SUPPLIER INFORMATION

(APPROVED BY AMA COUNCIL ON MEDICAL SERVICE8/88) *PLEASE PRINT OR TYPE* FORM HCFA-1500 (U2) (12-90) FORM OCWP-1500 FORM RRB-1500

Figure 11–21

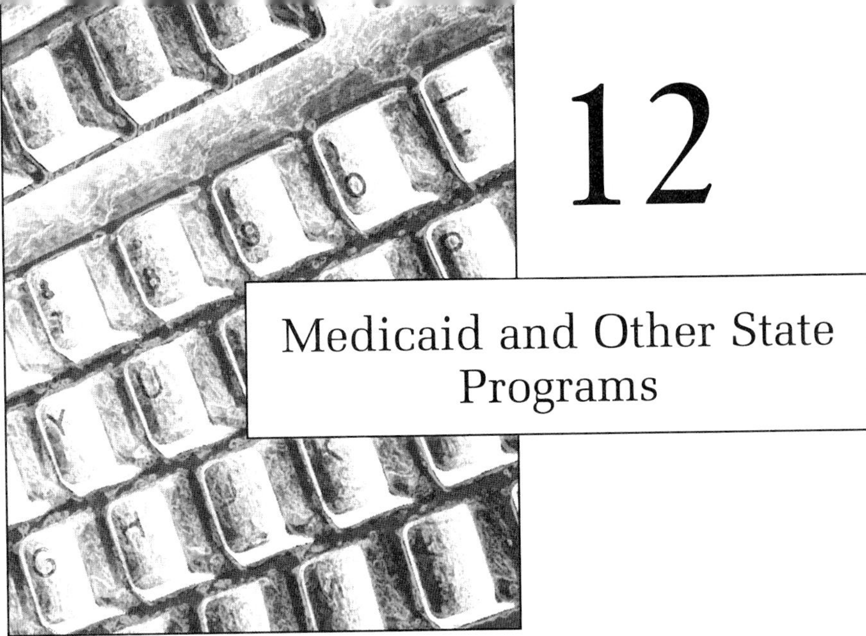

12

Medicaid and Other State Programs

KEY TERMS

Your instructor may wish to select some specific words pertinent to this chapter for a test. For definitions of the terms, further study, and/or reference, the words, phrases, and abbreviations may be found in the Glossary at the end of the Handbook. *Key terms for this chapter follow.*

categorically needy
covered services
Early and Periodic Screening, Diagnosis, and Treatment (EPSDT)
fiscal agent
Maternal and Child Health Programs (MCHP)
Medicaid (MCD)
Medi-Cal
medically needy (MN)
prior approval
recipient
share of cost
Supplemental Security Income (SSI)

PERFORMANCE OBJECTIVES

The student will be able to

- Define and spell the key terms for this chapter, given the information from the *Handbook* Glossary, within a reasonable period of time and with enough accuracy to obtain a satisfactory evaluation.
- Answer the self-study review questions after reading the chapter, with enough accuracy to obtain a satisfactory evaluation.
- Fill in the correct meaning of each abbreviation, given a list of common medical abbreviations and symbols that appear in chart notes, within a reasonable period of time and with enough accuracy to obtain a satisfactory evaluation.
- Complete each HCFA-1500 Health Insurance Claim Form for billing, given the patient's medical chart notes, ledger cards, and blank insurance claim forms, within a reasonable period of time and with enough accuracy to obtain a satisfactory evaluation.
- Correctly post payments, adjustments, and balances on the patient's ledger cards, using the Mock Fee Schedule in Appendix A, within a reasonable period of time and with enough accuracy to obtain a satisfactory evaluation.

STUDY OUTLINE

History
Medicaid Programs
  Maternal and Child Health Program
Low-Income Medicare Recipients
  Medicaid-Qualified Medicare Beneficiaries Program

Specified Low-Income Medicare Beneficiary Program
Qualifying Individuals Program
Medicaid Eligibility
Categorically Needy
Medically Needy
Maternal and Child Health Program Eligibility
Accepting Medicaid Patients
Identification Card
Retroactive Eligibility
Medicaid Benefits
Covered Services
Early and Periodic Screening, Diagnosis, and Treatment
Disallowed Services
Medicaid Managed Care
Claim Procedure
Copayment
Prior Approval
Time Limit
Reciprocity
Claim Form
Medicaid Managed Care
Maternal and Child Health Program
Medicaid and Other Plans
Government Programs and Medicaid
Group Health Insurance and Medicaid
Medicaid and Aliens
After Claim Submission
Remittance Advice
Appeals
Medicaid Fraud Control

SELF-STUDY 12–1 ▶ REVIEW QUESTIONS*

Review the objectives, key terms, glossary definitions to key terms, chapter information, and figures before completing the following review questions.

1. Medicaid is administered by state governments with partial federal funding.

2. Medicaid is not an insurance program. It is a/an assistance program.

3. In all other states the program is known as Medicaid but in California the program is called Medi-cal.

4. Because the federal government sets minimum requirements, states are free to enhance the Medicaid program. Name two ways Medicaid programs vary from state to state.
   a. coverage
   b. benefits

5. MCHP means Maternal and Child Health Programs and covers children of what age group? Under 21 years of age

6. What people might be eligible for Medicaid?
   a. certain needy and low-income people
   b. the aged (65 years or older)

*Review questions for Medi-Cal are provided in this *Workbook* in Appendix C.

c. the blind

d. the disabled

e. members of families with dependent

f. children (one parent) financially eligible).

7. Name two broad classifications of people eligible for Medicaid assistance.

a. catugorically needy

b. medically needy

8. When professional services are rendered, the Medicaid identification card or electronic verification must show eligibility for (circle one):

a. day of service b. year of service

c. month of service d. week of service

9. The name of the program for the prevention, early detection, and treatment of conditions of welfare children is known as Early and periodic screening, diagnosis and treatment. It is abbreviated as EPSDT.

10. Define these abbreviations.

a. MCD Medicaid

b. SSI supplement security income

c. AFDC Aid to families with dependent children

d. MI Medically indigent

11. Mrs. Ho suddenly experiences a pain in her right lower abdominal area and rushes to a local hospital for emergency care. Laboratory work verifies that she has a ruptured appendix and immediate surgery is recommended. Is prior authorization required in a bona fide emergency situation like this NO? What two blocks on the HCFA-1500 claim form need to be completed for emergency services? Block 24I and in Block 19 enter an emergency certification statement or include an attachment to the claim with this data

12. Your Medicaid patient seen today needs chronic hemodialysis services. You telephone for authorization to get verbal approval. Four important items to obtain are:

a. Date of authorization

b. name of the person who authorized

c. approximate time of day authorization is given

d. verbal number given by field office

13. The time limit for submitting a Medicaid claim varies from 2 months to 1 year from the date the service is rendered. In your state, the time limit is ________________.

14. The insurance claim form for submitting Medicaid claims in all states is Health insurance Claim form HCFA 1500.

15. Your Medicaid patient also has TRICARE. What billing procedure do you follow? Be exact in your steps for a dependent of an active military person.

    a. Bill tricare first
    b. Bill Medicaid second and attach an explanation of benefits from tricare to the billing form

16. When a Medicaid patient is injured in an automobile accident and the car has liability insurance, the insurance claim is sent to the (circle one):

    a. patient
    b. automobile insurance carrier (circled)
    c. Medicaid fiscal agent

17. Five categories of adjudicated claims that may appear on a Medicaid Remittance Advice document are

    a. adjustments
    b. approvals
    c. denials
    d. suspends
    e. audit/refund transactions

18. Name three levels of Medicaid appeals.

    a. regional fiscal intermediary or Medicaid bureau
    b. Department of welfare
    c. appellate court

To check your answers to this self-study assignment, see Appendix D.

ASSIGNMENT 12–2 ► COMPLETE A MEDICAID CLAIM FORM

Task: Complete a Medicaid HCFA-1500 claim form, post transactions to the ledger card, and define patient record abbreviations.

Conditions: Use the patient's record (Figure 12–1) and ledger (Figure 12–2), one health insurance claim form (Figure 12–3), typewriter or computer, procedural and diagnostic code books, and *Workbook* Appendixes A and B.

PATIENT RECORD NO. 1201

Clarkson,	Rose	–	03-09-44	F	013-487-2209
LAST NAME	FIRST NAME	MIDDLE NAME	BIRTH DATE	SEX	HOME PHONE

3408 Jackson Street,	Hempstead,	XY	11551-0300
ADDRESS	CITY	STATE	ZIP CODE

unemployed	
PATIENT'S OCCUPATION	NAME OF COMPANY

ADDRESS OF EMPLOYER	PHONE

SPOUSE OR PARENT	OCCUPATION

EMPLOYER	ADDRESS	PHONE

Medicaid	
NAME OF INSURANCE	INSURED OR SUBSCRIBER

POLICY NO.	GROUP NO.	EFFECTIVE DATE

	CC99756E**		030-87-9543
MEDICARE NO.	MEDICAID NO.	EFFECTIVE DATE	SOC. SEC. NO.

REFERRED BY: James Jackson, MD, 100 North Main Street, Hempstead, XY 11551 NPI#7201133720

DATE	PROGRESS
9-4-XX	New pt complains of cough & SOB. After an ECG and chest x-rays (2 views) the primary diagnosis
	was congestive heart disease. Pt to return in 2 wks for further observation. Perry Cardi, MD.
	**In some states, the Medicaid number may be as many as 14 digits in length.

Figure 12–1

Standards: Claim Productivity Measurement

Time: ______________ minutes

Accuracy: ________________

(Note: The time element and accuracy criteria may be given by your instructor.)

Directions:

1. Complete the Health Insurance Claim Form to Medicaid using OCR guidelines for Rose Clarkson by referring to her patient record and ledger card. Date the claim September 6. Refer to Appendix A to fill in the fees on the ledger card. Obtain the address of your Medicaid fiscal agent by referring to Appendix A in the *Handbook.* See Appendix A of this *Workbook* for Medicaid information. To complete the HCFA-1500 Claim Form for the Medi-Cal program, see Appendix C.
2. Refer to Chapter 6 of the *Handbook* for instructions on how to complete this claim form.
3. Refer to your *Current Procedural Terminology* code book to find the correct five-digit code number and modifiers for each professional service rendered.
4. Record on the ledger card when you have billed Medicaid.
5. A Performance Evaluation Checklist may be reproduced from the Instruction Guide to the Workbook chapter if your instructor wishes you to submit it to assist with scoring and comments.
6. After the instructor has returned your work to you, either make the necessary corrections and place it in a 3-ring notebook for future reference, or, if you receive a high score, place it in your portfolio for reference when applying for a job.

Abbreviations pertinent to this record:

ECG ______________ SOB ______________

Pt ______________ wks ______________

ASSIGNMENT 12–3 ▶ COMPLETE A MEDICAID CLAIM FORM

Task: Complete a Medicaid HCFA-1500 claim form, post transactions to the ledger card, and define patient record abbreviations.

Conditions: Use the patient's record (Figure 12–4) and ledger card (Figure 12–5), one health insurance claim form (Figure 12–6), typewriter or computer, procedural and diagnostic code books, and *Workbook* Appendixes A and B.

Standards: Claim Productivity Measurement

Time: ______________ minutes

Accuracy: ______________

(Note: The time element and accuracy criteria may be given by your instructor.)

Text continued on page 256

STATEMENT

College Clinic
4567 Broad Avenue
Woodland Hills, XY 12345-0001
Telephone: 013-486-9002
Fax: 013-487-8976

Miss Rose Clarkson
3408 Jackson Street
Hempstead, XY 11551-0300

DATE	PROFESSIONAL SERVICE DESCRIPTION	CHARGE		CREDITS				CURRENT BALANCE	
				PAYMENTS		ADJUSTMENTS			
9-4-xx	OV, D hx/exam, LC decision making								
9-4-xx	ECG 12 leads with interpretation and report								
9-4-xx	Chest x-rays (2 views)								

Due and payable within 10 days. **Pay last amount in balance column** 

Key:
PF: Problem-focused
EPF: Expanded problem-focused
D: Detailed
C: Comprehensive
SF: Straightforward
LC: Low complexity
MC: Moderate complexity
HC: High complexity
CON: Consultation
CPX: Complete phys exam
E: Emergency
ER: Emergency dept.
HCD: House call (day)
HCN: House call (night)
HV: Hospital visit
OV: Office visit

Figure 12–2

APPROVED OMB-0938-0008

PLEASE DO NOT STAPLE IN THIS AREA

CARRIER

PICA

HEALTH INSURANCE CLAIM FORM

PICA

1. MEDICARE (Medicare #) MEDICAID (Medicaid #) CHAMPUS (Sponsor's SSN) CHAMPVA (VA File #) GROUP HEALTH PLAN (SSN or ID) FECA BLK LUNG (SSN) OTHER (ID)

1a. INSURED'S I.D. NUMBER (FOR PROGRAM IN ITEM 1)

2. PATIENT'S NAME (Last Name, First Name, Middle Initial)

3. PATIENT'S BIRTH DATE MM | DD | YYYY SEX M F

4. INSURED'S NAME (Last Name, First Name, Middle Initial)

5. PATIENT'S ADDRESS (No., Street)

6. PATIENT RELATIONSHIP TO INSURED Self Spouse Child Other

7. INSURED'S ADDRESS (No., Street)

CITY STATE

8. PATIENT STATUS Single Married Other

CITY STATE

ZIP CODE TELEPHONE (Include Area Code)

Employed Full-Time Student Part-Time Student

ZIP CODE TELEPHONE (Include Area Code) ( )

9. OTHER INSURED'S NAME (Last Name, First Name, Middle Initial)

10. IS PATIENT'S CONDITION RELATED TO:

11. INSURED'S POLICY GROUP OR FECA NUMBER

a. OTHER INSURED'S POLICY OR GROUP NUMBER

a. EMPLOYMENT? (CURRENT OR PREVIOUS) YES NO

a. INSURED'S DATE OF BIRTH MM | DD | YY SEX M F

b. OTHER INSURED'S DATE OF BIRTH MM | DD | YY SEX M F

b. AUTO ACCIDENT? PLACE (State) YES NO

b. EMPLOYER'S NAME OR SCHOOL NAME

c. EMPLOYER'S NAME OR SCHOOL NAME

c. OTHER ACCIDENT? YES NO

c. INSURANCE PLAN NAME OR PROGRAM NAME

d. INSURANCE PLAN NAME OR PROGRAM NAME

10d. RESERVED FOR LOCAL USE

d. IS THERE ANOTHER HEALTH BENEFIT PLAN? YES NO *If yes, return to and complete item 9 a-d.*

READ BACK OF FORM BEFORE COMPLETING AND SIGNING THIS FORM.

12. PATIENT'S OR AUTHORIZED PERSON'S SIGNATURE I authorize the release of any medical or other information necessary to process this claim. I also request payment of government benefits either to myself or to the party who accepts assignment below.

SIGNED ______ DATE ______

13. INSURED'S OR AUTHORIZED PERSON'S SIGNATURE I authorize payment of medical benefits to the undersigned physician or supplier for services described below.

SIGNED ______

PATIENT AND INSURED INFORMATION

14. DATE OF CURRENT: MM | DD | YY ILLNESS (First symptom) OR INJURY (Accident) OR PREGNANCY (LMP)

15. IF PATIENT HAS HAD SAME OR SIMILAR ILLNESS GIVE FIRST DATE MM | DD | YY

16. DATES PATIENT UNABLE TO WORK IN CURRENT OCCUPATION FROM MM | DD | YY TO MM | DD | YY

17. NAME OF REFERRING PHYSICIAN OR OTHER SOURCE

17a. I.D. NUMBER OF REFERRING PHYSICIAN

18. HOSPITALIZATION DATES RELATED TO CURRENT SERVICES FROM MM | DD | YY TO MM | DD | YY

19. RESERVED FOR LOCAL USE

20. OUTSIDE LAB? YES NO $ CHARGES

21. DIAGNOSIS OR NATURE OF ILLNESS OR INJURY. (RELATE ITEMS 1,2,3 OR 4 TO ITEM 24E BY LINE)

1. ______ 3. ______

2. ______ 4. ______

22. MEDICAID RESUBMISSION CODE ORIGINAL REF. NO.

23. PRIOR AUTHORIZATION NUMBER

24. A DATE(S) OF SERVICE From MM DD YY To MM DD YY	B Place of Service	C Type of Service	D PROCEDURES, SERVICES, OR SUPPLIES (Explain Unusual Circumstances) CPT/HCPCS MODIFIER	E DIAGNOSIS CODE	F $ CHARGES	G DAYS OR UNITS	H EPSDT Family Plan	I EMG	J COB	K RESERVED FOR LOCAL USE

25. FEDERAL TAX I.D. NUMBER SSN EIN

26. PATIENT'S ACCOUNT NO.

27. ACCEPT ASSIGNMENT? (For govt. claims, see back) YES NO

28. TOTAL CHARGE $

29. AMOUNT PAID $

30. BALANCE DUE $

31. SIGNATURE OF PHYSICIAN OR SUPPLIER INCLUDING DEGREES OR CREDENTIALS (I certify that the statements on the reverse apply to this bill and are made a part thereof.)

SIGNED DATE

32. NAME AND ADDRESS OF FACILITY WHERE SERVICES WERE RENDERED (If other than home or office)

33. PHYSICIAN'S, SUPPLIER'S BILLING NAME, ADDRESS, ZIP CODE AND PHONE #

PIN# GRP#

PHYSICIAN OR SUPPLIER INFORMATION

(APPROVED BY AMA COUNCIL ON MEDICAL SERVICE 8/88) *PLEASE PRINT OR TYPE* FORM HCFA-1500 (U2) (12-90) FORM OCWP-1500 FORM RRB-1500

Figure 12–3

PATIENT RECORD NO. 1202

LAST NAME	FIRST NAME	MIDDLE NAME	BIRTH DATE	SEX	HOME PHONE
Drake,	Stephen	M.	04-03-91	M	013-277-5831

ADDRESS	CITY	STATE	ZIP CODE
2317 Charnwood Avenue,	Woodland Hills,	XY	12345

PATIENT'S OCCUPATION: student full time
NAME OF COMPANY:

ADDRESS OF EMPLOYER: PHONE:

SPOUSE OR PARENT: Mrs. Virginia B. Drake (mother)
OCCUPATION: none - family on welfare

EMPLOYER: ADDRESS: PHONE:

NAME OF INSURANCE: INSURED OR SUBSCRIBER:

POLICY NO.: GROUP NO.: EFFECTIVE DATE:

MEDICARE NO.: MEDICAID NO.: Child's identification number 19-37-1524033-1-62
EFFECTIVE DATE:
SOC. SEC. NO.: 566-09-0081

REFERRED BY: James B. Jeffers, MD, 100 S. Broadway, Woodland Hills, XY 12345 Provider No.1234506972

DATE	PROGRESS
5-1-XX	NP comes in complaining of severe sore throat since April 4. Exam shows much enlargement &
	inflam of tonsils. Temp 101.2. Did complete phys exam. Gave penicillin 5cc IM. Imp: Acute
	tonsillitis. Gerald Practon, MD
5-6-XX	Pt comes in again with severe sore throat. Mother states Stephen has had bouts of tonsillitis since age 6.
	Adv. tonsillectomy. Phoned for prior authorization 3 p.m.,Log #12, authorized by Mrs. Jane Michaels.
	Pt admitted to hosp for 2 days stay during which time surgery will be performed. Gerald Practon, MD
5-7-XX	Tonsillectomy and hospital visit. Pt doing well. Gerald Practon, MD
5-8-XX	Brief hospital visit made and pt discharged. To be seen in office in 10 days. Gerald Practon, MD
5-18-XX	No complaints. Temp 98.1. Return if necessary. Gerald Practon, MD

Figure 12–4

Directions:

1. Assume you have completed a *Medicaid treatment authorization request* form for Stephen M. Drake's hospital admission, and the prior authorization number is 45042. Complete the Medicaid form for Stephen M. Drake by referring to his patient record and ledger card. Refer to Appendix A to fill in the fees on the ledger card. Date the claim May 26. See Appendix A of this *Workbook* for Medicaid information. To complete the HCFA-1500 claim form for the Medi-Cal program, see Appendix C of the *Handbook*.

   Physicians' offices usually bill showing itemization of charges, such as for an office visit or admission to the hospital and the name of the surgery. However, many Medicaid programs do not pay for the office call or hospital admission. This is considered to be included in the surgical *global* fee when payment is issued to the attending physician.

   No charges (NC) do not necessarily have to be shown on the claim. However, postoperative - follow-up visits may be listed using a code number in the *CPT* medicine section. See if you can locate it.

   Remember the physician must ALWAYS sign all forms on Medicaid cases; stamped signatures are not allowed.

2. Use your *Current Procedural Terminology (CPT)* and *International Classification of Disease, 9th Revision, Clinical Modification (ICD-9-CM)* code books to determine the diagnostic codes and the correct five-digit code number and modifiers for each professional service rendered. If you do not have access to the *CPT* Code Book, refer to Appendix A of this *Workbook*.

3. Record on the ledger card when Medicaid has been billed.

4. Refer to Appendix A of this *Workbook* for the clinical and hospital provider numbers that are needed when completing Medicaid forms.

5. On July 1, Medicaid paid $200 on this claim. Post this payment (warrant/voucher no. 76L504) to the patient's ledger card and adjust off the balance.

6. A Performance Evaluation Checklist may be reproduced from the Instruction Guide to the *Workbook* chapter if your instructor wishes you to submit it to assist with scoring and comments.

7. After the instructor has returned your work to you, either make the necessary corrections and place it in a 3-ring notebook for future reference, or, if you receive a high score, place it in your portfolio for reference when applying for a job.

Abbreviations pertinent to this record:

adm ____________ imp ____________

adv ____________ inflam ____________

cc ____________ NC ____________

comp ____________ phys ____________

exam ____________ Pt ____________

hosp ____________ temp ____________

HV ____________ wk ____________

IM ____________

Text continued on page 262

STATEMENT

College Clinic
4567 Broad Avenue
Woodland Hills, XY 12345-0001
Telephone: 013-486-9002
Fax: 013-487-8976

Mrs. Virginia B. Drake
2317 Charnwood Avenue
Woodland Hills, XY 12345-0001

DATE	PROFESSIONAL SERVICE DESCRIPTION	CHARGE	CREDITS		CURRENT BALANCE
			PAYMENTS	ADJUSTMENTS	
5-1-xx	OV, comp hx/exam, HC decision making				
5-1-xx	Penicillin inj				
5-6-xx	Adm to hosp, C hx/exam initial hospital care, LC decision making				
5-7-xx	Tonsillectomy				
5-8-xx	Discharge				
5-18-xx	OV				

Due and payable within 10 days.

Pay last amount in balance column 

Key:							
PF:	Problem-focused	SF:	Straightforward	CON:	Consultation	HCD:	House call (day)
EPF:	Expanded problem-focused	LC:	Low complexity	CPX:	Complete phys exam	HCN:	House call (night)
D:	Detailed	MC:	Moderate complexity	E:	Emergency	HV:	Hospital visit
C:	Comprehensive	HC:	High complexity	ER:	Emergency dept.	OV:	Office visit

Figure 12–5

APPROVED OMB 0938-0008

PLEASE DO NOT STAPLE IN THIS AREA

CARRIER

PICA

HEALTH INSURANCE CLAIM FORM

PICA

1. MEDICARE (Medicare #) MEDICAID (Medicaid #) CHAMPUS (Sponsor's SSN) CHAMPVA (VA File #) GROUP HEALTH PLAN (SSN or ID) FECA BLK LUNG (SSN) OTHER (ID)

1a. INSURED'S I.D. NUMBER (FOR PROGRAM IN ITEM 1)

2. PATIENT'S NAME (Last Name, First Name, Middle Initial)

3. PATIENT'S BIRTH DATE MM DD YYYY SEX M F

4. INSURED'S NAME (Last Name, First Name, Middle Initial)

5. PATIENT'S ADDRESS (No., Street)

6. PATIENT RELATIONSHIP TO INSURED Self Spouse Child Other

7. INSURED'S ADDRESS (No., Street)

CITY STATE

8. PATIENT STATUS Single Married Other

CITY STATE

ZIP CODE TELEPHONE (Include Area Code) ( )

Employed Full-Time Student Part-Time Student

ZIP CODE TELEPHONE (include Area Code) ( )

9. OTHER INSURED'S NAME (Last Name, First Name, Middle Initial)

10. IS PATIENT'S CONDITION RELATED TO:

11. INSURED'S POLICY GROUP OR FECA NUMBER

a. OTHER INSURED'S POLICY OR GROUP NUMBER

a. EMPLOYMENT? (CURRENT OR PREVIOUS) YES NO

a. INSURED'S DATE OF BIRTH MM DD YY SEX M F

b. OTHER INSURED'S DATE OF BIRTH MM DD YY SEX M F

b. AUTO ACCIDENT? PLACE (State) YES NO

b. EMPLOYER'S NAME OR SCHOOL NAME

c. EMPLOYER'S NAME OR SCHOOL NAME

c. OTHER ACCIDENT? YES NO

c. INSURANCE PLAN NAME OR PROGRAM NAME

d. INSURANCE PLAN NAME OR PROGRAM NAME

10d. RESERVED FOR LOCAL USE

d. IS THERE ANOTHER HEALTH BENEFIT PLAN? YES NO *If yes, return to and complete item 9 a-d.*

READ BACK OF FORM BEFORE COMPLETING AND SIGNING THIS FORM.

12. PATIENT'S OR AUTHORIZED PERSON'S SIGNATURE I authorize the release of any medical or other information necessary to process this claim. I also request payment of government benefits either to myself or to the party who accepts assignment below.

SIGNED DATE

13. INSURED'S OR AUTHORIZED PERSON'S SIGNATURE I authorize payment of medical benefits to the undersigned physician or supplier for services described below.

SIGNED

PATIENT AND INSURED INFORMATION

14. DATE OF CURRENT: MM DD YY ILLNESS (First symptom) OR INJURY (Accident) OR PREGNANCY (LMP)

15. IF PATIENT HAS HAD SAME OR SIMILAR ILLNESS GIVE FIRST DATE MM DD YY

16. DATES PATIENT UNABLE TO WORK IN CURRENT OCCUPATION FROM MM DD YY TO MM DD YY

17. NAME OF REFERRING PHYSICIAN OR OTHER SOURCE

17a. I.D. NUMBER OF REFERRING PHYSICIAN

18. HOSPITALIZATION DATES RELATED TO CURRENT SERVICES FROM MM DD YY TO MM DD YY

19. RESERVED FOR LOCAL USE

20. OUTSIDE LAB? YES NO $ CHARGES

21. DIAGNOSIS OR NATURE OF ILLNESS OR INJURY. (RELATE ITEMS 1,2,3 OR 4 TO ITEM 24E BY LINE)

1. 3.

2. 4.

22. MEDICAID RESUBMISSION CODE ORIGINAL REF. NO.

23. PRIOR AUTHORIZATION NUMBER

24. A DATE(S) OF SERVICE From MM DD YY To MM DD YY	B Place of Service	C Type of Service	D PROCEDURES, SERVICES, OR SUPPLIES (Explain Unusual Circumstances) CPT/HCPCS MODIFIER	E DIAGNOSIS CODE	F $ CHARGES	G DAYS OR UNITS	H EPSDT Family Plan	I EMG	J COB	K RESERVED FOR LOCAL USE

25. FEDERAL TAX I.D. NUMBER SSN EIN

26. PATIENT'S ACCOUNT NO.

27. ACCEPT ASSIGNMENT? (For govt. claims, see back) YES NO

28. TOTAL CHARGE $

29. AMOUNT PAID $

30. BALANCE DUE $

31. SIGNATURE OF PHYSICIAN OR SUPPLIER INCLUDING DEGREES OR CREDENTIALS (I certify that the statements on the reverse apply to this bill and are made a part thereof.)

SIGNED DATE

32. NAME AND ADDRESS OF FACILITY WHERE SERVICES WERE RENDERED (if other than home or office)

33. PHYSICIAN'S, SUPPLIER'S BILLING NAME, ADDRESS, ZIP CODE AND PHONE #

PIN# GRP#

PHYSICIAN OR SUPPLIER INFORMATION

(APPROVED BY AMA COUNCIL ON MEDICAL SERVICE8/88) *PLEASE PRINT OR TYPE* FORM HCFA -1500 (U2) (12-90) FORM OCWP-1500 FORM RRB-1500

Figure 12–6

PATIENT RECORD NO. 1203

LAST NAME	FIRST NAME	MIDDLE NAME	BIRTH DATE	SEX	HOME PHONE
Brooke,	Barry	I.	02-03-85	M	013-487-9770

ADDRESS	CITY	STATE	ZIP CODE
3821 Ocean Drive,	Woodland Hills,	XY	12345-0001

PATIENT'S OCCUPATION: child full time student
NAME OF COMPANY:

ADDRESS OF EMPLOYER:
PHONE:

SPOUSE OR PARENT: Robert D. Brooke (father)
OCCUPATION: None- family on welfare (father totally disabled)

EMPLOYER:
ADDRESS:
PHONE:

NAME OF INSURANCE:
INSURED OR SUBSCRIBER:

POLICY NO.:
GROUP NO.:
EFFECTIVE DATE:

MEDICARE NO.:
MEDICAID NO.: Child's identification number 54-32-7681533-1-03
EFFECTIVE DATE:
SOC. SEC. NO.: 776-09-1931

REFERRED BY: Virginia B. Drake (friend)

DATE	PROGRESS
5-28-XX	11: 30 p.m Sunday new pt seen in ER at hosp. Pt twisted L knee while playing baseball at Grove Playground. X-rays were ordered - N for fx. Imp: effusion and ligament strain lt knee. Tx: aspirated lt knee and removed 5 cc. bloody fluid. Applied long leg cylinder walking cast. Pt to be seen in office in 2 wks. Raymond Skeleton, MD

Figure 12–7

ASSIGNMENT **12–4** ► **COMPLETE A MEDICAID CLAIM FORM**

Task: Complete a Medicaid HCFA-1500 claim form, post transactions to the ledger card, and define patient record abbreviations.

Conditions: Use the patient's record (Figure 12–7) and ledger card (Figure 12–8), one health insurance claim form (Figure 12–9), typewriter or computer, procedural and diagnostic code books, and *Workbook* Appendixes A and B.

Standards: Claim Productivity Measurement

Time: ________________ minutes

Accuracy: ________________

(Note: The time element and accuracy criteria may be given by your instructor.)

Directions:

1. Complete the Medicaid form for Barry I. Brook by referring to his patient record and ledger card. Refer to Appendix A to fill in the fees on the ledger card. Date the claim May 31. See Appendix A of this *Workbook* for Medicaid information. To complete the HCFA-1500 Claim Form for the Medi-Cal program, see Appendix C of the *Handbook*.

2. Use your *CPT* and *ICD-9-CM* code books to determine the diagnostic codes and the correct five-digit code number and modifiers for each professional service rendered. If you do not have access to the *CPT* code book, refer to Appendix A.

3. Record on the ledger card when you have billed Medicaid.

4. Refer to Appendix A of this *Workbook* for the facility provider number that is needed when completing Medicaid forms.

5. On July 1, Medicaid paid $75 (warrant/Voucher No. 32M670) on this claim. Post this payment to the patient's ledger card and adjust off the balance.

6. A Performance Evaluation Checklist may be reproduced from the Instruction Guide to the *Workbook* chapter if your instructor wishes you to submit it to assist with scoring and comments.

7. After the instructor has returned your work to you, either make the necessary corrections and place it in a 3-ring notebook for future reference, or, if you receive a high score, place it in your portfolio for reference when applying for a job.

Abbreviations pertinent to this record:

cc ________________ L ________________

ER ________________ lt ________________

Fx ________________ N ________________

hosp ________________ pt ________________

hist ________________ wks ________________

imp ________________ TX ________________

STATEMENT

College Clinic
4567 Broad Avenue
Woodland Hills, XY 12345-0001
Telephone: 013-486-9002
Fax: 013-487-8976

Mr. Robert D. Brooke
3821 Ocean Drive
Woodland Hills, XY 12345-0001

Re: Professional Services - Barry L. Brook

DATE	PROFESSIONAL SERVICE DESCRIPTION	CHARGE	CREDITS		CURRENT BALANCE
			PAYMENTS	ADJUSTMENTS	
5-28-xx	ER init, D hx/exam, MC decision making				
5-28-xx	Aspiration lt knee				
5-28-xx	Application long leg cylinder cast, lt leg , walker				
5-28-xx	Cast materials				

Due and payable within 10 days. **Pay last amount in balance column**

Key: PF: Problem-focused; EPF: Expanded problem-focused; D: Detailed; C: Comprehensive; SF: Straightforward; LC: Low complexity; MC: Moderate complexity; HC: High complexity; CON: Consultation; CPX: Complete phys exam; E: Emergency; ER: Emergency dept.; HCD: House call (day); HCN: House call (night); HV: Hospital visit; OV: Office visit

Figure 12–8

APPROVED OMB 0938-0008

PLEASE DO NOT STAPLE IN THIS AREA

CARRIER

PICA

HEALTH INSURANCE CLAIM FORM

PICA

1. MEDICARE (Medicare #) MEDICAID (Medicaid #) CHAMPUS (Sponsor's SSN) CHAMPVA (VA File #) GROUP HEALTH PLAN (SSN or ID) FECA BLK LUNG (SSN) OTHER (ID)

1a. INSURED'S I.D. NUMBER (FOR PROGRAM IN ITEM 1)

2. PATIENT'S NAME (Last Name, First Name, Middle Initial)

3. PATIENT'S BIRTH DATE MM DD YYYY SEX M F

4. INSURED'S NAME (Last Name, First Name, Middle Initial)

5. PATIENT'S ADDRESS (No., Street)

6. PATIENT RELATIONSHIP TO INSURED Self Spouse Child Other

7. INSURED'S ADDRESS (No., Street)

CITY STATE

8. PATIENT STATUS Single Married Other

CITY STATE

ZIP CODE TELEPHONE (Include Area Code) ( )

Employed Full-Time Student Part-Time Student

ZIP CODE TELEPHONE (include Area Code) ( )

9. OTHER INSURED'S NAME (Last Name, First Name, Middle Initial)

10. IS PATIENT'S CONDITION RELATED TO:

11. INSURED'S POLICY GROUP OR FECA NUMBER

a. OTHER INSURED'S POLICY OR GROUP NUMBER

a. EMPLOYMENT? (CURRENT OR PREVIOUS) YES NO

a. INSURED'S DATE OF BIRTH MM DD YY SEX M F

b. OTHER INSURED'S DATE OF BIRTH MM DD YY SEX M F

b. AUTO ACCIDENT? YES NO PLACE (State)

b. EMPLOYER'S NAME OR SCHOOL NAME

c. EMPLOYER'S NAME OR SCHOOL NAME

c. OTHER ACCIDENT? YES NO

c. INSURANCE PLAN NAME OR PROGRAM NAME

d. INSURANCE PLAN NAME OR PROGRAM NAME

10d. RESERVED FOR LOCAL USE

d. IS THERE ANOTHER HEALTH BENEFIT PLAN? YES NO *If yes, return to and complete item 9 a-d.*

READ BACK OF FORM BEFORE COMPLETING AND SIGNING THIS FORM.

12. PATIENT'S OR AUTHORIZED PERSON'S SIGNATURE I authorize the release of any medical or other information necessary to process this claim. I also request payment of government benefits either to myself or to the party who accepts assignment below.

SIGNED ______ DATE ______

13. INSURED'S OR AUTHORIZED PERSON'S SIGNATURE I authorize payment of medical benefits to the undersigned physician or supplier for services described below.

SIGNED ______

PATIENT AND INSURED INFORMATION

14. DATE OF CURRENT: MM DD YY ILLNESS (First symptom) OR INJURY (Accident) OR PREGNANCY (LMP)

15. IF PATIENT HAS HAD SAME OR SIMILAR ILLNESS GIVE FIRST DATE MM DD YY

16. DATES PATIENT UNABLE TO WORK IN CURRENT OCCUPATION FROM MM DD YY TO MM DD YY

17. NAME OF REFERRING PHYSICIAN OR OTHER SOURCE

17a. I.D. NUMBER OF REFERRING PHYSICIAN

18. HOSPITALIZATION DATES RELATED TO CURRENT SERVICES FROM MM DD YY TO MM DD YY

19. RESERVED FOR LOCAL USE

20. OUTSIDE LAB? YES NO $ CHARGES

21. DIAGNOSIS OR NATURE OF ILLNESS OR INJURY. (RELATE ITEMS 1,2,3 OR 4 TO ITEM 24E BY LINE)

1. ______ 3. ______

2. ______ 4. ______

22. MEDICAID RESUBMISSION CODE ORIGINAL REF. NO.

23. PRIOR AUTHORIZATION NUMBER

24. A DATE(S) OF SERVICE From MM DD YY To MM DD YY	B Place of Service	C Type of Service	D PROCEDURES, SERVICES, OR SUPPLIES (Explain Unusual Circumstances) CPT/HCPCS MODIFIER	E DIAGNOSIS CODE	F $ CHARGES	G DAYS OR UNITS	H EPSDT Family Plan	I EMG	J COB	K RESERVED FOR LOCAL USE

25. FEDERAL TAX I.D. NUMBER SSN EIN

26. PATIENT'S ACCOUNT NO.

27. ACCEPT ASSIGNMENT? (For govt. claims, see back) YES NO

28. TOTAL CHARGE $

29. AMOUNT PAID $

30. BALANCE DUE $

31. SIGNATURE OF PHYSICIAN OR SUPPLIER INCLUDING DEGREES OR CREDENTIALS (I certify that the statements on the reverse apply to this bill and are made a part thereof.)

SIGNED DATE

32. NAME AND ADDRESS OF FACILITY WHERE SERVICES WERE RENDERED (If other than home or office)

33. PHYSICIAN'S, SUPPLIER'S BILLING NAME, ADDRESS, ZIP CODE AND PHONE #

PIN# GRP#

PHYSICIAN OR SUPPLIER INFORMATION

(APPROVED BY AMA COUNCIL ON MEDICAL SERVICE8/88) *PLEASE PRINT OR TYPE* FORM HCFA -1500 (U2) (12-90) FORM OCWP-1500 FORM RRB-1500

Figure 12–9

13

TRICARE and CHAMPVA

KEY TERMS

Your instructor may wish to select some specific words pertinent to this chapter for a test. For definitions of the terms, further study, and/or reference, the words, phrases, and abbreviations may be found in the Glossary at the end of the Handbook. *Key terms for this chapter follow.*

active duty service member (ADSM)
allowable charge
authorized provider
beneficiaries
catastrophic cap
CHAMPVA
cooperative care
coordination of benefits
cost-share
Defense Enrollment Eligibility Reporting System (DEERS)
emergency
fiscal intermediary (FI)
health benefits advisor (HBA)
Health Care Finder (HCF)
medically (or psychologically) necessary
military treatment facility (MTF)
Nonavailability Statement (NAS)
nonparticipating provider (nonpar)
other health insurance (OHI)
participating provider (par)
partnership program
point-of-service (POS) option
preauthorization
primary care manager (PCM)
quality assurance program
service benefit program
service-connected injury
service retiree (military retiree)
sponsor
summary payment voucher
total, permanent, service-connected disability
TRICARE Extra
TRICARE Prime
TRICARE Service Center (TSC)
urgent care
veteran

PERFORMANCE OBJECTIVES

The student will be able to

- Define and spell the key terms for this chapter, given the information from the *Handbook* Glossary, within a reasonable period of time and with enough accuracy to obtain a satisfactory evaluation.

- Answer the self-study review questions after reading the chapter, with enough accuracy to obtain a satisfactory evaluation.
- Fill in the correct meaning of each abbreviation, given a list of common medical abbreviations and symbols that appear in chart notes, within a reasonable period of time and with enough accuracy to obtain a satisfactory evaluation.
- Complete each HCFA-1500 Health Insurance Claim Form for billing, given the patient's medical chart notes, ledger cards, and blank insurance claim forms, within a reasonable period of time and with enough accuracy to obtain a satisfactory evaluation.
- Correctly post payments, adjustments, and balances on the patients' ledger cards, using the Mock Fee Schedule in Appendix A, within a reasonable period of time and with enough accuracy to obtain a satisfactory evaluation.
- Compute mathematical calculations, given TRICARE problem situations, within a reasonable period of time and with enough accuracy to obtain a satisfactory evaluation.

STUDY OUTLINE

History of TRICARE
TRICARE Programs
- Eligibility
  - Defense Enrollment Eligibility Reporting System
- Nonavailability Statement
  - Catchment Area
  - Automated NAS System

TRICARE Standard
- Enrollment
- Identification Card
- Benefits
- Fiscal Year
- Authorized Providers of Health Care
- Preauthorization
- Payment
  - Deductible and Copayment
  - Spouses and Children of Active Duty Members
  - All Other Eligible Beneficiaries
  - Participating Provider
  - Nonparticipating Provider

TRICARE Extra
- Enrollment
- Identification Card
- Benefits
- Network Provider
- Preauthorization
- Payments
  - Deductible and Copayment
  - Spouses and Children of Active Duty Members
  - All Other Eligible Beneficiaries

TRICARE Prime
- Enrollment
- Identification Card
- Benefits
- Primary Care Manager
- Preauthorization
- Payments
  - Copayment

TRICARE Prime Remote Program
- Enrollment
- Identification Card
- Benefits
- Payments

Supplemental Health Care Program
- Enrollment
- Identification Card
- Benefits
- Payments

TRICARE Hospice Program
TRICARE and HMO Coverage
CHAMPVA Program
- Eligibility
- Enrollment
- Identification Card
- Benefits
- Provider
- Preauthorization

Medical Record Access
- Privacy Act of 1974
- Computer Matching and Privacy Protection Act of 1988

Claims Procedure
- Fiscal Intermediary
- TRICARE Standard and CHAMPVA
  - Time Limit
  - Claims Office
- TRICARE Extra and TRICARE Prime

Time Limit
Claims Office
TRICARE Prime Remote and Supplemental Health Care Program
Time Limit
Claims Office
TRICARE/CHAMPVA and Other Insurance
Medicaid and TRICARE/CHAMPVA
Medicare and TRICARE
Medicare and CHAMPVA
Dual or Double Coverage
Third Party Liability
Workers' Compensation
Internet
Procedure: Completing a CHAMPVA Claim Form
After Claim Submission
TRICARE Summary Payment Voucher
CHAMPVA Explanation of Benefits Document
Quality Assurance
Claims Inquiries and Appeals

SELF-STUDY 13–1 ▶ REVIEW QUESTIONS

Review the objectives, key terms, glossary definitions to key terms, chapter information, and figures before completing the following review questions.

1. CHAMPUS, the acronym for Civilian Health and Medical Program of the Uniformed Services, is now called Tricare and was organized to control escalating medical costs and to standardize benefits for active-duty families and military retirees.

2. An active duty service member is known as a/an Sponsor; once retired, this former member is called a/an service or military retired

3. Individuals who qualify for TRICARE are known as Beneficiaries.

4. A system for verifying an individual's TRICARE eligibility is called ________.
Defense Enrollment Eligibility Reporting System

5. Mrs. Hancock, a TRICARE beneficiary, lives two miles from a Uniformed Services Medical Treatment Facility and wishes to be hospitalized for surgery at Orlando Medical Center, a civilian hospital. What type of authorization does she require?
Inpatient nonavailability statement

6. TRICARE Standard and CHAMPVA beneficiary identification cards are issued to dependents 10 yrs of age and older and retirees. Information must be obtained from front and back of the card and placed on the health insurance claim form.

7. Programs that allow TRICARE Standard beneficiaries to receive treatment, services, or supplies from civilian providers are called cooperative care and partnership

8. The TRICARE Standard deductible for outpatient care is how much per patient? 150 Per family? 300

9. What percentage does TRICARE Standard pay on outpatient services after the deductible has been met for dependents of active duty members? 80%

   For retired members or their dependents? 75%

10. For retired members or their dependents on TRICARE Standard, what is their responsibility for outpatient services? 150 deductible plus 25% of Tricare allowable

11. A voluntary TRICARE health maintenance organization type of option is known as Tricare Prime.

12. CHAMPVA is the acronym for Civilian Health and Medical Program of the Veterans Administration, now known as the Department of Veterans affairs

13. Those individuals who serve in the United States Armed Forces, finish their service, and are honorably discharged are known as a/an Veteran.

14. CHAMPVA is not an insurance program but is considered as a/an service benefit program.

15. Name those individuals entitled to CHAMPVA medical benefits.

    a. husband, wife, or unmarried child of a veteran with a total disability, permanent in nature, from a service-connected disability

    b. husband, wife, or unmarried child of a veteran who died because of service connected disability - or who, at the time of death, had a total disability, permanent in nature, resulting from a service-connected injury.

    c. husband, wife, or unmarried child of an individual who died in the line of duty while on active service

16. The public law establishing a person's right to review and contest inaccuracies in personal medical records is known as Privacy act of 1974.

17. An organization that contracts with the government to process TRICARE and CHAMPVA health insurance claims is known as a/an Fiscal intermediary.

18. The time limit for submitting a TRICARE Standard or CHAMPVA claim for outpatient service is within 1 yr from date service is provided; for inpatient service, it is 1 yr from patient's discharge from Hospital.

19. If a patient has other insurance besides TRICARE and is the dependent of an active military person, whom do you bill first? Other insurance

20. If Jason Williams, a TRICARE beneficiary who became disabled at age 10 years and is also receiving Medicare Part A benefits, is seen for a consultation, whom do you bill first? Medicare

21. A patient is seen as an emergency in the office who is a CHAMPVA and Medicaid beneficiary. Whom do you bill first? Champva

To check your answers to this self-study assignment, see Appendix D.

ASSIGNMENT **13–2** ▶ **CALCULATE MATHEMATICAL PROBLEMS**

Task: Calculate and insert the correct amounts for three TRICARE scenarios.

Conditions: Use pen or pencil, description of problem, and calculation.

Standards: Time: ______ minutes

Accuracy: ______

(Note: The time element and accuracy criteria may be given by your instructor.)

Directions:

Problem 1: It is October 1. In consultation, your physician sees the wife of a Navy man who is stationed at Port Hueneme. Dr. Caesar orders her to the hospital with a suspected ectopic pregnancy. She has a laparotomy and salpingectomy. Here are her bills. Indicate what TRICARE Standard will pay.

Outpatient Services:	*TRICARE Standard*		
	Bill	**Payment**	**Patient Owes**
Consultation	$75	$______	$______
Inpatient Services:			
Salpingectomy	$600		
Assistant surgeon	$120		
Anesthesiologist	$400		
3-day stay (drugs, lab, OR)	$2500		
Total	$______		$______

Problem 2: Same situation as Problem 1, except that the patient is the wife of a retired military man and has TRICARE Standard.

Outpatient Services:	*TRICARE Standard*		
	Bill/ Allowable	**TRICARE payment**	**Patient Owes**
Consultation	$75	$______	$______

Inpatient services with separately billed professional charges

	Bill/ Allowable	**Payment**	**Patient Owes**
Salpingectomy	$600	$______	$______
Assistant surgeon	$120	$______	$______
Anesthesiologist	$400	$______	$______
Inpatient services billed by hospital			
3-day stay (drugs, lab, OR)	$2500	$______	
Total payment owed by patient to Dr. Caesar			$______

Problem 3: A TRICARE patient asks you to accept assignment on her medical care and Dr. Caesar agrees. She has not met her deductible. She is the wife of an active duty man. She has TRICARE Extra.

Your bill

Consultation	$ 50	Allowable: $ 50
CBC	20	20
Urinalysis	5	5
Blood serology and complement fixation	25	25
PA & Lt Lat chest x-ray	40	40
ECG	35	30
Spirometry	40	40
TOTAL	$215	$210

How much is your check from TRICARE Extra? $______________. The patient owes the doctor $______________. Dr. Caesar's courtesy adjustment is $____.

ASSIGNMENT 13–3 ▶ COMPLETE A CLAIM FORM FOR A TRICARE STANDARD CASE

Task: Complete a TRICARE HCFA-1500 claim form, post transactions to the ledger card, and define patient record abbreviations.

Conditions: Use the patient's record (Figure 13–1) and ledger card (Figure 13–2), one health insurance claim form (Figure 13–3), typewriter or computer, procedural and diagnostic code books, and *Workbook* Appendixes A and B.

Standards: Claim Productivity Measurement

Time: ______________ minutes

Accuracy: ______________

(Note: The time element and accuracy criteria may be given by your instructor.)

Directions:

1. Complete the HCFA-1500 Claim Form using OCR guidelines, directing it to your local TRICARE fiscal intermediary. Refer to Miss Rosa M. Sandoval's patient record and ledger card for information. Refer to Appendix A to fill in the fee on the ledger card. Date the claim May 31. Dr. Atrics is not accepting assignment on this TRICARE Standard case but is completing the claim for the patient's convenience. The family of this patient has not previously met its deductible. See Chapter 6 of the *Handbook* for help in completing the HCFA-1500 claim form and refer to Figure 6–13.
2. Use your *CPT* code book or Appendix A to determine the correct five-digit code number and modifiers for each professional service rendered.
3. On May 11 Mrs. Sandoval makes a partial payment by check (No. 4013) of $90. Record the proper information on the ledger card for the payment, and note when you have billed TRICARE (May 31).
4. A Performance Evaluation Checklist may be reproduced from the Instruction Guide to the *Workbook* chapter if your instructor wishes you to submit it to assist with scoring and comments.
5. After the instructor has returned your work to you, either make the necessary corrections and place it in a 3-ring notebook for future reference, or, if you received a high score, place it in your portfolio for reference when applying for a job.

Abbreviations pertinent to this record:

adv ______________	HV ______________
a.m. ______________	imp ______________
ER ______________	OC ______________
exam ______________	ofc ______________
FU ______________	PRN ______________
Pt ______________	T ______________
retn ______________	temp ______________
rt ______________	wk ______________
surg ______________	c̄ ______________

PATIENT RECORD NO. 1301

Sandoval,	Rosa	M.	11-01-91	F	013-456-3322
LAST NAME	FIRST NAME	MIDDLE NAME	BIRTH DATE	SEX	HOME PHONE

209 West Maple Street,	Woodland Hills,	XY	12345
ADDRESS	CITY	STATE	ZIP CODE

child full time student
PATIENT'S OCCUPATION NAME OF COMPANY

ADDRESS OF EMPLOYER PHONE

Maria B. Sandoval (mother) homemaker
SPOUSE OR PARENT OCCUPATION

Hernan J. Sandoval (father) Army Staff Sargeant, Active Status 2-10-70
BIRTH DATE

Service # 886-91-0999 Social Security # 886-91-0999, HHC, 3rd Batt., 25th Infantry

Grade 9, A.P.O., New York, New York 10030

*TRICARE I.D. Card # 73485	01-01-80	994-02-1164
TRICARE NO.	EFFECTIVE DATE	SOC. SEC. NO.

REFERRED BY: Hilda M. Mendez (friend) * This number in not required on the HCFA-1500 claim form

DATE	PROGRESS
5-1-xx	Sunday 3 a.m. pt seen in ER hosp complaining of pain rt ear for 3 days. Exam reveals fluid and
	pus rt ear. Temp 101. Adv mother a myringotomy was necessary. Imp: Rt otitis media.
	Surg: Rt myringotomy $\bar{c}$ aspiration performed in ER. To be seen in ofc for FU. Pedro Atrics, MD
5-3-xx	No pain rt ear. Pt progressing to retn in 1 wk. T 98. Pedro Atrics, MD
5-8-xx	T 98, no fluid or pus in rt ear. No pain. Retn prn. Pedro Atrics, MD

Figure 13–1

STATEMENT

College Clinic
4567 Broad Avenue
Woodland Hills, XY 12345-0001
Telephone: 013-486-9002
Fax: 013-487-8976

Mr. Hernan Sandoval
209 West Maple Street
Woodland Hills, XY 12345-0001

DATE	PROFESSIONAL SERVICE DESCRIPTION	CHARGE	CREDITS		CURRENT BALANCE
			PAYMENTS	ADJUSTMENTS	
5-1-xx	ER, EPF hx/exam, LC decision making				
5-1-xx	Rt myringotomy with aspiration				
5-3-xx	OV				
5-10-xx	OV, EPF hx/exam, LC decision making				

Due and payable within 10 days. **Pay last amount in balance column** 

Key:							
PF:	Problem-focused	SF:	Straightforward	CON:	Consultation	HCD:	House call (day)
EPF:	Expanded problem-focused	LC:	Low complexity	CPX:	Complete phys exam	HCN:	House call (night)
D:	Detailed	MC:	Moderate complexity	E:	Emergency	HV:	Hospital visit
C:	Comprehensive	HC:	High complexity	ER:	Emergency dept.	OV:	Office visit

Figure 13–2

APPROVED OMB 0938-0008

PLEASE DO NOT STAPLE IN THIS AREA

CARRIER

PICA

HEALTH INSURANCE CLAIM FORM

PICA

1. MEDICARE (Medicare #) MEDICAID (Medicaid #) CHAMPUS (Sponsor's SSN) CHAMPVA (VA File #) GROUP HEALTH PLAN (SSN or ID) FECA BLK LUNG (SSN) OTHER (ID)

1a. INSURED'S I.D. NUMBER (FOR PROGRAM IN ITEM 1)

2. PATIENT'S NAME (Last Name, First Name, Middle Initial)

3. PATIENT'S BIRTH DATE MM DD YYYY SEX M F

4. INSURED'S NAME (Last Name, First Name, Middle Initial)

5. PATIENT'S ADDRESS (No., Street)

6. PATIENT RELATIONSHIP TO INSURED Self Spouse Child Other

7. INSURED'S ADDRESS (No., Street)

CITY STATE

8. PATIENT STATUS Single Married Other

CITY STATE

ZIP CODE TELEPHONE (Include Area Code) ( )

Employed Full-Time Student Part-Time Student

ZIP CODE TELEPHONE (include Area Code) ( )

9. OTHER INSURED'S NAME (Last Name, First Name, Middle Initial)

10. IS PATIENT'S CONDITION RELATED TO:

11. INSURED'S POLICY GROUP OR FECA NUMBER

a. OTHER INSURED'S POLICY OR GROUP NUMBER

a. EMPLOYMENT? (CURRENT OR PREVIOUS) YES NO

a. INSURED'S DATE OF BIRTH MM DD YY SEX M F

b. OTHER INSURED'S DATE OF BIRTH MM DD YY SEX M F

b. AUTO ACCIDENT? PLACE (State) YES NO

b. EMPLOYER'S NAME OR SCHOOL NAME

c. EMPLOYER'S NAME OR SCHOOL NAME

c. OTHER ACCIDENT? YES NO

c. INSURANCE PLAN NAME OR PROGRAM NAME

d. INSURANCE PLAN NAME OR PROGRAM NAME

10d. RESERVED FOR LOCAL USE

d. IS THERE ANOTHER HEALTH BENEFIT PLAN? YES NO *If yes, return to and complete item 9 a-d.*

READ BACK OF FORM BEFORE COMPLETING AND SIGNING THIS FORM.

12. PATIENT'S OR AUTHORIZED PERSON'S SIGNATURE I authorize the release of any medical or other information necessary to process this claim. I also request payment of government benefits either to myself or to the party who accepts assignment below.

SIGNED DATE

13. INSURED'S OR AUTHORIZED PERSON'S SIGNATURE I authorize payment of medical benefits to the undersigned physician or supplier for services described below.

SIGNED

PATIENT AND INSURED INFORMATION

14. DATE OF CURRENT: MM DD YY ILLNESS (First symptom) OR INJURY (Accident) OR PREGNANCY (LMP)

15. IF PATIENT HAS HAD SAME OR SIMILAR ILLNESS GIVE FIRST DATE MM DD YY

16. DATES PATIENT UNABLE TO WORK IN CURRENT OCCUPATION FROM MM DD YY TO MM DD YY

17. NAME OF REFERRING PHYSICIAN OR OTHER SOURCE

17a. I.D. NUMBER OF REFERRING PHYSICIAN

18. HOSPITALIZATION DATES RELATED TO CURRENT SERVICES FROM MM DD YY TO MM DD YY

19. RESERVED FOR LOCAL USE

20. OUTSIDE LAB? YES NO $ CHARGES

21. DIAGNOSIS OR NATURE OF ILLNESS OR INJURY. (RELATE ITEMS 1,2,3 OR 4 TO ITEM 24E BY LINE)

1.

2.

3.

4.

22. MEDICAID RESUBMISSION CODE ORIGINAL REF. NO.

23. PRIOR AUTHORIZATION NUMBER

24. A DATE(S) OF SERVICE From MM DD YY To MM DD YY	B Place of Service	C Type of Service	D PROCEDURES, SERVICES, OR SUPPLIES (Explain Unusual Circumstances) CPT/HCPCS MODIFIER	E DIAGNOSIS CODE	F $ CHARGES	G DAYS OR UNITS	H EPSDT Family Plan	I EMG	J COB	K RESERVED FOR LOCAL USE

25. FEDERAL TAX I.D. NUMBER SSN EIN

26. PATIENT'S ACCOUNT NO.

27. ACCEPT ASSIGNMENT? (For govt. claims, see back) YES NO

28. TOTAL CHARGE $

29. AMOUNT PAID $

30. BALANCE DUE $

31. SIGNATURE OF PHYSICIAN OR SUPPLIER INCLUDING DEGREES OR CREDENTIALS (I certify that the statements on the reverse apply to this bill and are made a part thereof.)

SIGNED DATE

32. NAME AND ADDRESS OF FACILITY WHERE SERVICES WERE RENDERED (If other than home or office)

33. PHYSICIAN'S, SUPPLIER'S BILLING NAME, ADDRESS, ZIP CODE AND PHONE #

PIN# GRP#

PHYSICIAN OR SUPPLIER INFORMATION

(APPROVED BY AMA COUNCIL ON MEDICAL SERVICE 8/88) *PLEASE PRINT OR TYPE* FORM HCFA-1500 (U2) (12-90) FORM OCWP-1500 FORM RRB-1500

Figure 13–3

ASSIGNMENT 13–4 ▶ COMPLETE A CLAIM FORM FOR A TRICARE EXTRA CASE

Task: Complete a TRICARE HCFA-1500 claim form, post transactions to the ledger card, and define patient record abbreviations.

Conditions: Use the patient's record (Figure 13–4) and ledger card (Figure 13–5), one health insurance claim form (Figure 13–6), typewriter or computer, procedural and diagnostic code books, and *Workbook* Appendixes A and B.

Standards: Claim Productivity Measurement

Time: ______________ minutes

Accuracy: ______________

(Note: The time element and accuracy criteria may be given by your instructor.)

Directions:

1. Complete the HCFA-1500 Claim Form using OCR guidelines, directing it to your local TRICARE fiscal intermediary. See Chapter 6 of the Handbook for help in completing the HCFA-1500 claim form, and refer to Figure 6–13. Refer to Mrs. Darlene B. Drew's patient record and ledger card for information. Refer to Appendix A to fill in the fees on the ledger card. Date the claim February 3. Let us assume the patient brings in a hard copy of a signed Nonavailability Statement DD Form 1251, which shows approval of the physician to treat the patient. Dr. Ulibarri is accepting assignment on this TRICARE Extra case. This patient met her deductible last November when seen by a previous physician.
2. Use your CPT code book or Appendix A to determine the correct five-digit code number and modifiers for each professional service rendered.
3. Record the proper information on the ledger card when you have billed TRICARE Extra.
4. A Performance Evaluation Checklist may be reproduced from the Instruction Guide to the Workbook chapter if your instructor wishes you to submit it to assist with scoring and comments.
5. After the instructor has returned your work to you, either make the necessary corrections and place it in a 3-ring notebook for future reference, or, if you received a high score, place it in your portfolio for reference when applying for a job.

Abbreviations pertinent to this record:

adm ______________	PE ______________
BP ______________	Pt ______________
CC ______________	RBC ______________
cc ______________	rec ______________
DC ______________	retn ______________
Dx ______________	Rx ______________
Ex ______________	t.i.d ______________
FU ______________	UA ______________
hosp ______________	WBC ______________
I & D ______________	c̄ ______________

PATIENT RECORD NO. 1302

Drew,	Darlene	B.	12-22-41	F	013-466-1002
LAST NAME	FIRST NAME	MIDDLE NAME	BIRTH DATE	SEX	HOME PHONE

720 Ganley Street,	Woodland Hills,	XY	12345
ADDRESS	CITY	STATE	ZIP CODE

seamstress	J.B. Talon Company
PATIENT'S OCCUPATION	NAME OF COMPANY

2111 Ventura Road, Merck, XY 12346	013-733-0156
ADDRESS OF EMPLOYER	PHONE

Harry M. Drew	U.S. Navy Lieutenant Commander (L/C)	Active Status
SPOUSE OR PARENT	OCCUPATION	

Service # 221-96-0711	Social Security # 221-96-0711	Grade 12	4-15-37
			BIRTH DATE

P.O Box 2927, A.P.O.,New York, New York 09194

*TRICARE Extra I.D. Card # 67531	01-01-80	450-10-3762
TRICARE NO.	EFFECTIVE DATE	SOC. SEC. NO.

REFERRED BY: James B. Jeffers, MD, 100 S. Broadway, Woodland Hills, XY 12345 Tax ID# 776210740

* This number in not required on the HCFA-1500 claim form

DATE	PROGRESS
1-13-xx	CC new pt comes in complaining of very large, tender mass in periurethral orifice. Incision and
	drainage of deep periurethral abscess. Obtained 10 cc greenish pus. UA; WBC and RBC's
	loaded. Pt feels much better. Rx Terramycin 21 caps 1 t.i.d. Retn 5 days. Dx: Periurethral abscess
	in suburethral cyst. Took culture and sent to lab. Gene Ulibarri, MD
1-18-xx	Cyst is filled up again. Rec hospitalization to perform a marsupialization of urethral diverticulum.
	Culture shows pseudomonas organism. Gene Ulibarri, MD
1-19-xx	Adm to College Hosp. Surg: Marsupialization of urethral diverticulum and packing $\bar{c}$ Iodoform.
	Gene Ulibarri, MD
1-20-xx	DC from hosp. Renewed Rx Terramycin. To be seen in office next week for FU Ex. Gene Ulibarri, MD

Figure 13–4

STATEMENT

College Clinic
4567 Broad Avenue
Woodland Hills, XY 12345-0001
Telephone: 013-486-9002
Fax: 013-487-8976

Mr. Harry M. Drew
720 Ganley Street
Woodland Hills, XY 12345-0001

DATE	PROFESSIONAL SERVICE DESCRIPTION	CHARGE	CREDITS		CURRENT BALANCE
			PAYMENTS	ADJUSTMENTS	
1-13-xx	OV, D hx/exam, LC decision making				
1-13-xx	UA, non -auto c̄ microscopy				
1-13-xx	Drainage of deep periurethral abscess				
1-13-xx	Handling of culture				
1-18-xx	OV				
1-19-xx	Admit & initial hosp care, C hx/exam MC decision making				
1-19-xx	Marsupialization of urethral diverticulum				
1-20-xx	Discharge hosp.				

Due and payable within 10 days. **Pay last amount in balance column** 

Key:
PF: Problem-focused
EPF: Expanded problem-focused
D: Detailed
C: Comprehensive
SF: Straightforward
LC: Low complexity
MC: Moderate complexity
HC: High complexity
CON: Consultation
CPX: Complete phys exam
E: Emergency
ER: Emergency dept.
HCD: House call (day)
HCN: House call (night)
HV: Hospital visit
OV: Office visit

Figure 13–5

APPROVED OMB 0938-0008

CARRIER

PLEASE DO NOT STAPLE IN THIS AREA

PICA

HEALTH INSURANCE CLAIM FORM

PICA

1. MEDICARE (Medicare #) MEDICAID (Medicaid #) CHAMPUS (Sponsor's SSN) CHAMPVA (VA File #) GROUP HEALTH PLAN (SSN or ID) FECA BLK LUNG (SSN) OTHER (ID)

1a. INSURED'S I.D. NUMBER (FOR PROGRAM IN ITEM 1)

2. PATIENT'S NAME (Last Name, First Name, Middle Initial)

3. PATIENT'S BIRTH DATE MM DD YYYY SEX M F

4. INSURED'S NAME (Last Name, First Name, Middle Initial)

5. PATIENT'S ADDRESS (No., Street)

6. PATIENT RELATIONSHIP TO INSURED Self Spouse Child Other

7. INSURED'S ADDRESS (No., Street)

CITY STATE

8. PATIENT STATUS Single Married Other; Employed Full-Time Student Part-Time Student

CITY STATE

ZIP CODE TELEPHONE (Include Area Code) ( )

ZIP CODE TELEPHONE (include Area Code) ( )

9. OTHER INSURED'S NAME (Last Name, First Name, Middle Initial)

10. IS PATIENT'S CONDITION RELATED TO:

11. INSURED'S POLICY GROUP OR FECA NUMBER

a. OTHER INSURED'S POLICY OR GROUP NUMBER

a. EMPLOYMENT? (CURRENT OR PREVIOUS) YES NO

a. INSURED'S DATE OF BIRTH MM DD YY SEX M F

b. OTHER INSURED'S DATE OF BIRTH MM DD YY SEX M F

b. AUTO ACCIDENT? PLACE (State) YES NO

b. EMPLOYER'S NAME OR SCHOOL NAME

c. EMPLOYER'S NAME OR SCHOOL NAME

c. OTHER ACCIDENT? YES NO

c. INSURANCE PLAN NAME OR PROGRAM NAME

d. INSURANCE PLAN NAME OR PROGRAM NAME

10d. RESERVED FOR LOCAL USE

d. IS THERE ANOTHER HEALTH BENEFIT PLAN? YES NO *If yes*, return to and complete item 9 a-d.

READ BACK OF FORM BEFORE COMPLETING AND SIGNING THIS FORM.

12. PATIENT'S OR AUTHORIZED PERSON'S SIGNATURE I authorize the release of any medical or other information necessary to process this claim. I also request payment of government benefits either to myself or to the party who accepts assignment below.

SIGNED DATE

13. INSURED'S OR AUTHORIZED PERSON'S SIGNATURE I authorize payment of medical benefits to the undersigned physician or supplier for services described below.

SIGNED

PATIENT AND INSURED INFORMATION

14. DATE OF CURRENT: MM DD YY ILLNESS (First symptom) OR INJURY (Accident) OR PREGNANCY (LMP)

15. IF PATIENT HAS HAD SAME OR SIMILAR ILLNESS GIVE FIRST DATE MM DD YY

16. DATES PATIENT UNABLE TO WORK IN CURRENT OCCUPATION FROM MM DD YY TO MM DD YY

17. NAME OF REFERRING PHYSICIAN OR OTHER SOURCE

17a. I.D. NUMBER OF REFERRING PHYSICIAN

18. HOSPITALIZATION DATES RELATED TO CURRENT SERVICES FROM MM DD YY TO MM DD YY

19. RESERVED FOR LOCAL USE

20. OUTSIDE LAB? YES NO $ CHARGES

21. DIAGNOSIS OR NATURE OF ILLNESS OR INJURY. (RELATE ITEMS 1,2,3 OR 4 TO ITEM 24E BY LINE)

1.

2.

3.

4.

22. MEDICAID RESUBMISSION CODE ORIGINAL REF. NO.

23. PRIOR AUTHORIZATION NUMBER

24. A DATE(S) OF SERVICE From MM DD YY To MM DD YY	B Place of Service	C Type of Service	D PROCEDURES, SERVICES, OR SUPPLIES (Explain Unusual Circumstances) CPT/HCPCS MODIFIER	E DIAGNOSIS CODE	F $ CHARGES	G DAYS OR UNITS	H EPSDT Family Plan	I EMG	J COB	K RESERVED FOR LOCAL USE

25. FEDERAL TAX I.D. NUMBER SSN EIN

26. PATIENT'S ACCOUNT NO.

27. ACCEPT ASSIGNMENT? (For govt. claims, see back) YES NO

28. TOTAL CHARGE $

29. AMOUNT PAID $

30. BALANCE DUE $

31. SIGNATURE OF PHYSICIAN OR SUPPLIER INCLUDING DEGREES OR CREDENTIALS (I certify that the statements on the reverse apply to this bill and are made a part thereof.)

SIGNED DATE

32. NAME AND ADDRESS OF FACILITY WHERE SERVICES WERE RENDERED (if other than home or office)

33. PHYSICIAN'S, SUPPLIER'S BILLING NAME, ADDRESS, ZIP CODE AND PHONE #

PIN# GRP#

PHYSICIAN OR SUPPLIER INFORMATION

(APPROVED BY AMA COUNCIL ON MEDICAL SERVICE 8/88)

PLEASE PRINT OR TYPE

FORM HCFA -1500 (U2) (12-90)
FORM OCWP-1500 FORM RRB-1500

Figure 13–6

ASSIGNMENT 13–5 ▶ COMPLETE THREE CLAIM FORMS FOR A TRICARE STANDARD CASE

Task: Complete TRICARE HCFA-1500 claim forms, post transactions to the ledger card, and define patient record abbreviations.

Conditions: Use the patient's record (Figure 13–7) and ledger card (Figure 13–8), health insurance claim forms (Figures 13–9, 13–10, and 13–11), typewriter or computer, procedural and diagnostic code books, and *Workbook* Appendixes A and B.

Standards: Claim Productivity Measurement

Time: ______________ minutes

Accuracy: ______________

(Note: The time element and accuracy criteria may be given by your instructor.)

Directions:

1. Since this case requires three claim forms, make photocopies of the HCFA-1500 form or see Workbook Figures 13–10 and 13–11. Complete the HCFA-1500 Claim Form using OCR guidelines, directing it to your local TRICARE fiscal intermediary. See Chapter 13 of the *Handbook* for help in completing the HCFA-1500 claim form and refer to Figure 6–13. Refer to Mrs. Mae I. Abbreviate's patient record and ledger card for information. Refer to Appendix A to fill in the fees on the ledger card. Date the claim January 31. Assume that the patient brings in a hard copy of a signed Nonavailability Statement DD Form 1251, which shows approval of the physician to treat the patient. Dr. Coccidioides is not accepting assignment on this TRICARE Standard case but is completing the claim for the patient's convenience. This patient has not previously met her deductible.
2. Use your CPT code book or Appendix A to determine the correct five-digit code number and modifiers for each professional service rendered. X-rays in this case were taken at Speedy Radiology Service at 4300 Broad Avenue, Woodland Hills, XY 12345, provider No. 808491205, and laboratory work was sent to Laboratory Associates, 4100 Broad Avenue, Woodland Hills, XY 12345. The doctor is submitting the bill for x-rays.
3. Record the proper information on the ledger card when you have billed TRICARE.
4. A Performance Evaluation Checklist may be reproduced from the Instruction Guide to the Workbook chapter if your instructor wishes you to submit it to assist with scoring and comments.
5. After the instructor has returned your work to you, either make the necessary corrections and place it in a 3-ring notebook for future reference, or, if you received a high score, place it in your portfolio for reference when applying for a job.

Abbreviations pertinent to this record:

abdom ______________ D & C ______________

aet ______________ Dx ______________

BP ______________ EENT ______________

Ca ______________ FH ______________

CC ______________ GB ______________

Text continued on page 293

PATIENT RECORD NO. 1303

Abbreviate,	Mae	I.	01-02-42	F	013-986-7667
LAST NAME	FIRST NAME	MIDDLE NAME	BIRTH DATE	SEX	HOME PHONE

4667 Symbol Road,	Woodland Hills,	XY	12345
ADDRESS	CITY	STATE	ZIP CODE

administrative assistant	U.R. Wright Company
PATIENT'S OCCUPATION	NAME OF COMPANY

6789 Abridge Road , Woodland Hills, XY 12346	013-988-7540
ADDRESS OF EMPLOYER	PHONE

Shorty S. Abbreviate	Army Staff Sargeant, Active Status	3-25-40
SPOUSE OR PARENT	OCCUPATION	BIRTH DATE

Service # 023-19-7866 Social Security # 023-19-7866,HHC. 2nd Batt., 27th Infantry

Grade 12, A.P.O.,New York, New York 10030

*TRICARE Standard I.D. Card # 97600	1-1-9X	01-01-80	865-04-2311
TRICARE NO.	EXP. DATE	EFFECTIVE DATE	SOC. SEC. NO.

REFERRED BY: Jane B. Accurate (friend)

* This number in not required on the HCFA-1500 claim form

DATE	PROGRESS
1-4-xx	Pt 45 W♀in for complete PE; CC recent URI of 2 wk duration. PND, chest pain and cough;
	sweat, chills, and sputum c̄ pus X5 days. PH; Removal of T & A aet 6, UCHD; Para I, D & C
	aet 41;Surg on OS after accident last yr. FH:Father expired of c̄ Ca kidney aet 63; Mother L& W
	after GB surg. PX: 5'7", Wt 150#, EENT o except OS opaque; LMP 12-18-91; Chest: Dyspnea
	and rales, BP 120/80, TPR normal, Abdomen o. GGE; Lab rpt: WBC 14,800, RBC 4.2
	Prog; NYD. Chest x-rays reveal a cavity c̄ a fluid level. Sputum specimen sent for culture and
	sensitivity tests. Dx: Lung abscess. Rx penicillion G 10 million u/day IV for 5 days.
	Brady Coccidioides, MD
1-15-xx	Penicillin G 10 million units IV infusion. Pt doing well. Brady Coccidioides, MD
1-16-xx	Penicillin G 10 million units IV infusion. Ordered bilateral bronchography. Brady Coccidioides, MD
1-17-xx	Penicillin G 10 million units IV infusion. Brady Coccidioides, MD
1-18-xx	Penicillin G 10 million units IV infusion. Pt doing well. Few residual shadows on repeat of chest x-ray.
	PTR in 1 wk. Brady Coccidioides, MD

Figure 13–7

STATEMENT

College Clinic
4567 Broad Avenue
Woodland Hills, XY 12345-0001
Telephone: 013-486-9002
Fax: 013-487-8976

Mrs. Shorty S. Abbreviate
4667 Symbol Road
Woodland Hills, XY 12345-0001

DATE	PROFESSIONAL SERVICE DESCRIPTION	CHARGE		CREDITS PAYMENTS		CREDITS ADJUSTMENTS		CURRENT BALANCE	
1-14-xx	OV, C hx/exam, HC decision making								
1-14-xx	AP & lat chest x-rays								
1-14-xx	Handling of sputum specimen								
1-14-xx	Penicillin inj 10 mil U. IV								
1-15-xx	OV, PF hx/exam, SP decision making								
1-15-xx	Penicillin inj 10 mil U. IV								
1-16-xx	OV, PF hx/exam, SF decision making								
1-16-xx	Penicillin inj 10 mil U. IV								
1-16-xx	Bilateral bronchography								
1-17-xx	OV, PF hx/exam, SF decision making								
1-17-xx	Penicillin inj 10 mil U. IV								
1-18-xx	OV, PF hx/exam, SF decision making								
1-18-xx	Penicillin inj 10 mil U. IV								
1-18-xx	AP & lat chest x-rays								

Due and payable within 10 days.

Pay last amount in balance column 

Key:
PF: Problem-focused
EPF: Expanded problem-focused
D: Detailed
C: Comprehensive
SF: Straightforward
LC: Low complexity
MC: Moderate complexity
HC: High complexity
CON: Consultation
CPX: Complete phys exam
E: Emergency
ER: Emergency dept.
HCD: House call (day)
HCN: House call (night)
HV: Hospital visit
OV: Office visit

Figure 13–8

APPROVED OMB-0938-0008

PLEASE DO NOT STAPLE IN THIS AREA

CARRIER

PICA

HEALTH INSURANCE CLAIM FORM

PICA

1. MEDICARE (Medicare #) MEDICAID (Medicaid #) CHAMPUS (Sponsor's SSN) CHAMPVA (VA File #) GROUP HEALTH PLAN (SSN or ID) FECA BLK LUNG (SSN) OTHER (ID)

1a. INSURED'S I.D. NUMBER (FOR PROGRAM IN ITEM 1)

2. PATIENT'S NAME (Last Name, First Name, Middle Initial)

3. PATIENT'S BIRTH DATE MM DD YYYY SEX M F

4. INSURED'S NAME (Last Name, First Name, Middle Initial)

5. PATIENT'S ADDRESS (No., Street)

6. PATIENT RELATIONSHIP TO INSURED Self Spouse Child Other

7. INSURED'S ADDRESS (No., Street)

CITY STATE

8. PATIENT STATUS Single Married Other

CITY STATE

ZIP CODE TELEPHONE (Include Area Code)

Employed Full-Time Student Part-Time Student

ZIP CODE TELEPHONE (include Area Code) ( )

9. OTHER INSURED'S NAME (Last Name, First Name, Middle Initial)

10. IS PATIENT'S CONDITION RELATED TO:

11. INSURED'S POLICY GROUP OR FECA NUMBER

a. OTHER INSURED'S POLICY OR GROUP NUMBER

a. EMPLOYMENT? (CURRENT OR PREVIOUS) YES NO

a. INSURED'S DATE OF BIRTH MM DD YY SEX M F

b. OTHER INSURED'S DATE OF BIRTH MM DD YY SEX M F

b. AUTO ACCIDENT? YES NO PLACE (State)

b. EMPLOYER'S NAME OR SCHOOL NAME

c. EMPLOYER'S NAME OR SCHOOL NAME

c. OTHER ACCIDENT? YES NO

c. INSURANCE PLAN NAME OR PROGRAM NAME

d. INSURANCE PLAN NAME OR PROGRAM NAME

10d. RESERVED FOR LOCAL USE

d. IS THERE ANOTHER HEALTH BENEFIT PLAN? YES NO *If yes, return to and complete item 9 a-d.*

READ BACK OF FORM BEFORE COMPLETING AND SIGNING THIS FORM.

12. PATIENT'S OR AUTHORIZED PERSON'S SIGNATURE I authorize the release of any medical or other information necessary to process this claim. I also request payment of government benefits either to myself or to the party who accepts assignment below.

SIGNED ______ DATE ______

13. INSURED'S OR AUTHORIZED PERSON'S SIGNATURE I authorize payment of medical benefits to the undersigned physician or supplier for services described below.

SIGNED ______

PATIENT AND INSURED INFORMATION

14. DATE OF CURRENT: MM DD YY ILLNESS (First symptom) OR INJURY (Accident) OR PREGNANCY (LMP)

15. IF PATIENT HAS HAD SAME OR SIMILAR ILLNESS GIVE FIRST DATE MM DD YY

16. DATES PATIENT UNABLE TO WORK IN CURRENT OCCUPATION MM DD YY FROM MM DD YY TO

17. NAME OF REFERRING PHYSICIAN OR OTHER SOURCE

17a. I.D. NUMBER OF REFERRING PHYSICIAN

18. HOSPITALIZATION DATES RELATED TO CURRENT SERVICES MM DD YY FROM MM DD YY TO

19. RESERVED FOR LOCAL USE

20. OUTSIDE LAB? YES NO $ CHARGES

21. DIAGNOSIS OR NATURE OF ILLNESS OR INJURY. (RELATE ITEMS 1,2,3 OR 4 TO ITEM 24E BY LINE)

1. ______ 3. ______

2. ______ 4. ______

22. MEDICAID RESUBMISSION CODE ORIGINAL REF. NO.

23. PRIOR AUTHORIZATION NUMBER

24. A DATE(S) OF SERVICE From MM DD YY To MM DD YY	B Place of Service	C Type of Service	D PROCEDURES, SERVICES, OR SUPPLIES (Explain Unusual Circumstances) CPT/HCPCS MODIFIER	E DIAGNOSIS CODE	F $ CHARGES	G DAYS OR UNITS	H EPSDT Family Plan	I EMG	J COB	K RESERVED FOR LOCAL USE

25. FEDERAL TAX I.D. NUMBER SSN EIN

26. PATIENT'S ACCOUNT NO.

27. ACCEPT ASSIGNMENT? (For govt. claims, see back) YES NO

28. TOTAL CHARGE $

29. AMOUNT PAID $

30. BALANCE DUE $

31. SIGNATURE OF PHYSICIAN OR SUPPLIER INCLUDING DEGREES OR CREDENTIALS (I certify that the statements on the reverse apply to this bill and are made a part thereof.)

SIGNED DATE

32. NAME AND ADDRESS OF FACILITY WHERE SERVICES WERE RENDERED (If other than home or office)

33. PHYSICIAN'S, SUPPLIER'S BILLING NAME, ADDRESS, ZIP CODE AND PHONE #

PIN# GRP#

PHYSICIAN OR SUPPLIER INFORMATION

(APPROVED BY AMA COUNCIL ON MEDICAL SERVICE 8/88)

PLEASE PRINT OR TYPE

FORM HCFA-1500 (U2) (12-90)
FORM OCWP-1500 FORM RRB-1500

Figure 13–9

14. DATE OF CURRENT: MM | DD | YY — ILLNESS (First symptom) OR INJURY (Accident) OR PREGNANCY (LMP)

15. IF PATIENT HAS HAD SAME OR SIMILAR ILLNESS GIVE FIRST DATE MM | DD | YY

16. DATES PATIENT UNABLE TO WORK IN CURRENT OCCUPATION FROM MM | DD | YY TO MM | DD | YY

17. NAME OF REFERRING PHYSICIAN OR OTHER SOURCE

17a. I.D. NUMBER OF REFERRING PHYSICIAN

18. HOSPITALIZATION DATES RELATED TO CURRENT SERVICES FROM MM | DD | YY TO MM | DD | YY

19. RESERVED FOR LOCAL USE

20. OUTSIDE LAB? YES NO $ CHARGES

21. DIAGNOSIS OR NATURE OF ILLNESS OR INJURY. (RELATE ITEMS 1,2,3 OR 4 TO ITEM 24E BY LINE)

1. ____ 3. ____

2. ____ 4. ____

22. MEDICAID RESUBMISSION CODE | ORIGINAL REF. NO.

23. PRIOR AUTHORIZATION NUMBER

24. A DATE(S) OF SERVICE From MM DD YY To MM DD YY	B Place of Service	C Type of Service	D PROCEDURES, SERVICES, OR SUPPLIES (Explain Unusual Circumstances) CPT/HCPCS | MODIFIER	E DIAGNOSIS CODE	F $ CHARGES	G DAYS OR UNITS	H EPSDT Family Plan	I EMG	J COB	K RESERVED FOR LOCAL USE

25. FEDERAL TAX I.D. NUMBER SSN EIN

26. PATIENT'S ACCOUNT NO.

27. ACCEPT ASSIGNMENT? (For govt. claims, see back) YES NO

28. TOTAL CHARGE $

29. AMOUNT PAID $

30. BALANCE DUE $

31. SIGNATURE OF PHYSICIAN OR SUPPLIER INCLUDING DEGREES OR CREDENTIALS (I certify that the statements on the reverse apply to this bill and are made a part thereof.)

SIGNED DATE

32. NAME AND ADDRESS OF FACILITY WHERE SERVICES WERE RENDERED (if other than home or office)

33. PHYSICIAN'S, SUPPLIER'S BILLING NAME, ADDRESS, ZIP CODE AND PHONE #

PIN# GRP#

PHYSICIAN OR SUPPLIER INFORMATION

(APPROVED BY AMA COUNCIL ON MEDICAL SERVICE8/88) *PLEASE PRINT OR TYPE* FORM HCFA -1500 (U2) (12-90) FORM OCWP-1500 FORM F

Figure 13–10

14. DATE OF CURRENT: MM | DD | YY ◄ ILLNESS (First symptom) OR INJURY (Accident) OR PREGNANCY (LMP)

15. IF PATIENT HAS HAD SAME OR SIMILAR ILLNESS GIVE FIRST DATE MM | DD | YY

16. DATES PATIENT UNABLE TO WORK IN CURRENT OCCUPATION FROM MM | DD | YY TO MM | DD | YY

17. NAME OF REFERRING PHYSICIAN OR OTHER SOURCE

17a. I.D. NUMBER OF REFERRING PHYSICIAN

18. HOSPITALIZATION DATES RELATED TO CURRENT SERVICES FROM MM | DD | YY TO MM | DD | YY

19. RESERVED FOR LOCAL USE

20. OUTSIDE LAB? ☐ YES ☐ NO $ CHARGES

21. DIAGNOSIS OR NATURE OF ILLNESS OR INJURY. (RELATE ITEMS 1,2,3 OR 4 TO ITEM 24E BY LINE)

1. _____ 3. _____

2. _____ 4. _____

22. MEDICAID RESUBMISSION CODE | ORIGINAL REF. NO.

23. PRIOR AUTHORIZATION NUMBER

24. A DATE(S) OF SERVICE From MM DD YY To MM DD YY	B Place of Service	C Type of Service	D PROCEDURES, SERVICES, OR SUPPLIES (Explain Unusual Circumstances) CPT/HCPCS | MODIFIER	E DIAGNOSIS CODE	F $ CHARGES	G DAYS OR UNITS	H EPSDT Family Plan	I EMG	J COB	K RESERVED FOR LOCAL USE

25. FEDERAL TAX I.D. NUMBER SSN EIN ☐ ☐

26. PATIENT'S ACCOUNT NO.

27. ACCEPT ASSIGNMENT? (For govt. claims, see back) ☐ YES ☐ NO

28. TOTAL CHARGE $

29. AMOUNT PAID $

30. BALANCE DUE $

31. SIGNATURE OF PHYSICIAN OR SUPPLIER INCLUDING DEGREES OR CREDENTIALS (I certify that the statements on the reverse apply to this bill and are made a part thereof.)

SIGNED DATE

32. NAME AND ADDRESS OF FACILITY WHERE SERVICES WERE RENDERED (if other than home or office)

33. PHYSICIAN'S, SUPPLIER'S BILLING NAME, ADDRESS, ZIP CODE AND PHONE #

PIN# GRP#

PHYSICIAN OR SUPPLIER INFORMATION

(APPROVED BY AMA COUNCIL ON MEDICAL SERVICE8/88) *PLEASE PRINT OR TYPE* FORM HCFA -1500 (U2) (12-90) FORM OCWP-1500 FORM F

Figure 13–11

GGE ______________

GI ______________

Ht ______________

I ______________

LMP ______________

L & W ______________

NYD ______________

OS ______________

Para I ______________

PE ______________

PH ______________

PND ______________

Prog ______________

pt ______________

PTR ______________

PX ______________

RBC ______________

Rx ______________

surg ______________

T & A ______________

TPR ______________

u ______________

UCHD ______________

URI ______________

W ______________

WBC ______________

wk ______________

wt ______________

X ______________

yr ______________

c̄ ______________

♀ ______________

ō ______________

o ______________

COMPUTER EXERCISE

Case 7 TRICARE

Before proceeding, you may want to do an exercise based on the concepts you have learned. Additional practice material is on your computer diskette.

Directions: Insert the diskette into the computer and follow the instructions on the screen for Computer Exercise Case 7.

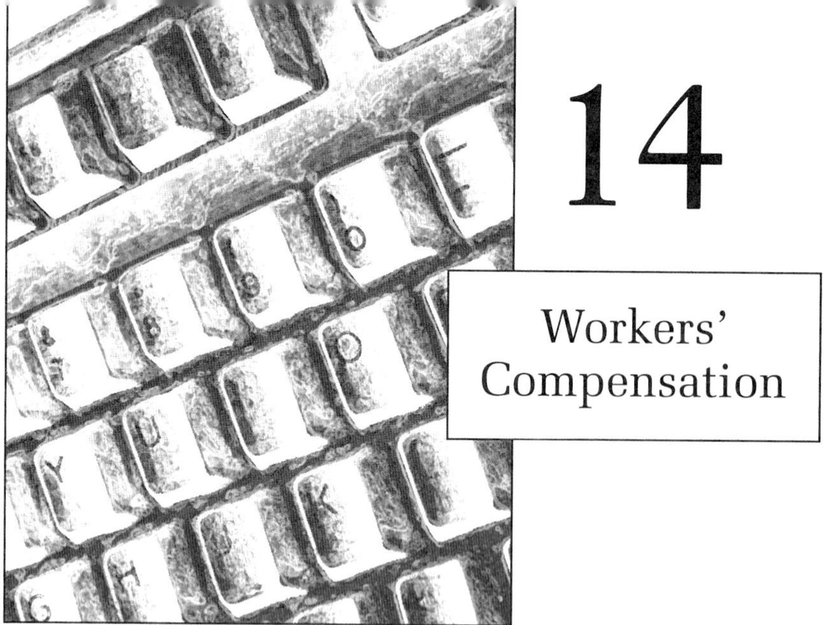

14

Workers' Compensation

KEY TERMS

Your instructor may wish to select some specific words pertinent to this chapter for a test. For definitions of the terms, further study, and/or reference, the words, phrases, and abbreviations may be found in the Glossary at the end of the Handbook. *Key terms for this chapter follow.*

accident
adjudication
by report (BR)
claims examiner
compromise and release (C and R)
deposition
ergonomic
extraterritorial
Federal Employees' Compensation Act (FECA)
fee schedule
independent medical examiner (IME)
injury
insurance adjuster
lien
medical service order
nondisability (ND) claim
occupational illness (or disease)
Occupational Safety and Health Administration (OSHA)
permanent and stationary (P and S)
permanent disability (PD)
petition
second injury fund
sequelae
sub rosa films
subsequent injury fund (SIF)
temporary disability (TD)
third party liability
third party subrogation
waiting period (WP)
work hardening
Workers' Compensation Appeals Board (WCAB)
workers' compensation (WC) insurance

PERFORMANCE OBJECTIVES

The student will be able to

- Define and spell the key terms for this chapter, given the information from the *Handbook* Glossary, with a reasonable period of time and with enough accuracy to obtain a satisfactory evaluation.
- Answer the self-study review questions after reading the chapter, with enough accuracy to obtain a satisfactory evaluation.
- Fill in the correct meaning of each abbreviation, given a list of common medical abbreviations and

symbols that appear in chart notes, within a reasonable period of time and with enough accuracy to obtain a satisfactory evaluation.

- Complete each workers' compensation form for billing, given the patients' medical chart notes, ledger cards, and blank insurance forms, within a reasonable period of time and with enough accuracy to obtain a satisfactory evaluation.
- Complete each HCFA-1500 Health Insurance Claim Form for submission to a workers' compensation insurance company, given the patients' medical chart notes, ledger cards, and blank insurance claim forms, within a reasonable period of time and with enough accuracy to obtain a satisfactory evaluation.
- Correctly post payments, adjustments, and balances on the patients' ledger cards, using the Mock Fee Schedule in Appendix A, within a reasonable period of time and with enough accuracy to obtain a satisfactory evaluation.

STUDY OUTLINE

History
- Workers' Compensation Statutes
- Workers' Compensation Reform

Workers' Compensation Laws and Insurance
- Purposes of Workers' Compensation Laws
- Self-Insurance
- Managed Care

Eligibility
- Industrial Accident
- Occupational Illness

Coverage
- Federal Laws
- State Laws
  - Minors
  - Interstate Laws
  - Volunteer Workers
  - Funding
  - Second-Injury Fund (Subsequent Injury Fund)
  - Minimum Number of Employees
  - Waiting Periods
- State Disability and Workers' Compensation

Benefits

Types of State Claims
- Nondisability Claim
- Temporary Disability Claim
  - Vocational Rehabilitation
  - Work Hardening
  - Ergonomics

Permanent Disability Claim
- Rating
- Surveillance

Fraud and Abuse

Occupational Safety and Health Administration (OSHA) Act of 1970
- Background
- Coverage
- Regulations
- Filing a Complaint
- Inspection
- Record Keeping and Reporting

Legal Situations
- Medical Evaluator
- Depositions
- Medical Testimony
- Liens
- Third Party Subrogation

Medical Reports
- Confidentiality
- Documentation
- Medical Record Keeping
- Terminology

Reporting Requirements
- Employer's Report
- Medical Service Order
- Physician's First Report

Procedure: Completing the Doctor's First Report of Occupational Injury or Illness Form
- Progress or Supplemental Report
- Final Report

Claim Submission
- Financial Responsibility
- Fee Schedules
  - Types of Fee Schedules
- Helpful Billing Tips
- Billing Claims
  - Electronic Claims Submission and Reports
- Out-of-State Claims

Delinquent Claims

SELF-STUDY 14–1 ► REVIEW QUESTIONS

Review the objectives, key terms, glossary definitions to key terms, chapter information, and figures before completing the following review questions.

1. Name two kinds of statutes under workers' compensation.

   a. Federal compensation laws

   b. State compensation laws

2. An unforeseen, unexpected, unintended event that occurs at a particular time and place, causing injury to an individual not of his or her own making, is called a/an accident.

3. Maria Cardoza works in a plastics manufacturing company and inhales some fumes that cause bronchitis. Since this condition is associated with her employment, it is called a/an occupational illness.

4. Name the federal workers' compensation acts that cover workers.

   a. Workmen's compensation Law of the district of columbia

   b. Federal Coal Mine Health and Safety Act

   c. Federal Employees' Compensation Act

   d. Longshoremen's and Harbor Worker's Compensation Act

5. State compensation laws that *require* each employer to accept its provisions and provide for specialized benefits for employees who are injured at work are called compulsory Laws.

6. State compensation laws that *may be accepted or rejected* by the employer are known as elective laws.

7. State five methods used for funding workers' compensation.

   a. monopolistic state or Provincial Fund

   b. employers may qualify as self insurers

   c. Territorial Fund

   d. competitive state fund

   e. private insurance companies

8. Who pays the workers' compensation insurance premiums? Employers

9. What is the time limit in your state for submitting the employers' and/or physicians' report of an industrial accident? ______

10. When an employee with a preexisting condition is injured at work and the injury produces a disability greater than that caused by the second injury alone, the benefits are derived from a/an Subsequent or secondary injury fund

11. Name jobs that may not be covered by workers' compensation insurance.

a. domestic or casual employees
b. laborers
c. babysitters
d. charity workers
e. Gardeners
f. Newspaper Vendors or distributors

12. What is the minimum number of employees per business needed in your state before workers' compensation statutes become effective? ______

13. What waiting period must elapse in your state before workers' compensation payments begin? ______

14. List five types of workers' compensation benefits.

a. Medical treatment
b. temporary disability indemnity
c. permanent disability indemnity
d. Death benefits
e. Rehabilitation benefits

15. Who can treat an industrial injury? Licensed physician, osteopath dentist or chiropractor

16. Three types of workers' compensation claims are

a. non disability
b. temporary disability
c. permanent disability

17. Explain the differences between these three types of claims.

a. Nondisability claim: Person is injured or ill, treated, and goes back to work. No disability from his or her job

b. Temporary disability claim: Person is injured or ill and cannot work at his or her job and is off work for a period of time

c. Permanent disability claim: Person is injured or ill, and cannot work at his or her job and is off work for a period of time

18. After suffering an industrial injury, Mr. Fields is in a treatment program in which he is given real work tasks for building strength and endurance. This form of therapy is called Work Hardening.

19. Define these abbreviations.

a. TD Temporary disability b. PD Permanent disability

c. P & S permanent and stationary d. C & R compromise and release

20. Weekly temporary disability payments are based on the employees earnings at the time of the injury or illness.

21. When an industrial case reaches the time for rating the disability, this is accomplished by the states industrial accident commission or worker's compensation board.

22. May an injured person appeal his or her case if not satisfied with the rating?

If so, to whom does he or she appeal? yes

or? Workers compensation Appeals board or Industrial Accident Commission

23. When a case of fraud or abuse is suspected in a workers' compensation case, the physician should report the situation to the insurance carrier.

24. Employers are required to meet health and safety standards for their employees under federal and state statutes known as the Occupational Safety and Health Administration (OSHA) Act of 1970.

25. A man takes his girlfriend to a roofing job and she is injured. Is she covered under workers' compensation insurance? No

26. A proceeding during which an attorney questions a witness who answers under oath but not in open court is called a/an Deposition.

27. The legal promise of a patient to satisfy a debt to the physician from proceeds received from a litigated case is termed a/an lien.

28. The process of carrying on a lawsuit is called litigation.

29. Explain third party subrogation. a third party is responsible for the injury (person is injured by an outside party).

30. What is the first thing an employee should do after he or she is injured?

Notify his or her employer or immediate supervisor

31. When an individual suffers a work-related injury or illness, the employer must complete and send a form to the insurance company and workers' compensation state offices called a/an Employers report of occupational injury or illness, and if the employee is sent to a physician's office for medical care, the employer must complete a form that authorizes the physician to treat the employee, called a/an Medical Service order.

32. When a physician treats an industrial injury, he or she must complete a/an First treatment Medical Report and send it to the following:

a. insurance carrier

b. employer

c. state workers' compensation office

d. retain a copy for the Physicians files

Is a stamped physician's signature acceptable on the form? NO Explain.

Each copy must be signed in ink because it is a legal document

33. If the physician feels the injured employee is capable of returning to work after having been on temporary disability, what does the physician do? Sends in a report to the Insurance company giving the date for return to work

34. In a workers' compensation case, bills should be submitted monthly or at the time of termination of treatment and a claim becomes delinquent after a time frame of 45 days.

35. If an individual seeks medical care for a workers' compensation injury from another state, which state's regulations are followed? The state (jurisdiction) Where the claim originated and the accident or injury occurred

To check your answers to this self-study assignment, see Appendix D.

ASSIGNMENT 14–2 ▶ COMPLETE A DOCTOR'S FIRST REPORT OF OCCUPATIONAL INJURY OR ILLNESS FORM

Task: Complete a Doctor's First Report of Occupational Injury or Illness form and define patient record abbreviations.

Conditions: Use the patient's record (Figure 14–1) and Doctor's First Report of Occupational Injury or Illness form (Figure 14–2), and typewriter or computer.

Standards: Claim Productivity Measurement

Time: ______________ minutes

Accuracy : ______________

(Note: The time element and accuracy criteria may be given by your instructor.)

Directions:

1. Complete the *Doctor's First Report of Occupational Injury or Illness* (Figure 14–2) for this nondisability type of claim.
2. Define abbreviations found in the patient's medical record.
3. After the instructor has returned your work to you, either make the necessary corrections and place it in a 3-ring notebook for future reference, or, if you receive a high score, place it in your portfolio for use when applying for a job.

Abbreviations pertinent to this record:

AP ______________

approx. ______________

apt ______________

CAT ______________

c/o ______________

DC ______________

Dr. ______________

Ex ______________

FU ______________

Hosp ______________

L ______________

lat ______________

lt ______________

neg ______________

PD ______________

pt ______________

reg ______________

RTW ______________

Tr ______________

Tx ______________

wks ______________

♂ ______________

PATIENT RECORD NO. 1401

Hiranuma,	Glen	M.	12-24-45	M	013-467-3383
LAST NAME	FIRST NAME	MIDDLE NAME	BIRTH DATE	SEX	HOME PHONE

4372 Hanley Avenue,	Woodland Hills,	XY	12345
ADDRESS	CITY	STATE	ZIP CODE

house painter	Pittsburgh Paint Company (commercial painting company)
PATIENT'S OCCUPATION	NAME OF COMPANY

3725 Bonfeld Avenue,	Woodland Hills, XY 12345	013-486-9070
ADDRESS OF EMPLOYER		PHONE

Esme M. Hiranuma	homemaker
SPOUSE OR PARENT	OCCUPATION

BIRTHDATE

State Compensation Insurance Fund, 14156 Magnolia Boulevard, Torres, XY 12349
NAME OF INSURANCE

016-2432-211		558-40-9960
POLICY NO.	EFFECTIVE DATE	SOC. SEC. NO.

REFERRED BY: Pittsburgh Paint Company

DATE	PROGRESS
5-22-XX	At 9:30 a.m. this ♂ pt was painting an apt ceiling. Pt slipped and fell from ladder & hit his head and lt side of body. Brief unconsciousness for approximately 15 minutes. Apt located at 3540 W. 87th Street, Woodland Hills, XY 12345. Pt c/o L shoulder pain and swelling; L leg and hip pain; neck and head pain. Pt notified employer immediately. Sent to College Hosp where x-rays of lt hip, lt femur, and cervical spine were taken (2 views AP & Lat)--all neg. CAT of brain. (Dr. was called to hosp at request of employer and saw pt at 5 p.m.).Ex & Tr for L shoulder sprain, L hip and leg abrasions. Pt to be admitted for overnight in hosp for concussion. Plan to DC 5-23-XX. No PD expected. Pt to FU in 2 wks. Approx. RTW 6-6-XX Gerald Procter, MD

Figure 14–1

ASSIGNMENT 14–3 ► COMPLETE A CLAIM FORM FOR A WORKERS' COMPENSATION CASE

Task: Complete a HCFA-1500 claim form and post transactions to the ledger card.

Conditions: Use the patient's record (Figure 14–1) and ledger card (Figure 14–3), HCFA-1500 claim form (Figure 14–4), typewriter or computer, procedural and diagnostic code books, and *Workbook* Appendix A.

Standards: Claim Productivity Measurement

Time: ________________ minutes

Accuracy: ________________

(Note: The time element and accuracy criteria may be given by your instructor.)

Directions:

1. Complete a HCFA-1500 claim form using OCR guidelines. Date the claim May 24 of the current year.
2. Determine the correct five-digit code number and modifiers for each professional service rendered.
3. Post transactions to the ledger card and indicate the proper information when you have billed the workers' compensation insurance company. X-rays would be billed by the hospital as inpatient diagnostic work-up.
4. A Performance Evaluation Checklist may be reproduced from the Instruction Guide to the *Workbook* chapter if your instructor wishes you to submit it to assist with scoring and comments.
5. After the instructor has returned your work to you, either make the necessary corrections and place it in a 3-ring notebook for future reference, or, if you received a high score, place it in your portfolio for reference when applying for a job.

ASSIGNMENT 14–4 ► COMPLETE A DOCTOR'S FIRST REPORT OF OCCUPATIONAL INJURY OR ILLNESS FORM

Task: Complete a Doctor's First Report of Occupational Injury or Illness form and define patient record abbreviations.

Conditions: Use the patient's record (Figure 14–5) and Doctor's First Report of Occupational Injury or Illness form (Figure 14–6), and typewriter or computer.

Standards: Claim Productivity Measurement

Time: ________________ minutes

Accuracy: ________________

(Note: The time element and accuracy criteria may be given by your instructor.)

Directions:

1. Complete the Doctor's First Report of Occupational Injury or Illness for this temporary disability type of claim. Refer to Carlos Giovanni's patient record for November 11 through November 15.
2. Define abbreviations found in the patient's medical record.

Text continued on page 313

DOCTOR'S FIRST REPORT OF OCCUPATIONAL INJURY OR ILLNESS

Within 5 days of initial examination, for every occupational injury or illness, send 2 copies of this report to the employers' workers' compensation insurance carrier or the self-insured employer. Failure to file a timely doctor's report may result in assessment of a civil penalty. In the case of diagnosed or suspected pesticide poisoning, send a copy of this report to Division of Labor Statistics and Research.

1. **INSURER NAME AND ADDRESS**

2. **EMPLOYER NAME** Policy No.

3. Address No. and Street City Zip

4. Nature of business(e.g., food manufacturing, building construction, retailer of women's clothes)

5. **PATIENT NAME** (first, middle initial, last name) | 6. Sex ☐Male ☐Female | 7. Date of Birth Mo. Day Yr.

8. Address No. and Street City Zip | 9. Telephone Number

10. Occupation (Specific job title) | 11. Social Security Number

12. Injured at: No. and Street City County

13. Date and hour of injury or onset or illness Mo. Day Yr. Hour _____a.m____p.m | 14. Date last worked Mo. Day Yr.

15. Date and hour of first examination or treatment Mo. Day Yr. Hour _____a.m____p.m | 16. Have you (or your office) previously treated patient? ☐Yes ☐No

Patient please complete this portion, if able to do so. Otherwise, doctor please complete immediately. Inability or failure of a patient to complete this portion shall not affect his/her rights to workers' compensation under the Labor Code.
17. DESCRIBE HOW THE ACCIDENT OR EXPOSURE HAPPENED (Give specific object, machinery or chemical.)

18. **SUBJECTIVE COMPLAINTS** (Describe fully.)

19. **OBJECTIVE FINDINGS**
   A. Physical examination
   B. X-ray and laboratory results (State if none or pending.)

20. **DIAGNOSIS** (If occupational illness specify etiologic agent and duration of exposure.) Chemical or toxic compound involved? ☐Yes ☐No ICD - 9 Code

21. Are your findings and diagnosis consistent with patient's account of injury or onset of illness? ☐Yes ☐No If "no" please explain

22. Is there any other current condition that will impede or delay patient's recovery? ☐Yes ☐No If "yes" please explain

23. **TREATMENT REQUIRED**

24. If further treatment required, specify treatment plan/estimated duration.

25. If hospitalized as inpatient, give hospital name and location Date admitted Mo. Day Yr. Estimated stay

26. **WORK STATUS** --Is patient able to perfom usual work? ☐ Yes ☐ No
   If "no," date when patient can return to: Regular work____/____/
   Modified work____/____/ Specify restrictions

Doctor's Signature __________ License Number __________
Doctor's Name and Degree __________ IRS Number __________
Address __________ Telephone Number __________

Figure 14–2

STATEMENT

College Clinic
4567 Broad Avenue
Woodland Hills, XY 12345-0001
Telephone: 013-486-9002
Fax: 013-487-8976

TO: State Compensation Insurance Fund
14156 Magnolia Boulevard
Torres, XY 12349-0218

RE: Inj: Glen M. Hiranuma
Date of Inj: 5-22-xx
Emp: Pittsburgh Paint Company
Policy No.: 016-2432-211

DATE	PROFESSIONAL SERVICE DESCRIPTION	CHARGE	CREDITS		CURRENT BALANCE
			PAYMENTS	ADJUSTMENTS	
5-22-xx	Hosp exam & initial treatment, C hx/exam, MC decision making				
5-22-xx	Medical report				
5-23-xx	Discharge hospital				

Due and payable within 10 days. **Pay last amount in balance column** 

Key:
PF: Problem-focused
EPF: Expanded problem-focused
D: Detailed
C: Comprehensive
SF: Straightforward
LC: Low complexity
MC: Moderate complexity
HC: High complexity
CON: Consultation
CPX: Complete phys exam
E: Emergency
ER: Emergency dept.
HCD: House call (day)
HCN: House call (night)
HV: Hospital visit
OV: Office visit

Figure 14–3

APPROVED OMB-0938-0008

PLEASE DO NOT STAPLE IN THIS AREA

CARRIER

PICA

HEALTH INSURANCE CLAIM FORM

PICA

1. MEDICARE (Medicare #) | MEDICAID (Medicaid #) | CHAMPUS (Sponsor's SSN) | CHAMPVA (VA File #) | GROUP HEALTH PLAN (SSN or ID) | FECA BLK LUNG (SSN) | OTHER (ID)

1a. INSURED'S I.D. NUMBER (FOR PROGRAM IN ITEM 1)

2. PATIENT'S NAME (Last Name, First Name, Middle Initial)

3. PATIENT'S BIRTH DATE MM | DD | YYYY SEX M ☐ F ☐

4. INSURED'S NAME (Last Name, First Name, Middle Initial)

5. PATIENT'S ADDRESS (No., Street)

6. PATIENT RELATIONSHIP TO INSURED Self ☐ Spouse ☐ Child ☐ Other ☐

7. INSURED'S ADDRESS (No., Street)

CITY | STATE

8. PATIENT STATUS Single ☐ Married ☐ Other ☐

CITY | STATE

ZIP CODE | TELEPHONE (Include Area Code)

Employed ☐ Full-Time Student ☐ Part-Time Student ☐

ZIP CODE | TELEPHONE (include Area Code) ( )

9. OTHER INSURED'S NAME (Last Name, First Name, Middle Initial)

10. IS PATIENT'S CONDITION RELATED TO:

11. INSURED'S POLICY GROUP OR FECA NUMBER

a. OTHER INSURED'S POLICY OR GROUP NUMBER

a. EMPLOYMENT? (CURRENT OR PREVIOUS) ☐ YES ☐ NO

a. INSURED'S DATE OF BIRTH MM | DD | YY SEX M ☐ F ☐

b. OTHER INSURED'S DATE OF BIRTH MM | DD | YY SEX M ☐ F ☐

b. AUTO ACCIDENT? ☐ YES ☐ NO PLACE (State)

b. EMPLOYER'S NAME OR SCHOOL NAME

c. EMPLOYER'S NAME OR SCHOOL NAME

c. OTHER ACCIDENT? ☐ YES ☐ NO

c. INSURANCE PLAN NAME OR PROGRAM NAME

d. INSURANCE PLAN NAME OR PROGRAM NAME

10d. RESERVED FOR LOCAL USE

d. IS THERE ANOTHER HEALTH BENEFIT PLAN? ☐ YES ☐ NO *If yes, return to and complete item 9 a-d.*

READ BACK OF FORM BEFORE COMPLETING AND SIGNING THIS FORM.

12. PATIENT'S OR AUTHORIZED PERSON'S SIGNATURE I authorize the release of any medical or other information necessary to process this claim. I also request payment of government benefits either to myself or to the party who accepts assignment below.

SIGNED ______ DATE ______

13. INSURED'S OR AUTHORIZED PERSON'S SIGNATURE I authorize payment of medical benefits to the undersigned physician or supplier for services described below.

SIGNED ______

PATIENT AND INSURED INFORMATION

14. DATE OF CURRENT: MM | DD | YY ◄ ILLNESS (First symptom) OR INJURY (Accident) OR PREGNANCY (LMP)

15. IF PATIENT HAS HAD SAME OR SIMILAR ILLNESS GIVE FIRST DATE MM | DD | YY

16. DATES PATIENT UNABLE TO WORK IN CURRENT OCCUPATION FROM MM | DD | YY TO MM | DD | YY

17. NAME OF REFERRING PHYSICIAN OR OTHER SOURCE

17a. I.D. NUMBER OF REFERRING PHYSICIAN

18. HOSPITALIZATION DATES RELATED TO CURRENT SERVICES FROM MM | DD | YY TO MM | DD | YY

19. RESERVED FOR LOCAL USE

20. OUTSIDE LAB? ☐ YES ☐ NO $ CHARGES

21. DIAGNOSIS OR NATURE OF ILLNESS OR INJURY. (RELATE ITEMS 1,2,3 OR 4 TO ITEM 24E BY LINE)

1. ______ 3. ______

2. ______ 4. ______

22. MEDICAID RESUBMISSION CODE | ORIGINAL REF. NO.

23. PRIOR AUTHORIZATION NUMBER

24. A DATE(S) OF SERVICE From MM DD YY To MM DD YY	B Place of Service	C Type of Service	D PROCEDURES, SERVICES, OR SUPPLIES (Explain Unusual Circumstances) CPT/HCPCS | MODIFIER	E DIAGNOSIS CODE	F $ CHARGES	G DAYS OR UNITS	H EPSDT Family Plan	I EMG	J COB	K RESERVED FOR LOCAL USE

25. FEDERAL TAX I.D. NUMBER SSN ☐ EIN ☐

26. PATIENT'S ACCOUNT NO.

27. ACCEPT ASSIGNMENT? (For govt. claims, see back) ☐ YES ☐ NO

28. TOTAL CHARGE $

29. AMOUNT PAID $

30. BALANCE DUE $

31. SIGNATURE OF PHYSICIAN OR SUPPLIER INCLUDING DEGREES OR CREDENTIALS (I certify that the statements on the reverse apply to this bill and are made a part thereof.)

SIGNED ______ DATE ______

32. NAME AND ADDRESS OF FACILITY WHERE SERVICES WERE RENDERED (if other than home or office)

33. PHYSICIAN'S, SUPPLIER'S BILLING NAME, ADDRESS, ZIP CODE AND PHONE #

PIN# | GRP#

PHYSICIAN OR SUPPLIER INFORMATION

(APPROVED BY AMA COUNCIL ON MEDICAL SERVICE8/88)

PLEASE PRINT OR TYPE

FORM HCFA-1500 (U2) (12-90)
FORM OCWP-1500 FORM RRB-1500

Figure 14–4

PATIENT RECORD NO. 1402

LAST NAME	FIRST NAME	MIDDLE NAME	BIRTH DATE	SEX	HOME PHONE
Giovanni,	Carlos	A.	10-24-45	M	013-677-3485

ADDRESS	CITY	STATE	ZIP CODE
89 Beaumont Court,	Woodland Hills,	XY	12345

PATIENT'S OCCUPATION	NAME OF COMPANY
TV repairman	Giant Television Co. (tv repair co)

ADDRESS OF EMPLOYER	PHONE
8764 Ocean Avenue, Woodland Hills, XY 12345	013-647-8851

SPOUSE OR PARENT	OCCUPATION
Maria B. Giovanni	homemaker

EMPLOYER	ADDRESS	PHONE

NAME OF INSURANCE	INSURED OR SUBSCRIBER
State Compensation Ins. Fund 600 S. Lafayette Park Pl., Ehrlich, XY 12350	

POLICY NO.	GROUP NO.	EFFECTIVE DATE
57780		

MEDICARE NO.	MEDICAID NO.	EFFECTIVE DATE	SOC. SEC. NO.
			556-48-9699

REFERRED BY: Giant Television Co.

DATE	PROGRESS
11-11-XX	Today at 2 p.m. fell from roof of private home (2231 Duarte St., Woodland Hills, XY 12345 in Woodland Hills county). States "When I was attaching the base of an antenna the weight of the antenna shifted and knocked me off the roof." Pt complains of head pain and indicates brief loss of consciousness. Adm. pt to College Hosp. at 5 p.m. Pt was referred by employer. Dg: X- rays showed fractured skull. Pt also suffered cerebral concussion and R subdural hematoma. No open wound. Astro Parkinson, MD
11-12-XX	Performed R infratentorial craniotomy & removed subdural hematoma. Pt will be seen q.d. TD: Pt will be able to return to work on 1-15-XX. Possible cranial defect & head disfigurement resulting. Pt to be hospitalized for approx 2 wks for further tr. Astro Parkinson, MD
11-13-XX	HV Pt improving; recommend consult with Dr. Graff for cranial defect. Astro Parkinson, MD
11-14-XX	Pt seen in cons by Dr. Cosmo Graff who stated unable to correct PO cranial defect. Astro Parkinson, MD
11-15-XX	through 11-29-XX Daily HV Astro Parkinson, MD
11-30-XX	DC from hosp. Permanant cranial defect resulting from surgery. Complete progress report submitted. Astro Parkinson, MD
12-29-XX	No further trt necessary. PT able to resume reg W on 1-15-XX. Final report submitted. Astro Parkinson, MD

Figure 14–5

DOCTOR'S FIRST REPORT OF OCCUPATIONAL INJURY OR ILLNESS

Within 5 days of initial examination, for every occupational injury or illness, send 2 copies of this report to the employers' workers' compensation insurance carrier or the self-insured employer. Failure to file a timely doctor's report may result in assessment of a civil penalty. In the case of diagnosed or suspected pesticide poisoning, send a copy of this report to Division of Labor Statistics and Research.

1. INSURER NAME AND ADDRESS

2. EMPLOYER NAME Policy No.

3. Address No. and Street City Zip

4. Nature of business(e.g., food manufacturing, building construction, retailer of woman's clothes)

5. PATIENT NAME (first, middle initial, last name) | 6. Sex ☐Male ☐Female | 7. Date of Birth mo. Day Yr.

8. Address No. and Street City Zip | 9. Telephone Number

10. Occupation (Specific job title) | 11. Social Security Number

12. Injured at: No. and Street City County

13. Date and hour of injury or onset or illness Mo. Day Yr. Hour _____a.m____p.m | 14. Date last worked Mo. Day Yr.

15. Date and hour of first examination or treatment Mo. Day Yr. Hour _____a.m____p.m | 16. Have you (or your office) previously treated patient? ☐Yes ☐No

Patient please complete this portion, if able to do so. Otherwise, doctor please complete immediately. Inability or failure of a patient to complete this portion shall not affect his/her rights to workers' compensation under the Labor Code.
17. DESCRIBE HOW THE ACCIDENT OR EXPOSURE HAPPENED (Give specific object, machinery or chemical.)

18. SUBJECTIVE COMPLAINTS (Describe fully.)

19. OBJECTIVE FINDINGS
A. Physical examination

B. X-ray and laboratory results (State if none or pending.)

20. DIAGNOSIS (if occupational illness specify etiologic agent and duration of exposure.) Chemical or toxic compound involved? ICD - 9 Code ☐Yes ☐No

21. Are your findings and diagnosis consistent with patient's account of injury or onset of illness? ☐Yes ☐No If "no" please explain

22. Is there any other current condition that will impede or delay patient's recovery? ☐Yes ☐No If "yes" please explain

23. TREATMENT REQUIRED

24. If further treatment required, specify treatment plan/estimated duration.

25. If hospitalized as inpatient, give hospital name and location Date admitted Mo. Day Yr. Estimated stay

26. WORK STATUS –is patient able to perfom usual work? ☐ Yes ☐ No
If "no," date when patient can return to: Regular work____/____/
Modified work____/____/ Specify restrictions

Doctor's Signature __________ License Number __________
Doctor's Name and Degree __________ IRS Number __________
Address __________ Telephone Number __________

Figure 14–6

3. After the instructor has returned your work to you, either make the necessary corrections and place it in a 3-ring notebook for future reference, or, if you receive a high score, place it in your portfolio for use when applying for a job.

Abbreviations pertinent to this record:

Adm. ______	P & S ______
approx ______	pt ______
cons ______	q.d. ______
DC ______	R ______
Dg ______	reg ______
Hosp. ______	TD ______
HV ______	tr ______
p.m. ______	W ______
PO ______	wks ______

ASSIGNMENT 14–5 ▸ COMPLETE A CLAIM FORM FOR A WORKERS' COMPENSATION CASE

Task: Complete a HCFA-1500 claim form and post transactions to the ledger card.

Conditions: Use the patient's record (Figure 14–5) and ledger card (Figure 14–7), HCFA-1500 claim form (Figure 14–8), typewriter or computer, procedural and diagnostic code books, and *Workbook* Appendix A.

Standards: Claim Productivity Measurement

Time: ______ minutes

Accuracy: ______

(Note: The time element and accuracy criteria may be given by your instructor.)

Directions:

1. Complete a HCFA-1500 claim form for November dates of service using OCR guidelines for this temporary disability type of claim. Note: A progress report is being submitted with this claim. Date the claim November 30 of the current year.
2. Determine the correct five-digit code number and modifiers for each professional service rendered.
3. Post transactions to the ledger card and indicate the proper information when you have billed the workers' compensation insurance company.
4. A Performance Evaluation Checklist may be reproduced from the Instruction Guide to the *Workbook* chapter if your instructor wishes you to submit it to assist with scoring and comments.
5. After the instructor has returned your work to you, either make the necessary corrections and place it in a 3-ring notebook for future reference, or, if you received a high score, place it in your portfolio for reference when applying for a job.

ASSIGNMENT 14–6 ► COMPLETE A CLAIM FORM FOR A WORKERS' COMPENSATION CASE

Task: Complete a HCFA-1500 claim form and post transactions to the ledger card.

Conditions: Use the patient's record (Figure 14–5) and ledger card (Figure 14–7), HCFA-1500 claim form (Figure 14–9), typewriter or computer, procedural and diagnostic code books, and *Workbook* Appendix A.

Standards: Claim Productivity Measurement

Time: ________________ minutes

Accuracy: ________________

(Note: The time element and accuracy criteria may be given by your instructor.)

Directions:

1. Complete a HCFA-1500 claim form for a final medical report using OCR guidelines for this temporary disability type of claim. Date the claim December 29 of the current year.
2. Determine the correct five-digit code number and modifiers for the final medical report.
3. Post transactions to the ledger card and indicate the proper information when you have billed the workers' compensation insurance company.
4. A Performance Evaluation Checklist may be reproduced from the Instruction Guide to the Workbook chapter if your instructor wishes you to submit it to assist with scoring and comments.
5. After the instructor has returned your work to you, either make the necessary corrections and place it in a 3-ring notebook for future reference, or, if you received a high score, place it in your portfolio for reference when applying for a job.

STATEMENT

College Clinic
4567 Broad Avenue
Woodland Hills, XY 12345-0001
Telephone: 013-486-9002
Fax: 013-487-8976

TO: State Compensation Insurance Fund
600 S. Lafayette Park Place
Ehrlich, XY 12350-8900

RE: Inj: Carlos A. Giovanni
Date of Inj: 11-11-xx
Emp: Giant Television Company
Policy No.: 57780

DATE	PROFESSIONAL SERVICE DESCRIPTION	CHARGE	CREDITS		CURRENT BALANCE
			PAYMENTS	ADJUSTMENTS	
11-11-xx	HV hx/exam, HC decision making				
11-12-xx	Craniotomy remove subdural hematoma				
11-13-xx	HV, PF hx/exam, LC decision making				
11-14-xx	HV, PF hx/exam, LC decision making				
11-15 to 11-29-xx	HV, PF hx/exam, LC decision making				
11-30-xx	Hosp discharge				
11-30-xx	Medical Report (Special Report)				
12-29-xx	OC,EPF hx/exam, LC decision making				
12-29-xx	Final medical report (Special Report)				

Due and payable within 10 days. **Pay last amount in balance column** 

Key: PF: Problem-focused
EPF: Expanded problem-focused
D: Detailed
C: Comprehensive
SF: Straightforward
LC: Low complexity
MC: Moderate complexity
HC: High complexity
CON: Consultation
CPX: Complete phys exam
E: Emergency
ER: Emergency dept.
HCD: House call (day)
HCN: House call (night)
HV: Hospital visit
OV: Office visit

Figure 14–7

APPROVED OMB-0938-0008

PLEASE DO NOT STAPLE IN THIS AREA

CARRIER

PICA

HEALTH INSURANCE CLAIM FORM

PICA

1. MEDICARE (Medicare #) MEDICAID (Medicaid #) CHAMPUS (Sponsor's SSN) CHAMPVA (VA File #) GROUP HEALTH PLAN (SSN or ID) FECA BLK LUNG (SSN) OTHER (ID)

1a. INSURED'S I.D. NUMBER (FOR PROGRAM IN ITEM 1)

2. PATIENT'S NAME (Last Name, First Name, Middle Initial)

3. PATIENT'S BIRTH DATE MM | DD | YYYY SEX M F

4. INSURED'S NAME (Last Name, First Name, Middle Initial)

5. PATIENT'S ADDRESS (No., Street)

CITY STATE

ZIP CODE TELEPHONE (Include Area Code)

6. PATIENT RELATIONSHIP TO INSURED Self Spouse Child Other

8. PATIENT STATUS Single Married Other

Employed Full-Time Student Part-Time Student

7. INSURED'S ADDRESS (No., Street)

CITY STATE

ZIP CODE TELEPHONE (include Area Code) ( )

9. OTHER INSURED'S NAME (Last Name, First Name, Middle Initial)

a. OTHER INSURED'S POLICY OR GROUP NUMBER

b. OTHER INSURED'S DATE OF BIRTH MM | DD | YY SEX M F

c. EMPLOYER'S NAME OR SCHOOL NAME

d. INSURANCE PLAN NAME OR PROGRAM NAME

10. IS PATIENT'S CONDITION RELATED TO:

a. EMPLOYMENT? (CURRENT OR PREVIOUS) YES NO

b. AUTO ACCIDENT? YES NO PLACE (State)

c. OTHER ACCIDENT? YES NO

10d. RESERVED FOR LOCAL USE

11. INSURED'S POLICY GROUP OR FECA NUMBER

a. INSURED'S DATE OF BIRTH MM | DD | YY SEX M F

b. EMPLOYER'S NAME OR SCHOOL NAME

c. INSURANCE PLAN NAME OR PROGRAM NAME

d. IS THERE ANOTHER HEALTH BENEFIT PLAN? YES NO *If yes, return to and complete item 9 a-d.*

READ BACK OF FORM BEFORE COMPLETING AND SIGNING THIS FORM.

12. PATIENT'S OR AUTHORIZED PERSON'S SIGNATURE I authorize the release of any medical or other information necessary to process this claim. I also request payment of government benefits either to myself or to the party who accepts assignment below.

SIGNED ______ DATE ______

13. INSURED'S OR AUTHORIZED PERSON'S SIGNATURE I authorize payment of medical benefits to the undersigned physician or supplier for services described below.

SIGNED ______

PATIENT AND INSURED INFORMATION

14. DATE OF CURRENT: MM | DD | YY ◀ ILLNESS (First symptom) OR INJURY (Accident) OR PREGNANCY (LMP)

15. IF PATIENT HAS HAD SAME OR SIMILAR ILLNESS GIVE FIRST DATE MM | DD | YY

16. DATES PATIENT UNABLE TO WORK IN CURRENT OCCUPATION FROM MM | DD | YY TO MM | DD | YY

17. NAME OF REFERRING PHYSICIAN OR OTHER SOURCE

17a. I.D. NUMBER OF REFERRING PHYSICIAN

18. HOSPITALIZATION DATES RELATED TO CURRENT SERVICES FROM MM | DD | YY TO MM | DD | YY

19. RESERVED FOR LOCAL USE

20. OUTSIDE LAB? YES NO $ CHARGES

21. DIAGNOSIS OR NATURE OF ILLNESS OR INJURY. (RELATE ITEMS 1,2,3 OR 4 TO ITEM 24E BY LINE)

1. ______ 3. ______

2. ______ 4. ______

22. MEDICAID RESUBMISSION CODE ORIGINAL REF. NO.

23. PRIOR AUTHORIZATION NUMBER

24. A DATE(S) OF SERVICE From MM DD YY To MM DD YY	B Place of Service	C Type of Service	D PROCEDURES, SERVICES, OR SUPPLIES (Explain Unusual Circumstances) CPT/HCPCS | MODIFIER	E DIAGNOSIS CODE	F $ CHARGES	G DAYS OR UNITS	H EPSDT Family Plan	I EMG	J COB	K RESERVED FOR LOCAL USE

25. FEDERAL TAX I.D. NUMBER SSN EIN

26. PATIENT'S ACCOUNT NO.

27. ACCEPT ASSIGNMENT? (For govt. claims, see back) YES NO

28. TOTAL CHARGE $

29. AMOUNT PAID $

30. BALANCE DUE $

31. SIGNATURE OF PHYSICIAN OR SUPPLIER INCLUDING DEGREES OR CREDENTIALS (I certify that the statements on the reverse apply to this bill and are made a part thereof.)

SIGNED DATE

32. NAME AND ADDRESS OF FACILITY WHERE SERVICES WERE RENDERED (If other than home or office)

33. PHYSICIAN'S, SUPPLIER'S BILLING NAME, ADDRESS, ZIP CODE AND PHONE #

PIN# GRP#

PHYSICIAN OR SUPPLIER INFORMATION

(APPROVED BY AMA COUNCIL ON MEDICAL SERVICE8/88) *PLEASE PRINT OR TYPE* FORM HCFA-1500 (U2) (12-90) FORM OCWP-1500 FORM RRB-1500

Figure 14–8

APPROVED OMB-0938-0008

PLEASE DO NOT STAPLE IN THIS AREA

CARRIER

PICA

HEALTH INSURANCE CLAIM FORM

PICA

1. MEDICARE (Medicare #) MEDICAID (Medicaid #) CHAMPUS (Sponsor's SSN) CHAMPVA (VA File #) GROUP HEALTH PLAN (SSN or ID) FECA BLK LUNG (SSN) OTHER (ID)

1a. INSURED'S I.D. NUMBER (FOR PROGRAM IN ITEM 1)

2. PATIENT'S NAME (Last Name, First Name, Middle Initial)

3. PATIENT'S BIRTH DATE MM DD YYYY SEX M F

4. INSURED'S NAME (Last Name, First Name, Middle Initial)

5. PATIENT'S ADDRESS (No., Street)

6. PATIENT RELATIONSHIP TO INSURED Self Spouse Child Other

7. INSURED'S ADDRESS (No., Street)

CITY STATE

8. PATIENT STATUS Single Married Other

CITY STATE

ZIP CODE TELEPHONE (Include Area Code)

Employed Full-Time Student Part-Time Student

ZIP CODE TELEPHONE (include Area Code) ( )

9. OTHER INSURED'S NAME (Last Name, First Name, Middle Initial)

10. IS PATIENT'S CONDITION RELATED TO:

11. INSURED'S POLICY GROUP OR FECA NUMBER

a. OTHER INSURED'S POLICY OR GROUP NUMBER

a. EMPLOYMENT? (CURRENT OR PREVIOUS) YES NO

a. INSURED'S DATE OF BIRTH MM DD YY SEX M F

b. OTHER INSURED'S DATE OF BIRTH MM DD YY SEX M F

b. AUTO ACCIDENT? PLACE (State) YES NO

b. EMPLOYER'S NAME OR SCHOOL NAME

c. EMPLOYER'S NAME OR SCHOOL NAME

c. OTHER ACCIDENT? YES NO

c. INSURANCE PLAN NAME OR PROGRAM NAME

d. INSURANCE PLAN NAME OR PROGRAM NAME

10d. RESERVED FOR LOCAL USE

d. IS THERE ANOTHER HEALTH BENEFIT PLAN? YES NO *If yes, return to and complete item 9 a-d.*

READ BACK OF FORM BEFORE COMPLETING AND SIGNING THIS FORM.

12. PATIENT'S OR AUTHORIZED PERSON'S SIGNATURE I authorize the release of any medical or other information necessary to process this claim. I also request payment of government benefits either to myself or to the party who accepts assignment below.

SIGNED ______ DATE ______

13. INSURED'S OR AUTHORIZED PERSON'S SIGNATURE I authorize payment of medical benefits to the undersigned physician or supplier for services described below.

SIGNED ______

PATIENT AND INSURED INFORMATION

14. DATE OF CURRENT: MM DD YY ILLNESS (First symptom) OR INJURY (Accident) OR PREGNANCY (LMP)

15. IF PATIENT HAS HAD SAME OR SIMILAR ILLNESS GIVE FIRST DATE MM DD YY

16. DATES PATIENT UNABLE TO WORK IN CURRENT OCCUPATION FROM MM DD YY TO MM DD YY

17. NAME OF REFERRING PHYSICIAN OR OTHER SOURCE

17a. I.D. NUMBER OF REFERRING PHYSICIAN

18. HOSPITALIZATION DATES RELATED TO CURRENT SERVICES FROM MM DD YY TO MM DD YY

19. RESERVED FOR LOCAL USE

20. OUTSIDE LAB? YES NO $ CHARGES

21. DIAGNOSIS OR NATURE OF ILLNESS OR INJURY. (RELATE ITEMS 1,2,3 OR 4 TO ITEM 24E BY LINE)

1. ______ 3. ______

2. ______ 4. ______

22. MEDICAID RESUBMISSION CODE ORIGINAL REF. NO.

23. PRIOR AUTHORIZATION NUMBER

24. A DATE(S) OF SERVICE From MM DD YY	To MM DD YY	B Place of Service	C Type of Service	D PROCEDURES, SERVICES, OR SUPPLIES (Explain Unusual Circumstances) CPT/HCPCS MODIFIER	E DIAGNOSIS CODE	F $ CHARGES	G DAYS OR UNITS	H EPSDT Family Plan	I EMG	J COB	K RESERVED FOR LOCAL USE

25. FEDERAL TAX I.D. NUMBER SSN EIN

26. PATIENT'S ACCOUNT NO.

27. ACCEPT ASSIGNMENT? (For govt. claims, see back) YES NO

28. TOTAL CHARGE $

29. AMOUNT PAID $

30. BALANCE DUE $

31. SIGNATURE OF PHYSICIAN OR SUPPLIER INCLUDING DEGREES OR CREDENTIALS (I certify that the statements on the reverse apply to this bill and are made a part thereof.)

SIGNED DATE

32. NAME AND ADDRESS OF FACILITY WHERE SERVICES WERE RENDERED (if other than home or office)

33. PHYSICIAN'S, SUPPLIER'S BILLING NAME, ADDRESS, ZIP CODE AND PHONE #

PIN# GRP#

PHYSICIAN OR SUPPLIER INFORMATION

(APPROVED BY AMA COUNCIL ON MEDICAL SERVICE8/88) *PLEASE PRINT OR TYPE* FORM HCFA-1500 (U2) (12-90) FORM OCWP-1500 FORM RRB-1500

Figure 14–9

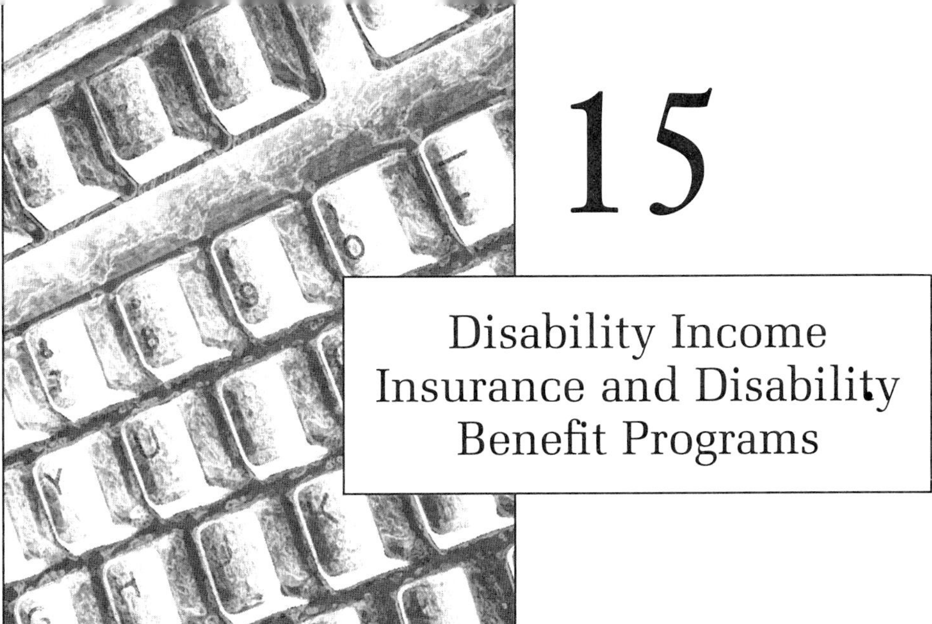

15

Disability Income Insurance and Disability Benefit Programs

KEY TERMS

Your instructor may wish to select some specific words pertinent to this chapter for a test. For definitions of the terms, further study, and/or reference, the words, phrases, and abbreviations may be found in the Glossary at the end of the Handbook. *Some of the insurance terms presented in this chapter are shown marked with an asterisk and may seem familiar from previous chapters. However, their meanings may or may not have a slightly different connotation when referring to disability income insurance. Key terms for this chapter follow:*

accidental death and dismemberment
Armed Services Disability
benefit period*
Civil Service Retirement System (CSRS)
consultative examiner (CE)
cost-of-living adjustment
Disability Determination Services (DDS)
disability income insurance
double indemnity
exclusions*
Federal Employees Retirement System (FERS)
future purchase option
guaranteed renewable*
hearing
long-term disability insurance
noncancelable clause*
partial disability*
reconsideration
regional office (RO)
residual benefits*
short-term disability income insurance
Social Security Administration (SSA)
Social Security Disability Insurance (SSDI) program
State Disability Insurance (SDI)
supplemental benefits
temporary disability*
temporary disability insurance (TDI)
total disability*
unemployment compensation disability (UCD)
Veterans Affairs (VA) disability program
Veterans Affairs (VA) outpatient clinics
voluntary disability insurance
waiting period*
waiver of premium*

PERFORMANCE OBJECTIVES

The student will be able to

- Define and spell the key terms for this chapter, given the information from the *Handbook* Glossary, within a reasonable period of time and with enough accuracy to obtain a satisfactory revaluation.
- Answer the self-study review questions after reading the chapter, with enough accuracy to obtain a satisfactory evaluation.
- Fill in the correct meaning of each abbreviation, given a list of common medical abbreviations and symbols that appear in chart notes, within a reasonable period of time and with enough accuracy to obtain a satisfactory evaluation.
- Complete each state disability form, given the patients' medical chart notes and blank state disability forms, within a reasonable period of time and with enough accuracy to obtain a satisfactory evaluation.

STUDY OUTLINE

Disability Claims
History
Disability Income Insurance
- Individual
  - Waiting Period
  - Benefit Period
  - Benefits
  - Types of Disability
  - Clauses
  - Exclusions
  - AIDS and HIV
- Group
  - Benefits
  - Exclusions

Federal Disability Programs
- Workers' Compensation
- Disability Benefit Programs
  - Social Security Disability Insurance Program
  - Supplemental Security Income
  - Civil Service and Federal Employees Retirement System Disability
  - Armed Services Disability
  - Veterans' Affairs Disability

State Disability Insurance
- Background
- State Programs
- Funding
- Eligibility
- Benefits
  - Limited Benefits
  - Reduced Benefits
- Time Limits
- Medical Examinations
- Restrictions

Voluntary Disability Insurance
Procedure: Claims Submission
- Disability Income Claims
- Federal Disability Claims
- Veterans' Affairs Disability Outpatient Clinic Claims
- State Disability Claims

SELF-STUDY **15–1** ▶ **REVIEW QUESTIONS**

Review the objectives, key terms, glossary definitions to key terms, chapter information, tables, and figures before completing the following review questions.

1. Health insurance that provides monthly or weekly income when an individual is unable to work because of a nonindustrial illness or injury is called Disability income insurance.
2. Another insurance term for *benefits* is indemnity.
3. Some insurance contracts that pay twice the face amount of the policy if accidental death occurs may have a provision entitled Double indemnity.
4. When an individual who is insured under a disability income insurance policy cannot perform *one or more* of his or her regular job duties, this is known as residual or partial disability.
5. When a person insured under a disability income insurance policy cannot perform *all functions* of his or her regular job duties for a limited period of time, this is known as temporary disability.
6. When investigating the purchase of insurance, the word(s) to look for in the insurance contract that mean the premium cannot be increased at renewal time is/are noncancelable clause.
7. When an individual becomes permanently disabled and cannot pay the insurance premium, a desirable provision in an insurance contract is waiver of premium.
8. Provisions that limit the scope of insurance coverage are known as exclusions.

9. Ezra Jackson has disability income insurance under a group policy paid for by his employer. One evening he goes roller blading and suffers a complex fracture of the patella requiring several months off work. Are his monthly disability benefits taxable?

Yes Why? Because he has not made any contribution toward the premiums

10. Two federal programs for individuals under 65 years of age who suffer from a severe disability are:

a. Social Security Disability Insurance (SSDI)

b. Supplemental Security Income (SSI)

11. To be eligible to apply for disability benefits under Social Security, an individual must be unable to do any type of work for a period of not less than 12 months.

12. Social Security may hire a physician to evaluate an applicant's disability. A physician's role may be any one of the following:

a. physician treating the patient

b. consultative examiner (CE)

c. Full- or part-time medical or psychologic consultant

13. A Social Security division that determines an individual's eligibility to be placed under the federal disability program is called Disability Determination Services.

14. Jamie Woods, a Navy petty officer, suffers an accident aboard the USS *Denebola* just before his honorable discharge. To receive veteran's benefits for this injury, the time limit in which a claim must be filed is within 1 year from date of sustaining the injury.

15. Name the states and territory that have nonindustrial state disability programs.

a. california

b. Hawaii

c. New Jersey

d. New York

e. Puerto Rico

f. Rhode Island

16. List two states where hospital benefits may be paid for nonoccupational illness or injury under a state's temporary disability benefit program.

a. Hawaii under a prepaid Health Care program

b. Puerto Rico under a prepaid Health care program

17. Temporary disability insurance claims must be filed within how many days in your state?

18. How long can a person continue to draw temporary disability insurance benefits?

19. After a claim begins, when do basic state disability benefits become payable if the patient is confined at home? on the eighth day of consecutive disability or the first day of hospital confinement In california, if disability extends 22 days or beyond, benefits are paid from the first day of disability.

If the patient is hospitalized? First day of hospital confinement only in Hawaii and Puerto Rico

20. Nick Tyson has recovered from a previous temporary disability and becomes ill again with the same ailment. Is he entitled to state disability benefits? yes if 15 days have elapsed.

21. John S. Thatcher stubbed his toe as he was leaving work. Since the injury was only slightly uncomfortable, he thought no more about it. The next morning he found that his foot was too swollen to fit in his shoe, so he stayed home. When the swelling did not subside after 3 days, John went to the doctor. X-rays showed a broken toe, which kept John home for 2 weeks. After 1 week he applied for temporary state disability benefits. Will he be paid? yes Why? Benefits become payable on the eighth day of consecutive disability (This also may depend on whether the injury is declared a work-related or industrial injury and whether the rate of worker's compensation is less than state disability benefits

22. Peggy Jonson has an ectopic pregnancy and is unable to work because of this complication of her pregnancy. Can she receive state temporary disability benefits?

yes

23. If a woman has an abnormal condition that arises out of her pregnancy (such as diabetes or varicose veins) and is unable to work because of the condition, can she receive state disability benefits? yes

Four states that allow for maternity benefits in normal pregnancy are:

a. California c. New Jersey

b. Hawaii d. Rhode Island

24. Betty T. Kraft had to stay home from her job because her 10-year-old daughter had measles. She applied for temporary state disability benefits. Will she be paid?

NO Why? Betty must be ill or injured to collect benefits

25. Vincent P. Michael was ill with a bad cold for 1 week. Will he receive temporary state disability benefits?

NO Why? He must be ill more than 1 week to collect state disability.

26. Betsy C. Palm had an emergency appendectomy and was hospitalized for 3 days. Will she receive state disability benefits?

yes Why? Because payment begins on the first day of hospital confinement

27. Frank E. Thompson is a box boy at a supermarket on Saturdays and Sundays while a full-time student at college. He broke his leg while skiing so he cannot work at the market, but he is able to attend classes with his leg in a cast. Can he collect state disability benefits for his part-time job?

yes Why? As long as he has met the quarterly amount that is required to be put into the fund in the state, he is eligible

28. Jerry L. Slate is out of a job and is receiving unemployment insurance benefits. He is now suffering from a severe case of intestinal flu. The employment office calls him to interview for a job, but he is too ill to go. Can he collect temporary state disability benefits for this illness when he might have been given a job?

Yes Why? Because at the time he gets the flu he can go on state disability as he is not able to go for a job interview

29. Joan T. Corman has diabetes, which sometimes makes her weak so that she has to leave work early in the afternoon. She loses pay for each hour she cannot work. Can she collect temporary state disability benefits?

No Why? Because she has not been off work continuously for 7 days.

30. While walking the picket line with other employees on strike, Gene J. Berry came down with pneumonia and was ill for 2 weeks. Can he collect temporary state disability benefits?

Yes Why? Because he might have become ill whether the strike was on or not.

Gene went back to work for 3 weeks and then developed a slight cold and cough, which again was diagnosed as pneumonia. The doctor told him to stay home from work. Would he be able to collect temporary disability benefits again?

Yes Why? Because more than 15 days have elapsed since his return to work and the recurrence of the illness.

31. A month after he retired, Roger Reagan had a gallbladder operation. Can he receive temporary state disability benefits?

NO Why? Because he is retired and has no state disability insurance

32. Jane M. Lambert fell in the backyard of her home and fractured her left ankle. She had a nonunion fracture and was out of work for 28 weeks. For how long will she collect temporary state disability benefits? ______

33. Dr. Kay examines Ben Yates and completes a claim form for state disability income due to a prolonged illness. On receiving the information, the insurance adjuster notices some conflicting data. Name other documents that may be requested to justify payment of benefits.

a. Employer's records

b. employee's wage statements and or tax forms

c. medical records of attending physician

34. Trent Walters, a permanently disabled individual, applies for federal disability benefits. To establish eligibility for benefits under this program, data allowed must be no more than 1 year(s) old.

35. A Veterans' Affairs patient is seen as an emergency by Dr. Onion. Name the two methods or options for billing this case.

a. physician may bill VA outpatient clinic

b. patient may pay physician and get reimbursed by the VA by following the instructions on the VA outpatient clinic card

36. When submitting a claim form for a patient applying for state disability benefits, the most important item required on the form is claimant's social Security number.

To check yours answers to this self-study assignment, see Appendix D.

ASSIGNMENT 15–2 ▶ COMPLETE TWO STATE DISABILITY INSURANCE FORMS

Task: Complete two state disability insurance forms and define patient record abbreviations.

Conditions: Use the patient's record (Figure 15–1), Claim Statement of Employee form (Figure 15–2), Doctor's Certificate form (Figure 15–3), and typewriter or computer.

Standards: Time: ______________ minutes

Accuracy: ______________

(Note: The time element and accuracy criteria may be given by your instructor.)

Directions:

1. To familiarize you with what information the employee must furnish, this assignment will encompass completing both the *Claim Statement of Employee* (Figure 15–2) and the *Doctor's Certificate* (Figure 15–3). Mr. Broussard (see Figure 15–1) is applying for state disability benefits, and he does not receive sick leave pay from his employer. Date the Claim Statement of Employee November 5, and date the Doctor's Certificate November 10. Remember that this is not a claim for payment to the physician, so no ledger card has been furnished for this patient.
2. After the instructor has returned your work to you, either make the necessary corrections and place it in a 3-ring notebook for future reference, or, if you received a high score, place it in your portfolio for reference when applying for a job.

Abbreviations pertinent to this record:

c/o ______________

exam ______________

hosp ______________

imp ______________

LBP ______________

lt ______________

MRI ______________

NP ______________

pt ______________

retn ______________

rt ______________

RTO ______________

SLR ______________

STAT ______________

wk ______________

WNL ______________

PATIENT RECORD NO. 1501

LAST NAME	FIRST NAME	MIDDLE NAME	BIRTH DATE	SEX	HOME PHONE
Broussard,	Jeff	L.	03-09-52	M	013-466-2490

ADDRESS	CITY	STATE	ZIP CODE
3577 Plain Street,	Woodland Hills,	XY	12345

PATIENT'S OCCUPATION: carpenter Payroll #2156
NAME OF COMPANY: Ace Construction Company

ADDRESS OF EMPLOYER: 4556 West Eighth Street, Dorland, XY 12347
PHONE: 013-447-8900

SPOUSE OR PARENT: Harriet M. Broussard
OCCUPATION: secretary

EMPLOYER: Merit Acounting Company
ADDRESS: 6743 Main Street, Woodland Hills, XY 12345
PHONE: 013-478-0980

NAME OF INSURANCE: Blue Cross
INSURED OR SUBSCRIBER: Jeff L. Broussard

POLICY NO.	GROUP NO.	EFFECTIVE DATE
466-23-9979	6131	1-1-80

MEDICARE NO.	MEDICAID NO.	EFFECTIVE DATE	SOC. SEC. NO.
			566-12-0090

REFERRED BY: Harold B. Hartburn (friend)

DATE	PROGRESS
10-21-XX	8:30 a.m. NP seen c/o ongoing LBP. On 8-15-XX after swinging a golf club, pt had
	sudden onset of severe pain in low back with radiation to lt side. Pt unable to work 8-16
	but resumed wk on 8-17 and has been working full time but doing no lifting while
	working. Pain is exacerbating affecting his work and reg duties. Exam showed SLR
	strongly positive on lt, on rt causes pain into lt side. Neurological exam WNL. Ordered
	STAT MRI. Off work. RTO. *Raymond Skeleton, MD*
10-23-XX	Pt returns for test results. MRI showed huge defect L4-5 on lt. Imp: acute herniated disc
	L4-5 on lt. Recommend laminotomy and discectomy L4-5. *Raymond Skeleton, MD*
11-1-XX	Admit to College Hospital. Operation: Lumbar laminotomy with exploration and
	decompression of spinal cord without diskectomy L4-5; lumbar anterior arthrodesis. Pt
	seen daily in hosp. *Raymond Skeleton, MD*
11-5-XX	At 3 p.m. pt discharged to home. Will retn to wk 12-15-XX. *Raymond Skeleton, MD*

Figure 15–1

CLAIM STATEMENT OF EMPLOYEE

COMPLETE ALL ITEMS. IF INCOMPLETE, THIS FORM WILL BE RETURNED, CAUSING A DELAY IN BENEFIT PAYMENTS

Do you need assistance in a language other than English? ☐ **No** ☐ **Yes** **If yes, write language here.**

¿Prefiere Ud. formularios escritos en Español? ☐ **No** ☐ **Sí**

1. Print your full name: FIRST INITIAL LAST

Other Names (including maiden, married and ethnic surnames) Used:

Your Mailing Address:
STREET ADDRESS, P.O. BOX OR RFD APT. NO. CITY OR TOWN STATE AND ZIP CODE

Your Home Address: (if different from mailing address)
STREET ADDRESS, OR SPECIFIC DIRECTIONS TO YOUR HOME IF P.O. BOX OR RFD.

2. **IMPORTANT: Enter your Social Security Account Number**

2A. If you have used another Social Security number, enter that number here.

3. What was the first day you were too sick to perform all the duties of your regular or customary work, even if it was a Saturday, Sunday, holiday or normal day off?

MONTH ☐ DAY ☐ YEAR ☐

MALE ☐ FEMALE ☐

Birthdate: Mo. Day Yr.

4. What was the last day you worked?

MONTH ☐ DAY ☐ YEAR ☐

5. Employer's Business Name: Telephone Number ( )
Employer's Business Address: NUMBER AND STREET CITY STATE AND ZIP CODE

6. Your occupation with this employer: Your Badge or Payroll number:

7. What is your usual occupation?

8. Are you self-employed? Yes ☐ No ☐

9. Did you lose any time from work because of this illness or injury during the two weeks before the last day you worked as shown in item (4) above? Yes ☐ No ☐

10. Did you stop work because of sickness, injury or pregnancy? If "No," please give reason: Yes ☐ No ☐

11. Have you filed for or received UNEMPLOYMENT INSURANCE benefits between the last day you worked and the first day you became disabled? Yes ☐ No ☐

12. a. Has, or will your employer continue your pay by means of sick leave, vacation, pension, gift or other means? Yes ☐ No ☐
    b. Do you authorize the Employment Development Department to disclose benefit eligibility information to your employer to be used only for the purpose of integrating your employer's wage continuation/ sick leave program with your benefits? (This information is limited to the claim effective date; the weekly and maximum benefit amounts; and the periods covered by benefit payments.) Yes ☐ No ☐

13. Was this disability or any other disability during this claim period caused by your work? If "Yes," please provide the name and address of any insurance carrier from whom you are claiming or receiving Workers' Compensation Benefits: Yes ☐ No ☐

14. Have you recovered from your disability? If "Yes," enter date of recovery: Yes ☐ No ☐

15. Have you returned to work for any day, part-time or full-time after the beginning date of your disability as shown in item (3) above? If "Yes," please enter such dates: Yes ☐ No ☐

16. Were you, as a result of an arrest, confined to a jail, detention center, prison, medical center or other correctional institution or any other place at any time during your disability? If "Yes," give dates: Yes ☐ No ☐

I hereby claim benefits and certify that for the period covered by this claim I was unemployed and disabled, that the foregoing statements including any accompanying statements are to the best of my knowledge and belief true, correct and complete. I hereby authorize my attending physician, practitioner, hospital and employer to furnish and disclose all facts concerning my disability and wages or earnings that are within their knowledge and to allow inspection of and provide copies of any hospital records concerning my disability that are under their control. I understand that authorizations contained in this claim statement are granted for a period of 18 months from the date of my signature or the effective date of the claim, whichever is later. I agree that a photocopy of this release shall be as valid as the original.

Claim signed on: MONTH DAY YEAR | Claimant's signature: (DO NOT PRINT) | Telephone Number ( )

Under Section 2101 of the California Unemployment Insurance Code, it is a violation to willfully make a false statement or knowingly conceal a material fact in order to obtain the payment of any benefits, such violation being punishable by imprisonment and/or a fine not exceeding $20,000 or both.

If your signature is made by mark (X) it must be attested by two witnesses with their addresses.

SIGNATURE-WITNESS	SIGNATURE-WITNESS
ADDRESS	ADDRESS

If an authorized agent is filing for benefits for an INCAPACITATED or DECEASED claimant, or a spouse is filing for a MENTALLY INCAPACITATED individual, contact the office below for the required forms and instructions.

Figure 15–2

DOCTOR'S CERTIFICATE

Certification may be made by a licensed medical or osteopathic physician and surgeon, chiropractor, dentist, optometrist, designated psychologist or an authorized medical officer of a United States Government facility. Certification may also be made by a licensed nurse-midwife or nurse practitioner for the purposes of disability related to normal pregnancy or childbirth. All items on this sheet must be completed legibly.

Patient File No.	Name	Social Security Number

17. I attended the patient for the present medical problem from: MONTH DAY YEAR To MONTH DAY YEAR At intervals of:

18. Are you completing this form for the sole purpose of referral or recommendation to an alcoholic recovery home or drug-free residential facility? Yes ☐ No ☐ If yes, please enter facility name and address in item #28.

19. History:

Diagnosis:

Findings (state nature, severity and bodily extent of the incapacitating disease or injury):

ICD Disease Code, Primary: (REQUIRED)

ICD Disease Code, Secondary:

Type of treatment and/or medication rendered to patient:

20. Diagnosis confirmed by: **(Specify type of test or X-ray)**

21. Is this patient now pregnant or has she been pregnant since the date of treatment as reported above? Yes ☐ No ☐
Is the pregnancy normal? Yes ☐ No ☐
If "Yes," date pregnancy terminated or future EDC.
If "No," state the abnormal and involuntary complication causing maternal disability.

22. Operation: Date performed or to be performed ☐ Type of Operation: ICD Procedure Code: (REQUIRED)

23. Has the patient at any time during your attendance for this medical problem, been incapable or performing his or her regular work? Yes ☐ No ☐ If "Yes" the disability commenced on:

24. APPROXIMATE date, based on your examination of patient, disability (if any) should end or has ended sufficiently to permit the patient to resume regular or customary work. Even if considerable question exists, make SOME "estimate." This is a requirement of the Code, and the claim will be delayed if such date is not entered. Such answers as "Indefinite" or "don't know" will not suffice. (ENTER DATE) ☐

25. Based on your examination of patient, is this disability the result of "occupation" either as an "industrial accident" or as an "occupational disease"?
Yes ☐ No ☐ (This should include aggravation of pre-existing condiitons by occupation.)

26. Have you reported this OR A CONCURRENT DISABILITY to any insurance carrier as a Workers' Compensation claim?
Yes ☐ No ☐ If "Yes,"to whom? (Name of carrier or firm)

27. Was patient in a hospital surgical unit, surgical unit, ambulatory surgical center certified to participate in the federal Medicare program or a postsurgical recovery care unit as designated by section 1250.9 of the Health and Safety Code? Yes ☐ No ☐
If "Yes," please provide name and address:

28. Was or is patient in an alcoholic recovery home or drug-free residential facility? Yes ☐ No ☐
If "Yes," please provide name and address:

29. Was or is patient confined as a registered bed patient in a hospital? Yes ☐ No ☐
If "Yes," please provide name and address:

Date and hour entered as a registered bed patient and discharged pursuant to your orders:

ENTERED	STILL CONFINED	DISCHARGED
on , 20XX , at A.M. P.M.	on , 20XX	on , 20XX , at A.M. P.M.

30. Would the disclosure of this information to your patient be medically or psychologically detrimental to the patient?
Yes ☐ No ☐

I hereby certify that, based on my examination, the above statements truly describes the patient's disability (if any) and the estimated duration thereof, and that I am a ____________ (TYPE OF DOCTOR) licensed to practice by the State of ____________

▶ PRINT OR TYPE DOCTOR'S NAME AS SHOWN ON LICENSE

▶ SIGNATURE OF ATTENDING DOCTOR

▶ NO. AND STREET CITY ZIP CODE

▶ STATE LICENSE NUMBER ( ) TELEPHONE NUMBER DATE OF SIGNING THIS FORM

"Under Section 2116 of the California Unemployment Insurance Code, it is a violation for any individual who, with the intent to defraud, falsely certifies the medical condition of any person in order to obtain disability insurance benefits, whether for the maker or for any other person, and is punishable by imprisonment and/or a fine not exceeding twenty thousand dollars.

Figure 15–3

ASSIGNMENT 15–3 ▶ COMPLETE TWO STATE DISABILITY INSURANCE FORMS

Task: Complete two state disability insurance forms and define patient record abbreviations..

Conditions: Use the patient's record (Figure 15–4), Doctor's Certificate form (Figure 15–5), First Claim Form (Figure 15–6), and typewriter or computer.

Standards: Time: ______________ minutes

Accuracy: ______________

(Note: The time element and accuracy criteria may be given by your instructor.)

Directions:

1. Let us assume that the Claim Statement of Employee has been completed satisfactorily by Mr. Fred E. Thorndike (Figure 15–4). Complete the *Doctor's Certificate* portion of the First Claim Form (Figure 15–5), and date it December 2. In completing this portion of the assignment, look at the first entry made by Dr. Practon on November 25 only.
2. Mr. Thorndike returns to see Dr. Practon on December 7, at which time his disability leave needs to be extended. Complete the *Physician's Supplementary Certificate* (Figure 15–6) by referring to the entry made during the second visit, and date the Certificate December 7. Remember that this is not a claim for payment to the physician, so no ledger card has been furnished for this patient.
3. After the instructor has returned your work to you, either make the necessary corrections and place it in a 3-ring notebook for future reference, or, if you received a high score, place it in your portfolio for reference when applying for a job.

Abbreviations pertinent to this record:

CXR ______________________

Dx ______________________

est pt ______________________

F/U ______________________

PE ______________________

Pt ______________________

Reg ______________________

RTO ______________________

SD ______________________

slt ______________________

wk ______________________

wks ______________________

PATIENT RECORD NO. 1502

LAST NAME	FIRST NAME	MIDDLE NAME	BIRTH DATE	SEX	HOME PHONE
Thorndike,	Fred	E.	02-17-44	M	013-465-7820

ADDRESS	CITY	STATE	ZIP CODE
5784 Helen Street,	Woodland Hills,	XY	12345

PATIENT'S OCCUPATION: salesman Payroll No. 6852
NAME OF COMPANY: Easy On Paint Company

ADDRESS OF EMPLOYER: 4586 West 20th Street, Woodland Hills, XY 12345
PHONE: 013-467-8898

SPOUSE OR PARENT: Jennifer B. Thorndike
OCCUPATION: homemaker

EMPLOYER: ADDRESS: PHONE:

NAME OF INSURANCE: Pacific Mutual Insurance Co.
INSURED OR SUBSCRIBER: Fred E. Thorndike

POLICY NO.: 120 South Main Street, Merck, XY 12346
GROUP NO.: 6709
EFFECTIVE DATE: 1-9-90

MEDICARE NO.: MEDICAID NO.: EFFECTIVE DATE: SOC. SEC. NO.: 549-23-8721

REFERRED BY: John Diehl (friend)

DATE	PROGRESS
11-25-XX	On or about 11-3-xx, pt began to have chest pain and much coughing. On 11-24-xx,
	pt too ill to work and decided to file for SDI benefits. Pt states illness is not work
	connected and he does not receive sick pay. PE: Pt examined and complained of productive
	cough of 3 wks duration and chest pain. Chest x-rays confirmed dx-mucopurulent
	chronic bronchitis. Cont home rest and prescribed antibiotic medication. RTO 12-7-xx.
	Pt will be capable of returning to wk 12-8-xx. Gerald Practon, MD
12-7-XX	Est pt returns for F/U c̄ bronchitis. Chest pain improved. Still running low grade temp
	c̄ productive cough. F/U CXR shows clearing. Recommended bed rest x 7d. Will
	extend disability to 12-15-xx at which time pt time can resume reg work. No complications
	anticipated. Gerald Practon, MD

Figure 15–4

DOCTOR'S CERTIFICATE

Certification may be made by a licensed medical or osteopathic physician and surgeon, chiropractor, dentist, optometrist, designated psychologist or an authorized medical officer of a United States Government facility. Certification may also be made by a licensed nurse-midwife or nurse practitioner for the purposes of disability related to normal pregnancy or childbirth. All items on this sheet must be completed legibly.

Patient File No.	Name	Social Security Number

17. I attended the patient for the present medical problem from: MONTH DAY YEAR To MONTH DAY YEAR At intervals of:

18. Are you completing this form for the sole purpose of referral or recommendation to an alcoholic recovery home or drug-free residential facility? Yes☐ No☐ If yes, please enter facility name and address in item #28.

19. History: Findings (state nature, severity and bodily extent of the incapacitating disease or injury):

Diagnosis:

ICD Disease Code, Primary: (REQUIRED) ICD Disease Code, Secondary:

Type of treatment and/or medication rendered to patient:

20. Diagnosis confirmed by: **(Specify type of test or X-ray)**

21. Is this patient now pregnant or has she been pregnant since the date of treatment as reported above? Yes☐ No☐ Is the pregnancy normal? Yes☐ No☐ If "Yes," date pregnancy terminated or future EDC. If "No," state the abnormal and involuntary complication causing maternal disability:

22. Operation: Date performed or to be performed ☐ Type of Operation: ICD Procedure Code: (REQUIRED)

23. Has the patient at any time during your attendance for this medical problem, been incapable of performing his or her regular work? Yes☐ No☐ If "Yes" the disability commenced on:

24. APPROXIMATE date, based on your examination of patient, disability (if any) should end or has ended sufficiently to permit the patient to resume regular or customary work. Even if considerable question exists, make SOME "estimate." This is a requirement of the Code, and the claim will be delayed if such date is not entered. Such answers as "Indefinite" or "don't know" will not suffice. (ENTER DATE) ☐

25. Based on your examination of patient, is this disability the result of "occupation" either as an "industrial accident" or as an "occuaptional disease"?
Yes☐ No☐ (This should include aggravation of pre-existing conditions by occupation.)

26. Have you reported this OR A CONCURRENT DISABILITY to any insurance carrier as a Workers' Compensation Claim?
Yes☐ No☐ If "Yes," to whom? (Name of carrier or firm)

27. Was patient in a hospital surgical unit, surgical unit, ambulatory surgical center certified to participate in the federal Medicare program or a postsurgical recovery care unit as designated by section 1250.9 of the Health and Safety Code? Yes☐ No☐
If "Yes," please provide name and address:

28. Was or is patient a resident in an alcoholic recovery home or drug-free residential facility? Yes☐ No☐
If "Yes," please provide name and address:

29. Was or is patient confined as a registered bed patient in a hospital? Yes☐ No☐
If "Yes," please provide name and address:

Date and hour entered as a registered bed patient and discharged pursuant to your orders:

ENTERED	STILL CONFINED	DISCHARGED
on , 20 , at A.M. P.M.	on , 20	on , 20 , at A.M. P.M.

30. Would the disclosure of this information to your patient be medically or psychologically detrimental to the patient?
Yes☐ No☐

I hereby certify that, based on my examination, the above statements truly descibe the patient's disability (if any) and the estimated duration thereof, and that I am a ______________ (TYPE OF DOCTOR) licensed to practice by the State of ______________

▶ PRINT OR TYPE DOCTOR'S NAME AS SHOWN ON LICENSE ▶ SIGNATURE OF ATTENDING DOCTOR

▶ NO. AND STREET CITY ZIP CODE ▶ STATE LICENSE NUMBER ( ) TELEPHONE NO. DATE OF SIGNING THIS FORM

"Under Section 2116 of the California Unemployment Insurance Code, it is a violation for any individual who, with the intent to defraud, falsely certifies the medical condition of any person in order to obtain disability insurance benefits, whether for the maker or for any other person, and is punishable by imprisonment and/or a fine not exceeding twenty thousand dollars.

Figure 15–5

NOTICE OF FINAL PAYMENT

The information contained in your claim for Disability Insurance indicates that you are now able to work, therefore, this is the final check that you will receive on this claim.

IF YOU ARE ***STILL*** DISABLED: You should complete the Claimant's Certification portion of this form and contact your doctor immediately to have him/her complete the Physician's Supplementary Certificate below.

IF YOU BECOME DISABLED ***AGAIN:*** File a new Disability Insurance claim form.

IF YOU ARE UNEMPLOYED AND AVAILABLE FOR WORK: Report to the nearest Unemployment Insurance office of the Department for assistance in finding work and to determine your entitlement to Unemployment Insurance Benefits.

This determination is final unless you file an appeal within twenty (20) days from the date of the mailing of this notification. You may appeal by giving a detailed statement as to why you believe the determination is in error. All communications regarding this Disability Insurance claim should include your Social Security Account Number and be addressed to the office shown.

CLAIMANT'S CERTIFICATION

I certify that I continue to be disabled and incapable of doing my regular work, and that I have reported all wages, Worker's Compensation benefits and other monies received during the claim period to the Employment Development Department.

ENTER YOUR SOCIAL SECURITY NUMBER 549 23 8721

Sign Your Name ______________ Fred E. Thorndike

Date Signed ______________ December 6, 20XX

PHYSICIAN'S SUPPLEMENTARY CERTIFICATE

Department Use Only	

1. Are you still treating patient? ________ Date of last treatment ______________, 20___.
2. What present condition continues to make the patient disabled?

____

____

____

3. Date patient recovered, or will recover sufficiently (even if under treatment) to be able to perform his/her regular and customary work ______________, 20_____. Please enter a specific or estimated recovery date.
4. Would the disclosure of this information to your patient be medically or psychologically detrimental to the patient?
   Yes ☐ No ☐

I hereby certify that the above statements in my opinion truly describe the claimant's condition and the estimated duration thereof.

Doctor's Signature ______________

______________, 20____
Date

Phone Number ______________

DE 2525XX Rev. 13 (3-86) – Versión en español en el dorso –

Figure 15–6

ASSIGNMENT 15-4 ► COMPLETE A STATE DISABILITY INSURANCE FORM

Task: Complete two state disability insurance forms and define patient record abbreviations.

Conditions: Use the patient's record (Figure 15–7), Doctor's Certificate form (Figure 15–8), and typewriter or computer.

Standards: Time: ________________ minutes

Accuracy: ________________

(Note: The time element and accuracy criteria may be given by your instructor.)

Directions:

1. Assume that the *Claim Statement of Employee* has been completed satisfactorily by Mr. James T. Fujita (Figure 15–7). Complete the *Doctor's Certificate* portion of the First Claim Form (Figure 15–8), and date it December 15. Remember that this is not a claim for payment to the physician, so no ledger card has been furnished for this patient.

2. After the instructor has returned your work to you, either make the necessary corrections and place it in a 3-ring notebook for future reference, or, if you received a high score, place it in your portfolio for reference when applying for a job.

Abbreviations pertinent to this record:

exam ________________________________

hx ________________________________

imp ________________________________

neg ________________________________

pt ________________________________

SD ________________________________

WBC ________________________________

wk ________________________________

PATIENT RECORD NO. 1503

Fujita,	James	T.	03-27-34	M	013-677-2881
LAST NAME	FIRST NAME	MIDDLE NAME	BIRTH DATE	SEX	HOME PHONE

3538 South A Street,	Woodland Hills,	XY	12345
ADDRESS	CITY	STATE	ZIP CODE

electrician Payroll No. 8834 — PATIENT'S OCCUPATION
Macy Electric Company — NAME OF COMPANY

2671 North C Street, Woodland Hills, XY 12345 — ADDRESS OF EMPLOYER
013-677-2346 — PHONE

Mary J. Fujita — SPOUSE OR PARENT
homemaker — OCCUPATION

EMPLOYER ADDRESS PHONE

Atlantic Mutual Insurance Company, 111 South Main Street, Woodland Hills, XY 12345 — NAME OF INSURANCE
James T. Fujita — INSURED OR SUBSCRIBER

F20015		1-3-90
POLICY NO.	GROUP NO.	EFFECTIVE DATE

			567-43-8898
MEDICARE NO.	MEDICAID NO.	EFFECTIVE DATE	SOC. SEC. NO.

REFERRED BY: Cherry Hotta (aunt)

DATE	PROGRESS
12-7-XX	Today pt could not go to work and came for exam complaining of pain in abdomen,
	nausea, and no vomiting. Pt has hx of mesentery adenopathy. Exam neg except abdomen
	showed tenderness all over with voluntary guarding. WBC 10,000. Imp: Mesenteric
	adenitis. Advised strict bed rest at home and bland diet. To return in 1 wk. Will file
	for SDI benefits. Pt states illness is not work connected and he receives sick leave
	pay of $150/wk. Gaston Input, MD
12-15-XX	Exam showed normal nontender abdomen. No nausea. Pt tolerating food well.
	WBC 7,500. Pt will be capable of returning to work 12-22-xx. Gaston Input, MD

Figure 15–7

DOCTOR'S CERTIFICATE

Certification may be made by a licensed medical or osteopathic physician and surgeon, chiropractor, dentist, podiatrist optometrist, designated psychologist or an authorized medical officer of a United States Government facility. Certification may also be made by a licensed nurse-midwife or nurse practitioner for the purposes of disability related to normal pregnancy or childbirth. All items on this sheet must be completed legibly.

Patient File No.	Name	Social Security Number

17. I attended the patient for the present medical problem from: MONTH DAY YEAR To MONTH DAY YEAR At intervals of:

18. Are you completing this form for the sole purpose of referral or recommendation to an alcoholic recovery home or drug-free residential facility? Yes☐ No☐ If yes, please enter facility name and address in item #28.

19. History: | Findings (state nature, severity and bodily extent of the incapacitating disease or injury):

Diagnosis:

ICD Disease Code, Primary: (REQUIRED) | ICD Disease Code, Secondary:

Type of treatment and/or medication rendered to patient:

20. Diagnosis confirmed by: **(Specify type of test or X-ray)**

21. Is this patient now pregnant or has she been pregnant since the date of treatment as reported above? Yes☐ No☐
Is the pregnancy normal? Yes☐ No☐
If "Yes," date pregnancy terminated or future EDC.
If "No," state the abnormal and involuntary complication causing maternal disability:

22. Operation: Date performed or to be performed ☐ | Type of Operation: | ICD Procedure Code: (REQUIRED)

23. Has the patient at any time during your attendance for this medical problem, been incapable of performing his or her regular work? Yes☐ No☐ If "Yes" the disability commenced on:

24. APPROXIMATE date, based on your examination of patient, disability (if any) should end or has ended sufficiently to permit the patient to resume regular or customary work. Even if considerable question exists, make SOME "estimate." This is a requirement of the Code, and the claim will be delayed if such date is not entered. Such answers as "Indefinite" or "don't know" will not suffice. (ENTER DATE) ☐

25. Based on your examination of patient, is this disability the result of "occupation" either as an "industrial accident" or as an "occuaptional disease"?
Yes☐ No☐ (This should include aggravation of pre-existing conditions by occupation.)

26. Have you reported this OR A CONCURRENT DISABILITY to any insurance carrier as a Workers' Compensation Claim?
Yes☐ No☐ If "Yes," to whom? (Name of carrier or firm)

27. Was patient in a hospital surgical unit, surgical unit, ambulatory surgical center certified to participate in the federal Medicare program or a postsurgical recovery care unit as designated by section 1250.9 of the Health and Safety Code? Yes☐ No☐
If "Yes," please provide name and address:

28. Was or is patient a resident in an alcoholic recovery home or drug-free residential facility? Yes☐ No☐
If "Yes," please provide name and address:

29. Was or is patient confined as a registered bed patient in a hospital? Yes☐ No☐
If "Yes," please provide name and address:

Date and hour entered as a registered bed patient and discharged pursuant to your orders:

ENTERED	STILL CONFINED	DISCHARGED
on , 20 , at A.M. P.M.	on , 20	on , 20 , at A.M. P.M.

30. Would the disclosure of this information to your patient be medically or psychologically detrimental to the patient?
Yes☐ No☐

I hereby certify that, based on my examination, the above statements truly descibe the patient's disability (if any) and the estimated duration thereof, and that I am a ______________ (TYPE OF DOCTOR) licensed to practice by the State of ______________

▶ ______________ PRINT OR TYPE DOCTOR'S NAME AS SHOWN ON LICENSE

▶ ______________ SIGNATURE OF ATTENDING DOCTOR

▶ ______________ NO. AND STREET CITY ZIP CODE

▶ ______________ STATE LICENSE NUMBER ( ) TELEPHONE NO. DATE OF SIGNING THIS FORM

"Under Section 2116 of the California Unemployment Insurance Code, it is a violation for any individual who, with the intent to defraud, falsely certifies the medical condition of any person in order to obtain disability insurance benefits, whether for the maker or for any other person, and is punishable by imprisonment and/or a fine not exceeding twenty thousand dollars.

Figure 15–8

ASSIGNMENT 15–5 ▸ COMPLETE A STATE DISABILITY INSURANCE FORM

Task: Complete two state disability insurance forms and define patient record abbreviations.

Conditions: Use the patient's record (Figure 15–9), Doctor's Certificate form (Figure 15–10), Request for Additional Medical Information Form (Figure 15–11), and typewriter or computer.

Standards: Time: ________________ minutes

Accuracy: ________________

(Note: The time element and accuracy criteria may be given by your instructor.)

Directions:

1. Mr. Jake J. Burrows (Figure 15–9) has previously applied for state disability benefits. After 2 months he is referred to another doctor for further care. Complete the form (Figure 15–10) and date it June 25. You will notice that this form is almost identical to the *Doctor's Certificate* and is mailed to the claimant to secure the certification of a new physician or to clarify a specific claimed period of disability. In completing this part of the assignment, look at the first three entries on the patient record only.

2. Complete the *Request for Additional Medical Information Form* (Figure 15–11) by looking at the last entry on Mr. Burrows' record, and date the report July 15. Remember that this is not a claim for payment to the physician, so no ledger card has been furnished for this patient.

3. After the instructor has returned your work to you, either make the necessary corrections and place it in a 3-ring notebook for future reference, or, if you received a high score, place it in your portfolio for reference when applying for a job.

Abbreviations pertinent to this record:

approx ________________

C 5/6 ________________

exam ________________

hosp ________________

imp ________________

Pt ________________

retn ________________

c̄ ________________

PATIENT RECORD NO. 1504

LAST NAME	FIRST NAME	MIDDLE NAME	BIRTH DATE	SEX	HOME PHONE
Burrows,	Jake	J.	04-26-50	M	013-478-9009

ADDRESS	CITY	STATE	ZIP CODE
319 Barry Street,	Woodland Hills,	XY	12345

PATIENT'S OCCUPATION: assembler
NAME OF COMPANY: Convac Electronics Company

ADDRESS OF EMPLOYER: 3440 West 7th Street, Woodland Hills, XY 12345
PHONE: 013/467-9008

SPOUSE OR PARENT: Jane B. Burrows
OCCUPATION: homemaker

EMPLOYER:
ADDRESS:
PHONE:

NAME OF INSURANCE: Blue Shield
INSURED OR SUBSCRIBER: Jake J. Burrows

POLICY NO.: T8471811A
GROUP NO.: 535537AT
EFFECTIVE DATE: 1-1-90

MEDICARE NO.:
MEDICAID NO.:
EFFECTIVE DATE:
SOC. SEC. NO.: 457-99-0801

REFERRED BY: Clarence Butler, MD, 300 Sixth Street, Woodland Hills, XY 12345 NPI#6201143529

DATE	PROGRESS
6-2-XX	Pt. referred by Dr. Butler. Pt states on 4-19-XX was wrestling c̄ son and jerked his neck the wrong way. 2 days later had much pain and muscle spasm in the cervical region. X-rays show degenerated disk C5/6. Exam: Limited range of neck motion and limited abduction both arms. Imp: Degenerated cervical disk C5/6. Pt unable to work as of this date. Myelogram ordered. Return for test results. Raymond Skeleton, MD
6-24-XX	Myelogram positive at C5/6. Scheduled for surgery the following day. Raymond Skeleton, MD
6-25-XX	Pt adm to College Hospital for disk excision and anterior cervical fusion at C5/6. Pt will be discharged from hosp on 6-29-xx. Approx date of retn to work 8-15-xx. Raymond Skeleton, MD
6-26 to 6-29	Pt seen daily in hospital. Discharged 6-29. RTO 2 weeks. Raymond Skeleton, MD
7-15-XX	Pt has some restriction of cervical motion. No muscle spasm. Very little cervical pain. Pt to be seen in 2 wks. To retn to work 8-15-xx. Raymond Skeleton, MD

Figure 15–9

In order that any disability insurance to which you may be entitled may be paid without undue delay, please have the physician who treats or treated you during the period indicated below complete this form and return it to us at his earliest convenience.

Para que cualquier beneficio del Segurdo de Incapacidad a que Ud. pueda tener derecho a recibir sea pagado sin demoras excesivas, haga el favor de hacer que el médicio que le atiende o atiendó, durante el periodo indicado abajo, complete este formulario y que lo regrese a nuestra oficina cuanto antes.

Henry B. Garcia
Disability Insurance Program Representative

6-2 thru 7-25-XX
Period Dates - Feches del Periodo

457-99-0801
S.S.A. – No. Des S.S.

1. I attended the patient for the present medical problem from: Month Day Year To: Month Day Year At intervals of:

2. History:
State the nature, severity and the bodily extent of the incapacitating disease or injury.
Findings:
Dianosis:
Type of treatment and/or medication rendered to patient:

3. Diagnosis confirmed by: (*Specify type of test or X-ray*)

4. Is this patient now pregnant or has she been pregnant since the date of treatment as reported above? Yes☐ No☐ If "Yes", date pregnancy terminated or future EDC:
Is the pregnancy normal? Yes☐ No☐ If "No", state the abnormal and involuntary complication causing maternal disability:

5. Operation: Date performed: ☐ Date to be performed: ☐ Type of Operation:

6. Has the patient at any time during your attendance for this medical problem, been incapable of performing his/her regular work? Yes☐ No☐ If "Yes", the disability commenced on:

7. APPROXIMATE date, based on your examination of patient, disability (if any) should end or has ended sufficiently to permit the patient to resume regular or customary work. Even if considerable question exists, make *SOME* "estimate." This is a requirement of the Code, and the claim will be delayed if such date is not entered. Such answers as "Indefinite" or "don't know" will not suffice. (ENTER DATE) ☐

8. Based on your examination of patient, is this disability the result of "occupation" either as an "industrial accident" or as an "occupational disease?"
(This should include aggravation of pre-existing conditions by occupation.) Yes☐ No☐

9. Have you reported this *OR A CONCURRENT DISABILITY* to any insurance carrier as a Workers' Compensation Claim?
Yes☐ No☐ If "Yes," to whom?

10. Was or is patient confined as a registered bed patient in a hospital? Yes☐ No☐
Was patient treated in the surgical unit of a hospital or surgical unit? Yes☐ No☐
If "Yes," please provide name and address:

11. Date and hour entered as a registered bed patient and discharged pursuant to your orders:

ENTERED	STILL CONFINED	DISCHARGED
on , 20 , at A.M. P.M.	on , 20	on , 20 , at A.M. P.M.

12. Would the disclosure of this information to your patient be medically or psychologically detrimental to the patient?
Yes☐ No☐

I hereby certify that, based on my examination, the above statements truly descibe the patient's disability (if any) and the estimated duration thereof, and that I am a ____________ (TYPE OF DOCTOR) licensed to practice by the State of ____________

PRINT OR TYPE DOCTOR'S NAME AS SHOWN ON LICENSE   SIGNATURE OF ATTENDING DOCTOR

NO. AND STREET   CITY   ZIP CODE   STATE LICENSE NUMBER   ( ) TELEPHONE NUMBER   DATE OF SIGNING THIS FORM

Certification may be made by a licensed physician and surgeon, osteopath, chiropractor, dentist, podiatrist, optometrist, designated psychologist, or an authorized medical officer of a United States Government facility. All items on this sheet must be completed.

Figure 15–10

STATE OF CALIFORNIA
EMPLOYMENT DEVELOPMENT DEPARTMENT

REQUEST FOR ADDITIONAL MEDICAL INFORMATION

457-99-0801 – Our file No,
Jake J. Burrows – Your patient
– Regular or Customary Work

Raymond Skeleton, M.D.
4567 Broad Avenue
Woodland Hills, XY 12345

The original basic information and estimate of duration of your patient's disability have been carefully evaluated. At the present time, the following additional information based upon the progress and present condition of this patient is requested. This will assist the Department in determining eligibilty for further disability insurance benefits. Return of the completed form as soon as possible will be appreciated.

WM. C. SCHMIDT, M.D., MEDICAL DIRECTOR

CLAIMS EXAMINER *DOCTOR: Please complete either part A or B, date and sign.*

PART A IF YOUR PATIENT HAS RECOVERED SUFFICIENTLY TO BE ABLE TO RETURN TO HIS/HER REGULAR OR CUSTOMARY WORK LISTED ABOVE, PLEASE GIVE THE DATE, ______ 20 ____

PART B THIS PART REFERS TO PATIENT WHO IS STILL DISABLED.

Are you still treating the patient? Yes☐ No☐ ______ 20 ____ .
DATE OF LAST TREATMENT

What are the medical circumstances which continue to make your patient disabled?

What is your present estimate of the date your patient will be able to perform his/her regular or customary work listed above? Date ______ 20 ____ .

Further comments:

Would the disclosure of this information to your patient be medically or physically detrimental to the patient? Yes☐ No☐

Date ______ 20 ____ ______
DOCTOR'S SIGNATURE

ENCLOSED IS A STAMPED PREADDRESSED ENVELOPE FOR YOUR CONVENIENCE.

DE 2547 Rev. 17 (4-84)

Figure 15–11

ASSIGNMENT 15–6 ► COMPLETE A STATE DISABILITY INSURANCE FORM

Task: Complete two state disability insurance forms and define patient record abbreviations.

Conditions: Use the patient's record (Figure 15–12), Doctor's Certificate form (Figure 15–13), and typewriter or computer.

Standards: Time: ______________ minutes

Accuracy: ______________

(Note: The time element and accuracy criteria may be given by your instructor.)

Directions:

1. Mr. Vincent P. Michael (Figure 15–12) is applying for state disability benefits. Complete the *Doctor's Certificate* portion of the form (Figure 15–13), and date it September 21. Assume that the *Claim Statement of Employee* has been completed satisfactorily by Mr. Michael. Remember that this is not a claim for payment to the physician, so no ledger card has been furnished for this patient.
2. After the instructor has returned your work to you, either make the necessary corrections and place it in a 3-ring notebook for future reference, or, if you received a high score, place it in your portfolio for reference when applying for a job.

Abbreviations pertinent to this record:

approx ______________________ imp ______________________

CVA ______________________ mm ______________________

ESR ______________________ pt ______________________

hr ______________________ retn ______________________

wk ______________________

PATIENT RECORD NO. 1505

LAST NAME	FIRST NAME	MIDDLE NAME	BIRTH DATE	SEX	HOME PHONE
Michael,	Vincent	P.	05-17-45	M	013-567-9001

ADDRESS	CITY	STATE	ZIP CODE
15291/2 Thompson Boulevard,	Woodland Hills,	XY	12345

PATIENT'S OCCUPATION	NAME OF COMPANY
assembler "A"	Burroughs Corporation

ADDRESS OF EMPLOYER	PHONE
5411 North Lindero Canyon Road, Woodland Hills, XY 12345	013/560-9008

SPOUSE OR PARENT	OCCUPATION
Helen J. Michael	homemaker

EMPLOYER	ADDRESS	PHONE

NAME OF INSURANCE	INSURED OR SUBSCRIBER
Blue Shield	Vincent P. Michael

POLICY NO.	GROUP NO.	EFFECTIVE DATE
T8411981A	677899AT	1-1-90

MEDICARE NO.	MEDICAID NO.	EFFECTIVE DATE	SOC. SEC. NO.
			562-90-8888

REFERRED BY: Robert T. Smith (friend)

DATE	PROGRESS
9-20-XX	Pt complains of having had the flu, headache, dizziness, and of being tired. Pt unable
	to go to work today. Exam shows weakness of L hand. Pt exhibits light dysphasia and
	confusion. Chest x-ray shows cardiomegaly and slight pulmonary congestion. ESR
	46 mm/hr. Imp: Post flu syndrome, transient ischemic attack, possible CVA. Prescribed
	medication for congestion and adv pt to take aspirin 1/day. Pt to stay off work and retn in
	1 wk. Approx date of retn to work 10-16-xx. Brady Coccidioides, MD

Figure 15–12

DOCTOR'S CERTIFICATE

Certification may be made by a licensed medical or osteopathic physician and surgeon, chiropractor, dentist, optometrist, designated psychologist or an authorized medical officer of a United States Government facility. Certification may also be made by a licensed nurse-midwife or nurse practitioner for the purposes of disability related to normal pregnancy or childbirth. All items on this sheet must be completed legibly.

Patient File No.	Name	Social Security Number

17. I attended the patient for the present medical problem from: MONTH DAY YEAR To MONTH DAY YEAR At intervals of:

18. Are you completing this form for the sole purpose of referral or recommendation to an alcoholic recovery home or drug-free residential facility? Yes No If yes, please enter facility name and address in item #28.

19. History: | Objective Findings/Detailed Statement of Symptoms

Diagnosis:

ICD Disease Code, Primary: (REQUIRED) | ICD Disease Code, Secondary:

Type of treatment and/or medication rendered to patient:

20. Diagnosis confirmed by: **(Specify type of test or X-ray)**

21. Is this patient now pregnant or has she been pregnant since the date of treatment as reported above? Yes☐ No☐
Is the pregnancy normal? Yes☐ No☐
If "Yes," date pregnancy terminated or future EDC.
If "No," state the abnormal and involuntary complication causing maternal disability.

22. Operation: Date performed or to be performed ☐ Type of Operation: ICD Procedure Code: (REQUIRED)

23. Has the patient at any time during your attendance for this medical problem, been incapable or performing his or her regular work? Yes☐ No☐ If "Yes" the disability commenced on:

24. APPROXIMATE date, based on your examination of patient, disability (if any) should ebd or has ended sufficiently to permit the patient to resume regular or customary work. Even if considerable question exists, make SOME "estimate." This is a requirement of the Code, and the claim will be delayed if if such date is not entered. Such answers as "Indefinite" or "don't know" will not suffice. (ENTER DATE) ☐

25. Based on your examination of patient, is this disability the result of "occupation" either as an "industrial accident" or as an "occuaptional disease"?
Yes☐ No☐ (This should include aggravation of pre-existing condiitons by occupation.)

26. Have you reported this OR A CONCURRENT DISABILITY to any insurance carrier as a Workers' Compensation claim?
Yes☐ No☐ If "Yes," to whom? (Name of carrier or firm)

27. Was patient in a hospital surgical unit, surgical unit, ambulatory surgical center certified to participate in the federal Medicare program or a postsurgical recovery care unit as designated by section 1250.9 of the Health and Safety Code? Yes☐ No☐
If "Yes," please provide name and address:

28. Was or is patient in an alcoholic recovery home or drug-free residential facility? Yes☐ No☐
If "Yes," please provide name and address:

29. Would the disclosure of this information to your patient be medically or psychologically detrimental to the patient? Yes☐ No☐
Yes☐ No☐

I hereby certify that, based on my examination, the above statements truly describe the patient's disability (if any) and the estimated deration thereof, and that I am a ____________ (TYPE OF DOCTOR) licensed to practice by the State of ____________

▶ ____________
PRINT OR TYPE DOCTOR'S NAME AS SHOWN ON LICENSE

▶ ____________
SIGNATURE OF ATTENDING DOCTOR

▶ ____________
NO. AND STREET   CITY   ZIP CODE

▶ ____________ ( )
STATE LICENSE NUMBER   TELEPHONE NUMBER   DATE OF SIGNING THIS FORM

"Under Section 2116 of the California Unemployment Insurance Code, it is a violation for any individual who, with the intent to defraud, falsely certifies the medical condition of any person in order to obtain disability insurance benefits, whether for the maker or or for any other person, and is punishable by imprisonment and/or a fine not exceeding twenty thousand dollars.

Figure 15–13

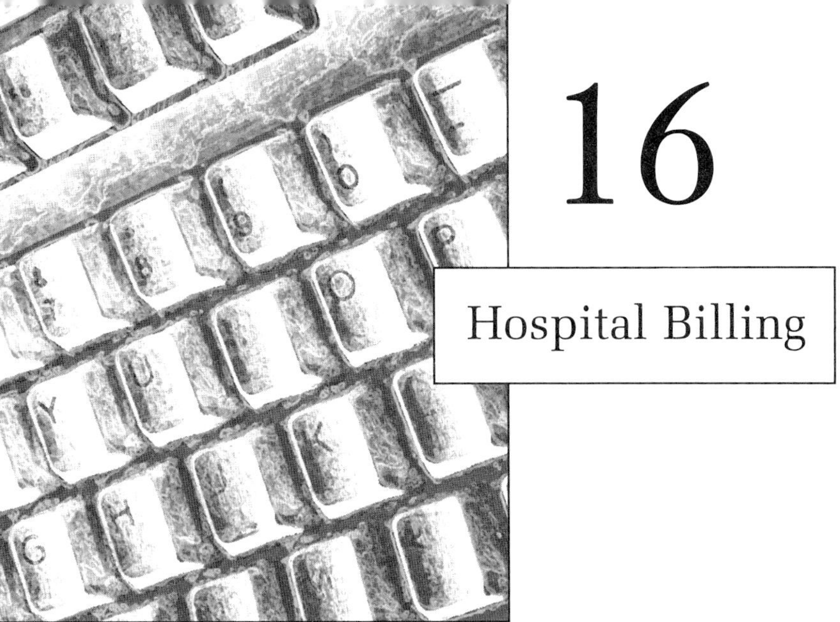

16 Hospital Billing

KEY TERMS

Your instructor may wish to select some specific words pertinent to this chapter for a test. For definitions of the terms, further study, and/or reference, the words, phrases, and abbreviations may be found in the Glossary at the end of the Handbook. *Key terms for this chapter follow.*

admission review
ambulatory payment classifications (APCs)
appropriateness evaluation protocol (AEP)
capitation
case rate
charge description master (CDM)
charges
clinical outliers
comorbidity
cost outlier
cost outlier review
day outlier review
diagnosis-related groups (DRGs)
DRG creep
elective surgery
grouper
inpatient
International Classification of Diseases, 9th Revision, Clinical Modification (ICD-9-CM)
looping
major diagnostic categories (MDCs)
outpatient
percentage of revenue
per diem
preadmission testing (PAT)
principal diagnosis
procedure review
professional review organizations (PROs)
readmission review
stop loss
transfer review
Uniform Bill (UB-92) claim form
utilization review (UR)

PERFORMANCE OBJECTIVES

The student will be able to

- Define and spell the key terms for this chapter, given the information from the *Handbook* Glossary, within a reasonable period of time and with enough accuracy to obtain a satisfactory evaluation.
- Answer the self-study review questions after reading the chapter, with enough accuracy to obtain a satisfactory evaluation.
- State the reasons why claims may be either rejected, delayed, or incorrect payment received, given computer-generated UB-92 claim forms,

within a reasonable period of time and with enough accuracy to obtain a satisfactory evaluation.

- Analyze, edit, and insert entries on computer-generated UB-92 claim forms so payment will be accurate, within a reasonable period of time and with enough accuracy to obtain a satisfactory evaluation.
- Answer questions about the UB-92 claim form to become familiar with the data it contains.
- Answer questions about the UB-92 claim form to learn which hospital departments input data for different blocks on this form.

STUDY OUTLINE

Patient Service Representative
- Qualifications
- Primary Functions and Competencies
- Principal Responsibilities

Medicolegal Confidentiality Issues
- Documents
- Verbal Communication
- Computer Security

Admission Procedures
- Appropriateness Evaluation Protocols
- Admitting Procedures for Major Insurance Programs
  - Private Insurance (Group or Individual)
  - Managed Care
  - Medicaid
  - Medicare
  - TRICARE and CHAMPVA
  - Worker's Compensation
- Preadmission Testing
  - Medicare 72-Hour Rule
  - Exceptions to 72-Hour Rule
  - Compliance Safeguards

Utilization Review
- Peer Review Organization

Coding Hospital Procedures
- Outpatient—Reason for Visit
- Inpatient—Principal Diagnosis
  - Rules for Coding Inpatient Diagnoses

Coding Inpatient Procedures
- ICD-9-CM Volume 3 Procedures
  - Tabular List
  - Alphabetic Index

Procedure: Coding from Volume 3

Coding Outpatient Procedures
- Current Procedural Terminology
- Health Care Finance Administration Common Procedure Coding System
- Modifiers

Inpatient Billing Process
- Admitting Clerk
- Insurance Verifier
- Attending Physician and Nursing Staff
- Discharge Analyst
- Charge Description Master
- Code Specialist
  - Coding Credentials
- Insurance Billing Editor

Procedure: Editing a Uniform Bill (UB-92) Claim Form
- Nurse Auditor

Reimbursement Process
- Reimbursement Methods
- Electronic Data Interchange
- Hard Copy Billing
- Receiving Payment

Outpatient Insurance Claims
- Hospital Professional Services

Billing Problems
- Duplicate Statements
- Double Billing
- Phantom Charges

Hospital Billing Claim Form
- Uniform Bill Inpatient and Outpatient Claim Form
- Instructions for Completing the UB-92 Claim Form

Diagnosis-Related Groups
- History
- The Diagnosis-Related Groups System
- Diagnosis-Related Groups and the Medical Assistant/Insurance Billing Specialist

Outpatient Classifications
- Ambulatory Payment Classification System
  - Hospital Prospective Payment System
  - APC Status
  - Types of APCs

SELF-STUDY **16–1** ► **REVIEW QUESTIONS**

Review the objectives, key terms, glossary definitions to key terms, chapter information, and figures before completing the following review questions.

1. You are reviewing a computer-generated insurance claim before it is sent to the insurance carrier and notice the patient's name as being an old friend. You quickly read the code for the diagnosis. Is this a breach of confidentiality? ____________________

2. You are coding in a medical records department when an agent from the Federal Bureau of Investigation walks in and asks for a patient's address. You ask, "Why do you need Mrs. Doe's address? Do you have a signed authorization from Mrs. Doe for release of information from our facility?" The FBI agent responds, "I'm trying to locate this person because of counterfeiting charges. No, I don't have a signed authorization form." Would there be any breach of confidentiality if you release the patient's address? Explain. ____________________

3. List three instances of breaching confidentiality in a hospital setting.

   a. ____________________

   b. ____________________

   c. ____________________

4. Name five different payment types under managed care contracts.

   a. ____________________

   b. ____________________

   c. ____________________

   d. ____________________

   e. ____________________

5. What is the purpose of appropriateness evaluation protocols (AEP)? ____________________

   ____

   ____

   ____

6. If a patient under a managed care plan goes to a hospital that is under contract with the plan for admission, what is necessary for inpatient admission? ____________________

   ____

7. In what type of situation would a patient not have an insurance identification card?

____

8. When a patient receives diagnostic tests and hospital outpatient services prior to admission to the hospital and these charges are combined with inpatient services becoming part of the diagnostic-related group payment, this regulation in hospital billing is known as ____

9. The diagnosis established after study and listed for admission to the hospital for an illness or injury is called a/an __________________ diagnosis.

10. When reviewing an inpatient medical record, terminology and/or phrases to look for that relate to uncertain diagnoses are ____

____

____

11. From the list of *ICD-9-CM* descriptions shown, place in correct sequential order (1, 2, 3) for billing purposes. In this case, the medical procedure is a repair of other hernia of the anterior abdominal wall, incisional hernia repair with prosthesis, *ICD-9-CM* code 53.61.

	Diagnosis	*ICD-9-CM Code*
_______	Chronic liver disease, liver damage unspecified	571.3
_______	Alcohol dependence syndrome (other and unspecified)	303.9
_______	Other hernia of abdominal cavity without mention of obstruction or gangrene (incisional hernia)	553.21

12. Mrs. Benson, a Medicare patient, is admitted by Dr. Dalton to the hospital on January 4 and is seen in consultation by Dr. Frank on January 5. On January 6, Mrs. Benson is discharged with a diagnosis of coronary atherosclerosis. State some of the problems regarding payment and Medicare policies that would affect this case.

____

____

____

13. Match the words or phrases used for managed care reimbursement methods in the first column with the definitions in the second column. Write the correct letters in the blanks.

sliding scales for discounts and per diems	_______	a. Reimbursement method that pays more for the first day in the hospital than subsequent days.

discounts in the form of sliding scale	_______	b. Reimbursement to the hospital on a per member per month basis.
stop loss	_______	c. Plan advances cash to cover expected claims to the hospital.
withhold	_______	d. Fixed percentage paid to the hospital to cover charges.
charges	_______	e. Single charge for a day in the hospital regardless of actual cost.
ambulatory payment classifications		
	_______	f. Interim per diem paid for each day in the hospital; based on total volume of business generated.
case rate		
diagnostic-related groups	_______	g. Classification system categorizing patients who are medically related with respect to diagnosis and treatment and statistically similar in lengths of hospital stay.
differential by service type		
periodic interim payments	_______	h. Hospital receives a flat per-admission payment for the particular service to which the patient is admitted.
bed leasing		
	_______	i. An averaging after a flat rate is given to certain categories of procedures.
differential by day in hospital		
capitation	_______	j. Outpatient classification based on procedures rather than on diagnoses
per diem		
	_______	k. Hospital buys insurance to protect against lost revenue and receives less of a capitation fee.
percentage of revenue		
	_______	l. Method in which part of plan's payment to the hospital may be withheld and paid at the end of the year.
	_______	m. When a managed care plan leases beds from a hospital and pays per bed whether used or not.
	_______	n. A percentage reduction in charges for total bed days per year.
	_______	o. Dollar amount a hospital bills a case for services rendered.

14. Define the term *outpatient*. ____

____

15. Define the term *elective surgery*. ____

____

____

16. Baby Stephens falls from a high stool, cutting his head. His mother rushes him to St. Joseph's Medical Center for emergency care. The physician examines the baby, takes two stitches closing the laceration, sends the child for skull x-rays, and then discharges him to home. Will the emergency care be billed as an inpatient or outpatient?

____

17. The inpatient and outpatient hospital billing department uses a summary form for submitting an insurance claim to an insurance plan called ______________________

____

18. You can determine whether a UB-92 claim form is for an inpatient or an outpatient by the following observations:

    a. When the inpatient block number 4 shows three-digit billing code(s) ________

    b. When the outpatient block number 4 shows three-digit billing code(s) ________

    c. When revenue codes and block number(s) ______________________ indicate type of service rendered

19. Describe the significance of Blocks 42, 43, 44, 46, and 47 of the UB-92 claim form.

    a. Block 42 ______________________

    b. Block 43 ______________________

    c. Block 44 ______________________

    d. Block 46 ______________________

    e. Block 47 ______________________

20. Why did Medicare implement the DRG-based system of reimbursement?

____

21. Name the six variables that affect Medicare reimbursement under the DRG system.

    a. ______________________

    b. ______________________

    c. ______________________

    d. ______________________

    e. ______________________

    f. ______________________

22. Define the following abbreviations.

AEP ______________________

PAT ______________________

MDC ______________________

PPS ______________________________

TEFRA ______________________________

UR ______________________________

IS ______________________________

SI ______________________________

APC ______________________________

23. Define cost outliers. ______________________________

____

24. Define comorbidity. ______________________________

____

____

To check your answers to this self-study assignment, see Appendix D.

ASSIGNMENT 16–2 ▶ LOCATE AND SEQUENCE DIAGNOSTIC CODES FOR CONDITIONS

Performance Objective

Task: Locate the correct diagnostic code for each diagnosis listed for five cases.

Conditions: Use pen or pencil and *International Classification of Diseases, Ninth Revision, Clinical Modification* diagnostic code book.

Standards: Time: ____________ minutes

Accuracy: ____________

(Note: The time element and accuracy criteria may be given by your instructor.)

Directions: These cases point out the value of proper versus improper coding regarding correct sequence and inclusion of specific codes, indicating the variance of payment. Assign the correct ICD-9-CM code numbers. Note how the same case was assigned different DRG codes listing different principal and secondary hospital diagnoses and that the DRG payment for each is substantially different. Also note the difference in the major diagnostic category (MDC).

Case 1

Age: 12 Sex: Male

MDC: Four diseases and disorders of the respiratory system

DRG: Code 98: Bronchitis and asthma age 0–17

Principal Diagnosis

Asthma w/o status asthmaticus____________

MDC: Four diseases and disorders of the respiratory system

DRG: Code 91: Simple pneumonia and pleurisy age 0–17

Principal Diagnosis

Pneumonia, organism NOS ____________

Secondary Diagnoses

Pneumonia, organism NOS ________________

Otitis media NOS ________________

DRG Payment: $2,705

Secondary Diagnoses

Asthma w/o status asthmaticus ________________

Otitis media NOS ________________

DRG Payment: $3,246

Case 2

Age: 77 Sex: Male
MDC: Five diseases and disorders of the circulatory system
DRG: Code 138: Cardiac arrhythmia and conduction disorders, age > 69 and/or CC

Principal Diagnosis

Atrial fibrillation ________________

Secondary Diagnoses

Fracture six ribs—closed ________________

Trans cereb ischemia NOS ________________

Syncope and collapse ________________

Fx scapula NOS—closed ________________

Fall NEC & NOS ________________

MDC: Four diseases and disorders of the respiratory system
DRG: Code 83: Major chest trauma, age > 69 and/or CC

Principal Diagnosis

Fracture six ribs—closed ________________

Secondary Diagnoses

Atrial fibrillation ________________

Trans cereb ischemia NOS ________________

Syncope and collapse ________________

Fx scapula NOS—closed ________________

Fall NEC & NOS ________________

Procedures

Contrast cerebr arteriogram ________________

CAT scan of head ________________

Dx ultrasound—heart ________________

Physical therapy NEC ________________

DRG Payment: $5,882

DRG Payment: $6,206

Note: Since this is a hospital case, *ICD-9-CM* Volume 3 should be used to code the procedures. However, Volume 3 is not used in the medical office.

Case 3

Age: 42 Sex: Male
MDC: Nineteen mental diseases and disorders
DRG: Code 426: Depressive neuroses

MDC: Five diseases and disorders of the circulatory systsem
DRG: Code 122: Circulatory disorders with ami w/o cv comp disch alive

Principal Diagnosis

Neurotic depression ____________________

Secondary Diagnoses

Acute myocardial infarction anterior wall

NEC ____________________

Chest pain NOS ____________________

Heart disease NOS____________________

Paranoid personality ____________________

Principal Diagnosis

Acute myocardial infarction anterior wall

NEC ____________________

Secondary Diagnoses

Neurotic depression ____________________

Chest pain NOS ____________________

Heart disease NOS____________________

Paranoid personality ____________________

Procedures

Dx ultrasound—heart ____________________

Other resp procedures ____________________

DRG Payment: $6,007

DRG Payment: $8,637

Note: Since this is a hospital case, *ICD-9-CM* Volume 3 should be used to code the procedures. However, Volume 3 is not used in the medical office.

Case 4

Age: 65 Sex: Male
MDC: Five diseases and disorders of the circulatory system
DRG: Code 468: Unrelated OR proc

Principal Diagnosis

Hypertensive heart disease NOS____________

Secondary Diagnoses

Hematuria ____________________

Hyperplasia of prostate ____________________

Hemiplegia NOS ____________________

Late eff cerebrovasc dis ____________________

Malign neopl prostate ____________________

MDC: Twelve diseases and disorders of the male reproductive system
DRG: Code 336: Transurethral prostatectomy, age > 69 and/or CC

Principal Diagnosis

Malig neopl prostate ____________________

Secondary Diagnoses

Hematuria ____________________

Hypertensive heart disease NOS __________

Hemiplegia NOS ____________________

Late eff cerebrovasc dis ____________________

Hyperplasia of prostate ____________________

Procedures

Transurethral prostatect ______________

Urethral dilation ____________________

Cystoscopy NEC ____________________

Intravenous pyelogram _______________

Nephrotomogram NEC ______________

DRG Payment: $13,311

DRG Payment: $6,377

Note: Since this is a hospital case, *ICD-9-CM* Volume 3 should be used to code the procedures. However, Volume 3 is not used in the medical office.

Case 5

Age: 62 Sex: Female

MDC: Six diseases and disorders of the digestive system
DRG: Code 188: Other digestive system diagnoses, age > 69 and/or CC

Principal Diagnosis

Descending colon inj—closed ________________

Secondary Diagnoses

Liver injury NOS—closed ___________________

Open wnd knee/leg—compl _________________

Firearm accident NOS ______________________

No procedures performed

DRG Payment: $4,710

MDC: Seven diseases and disorders of the hepatobiliary system and pancreas
DRG: Code 205: Disorders of the liver exc malig, cirr, alc hepa, age > 69 and/or CC

Principal Diagnosis

Liver injury NOS—closed _________________

Secondary Diagnoses

Atrial fibrillation ________________________

Urin tract infection NOS __________________

Descending colon inj—closed ______________

Open wnd knee/leg—compl ________________

Firearm accident NOS ____________________

E. coli infect NOS ________________________

DRG Payment: $6,847

ASSIGNMENT 16–3 ► IDENTIFY HOSPITAL DEPARTMENTS THAT INPUT DATA FOR THE UB-92 CLAIM FORM

Performance Objective

Task: Answer questions about the hospital departments that supply data for the UB-92 claim form.

Conditions: Use ink pen.

Standards: Time: ________________ minutes

Accuracy: ________________

(Note: The time element and accuracy criteria may be given by your instructor.)

Directions: Depending on your instructor's preference you may complete this exercise with or without notes or other material.

You have become familiar with the information in all 86 blocks of the UB-92 Claim Form. This assignment will help you learn which of six hospital departments input information into the computer system to be printed out in the various blocks.

This will enhance your understanding of how multiple employees in a large facility take part in helping produce a completed UB-92 Claim Form. It will also increase your understanding of where errors and omissions originate so you may amend them when you start the editing and correction process. Answer the following questions.

1. Which department is responsible for inputting the charges for a blood test?

____

2. Which department is responsible for inputting an insurance certificate or subscriber number?

____

3. Which department is responsible for inputting the procedure codes?_______________________

____

4. Which department is responsible for inputting the patient's name and address?________________

____

5. Which department is responsible for inputting the diagnostic codes?_______________________

____

ASSIGNMENT 16–4 ► STUDY UB-92 CLAIM FORM BLOCK DATA

Performance Objective

Task: Answer questions about the UB-92 claim form blocks.

Conditions: Use ink pen.

Standards: Time: ______________ minutes

Accuracy: ______________

(Note: The time element and accuracy criteria may be given by your instructor.)

Directions: Depending on your instructor's preference, you may complete this exercise with or without notes or other material.

You have learned about a number of reimbursement methods, confidentiality issues, evaluation protocols, and the utilization review process. This information is necessary to process an insurance claim to obtain maximum reimbursement. To learn the UB-92 Claim Form you must become familiar with the data it contains, including codes, and the location of various types of information. Answer the following questions.

1. In Block 4, state the correct billing codes for:

   a. Inpatient services ______________________________

   b. Outpatient Services ______________________________

2. What is listed in Block 7? ______________________________

3. What insurance carriers or programs require Block 9 to be completed? ______________________________

   ____

   ____

4. What format is required in Block 14 for the patient's date of birth? ______________________________

5. If a patient was in the hospital for the delivery of a premature infant, what code would be used in Block 20? ______________________________

6. If a patient was discharged from inpatient care at 2:15 p.m., how would this be noted in Block 21? ______________________________

7. What is the correct code to use in Block 22 if a patient was discharged to a home hospice situation? ______________________________

8. If neither the patient nor spouse was employed, what code would be used to indicate this in Blocks 24 through 30? ______

9. State the reason for the codes used in Blocks 32 through 35. ______

______

______

10. What revenue code must be shown on all bills as a final entry and in what block does it occur? ______

ASSIGNMENT 16–5 ▶ UNIFORM BILL (UB-92) CLAIM FORM QUESTIONS ABOUT EDITING

Performance Objective

Task: Answer questions about editing the Blocks on the Uniform Bill (UB-92) Claim Form

Conditions: Use ink pen.

Standards: Time: ______ minutes

Accuracy: ______

(Note: The time element and accuracy criteria may be given by your instructor.)

Directions: You are now ready to learn more about the critical editing process for determining errors and omissions on the UB-92 Claim Form. This important skill may help you secure a job in the claims processing department. Refer to the *Handbook* Figure 16–5 and answer the questions.

1. Where does the editing process begin on the Uniform Bill (UB-92) Claim form? ______

______

2. What block(s) is/are mandatory when verifying insurance information on the UB-92 Claim Form? ______

3. What block should the principal diagnostic code appear in? ______

______

4. For an inpatient claim, if Block 43 lists the hospital room, Block 44 lists the per day rate, and Block 46 lists the number of hospital days, what other block is used to verify this for accuracy? ______

5. Besides room rate and number of inpatient days, what is another important factor in reviewing the services shown in Blocks 42 through 47? ______________________________

____

____

____

6. For outpatient claims, what other item(s) is/are shown besides the date, description of the service rendered, and fee? ______________________________

7. Where can an insurance editor check when there is doubt about a service shown on a UB-92 Claim Form? ______________________________

8. Which block should show the estimated amount due from the insurance company? ______________________________

____

ASSIGNMENT 16–6 ▶ LOCATE ERRORS ON A COMPUTER-GENERATED UB-92 CLAIM FORM

Performance Objective

Task: Locate the blocks on the computer-generated insurance claim form that need completion of missing information or data that need to be corrected before submission to the insurance company.

Conditions: Use Mary J. Torre's completed insurance claim (Figure 16–1), checklist for editing a Uniform Bill (UB-92) Claim Form, and a red ink pen.

Standards: Time: ______________ minutes

Accuracy: ______________

(Note: The time element and accuracy criteria may be given by your instructor.)

Directions: Refer to the *Handbook* Figure 16–5 to employ the step-by-step approach while editing the computer-generated UB-92 Claim Form (Figure 16–1). Use the checklist to help you when reviewing the claim form. Locate the blocks on the claim form that need completion of missing information or that need data to be added before submission to the insurance company. Highlight all errors you discover. Insert all corrections and missing information in red. If you cannot locate the necessary information but know it is mandatory, write "NEED" in the corresponding block.

In addition, you notice that the second line entry for pharmacy shows a total of $6,806. However, you know from reviewing the case that one injection of a drug known as TPA (Revenue code 259 and fee $5,775), which dissolves clots and opens vessels when a patient has a cardiac infarct, was not broken out of the fee. Handwrite this final entry. On line 2, cross out the total charge $6,806 and insert the correct pharmacy reduced amount.

Text continued on page 365

013-487-6789
COLLEGE HOSPITAL
4500 BROAD AVENUE
WOODLAND HILLS XY 12345-0001

2

3 PATIENT CONTROL NO.: 10687127

4 TYPE OF BILL: 111

5 FED. TAX NO.: 95-0731067

6 STATEMENT COVERS PERIOD FROM: 071120XX THROUGH: 071420XX

7 COV D: 003 | 8 N-C D | 9 C-I D. | 10 L-R D | 11

12 PATIENT NAME: TORRE, MARY J.

13 PATIENT ADDRESS: 452 JEME STREET WOODLAND HILLS, XY 12345-0001

14 BIRTHDATE	15 SEX	16 MS	ADMISSION 17 DATE	18 HR	19 TYPE	20 SRC	21 D HR	22 STAT	23 MEDICAL RECORD NO.	CONDITION CODES 24	25	26	27	28	29	30	31
12031918	F	M	071120XX	21	2	7	17	01	2018856	C5	04						

	32 OCCURRENCE CODE	DATE	33 OCCURRENCE CODE	DATE	34 OCCURRENCE CODE	DATE	35 OCCURRENCE CODE	DATE	36 OCCURRENCE SPAN CODE	FROM	THROUGH	37
a	11	071120XX										A
b												B
												C

38
TORRE, MARY J.
452 JEME STREET
WOODLAND HILLS, XY 12345-0001

	39 VALUE CODES CODE	AMOUNT	40 VALUE CODES CODE	AMOUNT	41 VALUE CODES CODE	AMOUNT
a	01	650.00				
b						
c						
d						

	42 REV CD.	43 DESCRIPTION	44 HCPCS/RATES	45 SERV. DATE	46 SERV. UNITS	47 TOTAL CHARGES	48 NON-COVERED CHARGES	49	
1	210	ROOM AND CARE CCU	1600.00		3	4800.00			1
2	250	PHARMACY			121	6806.00			2
3	270	MED-SUR SUPPLIES			31	700.50			3
4	300	LABORATORY			45	1710.50			4
5	310	PATHOLOGY LABORATORY			1	99.50			5
6	320	RADIOLOGY			3	159.00			6
7	450	EMERGENCY ROOM SERVICE			5	196.00			7
8	730	ELECTROCARDIOLOGY			7	700.00			8
9	001	TOTAL				15171.50			9
10									10
11									11
12									12
13									13
14									14
15									15
16									16
17									17
18									18
19									19
20									20
21									21
22									22
23									23

	50 PAYER	51 PROVIDER NO.	52 REL INFO	53 ASG BEN	54 PRIOR PAYMENTS	55 EST. AMOUNT DUE	56
A	MEDPRIME - HPR		Y	Y			
B							
C							

57 DUE FROM PATIENT ▶

	58 INSURED'S NAME	59 P.REL	60 CERT.-SSN-HIC-ID. NO.	61 GROUP NAME	62 INSURANCE GROUP NO.	
A	TORRE, MARY J	01	54626897101		6500-0000	A
B						B
C						C

	63 TREATMENT AUTHORIZATION CODES	64 ESC	65 EMPLOYER NAME	66 EMPLOYER LOCATION	
A		9	RETIRED 080184		A
B					B
C					C

67 PRIN. DIAG. CD.	68 CODE	69 CODE	70 CODE	71 CODE	72 CODE	73 CODE	74 CODE	75 CODE	76 ADM. DIAG. CD.	77 E-CODE	78
41011	4589	5780	E9444	E9424	E8490	E9344	E8497		41011		

68 OTHER DIAG. FEES

79 P.C.: 9

80 PRINCIPAL PROCEDURE CODE / DATE; 81 OTHER PROCEDURE CODE / DATE; OTHER PROCEDURE CODE / DATE; OTHER PROCEDURE CODE / DATE; OTHER PROCEDURE CODE / DATE; OTHER PROCEDURE CODE / DATE

82 ATTENDING PHYS. ID: 642110670 CARDI PERRY

83 OTHER PHYS. ID

OTHER PHYS. ID

84 REMARKS

85 PROVIDER REPRESENTATIVE: X *Perry Cardi, MD*

86 DATE: 071620XX

I CERTIFY THE CERTIFICATION ON THE REVERSE APPLY TO THIS BILL AND ARE MADE A PART HEREOF.

UB-92 HCFA-1450

OCR/ORIGINAL

Figure 16–1

Checklist for Editing a Uniform Bill (UB-92) Claim Form

Assignment 16–6 Mary J. Torre

Steps	Blocks
1	Blocks 1 _______ and 5 _________
2	Block 4: Inpatient __________ Outpatient __________
3	Blocks 12 _________ 38 ______ 58 ______ and 59 ______
4	Block 14 _____________
5	Blocks 12 _____ and 15___________
6	Blocks 50 _______ 60 ______ 61 _____ 62 ______ 65 _______ and 66 ___________
7	Blocks 67 ____________ 76 _________ and 78 _______
8	Blocks 80 _______ __________ and 81 ___________
9	Blocks 82 ________ and 83 ___________
10	Blocks 6 _________ 17 __________ and 32 __________
11	**Inpatient**: Blocks 42–47: 7 ________ 18 _____ 21 _________ and 46 _________
12	Block 47 _________
13	Blocks 42 _________ and 46 ___________
14	**Outpatient**: Blocks 43 ___________ 44 ____________ and 45 _______________
15	Detailed record to be checked
16	Blocks 42 ___________ 43 _________ and 47 _______
17	Block 55 ____________
18	Blocks 85 _________________ and 86 ___________

ASSIGNMENT 16–7 ▸ LOCATE ERRORS ON A COMPUTER-GENERATED UB-92 CLAIM FORM

Performance Objective

Task: Locate the blocks on the computer-generated insurance claim form that need completion of missing information or data that need to be corrected before submission to the insurance company.

Conditions: Use Henry M. Cosby's completed insurance claim (Figure 16–2), checklist for editing a Uniform Bill (UB-92) Claim Form, and a red ink pen.

Standards: Time: _______________ minutes

Accuracy: _______________

(Note: The time element and accuracy criteria may be given by your instructor.)

Directions: Refer to the *Handbook* Figure 16–5 to employ the step-by-step approach while editing the computer-generated UB-92 Claim Form (Figure 16–2). Use the checklist to help you when reviewing the claim form. Locate the blocks on the claim form that need completion of missing information or that need data to be added before submission to the insurance company. Highlight all errors you discover. Insert all corrections and missing information in red. If you cannot locate the necessary information but know it is mandatory, write "NEED" in the corresponding block. State the reason(s) why the claim may be either rejected, delayed, or incorrect payment generated because of error(s) discovered.

Checklist for Editing a Uniform Bill (UB-92) Claim Form

Assignment 16–7 Henry M. Cosby

Steps	Blocks
1	Blocks 1_______ and 5 _______
2	Block 4: Inpatient _______ Outpatient
3	Blocks 12 _______ 38 _______ 58 _______ and 59 _______
4	Block 14 _______
5	Blocks 12 _______ and 15 _______
6	Blocks 50 _______ 60 _______ 61 _______ 62 _______ 65 _______ and 66 _______
7	Blocks 67 _______ 76 _______ and 78 _______
8	Blocks 80 _______ _______ and 81 _______
9	Blocks 82 _______ and 83 _______
10	Blocks 6 _______ 17 _______ and 32 _______
11	**Inpatient**: Blocks 42–47: 7 _______ 18 _______ 21 _______ and 46 _______
12	Block 47 _______
13	Blocks 42 _______ and 46 _______
14	**Outpatient**: Blocks 43 _______ 44 _______ and 45 _______
15	Detailed record to be checked
16	Blocks 42 _______ 43 _______ and 47 _______
17	Block 55 _______
18	Blocks 85 _______ and 86 _______

ASSIGNMENT 16–8 ▶ LOCATE ERRORS ON A COMPUTER-GENERATED UB-92 CLAIM FORM

Performance Objective

Task: Locate the blocks on the computer-generated insurance claim form that need completion of missing information or data that need to be corrected before submission to the insurance company.

Conditions: Use Harold M. McDonald's completed insurance claim (Figure 16–3), checklist for editing a Uniform Bill (UB-92) Claim Form, and a red ink pen.

Standards: Time: __________ minutes

Accuracy: __________

(Note: The time element and accuracy criteria may be given by your instructor.)

Directions: Refer to the *Handbook* Figure 16–5 to employ the step-by-step approach while editing the computer-generated UB-92 Claim Form (Figure 16–3). Use the checklist to help you when reviewing the claim form. Locate the blocks on the claim form that need completion of missing information or that need data to be added before submission to the insurance company. Highlight all errors you discover. Insert all corrections and missing information in red. If you cannot locate the necessary information but know it is mandatory, write "NEED" in the corresponding block.

You notice that the seventh *CPT*/HCPCS code 43450 for operating room is missing. On hospital claims, the entry for operating room is usually blank and must be handwritten in as this is the code for the surgical procedure.

Text continued on page 373

COLLEGE HOSPITAL 4500 BROAD AVENUE WOODLAND HILLS XY 12345-0001 013-487-6789	2	3 PATIENT CONTROL NO. 10687127	4 TYPE OF BILL 131

5 FED. TAX NO.	6 STATEMENT COVERS PERIOD FROM	THROUGH	7 COV D	8 N-C D	9 C-I D	10 L-R D	11
95-0731067	031520XX	031520XX					

12 PATIENT NAME	13 PATIENT ADDRESS
COSBY, HENRY M	1501 PACIFIC WAY WOODLAND HILLS, XY 12345-0001

14 BIRTHDATE	15 SEX	16 MS	ADMISSION 17 DATE	18 HR	19 TYPE	20 SRC	21 D HR	22 STAT	23 MEDICAL RECORD NO.	CONDITION CODES 24	25	26	27	28	29	30	31
03101956	M	M	031520XX	13	3	2	99	01	2084100	C5							

	32 OCCURRENCE CODE	DATE	33 OCCURRENCE CODE	DATE	34 OCCURRENCE CODE	DATE	35 OCCURRENCE CODE	DATE	36 OCCURRENCE SPAN CODE	FROM	THROUGH	37
a	05	072119XX										A
b												B
												C

38
COSBY, HENRY M
1501 PACIFIC WAY
WOODLAND HILLS XY 12345

	39 VALUE CODES CODE	AMOUNT	40 VALUE CODES CODE	AMOUNT	41 VALUE CODES CODE	AMOUNT
a						
b						
c						
d						

	42 REV CD.	43 DESCRIPTION	44 HCPCS/RATES	45 SERV. DATE	46 SERV. UNITS	47 TOTAL CHARGES	48 NON-COVERED CHARGES	49
1	110	ROOM-BOARD/SEMI/PVT	650.00		1	650 00		
2	250	PHARMACY			11	207 20		
3	270	MED-SUR SUPPLIES			4	1041 28		
4	360	OPERATING ROOM				865 00		
5	370	ANESTHESIA				64 50		
6	730	ELECTROCARDIOGRAM	93000	031320XX	031320XX	100 00		
7	001	Total				2927 98		

	50 PAYER	51 PROVIDER NO.	52 REL INFO	53 ASG BEN	54 PRIOR PAYMENTS	55 EST. AMOUNT DUE	56
A	BLUE SHIELD OF CA	Z22C49122	Y	Y			
B							
C							

57 DUE FROM PATIENT ▶

	58 INSURED'S NAME	59 P.REL	60 CERT.-SSN-HIC-ID. NO.	61 GROUP NAME	62 INSURANCE GROUP NO.
A	COSBY, HENRY M	01	564729922		PA 0132
B					
C					

	63 TREATMENT AUTHORIZATION CODES	64 ESC	65 EMPLOYER NAME	66 EMPLOYER LOCATION
A		4	DBA: COSBY AUTO BODY	
B				
C				

67 PRIN. DIAG. CD.	68 CODE	69 CODE	70 CODE	71 CODE	72 CODE	73 CODE	74 CODE	75 CODE	76 ADM. DIAG. CD.	77 E-CODE	78
8408											

(68 OTHER DIAG. FEES)

79 P.C.	80 PRINCIPAL PROCEDURE CODE	DATE	81 OTHER PROCEDURE CODE	DATE	OTHER PROCEDURE CODE	DATE
9	8301	031520XX				
	OTHER PROCEDURE CODE	DATE	OTHER PROCEDURE CODE	DATE	OTHER PROCEDURE CODE	DATE

82 ATTENDING PHYS. ID
126785470 SKELETON RAYMOND

83 OTHER PHYS. ID

OTHER PHYS. ID

84 REMARKS
FELL WATERSKIING 7/21/20XX

85 PROVIDER REPRESENTATIVE: X SIGNATURE ON FILE
86 DATE: 031620XX

I CERTIFY THE CERTIFICATION ON THE REVERSE APPLY TO THIS BILL AND ARE MADE A PART HEREOF.

UB-92 HCFA-1450 OCR/ORIGINAL

Figure 16–2

1.	2	3 PATIENT CONTROL NO.	4 TYPE OF BILL
COLLEGE HOSPITAL 4500 BROAD AVENUE WOODLAND HILLS XY 12345-0001 013-487-6789		10670685	131

5 FED. TAX NO.	6 STATEMENT COVERS PERIOD FROM	THROUGH	7 COV D	8 N-C D	9 C-I D.	10 L-R D	11
95-0731067	070520XX	070520XX					

12 PATIENT NAME	13 PATIENT ADDRESS
MCDONALD HAROLD M	22 BEACON ROAD WOODLAND HILLS, XY 12345-0001

14. BIRTHDATE	15.SEX	16 MS	ADMISSION 17 DATE	18 HR	19 TYPE	20 SRC	21 D HR	22 STAT	23 MEDICAL RECORD NO.	CONDITION CODES 24	25	26	27	28	29	30	31
04261929	M	M	070520XX	12	3	1	99	01	2071307	C5							

	32 CODE	OCCURRENCE DATE	33 CODE	OCCURRENCE DATE	34 CODE	OCCURRENCE DATE	35 CODE	OCCURRENCE DATE	36 CODE	OCCURRENCE SPAN FROM	THROUGH	37
a												A
b												B
												C

38
MCDONALD HAROLD M
22 BEACON ROAD
WOODLAND HILLS XY 12345-0001

	39 CODE	VALUE CODES AMOUNT	40 CODE	VALUE CODES AMOUNT	41 CODE	VALUE CODES AMOUNT
a						
b						
c						
d						

	42 REV CD.	43 DESCRIPTION	44 HCPCS/RATES	45 SERV. DATE	46 SERV. UNITS	47 TOTAL CHARGES	48 NON-COVERED CHARGES	49	
1	250	PHARMACY			5	90 90			1
2	270	MED - SUR SUPPLIES			16	2519 50			2
3	300	DRAWING BLOOD	36415	070520XX	1	8 50			3
4	300	13-16 BLOOD/URINE TESTS	80016	070520XX	1	28 00			4
5	300	CREATININE CLEARANCE TEST	82575	070520XX	1	20 00			5
6	300	CBC	85025 24	070520XX	1	16 50			6
7	320	CONTRAST XRAY EXAM, ESOPH	74220	070520XX	1	114 00			7
8	320	X-RAY GUIDE, GI DILATION	74360	070520XX	1	750 00			8
9	360	OPERATING ROOM				500 00			9
10	410	CONT OXIMETER HOURS	82805 22	070520XX	1	8 00			10
11	001	Total				4055 40			11
12									12
13									13
14									14
15									15
16									16
17									17
18									18
19									19
20									20
21									21
22									22
23									23

	50 PAYER	51 PROVIDER NO.	52 REL INFO	53 ASG BEN	54 PRIOR PAYMENTS	55 EST. AMOUNT DUE	56
A	HEALTH PLAN REDWOOD	278654901	Y	Y			
B							
C							

57 **DUE FROM PATIENT ▶**

	58 INSURED'S NAME	59 P.REL	60 CERT.-SSN-HIC-ID. NO.	61 GROUP NAME	62 INSURANCE GROUP NO.	
A	MCDONALD HAROLD M	01	31424435401		1320-0000 PLAN GO	A
B						B
C						C

	63 TREATMENT AUTHORIZATION CODES	64 ESC	65 EMPLOYER NAME	66 EMPLOYER LOCATION	
A		9	WC PEDERSON FORD		A
B					B
C					C

67 PRIN. DIAG. CD.	68 OTHER DIAG. FEES 68 CODE	69 CODE	70 CODE	71 CODE	72 CODE	73 CODE	74 CODE	75 CODE	76 ADM. DIAG. CODE	77 E-CODE	78
1509	V725										

79 P.C.	80 PRINCIPAL PROCEDURE CODE	DATE	81 OTHER PROCEDURE CODE	DATE	OTHER PROCEDURE CODE	DATE
9						
	OTHER PROCEDURE CODE	DATE	OTHER PROCEDURE CODE	DATE	OTHER PROCEDURE CODE	DATE

82 ATTENDING PHYS. ID
124589770 ANTRUM, CONCHA

83 OTHER PHYS. ID

OTHER PHYS. ID

84 REMARKS
HPR

85 PROVIDER REPRESENTATIVE: X *Concha Antrum, MD*
86 DATE: 070620XX

I CERTIFY THE STATEMENTS ON THE REVERSE APPLY TO THIS BILL AND ARE MADE A PART HEREOF.

UB-92 HCFA-1450 OCR/ORIGINAL

Figure 16–3

COLLEGE HOSPITAL
4500 BROAD AVENUE
WOODLAND HILLS XY 12345-0001
013-487-6789

2

3 PATIENT CONTROL NO. 10630911

4 TYPE OF BILL 111

5 FED. TAX NO. 95-0731067

6 STATEMENT COVERS PERIOD FROM 06120XX THROUGH 06120XX

7 COV D 010 | 8 N-C D | 9 C-I D. | 10 L-R D | 11

12 PATIENT NAME MARTINEZ PEDRO

13 PATIENT ADDRESS 7821 SENSOR AVE WOODLAND HILLS, XY 12345-0001

14. BIRTHDATE	15.SEX	16 MS	ADMISSION 17 DATE	18 HR	19 TYPE	20 SRC	21 D HR	22 STAT	23 MEDICAL RECORD NO.	CONDITION CODES 24	25	26	27	28	29	30	31
092218	M	W	061120XX	20	1	7	19	03	3567811	C5	04						

32 OCCURRENCE CODE DATE | 33 OCCURRENCE CODE DATE | 34 OCCURRENCE CODE DATE | 35 OCCURRENCE CODE DATE | 36 OCCURRENCE SPAN CODE FROM THROUGH | 37 A B C

38 MARTINEZ PEDRO
7821 SENSOR AVENUE
WOODLAND HILLS XY 12345-0001

39 VALUE CODES CODE AMOUNT: a 01 650 00

40 | 41 VALUE CODES CODE AMOUNT

	42 REV CD.	43 DESCRIPTION	44 HCPCS/RATES	45 SERV. DATE	46 SERV. UNITS	47 TOTAL CHARGES	48 NON-COVERED CHARGES	49
1	110	ROOM - BOARD/SEMI/PVT	650.00		1	650 00		
2	120	ROOM AND CARE SEMI	650.00		1	650 00		
3	210	ROOM AND CARE CCU	1600.00		8	12800 00		
4	250	PHARMACY			500	7133 90		
5	270	MED - SUR SUPPLIES			149	3689 50		
6	300	LABORATORY			97	5399 33		
7	320	RADIOLOGY			27	1544 00		
8	350	CT SCAN			1	622 00		
9	410	RESPIRATORY THERAPY			240	6698 50		
10	420	PHYSICAL THERAPY			9	470 00		
11	450	EMERGENCY ROOM SERV			6	197 00		
12	460	PULMONARY FUNCTION				29 00		
13	730	ELECTROCARDIOLOGY			1	100 00		
14	942	EDUCATION			6	82 50		
15	001	Total				40065 73		

	50 PAYER	51 PROVIDER NO.	52 REL INFO	53 ASG BEN	54 PRIOR PAYMENTS	55 EST. AMOUNT DUE	56
A	MEDIPRIME-HPR		Y	Y			
B							
C							

57 **DUE FROM PATIENT ▶**

	58 INSURED'S NAME	59 P.REL	60 CERT.-SSN-HIC-ID. NO.	61 GROUP NAME	62 INSURANCE GROUP NO.
A	MARTINEZ PEDRO	01	55025897001		6500-0000
B					
C					

	63 TREATMENT AUTHORIZATION CODES	64 ESC	65 EMPLOYER NAME	66 EMPLOYER LOCATION
A		5	RETIRED 1975	
B				
C				

67 PRIN. DIAG. CD.	68 CODE	69 CODE	70 CODE	71 CODE	72 CODE	73 CODE	74 CODE	75 CODE	76 ADM. DIAG. CODE	77 E-CODE	78
4169	51881	49121									

68 OTHER DIAG. FEES

79 P.C. 9 | 80 PRINCIPAL PROCEDURE CODE DATE | 81 OTHER PROCEDURE CODE DATE | OTHER PROCEDURE CODE DATE

OTHER PROCEDURE CODE DATE | OTHER PROCEDURE CODE DATE | OTHER PROCEDURE CODE DATE

82 ATTENDING PHYS. ID 642110670 COCCIDIOIDES BRADY

83 OTHER PHYS. ID

OTHER PHYS. ID

84 REMARKS

85 PROVIDER REPRESENTATIVE X

86 DATE

I CERTIFY THE CERTIFICATION ON THE REVERSE APPLY TO THIS BILL AND ARE MADE A PART HEREOF

UB-92 HCFA-1450 OCR/ORIGINAL

Figure 16–4

Checklist for Editing a Uniform Bill (UB-92) Claim Form

Assignment 16–8 Harold M. McDonald

Steps	Blocks
1	Blocks 1 ________ and 5 _________
2	Block 4: Inpatient ___________ Outpatient _________
3	Blocks 12 __________ 38 _______ 58 ______ and 59 _________
4	Block 14 ________
5	Blocks 12 _________ and 15 ________
6	Blocks 50 _________ 60 _______ 61 _____ 62 __________
	65 _______ and 66 ___________
7	Blocks 67 _________ 76 ___________ and 78 _________
8	Blocks 80 _________ ___________ and 81 ___________
9	Blocks 82 _________ and 83 _________
10	Blocks 6 ____________ 17 _________ and 32 _______
11	**Inpatient**: Blocks 42–47: 7 _______ 18 ________ 21 _______ and 46 _________
12	Block 47 __________
13	Blocks 42 __________ and 46 __________
14	**Outpatient**: Blocks 43 ______ 44 ______ and 45 ________
15	Detailed record to be checked
16	Blocks 42 _______ 43 ______ and 47 ________
17	Block 55 ____________
18	Blocks 85 _________________ and 86 ____________

ASSIGNMENT 16–9 ▸ LOCATE ERRORS ON A COMPUTER-GENERATED UB-92 CLAIM FORM

Performance Objective

Task: Locate the blocks on the computer-generated insurance claim form that need completion of missing information or data that need to be corrected before submission to the insurance company.

Conditions: Use Pedro Martinez's completed insurance claim (Figure 16–4), checklist for editing a Uniform Bill (UB-92) Claim Form, and a red ink pen.

Standards: Time: ______________ minutes

Accuracy: ______________

(Note: The time element and accuracy criteria may be given by your instructor.)

Directions: Refer to the *Handbook* Figure 16–5 to employ the step-by-step approach while editing the computer-generated UB-92 Claim Form (Figure 16–4). Use the checklist to help you when reviewing the claim form. Locate the blocks on the claim form that need completion of missing information or that need data to be added before submission to the insurance company. Highlight all errors you discover. Insert all corrections and missing information in red. If you cannot locate the necessary information but know it is mandatory, write "NEED" in the corresponding block. Then write a list of reasons why the claim may be either rejected, delayed, or incorrect payment generated because of errors discovered.

Checklist for Editing a Uniform Bill (UB-92) Claim Form

Assignment 16–9 Pedro Martinez

Steps	Blocks
1	Blocks 1 ________ and 5 ___________
2	Block 4: Inpatient _________ Outpatient _________
3	Blocks 12 ________ 38 _________ 58 ______ and 59 __________
4	Block 14 __________
5	Blocks 12 ________ and 15 ___________
6	Blocks 50 __________ 60 ______ 61 _________ 62 __________
	65 __________ and 66 _______
7	Blocks 67 ________ 76 _________ and 78 _________
8	Blocks 80 _______ ______________ and 81 _______
9	Blocks 82 _________ and 83 _____________
10	Blocks 6 __________ 17 _________ and 32 ___________
11	**Inpatient**: Blocks 42–47: 7 ______ 18_______ 21 _________ and 46 _________
12	Block 47 _______
13	Blocks 42 _________ and 46 _________
14	**Outpatient**: Blocks 43 ________ 44 _______ and 45 ________
15	Detailed record to be checked
16	Blocks 42 ______ 43 _______ and 47 ________
17	Block 55 __________
18	Blocks 85 __________________________ and 86 __________

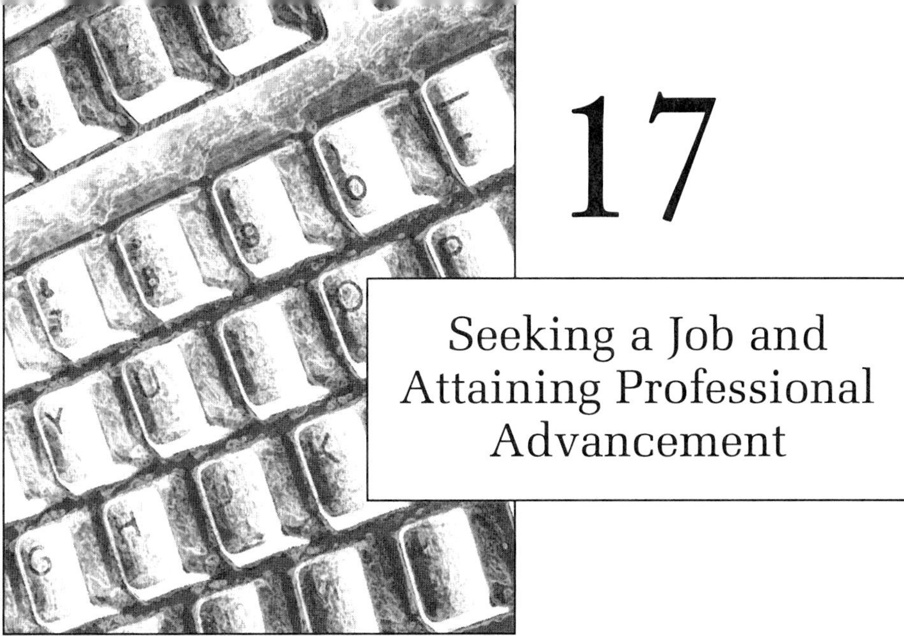

17

Seeking a Job and Attaining Professional Advancement

KEY TERMS

Your instructor may wish to select some specific words pertinent to this chapter for a test. For definitions of the terms, further study, and/or reference, the words, phrases, and abbreviations may be found in the Glossary at the end of the Handbook. *Key terms for this chapter follow.*

alien
application form
blind mailing
certification
Certified Claims Assistance Professional (CCAP)
Certified Coding Specialist (CCS)
Certified Coding Specialist–Physician (CCS–P)
Certified Electronic Claims Professional (CECP)
Certified Medical Assistant (CMA)
Certified Professional Coder (CPC)
chronologic resume
claims assistance professional (CAP)
coding specialist
combination resume
continuing education
cover letter
electronic claims processor (ECP)
employment agency
freelance
functional resume
interview
mentor
Nationally Certified Insurance Coding Specialist (NCICS)
networking
portfolio
Professional Association of Health Care Office Managers (PAHCOM)
recertification
Registered Medical Assistant (RMA)
Registered Medical Coder (RMC)
registration
resume
self-employment

PERFORMANCE OBJECTIVES

The student will be able to

- Define and spell the key terms for this chapter, given the information from the *Handbook* Glossary, within a reasonable period of time and with enough accuracy to obtain a satisfactory evaluation.
- Answer the self-study review questions after reading the chapter, with enough accuracy to obtain a satisfactory evaluation.
- Research information in preparation for typing a resume, given a worksheet to complete within a

reasonable period of time, and with enough accuracy to obtain a satisfactory evaluation.

- Type an accurate resume in attractive format, using plain typing paper, within a reasonable period of time, to obtain a satisfactory evaluation.
- Compose and type a letter of introduction to go with the resume and place in a typed envelope, using one sheet of plain typing paper and a number 10 envelope, within a reasonable period of time, to obtain a satisfactory evaluation.
- Complete an application form for a job, given an application for position form, within a reasonable period of time, and with enough accuracy to obtain a satisfactory evaluation.
- Compose and type a follow-up thank you letter and place in a typed envelope, using one sheet of plain typing paper and a number 10 envelope, within a reasonable period of time, to obtain a satisfactory evaluation.
- Access the Internet and visit web sites to research and/or obtain data.

STUDY OUTLINE

Employment Opportunities
- Insurance Billing Specialist
- Claims Assistance Professional

Job Search
- On-line Job Search
    - Internet
- Job Fairs
- Application
- Letter of Introduction
- Resume

Procedure: Creating an Electronic Resume

Procedure: Preparing a Resume in ASCII
- Interview
    - Portfolio
    - Alien
- Follow-up Letter

Self-Employment
- Setting up an Office
- Finances
- Equipment
- Insurance
- Marketing, Advertising, Promotion, and Public Relations
- Contracts or Agreements
- Documentation
- Statements and Pricing

Professional Associations: Certification and Registration
- American Association of Medical Assistants
- American Medical Technologists
- National Electronic Biller's Alliance
- Nationally Certified Insurance Coding Specialist
- American Association of Medical Billers
- International Billing Association
- American Academy of Professional Coders
- American Health Information Management Association
- Medical Management Institute
- Alliance of Claims Assistance Professionals
- American Guild of Patient Account Management
- Professional Association of Health Care Office Managers
- Medical Group Management Association

Keeping Current
- Mentor
- Networking

SELF-STUDY 17–1 ► REVIEW QUESTIONS

Review the objectives, key terms, glossary definitions to key terms, chapter information, and figures before completing the following review questions.

1. Read the job descriptions in *Handbook* Chapter 17. An ability to read handwritten and transcribed documents in the medical record, interpret information, and enter accurate code data in the computer system are technical skills required in the job of

   a/an ____

2. You have just completed a 1-year medical insurance billing course at a college. Name some preliminary job search contacts to make on campus.

   a. ______________________________

   b. ______________________________

   c. ______________________________

   d ______________________________

3. Name skills that may be listed on an application form or in a resume when seeking a position as an insurance billing specialist.

   a. ______________________________

   b. ______________________________

   c. ______________________________

   d ______________________________

   e. ______________________________

   f. ______________________________

4. A question appears on a job application form about salary. Two ways in which to handle this question are

   a. ______________________________

   b. ______________________________

5. State the chief purpose of a cover letter when sending a resume to a prospective employer. ______________________________

   ____

6. A resume style that emphasizes work experience dates is known as a/an ______________ format; the ______________ format stresses job skills.

7. When job applicants have similar skills and education, surveys have shown that hiring by employers has been based on ______________________________

   ____

8. List the items to be compiled in a portfolio.

   a. ______________________________

   b. ______________________________

   c. ______________________________

d. ______________________________

e. ______________________________

f. ______________________________

g. ______________________________

h. ______________________________

i. ______________________________

j. ______________________________

9. You are being interviewed for a job and the interviewer asks this question: "What is your religious preference?" What would you respond? ______________________________

____

10. If a short period of time elapses after an interview and the applicant has received no word from the prospective employer, what follow-up steps may be taken?

a. ______________________________

b. ______________________________

11. When planning to start an insurance reimbursement business, enough funds to operate the business for a period of ____________________ is vital.

12. Once an individual has begun his or her own business, the most common reason that a business might fail is ______________________________.

13. In regard to the Internal Revenue Service, estimated tax payments must be made ____________ when the net income is ____________ or more.

14. Hugh Beason was the owner of XYZ Medical Reimbursement Service. A fire occurred, damaging some of the equipment and part of the office premises, requiring him to stop his work for a month so that repairs could be made. What type(s) of insurance would be helpful for this type of problem? ______________________________

15. Name three situations in which an established insurance reimbursement service may require additional help.

a. ______________________________

b. ______________________________

c. ______________________________

16. Jerry Hahn is pursuing a career as a claims assistance professional. When marketing his business, the target audience should be ______________ and ______________.

17. Jennifer Inouye has been hired as a coding specialist by a hospital and needs to keep documentation when working. This may consist of

    a. ______________________________

    b. ______________________________

    c. ______________________________

18. List various methods used for pricing services as a self-employed insurance billing specialist.

    a. ______________________________

    b. ______________________________

19. A statement issued by a board or association verifying that an individual meets professional standards is called ______________________________.

20. Professional registration may be done in either of two ways. They are:

    a. ______________________________

    ____

    b. ______________________________

21. Define the following abbreviations that stand for validations of professionalism.

    CCAP ______________________________

    CPC ______________________________

    CCS ______________________________

    HRS ______________________________

    CMB ______________________________

    NCICS ______________________________

22. Read each statement and indicate whether True (T) or False (F).

    _______ a. Enhancing knowledge and keeping up-to-date are responsibilities of an insurance billing specialist.

    _______ b. Professional status of an insurance billing specialist may be obtained by passing a national examination for an HRS.

    _______ c. Professional status of a claims assistance professional may be obtained by passing a national examination as a CCS.

23. Name some ways an insurance billing specialist may seek to keep knowledge current.

 a. ______________________________

 b. ______________________________

 c. ______________________________

 d. ______________________________

24. Give the names of two national organizations that certify coders.

 a. ______________________________

 b. ______________________________

ASSIGNMENT 17–2 ► CONSTRUCT A RESUME WORKSHEET

Performance Objective

Task: Complete a worksheet in preparation for typing your resume.

Conditions: Use one sheet of plain typing paper and computer or typewriter.

Standards: Time: ____________ minutes

Accuracy: ____________

(Note: The time element and accuracy criteria may be given by your instructor.)

Directions: Complete a worksheet in preparation for typing your resume. Some of the information requested on the worksheet should not appear on the resume but should be available if you are asked to provide it.

ASSIGNMENT 17–3 ► TYPE A RESUME

Performance Objective

Task: Respond to a job advertisement and type a resume by abstracting data from your worksheet developed in Assignment 17–2.

Conditions: Use one sheet of plain typing paper, newspaper advertisement (Figure 17–1), and computer or typewriter.

Standards: Time: ____________ minutes

Accuracy: ____________

(Note: The time element and accuracy criteria may be given by your instructor.)

Directions: An advertisement appeared in your local newspaper (Figure 17–1). You decide to apply for the position. Abstract data you think are relevant from your information worksheet and type a resume in rough draft. Ask the instructor for suggestions to improve the rough draft. Refer to *Handbook* Chapter 17, Figure 17–10, to help organize your resume into an attractive format before typing the final copy.

MEDICAL INSURANCE CODING/REIMBURSEMENT SPECIALIST

Mid-Atlantic Clinic, a 20-physician, multi-specialty group practice in Chicago, Illinois, has a need for a coding and reimbursement specialist. Knowledge of medical terminology, CPT and ICD-9-CM coding systems, Medicare regulations, third-party insurance reimbursement and physician billing procedures required. Proficiency in the interpretation and coding of procedural and diagnostic codes is strongly preferred. Successful candidates must have excellent communication and problem-solving skills. This position offers a competitive salary and superior benefits. Please send resume to:

George B. Pason, Personnel Director
Mid-Atlantic Clinic
1230 South Main Street
Chicago, IL 60611

Figure 17–1

ASSIGNMENT 17–4 ► COMPOSE A COVER LETTER

Performance Objective

Task: Compose a cover letter to accompany your resume.

Conditions: Use one sheet of plain typing paper, Number 10 envelope, and computer or typewriter.

Standards: Time: ______________ minutes

Accuracy: ______________

(Note: The time element and accuracy criteria may be given by your instructor.)

Directions: Compose a cover letter introducing yourself, and type a rough draft. Consult the instructor for suggestions. Type the cover letter on plain bond paper in mailable form. Refer to the sample letter in *Handbook* Chapter 17, Figure 17–9 as a guide to help organize thoughts. Type a number 10 envelope and insert the letter with the resume from Assignment 17–3.

ASSIGNMENT 17–5 ► COMPLETE A JOB APPLICATION FORM

Performance Objective

Task: Complete a job application form by using data from your resume.

Conditions: Use application form (Figures 17–2*A* and *B*), your resume, and computer or typewriter.

Text continued on page 384

APPLICATION FOR POSITION/ Medical or Dental Office
AN EQUAL OPPORTUNITY EMPLOYER

(In answering questions, use extra blank sheet if necessary)

No employee, applicant, or candidate for promotion training or other advantage shall be discriminated against (or given preference) because of race, color, religion, sex, age, physical handicap, veteran status, or national origin.
PLEASE READ CAREFULLY AND WRITE OR PRINT ANSWERS TO ALL QUESTIONS. DO NOT TYPE

Date of application

A. PERSONAL INFORMATION

Name- Last First Middle	Social Security No.	Area Code/Phone No. ( )
Present Address: -Street (Apt. #) City State Zip		How long at this address?
Previous Address: -Street City State Zip From: To:	Person to notify in case of Emergency or Accident - Name: Address: Telephone:	

B. EMPLOYMENT INFORMATION

For what position are you applying?	☐ Full-time ☐ Part-time ☐ Either	Date available for employment?:	Wage/Salary Expectations:
List hrs./days you prefer to work:	List any hrs./days you are not available: (Except for times required for religious practices or observances)		Can you work overtime, if necessary? ☐ Yes ☐ No
Are you employed now?: ☐ Yes ☐ No	If so, may we inquire of your present employer?: ☐ No ☐ Yes, If yes: Name of employer: Phone number: ( )		
Have you ever been bonded?: ☐ Yes ☐ No	If required for position, are you bondable? ☐ Yes ☐ No ☐ Uncertain	Have you applied for a position with this office before? ☐ No ☐ Yes, If yes, when?:	
Referred by/ or where did you hear of this job?:			
Can you, upon employment, submit verification of your legal right to work in the United States? ☐ Yes ☐ No Submit proof that you meet legal age requirement for employment? ☐ Yes ☐ No	Language(s) applicant speaks or writes (if use of a language other than English is relevant to the job for which applicant is applying):		

C. EDUCATIONAL HISTORY

Name and address of schools attended (Include current)	Dates From	Thru	Highest grade/level completed	Diploma/degree(s) obtained/areas of study:
High school				
College				Degree/Major
Post graduate				Degree/Major
Other				Course/Diploma/License Certificate

Specific training, education, or experiences which will assist you in the job for which you have applied:

Future educational plans:

D. SPECIAL SKILLS

CHECK BELOW THE KINDS OF WORK YOU HAVE DONE:

		☐ MEDICAL INSURANCE FORMS	☐ RECEPTIONIST
☐ BLOOD COUNTS	☐ DENTAL ASSISTANT	☐ MEDICAL TERMINOLOGY	☐ TELEPHONES
☐ BOOKKEEPING	☐ DENTAL HYGIENIST	☐ MEDICAL TRANSCRIPTION	☐ TYPING
☐ COLLECTIONS	☐ FILING	☐ NURSING	☐ STENOGRAPHY
☐ COMPOSING LETTERS	☐ INJECTIONS	☐ PHLEBOTOMY (Draw Blood)	☐ URINALYSIS
☐ COMPUTER INPUT	☐ INSTRUMENT STERILIZATION	☐ POSTING	☐ X-RAY
OFFICE EQUIPMENT USED: ☐ COMPUTER	☐ DICTATING EQUIPMENT	☐ WORD PROCESSOR	☐ OTHER:
Other kinds of tasks performed or skills that may be applicable to position:		Typing speed:	Shorthand speed:

RM NO. 72-110 ©1976 BIBBERO SYSTEMS INC. PETALUMA, CA (MB-CO) # 2-5 (REV. 10/92)
REORDER CALL 800-BIBBERO (800) 242-2376

(PLEASE COMPLETE OTHER SIDE)

Figure 17–2*A*

E. EMPLOYMENT RECORD

LIST MOST RECENT EMPLOYMENT FIRST — May we contact your previous Employer(s) for a reference? ☐ yes ☐ no

1) Employer — Work performed. Be specific.

Address Street City State Zip code

Phone number ( )

Type of business — Dates From Mo. Yr. To Mo. Yr.

Your position — Hourly rate/Salary Starting Final

Supervisor's name

Reason for leaving

2) Employer — Work performed. Be specific:

Address Street City State Zip code

Phone number ( )

Type of business — Dates From Mo. Yr. To Mo. Yr.

Your position — Hourly rate/Salary Starting Final

Supervisor's name

Reason for leaving

3) Employer — Work performed. Be specific:

Address Street City State Zip code

Phone number ( )

Type of business — Dates From Mo. Yr. To Mo. Yr.

Your position — Hourly rate/Salary Starting Final

Supervisor's name

Reason for leaving

F. REFERENCES: FRIENDS/ACQUAINTANCES NON-RELATED

1) Name Address Telephone Number (☐Work ☐Home) Occupation Years acquainted

2) Name Address Telephone Number (☐Work ☐Home) Occupation Years acquainted

Please feel free to add any information which you feel will help us consider you for employment.

READ THE FOLLOWING CAREFULLY, THEN SIGN AND DATE THE APPLICATION

I certify that all answers given by me on this application are true, correct and complete to the best of my knowledge. I acknowledge notice that the information contained in this application is subject to check. I agree that, if hired, my continued employment may be contingent upon the accuracy of that information. If employed, I further agree to comply with company/office rules and regulations.

Signature ______________________ Date: ______________

RM NO. 72-110 ©1976 BIBBERO SYSTEMS INC. PETALUMA, CA (MB-CO) # 6-7 (REV. 4/92) TO REORDER CALL 800-BIBBERO (800) 242-2376

B

Figure 17–2*B*

Standards: Time: ______________ minutes

Accuracy: ______________

(Note: The time element and accuracy criteria may be given by your instructor.)

Directions: Assume the employer asked you to come to his or her place of business to complete an application form and make an appointment for an interview. Using your data and resume, complete an application form (Figures 17–2*A* and *B*).

ASSIGNMENT 17–6 ▶ PREPARE A FOLLOW-UP THANK YOU LETTER

Performance Objective

Task: Prepare a follow-up thank you letter after the interview, sending it to the interviewer.

Conditions: Use one sheet of plain typing paper, Number 10 envelope, and computer or typewriter.

Standards: Time: ______________ minutes

Accuracy: ______________

(Note: The time element and accuracy criteria may be given by your instructor.)

Directions: After the interview, you decide to send a follow-up thank you letter to the person who interviewed you. Type a letter and address a number 10 envelope. Refer to *Handbook* Chapter 17, Figure 17–16, to help organize your thoughts.

ASSIGNMENT 17–7 ▶ VISIT WEB SITES FOR JOB OPPORTUNITIES

Performance Objective

Task: Access the Internet and visit several web sites of the World Wide Web.

Conditions: Use a computer with printer and/or pen or pencil to make notes.

Standards: Time: ______________ minutes

Accuracy: ______________

(Note: The time element and accuracy criteria may be given by your instructor.)

Directions: If you have access to the Internet, visit the World Wide Web and do some job searching. After obtaining the web site data, take them to share for class discussion. Note that some sites may not be accessible if you attempt to visit them during peak hours.

1. Visit the American Association of Medical Assistants' web site, www.aama-ntl.org, and click on AAMA Job Source. See if there are any new job opportunities in your state. Print a hard copy of the names, addresses, and telephone numbers of participating employers near your region while remaining online.

2. Connect to the Allied Health Opportunities for Healthcare Professionals' web site http://www.gvpub.com. Click on "Employment Opportunities." After you get to that screen, click on "Allied Health Opportunities," and at the next screen, click on "Medical Assistants" or "Health Information Management Professionals." Then see if you can locate any listings for billing or coding positions. Print out some of the listings that appeal to you and take them to class for discussion.

3. Check out an online resource, hcPro's Health Information Management Supersite, www.himinfo.com. This site has job postings for many medical job titles for those involved in health information management. Click on the Career Center under the Interactive site features to see job postings. Then click on HIM Job Listings. Enter a job title to do a search, e.g., coder or biller, and see if you can locate any job openings. Print some of these listings to share and discuss during class.

4. Visit the JustCoding Web site, www.justcoding.com, and click the Link to Coding Career Center. Then click on Search for a Job under the For Employees heading. Enter a key word, e.g., coder, and see if you can obtain any search results. Print some of these listings to share and discuss during class.

5. Access the Internet and use a search engine (Yahoo, Excite, Alta Vista). Key in "Yahoo insurance billers" to search for job opportunities. See if you can locate any jobs that are in your region or state. List three web site addresses that you find and take them to share for class discussion.

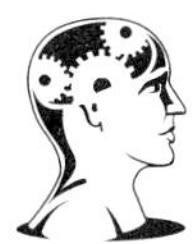

ASSIGNMENT 17–8 ► CRITICAL THINKING

Performance Objective

Task: Write a paragraph describing the benefits of becoming certified.

Conditions: Use a computer with printer and/or pen or pencil.

Standards: Time: ______________ minutes

Accuracy: ________________

(Note: The time element and accuracy criteria may be given by your instructor.)

Directions: Write a paragraph or two describing why you would like to become certified and incorporate a numbered list of benefits. Make sure grammar, punctuation, and spelling are correct.

Tests

Test 1: Procedure (E/M and Medicine Sections) and Diagnostic Procedure Code Test

Directions: Using a *Current Procedural Terminology (CPT)* code book or Appendix A, insert the correct code numbers and modifiers for each service rendered. Give a brief description for each professional service rendered, although this is not needed when completing the HCFA-1500 claim form. An additional optional exercise is to abstract the pertinent data from each case, use your *ICD-9-CM* code-book, and insert the diagnosis code.

Insert year of the *CPT* code book used ________________

Insert year of the *ICD-9-CM* code book used ________________

1. Dr. Input sees a new patient, Mrs. Post, in the office for acute abdominal distress. The physician spends approximately 1 hour doing a comprehensive history and physical examination with high-complexity decision making. Several diagnostic studies are ordered, and she is given an appointment to return in 1 week.
   Description

   ____ *CPT #* _______

   ____ *ICD #* _______

2. Mr. Nakahara, an established patient, sees Dr. Practon in the office on January 11 for a re-evaluation of his diabetic condition. Dr. Practon takes a detailed history and performs a detailed examination. Decision making is moderately complex.
   Description

   ____ *CPT #* _______

   ____ *ICD #* _______

3. Dr. Cardi sees Mrs. Franklin for a follow-up office visit for her hypertension. A problem-focused history and examination of her cardiovascular system were done, revealing BP 140/100. Straightforward decision making with medication being

prescribed. Patient advised to return in 2 weeks to have her blood pressure checked by the nurse. Mrs. Franklin returns 2 weeks later, and the nurse checks her blood pressure.
Description

____ *CPT #* ______

____ *ICD #* ______

____ *CPT #* ______

____ *ICD #* ______

4. Dr. Skeleton receives a call at 7 p.m. from Mrs. Snyder. Her husband, a patient of Dr. Skeleton's, has been very ill for 2 hours with profuse vomiting. Dr. Skeleton goes to their home to see Mr. Snyder and spends considerable time doing a detailed history and examination. The medical decision making was of a highly complex nature. Physician administered an injection of Compazine.
Description

____ *CPT #* ______

____ *CPT #* ______

____ *ICD #* ______

5. Dr. Cutis sees an established patient, a registered nurse, for determination of pregnancy. Detailed hx & exam are done, with moderate complexity medical decision making. A Papanicolaou smear is taken, a blood sample is drawn, and the specimens are sent to an independent laboratory for a qualitative hCG (human chorionic gonadotropin) test. The patient also complains of something she has discovered under her armpit. On examination, there is a furuncle of the left axilla, which is incised and drained during this visit. The laboratory requires *CPT* coding on the lab requisition. List how these lab procedures would appear on the requisition sheet. The Pap smear is processed using the Bethesda System and done under physician supervision.
Professional Service Rendered by Dr. Cutis

____ *CPT #* ______

____ *CPT #* ______

____ *CPT #* ______

____ *CPT #* ______

____ *ICD #* ______

____ *ICD #* ______

Laboratory Service on Requisition Sheet

____ *CPT #* ______

____ *CPT #* ______

6. Dr. Antrum makes a house call on Betty Mason, an established patient, for a problem-focused history of acute otitis media. A problem-focused examination is performed, with straightforward medical decision making. While there, she also sees Betty's younger sister, Sandra, whom she has seen previously in the office, for acute tonsillitis. A problem-focused hx & exam is performed with low-complexity decision making. In addition to the examinations, she gives both children injections of penicillin.
Professional Service Rendered to Betty

_______________ *CPT #* _______

_______________ *CPT #* _______

_______________ *ICD #* _______

Professional Service Rendered to Sandra

_______________ *CPT #* _______

_______________ *CPT #* _______

_______________ *ICD #* _______

7. Two weeks later Dr. Antrum is called to the emergency department at College Hospital at 2 a.m. on Sunday to see Betty Mason for recurrent chronic otitis media with suppuration. A problem-focused hx & exam is performed with straightforward decision making. Dr. Antrum administers a second injection of penicillin.
Description

_______________ *CPT #* _______

_______________ *CPT #* _______

_______________ *ICD #* _______

8. While at the hospital, Dr. Antrum is asked to see another patient in the emergency department, who is new to her. A problem-focused history is taken. She does a problem-focused examination and straightforward decision making for an intermediate 3.5-cm laceration of the scalp. It is sutured and patient is advised to come to the office in 4 days for a dressing change. Four days later the patient comes into the office for a dressing change by the nurse.
Description

_______________ *CPT #* _______

_______________ *CPT #* _______

_______________ *CPT #* _______

_______________ *ICD #* _______

9. Dr. Menter, a psychiatrist, sees the following patients in the hospital. Code the procedures.
Ms. Blake: Consultation, expanded problem-focused hx & exam and straightforward decision making. Referred by Dr. Practon. *CPT #* _______

Mrs. Clark: Group psychotherapy (50 min) *CPT #* ______

Mrs. Samson: Group psychotherapy (50 min) *CPT #* ______

Mr. Shoemaker: Group psychotherapy (50 min) *CPT #* ______

Miss James: Individual psychotherapy (25 min) *CPT #* ______

10. Dr. Input, a gastroenterologist, sees Mrs. Chan in the hospital at the request of Dr. Practon for an esophageal ulcer. In addition to the detailed history/examination and low-complexity decision making, he does an esophageal intubation and washings and prepares slides for cytology. Two days later he sees Mrs. Chan in follow-up inpatient consultation and does a problem-focused interval hx & exam and low-complexity decision making. He performs a gastric intubation and collects washings for cytology for a gastric ulcer.
    Description

______________________________ *CPT #* ______

______________________________ *CPT #* ______

______________________________ *ICD #* ______

______________________________ *CPT #* ______

______________________________ *CPT #* ______

______________________________ *ICD #* ______

11. Mrs. Galati, a new patient, goes to Dr. Cardi because of chest pain (moderate to severe), weakness, fatigue, and dizziness. Dr. Cardi takes a comprehensive history and does a comprehensive examination, including ECG with interpretation and report, followed by a treadmill ECG. He also performs a vital capacity test and dipstick urinalysis, and draws blood for a SMA-C (16 panel tests including CBC) and T-3 that are sent to and billed by a laboratory. Medical decision making was of high complexity.
    Description

______________________________ *CPT #* ______

______________________________ *CPT #* ______

______________________________ *CPT #* ______

______________________________ *CPT #* ______

______________________________ *CPT #* ______

______________________________ *CPT #* ______

______________________________ *ICD #* ______

______________________________ *ICD #* ______

______________________________ *ICD #* ______

12. Jake Wonderhill has not had his eyes examined by Dr. Lenser for about 5 years. He is seen by Dr. Lenser, who performs the following ophthalmologic procedures in addition to a comprehensive eye examination: fluorescein angioscopy and electroretinography. He is diagnosed with retinitis pigmentosa.
Description

_______________ *CPT #* ______

_______________ *CPT #* ______

_______________ *CPT #* ______

_______________ *ICD #* ______

13. Dr. Practon is making rounds at the College Hospital and answers an urgent call on 3rd Floor East. He performs resuscitation on Mr. Sanchez for cardiac arrest and orders the patient taken to the critical care unit. Chest x-rays, lab work, blood gases, and ECG are performed. The physician is detained 2 hours in constant attendance on the patient.
Description

_______________ *CPT #* ______

_______________ *CPT #* ______

_______________ *ICD #* ______

14. Mrs. Powers, new patient, sees Dr. Skeleton for low sciatica. Dr. Skeleton takes a detailed history and does a detailed examination of her lower back and extremities. Medical decision making is of low complexity. Diathermy (30 min) is given. The next day she comes in for therapeutic exercises in the Hubbard tank (30 min).
Description

_______________ *CPT #* ______

_______________ *CPT #* ______

_______________ *ICD #* ______

_______________ *CPT #* ______

_______________ *ICD #* ______

15. A. Mrs. Garcia, a new patient, is seen by Dr. Caesar for occasional vaginal spotting (detailed hx/exam and low-complexity decision making). The doctor determines the bleeding is coming from the cervix and asks her to return in 3 days for cryocauterization of the cervix. During the initial examination, Mrs. Garcia asks for an evaluation for possible infertility. Dr. Caesar advises her to wait 2 to 3 weeks and make an appointment for two infertility tests.
    B. When the patient returns in 3 days for cryocauterization, the doctor also takes a wet mount for bacteria/fungi, which is sent to and billed by a laboratory.
    C. Three weeks later, an injection procedure for hysterosalpingography and endometrial biopsy are performed.

A. _______________ *CPT #* ______

_______________ *ICD #* ______

B. ______________________________ CPT # ______

______________________________ CPT # ______

______________________________ ICD # ______

C. ______________________________ CPT # ______

______________________________ CPT # ______

______________________________ ICD # ______

Multiple Choice. After reading the boxed codes with descriptions, select the answer(s) that is/are best in each case.

59120	Surgical treatment of ectopic pregnancy; tubal or ovarian, requiring salpingectomy and/or oophorectomy, abdominal or vaginal approach.
59121	tubal or ovarian, without salpingectomy and/or oophorectomy
59130	abdominal pregnancy
59135	interstitial, uterine pregnancy requiring total hysterectomy
59136	interstitial, uterine pregnancy with partial resection of uterus
59140	cervical, with evacuation

16. In regard to this section of *CPT* codes, which of the following statements is true about codes 59120 through 59140 (mark all that apply):

    a. they refer to abdominal hysterotomy

    b. they involve laparoscopic treatment of ectopic pregnancy

    c. they refer to treatment of ectopic pregnancy by surgery

    d. they involve tubal ligation

17. In regard to this section of *CPT* codes, for treatment of an ectopic pregnancy, tubal, requiring oophorectomy, the code to select is:

    a. 59121

    b. 59120

    c. 59135

    d. 59136

    e. 59130

18. In regard to this section of *CPT* codes, for treatment of an ectopic pregnancy (interstitial, uterine) requiring a total hysterectomy, the code(s) to select is/are:

    a. 59135

    b. 59135 and 59120

c. 59120

d. 59130 and 59120

e. 59121

Test 2: Procedure Code with Modifiers and Diagnostic Code Test

Match the description given in the right column with the procedure code/modifier combination in the left column. Write the letter in the blank.

Procedure with Modifier		*Description*
1. 99245–21	_______	a. Dr. Practon assisted Dr. Caesar with a total abdominal hysterectomy and bilateral salpingo-oophorectomy.
2. 31540–57	_______	b. Dr. Skeleton interprets a thoracolumbar x-ray film that was taken at College Hospital.
3. 58150–80	_______	c. Mrs. Ulwelling saw Dr. Antrum as a new patient, and he recommended that the patient have a laryngoscopy with stripping of vocal cords to be done the following day.
4. 32440–55	_______	d. Mrs. Gillenbach walked through a plate glass window and had a rhinoplasty performed by Dr. Graff on 2/16/XX. On 2/26/XX she came to see Dr. Graff for a consultation regarding reconstructive surgery on her right leg.
5. 72080–26	_______	e. Mr. Mercado was seen by Dr. Langerhans in the office for a complicated diabetic consultation. A comprehensive history and examination was done, with high-complexity medical decision making; however, the physician spent a total of 2 hours with the patient.
6. 29425–58	_______	f. Dr. Cutler performed a bilateral orchiopexy (inguinal approach) on baby Kozak.
(50/51) 7. 54640–99	_______	g. Dr. Skeleton applied a short leg walking cast to Mrs. Belchere's right leg 4 weeks after his initial treatment of her fractured tibia.
8. 99253–24	_______	h. Dr. Cutler went on vacation and Dr. Coccidioides took care of Mrs. Ash during her postoperative period after her total pneumonectomy.

Directions: Using a *Current Procedural Terminology (CPT)* code book or Appendix A, insert the correct code numbers and modifiers for each service rendered. Give a brief description for each professional service rendered, although this is not needed when completing the HCFA-1500 claim form.

9. Dr. Input performs a gastrojejunostomy for carcinoma in situ of the duodenum and calls in Dr. Scott to do the anesthesia and Dr. Cutler to assist. This intraperitoneal surgery takes 2 hours, 30 minutes. The patient is normal and healthy. List the procedure and diagnostic code numbers with appropriate modifiers for each physician.
   Professional Service Rendered by Dr. Input

   ______________________________________ *CPT #* _______

   ______________________________________ *ICD #* _______

Professional Service Rendered by Dr. Scott

______________________________ *CPT #* ______

______________________________ *ICD #* ______

Professional Service Rendered by Dr. Cutler

______________________________ *CPT #* ______

______________________________ *ICD #* ______

10. Dr. Rumsey assists Dr. Cutler with a total colectomy (intraperitoneal procedure) with ileostomy. Dr. Scott is the anesthesiologist. Surgery takes 2 hours, 55 minutes. The patient has a secondary malignant neoplasm of the colon (severe systemic disease). List the procedure code numbers with appropriate modifiers and diagnostic code numbers for each physician.
    Professional Service Rendered by Dr. Rumsey

    ______________________________ *CPT #* ______

    ______________________________ *ICD #* ______

    Professional Service Rendered by Dr. Scott

    ______________________________ *CPT #* ______

    ______________________________ *ICD #* ______

    Professional Service Rendered by Dr. Cutler

    ______________________________ *CPT #* ______

    ______________________________ *ICD #* ______

11. Dr. Cutis removes a malignant lesion from a patient's back (1.5 cm) and does the local anesthesia herself.
    Description

    ______________________________ *CPT #* ______

    ______________________________ *ICD #* ______

12. Dr. Skeleton sees Mr. Richmond, a new patient worked into the office schedule as an emergency following an automobile accident. He has multiple lacerations of the face, arm, and chest and a fracture of the left tibia. The physician takes a comprehensive history and does a comprehensive examination. Decision making is moderately complex. He orders bilateral x-rays of the tibia and fibula and two views of the chest and left wrist to be taken in his office. Then he closes the following lacerations: 2.6 cm, simple, face; 2.0 cm, intermediate, face; 7.5 cm, intermediate, right arm; 4.5 cm, intermediate, chest. All x-rays are negative except

the left tibia. Dr. Skeleton performs a manipulative reduction of the left tibial shaft and applies a cast.
Description

____ *CPT #* _______

____ *ICD #* _______

____ *CPT #* _______

____ *CPT #* _______

____ *CPT #* _______

____ *CPT #* _______

____ *CPT #* _______

____ *CPT #* _______

____ *CPT #* _______

____ *CPT #* _______

____ *ICD #* _______

____ *ICD #* _______

____ *ICD #* _______

____ *ICD #* _______

Six weeks later Dr. Skeleton sees the same patient for an office visit and takes x-rays (2 views) of the left tibia and fibula. Treatment involves application of a cast below the left knee to the toes, including a walking heel.
Description

____ *CPT #* _______

____ *CPT #* _______

____ *CPT #* _______

____ *ICD #* _______

13. Dr. Cutler performs an incisional biopsy of the breast for a breast lump, requiring 40 minutes of anesthesia. Dr. Scott is the anesthesiologist. The patient is normal and healthy. List the procedure and diagnostic code numbers for each physician.

Professional Service Rendered by Dr. Cutler

_______________ *CPT #* _______

_______________ *ICD #* _______

Professional Service Rendered by Dr. Scott

_______________ *CPT #* _______

_______________ *ICD #* _______

14. Mrs. DeBeau is aware that Dr. Input will be out of town for 6 weeks; however, she decides to have him perform the recommended combined anterior-posterior colporrhaphy with enterocele repair for vaginal enterocele. Dr. Practon agrees to do the follow-up care and assist. Dr. Scott is the anesthesiologist. The anesthesia time is 2 hours, 15 minutes. The patient is normal and healthy. List the procedure and diagnostic code numbers for each physician.
Professional Service Rendered by Dr. Input

_______________ *CPT #* _______

_______________ *ICD #* _______

Professional Service Rendered by Dr. Practon

_______________ *CPT #* _______

_______________ *CPT #* _______

_______________ *CPT #* _______

_______________ *ICD #* _______

Professional Service Rendered by Dr. Scott

_______________ *CPT #* _______

_______________ *ICD #* _______

15. Mr. Wong, a new patient, is seen in the College Hospital and undergoes a comprehensive H & P with moderately complex decision making. Dr. Coccidioides performs a bronchoscopy with biopsy. Results of the biopsy confirm the diagnosis: malignant neoplasm of upper left lobe of lung. The following day he performs a total pneumonectomy. Dr. Cutler assists on the total pneumonectomy (pulmonary resection), and Dr. Scott is the anesthesiologist. Surgery takes 3 hours, 45 minutes. Patient has mild systemic disease. List the procedure and diagnostic code numbers for each physician.
Professional Service Rendered by Dr. Coccidioides

_______________ *CPT #* _______

_______________ *CPT #* _______

_______________ *CPT #* _______

_______________ *ICD #* _______

Professional Service Rendered by Dr. Cutler

______________________________ *CPT #* ______

______________________________ *ICD #* ______

Professional Service Rendered by Dr. Scott

______________________________ *CPT #* ______

______________________________ *ICD #* ______

When completing the HCFA-1500 claim form for Dr. Scott, in which block would

you list anesthesia minutes? ______________________________

Test 3: Procedure (Radiology and Pathology Sections) and Diagnostic Code Test

Directions: Using a *Current Procedural Terminology (CPT)* code book or Appendix A, insert the correct procedure code numbers and modifiers and diagnostic codes for each service rendered. Give a brief description for each professional service rendered, although this is not needed when completing the HCFA-1500 claim form.

1. Mrs. Cahn sees Dr. Skeleton because of severe pain in her right shoulder. She is a new patient. Dr. Skeleton takes a detailed history and performs a detailed examination. A complete x-ray study of the right shoulder is done. Decision making is of low complexity. Diagnosis of bursitis is made, and an injection of the bursa is administered.
   Description

   ______________________________ *CPT #* ______

   ______________________________ *CPT #* ______

   ______________________________ *CPT #* ______

   ______________________________ *ICD #* ______

2. John Murphy comes into the Broxton Radiologic Group, Inc., for an extended radiation therapy consultation for prostatic cancer. The radiologist takes a detailed history and does a detailed examination. Decision making is of low complexity. The physician determines a simple treatment plan involving simple simulation-aided field settings. Basic dosimetry calculations are done, and the patient returns the following day and receives radiation therapy to a single treatment area (6–10 MeV).
   Description

   ______________________________ *CPT #* ______

   ______________________________ *CPT #* ______

   ______________________________ *CPT #* ______

__________ *CPT #* ______

__________ *CPT #* ______

Diagnosis: __________ *ICD #* ______

3. Dr. Input refers Mrs. Horner to the Nuclear Medicine department of the Broxton Radiologic Group, Inc., for a bone marrow imaging of the whole body and imaging of the liver and spleen. List the procedure code numbers after each radiologic procedure to show how the radiology group would bill. Also list the diagnosis of malignant neoplasm of the bone marrow.
   Description

   Total body bone marrow, imaging *CPT #* ______

   Radiopharmaceuticals, diagnostic *CPT #* ______

   Liver and spleen imaging *CPT #* ______

   Radiopharmaceuticals, diagnostic *CPT #* ______

   Diagnosis: __________ *ICD #* ______

4. Dr. Input also refers Mrs. Homer to XYZ Laboratory for the following tests. List the procedure code numbers to indicate how the laboratory would bill.
   Description

   CBC, automated with manual differential *CPT #* ______

   Urinalysis, automated with microscopy *CPT #* ______

   Urine culture (quantitative, colony count) *CPT #* ______

   Urine antibiotic sensitivity (microtiter) *CPT #* ______

5. The general laboratory at College Hospital receives a surgical tissue specimen (ovarian biopsy) for gross and microscopic examination from a patient with Stein-Leventhal syndrome. List the procedure and diagnostic code numbers to indicate what the hospital pathology department would bill.
   Description

   __________ *CPT #* ______

   Diagnosis: __________ *ICD #* ______

6. Dr. Langerhans refers Jerry Cramer to XYZ Laboratory for a lipid panel. He has a family history of cardiovascular disease. List the procedure and diagnostic code number(s) to indicate how the laboratory would bill.
   Description

   __________ *CPT #* ______

   Diagnosis: __________ *ICD #* ______

7. Dr. Caesar is an Ob-Gyn specialist who has her own ultrasound machine. Carmen Cardoza, age 45, is referred to Dr. Caesar for an obstetric consultation and an amniocentesis using ultrasonic guidance. The diagnosis is Rh incompatibility. The doctor performs a detailed history and physical exam and decision making of low complexity.
   Description

   ______________________________ *CPT #* ______

   ______________________________ *CPT #* ______

   ______________________________ *CPT #* ______

   Diagnosis: ______________________________ *ICD #* ______

8. Mr. Marcos' medical record indicates that a retrograde pyelogram followed by a percutaneous nephrostolithotomy, with basket extraction of a stone 1 cm in size, was performed by Dr. Ulibarri for nephrolithiasis.
   Description

   ______________________________ *CPT #* ______

   ______________________________ *CPT #* ______

   Diagnosis: ______________________________ *ICD #* ______

9. Broxton Radiologic Group, Inc., performs the following procedures on Mrs. Stephens at the request of Dr. Input. List the procedure code numbers after each radiologic procedure. On the laboratory slip the following congenital diagnoses are listed: Diverticulum of the stomach and colon; cystic lung. Locate the corresponding diagnostic codes.

   Barium enema *CPT #* ______

   Upper GI tract with small bowel *CPT #* ______

   Complete chest x-ray *CPT #* ______

   Diagnosis: ______________________________ *ICD #* ______

   Diagnosis: ______________________________ *ICD #* ______

   Diagnosis: ______________________________ *ICD #* ______

10. Two weeks later Mrs. Stephens is referred again for further radiologic studies for flank pain. List the procedure and diagnostic code numbers after each radiologic procedure.

    IVP (intravenous pyelogram) with drip infusion *CPT #* ______

    Oral cholecystography *CPT #* ______

    Diagnosis: ______________________________ *ICD #* ______

Test 4: Completing a HCFA-1500 Claim Form for a Private Plan

Performance Objective

Task: Complete a health insurance claim form using OCR guidelines and post the information to the patient's ledger card.

Conditions: Use Jennifer Lacey's patient record (Figure 1), ledger card (Figure 2), one health insurance claim form (Figure 3), typewriter, computer, or pen, procedural and diagnostic code books, and *Workbook* Appendixes A and B.

Standards: Claim Productivity Management

Time: ______________ minutes

Accuracy: ______________

(Note: The time element and accuracy criteria may be given by your instructor.)

Directions: Complete a HCFA-1500 claim form on Jennifer Lacey using OCR guidelines. Use your *CPT* code book or Appendix A to determine the correct five-digit code numbers and fees for each professional service rendered. Remember to include modifiers if necessary. Use your diagnostic code book to code each active diagnosis. Dr. Caesar is accepting assignment. Date the claim August 15 and record on the ledger card when you have submitted the claim to the insurance company.

American Commercial Insurance Company sent a check (Voucher number 5586) on November 17 in the amount of $880. The patient's responsibility is $220. Post the payment and write off (adjust) the remaining balance. Circle the amount billed to the patient.

PATIENT RECORD NO. T0004

LAST NAME	FIRST NAME	MIDDLE NAME	BIRTH DATE	SEX	HOME PHONE
Lacey,	Jennifer	T.	11-12-45	F	013-549-0098

ADDRESS	CITY	STATE	ZIP CODE
451 Roberts Street,	Woodland Hills,	XY	12345

PATIENT'S OCCUPATION: Legal secretary
NAME OF COMPANY: Attorneys Higgins and Higgins

ADDRESS OF EMPLOYER: 430 Second Avenue, Woodland Hills, XY 12345
PHONE: 013-540-6675

SPOUSE OR PARENT OCCUPATION

EMPLOYER ADDRESS PHONE

NAME OF INSURANCE: American Commercial Insurance, 5682 Bendix Boulevard, Woodland Hills, XY 12345

OTHER INSURANCE

POLICY NO.	GROUP NO.	EFFECTIVE DATE	SOC. SEC. NO.
5789022			430-98-7709

REFERRED BY: Clarence Cutler, MD 4567 Broad Avenue, Woodland Hills, XY 12345

DATE	PROGRESS
8-1-XX	New pt came in for consultation and additional opinion referred by Dr. Cutler. CC: full feeling in stomach. BM difficulty for 5 days. Sometimes difficulty c̄ urination. Ultrasonic report showed rt ovarian mass and leiomyomata uteri. Pap smear Class 1. PE confirmed 1g tumor extending out of pelvis and felt halfway to umbilicus. Adv additional tests and expl. laparotomy with abdominal hysterectomy; possible bilateral salpingo-oophorectomy and pelvic exenteration for malignancy. Bertha Caesar, MD
8-2-XX	Adm to College Hosp. Ordered IVP, barium enema and bone scan; scheduled surgery next day. Bertha Caesar, MD
8-3-XX	Perf abdominal hysterectomy with bilateral salpingo-oophorectomy. Path report revealed leiomyomata uteri and cystoma of rt ovary. Bertha Caesar, MD
8-4-XX	Hosp. visit. Mild PO pain. Otherwise doing well. Bertha Caesar, MD
8-5-XX	Hosp. visit. Improving and less pain. Bertha Caesar, MD
8-6-XX	Hosp. visit. Ambulating well. Dressing changed. Bertha Caesar, MD
8-7-XX	Hosp. visit. No pain, ambulating without assistance. Plan to DC tomorrow. Bertha Caesar, MD
8-8-XX	Pt doing well; DC to home. Bertha Caesar, MD

Figure 1

STATEMENT

College Clinic
4567 Broad Avenue
Woodland Hills, XY 12345-0001
Telephone: 013-486-9002
Fax: 013-487-8976

Miss Jennifer T. Lacey
451 Roberts Street
Woodland Hills, XY 12345

DATE	PROFESSIONAL SERVICE DESCRIPTION	CHARGE	CREDITS		CURRENT BALANCE
			PAYMENTS	ADJUSTMENTS	
8-1-xx	Consultation, EPF hx/exam, SF decision making				
8-2-xx	Init hosp care: comp hx/exam, hist incl prep of hosp documents & adm, HC decision making				
8-3-xx	Total abdominal hysterectomy with salpingo-oophorectomy				
8-4-xx	HV				
8-5-xx	HV				
8-6-xx	HV				
8-7-xx	HV				
8-8-xx	Hosp discharge				

Due and payable within 10 days. **Pay last amount in balance column** 

Key:
- PF: Problem-focused
- EPF: Expanded problem-focused
- D: Detailed
- C: Comprehensive
- SF: Straightforward
- LC: Low complexity
- MC: Moderate complexity
- HC: High complexity
- CON: Consultation
- CPX: Complete phys exam
- E: Emergency
- ER: Emergency dept.
- HCD: House call (day)
- HCN: House call (night)
- HV: Hospital visit
- OV: Office visit

Figure 2

APPROVED OMB 0938-0008

PLEASE DO NOT STAPLE IN THIS AREA

CARRIER

PICA

HEALTH INSURANCE CLAIM FORM

PICA

1. MEDICARE (Medicare #) MEDICAID (Medicaid #) CHAMPUS (Sponsor's SSN) CHAMPVA (VA File #) GROUP HEALTH PLAN (SSN or ID) FECA BLK LUNG (SSN) OTHER (ID)

1a. INSURED'S I.D. NUMBER (FOR PROGRAM IN ITEM 1)

2. PATIENT'S NAME (Last Name, First Name, Middle Initial)

3. PATIENT'S BIRTH DATE MM | DD | YYYY SEX M F

4. INSURED'S NAME (Last Name, First Name, Middle Initial)

5. PATIENT'S ADDRESS (No., Street)

6. PATIENT RELATIONSHIP TO INSURED Self Spouse Child Other

7. INSURED'S ADDRESS (No., Street)

CITY STATE

8. PATIENT STATUS Single Married Other; Employed Full-Time Student Part-Time Student

CITY STATE

ZIP CODE TELEPHONE (Include Area Code)

ZIP CODE TELEPHONE (include Area Code) ( )

9. OTHER INSURED'S NAME (Last Name, First Name, Middle Initial)

10. IS PATIENT'S CONDITION RELATED TO:

11. INSURED'S POLICY GROUP OR FECA NUMBER

a. OTHER INSURED'S POLICY OR GROUP NUMBER

a. EMPLOYMENT? (CURRENT OR PREVIOUS) YES NO

a. INSURED'S DATE OF BIRTH MM | DD | YY SEX M F

b. OTHER INSURED'S DATE OF BIRTH MM | DD | YY SEX M F

b. AUTO ACCIDENT? YES NO PLACE (State)

b. EMPLOYER'S NAME OR SCHOOL NAME

c. EMPLOYER'S NAME OR SCHOOL NAME

c. OTHER ACCIDENT? YES NO

c. INSURANCE PLAN NAME OR PROGRAM NAME

d. INSURANCE PLAN NAME OR PROGRAM NAME

10d. RESERVED FOR LOCAL USE

d. IS THERE ANOTHER HEALTH BENEFIT PLAN? YES NO *If yes, return to and complete item 9 a-d.*

READ BACK OF FORM BEFORE COMPLETING AND SIGNING THIS FORM.

12. PATIENT'S OR AUTHORIZED PERSON'S SIGNATURE I authorize the release of any medical or other information necessary to process this claim. I also request payment of government benefits either to myself or to the party who accepts assignment below.

SIGNED ______ DATE ______

13. INSURED'S OR AUTHORIZED PERSON'S SIGNATURE I authorize payment of medical benefits to the undersigned physician or supplier for services described below.

SIGNED ______

PATIENT AND INSURED INFORMATION

14. DATE OF CURRENT: MM | DD | YY ◀ ILLNESS (First symptom) OR INJURY (Accident) OR PREGNANCY (LMP)

15. IF PATIENT HAS HAD SAME OR SIMILAR ILLNESS GIVE FIRST DATE MM | DD | YY

16. DATES PATIENT UNABLE TO WORK IN CURRENT OCCUPATION FROM MM | DD | YY TO MM | DD | YY

17. NAME OF REFERRING PHYSICIAN OR OTHER SOURCE

17a. I.D. NUMBER OF REFERRING PHYSICIAN

18. HOSPITALIZATION DATES RELATED TO CURRENT SERVICES FROM MM | DD | YY TO MM | DD | YY

19. RESERVED FOR LOCAL USE

20. OUTSIDE LAB? YES NO $ CHARGES

21. DIAGNOSIS OR NATURE OF ILLNESS OR INJURY. (RELATE ITEMS 1,2,3 OR 4 TO ITEM 24E BY LINE)

1. ______ 3. ______

2. ______ 4. ______

22. MEDICAID RESUBMISSION CODE ORIGINAL REF. NO.

23. PRIOR AUTHORIZATION NUMBER

24. A DATE(S) OF SERVICE From MM DD YY To MM DD YY	B Place of Service	C Type of Service	D PROCEDURES, SERVICES, OR SUPPLIES (Explain Unusual Circumstances) CPT/HCPCS | MODIFIER	E DIAGNOSIS CODE	F $ CHARGES	G DAYS OR UNITS	H EPSDT Family Plan	I EMG	J COB	K RESERVED FOR LOCAL USE

25. FEDERAL TAX I.D. NUMBER SSN EIN

26. PATIENT'S ACCOUNT NO.

27. ACCEPT ASSIGNMENT? (For govt. claims, see back) YES NO

28. TOTAL CHARGE $

29. AMOUNT PAID $

30. BALANCE DUE $

31. SIGNATURE OF PHYSICIAN OR SUPPLIER INCLUDING DEGREES OR CREDENTIALS (I certify that the statements on the reverse apply to this bill and are made a part thereof.)

SIGNED DATE

32. NAME AND ADDRESS OF FACILITY WHERE SERVICES WERE RENDERED (If other than home or office)

33. PHYSICIAN'S, SUPPLIER'S BILLING NAME, ADDRESS, ZIP CODE AND PHONE #

PIN# GRP#

PHYSICIAN OR SUPPLIER INFORMATION

(APPROVED BY AMA COUNCIL ON MEDICAL SERVICE8/88) *PLEASE PRINT OR TYPE* FORM HCFA-1500 (U2)(12-90) FORM OCWP-1500 FORM RRB-1500

Figure 3

Test 5: Completing a HCFA-1500 Claim Form for a Private Plan

Performance Objective

Task: Complete a health insurance claim form using OCR guidelines and post the information to the patient's ledger card.

Conditions: Use Hortense N. Hope's patient record (Figure 4), ledger card (Figure 5), one health insurance claim form (Figure 6), typewriter, computer or pen, procedural and diagnostic code books, and *Workbook* Appendixes A and B.

Standards: Claim Productivity Management

Time: ________________ minutes

Accuracy: ________________

(Note: The time element and accuracy criteria may be given by your instructor.)

Directions: Complete a HCFA-1500 claim form using OCR guidelines and date it July 31. Use your *CPT* code book or Appendix A to determine the correct five-digit code numbers and fees for each professional service rendered. Remember to include modifiers if necessary. Use your diagnostic code book to code each active diagnosis. Dr. Practon is accepting assignment. Record on the ledger card when you have submitted the claim to the insurance company.

PATIENT RECORD NO. T0005

LAST NAME	FIRST NAME	MIDDLE NAME	BIRTH DATE	SEX	HOME PHONE
Hope,	Hortense	N.	04-12-46	F	013-666-7821

ADDRESS	CITY	STATE	ZIP CODE
247 Lantern Pike,	Woodland Hills,	XY	12345

PATIENT'S OCCUPATION	NAME OF COMPANY
clerk typist	R and S Manufacturing Company

ADDRESS OF EMPLOYER	PHONE
2271 West 74 Street, Torres, XY 12349	013-466-5890

SPOUSE OR PARENT	OCCUPATION
Harry J. Hope	carpenter

EMPLOYER	ADDRESS	PHONE
Jesse Construction Company,	3861 South Orange Street, Torres, XY 12349	013-765-2318

NAME OF INSURANCE
Ralston Insurance Company, 2611 Hanley Street, Woodland Hills, XY 12345

POLICY NO.	GROUP NO.
ATC32145 8809	T8471811A

MEDICARE NO.	MEDICAID NO.	EFFECTIVE DATE	SOC. SEC. NO.
			321-45-8809

REFERRED BY: husband

DATE	PROGRESS
07-01-xx	New ♀ pt comes in complaining of lt great toe pain. Exam reveals slight infection of lt great toe.
	Drained and cleaned nail lt great toe. Adv to retn in 2 days. *Gerald Practon, MD*
07-03-xx	Excised entire lt great toenail under total toe procaine block. Drs applied. PTR in 5 days for
	checkup. *Gerald Practon, MD*
07-07-xx	Nail bed healing well. Retn PRN. *Gerald Practon, MD*

Figure 4

STATEMENT

College Clinic
4567 Broad Avenue
Woodland Hills, XY 12345-0001
Telephone: 013-486-9002
Fax: 013-487-8976

Mrs. Hortense N. Hope
247 Lantern Pike
Woodland Hills, XY 12345-0001

DATE	PROFESSIONAL SERVICE DESCRIPTION	CHARGE		CREDITS				CURRENT BALANCE	
				PAYMENTS		ADJUSTMENTS			
7-1-xx	OV, initial new pt								
7-1-xx	Drainage lt great toenail								
7-3-xx	Excision entire lt great toenail under total toe procaine block								
7-7-xx	OV, PF hx/exam, SF decision making								

Due and payable within 10 days. **Pay last amount in balance column** 

Key: PF: Problem-focused
EPF: Expanded problem-focused
D: Detailed
C: Comprehensive
SF: Straightforward
LC: Low complexity
MC: Moderate complexity
HC: High complexity
CON: Consultation
CPX: Complete phys exam
E: Emergency
ER: Emergency dept.
HCD: House call (day)
HCN: House call (night)
HV: Hospital visit
OV: Office visit

Figure 5

APPROVED OMB 0938-0008

PLEASE DO NOT STAPLE IN THIS AREA

CARRIER

PICA

HEALTH INSURANCE CLAIM FORM

PICA

1. MEDICARE (Medicare #) MEDICAID (Medicaid #) CHAMPUS (Sponsor's SSN) CHAMPVA (VA File #) GROUP HEALTH PLAN (SSN or ID) FECA BLK LUNG (SSN) OTHER (ID)

1a. INSURED'S I.D. NUMBER (FOR PROGRAM IN ITEM 1)

2. PATIENT'S NAME (Last Name, First Name, Middle Initial)

3. PATIENT'S BIRTH DATE MM | DD | YYYY SEX M F

4. INSURED'S NAME (Last Name, First Name, Middle Initial)

5. PATIENT'S ADDRESS (No., Street)

6. PATIENT RELATIONSHIP TO INSURED Self Spouse Child Other

7. INSURED'S ADDRESS (No., Street)

CITY STATE

8. PATIENT STATUS Single Married Other

CITY STATE

ZIP CODE TELEPHONE (Include Area Code)

Employed Full-Time Student Part-Time Student

ZIP CODE TELEPHONE (Include Area Code) ( )

9. OTHER INSURED'S NAME (Last Name, First Name, Middle Initial)

10. IS PATIENT'S CONDITION RELATED TO:

11. INSURED'S POLICY GROUP OR FECA NUMBER

a. OTHER INSURED'S POLICY OR GROUP NUMBER

a. EMPLOYMENT? (CURRENT OR PREVIOUS) YES NO

a. INSURED'S DATE OF BIRTH MM | DD | YY SEX M F

b. OTHER INSURED'S DATE OF BIRTH MM | DD | YY SEX M F

b. AUTO ACCIDENT? YES NO PLACE (State)

b. EMPLOYER'S NAME OR SCHOOL NAME

c. EMPLOYER'S NAME OR SCHOOL NAME

c. OTHER ACCIDENT? YES NO

c. INSURANCE PLAN NAME OR PROGRAM NAME

d. INSURANCE PLAN NAME OR PROGRAM NAME

10d. RESERVED FOR LOCAL USE

d. IS THERE ANOTHER HEALTH BENEFIT PLAN? YES NO *If yes, return to and complete item 9 a-d.*

READ BACK OF FORM BEFORE COMPLETING AND SIGNING THIS FORM.

12. PATIENT'S OR AUTHORIZED PERSON'S SIGNATURE I authorize the release of any medical or other information necessary to process this claim. I also request payment of government benefits either to myself or to the party who accepts assignment below.

SIGNED ______ DATE ______

13. INSURED'S OR AUTHORIZED PERSON'S SIGNATURE I authorize payment of medical benefits to the undersigned physician or supplier for services described below.

SIGNED ______

PATIENT AND INSURED INFORMATION

14. DATE OF CURRENT: MM | DD | YY ◀ ILLNESS (First symptom) OR INJURY (Accident) OR PREGNANCY (LMP)

15. IF PATIENT HAS HAD SAME OR SIMILAR ILLNESS GIVE FIRST DATE MM | DD | YY

16. DATES PATIENT UNABLE TO WORK IN CURRENT OCCUPATION FROM MM | DD | YY TO MM | DD | YY

17. NAME OF REFERRING PHYSICIAN OR OTHER SOURCE

17a. I.D. NUMBER OF REFERRING PHYSICIAN

18. HOSPITALIZATION DATES RELATED TO CURRENT SERVICES FROM MM | DD | YY TO MM | DD | YY

19. RESERVED FOR LOCAL USE

20. OUTSIDE LAB? YES NO $ CHARGES

21. DIAGNOSIS OR NATURE OF ILLNESS OR INJURY. (RELATE ITEMS 1,2,3 OR 4 TO ITEM 24E BY LINE)

1. ______ 3. ______

2. ______ 4. ______

22. MEDICAID RESUBMISSION CODE ORIGINAL REF. NO.

23. PRIOR AUTHORIZATION NUMBER

24. A DATE(S) OF SERVICE From MM DD YY To MM DD YY	B Place of Service	C Type of Service	D PROCEDURES, SERVICES, OR SUPPLIES (Explain Unusual Circumstances) CPT/HCPCS | MODIFIER	E DIAGNOSIS CODE	F $ CHARGES	G DAYS OR UNITS	H EPSDT Family Plan	I EMG	J COB	K RESERVED FOR LOCAL USE

25. FEDERAL TAX I.D. NUMBER SSN EIN

26. PATIENT'S ACCOUNT NO.

27. ACCEPT ASSIGNMENT? (For govt. claims, see back) YES NO

28. TOTAL CHARGE $

29. AMOUNT PAID $

30. BALANCE DUE $

31. SIGNATURE OF PHYSICIAN OR SUPPLIER INCLUDING DEGREES OR CREDENTIALS (I certify that the statements on the reverse apply to this bill and are made a part thereof.)

SIGNED DATE

32. NAME AND ADDRESS OF FACILITY WHERE SERVICES WERE RENDERED (If other than home or office)

33. PHYSICIAN'S, SUPPLIER'S BILLING NAME, ADDRESS, ZIP CODE AND PHONE #

PIN# GRP#

PHYSICIAN OR SUPPLIER INFORMATION

(APPROVED BY AMA COUNCIL ON MEDICAL SERVICE 8/88) *PLEASE PRINT OR TYPE* FORM HCFA-1500 (U2)(12-90) FORM OCWP-1500 FORM RRB-1500

Figure 6

Test 6: Completing a HCFA-1500 Claim Form for a Medicare Case

Performance Objective

Task: Complete a health insurance claim form using OCR guidelines and post the information to the patient's ledger card.

Conditions: Use Frances F. Foote's patient record (Figure 7), ledger card (Figure 8), one health insurance claim form (Figure 9), typewriter, computer or pen, procedural and diagnostic code books, and *Workbook* Appendixes A and B.

Standards: Claim Productivity Management

Time: ________________ minutes

Accuracy: ________________

(Note: The time element and accuracy criteria may be given by your instructor).

Directions: Complete a HCFA-1500 claim form using OCR guidelines, directing it to your local fiscal intermediary whose name and address may be found in Appendix A of the *Handbook*. Use your *CPT* code book or Appendix A to determine the correct five-digit code numbers and fees for each professional service rendered. Date the claim October 31. Remember to include modifiers if necessary. Use your diagnostic code book to code each active diagnosis. Dr. Pedro is accepting assignment. Record on the ledger card when you have submitted the claim to the insurance company.

PATIENT RECORD NO. T0006

LAST NAME	FIRST NAME	MIDDLE NAME	BIRTH DATE	SEX	HOME PHONE
Foote,	Frances	F.	08-10-32	F	013-678-0943

ADDRESS	CITY	STATE	ZIP CODE
984 North A Street,	Woodland Hills,	XY	12345

PATIENT'S OCCUPATION: retired legal secretary
NAME OF COMPANY:

ADDRESS OF EMPLOYER:
PHONE:

SPOUSE OR PARENT: Harry L. Foote
OCCUPATION: roofer

EMPLOYER / ADDRESS: BDO Construction Company, 340 North 6th Street, Woodland Hills, XY 12345
PHONE: 013-478-9083

NAME OF INSURANCE GROUP: Medicare
INSURED OR SUBSCRIBER: self

POLICY NO.:
GROUP NO.:

MEDICARE NO.	MEDICAID NO.	EFFECTIVE DATE	SOC. SEC. NO.	UPIN/NPI
578-78-8924A			578-78-8924	

REFERRED BY: G.U. Curette, MD, 4780 Main St., Ehrlich, XY 12350 Tel: 013-430-8788 #3421660012

DATE	PROGRESS
10-11-XX	CC: Discomfort around lt great toe. Exam: severe overgrowth of nail into surrounding tissues. AP and lat. x-rays taken & interp shows lt foot essentially neg. No gout or arthritis seen. DX: severe onychocryptosis both margins of lt hallux. Adv to retn as OP to hosp for surgery on lt hallux. No disability from work. Nick Pedro, DPM
10-13-XX	Op: Complete wedge resection for repair of lt hallux ingrown nail. Retn 1 wk for PO re ch. Pt may continue to work. No disability. Nick Pedro, DPM
10-20-XX	Lt hallux healing well. RTC as necessary. Nick Pedro, DPM

Figure 7

STATEMENT

College Clinic
4567 Broad Avenue
Woodland Hills, XY 12345-0001
Telephone: 013-486-9002
Fax: 013-487-8976

Mrs. Frances F. Foote
984 North A Street
Woodland Hills, XY 12345-0001

DATE	PROFESSIONAL SERVICE DESCRIPTION	CHARGE	CREDITS PAYMENTS	CREDITS ADJUSTMENTS	CURRENT BALANCE
10-11-xx	OV, PF hx/exam, SF decision making				
10-11-xx	AP & lat x-rays lt foot with interpret				
10-13-xx	Exc nail & matrix. compl				
10-20-xx	OV, PF hx/exam, SF decision making				

Due and payable within 10 days. **Pay last amount in balance column** 

Key:
PF: Problem-focused
EPF: Expanded problem-focused
D: Detailed
C: Comprehensive
SF: Straightforward
LC: Low complexity
MC: Moderate complexity
HC: High complexity
CON: Consultation
CPX: Complete phys exam
E: Emergency
ER: Emergency dept.
HCD: House call (day)
HCN: House call (night)
HV: Hospital visit
OV: Office visit

Figure 8

APPROVED OMB 0938-0008

PLEASE DO NOT STAPLE IN THIS AREA

CARRIER

PICA

HEALTH INSURANCE CLAIM FORM

PICA

1. MEDICARE (Medicare #) MEDICAID (Medicaid #) CHAMPUS (Sponsor's SSN) CHAMPVA (VA File #) GROUP HEALTH PLAN (SSN or ID) FECA BLK LUNG (SSN) OTHER (ID)

1a. INSURED'S I.D. NUMBER (FOR PROGRAM IN ITEM 1)

2. PATIENT'S NAME (Last Name, First Name, Middle Initial)

3. PATIENT'S BIRTH DATE MM | DD | YYYY SEX M F

4. INSURED'S NAME (Last Name, First Name, Middle Initial)

5. PATIENT'S ADDRESS (No., Street)

6. PATIENT RELATIONSHIP TO INSURED Self Spouse Child Other

7. INSURED'S ADDRESS (No., Street)

CITY STATE

8. PATIENT STATUS Single Married Other

CITY STATE

ZIP CODE TELEPHONE (Include Area Code)

Employed Full-Time Student Part-Time Student

ZIP CODE TELEPHONE (Include Area Code) ( )

9. OTHER INSURED'S NAME (Last Name, First Name, Middle Initial)

10. IS PATIENT'S CONDITION RELATED TO:

11. INSURED'S POLICY GROUP OR FECA NUMBER

a. OTHER INSURED'S POLICY OR GROUP NUMBER

a. EMPLOYMENT? (CURRENT OR PREVIOUS) YES NO

a. INSURED'S DATE OF BIRTH MM | DD | YY SEX M F

b. OTHER INSURED'S DATE OF BIRTH MM | DD | YY SEX M F

b. AUTO ACCIDENT? PLACE (State) YES NO

b. EMPLOYER'S NAME OR SCHOOL NAME

c. EMPLOYER'S NAME OR SCHOOL NAME

c. OTHER ACCIDENT? YES NO

c. INSURANCE PLAN NAME OR PROGRAM NAME

d. INSURANCE PLAN NAME OR PROGRAM NAME

10d. RESERVED FOR LOCAL USE

d. IS THERE ANOTHER HEALTH BENEFIT PLAN? YES NO *If yes, return to and complete item 9 a-d.*

READ BACK OF FORM BEFORE COMPLETING AND SIGNING THIS FORM.

12. PATIENT'S OR AUTHORIZED PERSON'S SIGNATURE I authorize the release of any medical or other information necessary to process this claim. I also request payment of government benefits either to myself or to the party who accepts assignment below.

SIGNED ____ DATE ____

13. INSURED'S OR AUTHORIZED PERSON'S SIGNATURE I authorize payment of medical benefits to the undersigned physician or supplier for services described below.

SIGNED ____

PATIENT AND INSURED INFORMATION

14. DATE OF CURRENT: MM | DD | YY ◀ ILLNESS (First symptom) OR INJURY (Accident) OR PREGNANCY (LMP)

15. IF PATIENT HAS HAD SAME OR SIMILAR ILLNESS GIVE FIRST DATE MM | DD | YY

16. DATES PATIENT UNABLE TO WORK IN CURRENT OCCUPATION FROM MM | DD | YY TO MM | DD | YY

17. NAME OF REFERRING PHYSICIAN OR OTHER SOURCE

17a. I.D. NUMBER OF REFERRING PHYSICIAN

18. HOSPITALIZATION DATES RELATED TO CURRENT SERVICES FROM MM | DD | YY TO MM | DD | YY

19. RESERVED FOR LOCAL USE

20. OUTSIDE LAB? YES NO $ CHARGES

21. DIAGNOSIS OR NATURE OF ILLNESS OR INJURY. (RELATE ITEMS 1,2,3 OR 4 TO ITEM 24E BY LINE)

1. ____ 3. ____

2. ____ 4. ____

22. MEDICAID RESUBMISSION CODE ORIGINAL REF. NO.

23. PRIOR AUTHORIZATION NUMBER

24. A DATE(S) OF SERVICE From MM DD YY To MM DD YY	B Place of Service	C Type of Service	D PROCEDURES, SERVICES, OR SUPPLIES (Explain Unusual Circumstances) CPT/HCPCS | MODIFIER	E DIAGNOSIS CODE	F $ CHARGES	G DAYS OR UNITS	H EPSDT Family Plan	I EMG	J COB	K RESERVED FOR LOCAL USE

25. FEDERAL TAX I.D. NUMBER SSN EIN

26. PATIENT'S ACCOUNT NO.

27. ACCEPT ASSIGNMENT? (For govt. claims, see back) YES NO

28. TOTAL CHARGE $

29. AMOUNT PAID $

30. BALANCE DUE $

31. SIGNATURE OF PHYSICIAN OR SUPPLIER INCLUDING DEGREES OR CREDENTIALS (I certify that the statements on the reverse apply to this bill and are made a part thereof.)

SIGNED DATE

32. NAME AND ADDRESS OF FACILITY WHERE SERVICES WERE RENDERED (If other than home or office)

33. PHYSICIAN'S, SUPPLIER'S BILLING NAME, ADDRESS, ZIP CODE AND PHONE #

PIN# GRP#

PHYSICIAN OR SUPPLIER INFORMATION

(APPROVED BY AMA COUNCIL ON MEDICAL SERVICE 8/88) *PLEASE PRINT OR TYPE* FORM HCFA-1500 (U2) (12-90) FORM OCWP-1500 FORM RRB-1500

Figure 9

Test 7: Completing a HCFA-1500 Claim Form for a Medicare Case

Performance Objective

Task: Complete three health insurance claim forms using OCR guidelines and post the information to the patient's ledger card.

Conditions: Use Charles B. Kamb's patient record (Figure 10), ledger card (Figure 11), three health insurance claim forms (Figures 12, 13, and 14), typewriter, computer, or pen, procedural and diagnostic code books, and *Workbook* Appendixes A and B.

Standards: Claim Productivity Management

Time: ________________ minutes

Accuracy: ________________

(Note: The time element and accuracy criteria may be given by your instructor.)

Directions: Complete three HCFA-1500 claim forms using OCR guidelines, directing it to your local fiscal intermediary whose name and address may be found in Appendix A of the *Handbook*. Use your *CPT* code book or Appendix A to determine the correct five-digit code numbers and fees for each professional service rendered. Date the claim June 30. Remember to include modifiers if necessary. Use your diagnostic code book to code each active diagnosis. Dr. Practon is accepting assignment. Record on the ledger card when you have submitted the claim to the insurance company.

PATIENT RECORD NO. T0007

LAST NAME	FIRST NAME	MIDDLE NAME	BIRTH DATE	SEX	HOME PHONE
Kamb,	Charles	B.	01-26-27	M	013-467-2601

ADDRESS	CITY	STATE	ZIP CODE
2600 West Nautilus Street,	Woodland Hills,	XY	12345

PATIENT'S OCCUPATION	NAME OF COMPANY
retired TV actor	Amer. Federation of TV & Radio Artists (AFTRA)

ADDRESS OF EMPLOYER	PHONE
30077 Ventura Boulevard, Woodland Hills, XY 12345	013-466-3331

SPOUSE OR PARENT	OCCUPATION
Jane C. Kamb	homemaker

EMPLOYER	ADDRESS	PHONE

NAME OF INSURANCE	INSURED OR SUBSCRIBER
Medicare	self

MEDICARE NO.	MEDICAID NO.	EFFECTIVE DATE	SOC. SEC. NO.
454-01-9569A			454-01-9569

REFERRED BY: Mrs. O. S. Tomy (friend)

DATE	PROGRESS
06-01-XX	New pt W ♂ comes in complaining of nasal bleeding for two and a half mo c̄ headaches and
	nasal congestion. Pt has had HBP for 1 yr. Taking med Serpasil prescribed by dr in Ohio.
	Coagulation time and platelet count done in ofc--normal. Exam revealed nasal hemorrhage.
	BP 200/120. Gave inj IM carbazochrome salicylate 5 mg/1cc, used cautery, postnasal packs. Adv
	retn tomorrow. Ordered previous med records from dr in Ohio. D: Recurrent epistaxis due to
	hypertension. No disability from work. Gerald Practon, MD
06-02-XX	Removed nasal packs, replaced postnasal pack. Inj IM 5 mg/1 cc carbazochrome salicylate. BP
	180/100. Adv retn in 3 days. Gerald Practon, MD
06-05-XX	Removed post pack and replaced. BP 200/100. Adv retn in 4 days for recheck. Gerald Practon, MD
06-09-XX	Removed post pack. BP 200/120. Adv retn 3 days. Gerald Practon, MD
06-12-XX	Rev previous med records. Pt referred to Dr. Perry Cardi (int) for future care re HBP. No dis
	from work. Gerald Practon, MD

Figure 10

STATEMENT

College Clinic
4567 Broad Avenue
Woodland Hills, XY 12345-0001
Telephone: 013-486-9002
Fax: 013-487-8976

Mr. Charles B. Kamb
2600 West Nautilus Street
Woodland Hills, XY 12345-0001

DATE	PROFESSIONAL SERVICE DESCRIPTION	CHARGE	CREDITS		CURRENT BALANCE
			PAYMENTS	ADJUSTMENTS	
6-1-xx	Initial OV new pt				
6-1-xx	Coagulation time/Lee and White				
6-1-xx	Platelet count manual				
6-1-xx	Inj 5 mg/1cc carbazochrome salicylate				
6-1-xx	Post nasal packs with cauterization				
6-2-xx	OV PF Hx/exam SF decision making				
6-2-xx	Subsequent post packing				
6-2-xx	Inj 5 mg/1 cc carbazochrome salicylate				
6-5-xx	OV PF Hx/exam SF decision making				
6-5-xx	Subsequent post packing				
6-9-xx	OV, PF hx/exam, LC decision making removal post packs				
6-12-xx	OV, D hx/exam, MC decision making				
					⇧

Due and payable within 10 days. **Pay last amount in balance column**

Key: PF: Problem-focused
EPF: Expanded problem-focused
D: Detailed
C: Comprehensive
SF: Straightforward
LC: Low complexity
MC: Moderate complexity
HC: High complexity
CON: Consultation
CPX: Complete phys exam
E: Emergency
ER: Emergency dept.
HCD: House call (day)
HCN: House call (night)
HV: Hospital visit
OV: Office visit

Figure 11

APPROVED OMB 0938-0008

PLEASE DO NOT STAPLE IN THIS AREA

CARRIER

PICA

HEALTH INSURANCE CLAIM FORM

PICA

1. MEDICARE (Medicare #) MEDICAID (Medicaid #) CHAMPUS (Sponsor's SSN) CHAMPVA (VA File #) GROUP HEALTH PLAN (SSN or ID) FECA BLK LUNG (SSN) OTHER (ID)

1a. INSURED'S I.D. NUMBER (FOR PROGRAM IN ITEM 1)

2. PATIENT'S NAME (Last Name, First Name, Middle Initial)

3. PATIENT'S BIRTH DATE MM DD YYYY SEX M F

4. INSURED'S NAME (Last Name, First Name, Middle Initial)

5. PATIENT'S ADDRESS (No., Street)

6. PATIENT RELATIONSHIP TO INSURED Self Spouse Child Other

7. INSURED'S ADDRESS (No., Street)

CITY STATE

8. PATIENT STATUS Single Married Other; Employed Full-Time Student Part-Time Student

CITY STATE

ZIP CODE TELEPHONE (Include Area Code)

ZIP CODE TELEPHONE (Include Area Code) ( )

9. OTHER INSURED'S NAME (Last Name, First Name, Middle Initial)

10. IS PATIENT'S CONDITION RELATED TO:

11. INSURED'S POLICY GROUP OR FECA NUMBER

a. OTHER INSURED'S POLICY OR GROUP NUMBER

a. EMPLOYMENT? (CURRENT OR PREVIOUS) YES NO

a. INSURED'S DATE OF BIRTH MM DD YY SEX M F

b. OTHER INSURED'S DATE OF BIRTH MM DD YY SEX M F

b. AUTO ACCIDENT? PLACE (State) YES NO

b. EMPLOYER'S NAME OR SCHOOL NAME

c. EMPLOYER'S NAME OR SCHOOL NAME

c. OTHER ACCIDENT? YES NO

c. INSURANCE PLAN NAME OR PROGRAM NAME

d. INSURANCE PLAN NAME OR PROGRAM NAME

10d. RESERVED FOR LOCAL USE

d. IS THERE ANOTHER HEALTH BENEFIT PLAN? YES NO *If yes, return to and complete item 9 a-d.*

READ BACK OF FORM BEFORE COMPLETING AND SIGNING THIS FORM.

12. PATIENT'S OR AUTHORIZED PERSON'S SIGNATURE I authorize the release of any medical or other information necessary to process this claim. I also request payment of government benefits either to myself or to the party who accepts assignment below.

SIGNED ____ DATE ____

13. INSURED'S OR AUTHORIZED PERSON'S SIGNATURE I authorize payment of medical benefits to the undersigned physician or supplier for services described below.

SIGNED ____

PATIENT AND INSURED INFORMATION

14. DATE OF CURRENT: MM DD YY ILLNESS (First symptom) OR INJURY (Accident) OR PREGNANCY (LMP)

15. IF PATIENT HAS HAD SAME OR SIMILAR ILLNESS GIVE FIRST DATE MM DD YY

16. DATES PATIENT UNABLE TO WORK IN CURRENT OCCUPATION FROM MM DD YY TO MM DD YY

17. NAME OF REFERRING PHYSICIAN OR OTHER SOURCE

17a. I.D. NUMBER OF REFERRING PHYSICIAN

18. HOSPITALIZATION DATES RELATED TO CURRENT SERVICES FROM MM DD YY TO MM DD YY

19. RESERVED FOR LOCAL USE

20. OUTSIDE LAB? YES NO $ CHARGES

21. DIAGNOSIS OR NATURE OF ILLNESS OR INJURY. (RELATE ITEMS 1,2,3 OR 4 TO ITEM 24E BY LINE)

1. ____ 3. ____

2. ____ 4. ____

22. MEDICAID RESUBMISSION CODE ORIGINAL REF. NO.

23. PRIOR AUTHORIZATION NUMBER

24. A DATE(S) OF SERVICE From MM DD YY To MM DD YY	B Place of Service	C Type of Service	D PROCEDURES, SERVICES, OR SUPPLIES (Explain Unusual Circumstances) CPT/HCPCS MODIFIER	E DIAGNOSIS CODE	F $ CHARGES	G DAYS OR UNITS	H EPSDT Family Plan	I EMG	J COB	K RESERVED FOR LOCAL USE

25. FEDERAL TAX I.D. NUMBER SSN EIN

26. PATIENT'S ACCOUNT NO.

27. ACCEPT ASSIGNMENT? (For govt. claims, see back) YES NO

28. TOTAL CHARGE $

29. AMOUNT PAID $

30. BALANCE DUE $

31. SIGNATURE OF PHYSICIAN OR SUPPLIER INCLUDING DEGREES OR CREDENTIALS (I certify that the statements on the reverse apply to this bill and are made a part thereof.)

SIGNED DATE

32. NAME AND ADDRESS OF FACILITY WHERE SERVICES WERE RENDERED (If other than home or office)

33. PHYSICIAN'S, SUPPLIER'S BILLING NAME, ADDRESS, ZIP CODE AND PHONE #

PIN# GRP#

PHYSICIAN OR SUPPLIER INFORMATION

(APPROVED BY AMA COUNCIL ON MEDICAL SERVICE 8/88) *PLEASE PRINT OR TYPE* FORM HCFA-1500 (U2) (12-90) FORM OCWP-1500 FORM RRB-1500

Figure 12

APPROVED OMB 0938-0008

PLEASE DO NOT STAPLE IN THIS AREA

CARRIER

PICA

HEALTH INSURANCE CLAIM FORM

PICA

1. MEDICARE (Medicare #) MEDICAID (Medicaid #) CHAMPUS (Sponsor's SSN) CHAMPVA (VA File #) GROUP HEALTH PLAN (SSN or ID) FECA BLK LUNG (SSN) OTHER (ID)

1a. INSURED'S I.D. NUMBER (FOR PROGRAM IN ITEM 1)

2. PATIENT'S NAME (Last Name, First Name, Middle Initial)

3. PATIENT'S BIRTH DATE MM | DD | YYYY SEX M F

4. INSURED'S NAME (Last Name, First Name, Middle Initial)

5. PATIENT'S ADDRESS (No., Street)

6. PATIENT RELATIONSHIP TO INSURED Self Spouse Child Other

7. INSURED'S ADDRESS (No., Street)

CITY STATE

8. PATIENT STATUS Single Married Other

CITY STATE

ZIP CODE TELEPHONE (Include Area Code)

Employed Full-Time Student Part-Time Student

ZIP CODE TELEPHONE (include Area Code) ( )

9. OTHER INSURED'S NAME (Last Name, First Name, Middle Initial)

10. IS PATIENT'S CONDITION RELATED TO:

11. INSURED'S POLICY GROUP OR FECA NUMBER

a. OTHER INSURED'S POLICY OR GROUP NUMBER

a. EMPLOYMENT? (CURRENT OR PREVIOUS) YES NO

a. INSURED'S DATE OF BIRTH MM | DD | YY SEX M F

b. OTHER INSURED'S DATE OF BIRTH MM | DD | YY SEX M F

b. AUTO ACCIDENT? PLACE (State) YES NO

b. EMPLOYER'S NAME OR SCHOOL NAME

c. EMPLOYER'S NAME OR SCHOOL NAME

c. OTHER ACCIDENT? YES NO

c. INSURANCE PLAN NAME OR PROGRAM NAME

d. INSURANCE PLAN NAME OR PROGRAM NAME

10d. RESERVED FOR LOCAL USE

d. IS THERE ANOTHER HEALTH BENEFIT PLAN? YES NO *If yes, return to and complete item 9 a-d.*

READ BACK OF FORM BEFORE COMPLETING AND SIGNING THIS FORM.

12. PATIENT'S OR AUTHORIZED PERSON'S SIGNATURE I authorize the release of any medical or other information necessary to process this claim. I also request payment of government benefits either to myself or to the party who accepts assignment below.

SIGNED ____________ DATE ________

13. INSURED'S OR AUTHORIZED PERSON'S SIGNATURE I authorize payment of medical benefits to the undersigned physician or supplier for services described below.

SIGNED ____________

PATIENT AND INSURED INFORMATION

14. DATE OF CURRENT: MM | DD | YY ILLNESS (First symptom) OR INJURY (Accident) OR PREGNANCY (LMP)

15. IF PATIENT HAS HAD SAME OR SIMILAR ILLNESS GIVE FIRST DATE MM | DD | YY

16. DATES PATIENT UNABLE TO WORK IN CURRENT OCCUPATION FROM MM | DD | YY TO MM | DD | YY

17. NAME OF REFERRING PHYSICIAN OR OTHER SOURCE

17a. I.D. NUMBER OF REFERRING PHYSICIAN

18. HOSPITALIZATION DATES RELATED TO CURRENT SERVICES FROM MM | DD | YY TO MM | DD | YY

19. RESERVED FOR LOCAL USE

20. OUTSIDE LAB? YES NO $ CHARGES

21. DIAGNOSIS OR NATURE OF ILLNESS OR INJURY. (RELATE ITEMS 1,2,3 OR 4 TO ITEM 24E BY LINE)

1. ______ 3. ______

2. ______ 4. ______

22. MEDICAID RESUBMISSION CODE ORIGINAL REF. NO.

23. PRIOR AUTHORIZATION NUMBER

24. A DATE(S) OF SERVICE From MM DD YY To MM DD YY	B Place of Service	C Type of Service	D PROCEDURES, SERVICES, OR SUPPLIES (Explain Unusual Circumstances) CPT/HCPCS | MODIFIER	E DIAGNOSIS CODE	F $ CHARGES	G DAYS OR UNITS	H EPSDT Family Plan	I EMG	J COB	K RESERVED FOR LOCAL USE

25. FEDERAL TAX I.D. NUMBER SSN EIN

26. PATIENT'S ACCOUNT NO.

27. ACCEPT ASSIGNMENT? (For govt. claims, see back) YES NO

28. TOTAL CHARGE $

29. AMOUNT PAID $

30. BALANCE DUE $

31. SIGNATURE OF PHYSICIAN OR SUPPLIER INCLUDING DEGREES OR CREDENTIALS (I certify that the statements on the reverse apply to this bill and are made a part thereof.)

SIGNED DATE

32. NAME AND ADDRESS OF FACILITY WHERE SERVICES WERE RENDERED (If other than home or office)

33. PHYSICIAN'S, SUPPLIER'S BILLING NAME, ADDRESS, ZIP CODE AND PHONE #

PIN# GRP#

PHYSICIAN OR SUPPLIER INFORMATION

(APPROVED BY AMA COUNCIL ON MEDICAL SERVICE8/88) *PLEASE PRINT OR TYPE* FORM HCFA-1500 (U2) (12-90) FORM OCWP-1500 FORM RRB-1500

Figure 13

APPROVED OMB 0938-0008

PLEASE DO NOT STAPLE IN THIS AREA

CARRIER

PICA

HEALTH INSURANCE CLAIM FORM

PICA

1. MEDICARE (Medicare #) MEDICAID (Medicaid #) CHAMPUS (Sponsor's SSN) CHAMPVA (VA File #) GROUP HEALTH PLAN (SSN or ID) FECA BLK LUNG (SSN) OTHER (ID)

1a. INSURED'S I.D. NUMBER (FOR PROGRAM IN ITEM 1)

2. PATIENT'S NAME (Last Name, First Name, Middle Initial)

3. PATIENT'S BIRTH DATE MM | DD | YYYY SEX M F

4. INSURED'S NAME (Last Name, First Name, Middle Initial)

5. PATIENT'S ADDRESS (No., Street)

6. PATIENT RELATIONSHIP TO INSURED Self Spouse Child Other

7. INSURED'S ADDRESS (No., Street)

CITY STATE

8. PATIENT STATUS Single Married Other

CITY STATE

ZIP CODE TELEPHONE (Include Area Code)

Employed Full-Time Student Part-Time Student

ZIP CODE TELEPHONE (include Area Code) ( )

9. OTHER INSURED'S NAME (Last Name, First Name, Middle Initial)

10. IS PATIENT'S CONDITION RELATED TO:

11. INSURED'S POLICY GROUP OR FECA NUMBER

a. OTHER INSURED'S POLICY OR GROUP NUMBER

a. EMPLOYMENT? (CURRENT OR PREVIOUS) YES NO

a. INSURED'S DATE OF BIRTH MM | DD | YY SEX M F

b. OTHER INSURED'S DATE OF BIRTH MM | DD | YY SEX M F

b. AUTO ACCIDENT? PLACE (State) YES NO

b. EMPLOYER'S NAME OR SCHOOL NAME

c. EMPLOYER'S NAME OR SCHOOL NAME

c. OTHER ACCIDENT? YES NO

c. INSURANCE PLAN NAME OR PROGRAM NAME

d. INSURANCE PLAN NAME OR PROGRAM NAME

10d. RESERVED FOR LOCAL USE

d. IS THERE ANOTHER HEALTH BENEFIT PLAN? YES NO *If yes*, return to and complete item 9 a-d.

READ BACK OF FORM BEFORE COMPLETING AND SIGNING THIS FORM.

12. PATIENT'S OR AUTHORIZED PERSON'S SIGNATURE I authorize the release of any medical or other information necessary to process this claim. I also request payment of government benefits either to myself or to the party who accepts assignment below.

SIGNED ______ DATE ______

13. INSURED'S OR AUTHORIZED PERSON'S SIGNATURE I authorize payment of medical benefits to the undersigned physician or supplier for services described below.

SIGNED ______

PATIENT AND INSURED INFORMATION

14. DATE OF CURRENT: MM | DD | YY ILLNESS (First symptom) OR INJURY (Accident) OR PREGNANCY (LMP)

15. IF PATIENT HAS HAD SAME OR SIMILAR ILLNESS GIVE FIRST DATE MM | DD | YY

16. DATES PATIENT UNABLE TO WORK IN CURRENT OCCUPATION FROM MM | DD | YY TO MM | DD | YY

17. NAME OF REFERRING PHYSICIAN OR OTHER SOURCE

17a. I.D. NUMBER OF REFERRING PHYSICIAN

18. HOSPITALIZATION DATES RELATED TO CURRENT SERVICES FROM MM | DD | YY TO MM | DD | YY

19. RESERVED FOR LOCAL USE

20. OUTSIDE LAB? YES NO $ CHARGES

21. DIAGNOSIS OR NATURE OF ILLNESS OR INJURY. (RELATE ITEMS 1,2,3 OR 4 TO ITEM 24E BY LINE)

1. ______ 3. ______

2. ______ 4. ______

22. MEDICAID RESUBMISSION CODE ORIGINAL REF. NO.

23. PRIOR AUTHORIZATION NUMBER

24. A DATE(S) OF SERVICE From MM DD YY To MM DD YY	B Place of Service	C Type of Service	D PROCEDURES, SERVICES, OR SUPPLIES (Explain Unusual Circumstances) CPT/HCPCS | MODIFIER	E DIAGNOSIS CODE	F $ CHARGES	G DAYS OR UNITS	H EPSDT Family Plan	I EMG	J COB	K RESERVED FOR LOCAL USE

25. FEDERAL TAX I.D. NUMBER SSN EIN

26. PATIENT'S ACCOUNT NO.

27. ACCEPT ASSIGNMENT? (For govt. claims, see back) YES NO

28. TOTAL CHARGE $

29. AMOUNT PAID $

30. BALANCE DUE $

31. SIGNATURE OF PHYSICIAN OR SUPPLIER INCLUDING DEGREES OR CREDENTIALS (I certify that the statements on the reverse apply to this bill and are made a part thereof.)

SIGNED DATE

32. NAME AND ADDRESS OF FACILITY WHERE SERVICES WERE RENDERED (if other than home or office)

33. PHYSICIAN'S, SUPPLIER'S BILLING NAME, ADDRESS, ZIP CODE AND PHONE #

PIN# GRP#

PHYSICIAN OR SUPPLIER INFORMATION

(APPROVED BY AMA COUNCIL ON MEDICAL SERVICE8/88) *PLEASE PRINT OR TYPE* FORM HCFA-1500 (U2) (12-90) FORM OCWP-1500 FORM RRB-1500

Figure 14

Test 8: Completing a HCFA-1500 Claim Form for a Medicaid Case

Performance Objective

Task: Complete a health insurance claim form using OCR guidelines and post the information to the patient's ledger card.

Conditions: Use Louise K. Herman's patient record (Figure 15), ledger card (Figure 16), one health insurance claim form (Figure 17), typewriter, computer or pen, procedural and diagnostic code books, and *Workbook* Appendixes A and B.

Standards: Claim Productivity Management

Time: ______________ minutes

Accuracy: ______________

(Note: The time element and accuracy criteria may be given by your instructor.)

Directions: Complete a HCFA-1500 claim form using OCR guidelines, directing it to your local fiscal intermediary whose name and address may be found in Appendix A of the *Handbook*. Use your *CPT* code book or Appendix A to determine the correct five-digit code numbers and fees for each professional service rendered. Date the claim May 31. Remember to include modifiers if necessary. Use your diagnostic code book to code each active diagnosis. Dr. Rumsey is accepting assignment. Record on the ledger card when you have submitted the claim to the insurance company.

Post a payment from the insurance company of $350, check No. 4300, 40 days after claim submission.

PATIENT RECORD NO. T0008

LAST NAME	FIRST NAME	MIDDLE NAME	BIRTH DATE	SEX	HOME PHONE
Herman,	Louise	K.	11-04-46	F	013-266-9085

ADDRESS	CITY	STATE	ZIP CODE
13453 Burbank Boulevard,	Woodland Hills,	XY	12345

PATIENT'S OCCUPATION	NAME OF COMPANY
retired budget analyst	

ADDRESS OF EMPLOYER	PHONE

SPOUSE OR PARENT	OCCUPATION
Harold D. Herman	retired salesman

EMPLOYER	ADDRESS	PHONE

NAME OF INSURANCE	INSURED OR SUBSCRIBER
Medicaid	self

MEDICARE NO.	MEDICAID NO.	EFFECTIVE DATE	SOC. SEC. NO.
	00519360018		519-36-0018

REFERRED BY: Raymond Skeleton, MD

DATE	PROGRESS
05-06-XX	Pt referred by Dr. Skeleton. CC: Bleeding hemorrhoids. Anoscopy exam revealed Dx int and ext
	hemorrhoids and 2 infected rectal polyps. Adv. retn 2 days for removal of hemorrhoids and polyps.
	Rex Rumsey, MD
05-08-XX	In ofc perf int and ext hemorrhoidectomy: proctosigmoidoscopy perf for removal of polyps. Adv.
	sitz baths daily. Pt adv to retn 1 wk. Will be off wk from 5-8 through 5-15. Rex Rumsey, MD
05-15-XX	DNS
05-17-XX	Progressing well. No pain. No discomfort. Retn PRN. Rex Rumsey, MD

Figure 15

STATEMENT

College Clinic
4567 Broad Avenue
Woodland Hills, XY 12345-0001
Telephone: 013-486-9002
Fax: 013-487-8976

Mrs. Louise K. Herman
13453 Burbank Boulevard
Woodland Hills, XY 12345-0001

DATE	PROFESSIONAL SERVICE DESCRIPTION	CHARGE	CREDITS		CURRENT BALANCE
			PAYMENTS	ADJUSTMENTS	
5-6-xx	C hx/exam, HC decision making				
5-6-xx	Anoscopy, diag				
5-8-xx	Int & ext hemorrhoidectomy				
5-8-xx	Proctosigmoidoscopy exc rectal polyps, complicated				
5-17-xx	PO follow-up visit				

Due and payable within 10 days. **Pay last amount in balance column** 

Key: PF: Problem-focused
EPF: Expanded problem-focused
D: Detailed
C: Comprehensive
SF: Straightforward
LC: Low complexity
MC: Moderate complexity
HC: High complexity
CON: Consultation
CPX: Complete phys exam
E: Emergency
ER: Emergency dept.
HCD: House call (day)
HCN: House call (night)
HV: Hospital visit
OV: Office visit

Figure 16

APPROVED OMB 0938-0008

PLEASE DO NOT STAPLE IN THIS AREA

CARRIER

PICA

HEALTH INSURANCE CLAIM FORM

PICA

1. MEDICARE (Medicare #) MEDICAID (Medicaid #) CHAMPUS (Sponsor's SSN) CHAMPVA (VA File #) GROUP HEALTH PLAN (SSN or ID) FECA BLK LUNG (SSN) OTHER (ID)

1a. INSURED'S I.D. NUMBER (FOR PROGRAM IN ITEM 1)

2. PATIENT'S NAME (Last Name, First Name, Middle Initial)

3. PATIENT'S BIRTH DATE MM | DD | YYYY SEX M F

4. INSURED'S NAME (Last Name, First Name, Middle Initial)

5. PATIENT'S ADDRESS (No., Street)

6. PATIENT RELATIONSHIP TO INSURED Self Spouse Child Other

7. INSURED'S ADDRESS (No., Street)

CITY STATE

8. PATIENT STATUS Single Married Other

CITY STATE

ZIP CODE TELEPHONE (Include Area Code)

Employed Full-Time Student Part-Time Student

ZIP CODE TELEPHONE (Include Area Code) ( )

9. OTHER INSURED'S NAME (Last Name, First Name, Middle Initial)

10. IS PATIENT'S CONDITION RELATED TO:

11. INSURED'S POLICY GROUP OR FECA NUMBER

a. OTHER INSURED'S POLICY OR GROUP NUMBER

a. EMPLOYMENT? (CURRENT OR PREVIOUS) YES NO

a. INSURED'S DATE OF BIRTH MM | DD | YY SEX M F

b. OTHER INSURED'S DATE OF BIRTH MM | DD | YY SEX M F

b. AUTO ACCIDENT? YES NO PLACE (State)

b. EMPLOYER'S NAME OR SCHOOL NAME

c. EMPLOYER'S NAME OR SCHOOL NAME

c. OTHER ACCIDENT? YES NO

c. INSURANCE PLAN NAME OR PROGRAM NAME

d. INSURANCE PLAN NAME OR PROGRAM NAME

10d. RESERVED FOR LOCAL USE

d. IS THERE ANOTHER HEALTH BENEFIT PLAN? YES NO *If yes, return to and complete item 9 a-d.*

READ BACK OF FORM BEFORE COMPLETING AND SIGNING THIS FORM.

12. PATIENT'S OR AUTHORIZED PERSON'S SIGNATURE I authorize the release of any medical or other information necessary to process this claim. I also request payment of government benefits either to myself or to the party who accepts assignment below.

SIGNED ______ DATE ______

13. INSURED'S OR AUTHORIZED PERSON'S SIGNATURE I authorize payment of medical benefits to the undersigned physician or supplier for services described below.

SIGNED ______

PATIENT AND INSURED INFORMATION

14. DATE OF CURRENT: MM | DD | YY ILLNESS (First symptom) OR INJURY (Accident) OR PREGNANCY (LMP)

15. IF PATIENT HAS HAD SAME OR SIMILAR ILLNESS GIVE FIRST DATE MM | DD | YY

16. DATES PATIENT UNABLE TO WORK IN CURRENT OCCUPATION FROM MM | DD | YY TO MM | DD | YY

17. NAME OF REFERRING PHYSICIAN OR OTHER SOURCE

17a. I.D. NUMBER OF REFERRING PHYSICIAN

18. HOSPITALIZATION DATES RELATED TO CURRENT SERVICES FROM MM | DD | YY TO MM | DD | YY

19. RESERVED FOR LOCAL USE

20. OUTSIDE LAB? YES NO $ CHARGES

21. DIAGNOSIS OR NATURE OF ILLNESS OR INJURY. (RELATE ITEMS 1,2,3 OR 4 TO ITEM 24E BY LINE)

1. ______ 3. ______

2. ______ 4. ______

22. MEDICAID RESUBMISSION CODE ORIGINAL REF. NO.

23. PRIOR AUTHORIZATION NUMBER

24. A DATE(S) OF SERVICE From MM DD YY To MM DD YY	B Place of Service	C Type of Service	D PROCEDURES, SERVICES, OR SUPPLIES (Explain Unusual Circumstances) CPT/HCPCS | MODIFIER	E DIAGNOSIS CODE	F $ CHARGES	G DAYS OR UNITS	H EPSDT Family Plan	I EMG	J COB	K RESERVED FOR LOCAL USE

25. FEDERAL TAX I.D. NUMBER SSN EIN

26. PATIENT'S ACCOUNT NO.

27. ACCEPT ASSIGNMENT? (For govt. claims, see back) YES NO

28. TOTAL CHARGE $

29. AMOUNT PAID $

30. BALANCE DUE $

31. SIGNATURE OF PHYSICIAN OR SUPPLIER INCLUDING DEGREES OR CREDENTIALS (I certify that the statements on the reverse apply to this bill and are made a part thereof.)

SIGNED DATE

32. NAME AND ADDRESS OF FACILITY WHERE SERVICES WERE RENDERED (If other than home or office)

33. PHYSICIAN'S, SUPPLIER'S BILLING NAME, ADDRESS, ZIP CODE AND PHONE #

PIN# GRP#

PHYSICIAN OR SUPPLIER INFORMATION

(APPROVED BY AMA COUNCIL ON MEDICAL SERVICE 8/88) *PLEASE PRINT OR TYPE* FORM HCFA-1500 (U2) (12-90) FORM OWCP-1500 FORM RRB-1500

Figure 17

Test 9: Completing a HCFA-1500 Claim Form for a TRICARE Case

Performance Objective

Task: Complete a health insurance claim form using OCR guidelines and post the information to the patient's ledger card.

Conditions: Use Darlene M. Cash's patient record (Figure 18), ledger card (Figure 19), one health insurance claim form (Figure 20), typewriter, computer or pen, procedural and diagnostic code books, and *Workbook* Appendixes A and B.

Standards: Claim Productivity Management

Time: ________________ minutes

Accuracy: ________________

(Note: The time element and accuracy criteria may be given by your instructor.)

Directions: Complete a HCFA-1500 claim form using OCR guidelines, directing it to your local fiscal intermediary whose name and address may be found in Appendix A of the *Handbook*. Use your *CPT* code book or Appendix A to determine the correct five-digit code numbers and fees for each professional service rendered. Date the claim February 27. Remember to include modifiers if necessary. Use your diagnostic code book to code each active diagnosis. Dr. Cutler is accepting assignment. Record on the ledger card when you have submitted the claim to the insurance company.

Test 10: Completing a HCFA-1500 Claim Form for a Private Plan

Performance Objective

Task: Complete two health insurance claim forms using OCR guidelines and post the information to the patient's ledger card.

Conditions: Use Gertrude Hamilton's patient record (Figure 21), ledger card (Figure 22), two health insurance claim forms (Figures 23 and 24), typewriter, computer or pen, procedural and diagnostic code books, and *Workbook* Appendixes A and B.

Standards: Claim Productivity Management

Time: ________________ minutes

Accuracy: ________________

(Note: The time element and accuracy criteria may be given by your instructor.)

Directions: Complete two HCFA-1500 claim forms using OCR guidelines and date the first one August 15 and the second one October 15. Use your *CPT* code book or Appendix A to determine the correct five-digit code numbers and fees for each professional service rendered. Remember to include modifiers if necessary. Use your diagnostic code books to code each active diagnosis. Dr. Cardi is accepting assignment. Record on the ledger card when you have submitted the claim to the insurance company.

Mrs. Hamilton makes a payment of $200, check No. 5362, on October 26. Post the proper entry for this transaction.

PATIENT RECORD NO. T0009

Cash,	Darlene	M.	03-15-70	F	013-666-8901
LAST NAME	FIRST NAME	MIDDLE NAME	BIRTH DATE	SEX	HOME PHONE

5729 Redwood Avenue,	Woodland Hills,	XY	12345
ADDRESS	CITY	STATE	ZIP CODE

teacher	City Unified School District	298-34-6754
PATIENT'S OCCUPATION	NAME OF COMPANY	PATIENT'S SOC SEC NO.

Century High School, 2031 West Olympic Boulevard, Dorland, XY 12345	013-678-0176
ADDRESS OF EMPLOYER	PHONE

David F. Cash	Navy Petty Officer	Active Status	4-22-70
SPOUSE	OCCUPATION		BIRTHDATE

U.S. Navy Grade 8,	A.P. O., New York, New York 10030	HHC, 2nd Batt, 26th Infantry
EMPLOYER	ADDRESS	PHONE

TRICARE Standard
NAME OF INSURANCE

767-32-9080	767-32-9080
SPONSOR'S SERVICE NO.	SPONSOR'S SOC SEC NO

67540	01-01-90
TRICARE ID CARD NO.	EFFECTIVE DATE

REFERRED BY: Hugh R. Foot, MD, 2010 Main St., Woodland Hills, XY 12345 Fed Tax ID #61 2509996

DATE	PROGRESS
1-4-XX	Pt comes in complaining of slt pain in parietal area of skull which began earlier today. Exam N. Some
	slt redness of parietal area of scalp. Retn in 1 wk for observation. Imp: head pain undetermined. No
	disability from work. *Clarence Cutler, MD*
1-11-XX	Some slt elevation of skin in parietal area of scalp. Otherwise essentially neg. No warmth over area.
	Slt pain on pressure. *Clarence Cutler, MD*
2-3-XX	Elevation of skin still persisting. Imp: inflammatory cystic lesion of scalp 1.5 cm. Tr: excision of
	inflammatory cystic lesion of skin 1.5 dia on parietal scalp area. Removed cyst under procaine
	block: knife dissection: closure of wound c̄ six #000 black silk sutures. Adv to retn in 5 days for
	removal of sutures. *Clarence Cutler, MD*
2-9-XX	Sutures removed & dressed. To retn in 1 wk. *Clarence Cutler, MD*
2-15-XX	Parietal area well healed. RTO prn. *Clarence Cutler, MD*

Figure 18

STATEMENT

College Clinic
4567 Broad Avenue
Woodland Hills, XY 12345-0001
Telephone: 013-486-9002
Fax: 013-487-8976

Ms. Darlene M. Cash
5729 Redwood Avenue
Woodland Hills, XY 12345-0001

DATE	PROFESSIONAL SERVICE DESCRIPTION	CHARGE	CREDITS		CURRENT BALANCE
			PAYMENTS	ADJUSTMENTS	
1-4-xx	OV, EPF hx and exam, SF decision making				
1-11-xx	OV, PF hx/exam, LC decision making				
2-3-xx	OV, EPF hx/exam, LC decision making				
2-3-xx	Exc inflammatory cystic lesion scalp 1.5 cm dia				
2-9-xx	OV, minimal (5 min)				
2-15-xx	OV, minimal (5 min)				

Due and payable within 10 days. **Pay last amount in balance column** 

Key:
PF: Problem-focused
EPF: Expanded problem-focused
D: Detailed
C: Comprehensive
SF: Straightforward
LC: Low complexity
MC: Moderate complexity
HC: High complexity
CON: Consultation
CPX: Complete phys exam
E: Emergency
ER: Emergency dept.
HCD: House call (day)
HCN: House call (night)
HV: Hospital visit
OV: Office visit

Figure 19

APPROVED OMB 0938-0008

PLEASE DO NOT STAPLE IN THIS AREA

CARRIER

PICA

HEALTH INSURANCE CLAIM FORM

PICA

PATIENT AND INSURED INFORMATION

1. MEDICARE (Medicare #) MEDICAID (Medicaid #) CHAMPUS (Sponsor's SSN) CHAMPVA (VA File #) GROUP HEALTH PLAN (SSN or ID) FECA BLK LUNG (SSN) OTHER (ID)

1a. INSURED'S I.D. NUMBER (FOR PROGRAM IN ITEM 1)

2. PATIENT'S NAME (Last Name, First Name, Middle Initial)

3. PATIENT'S BIRTH DATE MM | DD | YYYY SEX M F

4. INSURED'S NAME (Last Name, First Name, Middle Initial)

5. PATIENT'S ADDRESS (No., Street)

6. PATIENT RELATIONSHIP TO INSURED Self Spouse Child Other

7. INSURED'S ADDRESS (No., Street)

CITY STATE

8. PATIENT STATUS Single Married Other Employed Full-Time Student Part-Time Student

CITY STATE

ZIP CODE TELEPHONE (Include Area Code)

ZIP CODE TELEPHONE (Include Area Code) ( )

9. OTHER INSURED'S NAME (Last Name, First Name, Middle Initial)

10. IS PATIENT'S CONDITION RELATED TO:

11. INSURED'S POLICY GROUP OR FECA NUMBER

a. OTHER INSURED'S POLICY OR GROUP NUMBER

a. EMPLOYMENT? (CURRENT OR PREVIOUS) YES NO

a. INSURED'S DATE OF BIRTH MM | DD | YY SEX M F

b. OTHER INSURED'S DATE OF BIRTH MM | DD | YY SEX M F

b. AUTO ACCIDENT? YES NO PLACE (State)

b. EMPLOYER'S NAME OR SCHOOL NAME

c. EMPLOYER'S NAME OR SCHOOL NAME

c. OTHER ACCIDENT? YES NO

c. INSURANCE PLAN NAME OR PROGRAM NAME

d. INSURANCE PLAN NAME OR PROGRAM NAME

10d. RESERVED FOR LOCAL USE

d. IS THERE ANOTHER HEALTH BENEFIT PLAN? YES NO *If yes*, return to and complete item 9 a-d.

READ BACK OF FORM BEFORE COMPLETING AND SIGNING THIS FORM.

12. PATIENT'S OR AUTHORIZED PERSON'S SIGNATURE I authorize the release of any medical or other information necessary to process this claim. I also request payment of government benefits either to myself or to the party who accepts assignment below.

SIGNED ______ DATE ______

13. INSURED'S OR AUTHORIZED PERSON'S SIGNATURE I authorize payment of medical benefits to the undersigned physician or supplier for services described below.

SIGNED ______

PHYSICIAN OR SUPPLIER INFORMATION

14. DATE OF CURRENT: MM | DD | YY ILLNESS (First symptom) OR INJURY (Accident) OR PREGNANCY (LMP)

15. IF PATIENT HAS HAD SAME OR SIMILAR ILLNESS GIVE FIRST DATE MM | DD | YY

16. DATES PATIENT UNABLE TO WORK IN CURRENT OCCUPATION FROM MM | DD | YY TO MM | DD | YY

17. NAME OF REFERRING PHYSICIAN OR OTHER SOURCE

17a. I.D. NUMBER OF REFERRING PHYSICIAN

18. HOSPITALIZATION DATES RELATED TO CURRENT SERVICES FROM MM | DD | YY TO MM | DD | YY

19. RESERVED FOR LOCAL USE

20. OUTSIDE LAB? YES NO $ CHARGES

21. DIAGNOSIS OR NATURE OF ILLNESS OR INJURY. (RELATE ITEMS 1,2,3 OR 4 TO ITEM 24E BY LINE)

1. ______ 3. ______

2. ______ 4. ______

22. MEDICAID RESUBMISSION CODE ORIGINAL REF. NO.

23. PRIOR AUTHORIZATION NUMBER

24. A DATE(S) OF SERVICE From MM DD YY To MM DD YY	B Place of Service	C Type of Service	D PROCEDURES, SERVICES, OR SUPPLIES (Explain Unusual Circumstances) CPT/HCPCS | MODIFIER	E DIAGNOSIS CODE	F $ CHARGES	G DAYS OR UNITS	H EPSDT Family Plan	I EMG	J COB	K RESERVED FOR LOCAL USE

25. FEDERAL TAX I.D. NUMBER SSN EIN

26. PATIENT'S ACCOUNT NO.

27. ACCEPT ASSIGNMENT? (For govt. claims, see back) YES NO

28. TOTAL CHARGE $

29. AMOUNT PAID $

30. BALANCE DUE $

31. SIGNATURE OF PHYSICIAN OR SUPPLIER INCLUDING DEGREES OR CREDENTIALS (I certify that the statements on the reverse apply to this bill and are made a part thereof.)

SIGNED DATE

32. NAME AND ADDRESS OF FACILITY WHERE SERVICES WERE RENDERED (If other than home or office)

33. PHYSICIAN'S, SUPPLIER'S BILLING NAME, ADDRESS, ZIP CODE AND PHONE #

PIN# GRP#

(APPROVED BY AMA COUNCIL ON MEDICAL SERVICE 8/88)

PLEASE PRINT OR TYPE

FORM HCFA-1500 (U2)(12-90)
FORM OCWP-1500 FORM RRB-1500

Figure 20

PATIENT RECORD NO. T0004

LAST NAME	FIRST NAME	MIDDLE NAME	BIRTH DATE	SEX	HOME PHONE
Hamilton,	Gertrude	C.	03-06-43	F	013-798-3321

ADDRESS	CITY	STATE	ZIP CODE
5320 Phillips Street,	Woodland Hills,	XY	12345

PATIENT'S OCCUPATION: retired secretary
NAME OF COMPANY:

ADDRESS OF EMPLOYER:
PHONE:

SPOUSE OR PARENT: deceased
OCCUPATION:

EMPLOYER:
ADDRESS:
PHONE:

NAME OF INSURANCE: Colonial Health Insurance, 1011 Main Street, Woodland Hills, XY 12345
INSURED OR SUBSCRIBER:

OTHER INSURANCE:

POLICY NO.	GROUP NO.	EFFECTIVE DATE	SOC. SEC. NO.
540987677	4566		540-98-7677

REFERRED BY: Gerald Practon, MD 4567 Broad Avenue, Woodland Hills, XY 12345

DATE	PROGRESS
7-29-XX	This 57-year-old pt adm to College Hosp today by Dr. Practon c̄ an adm Dx of bilateral carotid stenosis.
	Dr. Practon asked me to see patient in consultation. Hx: suffered CVA lt hemisphere 1 yr prior to adm.
	Marked rt arm & leg weakness c̄ weakness of rt face and slurring of speech. PE reveals lt carotid bruit,
	II/IV, & right carotid bruit, II/IV. Adv brain scan, lt carotid thromboendarterectomy, and adv rt carotid
	thromboendarterectomy at a later date. Will follow patient's progress and take over care of pt. P Cardi, MD
7-30-XX	Hosp visit. Had brain scan done today, ECG, and lab workup. Perry Cardi, MD
7-31-XX	Hosp visit. Discussed results of brain scan with Ms. Hamilton. Perry Cardi, MD
8-1-XX	Hosp visit. Decision made for surgery tomorrow. Perry Cardi, MD
8-2-XX	Lt carotid thromboendarterectomy. See op report. Perry Cardi, MD
8-3-XX	Hosp visit. Nothing unusual noted at operative site. Perry Cardi, MD
8-4-XX	DC hosp. To be seen in office in 1 week. Perry Cardi, MD
8-12-XX	PO visit. Making satisfactory PO progress. Adv rt carotid arterectomy. Perry Cardi, MD
9-16-XX	Adm College Hosp. Rt. carotid thromboendarterectomy performed. DX: carotid stenosis, status post-
	operative & HCVD. Perry Cardi, MD
9-17-XX	Hospital visit. No weeping at operative site. Perry Cardi, MD
9-18-XX	DC hosp. Perry Cardi, MD
10-4-XX	PO visit. Making satisfactory PO recovery. Retn 1 month. Perry Cardi, MD

Figure 21

STATEMENT

College Clinic
4567 Broad Avenue
Woodland Hills, XY 12345-0001
Telephone: 013-486-9002
Fax: 013-487-8976

Mrs. Gertrude C. Hamilton
5320 Phillips Street
Woodland Hills, XY 12345-0001

DATE	PROFESSIONAL SERVICE DESCRIPTION	CHARGE	CREDITS		CURRENT BALANCE
			PAYMENTS	ADJUSTMENTS	
7-29-xx	Consult, comp hx/exam, HC decision making				
7-30-xx	HV, PF hx/exam, LC decision making				
7-31-xx	HV, PF hx/exam, LC decision making				
8-1-xx	HV, EPF hx, exam, MC decision making				
8-2-xx	L carotid thromboendarterectomy				
8-3-xx	HV				
8-4-xx	Discharge				
8-12-xx	OV				
9-16-xx	Hosp adm, D hx/exam, LC decision making				
9-16-xx	Rt carotid thromboendarterectomy				
9-17-xx	HV				
9-18-xx	Discharge				
10-4-xx	OV				

Due and payable within 10 days. **Pay last amount in balance column** 

Key:							
PF:	Problem-focused	SF:	Straightforward	CON:	Consultation	HCD:	House call (day)
EPF:	Expanded problem-focused	LC:	Low complexity	CPX:	Complete phys exam	HCN:	House call (night)
D:	Detailed	MC:	Moderate complexity	E:	Emergency	HV:	Hospital visit
C:	Comprehensive	HC:	High complexity	ER:	Emergency dept.	OV:	Office visit

Figure 22

APPROVED OMB 0938-0008

PLEASE DO NOT STAPLE IN THIS AREA

CARRIER

PICA

HEALTH INSURANCE CLAIM FORM

PICA

PATIENT AND INSURED INFORMATION

1. MEDICARE (Medicare #) MEDICAID (Medicaid #) CHAMPUS (Sponsor's SSN) CHAMPVA (VA File #) GROUP HEALTH PLAN (SSN or ID) FECA BLK LUNG (SSN) OTHER (ID)

1a. INSURED'S I.D. NUMBER (FOR PROGRAM IN ITEM 1)

2. PATIENT'S NAME (Last Name, First Name, Middle Initial)

3. PATIENT'S BIRTH DATE MM DD YYYY SEX M F

4. INSURED'S NAME (Last Name, First Name, Middle Initial)

5. PATIENT'S ADDRESS (No., Street)

6. PATIENT RELATIONSHIP TO INSURED Self Spouse Child Other

7. INSURED'S ADDRESS (No., Street)

CITY STATE

8. PATIENT STATUS Single Married Other

CITY STATE

ZIP CODE TELEPHONE (Include Area Code)

Employed Full-Time Student Part-Time Student

ZIP CODE TELEPHONE (Include Area Code) ( )

9. OTHER INSURED'S NAME (Last Name, First Name, Middle Initial)

10. IS PATIENT'S CONDITION RELATED TO:

11. INSURED'S POLICY GROUP OR FECA NUMBER

a. OTHER INSURED'S POLICY OR GROUP NUMBER

a. EMPLOYMENT? (CURRENT OR PREVIOUS) YES NO

a. INSURED'S DATE OF BIRTH MM DD YY SEX M F

b. OTHER INSURED'S DATE OF BIRTH MM DD YY SEX M F

b. AUTO ACCIDENT? YES NO PLACE (State)

b. EMPLOYER'S NAME OR SCHOOL NAME

c. EMPLOYER'S NAME OR SCHOOL NAME

c. OTHER ACCIDENT? YES NO

c. INSURANCE PLAN NAME OR PROGRAM NAME

d. INSURANCE PLAN NAME OR PROGRAM NAME

10d. RESERVED FOR LOCAL USE

d. IS THERE ANOTHER HEALTH BENEFIT PLAN? YES NO *If yes, return to and complete item 9 a-d.*

READ BACK OF FORM BEFORE COMPLETING AND SIGNING THIS FORM.

12. PATIENT'S OR AUTHORIZED PERSON'S SIGNATURE I authorize the release of any medical or other information necessary to process this claim. I also request payment of government benefits either to myself or to the party who accepts assignment below.

SIGNED ______ DATE ______

13. INSURED'S OR AUTHORIZED PERSON'S SIGNATURE I authorize payment of medical benefits to the undersigned physician or supplier for services described below.

SIGNED ______

PHYSICIAN OR SUPPLIER INFORMATION

14. DATE OF CURRENT: MM DD YY ILLNESS (First symptom) OR INJURY (Accident) OR PREGNANCY (LMP)

15. IF PATIENT HAS HAD SAME OR SIMILAR ILLNESS GIVE FIRST DATE MM DD YY

16. DATES PATIENT UNABLE TO WORK IN CURRENT OCCUPATION FROM MM DD YY TO MM DD YY

17. NAME OF REFERRING PHYSICIAN OR OTHER SOURCE

17a. I.D. NUMBER OF REFERRING PHYSICIAN

18. HOSPITALIZATION DATES RELATED TO CURRENT SERVICES FROM MM DD YY TO MM DD YY

19. RESERVED FOR LOCAL USE

20. OUTSIDE LAB? YES NO $ CHARGES

21. DIAGNOSIS OR NATURE OF ILLNESS OR INJURY (RELATE ITEMS 1,2,3 OR 4 TO ITEM 24E BY LINE)

1. ______ 3. ______

2. ______ 4. ______

22. MEDICAID RESUBMISSION CODE ORIGINAL REF. NO.

23. PRIOR AUTHORIZATION NUMBER

24. A DATE(S) OF SERVICE From MM DD YY To MM DD YY	B Place of Service	C Type of Service	D PROCEDURES, SERVICES, OR SUPPLIES (Explain Unusual Circumstances) CPT/HCPCS MODIFIER	E DIAGNOSIS CODE	F $ CHARGES	G DAYS OR UNITS	H EPSDT Family Plan	I EMG	J COB	K RESERVED FOR LOCAL USE

25. FEDERAL TAX I.D. NUMBER SSN EIN

26. PATIENT'S ACCOUNT NO.

27. ACCEPT ASSIGNMENT? (For govt. claims, see back) YES NO

28. TOTAL CHARGE $

29. AMOUNT PAID $

30. BALANCE DUE $

31. SIGNATURE OF PHYSICIAN OR SUPPLIER INCLUDING DEGREES OR CREDENTIALS (I certify that the statements on the reverse apply to this bill and are made a part thereof.)

SIGNED DATE

32. NAME AND ADDRESS OF FACILITY WHERE SERVICES WERE RENDERED (If other than home or office)

33. PHYSICIAN'S, SUPPLIER'S BILLING NAME, ADDRESS, ZIP CODE AND PHONE #

PIN# GRP#

(APPROVED BY AMA COUNCIL ON MEDICAL SERVICE 8/88)

PLEASE PRINT OR TYPE

FORM HCFA-1500 (U2)(12-90)
FORM OCWP-1500 FORM RRB-1500

Figure 23

APPROVED OMB 0938-0008

CARRIER

PLEASE
DO NOT
STAPLE
IN THIS
AREA

PICA

HEALTH INSURANCE CLAIM FORM

PICA

1. MEDICARE (Medicare #) MEDICAID (Medicaid #) CHAMPUS (Sponsor's SSN) CHAMPVA (VA File #) GROUP HEALTH PLAN (SSN or ID) FECA BLK LUNG (SSN) OTHER (ID)

1a. INSURED'S I.D. NUMBER (FOR PROGRAM IN ITEM 1)

2. PATIENT'S NAME (Last Name, First Name, Middle Initial)

3. PATIENT'S BIRTH DATE MM | DD | YYYY SEX M F

4. INSURED'S NAME (Last Name, First Name, Middle Initial)

5. PATIENT'S ADDRESS (No., Street)

6. PATIENT RELATIONSHIP TO INSURED Self Spouse Child Other

7. INSURED'S ADDRESS (No., Street)

CITY STATE

8. PATIENT STATUS Single Married Other

CITY STATE

ZIP CODE TELEPHONE (Include Area Code)

Employed Full-Time Student Part-Time Student

ZIP CODE TELEPHONE (Include Area Code) ( )

9. OTHER INSURED'S NAME (Last Name, First Name, Middle Initial)

10. IS PATIENT'S CONDITION RELATED TO:

11. INSURED'S POLICY GROUP OR FECA NUMBER

a. OTHER INSURED'S POLICY OR GROUP NUMBER

a. EMPLOYMENT? (CURRENT OR PREVIOUS) YES NO

a. INSURED'S DATE OF BIRTH MM | DD | YY SEX M F

b. OTHER INSURED'S DATE OF BIRTH MM | DD | YY SEX M F

b. AUTO ACCIDENT? YES NO PLACE (State)

b. EMPLOYER'S NAME OR SCHOOL NAME

c. EMPLOYER'S NAME OR SCHOOL NAME

c. OTHER ACCIDENT? YES NO

c. INSURANCE PLAN NAME OR PROGRAM NAME

d. INSURANCE PLAN NAME OR PROGRAM NAME

10d. RESERVED FOR LOCAL USE

d. IS THERE ANOTHER HEALTH BENEFIT PLAN? YES NO *If yes, return to and complete item 9 a-d.*

READ BACK OF FORM BEFORE COMPLETING AND SIGNING THIS FORM.

12. PATIENT'S OR AUTHORIZED PERSON'S SIGNATURE I authorize the release of any medical or other information necessary to process this claim. I also request payment of government benefits either to myself or to the party who accepts assignment below.

SIGNED ____________ DATE ____________

13. INSURED'S OR AUTHORIZED PERSON'S SIGNATURE I authorize payment of medical benefits to the undersigned physician or supplier for services described below.

SIGNED ____________

PATIENT AND INSURED INFORMATION

14. DATE OF CURRENT: MM | DD | YY ◀ ILLNESS (First symptom) OR INJURY (Accident) OR PREGNANCY (LMP)

15. IF PATIENT HAS HAD SAME OR SIMILAR ILLNESS GIVE FIRST DATE MM | DD | YY

16. DATES PATIENT UNABLE TO WORK IN CURRENT OCCUPATION FROM MM | DD | YY TO MM | DD | YY

17. NAME OF REFERRING PHYSICIAN OR OTHER SOURCE

17a. I.D. NUMBER OF REFERRING PHYSICIAN

18. HOSPITALIZATION DATES RELATED TO CURRENT SERVICES FROM MM | DD | YY TO MM | DD | YY

19. RESERVED FOR LOCAL USE

20. OUTSIDE LAB? YES NO $ CHARGES

21. DIAGNOSIS OR NATURE OF ILLNESS OR INJURY. (RELATE ITEMS 1,2,3 OR 4 TO ITEM 24E BY LINE)

1. ____ 3. ____

2. ____ 4. ____

22. MEDICAID RESUBMISSION CODE ORIGINAL REF. NO.

23. PRIOR AUTHORIZATION NUMBER

24. A DATE(S) OF SERVICE From MM DD YY To MM DD YY	B Place of Service	C Type of Service	D PROCEDURES, SERVICES, OR SUPPLIES (Explain Unusual Circumstances) CPT/HCPCS | MODIFIER	E DIAGNOSIS CODE	F $ CHARGES	G DAYS OR UNITS	H EPSDT Family Plan	I EMG	J COB	K RESERVED FOR LOCAL USE

25. FEDERAL TAX I.D. NUMBER SSN EIN

26. PATIENT'S ACCOUNT NO.

27. ACCEPT ASSIGNMENT? (For govt. claims, see back) YES NO

28. TOTAL CHARGE $

29. AMOUNT PAID $

30. BALANCE DUE $

31. SIGNATURE OF PHYSICIAN OR SUPPLIER INCLUDING DEGREES OR CREDENTIALS (I certify that the statements on the reverse apply to this bill and are made a part thereof.)

SIGNED DATE

32. NAME AND ADDRESS OF FACILITY WHERE SERVICES WERE RENDERED (if other than home or office)

33. PHYSICIAN'S, SUPPLIER'S BILLING NAME, ADDRESS, ZIP CODE AND PHONE #

PIN# GRP#

PHYSICIAN OR SUPPLIER INFORMATION

(APPROVED BY AMA COUNCIL ON MEDICAL SERVICE 8/88) *PLEASE PRINT OR TYPE* FORM HCFA-1500 (U2)(12-90) FORM OCWP-1500 FORM RRB-1500

Figure 24

Appendix A

College Clinic

You are employed as an insurance billing specialist for an incorporated group of medical doctors, other allied health specialists, and podiatrists. These doctors are on the staff of a nearby hospital, College Hospital. Reference information to complete insurance claim forms for each assignment follows.

Office address:
College Clinic
4567 Broad Avenue
Woodland Hills, XY 12345–0001
telephone: 013–486–9002
FAX: 013–487–8976
Group practice (employer) tax identification number: 3664021CC
Clinic's Medicaid provider number: HSC 12345F
Medicare Durable Medical Equipment (DME) supplier number: 3400760001

Hospital address:
College Hospital
4500 Broad Avenue
Woodland Hills, XY 12345–0001
telephone: 013–487–6789
FAX: 013–486–8900
Hospital provider number: 95–0731067
Hospital's Medicaid provider number: HSC43700F
Hospital's Medicare provider number: HSP43700F

College Clinic Staff (Table 1)

Patient records in this *Workbook* include the doctors' names, specialties, subspecialties, and physicians' identification numbers of the College Clinic staff (see Table 1).

Table 1. College Clinic Staff

Name	Specialty (abbr)	Soc. Sec. #	State License #	EIN # or Federal Tax ID #	Medicare HCFA-Assigned National Provider Identifier (NPI)*
Concha Antrum, MD	Otolaryngologist (OTO) or Ear, Nose, and Throat Specialist (ENT)	082–19–1707	C 016021	74–1064090	1245897700
Pedro Atrics, MD	Pediatrician (PD)	134–80–7600	D 060123	71–3206151	3764001700
Bertha Caesar, MD	Obstetrician and Gynecologist (OBG)	230–80–6700	A 018174	72–5713051	4305675700
Perry Cardi, MD	Internist (I) *Subspecialty:* Cardiovascular Disease (CD)	557–46–9980	C 021400	70–6421710	6780502700
Brady Coccidioides, MD	Internist (I) *Subspecialty:* Pulmonary Disease (PUD)	670–54–0874	C 048211	75–6732101	6421106700
Vera Cutis, MD	Dermatologist (D)	409–19–8620	C 060021	71–8056112	7056871700
Clarence Cutler, MD	General Surgeon (GS)	410–23–5630	B 076005	71–5737291	4305004700
Dennis Drill, DDS	Dentist	240–47–8960	706100	72–4650312	7430108700
Max Glutens, RPT	Physical Therapist (PT)	507–40–4300	876100	79–3650028	6513227700
Cosmo Graff, MD	Plastic Surgeon (PS)	452–57–9899	C 081046	74–6078992	5030711700
Malvern Grumose, MD	Pathologist (Path)	470–67–2301	A 016025	72–7365114	
Gaston Input, MD	Internist (I) *Subspecialty:* Gastroenterologist (GE)	211–09–6734	C 080016	75–6721022	3278312700
Adam Langerhans, MD	Endocrinologist	447–90–6720	C 060511	60–5783128	4768065700
Cornell Lenser, MD	Ophthalmologist (OPH)	322–75-8963	C 060466	61–7894119	5403721700
Michael Menter, MD	Psychiatrist (P)	210–60–5302	C 071402	73–6657712	6730123700
Arthur O. Dont, DDS	Orthodontist	102–30–4566	805300	90–5117821	4537824700
Astro Parkinson, MD	Neurosurgeon (NS)	210–42–8533	C 026002	75–4453014	4678937700
Nick Pedro, DPM	Podiatrist	233–08–4300	E 083400	62–7410931	5402228700
Gerald Practon, MD	General Practitioner (GP) or Family Practitioner (FP)	123–45–6789	C 014021	70–3459766	4627889700
Walter Radon, MD	Radiologist (R)	344–09–6540	C 050013	95–4613782	4003722700
Rex Rumsey, MD	Proctologist (Proct)	337–88–9743	C 030421	95–3260111	0199904700
Sensitive E. Scott, MD	Anesthesiologist (Anes)	220–45–5655	C 020411	72–5420305	9999926700
Raymond Skeleton, MD	Orthopedist (ORS, Orthop)	432–11–4589	C 045612	74–6541270	1267854700
Gene Ulibarri, MD	Urologist (U)	990–70–3245	C 064303	77–8653124	2567883100

*At press time, official adoption of NPI numbers has not occurred. In most regions UPIN and PIN numbers are being used. Thus the column indicating NPI numbers is to be used for UPIN or PIN numbers for the simulation.

Abbreviations and Symbols

Abbreviations and symbols may appear on patient records, prescriptions, hospital charts, and patient ledger cards. Abbreviation styles differ, but the current trend is to omit periods in capital letter abbreviations except for doctors' academic degrees. For information on official American Hospital Association policy, refer to page 66 in the *Handbook*. Following is a list of abbreviations and symbols used in this *Workbook* and their meanings.

Abbreviations

A	allergy
Abdom	abdomen
abt	about
a.c.	before meals
Adj*	adjustment
adm	admit, admission, admitted
adv	advise
aet	at the age of
agit	shake or stir
$AgNO_3$	silver nitrate
ALL	allergy
AM, a.m.	ante meridiem (time—before noon)
ant	anterior
ante	before
AP	anterior-posterior, anteroposterior
approx	approximate
appt	appointment
apt	apartment
ASA	acetylsalicylic acid (aspirin)
ASAP	as soon as possible
ASCVD	arteriosclerotic cardiovascular disease
ASHD	arteriosclerotic heart disease
asst	assistant
auto	automobile
AV	atrioventricular
Ba	barium (enema)
Bal/fwd*	balance forward
B /F*	balance forward; brought forward
BI	biopsy
b.i.d.	2 times daily
BMR	basal metabolic rate
BP	blood pressure
Brev	sodium brevital
C	cervical (vertebrae); comprehensive (history/exam)
Ca, CA	cancer, carcinoma
c/a*	cash on account
CABG	coronary artery bypass graft
CAT	computed axial tomography
cau	Caucasian
CBC	complete blood count
CBS	chronic brain syndrome
cc	cubic centimeter
CC	chief complaint
chr	chronic
ck*	check
cm	centimeter
CO, c/o	complains of
compl, comp	complete, comprehensive
Con, CON, Cons	consultation
Cont	continue
CPX	complete physical examination
Cr*	credit
cs, CS*	cash on account
C-section	cesarean section
CVA	cardiovascular accident; cerebrovascular accident
CXR	chest x-ray
Cysto	cystoscopy
D	diagnosis; detailed (history/exam)
D & C	dilatation and curettage
dc	discontinue
DC	discharge
DDS	Doctor of Dental Surgery
def*	charge deferred
Del	delivery, OB
Dg	diagnosis
dia	diameter
diag	diagnosis, diagnostic
dil	dilate (stretch, expand)
Disch	discharge
DM	diabetes mellitus
DNA	does not apply
DNS	did not show
DPM	Doctor of Podiatric Medicine
DPT	diphtheria, pertussis, and tetanus
Dr	Doctor
Dr*	debit
DRG	diagnosis-related group
Drs	dressing
Dx	diagnosis
E	emergency
EC*	error corrected
ECG, EKG	electrocardiogram, electrocardiograph

*Bookkeeping abbreviation

ED	emergency department
EDC	estimated date of confinement
EEG	electroencephalograph
EENT	eye, ear, nose, and throat
EGD	esophagogastroduodenoscopy
EKG, ECG	electrocardiogram, electrocardiograph
E/M	Evaluation and Management (CPT code)
EMG	electromyogram
EPF	expanded problem-focused (history/exam)
epith	epithelial
ER	emergency room
Er, ER*	error corrected
ESR	erythrocyte sedimentation rate
est	established (patient)
Ex, exam	examination
exc	excision
Ex MO*	express money order
ext	external
24F, 28F	French (size of catheter)
FBS	fasting blood sugar
FH	family history
ft	foot, feet
FU	follow-up (examination)
fwd*	forward
Fx	fracture
gb, GB	gallbladder
GGE	generalized glandular enlargement
GI	gastrointestinal
Grav, grav	gravida, a pregnant woman; used with Roman numerals (I, II, III) to indicate the number of pregnancies
GU	genitourinary
H	hospital call
HBP	high blood pressure
HC	hospital call or consultation; high-complexity (decision making)
HCD	house call (day)
HCN	house call (night)
Hct	hematocrit
HCVD	hypertensive cardiovascular disease
Hgb	hemoglobin
hist	history
hosp	hospital
H & P	history and physical
hr, hrs	hour, hours
h.s.	before bedtime
HS	hospital surgery
Ht	height
HV	hospital visit
HX, hx	history
HX PX	history and physical examination
I	injection
IC	initial consultation
I & D	incision and drainage
I/f*	in full
IM	intramuscular (injection)
imp, imp.	impression (diagnosis)
inflam	inflammation
init	initial (office visit)
inj, INJ	injection
ins, INS*	insurance
int	internal
intermed	intermediate (office visit)
interpret	interpretation
IUD	intrauterine device
IV	intravenous (injection)
IVP	intravenous pyelogram
K 35	Kolman (instrument used in urology)
KUB	kidneys, ureters, bladder
L	left; laboratory
Lab, LAB	laboratory
lat	lateral; pertaining to the side
LC	low complexity (decision making)
LMP	last menstrual period
LS	lumbosacral
lt	left
ltd	limited (office visit)
L & W	living and well
M	medication; married
MC	moderate complexity (decision making)
med	medicine
mg	milligram(s)
mg/dL	milligrams per deciliter
MI	myocardial infarction
mL, ml	milliliter
mo	month(s)
MO*	money order
N	negative
NA	not applicable

*Bookkeeping abbreviation

NAD no appreciable disease
NC, N/C* no charge
NEC not elsewhere classifiable
neg negative
NOS not otherwise specified
NP new patient
NYD not yet diagnosed
OB, Ob-Gyn obstetrics and gynecology
OC office call
occ occasional
OD right eye
ofc office
OP outpatient
Op, op operation
OR operating room
orig original
OS office surgery; left eye
OV office visit
oz ounce
PA posterior-anterior, posteroanterior
Pap Papanicolaou (smear, stain, test)
Para I woman having borne one child
PC present complaint
p.c. after meals
PCP primary care physician
PD permanent disability
Pd, PD* professional discount
PE physical examination
perf performed
PF problem-focused (history/exam)
PH past history
Ph ex physical examination
phys physical
PID pelvic inflammatory disease
PM, p.m. post meridiem (time—after noon)
PND postnasal drip
PO, P Op postoperative
p.o. per os (Latin), by mouth
post posterior
postop postoperative
PPD purified protein derivative (such as in tuberculin test)
preop preoperative
prep prepared
PRN as necessary *(pro re nata)*
Proc procedure
Prog prognosis
P & S permanent and stationary
PSA prostate-specific antigen; blood test to determine cancer in prostate gland
Pt, pt patient
PT physical therapy
PTR patient to return
PVC premature ventricular contraction
PVT ck* private check received
PX physical examination
q every
qd one time daily, every day
qh every hour
q.i.d. four times daily
QNS insufficient quantity
qod every other day
R right; residence call; report
RBC, rbc red blood cell (count)
rec recommend
rec'd received
re ch recheck
re-exam re-examination
Reg regular
ret, retn, rtn return
rev review
RHD rheumatic heart disease
RN registered nurse
R/O rule out
ROA* received on account
RPT registered physical therapist
rt right
RTC return to clinic
RTO return to office
RTW return to work
RX, Rx, R_x prescribe, prescription; any medication or treatment ordered
S surgery
SC subcutaneous
sched. scheduled
SD state disability
SE special examination
SF straightforward (decision making)
Sig directions on prescription
SLR straight leg raising
slt slight
Smr smear
SOB shortness of breath
Sp gr specific gravity

*Bookkeeping abbreviation

SQ subcutaneous (injection)
STAT immediately
surg surgery
T temperature
T & A tonsillectomy and adenoidectomy
Tb, tb tuberculosis
TD temporary disability
temp temperature
tet. tox. tetanus toxoid
t.i.d. three times daily
TPR temperature, pulse, and respiration
Tr, trt treatment
TURB transurethral resection of bladder
TURP transurethral resection of prostate
TX treatment
u units
UA, ua urinalysis
UCHD usual childhood diseases
UCR usual, customary, and reasonable (fees)
UGI upper gastrointestinal
UPJ ureteropelvic junction or joint
UR urinalysis
URI upper respiratory infection
Urn urinalysis
UTI urinary tract infection
W work; white
WBC, wbc white blood cell (count); well baby care
wk week; work
wks weeks
WNL within normal limits
Wr Wassermann reaction (test for syphilis)
Wt, wt weight
X xray, x-ray(s); times (e.g., 3X = 3 times)
XR xray, x-ray(s)
yr year

Symbols

c̄,/c with
s̄,/s without
c̄c, c̄/c with correction (eye glasses)
s̄c, s̄/c without correction (eye glasses)
− negative
ō negative
⊕ positive
Ⓛ left
® right
♂ male
♀ female
−* charge already made
Θ* no balance due
✔* posted
($0.00)* credit

*Bookkeeping abbreviation

Laboratory Abbreviations

Abbreviation	Definition
AcG	factor V (AcG or proaccelerin); a factor in coagulation that converts prothrombin to thrombin
ACTH	adrenocorticotroic hormone
AFB	acid-fast bacilli
A/C ratio	albumin-coagulin ratio
AHB	alpha-hydroxybutyric [dehydrogenase]
AHG	antihemophilic globulin; antihemolytic globulin (factor)
ALA	aminolevulinic acid
ALT	alanine aminotransferase (see SGPT)
AMP	adenosine monophosphate
APT test	aluminum-precipitated toxoid test
AST	aspartate aminotransferase (see SGOT)
ATP	adenosine triphosphate
BSP	bromsulfonphthalein (Bromsulphalein; sodium sulfobromophthalein) [test]
BUN	blood urea nitrogen
CBC	complete blood count
CNS	central nervous system
CO	carbon monoxide
CPB	competitive protein binding: plasma
CPK	creatine phosphokinase
CSF	cerebrospinal fluid
D hemoglobin	hemoglobin fractionation by electrophoresis for hemoglobin D
DAP	direct agglutination pregnancy (Gravindex and DAP)
DEAE	diethylaminoethanol
DHT	dihydrotestosterone
DNA	deoxyribonucleic acid
DRT	test for syphilis
EACA	EACA control (epsilon-aminocaproic acid is a fibrinolysin)
EMIT	enzyme-multiplied immunoassay technique (for drugs)
ENA	extractable nuclear antigen
esr, ESR	erythrocyte sedimentation rate (sed rate)
FDP	fibrin degradation products
FIGLU	formiminoglutamic acid
FRAT	free radical assay technique (for drugs)
FSH	follicle-stimulating hormone
FSP	fibrinogen split products
FTA	fluorescent-absorbed treponema antibodies
Gc, Gm, Inv	immunoglobulin typing
GG, gamma G, A, D, G, M	gamma-globulin (immunoglobulin fractionation by electrophoresis)
GG, gamma G E, RIA	immunization E fractionation by radioimmunoassay
GGT	gamma-glutamyl transpeptidase
GLC	gas liquid chromatography
GMP	guanosine monophosphate
G6PD	glucose-6-phosphate dehydrogenase
HAA	hepatitis-associated agent (antigen)

Continued on following page

Laboratory Abbreviations *(continued)*

Abbreviation	Definition
HBD, HBDH	hydroxybutyrate dehydrogenase
HCT	hematocrit
hemoglobin, electrophoresis	letters of the alphabet used for different types or factors of hemoglobins (includes A_2, S, C, etc.)
Hgb	hemoglobin, qualitative
HGH	human growth hormone
HI	hemagglutination inhibition
HIA	hemagglutination inhibition antibody
HIAA	hydroxyindoleacetic acid (urine), 24-hour specimen
HIV	human immunodeficiency virus
HLA	human leukocyte antigen (tissue typing)
HPL	human placental lactogen
HTLV-III	antibody detection; confirmatory test
HVA	homovanillic acid
ICSH	interstitial cell–stimulating hormone
IFA	intrinsic factor, antibody (fluorescent screen)
IgA, IgE, IgG, IgM	immunoglobulins: quantitative by gel diffusion
INH	isonicotinic hydrazide, isoniazid
LAP	leucine aminopeptidase
LATS	long-acting thyroid-stimulating [hormone]
LDH	lactic dehydrogenase
LE Prep	lupus erythematosus cell preparation
L.E. factor	antinuclear antibody
LH	luteinizing hormone
LSD	lysergic acid diethylamide
L/S ratio	lecithin-sphingomyelin ratio
MC *(Streptococcus)*	antibody titer
MIC	minimum inhibitory concentration
NBT	nitro-blue tetrazolium [test]
OCT	ornithine carbamyl transferase
PAH	para-aminohippuric acid
PBI	protein-bound iodine
pCO_2	arterial carbon dioxide pressure (or tension)
PCP	phencyclidine piperidine
pcv	packed cell volume
pH	symbol for expression of concentration of hydrogen ions (degree of acidity)
PHA	phenylalanine
PIT	prothrombin inhibition test
PKU	phenylketonuria—a metabolic disease affecting mental development
PO_2	oxygen pressure
P & P	prothrombin-proconvertin
PSP	phenolsulfonphthalein
PT	prothrombin time
PTA	plasma thromboplastin antecedent
PTC	plasma thromboplastin component; phenylthiocarbamide
PTT	prothrombin time; partial thromboplastin time (plasma or whole blood)
RBC, rbc	red blood cells (count)

Laboratory Abbreviations *(continued)*

Abbreviation	Definition
RIA	radioimmunoassay
RISA	radioiodinated human serum albumin
RIST	radioimmunosorbent test
RPR	rapid plasma reagin [test]
RT_3U	resin triiodothyronine uptake
S-D	strength-duration (curve)
SGOT	serum glutamic oxaloacetic transaminase
SGPT	serum glutamic pyruvic transaminase
STS	serologic test for syphilis
T_3	triiodothyronine (uptake)
TB	tubercle bacillus, tuberculosis
TBG	thyroxine-binding globulin
T & B differentiation, lymphocytes	thymus-dependent lymphs and bursa-dependent lymphs
THC	tetrahydrocannabinol (marijuana)
TIBC	total iron-binding capacity, chemical
TLC screen	thin-layer chromatography screen
TRP	tubular reabsorption of phosphates
UA	urinalysis
VDRL	Venereal Disease Research Laboratory (agglutination test for syphilis)
VMA	vanillylmandelic acid
WBC, wbc	white blood cells (count)

Mock Fee Schedule

Refer to the following mock fee schedule (Table 2) to complete the ledger cards and claim forms in this *Workbook*. The fees listed are hypothetical and are intended only for use in completing the questions. For the cases that are private, Medicaid, TRICARE, and workers' compensation, use the amounts in the column labeled Mock Fees. For Medicare cases, refer to the three columns pertaining to Medicare and use the amounts in the column labeled Limiting Charge.

When completing the insurance claim forms, use the latest edition of *Current Procedural Terminology (CPT)*, the professional code book published by the American Medical Association, to find the correct code numbers and modifiers for the services rendered. If you do not have access to the latest edition of *CPT*, you may use the code numbers provided in the mock fee schedule; however, do so with the understanding that the code numbers and descriptions provided in this schedule are not comprehensive. They are based on the information found in *CPT*; however, students are cautioned not to use it as a substitute for *CPT*. Because the code numbers are subject to change, every medical office must have on hand the most recent edition of *CPT*.

The mock fee schedule (Tables 2 and 3) is arranged in the same sequence as the six *CPT* code book sections (i.e., Evaluation and Management; Anesthesia; Surgery; Radiology, Nuclear Medicine, and Diagnostic Ultrasound; Pathology and Laboratory; and Medicine), with a comprehensive list of modifiers placed at the beginning. An index at the end of the mock fee schedule can assist you in locating code numbers. Mock fees for the modifiers are not listed, since these can vary from one claim to another depending on the circumstances.

Remember that fees can vary with the region of the United States (West, Midwest, South, and East), the specialty of the practitioner, the type of community (urban, suburban, or rural), the type of practice (incorporated or unincorporated–solo, partners or shareholders), the overhead, and a number of other factors.

Table 2. College Clinic Mock Fee Schedule

Modifier Code No.	Description	Mock Fee ($)
-21	*Prolonged Evaluation and Management Services:* When the face-to-face or floor/unit service(s) provided is prolonged or otherwise greater than that usually required for the highest level of evaluation and management service within a given category, it may be identified by adding modifier -21 to the evaluation and management code number or by use of the separate five-digit modifier code 09921. A report may also be appropriate.	Increase fee
-22	*Unusual Services:* When the service(s) provided is greater than that usually required for the listed procedure, it may be identified by adding modifier -22 to the usual procedure code number or by using the separate five-digit modifier code number 09922. A report may also be appropriate.	Increase fee
-23	*Unusual Anesthesia:* Occasionally, a procedure that usually requires either no anesthesia or local anesthesia must be done under general anesthesia because of unusual circumstances. These circumstances may be reported by adding the modifier -23 to the procedure code number of the basic service or by using the separate five-digit modifier code number 09923.	Increase fee
-24	*Unrelated Evaluation and Management Service by the Same Physician During a Postoperative Period:* The physician may need to indicate that an evaluation and management service was performed during a postoperative period for a reason(s) unrelated to the original procedure. This circumstance may be reported by adding the modifier -24 to the appropriate level of E/M service, or the separate five-digit modifier 09924 may be used.	Variable per E/M fee
-25	*Significant, Separately Identifiable Evaluation and Management Service by the Same Physician on the Same Day of a Procedure or Other Service:* The physician may need to indicate that on the day a procedure or service identified by a CPT code was performed, the patient's condition required a significant, separately identifiable E/M service above and beyond the other service provided or beyond the usual preoperative and postoperative care associated with the procedure that was performed. The E/M service may be prompted by the symptom or condition for which the procedure and/or service was provided. As such, different diagnoses are not required for reporting of the E/M services on the same date. This circumstance may be reported by adding the modifier -25 to the appropriate level of E/M service, or the separate five-digit modifier 09925 may be used. NOTE: This modifier is not used to report an E/M service that resulted in a decision to perform surgery. See modifier -57.	Variable per E/M fee
-26	*Professional Component:* Certain procedures are a combination of a physician component and a technical component. When the physician component is reported separately, the service may be identified by adding the modifier -26 to the usual procedure code number, or the service may be reported by using the five-digit modifier code number 09926.	Decrease fee
-27	*Multiple Outpatient Hospital E/M Encounters on the Same Date:* For hospital outpatient reporting purposes, utilization of hospital resources related to separate and distinct E/M encounters performed in multiple outpatient hospital settings on the same date may be reported by adding the modifier -27 to each appropriate level outpatient and/or emergency department E/M code(s). This modifier provides a means of reporting circumstances involving E/M services provided by physician(s) in more than one	Variable

Table 2. College Clinic Mock Fee Schedule *Continued*

Modifier Code No.	Description	Mock Fee ($)
	(multiple) outpatient hospital setting(s) (e.g., hospital emergency department, clinic). Do not use this modifier for physician reporting of multiple E/M services performed by the same physician on the same date. See E/M, emergency department, or preventive medicine services codes.	
-32	*Mandated Services:* Services related to mandated consultation and/or related services (e.g., PRO, 3rd party payer) may be identified by adding the modifier -32 to the basic procedure, or the service may be reported by use of the five-digit modifier 09932.	Use standard fee
-47	*Anesthesia by Surgeon:* Regional or general anesthesia provided by the surgeon may be reported by adding the modifier -47 to the basic service or by using the separate five-digit modifier code number 09947 (this does not include local anesthesia). Note: Modifier -47 or code number 09947 would not be used as a modifier for the anesthesia procedures 00100 through 01999.	Increase fee
-50	*Bilateral Procedure:* Unless otherwise identified in the listings, bilateral procedures that are performed at the same operative session should be identified by the appropriate five-digit code number describing the first procedure. The second (bilateral) procedure is identified either by adding modifier -50 to the procedure code number or by using the separate five-digit modifier code 09950.	Paid at 50% of standard fee
-51	*Multiple Procedures:* When multiple procedures other than E/M services are performed at the same session by the same provider, the primary procedure or service may be reported as listed. The additional procedure(s) or service(s) may be identified by adding the modifier -51 to the additional procedure or service code(s) or by using the separate five-digit modifier code 09951. Note: This modifier should not be appended to designated "add-on" codes.	Second procedure usually paid at 50% of fee. Third procedure usually paid at 25% of fee. Fourth and subsequent procedures usually paid at 10% of fee.
-52	*Reduced Services:* Under certain circumstances a service or procedure is partially reduced or eliminated at the physician's discretion. Under these circumstances the service provided can be identified by its usual procedure number and the addition of the modifier -52, signifying that the service is reduced. This provides a means of reporting reduced services without disturbing the identification of the basic service. Modifier code 09952 may be used as an alternative to modifier -52. Note: For hospital outpatient reporting of a previously scheduled procedure/service that is partially reduced or canceled as a result of extenuating circumstances or those that threaten the well-being of the patient prior to or after administration of anesthesia, see modifiers -73 and -74.	Decrease fee
-53	*Discontinued Procedure:* Under certain circumstances, the physician may elect to terminate a surgical or diagnostic procedure. Due to extenuating circumstances or those that threaten the well-being of the patient, it may be necessary to indicate that a surgical or diagnostic procedure was started but discontinued. This circumstance may be reported by adding modifier -53 to the code reported by the physician for the discontinued procedure or by use of the separate five-digit modifier code 09953. Note: This modifier is not used to report the elective cancellation of a procedure prior to the patient's anesthesia induction and/or surgical preparation in the operating suite. For outpatient hospital/ambulatory surgery center (ASC) reporting of a previously scheduled procedure/service that	Decrease fee

Table continued on following page

Table 2. College Clinic Mock Fee Schedule *Continued*

Modifier Code No.	Description	Mock Fee ($)
	is partially reduced or canceled as a result of extenuating circumstances or those that threaten the well-being of the patient prior to or after administration of anesthesia, see modifiers -73 and -74 (see modifiers approved for ASC hospital outpatient use).	
-54	*Surgical Care Only:* When one physician performs a surgical procedure and another provides preoperative and/or postoperative management, surgical services may be identified by adding the modifier -54 to the usual procedure number or by using the separate five-digit modifier code 09954.	Decrease fee
-55	*Postoperative Management Only:* When one physician performs the postoperative management and another physician performs the surgical procedure, the postoperative component may be identified by adding modifier -55 to the usual procedure number or by using the separate five-digit modifier code 09955.	Decrease fee
-56	*Preoperative Management Only:* When one physician performs the preoperative care and evaluation and another physician performs the surgical procedure, the preoperative component may be identified by adding the modifier -56 to the usual procedure number or by using the separate five-digit modifier code 09956.	Decrease fee
-57	*Decision for Surgery:* An evaluation and management service that resulted in the initial decision to perform the surgery may be identified by adding the modifier -57 to the appropriate level of E/M service, or the separate five-digit modifier 09957 may be used.	Use standard fee
-58	*Staged or Related Procedure or Service by the Same Physician During the Postoperative Period:* The physician may need to indicate that the performance of a procedure or service during the postoperative period was: (a) planned prospectively at the time of the original procedure (staged); (b) more extensive than the original procedure; or (c) for therapy following a diagnostic surgical procedure. This circumstance may be reported by adding the modifier -58 to the staged or related procedure, or the separate five-digit modifier 09958 may be used. NOTE: This modifier is not used to report the treatment of a problem that requires a return to the operating room. See modifier -78.	Variable
-59	*Distinct Procedural Service:* Under certain circumstances, the physician may need to indicate that a procedure or service was distinct or independent from other services performed on the same day. Modifier -59 is used to identify procedures/services that are not normally reported together, but are appropriate under the circumstances. This may represent a different session or patient encounter, different procedure or surgery, different site or organ system, separate incision/excision, separate lesion, or separate injury (or area of injury in extensive injuries) not ordinarily encountered or performed on the same day by the same physician. However, when another already established modifier is appropriate it should be used rather than modifier -59. Only if no more descriptive modifier is available, and the use of modifier -59 best explains the circumstances, should modifier -59 be used. Modifier code 09959 may be used as an alternative to modifier -59.	Variable
-60	*Altered Surgical Field:* Certain procedures involve significantly increased operative complexity and/or time in a significantly altered surgical field resulting from the effects of prior surgery, marked scarring, adhesions, inflammation or distorted anatomy, irradiation, infection, very low weight (i.e., neonates and small	Increase fee

Table 2. College Clinic Mock Fee Schedule *Continued*

Modifier Code No.	Description	Mock Fee ($)
	infants less than 10 kg) and/or trauma (as documented in the patient's medical record). These circumstances should be reported by adding the modifier -60 to the procedure number or by use of the separate five-digit modifier code 09960. Note: For unusual procedural services not involving an altered surgical field due to the late effects of previous surgery, irradiation, infection, very low weight (i.e., neonates and infants less than 10 kg) and/or trauma, append the modifier -22 or use the separate five-digit code 09922.	
-62	*Two Surgeons:* Under certain circumstances the skills of two surgeons (usually with different skills) may be required in the management of a specific surgical procedure. Under such circumstances the separate services may be identified by adding the modifier -62 to the procedure number used by each surgeon for reporting his or her services. Modifier code 09962 may be used as an alternative to modifier -62. Note: If a co-surgeon acts as an assistant in the performance of additional procedure(s) during the same surgical session, those services may be reported using separate procedure code(s) with the modifier -80 or modifier -81 added, as appropriate.	Use standard fee
-66	*Surgical Team:* Under some circumstances, highly complex procedures (requiring the concomitant services of several physicians, often of different specialties, plus other highly skilled, specially trained personnel and various types of complex equipment) are carried out under the "surgical team" concept. Such circumstances may be identified by each participating physician with the addition of the modifier -66 to the basic procedure code number used for reporting services. Modifier code 09966 may be used as as alternative to modifier -66.	Variable
-73	*Discontinued Outpatient Hospital/Ambulatory Surgery Center (ASC) Procedure Prior to the Administration of Anesthesia:* Due to extenuating circumstances or those that threaten the well being of the patient, the physician may cancel a surgical or diagnostic procedure subsequent to the patient's surgical preparation (including sedation when provided, and being taken to the room where the procedure is to be performed), but prior to the administration of anesthesia (local, regional block[s] or general). Under these circumstances, the intended service that is prepared for but cancelled can be reported by its usual procedure number and the addition of the modifier -73 or by use of the separate five-digit modifier code 09973. Note: The elective cancellation of a service prior to the administration of anesthesia and/or surgical preparation of the patient should not be reported. For physician reporting of a discontinued procedure, see modifier -53.	Decrease fee
-74	*Discontinued Outpatient Hospital/Ambulatory Surgery Center (ASC) Procedure After Administration of Anesthesia:* Due to extenuating circumstances or those that threaten the well being of the patient, the physician may terminate a surgical or diagnostic procedure after the administration of anesthesia (local, regional block[s] or general) or after the procedure was started (incision made, intubation started, scope inserted, etc.) Under these circumstances, the procedure started but terminated can be reported by its usual procedure number and the addition of the modifier -74 or by use of the separate five-digit modifier code 09974.	Decrease fee

Table continued on following page

Table 2. College Clinic Mock Fee Schedule *Continued*

Modifier Code No.	Description	Mock Fee ($)
	Note: The elective cancellation of a service prior to the administration of anesthesia and/or surgical preparation of the patient should not be reported. For physician reporting of a discontinued procedure, see modifier -53.	
-76	*Repeat Procedure by Same Physician:* The physician may need to indicate that a procedure or service was repeated subsequent to the original procedure or service. This circumstance may be reported by adding modifier -76 to the repeated service/procedure or separate five-digit modifier code 09976 may be used.	Decrease fee
-77	*Repeat Procedure by Another Physician:* The physician may need to indicate that a basic procedure or service performed by another physician had to be repeated. This situation may be reported by adding modifier -77 to the repeated procedure/service, or the separate five-digit modifier code 09977 may be used.	Decrease fee
-78	*Return to the Operating Room for a Related Procedure During the Postoperative Period:* The physician may need to indicate that another procedure was performed during the postoperative period of the initial procedure. When this subsequent procedure is related to the first and requires the use of the operating room, it may be reported by adding the modifier -78 to the related procedure, or by using the separate five-digit modifier 09978. (For repeat procedures on the same day, see -76.)	Decrease fee
-79	*Unrelated Procedure or Service by the Same Physician During the Postoperative Period:* The physician may need to indicate that the performance of a procedure or service during the postoperative period was unrelated to the original procedure. This circumstance may be reported by using the modifier -79 or by using the separate five-digit modifier 09979. (For repeat procedures on the same day, see -76.)	Use standard fee
-80	*Assistant Surgeon:* Surgical assistant services may be identified by adding the modifier -80 to the usual procedure number(s) or by using the separate five-digit modifier code 09980.	Billed and/or paid at approximately 20% of surgeon's fee
-81	*Minimum Assistant Surgeon:* Minimum surgical assistant services are identified by adding the modifier -81 to the usual procedure number or by using the separate five-digit modifier code 09981.	Billed and/or paid at approximately 10% of surgeon's fee
-82	*Assistant Surgeon when qualified resident surgeon not available:* The unavailability of a qualified resident surgeon is a prerequisite for use of modifier -82 appended to the usual procedure code number(s) or by use of the separate five-digit modifier code 09982.	Decrease fee
-90	*Reference (Outside) Laboratory:* When laboratory procedures are performed by a party other than the treating or reporting physician and billed by the treating physician, the procedure may be identified by adding the modifier -90 to the usual procedure number or by using the separate five-digit modifier code 09990.	Fee according to contract
-91	*Repeat Clinical Diagnostic Laboratory Test:* In the course of treatment of the patient, it may be necessary to repeat the same laboratory test on the same day to obtain subsequent (multiple) test results. Under these circumstances, the laboratory test performed can be identified by its usual procedure number and the addition of modifier -91. Note: This modifier may not be used when tests are rerun to confirm initial results; due to testing problems with specimens or equipment; or for any other reason when a normal, one-time, reportable result is all that is required. This modifier may not be used when other code(s) describe a series of test results (e.g.,	Decrease fee

Table 2. College Clinic Mock Fee Schedule *Continued*

Modifier Code No.	Description	Mock Fee ($)
	glucose tolerance tests, evocative/suppression testing). This modifier may only be used for laboratory test(s) performed more than once on the same day on the same patient.	
-99	*Multiple Modifiers:* Under certain circumstances two or more modifiers may be necessary to completely delineate a service. In such situations modifier -99 should be added to the basic procedure, and other applicable modifiers may be listed as part of the description of the service. Modifier code 09999 may be used as an alternative to modifier -99.	Variable

Table 3. Mock Fee Schedule

Code No. and Description		Mock Fees	Medicare Participating	Medicare Non-participating	Medicare Limiting Charge
EVALUATION AND MANAGEMENT*					
OFFICE New Patient					
99201	Level I	33.25	30.43	28.91	33.25
99202	Level II	51.91	47.52	45.14	51.91
99203	Level III	70.92	64.92	61.67	70.92
99204	Level IV	106.11	97.13	92.27	106.11
99205	Level V	132.28	121.08	115.03	132.38
Established Patient					
99211	Level I	16.07	14.70	13.97	16.07
99212	Level II	28.55	26.14	24.83	28.55
99213	Level III	40.20	36.80	34.96	40.20
99214	Level IV	61.51	56.31	53.49	61.51
99215	Level V	96.97	88.76	84.32	96.97
HOSPITAL Observation Services (new or est pt)					
99217	Discharge	66.88	61.22	58.16	66.88
99218	Dhx/exam SF/LC DM	74.22	67.94	64.54	74.22
99219	Chx/exam MC DM	117.75	107.78	102.39	117.75
99220	Chx/exam HC DM	147.48	134.99	128.24	147.48
Inpatient Services (new or est pt)					
99221	30 min	73.00	66.82	63.48	73.00
99222	50 min	120.80	110.57	105.04	120.80
99223	70 min	152.98	140.03	133.03	152.98
Subsequent Hospital Care					
99231	15 min	37.74	34.55	32.82	37.74
99232	25 min	55.56	50.85	48.31	55.56
99233	35 min	76.97	70.45	66.93	76.97
99238	Discharge	65.26	59.74	56.75	65.26
CONSULTATIONS Office (new/est Pt)					
99241	Level I	51.93	47.54	45.16	51.93
99242	Level II	80.24	73.44	69.77	80.24
99243	Level III	103.51	94.75	90.01	103.51
99244	Level IV	145.05	132.77	126.13	145.05
99245	Level V	195.48	178.93	169.98	195.48

*See Tables 5-1 and 5-2 in the *Handbook* for more descriptions of E/M codes 99201 through 99275.

Table continued on following page

Table 3. Mock Fee Schedule *Continued*

Code No. and Description		Mock Fees	Medicare* Participating	Non-participating	Limiting Charge
Inpatient (new/est Pt)					
99251	Level I	53.29	48.78	46.34	53.29
99252	Level II	80.56	73.74	70.05	80.56
99253	Level III	106.10	97.12	92.26	106.10
99254	Level IV	145.26	132.96	126.31	145.26
99255	Level V	196.55	179.91	170.91	196.55
Follow-up Inpatient (new/est pt)					
99261	Focused	29.66	27.15	25.79	29.66
99262	Expanded	50.57	46.28	43.97	50.57
99263	Detailed	76.36	69.90	66.40	76.36
Confirmatory 2nd-3rd opinion (new/est pt)					
99271	Focused	45.47	41.62	39.54	45.47
99272	Expanded	67.02	61.35	58.28	67.02
99273	Detailed	95.14	87.08	82.73	95.14
99274	Comprehensive	125.15	114.56	108.83	125.15
99275	Comprehensive	172.73	158.10	150.20	172.73
EMERGENCY DEPARTMENT (new/est pt)					
99281	PF hx/exam SF DM	24.32	22.26	21.15	24.32
99282	EPF hx/exam LC DM	37.02	33.88	32.19	37.02
99283	EPF hx/exam MC DM	66.23	60.62	57.59	66.23
99284	D hx/exam MC DM	100.71	92.18	87.57	100.71
99285	C hx/exam HC DM	158.86	145.41	138.14	158.86
CRITICAL CARE SERVICES					
99291	First hour	208.91	191.22	181.66	208.91
99292	Each addl. 30 min	102.02	92.46	87.84	102.02
NEONATAL INTENSIVE CARE					
99295	Initial	892.74	817.16	776.30	892.74
99296	Subsequent unstable case	418.73	383.27	364.11	418.73
99297	Subsequent stable case	214.68	196.50	186.68	214.68
NURSING FACILITY					
99301	30 min	64.11	58.68	55.75	64.11
99302	40 min	90.55	82.88	78.74	90.55
99303	50 min	136.76	125.18	118.92	136.76
Subsequent (new/est pt)					
99311	15 min	37.95	34.74	33.00	37.95
99312	25 min	55.11	50.44	47.92	55.11
99313	35 min	69.61	63.72	60.53	69.61
DOMICILIARY, REST HOME, CUSTODIAL CARE New patient					
99321	PF hx/exam LC DM	46.10	42.20	40.09	46.10
99322	EPF hx/exam MC DM	65.02	59.52	56.54	65.02
99323	D hx/exam HC DM	86.18	78.88	74.94	86.18
Established patient					
99331	PF hx/exam LC DM	37.31	34.15	32.44	37.31
99332	EPF hx/exam MC DM	49.22	45.05	42.80	49.22
99333	D hx/exam HC DM	60.61	55.47	52.70	60.61
HOME SERVICES New patient					
99341	PF hx/exam SF DM	70.32	64.37	61.15	70.32
99342	EPF hx/exam LC DM	91.85	84.07	79.87	91.85
99343	D hx/exam MC DM	120.24	110.06	104.56	120.24

*Some services and procedures may not be considered a benefit under the Medicare program and when listed on a claim form, no reimbursement may be received. However, it is important to include these codes when billing because Medicare policies may change without an individual knowing of a new benefit. For this reason, some of the services shown in this mock fee schedule do not have any amounts listed under the three Medicare columns.

Table 3. Mock Fee Schedule *Continued*

Code No. and Description		Mock Fees	Medicare* Participating	Medicare* Non-participating	Medicare* Limiting Charge
Established patient					
99347	PF hx/exam SF DM	54.83	50.19	47.68	54.83
99348	EPF hx/exam LC DM	70.06	64.13	60.92	70.06
99349	D hx/exam MC DM	88.33	80.85	76.81	88.33
PROLONGED SERVICES WITH CONTACT Outpatient					
99354	First hour	96.97	88.76	84.32	96.97
99355	Each addl. 30 min	96.97	88.76	84.32	96.97
Inpatient					
99356	First hour	96.42	88.25	83.84	96.42
99357	Each addl. 30 min	96.42	88.25	83.84	96.42
PROLONGED SERVICES WITHOUT DIRECT CONTACT					
99358	First hour	90.00			
99359	Each addl. 30 min	90.00			
PHYSICIAN STANDBY SERVICE					
99360	Each 30 min	95.00			
CASE MANAGEMENT SERVICES Team Conferences					
99361	30 mm	85.00			
99362	60 min	105.00			
Telephone Calls					
99371	Simple or brief	30.00			
99372	Intermediate	40.00			
99373	Complex	60.00			
CARE PLAN OVERSIGHT SERVICES					
99375	30 min or more	93.40	85.49	81.22	93.40
PREVENTIVE MEDICINE New patient					
99381	Infant under 1 age year	50.00			
99382	1-4 years	50.00			
99383	5-11 years	45.00			
99384	12-17 years	45.00			
99385	18-39 years	50.00			
99386	40-64 years	50.00			
99387	65 yrs and over	55.00			
Established patient					
99391	Infant under age 1 year	35.00			
99392	1-4 years	35.00			
99393	5-11 years	30.00			
99394	12-17 years	30.00			
99395	18-39 years	35.00			
99396	40-64 years	35.00			
99397	65 yrs and over	40.00			
COUNSELING (new/est pt)					
Individual					
99401	15 min	35.00			
99402	30 min	50.00			
99403	45 min	65.00			
99404	60 min	80.00			
Group					
99411	30 min	30.00			
99412	60 min	50.00			

*Some services and procedures may not be considered a benefit under the Medicare program and when listed on a claim form, no reimbursement may be received. However, it is important to include these codes when billing because Medicare policies may change without an individual knowing of a new benefit. For this reason, some of the services shown in this mock fee schedule do not have any amounts listed under the three Medicare columns.

Table continued on following page

Table 3. Mock Fee Schedule *Continued*

Code No. and Description		Mock Fees	Medicare* Participating	Medicare* Non-participating	Medicare* Limiting Charge
Other preventive medicine services					
99420	Health hazard appraisal	50.00			
99429	Unlisted preventive med serv	variable			
NEWBORN CARE					
99431	Birthing room delivery	102.50	93.50	88.83	102.15
99432	Other than birthing room	110.16	100.83	95.79	110.16
99433	Subsequent hospital care	54.02	49.44	46.97	54.02
99440	Newborn resuscitation	255.98	234.30	222.59	255.98
99499	Unlisted E/M service	variable			
ANESTHESIOLOGY					
Anesthesiology fees are presented here for CPT codes. However, each case would require a fee for time, e.g., every 15 minutes would be worth $55. This fee is determined according to the relative value system, calculated, and added into the anesthesia (CPT) fee. Some anesthetists may list a surgical code using an anesthesia modifier on a subsequent line for carriers that do not acknowledge anesthesia codes.					
99100	Anes for pt under 1 yr/over 70	55.00			
99116	Anes complicated use total hypothermia	275.00			
99135	Anes complicated use hypotension	275.00			
99140	Anes complicated emer cond	110.00			
Physician Status Modifier Codes					
P-1	Normal healthy patient	00.00			
P-2	Patient with mild systemic disease	00.00			
P-3	Patient with severe systemic disease	55.00			
P-4	Patient with severe systemic disease (constant threat to life)	110.00			
P-5	Moribund pt not expected to survive for 24 hr with or without operation	165.00			
P-6	Declared brain-dead pt, organs being removed for donor	00.00			
Head					
00160	Anes for proc nose & accessory sinuses: NOS	275.00			
00172	Anes repair cleft palate	165.00			
Thorax					
00400	Anes for proc ant integumentary system of chest, incl SC tissue	165.00			
00402	Anes breast reconstruction	275.00			
00546	Anes pulmonary resection with thoracoplasty	275.00			
00600	Anes cervical spine and cord	550.00			
Lower Abdomen					
00800	Anes for proc lower ant abdominal wall	165.00			
00840	Anes intraperitoneal proc lower abdomen: NOS	330.00			
00842	Amniocentesis	220.00			
00914	Anes TURP	275.00			

*Some services and procedures may not be considered a benefit under the Medicare program and when listed on a claim form, no reimbursement may be received. However, it is important to include these codes when billing because Medicare policies may change without an individual knowing of a new benefit. For this reason, some of the services shown in this mock fee schedule do not have any amounts listed under the three Medicare columns.

Table 3. Mock Fee Schedule *Continued*

Code No. and Description		Mock Fees	Medicare*		
			Participating	Non-participating	Limiting Charge
00942	Anes colporrhaphy, colpotomy, colpectomy	220.00			
Upper Leg					
01210	Anes open proc hip joint; NOS	330.00			
01214	Total hip replacement	440.00			
Upper Arm and Elbow					
01740	Anes open proc humerus/elbow; NOS	220.00			
01758	Exc cyst/tumor humerus	275.00			
Radiologic Procedures					
01922	Anes CAT scan	385.00			
Miscellaneous Procedure(s)					
01999	Unlisted anes proc	variable			
Neurology					
95812	Electroencephalogram	129.32	118.37	112.45	129.32
95819	Electroencephalogram—awake and asleep	126.81	116.07	110.27	126.81
95860	Electromyography, 1 extremity	88.83	81.31	77.24	88.83
95864	Electromyography, 4 extremities	239.99	219.67	208.69	239.99
96100	Psychological testing (per hour)	80.95	74.10	70.39	80.95
Physical Medicine					
97024	Diathermy	14.27	13.06	12.41	14.27
97036	Hubbard tank, each 15 min	24.77	22.67	21.54	24.77
97110	Physical therapy, initial 30 min	23.89	21.86	20.77	23.89
97260	Manipulation (cervical, thoracic, lumbosacral, sacroiliac, hand, wrist), one area	16.93	15.49	14.72	16.93
Special Services and Reports					
99000	Handling of specimen (transfer from Dr.'s office to lab)	5.00			
99025	Initial surg eval (new pt) with starred procedure	50.00			
99050	Services requested after office hours in addition to basic service	25.00			
99052	Services between 10 p.m. and 8 a.m. in addition to basic service	35.00			
99054	Services on Sundays and holidays in addition to basic service	35.00			
99056	Services normally provided in office requested by pt in location other than office	20.00			
99058	Office services provided on an emergency basis	65.00			
99070	Supplies and materials (itemize drugs and materials provided)	25.00			
99080	Special reports:				
	Insurance forms	10.00			
	Review of data to clarify pt's status	20.00			
	WC reports	50.00			
	WC extensive review report	250.00			

*Some services and procedures may not be considered a benefit under the Medicare program and when listed on a claim form, no reimbursement may be received. However, it is important to include these codes when billing because Medicare policies may change without an individual knowing of a new benefit. For this reason, some of the services shown in this mock fee schedule do not have any amounts listed under the three Medicare columns.

Code No.	Description	Mock Fees	Medicare Participating	Medicare Non-participating	Medicare Limiting Charge	Medicare Follow-up Days[1]
10060*	I & D furuncle, onychia, paronychia; single	75.92	69.49	66.02	75.92	10
11040*	Debridement; skin, partial thickness	79.32	75.60	68.97	79.32	10
11044	Debridement; skin, subcu. muscle, bone	269.28	246.48	234.16	269.28	
11100	Biopsy of skin, SC tissue &/or mucous membrane; 1 lesion	65.43	59.89	56.90	65.43	10
11200*	Exc, skin tags; up to 15	55.68	50.97	48.42	55.68	10
11401	Exc, benign lesion, 0.6–1.0 cm trunk, arms, legs	95.62	87.53	83.15	96.62	10
11402	1.1–2.0 cm	121.52	111.23	105.67	121.52	10
11403	2.1–3.0 cm	151.82	138.97	132.02	151.82	10
11420	Exc, benign lesion, 0.5 cm or less scalp, neck, hands, feet, genitalia	75.44	69.05	65.60	75.44	10
11422	Exc, benign lesion scalp, neck, hands, feet, or genitalia; 1.1–2.0 cm	131.35	120.23	114.22	131.35	10
11441	Exc, benign lesion face, ears, eyelids, nose, lips, or mucous membrane; 0.6–1.0 cm dia or less	119.08	109.00	103.55	119.08	10
11602	Exc, malignant lesion, trunk, arms, or legs; 1.1–2.0 cm dia	195.06	178.55	169.62	195.06	10
11719	Trimming of nondystrophic nails, any number	30.58	27.82	26.33	30.58	0
11720*	Debridement of nails, any method, 1–5	32.58	29.82	28.33	32.58	0
11721*	6 or more	32.58	29.82	28.33	32.58	0
11730*	Avulsion nail plate, partial or complete, simple repair; single	76.91	70.40	66.88	76.91	0
11750	Exc, nail or nail matrix, partial or complete	193.45	177.07	168.22	193.45	10
11765	Wedge excision of nail fold	57.95	53.04	50.39	57.95	10
12001*	Simple repair (scalp, neck, axillae, ext genitalia, trunk, or extremities incl hands & feet); 2.5 cm or less	91.17	83.45	79.28	91.17	10
12011*	Simple repair (face, ears, eyelids, nose, lips, or mucous membranes); 2.5 cm or less	101.44	92.85	88.21	101.44	10
12013*	2.6–5.0 cm	123.98	113.48	107.81	123.98	10
12032*	Repair, scalp, axillae, trunk (intermediate)	169.73	155.36	147.59	169.73	10
12034	Repair, intermediate, layer closure of wounds (scalp, axillae, trunk, or extremities) excl hands or feet; 7.6–12.5 cm	214.20	196.06	186.26	214.20	10
12051*	Repair, intermediate, layer closure of wounds (face, ears, eyelids, nose, lips, or mucous membranes); 2.5 cm	167.60	153.41	145.74	167.60	10
17000*	Cauterization, 1 lesion	52.56	48.11	45.70	52.56	10

17003	Second through fourteen lesions, each	15.21	17.77	16.88	15.21	10
17100*	Destruction, any method, skin lesion (benign) any area except face—one	44.86	41.06	39.01	44.86	10
19020	Mastotomy, drainage/exploration deep abscess	237.36	217.26	206.40	237.36	90
19100*	Biopsy, breast, needle	96.17	88.03	83.63	96.17	0
19101	Biopsy, breast, incisional	281.51	257.67	244.79	281.51	10
20610*	Arthrocentesis, aspiration or injection joint (should, hip, knee) or bursa	52.33	47.89	45.50	52.33	0
21330	Nasal fracture, open treatment complicated	599.46	548.71	521.27	599.46	90
24066	Biopsy, deep, soft tissue, upper arm, elbow	383.34	350.88	333.34	383.34	90
27455	Osteotomy, proximal tibia	1248.03	1142.36	1085.24	1248.03	90
27500	Treatment closed femoral shaft fracture without manipulation	554.90	507.92	482.52	554.90	90
27530	Treatment closed tibial fracture, proximal, without manipulation	344.24	315.09	299.34	344.24	90
27750	Treatment closed tibial shaft fracture without manipulation	400.94	366.99	348.64	400.94	90
27752	With manipulation	531.63	486.62	462.29	531.63	90
29280	Strapping of hand	35.13	31.36	29.79	35.13	0
29345	Appl long leg cast (thigh to toes)	123.23	112.80	107.16	123.23	0
29355	Walker or ambulatory type	133.75	122.42	116.30	133.75	0
29425	Appl short leg walking cast	102.10	93.45	88.78	102.10	0
30110	Excision, simple nasal polyp	145.21	132.92	126.27	145.21	10
30520	Septoplasty	660.88	604.93	574.68	660.88	90
30903*	Control nasal hemorrhage; unilateral	118.17	108.17	102.76	118.17	0
30905*	Control nasal hemorrhage, posterior with posterior nasal packs; initial	190.57	174.43	165.71	190.57	0
30906*	Subsequent	173.01	158.36	150.44	173.01	
31540	Laryngoscopy with excision of tumor and/or stripping of vocal cords	488.95	447.55	425.17	488.95	0
31541	With operating microscope	428.33	392.06	372.46	428.33	0

[1] Data for the surgical follow-up days from St. Anthony's *CPT '96 Companion: A Guide to Medicare Billing.*
* Codes marked with an asterisk appear in *CPT* marked as shown. See *Handbook* Chapter 5 for detailed information.

Table continued on following page

Code No.	Description	Mock Fees	Medicare Participating	Medicare Non-participating	Medicare Limiting Charge	Medicare Follow-up Days[1]
31575	Laryngoscopy, flexible fiberoptic; diagnostic	138.48	126.76	120.42	138.48	0
31625	Bronchoscopy with biopsy	312.87	286.38	272.06	312.87	0
32310	Pleurectomy	1234.79	1130.24	1073.73	1234.79	90
32440	Pneumonectomy, total	1972.10	1805.13	1714.87	1972.10	90
33020	Pericardiotomy	1289.25	1180.09	1121.09	1289.25	90
33206	Insertion of pacemaker; atrial	728.42	666.75	633.41	728.42	90
33208	AV sequential	751.57	687.89	653.50	751.57	90
35301	Thromboendarterectomy, with or without patch graft; carotid, vertebral, subclavian, by neck incision	1585.02	1450.82	1378.28	1585.02	90
36005	Intravenous injection for contrast venography	59.18	54.17	51.46	59.18	0
36248	Catheter placement (selective) arterial system, 2nd, 3rd and beyond	68.54	62.74	59.60	68.54	0
36415*	Routine venipuncture for collection of specimen(s)	10.00	—	—	—	XXX
38101	Splenectomy, partial	994.44	910.24	864.73	994.44	90
38510	Biopsy/excision deep cervical node/s	327.42	299.69	284.71	327.42	90
39520	Excision tumor, mediastinal	1436.50	1314.87	1249.13	1436.50	90
42820	T & A under age 12 years	341.63	312.71	297.07	341.63	90
42821	T & A over age 12 years	410.73	375.96	357.16	410.73	90
43234	Upper GI endoscopy, simple primary exam	201.86	184.77	175.53	201.86	0
43235	Upper GI endoscopy incl esophagus, stomach, duodenum, or jejunum; complex	238.92	218.69	207.76	238.92	0
43456	Dilation esophagus	254.52	232.97	221.32	254.52	0
43820	Gastrojejunostomy	971.86	889.58	845.10	971.86	90
44150	Colectomy, total, abdominal	1757.81	1608.98	1528.53	1757.81	90
44320	Colostomy or skin level cecostomy	966.25	884.44	840.22	966.25	90
44950	Appendectomy	568.36	520.24	494.23	568.36	90
45308	Proctosigmoidoscopy for removal of polyp	135.34	123.88	117.69	135.34	0
45315	Multiple polyps	185.12	169.44	160.97	185.12	0
45330	Sigmoidoscopy, diagnostic (for biopsy or collection of specimen by brushing or washing)	95.92	87.80	83.41	95.92	0
45380	Colonoscopy with biopsy	382.35	349.98	332.48	382.35	0
46255	Hemorrhoidectomy int & ext, simple	503.57	460.94	437.89	503.57	90
46258	Hemorrhoidectomy with fistulectomy	636.02	582.17	553.06	636.02	90
46600	Anoscopy; diagnostic	32.86	30.07	28.57	32.86	0
46614	With coagulation for control of hemorrhage	182.10	166.68	158.35	182.10	0

46700	Anoplastic, for stricture, adult	657.39	601.73	571.64	657.39	90
47600	Cholecystectomy	937.74	858.35	815.43	937.74	90
49505	Inguinal hernia repair, age 5 or over	551.07	504.41	479.19	551.07	90
49520	Repair, inguinal hernia, any age; recurrent	671.89	615.00	584.25	671.89	90
50080	Nephrostolithotomy, percutaneous	1323.93	1211.83	1151.24	1323.93	90
50780	Ureteroneocystostomy	1561.23	1429.84	1357.59	1561.23	90
51900	Closure of vesicovaginal fistula, abdominal approach	1196.82	1095.48	1040.71	1196.82	90
52000	Cystourethroscopy	167.05	152.90	145.26	167.05	0
52601	Transurethral resection of prostate	1193.53	1092.47	1037.85	1193.53	90
53040	Drainage of deep periurethral abscess	379.48	347.35	329.98	379.48	90
53230	Excision, female diverticulum (urethral)	859.69	786.91	747.56	859.69	90
53240	Marsupialization of urethral diverticulum, M or F	520.11	476.07	452.27	520.11	90
53620*	Dilation, urethra, male	100.73	92.20	87.59	100.73	0
53660*	Dilation urethra, female	48.32	44.23	42.02	48.32	0
54150	Circumcision–newborn	111.78	102.32	97.20	111.78	10
54520	Orchiectomy, simple	523.92	479.56	455.58	523.92	90
55700	Biopsy of prostate, needle or punch	156.22	142.99	135.84	156.22	0
55801	Prostatectomy, perineal subtotal	1466.56	1342.39	1275.27	1466.56	90
57265	Colporrhaphy AP with enterocele repair	902.24	825.85	784.56	902.24	90
57452*	Colposcopy	84.18	77.05	73.20	84.18	0
57510	Cauterization of cervix, electro or thermal	115.15	105.40	100.13	115.15	10
57520	Circumferential (cone) of cervix with or without D & C, with or without Sturmdorff-type repair	387.08	354.30	336.59	387.08	90
58100*	Endometrial biopsy	71.88	65.79	62.50	71.88	0
58120	D & C, diagnostic and/or therapeutic (nonOB)	272.83	249.73	237.24	272.83	10
58150	TAH w/without salpingo-oophorectomy	1167.72	1068.85	1015.41	1167.72	90
58200	Total hysterectomy, extended, corpus cancer, including partial vaginectomy	1707.24	1562.69	1484.56	1707.24	90
58210	With bilateral radical pelvic lymphadenectomy	2160.78	1977.83	1878.94	2160.78	90
58300*	Insertion of intrauterine device	100.00				0
58340*	Hysterosalpingography, inj proc for	73.06	66.87	63.53	73.06	0
58720	Salpingo-oophorectomy, complete or partial, unilateral or bilateral	732.40	670.39	636.87	732.40	90
	Surgical treatment of ectopic pregnancy					
59120	Salpingectomy and/or oophorectomy	789.26	722.43	686.31	789.26	90

[1] Data for the surgical follow-up days from St. Anthony's *CPT '96 Companion: A Guide to Medicare Billing.*

* Codes marked with an asterisk appear in *CPT* marked as shown. See *Handbook* Chapter 5 for detailed information.

Table continued on following page

Code No.	and Description	Mock Fees	Medicare Participating	Medicare Non-participating	Medicare Limiting Charge	Medicare Follow-up Days[1]
59121	Without salpingectomy and/or oophorectomy	638.84	584.75	555.51	638.84	90
59130	Abdominal pregnancy	699.12	639.93	607.93	699.12	90
59135	Total hysterectomy, interstitial, uterine pregnancy	1154.16	1056.44	1003.62	1154.16	90
59136	Partial uterine resection, interstitial uterine pregnancy	772.69	707.26	671.90	772.69	90
59140	Cervical, with evacuation	489.68	448.22	425.81	489.68	90
59160	D & C postpartum hemorrhage (separate proc)	293.46	268.61	255.18	293.46	10
59400	OB Care—routine, inc. antepartum/ postpartum care	1864.30	1706.45	1621.13	1864.30	N/A
59515	C-section, low cervical, incl in-hosp postpartum care (separate proc)	1469.80	1345.36	1278.09	1469.80	N/A
59510	Including antepartum and postpartum care	2102.33	1924.33	1828.11	2102.33	N/A
59812	Treatment of incompl abortion, any trimester; completed surgically	357.39	327.13	310.77	357.39	90
61314	Craniotomy infratentorial	2548.09	2332.35	2215.73	2548.09	90
62270*	Spinal puncture, lumbar; diagnostic	77.52	70.96	67.41	77.52	0
65091	Excision of eye, without implant	708.22	648.25	615.84	708.22	90
65205*	Removal of foreign body, ext eye	56.02	51.27	48.71	56.02	0
65222*	Corneal, with slit lamp	73.81	67.56	64.18	73.81	0
69420*	Myringotomy	97.76	89.48	85.01	97.76	10

[1] Data for the surgical follow-up days from St. Anthony's *CPT '96 Companion: A Guide to Medicare Billing.*
*Codes marked with an asterisk appear in *CPT* marked as shown. See *Handbook* Chapter 5 for detailed information.

Table continued on following page

Code No. and Description		Mock Fees	Medicare		
			Participating	Non-participating	Limiting Charge
RADIOLOGY, NUCLEAR MEDICINE, AND DIAGNOSTIC ULTRASOUND					
70120	X-ray mastoids, 2 views per side	38.96	35.66	33.88	38.96
70130	X-ray mastoids, 3 views per side	56.07	51.33	48.76	56.07
71010	X-ray chest, 1 view	31.95	29.24	27.78	31.95
71020	Chest x-ray, 2 views	40.97	37.50	35.63	40.97
71030	Chest x-ray, compl, 4 views	54.02	49.44	46.97	54.02
71060	Bronchogram, bilateral	143.75	131.58	125.00	143.75
72100	X-ray spine, LS; AP & lat views	43.23	39.57	37.59	43.23
72114	Complete, incl bending views	74.97	68.62	65.19	74.97
73100	X-ray wrist, 2 views	31.61	28.94	27.49	31.61
73500	X-ray hip, 1 view	31.56	28.88	27.44	31.56
73540	X-ray pelvis & hips, infant or child, 2 views	37.94	34.73	32.99	37.94
73590	X-ray tibia & fibula, 2 views	33.35	30.53	29.00	33.35
73620	Radiologic exam, foot; AP & lat views	31.61	28.94	27.49	31.61
73650	X-ray calcaneus, 2 views	30.71	28.11	26.70	30.71
74241	Radiologic exam, upper gastrointestinal tract, with/without delayed films with KUB	108.93	99.71	94.72	108.93
74245	Upper GI tract with small bowel	161.70	148.01	140.61	161.70
74270	Barium enema	118.47	108.44	103.02	118.47
74290	Oral cholecystography	52.59	48.14	45.73	52.59
74400	Urography (pyelography), intravenous, with or without KUB	104.78	95.90	91.11	104.78
74405	Urography (pyelography), intravenous with spec hypertensive contrast concentration	118.36	108.34	102.92	118.36
74410	Urography, infusion	116.76	106.87	101.53	116.76
74420	Urography, retrograde	138.89	127.13	120.77	138.89
75982	Percutaneous placement of drainage catheter	359.08	328.67	312.24	359.08
76090	Mammography, unilateral	62.57	57.27	54.41	62.57
76091	Mammography, bilateral	82.83	75.82	72.03	82.83
76805	Echography, pregnant uterus, B-scan or real time; complete	154.18	141.13	134.07	154.18
76810	Echography, pregnant uterus, complete: multiple gestation, after first trimester	306.54	280.59	266.56	306.54
76946	Ultrasonic guidance for amniocentesis	91.22	83.49	79.32	91.22
77300	Radiation dosimetry	97.58	89.32	84.85	97.58
77315	Teletherapy, isodose plan, complex	213.59	195.51	185.73	213.59
78104	Bone marrow imaging, whole body	230.56	211.04	200.49	230.56
78215	Liver and spleen imaging	160.44	146.85	139.51	160.44
78800	Tumor localization, limited area	191.53	175.32	166.55	191.53

PATHOLOGY AND LABORATORY[1]

Laboratory tests done as groups or combination "profiles" performed on multichannel equipment should be billed using the appropriate code number (80002 through 80019). Following is a list of the tests. The subsequent listing illustrates how to find the correct code.

Alanine aminotransferase (ALT, SGPT)
Albumin
Aspartate aminotransferase (AST, SGOT)
Bilirubin, direct
Bilirubin, total
Calcium
Carbon dioxide content
Chloride
Cholesterol
Creatinine
Glucose (sugar)
Lactate dehydrogenase (LD)
Phosphatase, alkaline
Phosphorus (inorganic phosphate)
Potassium
Protein, total
Sodium
Urea nitrogen (BUN)
Uric acid

[1] Mock fees for laboratory tests presented in this schedule may not be representative of fees in your region due to the variety of capitation and managed care contracts, as well as discount policies made by laboratories. At the time of this edition, Medicare guidelines may or may not pay for automatic multichannel tests where a large number of tests are performed per panel. Some cases require documentation and a related diagnostic code for each test performed. Provider must have the CLIA level of licensure to bill for tests, and test results must be documented.

Code No. and Description		Mock Fees	Medicare Participating	Medicare Non-participating	Medicare Limiting Charge
ORGAN OR DISEASE-ORIENTED PANELS					
80049	Basic metabolic panel	15.00	14.60	13.87	16.64
80050	General health panel	20.00	19.20	15.99	21.87
80051	Electrolyte panel	20.00	19.20	15.99	21.87
80054	Comprehensive metabolic panel	25.00	20.99	19.94	23.93
80055	Obstetric panel	25.00	20.99	19.94	23.93
80058	Hepatic function panel	27.00	25.00	20.88	24.98
80059	Hepatitis panel	27.00	25.00	20.88	24.98
80061	Lipid panel	30.00	28.60	25.97	32.16
80072	Arthritis panel	30.00	28.60	25.97	32.16
80090	TORCH antibody panel	32.00	30.70	27.54	34.15
80091	Thyroid panel	32.00	30.70	27.54	34.15
81000	Urinalysis, non-automated, with microscopy	8.00	7.44	5.98	8.84
81001	Urinalysis, automated, with microscopy	8.00	7.44	5.98	8.84
81002	Urinalysis, non-automated without microscopy	8.00	7.44	5.98	8.84
81015	Urinalysis, microscopy only	8.00	7.44	5.98	8.84
82270	Blood, occult; feces screening 1–3	4.05	3.56	3.31	4.05
82565	Creatinine; blood	10.00	9.80	8.88	12.03
82947	Glucose; quantitative	15.00			
82951	Glucose tol test, 3 spec	40.00	41.00	36.80	45.16
82952	Each add spec beyond 3	30.00	28.60	25.97	32.16
83020	Hemoglobin, electrophoresis	25.00	20.00	19.94	23.93
83715	Lipoprotein, blood; electrophoretic separation	25.00	20.00	19.94	23.93
84478	Triglycerides, blood	20.00	19.20	15.99	21.87
84479	Triiodothyronine (T–3)	20.00	19.20	15.99	21.87
84520	Urea nitrogen, blood (BUN); quantitative	25.00	20.99	19.94	23.93
84550	Uric acid, blood chemical	20.00	19.20	15.99	21.87
84702	Gonadotropin, chorionic; quantitative	20.00	19.20	15.99	21.87
84703	Qualitative	20.00	19.20	15.99	21.87
85022	Complete blood count, manual, diff with WBC count	20.00	19.20	15.99	21.87
85025	Complete blood count (hemogram), platelet count, automated, differential WBC count	25.00	20.00	19.94	23.93
85031	Complete blood count, manual	25.00	20.00	19.94	23.93
85095	Bone marrow, aspiration only	73.52	67.29	63.93	73.52
85102	Bone marrow aspiration (biopsy)	90.65	82.98	78.83	90.65
85345	Coagulation time; Lee & White	20.00	19.20	15.99	21.87
85590	Platelet count (Rees-Ecker)	20.00	19.20	15.99	21.87
86038	Antinuclear antibodies	25.00	20.00	19.94	23.93
86580	Skin test; TB, intradermal	11.34	10.38	9.86	11.34
87081	Culture, bacterial, screening for single organisms	25.00	20.00	19.94	23.93
87181	Sensitivity studies, antibiotic; per antibiotic	20.00	19.20	15.99	21.87
87184	Disk method, per plate (12 disks or less)	20.00	19.20	15.99	21.87
87210	Smear, primary source, wet mount with simple stain, for bacteria, fungi, ova, and/or parasites	35.00	48.35	45.93	55.12
88150	Papanicolaou, cytopath	35.00	48.35	45.93	55.12
88302	Surgical pathology, gross & micro exam (skin, fingers, nerve, testis)	24.14	22.09	20.99	24.14
88305	Bone marrow, interpret	77.69	71.12	67.56	77.69

Code No. and Description		Mock Fees	Medicare* Participating	Medicare* Non-participating	Medicare* Limiting Charge
MEDICINE PROCEDURES					
Immunization Injections					
90701	Diphtheria, tetanus, pertussis	34.00			
90703	Tetanus toxoid	28.00			
90712	Poliovirus vaccine, oral	28.00			
Therapeutic Injections					
90782	IM or SC medication	4.77	4.37	4.15	4.77
90784	IV	21.33	19.53	18.55	21.33
90788	IM antibiotic	5.22	4.78	4.54	5.22
Psychiatry					
90816	Individual psychotherapy 20–30 min	60.25	55.15	52.39	60.25
90853	Group therapy	29.22	26.75	25.41	29.22
Hemodialysis					
90935	Single phys evaluation	117.23	107.31	101.94	117.23
90937	Repeat evaluation	206.24	188.78	179.34	206.24
Gastroenterology					
91000	Esophageal incubation	69.82	63.91	60.71	69.82
91055	Gastric incubation	87.41	80.01	76.01	87.41
Ophthalmologic Services					
92004	Comprehensive eye exam	90.86	83.17	79.01	90.86
92100	Tonometry	47.31	43.31	41.14	47.31
92230	Fluorescein angioscopy	55.49	50.79	48.25	55.49
92275	Electroretinography	81.17	74.29	70.58	81.17
92531	Spontaneous nystagmus	26.00			
Audiologic Function Tests					
92557	Basic comprehensive audiometry	54.33	49.73	47.24	54.33
92596	Ear measurements	26.81	24.54	23.31	26.81
Cardiovascular Therapeutic Services					
93000	Electrocardiogram (ECG)	34.26	31.36	29.79	34.26
93015	Treadmill ECG	140.71	128.80	122.36	140.71
93040	Rhythm ECG, 1–3 leads	18.47	16.90	16.06	18.47
Pulmonary					
94010	Spirometry	38.57	35.31	33.54	38.57
94060	Spirometry before and after bronchodilator	71.67	65.60	62.32	71.67
94150	Vital capacity, total	13.82	12.65	12.02	13.82
Allergy and Clinical Immunology					
95024	Intradermal tests	6.58	6.02	5.72	6.58
95044	Patch tests	8.83	8.08	7.68	8.83
95115	Treatment for allergy, corticosteroids, single inj.	17.20	15.75	14.96	17.20
95117	Treatment for allergy, 2 or more inj.	22.17	20.29	19.28	22.17
95165	Allergen immunotherapy, single or multiple antigens, multiple-dose vials		6.50	6.18	7.11
Neurology					
95812	Electroencephalogram, Up to 1 hr.	129.32	118.37	112.45	129.32
95819	Electroencephalogram—awake and asleep	126.81	116.07	110.27	126.81

*Some services and procedures may not be considered a benefit under the Medicare program, and when listed on a claim form, no reimbursement may be received. However, it is important to include these codes when billing because Medicare policies may change without an individual knowing of a new benefit. For this reason, some of the services shown in this mock fee schedule do not have any amounts listed under the three Medicare columns.

Table continued on following page

Code No. and Description		Mock Fees	Medicare* Participating	Medicare* Non-participating	Medicare* Limiting Charge
95860	Electromyography, 1 extremity	88.83	81.31	77.24	88.83
95864	Electromyography, 4 extremities	239.99	219.67	208.69	239.99
96100	Psychological testing (per hour)	80.95	74.10	70.39	80.95
Physical Medicine					
97024	Diathermy	14.27	13.06	12.41	14.27
97036	Hubbard tank, each 15 min	24.77	22.67	21.54	24.77
97110	Physical therapy, initial 30 min	23.89	21.86	20.77	23.89
97260	Manipulation (cervical, thoracic, lumbosacral, sacroiliac, hand, wrist), one area	16.93	15.49	14.72	16.93
Special Services and Reports					
99000	Handling of specimen (transfer from Dr.'s office to lab)	5.00			
99025	Initial surg eval (new pt) with starred procedure	50.00			
99050	Services requested after office hours in addition to basic service	25.00			
99052	Services between 10 p.m. and 8 a.m. in addition to basic service	35.00			
99054	Services on Sundays and holidays in addition to basic service	35.00			
99056	Services normally provided in office requested by pt in location other than office	20.00			
99058	Office services provided on an emergency basis	65.00			
99070	Supplies and materials (itemize drugs and materials provided)	25.00			
99080	Special reports:				
	Insurance forms	10.00			
	Review of data to clarify pt's status	20.00			
	WC reports	50.00			
	WC extensive review report	250.00			

*Some services and procedures may not be considered a benefit under the Medicare program, and when listed on a claim form, no reimbursement may be received. However, it is important to include these codes when billing because Medicare policies may change without an individual knowing of a new benefit. For this reason, some of the services shown in this mock fee schedule do not have any amounts listed under the three Medicare columns.

Index to table continued on following page

Index

Pneumonectomy	32440–32450
Preventive medicine	
established patient	99391–99397
health hazard appraisal	99420
new patient	99381–99387
unlisted	99429
Proctosigmoidoscopy	45300–45321
Prolonged services	
hospital inpatient	99356–99359
office/outpatient	99354, 99355, 99358, 99359
Prostatectomy, perineal, subtotal	55801
Psychiatric evaluation of records, reports, and/or tests	90825
Psychological testing	96100
Psychotherapy	
pharmocologic management	90862
family (conjoint)	90847
group medical	90853
individual	90816
multiple-family	90849
Puncture	
lumbar spine	62270, 62272

Q

Quadriceps repair	27430

R

Radiology	
dosimetry	77300, 77331
teletherapy	77305–77315, 77321
therapeutic	77261–77799
treatment delivery	77401–77417
Repair: see procedure, organ, structure, or region involved	
Reports, special	99080
Resection, prostate, transurethral	52601–54640

S

Salpingo-oophorectomy	58720
Salpingectomy and/or oophorectomy	59120–59140
excision, benign lesion	11420–11422
layer closure, wounds	12031–12037
simple repair, wounds	12001–12007
Sensitivity studies, antibiotic	87181–87192
Septum, nasal septoplasty	30520
Skin excision, skin tags	11200, 11201
Splenectomy	38100–38115
Smear, primary source	87205–87211
Spine, radiologic exam	72010–72120
Spirometry	94010–94070
Standby services	99360
Supplies and materials	99070, 99071

T

TB skin test	86580
Teletherapy	77305–77321
Thromboendarterectomy	35301–35381
Tibia, radiologic exam	73590
Tonometry	92100

Appendix B: Medicare Level II HCPCS Codes

The following pages provide a partial alphanumeric list of the Health Care Financing Administration's Common Procedure Coding System, referred to as HCPCS (pronounced "hick-picks"). These Level II codes and modifiers were adopted by the Medicare program in 1984; additional codes and modifiers are added and deleted every year. This system was developed to code procedures not listed in the American Medical Association's *Current Procedural Terminology (CPT)* code book. This second level is a national standard used by all regional Medicare carriers.

For fees, refer to a comparable procedure in Appendix A. *Example:* J2510, penicillin procaine injection, would be comparable to 90788, IM injection, so the fee is $5.22.

Partial List of the Medicare Health Care Financing Administration's Common Procedure Coding System (HCPCS)

In certain circumstances, a code may need a modifier to show that the procedure has been changed by a specific situation. Remember that CPT and national modifiers apply to both CPT and HCPCS code systems. When applicable, indicate the appropriate modifier on the insurance claim form. Sometimes a special report may be needed to clarify the use of the modifier to the insurance company.

Table 1. Medicare HCPCS Modifiers

Modifier	Description
These one-letter modifiers may be used most often with A codes, transportation services, including ambulance, chiropractic services, medical and surgical supplies, and miscellaneous.	
-D	Diagnostic or therapeutic site other than "H" or "P" when these are used as origin codes
-E	Residential, domiciliary, custodial facility (other than an 1819 facility)
-H	Hospital
-N	Skilled nursing facility (NF) (1819 facility)
-P	Physician's office
-R	Residence
-S	Scene of accident or acute event
-X	(destination code only) Intermediate stop at physician's office on the way to the hospital
A list of two-letter modifiers follows.	
-AA	Anesthesia service personally furnished by anesthesiologist. This modifier affects the fee schedule payment amount received.
-AB	Medical direction of own employee(s) by anesthesiologist (not more than four employees).
-AC	Medical direction of other than own employees by anesthesiologist (not more than four individuals).
-AD	Medical supervision by a physician; more than four concurrent anesthesia procedures. This modifier affects the fee schedule payment amount received.
-AE	Direction of residents in furnishing not more than two concurrent anesthesia services—attending physician relationship met.

Table 1. Medicare HCPCS Modifiers *Continued*

Modifier	Description
-AF	Anesthesia complicated by total body hypothermia. For therapeutic hypothermia, see CPT code numbers 99185 and 99186.
-AG	Anesthesia for emergency surgery on a patient who is moribund or who has an incapacitating system, i.e. disease that is a constant threat to life (may warrant additional fee).
-AH	Clinical psychologist.
-AJ	Clinical social worker.
-AK	Nurse practitioner, rural, team member
-AL	Nurse practitioner, non-rural, team member
-AM	Physician, team member service.
-AN	PA services for other than assistant-at-surgery, nonteam member.
-AP	Determination of refractive state not performed in the course of diagnostic ophthalmologic examination.
-AR	Return ambulance trip (when filing for a return trip, the appropriate procedure code should be followed by -AR).
-AS	PA services for assistant-at-surgery (nonteam member).
-AT	Acute treatment (this modifier should be used when reporting service A2000 for acute treatment).
-AU	PA for other than assistant-at-surgery team member.
-AV	Nurse practitioner, rural, nonteam member.
-AW	Clinical nurse specialist, nonteam member.
-AY	Clinical nurse specialist, team member.
-BP	The beneficiary has been informed of the purchase and rental options and has elected to purchase the item.
-BR	The beneficiary has been informed of the purchase and rental options and has elected to rent the item.
-BU	The beneficiary has been informed of the purchase and rental options and after 30 days has not informed the supplier of his/her decision.
-CC	Procedure code change. Use modifier when the procedure code submitted was changed either for administrative reasons or when an incorrect code was filed.
-DD	Powdered enteral formulae. Use modifier when enteral powdered products are supplied.
-EJ	Subsequent claim (for epoetin alfa-epo-infection claim only).
-EM	Emergency reserve supply (for end-stage renal disease [ESRD] benefit only).
-EP	Service provided as part of Medicaid Early Periodic Screening Diagnosis and Treatment (EPSDT) program.
-ET	Emergency treatment (dental procedures performed in emergency situation should show the modifier -ET). This modifier has no direct effect on reimbursement.
-E1	Upper left, eyelid
-E2	Lower left, eyelid
-E3	Upper right, eyelid
-E4	Lower right, eyelid
-FA	Left hand, thumb
-FP	Service provided as part of Medicaid family planning program.
-F1	Left hand, second digit
-F2	Left hand, third digit
-F3	Left hand, fourth digit
-F4	Left hand, fifth digit
-F5	Right hand, thumb
-F6	Right hand, second digit
-F7	Right hand, third digit
-F8	Right hand, fourth digit
-F9	Right hand, fifth digit
-GA	Waiver of liability statement on file.
-KA	Add-on option/accessory for wheelchair.
-KH	DMEPOS item, initial claim, purchase of first-month rental.
-KI	DMEPOS item, second or third rental.
-KJ	DMEPOS item, parenteral enteral nutrition (PEN) pump or capped rental, months 4 to 15.
-KK	Inhalation solution compounded from an FDA-approved formulation.
-KL	Product characteristics defined in medical policy are met.
-KO	Lower-extremity prosthesis functional level 0—does not have the ability or potential to ambulate or transfer safely with or without assistance and a prosthesis does not enhance the quality of life or mobility.
-K1	Lower-extremity prosthesis functional level 1—has the ability or potential to use a prosthesis for transfers or ambulation on level surfaces at fixed cadence; typical of the limited and unlimited household ambulator.

Table continued on following page

Table 1. Medicare HCPCS Modifiers *Continued*

Modifier	Description
-K2	Lower-extremity prosthesis functional level 2—has the ability or potential for ambulation with the ability to traverse low-level environmental barriers such as curbs, stairs, or uneven surfaces; typical of the limited community ambulator.
-K3	Lower-extremity prosthesis functional level 3—has the ability or potential for ambulation with variable cadence; typical of the community ambulator who has the ability to traverse most environmental barriers and may have vocational, therapeutic, or exercise activity that demands prosthetic utilization beyond simple locomotion.
-K4	Lower-extremity prosthesis functional level 4—has the ability or potential for prosthetic ambulation that exceeds the basic ambulation skills, exhibiting high impact stress or energy levels; typical of the prosthetic demands of the child, active adult, or athlete.
-LC	Left circumflex coronary artery.
-LD	Left anterior descending coronary artery.
-LL	Lease/rental. Use the -LL modifier when durable medical equipment (DME) rental is to be applied against the purchase price.
-LR	Laboratory round trip.
-LS	FDA-monitored intraocular lens implant.
-LT	Left side. Used to identify procedures performed on the left side of the body. This modifier has no direct effect on payment.
-MS	Six-month maintenance and servicing fee for reasonable and necessary parts and labor that are not covered under any manufacturer or supplier warranty.
-NR	New when rented. Use the -NR modifier when DME that was new at the time or rental is subsequently purchased.
-NU	New equipment.
-PL	Progressive addition lenses.
-QB	Physician providing service in a rural HPSA. The -QB and -QU modifiers describe covered Medicare services performed by a physician within the geographic boundaries of a rural or urban health professional shortage area (HPSA).
-QC	Single channel monitoring.
-QD	Recording and storage in solid state memory by a digital recorder.
-QE	Prescribed amount of oxygen less than 1 liter per minute (LPM).
-QF	Prescribed amount of oxygen exceeds 4 liters per minute (LPM), and portable oxygen is prescribed.
-QG	Prescribed amount of oxygen greater than 4 liters per minute (LPM).
-QH	Oxygen-conserving device is being used with an oxygen delivery system.
-QK	Medical direction of two, three, or four concurrent anesthesia procedures involving qualified individuals.
-QM	Ambulance service provided under arrangement by hospital.
-QN	Ambulance service furnished directly by a provider of services.
-QR	Repeat laboratory test performed on the same day.
-QS	Monitored anesthesia care service.
-QT	Recording and storage on tape by an analog tape recorder.
-QU	Physician providing service in urban HPSA. The -QB and -QU modifiers describe covered Medicare services performed by a physician within the geographic boundaries of a rural or urban health professional shortage area (HPSA).
-QX	CRNA service: With medical direction by a physician.
-QZ	CRNA service: Without medical direction by a physician.
-Q1	Certifies evidence of mycosis of the toenail, which causes marked limitation of ambulation
-Q2	HCFA/ORD demonstration project procedure service.
-Q3	Live kidney donor: services associated with postoperative medical complications directly related to the donation.
-Q4	Service for ordering/referring physician qualifies as a service exemption.
-Q5	Service furnished by a substitute physician under a reciprocal billing arrangement.
-Q6	Service furnished by a locum tenens physician.
-Q7	One Class A finding
-Q8	Two Class B findings
-Q9	One Class B and two Class C findings
-RC	Right coronary artery
-RP	Replacement and repair, -RP, may be used to indicate replacement of durable medical equipment, orthotic and prosthetic devices that have been in use for some time. On the claim, show the code for the part, followed by the -RP modifier and the fee for the part.

Table 1. Medicare HCPCS Modifiers *Continued*

Modifier	Description
-RR	Rental. Use this modifier when durable medical equipment is to be rented.
-RT	Right side. Used to identify procedures performed on the right side of the body. This modifier has no direct effect on payment.
-SF	Second opinion ordered by a professional review organization (PRO). 100% reimbursement; no Medicare deductible or coinsurance.
-SG	Ambulatory surgical center facility service.
-TA	Left foot, great toe
-TC	Technical component: Under certain circumstances a charge may be made for the technical component alone. Under those circumstances the technical component charge is identified by adding modifier -TC to the usual procedure number. Technical component charges are institution charges and not billed separately by physicians. However, portable x-ray suppliers only bill for the technical component and should use modifier -TC. The charge data from portable x-ray suppliers will then be used to build customary and prevailing profiles.
-Tl	Left foot, second digit
-T2	Left foot, third digit
-T3	Left foot, fourth digit
-T4	Left foot, fifth digit
-T5	Right foot, great toe
-T6	Right foot, second digit
-T7	Right foot, third digit
-T8	Right foot, fourth digit
-T9	Right foot, fifth digit
-UE	Used durable medical equipment.
-VP	Aphakic patient.

Table 2. HCPCS Alpha/Numeric Index

Description	Code
A	
above elbow endoskeletal prostheses	L6500
above elbow prostheses	L6250
above knee endoskeletal prostheses	L5320
acetazolamide sodium (Diamox sodium), injection	J1120
Achromycin, injection	J0120
Actinomycin D, injection	J9120
adjustable arms, wheelchair	E0973
adjustable chair, dialysis	E1570
adrenaline, injection	J0170
Adriamycin, injection	J9000
air ambulance	A0030
air bubble detector, dialysis	E1530
air travel and nonemergency transport	A0140
alarm, pressure dialysis	E1540
alcohol	A4244
alcohol wipes	A4245
alternating pressure pad	E0180
aminophylline injection	J0280
amitriptyline (Elavil), injection	J1320
ammonia test paper	A4774
amobarbital (Amytal sodium), injection	J0300
ampicillin, injection	J0290

Table continued on following page

Table 2. HCPCS Alpha/Numeric Index *Continued*

Description	Code
amputee adapter, wheelchair	E0959
amputee wheelchair, detachable elevating leg rests	E1170
amputee wheelchair, detachable foot rests	E1200
amygdalin, injection	J3570
anesthetics for dialysis	A4735
ankle prostheses, Symes, metal frame	L5060
ankle prostheses, Symes, molded socket	L5050
antineoplastic drugs, NOC	J9999
antitipping device, wheelchair	E0971
apnea monitor	E0608
appliance, pneumatic	E0655
Aralene HCl, injection	J0390
arm rest, wheelchair	E0994
arms, adjustable, wheelchair	E0973
asparaginase (Elspar), injection	J9020
atropine sulfate, injection	J0460
aurothioglucose (Solganal), injection	J2910
axillary crutch extension	L0978
B	
back, upholstery, wheelchair	E0993
bacterial sensitivity study	P7001
bandage, elastic	A4460
bandages, gauze	A4202
bath conductivity meter, dialysis	E1550
bathroom equipment, miscellaneous	E0179
batteries, wheelchair, deep cycle	E1069
battery charger, wheelchair	E1066
BCNU (carmustine, bischlorethyl nitrosourea), injection	J9050
bed accessories: boards, tables	E0315
bed pan	E0276
below elbow endoskeletal prostheses	L6400
below knee endoskeletal prostheses	L5300
belt, extremity	E0945
belt, ostomy	A4367
belt, pelvic	E0944
bench, bathtub	E0245
benzquinamide HCl (Emete-con), injection	J0510
benztropine, injection	J0515
bethanechol chloride, injection	J0520
bicarbonate dialysate	A4705
bilirubin (phototherapy) light	E0202
biperiden (Akineton), injection	J0190
bischlorethyl nitrosourea, injection	J9050
bleomycin sulfate, injection	J9040
blood, mucoprotein	P2038
blood (split unit), specify amount	P9011
blood (whole), for transfusion, per unit	P9010
blood leak detector, dialysis	El560
blood pressure monitor	A4670
blood pump, dialysis	El620
blood strips	A4253
blood testing supplies	A4770
bond or cement, ostomy skin	A4364
brompheniramine maleate (Dehist)	J0945
C	
calcimar, calcitoninsalmon, injection	J0630
calcium disodium edetate (Versenate), injection	J0600

Table 2. HCPCS Alpha/Numeric Index *Continued*

Description	Code
calcium gluconate, injection	J0610
calcium glycerophosphate and calcium lactate (Calphosan), injection	J0620
calcium leucovorin, injection	J0640
calf rest, wheelchair	E0995
calibrator solution	A4256
canes	E0100
carbon filters	A4680
carmustine, injection	J9050
catheter caps, disposable (dialysis)	A4860
catheter insertion tray	A4354
catheter irrigation set	A4355
CCPD supply kit	A4901
cefazolin sodium, injection	J0690
cefonicid sodium, 1 gm, injection	J0695
cellular therapy	M0075
cement, ostomy	A4364
centrifuge	A4650
cephalin flocculation, blood	P2028
cephalothin sodium (Keflin), injection	J1890
cephapirin sodium, injection	J0710
cervical head harness/halter	E0942
cervical pillow	E0943
chair, adjustable, dialysis	E1570
chelation therapy, IV (chemical endarterectomy)	M0300
chin cup, cervical	L0150
chiropractor, manipulation of spine	A2000
chloramphenicol (chloromycetin sodium succinate), injection	J0720
chlordiazepoxide HCl (Librium), injection	J1990
chloroprocaine HCl (Nesacaine), injection	J2400
chlorothiazide sodium (Diuril), injection	J1205
chlorpheniramine maleate (Chlor-Trimeton), injection	J0730
chlorpromazine (Thorazine), injection	J3230
chlorprothixene (Taractan), injection	J3080
chorionic gonadotropin, injection	J0725
clamps, dialysis, venous pressure	A4918
clamps, Harvard pressure	A4920
cleansing agent, dialysis equipment	A4790
clotting time tube	A4771
codeine phosphate, injection	J0745
colchicine, injection	J0760
colistimethate sodium (Coly-Mycin M), injection	J0770
commode seat, wheelchair	E0968
compressor	E0565
compressor, pneumatic	E0650
conductive paste or gel	A4558
Congo red blood	P2029
contracts, repair and maintenance, ESRD	A4890
corticotropin, injection	J0800
cortisone, injection	J0810
crutches	E0110
cryoprecipitate, each unit	P9012
culture sensitivity study	P7001
Cycler, hemodialysis	E1590
Cycler dialysis machine	E1594
cyclophosphamide, injection	J9070

Table continued on following page

Table 2. HCPCS Alpha/Numeric Index *Continued*

Description	Code
D	
D.H.E. 45, injection	J1110
dactinomycin or actinomycin (Cosmegen), injection	J9120
daunorubicin HCl, injection	J9150
decubitus care pad	E0185
deionizer, water purification system	El615
Depo-Estradiol, injection	J1000
Depo-Testosterone, injection	J1070
detector, blood leak, dialysis	El560
dexamethasone sodium phosphate, injection	J1100
dextrose/normal saline, solution	J7042
Dextrostix	A4772
dialysate concentrate additives	A4765
dialysate testing solution	A4760
dialysis, bath conductivity, meter	E1550
dialyzer holder	A4919
dialyzers	A4690
dialysis supplies, miscellaneous	A4913
diazepam (Valium), injection	J3360
diazoxide (Hyperstat), injection	J1730
DIC (dacarbazine, DTIC, DOME), 100-mg vial	J9130
dicyclomine (Bentyl), injection	J0500
digoxin, injection	J1160
dimenhydrinate (Dramamine), injection	J1240
dimercaprol (BAL in oil), injection	J0470
dimethyl sulfoxide, injection	J1212
diphenhydramine HCl (Benadryl), injection	J1200
disarticulation, elbow, prostheses	L6200
DME medical supplies	A4610
DMSO, dimethyl sulfoxide (Rimso-50), injection	J1212
drainage bag	A4358
drainage board	E0606
droperidol (Inapsine), injection	J1790
droperidol and fentanyl citrate (Innovar), injection	J1810
drugs, nonprescription	A9150
drugs, prescription, oral chemotherapy	J7150
dyphylline (Dilor), injection	J1180
E	
elbow protector	E0191
electrical work or plumbing, home, dialysis equipment	A4870
electrodes	A4556
elevating leg rest, wheelchair	E0990
endarterectomy, chemical	M0300
Endrate, ethylenediamine tetra-acetic acid (EDTA), injection	J3520
epinephrine, injection	J0170
ergonovine maleate (Ergotrate), injection	J1330
estradiol valerate (Delestrogen), injection	J0970
estradiol valerate, up to 20 mg (Estraval-2X), injection	J1390
estradiol valerate, up to 10 mg (Estraval P.A.), injection	J1380
estrone, injection	J1435
ethylnorepinephrine HCl (Bronkephrine HCl), injection	J0590
etoposide, 50 mg, injection	J9181
external ambulatory infusion pump with adm equip	E0781
extremity belt-harness	E0945
F	
faceplate, ostomy	A4361
fentanyl citrate (Sublimaze), injection	J3010

Table 2. HCPCS Alpha/Numeric Index *Continued*

Description	Code
fibrinogen unit	P9013
fistula cannulation set	A4730
flotation mattress	E0184
flotation pad gel pressure	E0185
floxuridine, 500 mg, injection	J9200
fluid barriers, dialysis	E1575
fluorouracil, injection	J9190
fluphenazine decanoate (Prolixin Decanoate), injection	J2680
footplates, wheelchair	E0970
foot rest, for use with commode chair	E0175
forearm crutches	E0110
furosemide (Lasix), injection	J1940
G	
gamma globulin, 1 ml, injection	P9014
Garamycin, injection	J1580
gauze bandages (gauze elastic)	A4202
gauze pads	A4200
gel, conductive	A4558
gel flotation pad	E0185
gentamicin, injection	J1580
globulin, gamma, 1 ml, injection	P9014
globulin, Rh immune, 1 ml, injection	P9015
gloves, dialysis	A4927
glucose test strips	A4772
gold sodium thiosulfate, injection	J1600
Gomco drain bottle	A4912
Grade-Aid, wheelchair	E0974
gravity traction device	E0941
Gravlee jet washer	A4470
H	
hair analysis	P2031
hallux-valgus dynamic splint	L3100
haloperidol (Haldol), injection	J1630
halter, cervical head	E0942
hand rims, wheelchair	E0967
harness, extremity	E0945
harness, pelvic	E0944
harness/halter, cervical head	E0942
Harvard pressure clamp, dialysis	A4920
head rest extension, wheelchair	E0966
heater for nebulizer	E1372
heel or elbow protector	E0191
heel stabilizer	L3170
helicopter ambulance	A0040
hemipelvectomy, endoskeletal prostheses	L5340
hemipelvectomy prostheses	L5280
hemodialysis, monthly capitation	E0945
hemodialysis kit	A4820
hemodialysis unit	E1590
hemostats	A4850
Hemostix	A4773
heparin	A4800
heparin infusion pump, dialysis	E1520
Hexcelite, cast material	A4590

Table continued on following page

Table 2. HCPCS Alpha/Numeric Index *Continued*

Description	Code
HN_2 (nitrogen mustard)	J9230
hot water bottle	E0220
hyaluronidase (Wyddase), injection	J3470
hydralazine (Apresoline HCl), injection	J0360
hydrochlorides of opium alkaloids (Pantopon), injection	J2480
hydrocortisone, injection	J1720
hydrocortisone acetate, up to 25 mg, injection	J1700
hydrocortisone phosphate, injection	J1710
hydrocortisone sodium succinate (Solu-Cortef), injection	J1720
hydromorphone (Dilaudid), injection	J1170
hydroxyzine HCl (Vistaril), injection	J3410
hyoscyamine sulfate (Levsin), injection	J1980
hypertonic saline solution	J7130
I	
ice cap or collar	E0230
imipramine HCl (Tofranil), injection	J3270
incontinence clamp	A4356
infusion pump, external ambulatory with adm equip	E0781
infusion pump, heparin, dialysis	E1520
infusion pump, implantable	E0782
installation and/or delivery charges for ESRD equip	E1600
insulin, injection	J1820
intercapsular thoracic endoskeletal prostheses	L6570
interferon, injection	J9213
intermittent peritoneal dialysis (IPD) supply kit	A4905
intermittent peritoneal dialysis (IPD) system, automatic	E1592
intraocular lenses, anterior chamber	V2630
intraocular lenses, iris supported	V2631
intraocular lenses, posterior chamber	V2632
iodine swabs/wipes	A4247
IPPB machine	E0500
iron dextran (Imferon), injection	J1760
irrigation kits, ostomy	A4400
irrigation set, catheter	A4355
IV pole	E0776
J	
jacket, Risser	A4581
K	
kanamycin sulfate, injection	J1840
kanamycin sulfate, up to 75 mg (Kantrex) pediatric, injection	J1850
Kartop patient list, toilet or bathroom	E0625
kit, CAPD supply	A4900
kit, CCPD supply	A4901
kit, hemodialysis	A4820
Kutapressin, injection	J1910
L	
Laetrile, amygdalin (vitamin B_{17}), injection	J3570
lancets	A4259
lead wires	A4557
leg extension, walker	E1058
leg rest, wheelchair, elevating	E0990
leukocyte-poor blood, each unit	P9016
levorphanol tartrate (Levo-Dromoran), injection	J1960
lidocaine (Xylocaine), injection	J2000
lightweight wheelchair	E1087
lincomycin, injection	J2010

Table 2. HCPCS Alpha/Numeric Index *Continued*

Description	Code
liquid barrier, ostomy	A4363
liver injection	J2050
lubricant, ostomy	A4402
M	
manipulation, of spine, by chiropractor	A2000
mannitol, injection	J2150
measuring cylinder, dialysis	A4921
mechlorethamine, injection	J9230
medical supplies used in DME	A4610
medroxyprogesterone acetate (Depo-Provera), injection	J1050
meperidine, injection	J2175
meperidine and promethazine HCl (Mepergan), injection	J2180
mephentermine sulfate (Wyamine), injection	J3450
mepivacaine (Carbocaine), injection	J0670
metaraminol (Aramine), injection	J0380
meter, bath conductivity, dialysis	E1550
methadone HCl, injection	J1230
methicillin sodium (Staphcillin), injection	J2970
methocarbamol (Robaxin), injection	J2800
methotrimeprazine (Levoprom), injection	J1970
methoxamine (Vasoxyl), injection	J3390
methyldopate (Aldomet ester HCl)	J0210
methylergonovine maleate (Methergine), injection	J2210
methylprednisolone acetate (Depo-Medrol), injection	J1020
methylprednisolone sodium succinate (Solu-Medrol), injection	
up to 40 mg	J2920
up to 125 mg	J2930
metoclopramide HCl (Reglan)	J2765
metocurine iodide (Metubine), injection	J2240
microbiology tests	P7001
mini-bus, nonemergency transportation	A0120
miscellaneous dialysis supplies	A4913
mithramycin, injection	J9270
mitomycin (Mutamycin), injection	J9280
monitor, apnea	E0608
monitor, blood pressure	A4670
morphine, injection	J2270
mucoprotein, blood	P2038
Mustargen, injection	J9230
Myotonachol, injection	J0520
N	
nandrolone decanoate, injection, up to 50 mg	J2320
nandrolone decanoate, injection, up to 200 mg	J2322
nandrolone phenpropionate (Anabolin), injection	J0340
narrowing device, wheelchair	E0969
nasal vaccine inhalation	J3530
nebulizer, portable	E1375
nebulizer, with compressor	E0570
nebulizer heater	E1372
needle with syringe	A4206
needles	A4215
needles, dialysis	A4655
neonatal transport, ambulance, base rate	A0225
neostigmine methylsulfate (Prostigmin), injection	J2710
neuromuscular stimulator	E0745

Table continued on following page

Table 2. HCPCS Alpha/Numeric Index *Continued*

Description	Code
niacin, injection	J2350
nikethamide (Coramine), injection	J3490
nitrogen mustard, injection	J9230
noncovered procedure	A9270
nonmedical supplies for dialysis (i.e., scale, scissors, stopwatch, etc.)	A4910
nonprescription drugs	A9150
nonprofit transport, nonemergency	A0120
O	
occipital/mandibular support, cervical	L0160
occupational therapy	H5300
Omnipen-N, injection	J2430
opium, injection	J2480
orphenadrine (Norflex), injection	L2360
orthoses, thoracic-lumbar-sacral (scoliosis)	L1200
ostomy supplies	A4421
oxacillin sodium (Prostaphlin), injection	J2410
oxymorphone HCl (Numorphan), injection	J2700
oxytetracycline, injection	J2460
oxytocin (Pitocin), injection	J2590
P	
pacemaker monitor, includes audible/visible check systems	E0610
pacemaker monitor, includes digital/visible check systems	E0615
pad for water circulating heat unit	E0249
pads, flotation, electric, standard	E0192
pail or pan for use with commode chair	E0167
papaverine HCl, injection	J2440
paraffin	A4265
paraffin bath unit	E0235
paste, conductive	A4558
pelvic belt/harness/boot	E0944
penicillin G banzathine (Bicillin), injection	J0540
penicillin G potassium (Pfizerpen), injection	J2540
penicillin procaine, aqueous, injection	J2510
pentazocine HCl (Talwin), injection	J3070
Percussor	E0480
peritoneal straps	L0980
peroxide	A4244
perphenazine (Trilafon), injection	J3310
personal items	A9190
pessary	A4560
phenobarbital, injection	J2560
phenobarbital sodium, injection	J2515
phentolamine mesylate (Regitine), injection	J2760
phenylephrine HCl (Neo-Synephrine), injection	J2370
phenytoin sodium (Dilantin), injection	J1165
pHisoHex solution	A4246
phototherapy, light	E0202
phytonadione (AquaMEPHYTON), injection, vitamin K	J3430
pillow, cervical	E0943
plasma, protein fraction, each unit	P9018
plasma, single donor, fresh frozen, each unit	P9017
platelet concentrate, each unit	P9019
platelet-rich plasma, each unit	P9020
podiatric services, noncovered	A9160
portable hemodialyzer system	E1635
portable nebulizer	E1375
postural drainage board	E0606

Table 2. HCPCS Alpha/Numeric Index *Continued*

Description	Code
pralidoxine chloride (Protopam), injection	J2730
prednisolone acetate, injection	J2650
preparation kits, dialysis	A4914
prescription drug, oral	J7140
prescription drug, oral chemotherapy	J7150
pressure alarm, dialysis	E1540
procainamide HCl (Pronestyl), injection	J2690
prochlorperazine (Compazine), injection	J0780
progesterone, injection	J2675
prolotherapy	M0076
promazine HCl (Sparine), injection	J2950
promethazine HCl (Phenergan), injection	J2550
propiomazine (Largon), injection	J1930
propranolol HCl (Inderal), injection	J1800
prostheses, above albow, endoskeletal	L6500
prostheses, below elbow, endoskeletal	L6400
prostheses, hemipelvectomy	L5280
prostheses, intercapsular thoracic, endoskeletal	L6570
prostheses, knee, endoskeletal	L5300
prostheses, lower extremity, NOC	L5999
prosthetic services, NOC	L8499
protamine sulfate, injection	J2720
protector, heel or elbow	E0191
Q	
Quad cane	E0105
R	
rack/stand, oxygen	E1355
reciprocating peritoneal dialysis system	E1630
red blood cells, each unit	P9021
regulator, oxygen	E1353
replacement components, ESRD machines	E1640
replacement tanks, dialysis	A4880
restraints, any type	E0710
reverse osmosis water purification, ESRD	E1610
Rh_o (D) immune globulin, injection	J2790
rib belt	A4572
rims, hand (wheelchair)	E0967
Ringer's, injection	J7120
rings, ostomy	A4404
Risser jacket	A4581
S	
safety equipment	E0700
safety visit, wheelchair	E0980
sales tax, orthotic/prosthetic/other	L9999
Sandril, injection	J2820
scale or scissors, dialysis	A4910
seat attachment, walker	E0156
seat insert, wheelchair	E0992
Seconal sodium, injection	J2860
sensitivity study	P7001
serum clotting time tube	A4771
shunt accessories, for dialysis	A4740
sitz bath, portable	E0160

Table continued on following page

Table 2. HCPCS Alpha/Numeric Index *Continued*

Description	Code
skin barrier, ostomy	A4362
skin bond or cement, ostomy	A4364
sling, patient lift	E0621
slings	A4565
social worker, nonemergency transport	A0160
sodium chloride, injection	J2912
sodium succinate, injection	J1720
sorbent cartridges, ESRD	E1636
spectinomycin dihydrochloride (Trobicin), injection	J3320
sphygmomanometer with cuff and stethoscope	A4660
spinal orthosis, NOC	L1499
splint	A4570
splint, hallux-valgus, night, dynamic	L3100
stand/rack, oxygen	E1355
sterilizing agent, dialysis	A4780
streptokinase-streptodornase, injection	J2995
streptomycin, injection	J3000
streptozocin, injection	J9320
succinylcholine chloride (Anectine), injection	J0330
suction pump, portable	E0600
surgical brush, dialysis	A4910
surgical stockings, above-knee length	A4490
surgical supplies, miscellaneous	A4649
surgical trays	A4550
swabs, Betadine or iodine	A4247
syringe	A4213
syringes, dialysis	A4655
T	
tape, all types, all sizes	A4454
taxes, orthotic/prosthetic/other	L9999
taxi, nonemergency transportation	A0100
tent, oxygen	E0455
terbutaline sulfate, 0.5 mg, injection	J3105
terminal devices	L6700
testosterone cypionate (Depo-Testadiol), injection	J1060
testosterone enanthate (Deladumone), injection	L0900
testosterone propionate, injection	J3150
testosterone suspension, injection	J3140
tetanus immune globulin (Homo-Tet), injection	J1670
tetracycline, injection	J0120
theophylline (Salyrgan-theophylline), injection	J2810
thermometer, dialysis	A4910
thiethylperazine maleate (Torecan), injection	J3280
thiotepa (triethylenethiophosphoramide), injection	J9340
thiothixene (Navane IM), injection	J2330
thymol turbidity, blood	P2033
thyrotropin (TSH), exogenous, up to 10 IU, injection	J3240
tobramycin sulfate (Nebcin), injection	J3260
toilet rail	E0243
toilet seat, raised	E0244
tolazoline HCl (Priscoline), injection	J2670
tolls, nonemergency transport	A0170
tool kit, dialysis	A4910
tourniquet, dialysis	A4910
tracheotomy collar or mask	A4621
traction device, gravity-assisted	E0941
traction equipment, overdoor	E0860

Table 2. HCPCS Alpha/Numeric Index *Continued*

Description	Code
travel hemodialyzer system	E1635
trays, surgical	A4550
triflupromazine HCl (Vesprin), injection	J3400
trimethaphan camsylate (Arfonad)	J0400
trimethobenzamide HCl (Tigan), injection	J3250
tube-occluding forceps/clamps, dialysis	A4910
U	
ultraviolet cabinet	E0690
unclassified drugs (contraceptives)	J3490
underarm crutches, wood	E0112
unipuncture control system, dialysis	E1580
upholstery, reinforced seat, wheelchair	E0975
upholstery seat, wheelchair	E0991
Ureaphil, injection	J3350
Urecholine, injection	J0520
urinary drainage bag	A4357
urinary leg bag	A4358
urinary suspensory	A4359
urine control strips or tablets	A4253
urine sensitivity study	P7001
V	
vancomycin (Vancocin), injection	J3370
vaporizer	E0605
vascular catheters	A4300
vinblastine sulfate, injection	J9360
venous pressure clamps, dialysis	A4918
ventilator, volume	E0450
vest, safety, wheelchair	E0980
vinblastine sulfate (Velban), injection	J9360
vitamin B_{12}, injection	J3420
vitamin K, injection	J3430
volume ventilator, stationary or portable	E0450
W	
WAK (wearable artificial kidney)	E1632
walker, wheeled, without seat	E0141
walker attachments, platform	E0154
warfarin sodium (Coumadin), injection—unclassified	J3490
washed red blood cells, each unit	P9022
water, ambulance	A0050
water softening system, ESRD	E1625
water tanks, dialysis	A4880
wearable artificial kidney	E1632
wheel attachment, walker	E0977
wrist disarticulation prosthesis	L6060
Y	
youth wheelchair	E1091

Appendix C: Medi-Cal

KEY TERMS

Your instructor may wish to select some words and abbreviations pertinent to the Medi-Cal program for a test. For definitions of the terms, further study, and/or reference, the words, phrases, and abbreviations may be found in the Glossary at the end of the Handbook. *Additional key terms are given in Chapter 12, Medicaid and Other State Programs. Key terms and abbreviations for this Appendix follow.*

accounts receivable (A/R) transaction
Aid to the Blind (AB)
Aid to Families with Dependent Children (AFDC)
Aid to the (permanently) Disabled (ATD)
automated eligibility verification system (AEVS)
benefits identification card (BIC)
California Children's Services (CCS)
Child Health and Disability Prevention Program (CHDP)
claim control number (CCN)
Claims and eligibility real-time software (CERTS)
Claims Inquiry Form (CIF)
Comprehensive Perinatal Services Program (CPSP)
computer media claims (CMC)
County Medical Services Program (CMSP)
Department of Health Services (DHS)
durable medical equipment (DME)
Electronic Data Systems (EDS) Corporation
electronic funds transfer (EFT)
eligibility verification confirmation (EVC)
Genetically Handicapped Persons Program (GHPP)
medically indigent (MI)
medically needy (MN)
nursing facility (NF)
Old Age Survivors, Health and Disability Insurance (OASHDI) Program
point of service (POS) device or network
presumptive eligibility (PE)
Provider Telecommunications Network (PTN)
Remittance Advice Details (RAD)
Resubmission Turnaround Document (RTD)
share of cost (SOF)
Treatment Authorization Request (TAR) form
Voice Drug TAR System (VDTS)

PERFORMANCE OBJECTIVES

The student will be able to

- Define and spell the key terms and abbreviations for this chapter, given the information from the *Handbook* Glossary, within a reasonable period of time and with enough accuracy to obtain a satisfactory evaluation.

- Answer the self-study review questions after reading the chapter, with enough accuracy to obtain a satisfactory evaluation.

Note: See Chapter 12, Medicaid and Other State Programs, and complete Assignments 12–2, 12–3, and 12–4 using Medi-Cal OCR guidelines and block-by-block requirements found in Appendix C of the *Handbook*. Additional performance objectives will be met by completing HCFA-1500 insurance claim forms for billing and posting to ledger cards.

STUDY OUTLINE

Types of Medi-Cal Plans
- Managed Care Plans
- Descriptions of Managed Care Plans

Medi-Cal Eligibility
- Share of Cost
- Identification Card
- Eligibility Verification
  - Verification Methods

Medi-Cal Benefits
- Medi-Services

Prior Approval
- Telecommunications Networks
- Treatment Authorization Request

Procedure: Completing the Treatment Authorization Request Form 50–1

Claim Procedure
- Fiscal Intermediaries
- Copayment
- Time Limit
- Helpful Billing Tips
- Medi-Cal and Other Coverage
  - Medi-Cal and Private Insurance
  - Medi-Cal and Medicare
  - Medi-Cal and TRICARE
- Computer Media Claims

Health Insurance Claim Form, HCFA-1500
- Instructions for Completing the HCFA-1500 Claim Form for the Medi-Cal Program

Uniform Bill (UB-92) Outpatient Claim Form
- Instructions for Completing the UB-92 Claim Form

After Claim Submission
- Remittance Advice Details
  - Adjustments
  - Approvals for Payment
  - Electronic Fund Transfer
  - Denials
  - Suspends
  - Accounts Receivable Transactions
- Resubmission Turnaround Document

Procedure: Completing the Resubmission Turnaround Document
- Claims Inquiry Form

Procedure: Completing the Claims Inquiry Form

Appeal Process

Procedure: Completing an Appeal Form

SELF-STUDY A–1 ▸ REVIEW QUESTIONS

Review the objectives, key terms and abbreviations, chapter information, and figures in *Handbook* Appendix C before completing the following review questions.

1. List the Medi-Cal program managed care plan models.

   a. ______________________________

   b. ______________________________

   c. ______________________________

   d. ______________________________

e. ______________________________

f. ______________________________

g. ______________________________

2. Mrs. Benson is a Medi-Cal recipient and injures her right leg in a fall. She is taken by ambulance to the emergency department of a local hospital. Must she seek treatment from a facility contracted under the Medi-Cal managed care plan or can she be treated wherever the ambulance takes her? ______________________________

____

3. If a Medi-Cal patient receives services from outside of his or her Medi-Cal managed care plan, what must the out-of-plan physician submit with the claim form for services?

____

____

4. Medically indigent individuals who are unable to provide mainstream medical care for themselves and whose incomes are above the assistance level are classified under a group called ______________________________.

5. Name the entity that issues an identification card to each Medi-Cal recipient who is eligible for benefits. ______________________________

____

6. Name the two most important verifications that are the provider's responsibilities to obtain.

a. ______________________________

b. ______________________________

7. List four methods used to verify eligibility.

a. ______________________________

b. ______________________________

c. ______________________________

d. ______________________________

8. Medical services to pregnant Medi-Cal recipients are available through the ________ ______________________________ program.

9. The name of the program that offers temporary coverage for prenatal care before a woman is officially a Medi-Cal recipient is called ______________________________.

10. Medi-Cal recipients may receive ______________________ Medi-Services per calendar month.

11. An automated voice-response system for a provider to obtain prior authorization for a Medi-Cal service is called ______________________.

12. Name two additional methods for obtaining prior approval for a Medi-Cal service.

    a. ______________________

    b. ______________________

13. To track a submitted Treatment Authorization Request, complete a/an ______________________.

14. A Medi-Cal patient seen today needs chronic hemodialysis services. You telephone for a TAR to get verbal approval. What four important items must you obtain to complete the written TAR?

    a. ______________________

    b. ______________________

    c. ______________________

    d. ______________________

15. A Medi-Cal patient came in for an office visit and the physician said the patient needed to have a cholecystectomy within the next 6 weeks to 2 months and that it needed to be scheduled when convenient (aka elective surgery). Before scheduling surgery, what do you do? ______________________

    ____

    After you have completed this procedure, the patient is scheduled for the cholecystectomy. After surgery, you bill Medi-Cal, noting ______________________ and ______________________ on the claim form. Do you need to send any information to the hospital? ______________________

16. The Medi-Cal copayment fee when a Medi-Cal patient seeks professional medical services from a physician is $______________________.

17. The Medi-Cal copayment fee when a patient has a prescription refilled is $ ______________________.

18. The time limit for submission of a Medi-Cal claim to receive 100% of the maximum allowable is ______________________.

A claim submitted within 8 months after service is rendered is reimbursed at __________ %. A claim sent within 12 months after service is given is paid at __________ %. A claim submitted over 1 year from the month service is received is paid __________ %.

19. State the difference in policy between the Medi-Cal global fee and the Medicare global package.

____

____

20. When a Medi-Cal patient has a private health insurance policy, who do you submit the initial claim to? __________

21. Claims for patients who are recipients of Medicare and Medi-Cal are referred to as __________ claims and the claim __________ assigned.

22. A Medi-Cal patient also has TRICARE. What billing procedure do you follow? Be exact in your steps for a dependent of an active military man.

   a. __________

   b. __________

23. Name the five categories of Medi-Cal adjudicated (resolution process) claims that appear on a Remittance Advice Details document.

   a. __________

   b. __________

   c. __________

   d. __________

   e. __________

24. When posting dollar amounts from a Remittance Advice Details document to the patient's ledger, payments are shown as __________, and negative adjustments are posted as __________.

25. When the Medi-Cal fiscal intermediary makes a direct deposit into a provider's bank account, this is known as __________.

26. If a provider feels a claim was denied in error, he or she should submit a/an __________ __________ for reconsideration.

27. On a Resubmission Turnaround Document, correct data are inserted into ______________________________ ______________________________ of the form.

28. Dr. Practon requests an adjustment for an underpaid claim by submitting a/an ______________________________.

29. A complaint about a Medi-Cal payment must be directed to the fiscal intermediary within ______________________________ of the action that caused the complaint.

30. Define these Medi-Cal abbreviations.

a. PE ______________________________
b. RAD ______________________________
c. BIC ______________________________
d. TAR ______________________________
e. MN ______________________________
f. POS ______________________________
g. CIF ______________________________
h. RTD ______________________________
i. SOC ______________________________
j. AEVS ______________________________

To check your answers to this self-study assignment, see Appendix D.

ASSIGNMENT 12–2 ► COMPLETE A MEDICAID CLAIM FORM

Directions: To complete this assignment for Medi-Cal, you will need the following information in addition to that given in *Workbook* Chapter 12. Rose Clarkson has a Share of Cost of $70. Dr. James Jackson's nine-digit Medi-Cal provider number is 00G5344722. Dr. Perry Cardi's nine-digit Medi-Cal provider number is 00A286950. The College Clinic's nine-digit Medi-Cal group number is ZZR12005F.

ASSIGNMENT 12–3 ► COMPLETE A MEDICAID CLAIM FORM

Directions: To complete this assignment for Medi-Cal, you will need the following information in addition to that given in *Workbook* Chapter 12. Dr. James B. Jeffers' nine-digit Medi-Cal provider number is 00C282870. Dr. Gerald Practon's nine-digit Medi-Cal provider number is 020A23651. The College Hospital's Medi-Cal facility number is HSC43700F. The College Clinic's nine-digit Medi-Cal group number is ZZR12005F.

ASSIGNMENT 12–4 ► COMPLETE A MEDICAID CLAIM FORM

Directions: To complete this assignment for Medi-Cal, you will need the following information in addition to that given in *Workbook* Chapter 12. Dr. Raymond Skeleton's nine-digit Medi-Cal provider number is 000G61310. The College Hospital's Medi-Cal facility number is HSC43700F. The College Clinic's nine-digit Medi-Cal group number is ZZR12005F.

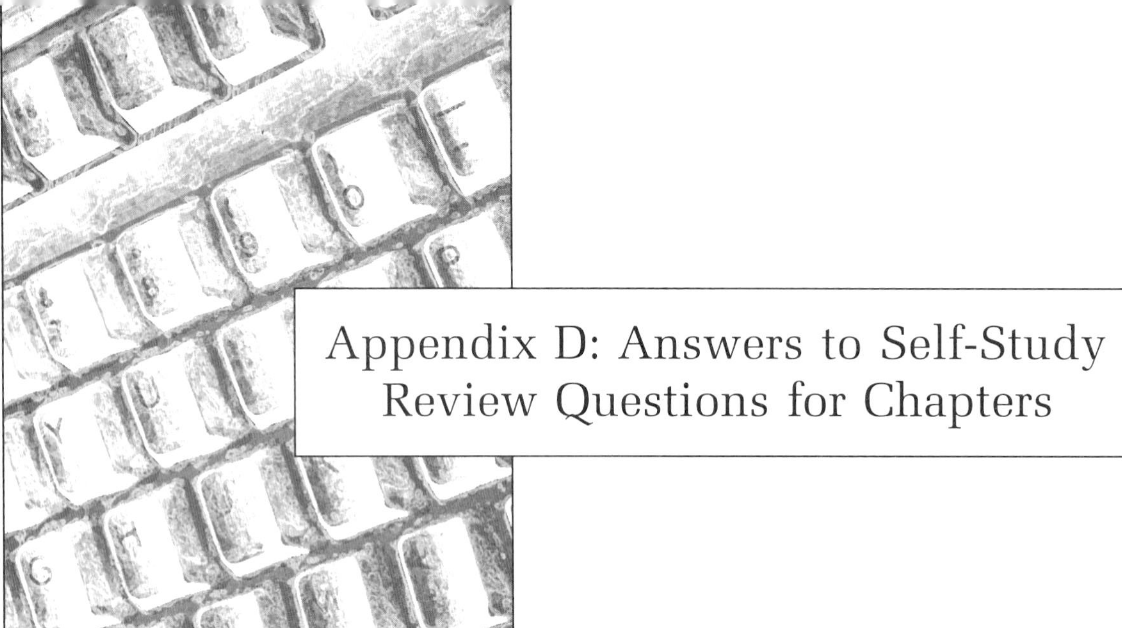

Appendix D: Answers to Self-Study Review Questions for Chapters

Self-Study 1–1 Review Questions

1. Identify three career opportunities (job titles) available after training in diagnostic and procedural coding and insurance claims completion. *Answers may vary but may consist of any three of the following:*
   a. **insurance billing specialist, medical biller, reimbursement specialist, insurance counselor, collection manager, coding specialist**
   b. **electronic claims professional**
   c. **claims assistance professional**
2. List the duties an insurance billing specialist might perform. *Answers may vary but should include the following comments:*
   a. **Review diagnostic and procedural codes for correctness and completeness**
   b. **Submit insurance claims promptly**
   c. **Collect data from hospitals, laboratories, and other physicians involved in a case**
   d. **Discuss patient's treatment plan and insurance coverage and negotiate a payment plan**
   e. **Answer routine inquiries related to account balances and insurance submission dates**
   f. **Assist patients in budgeting**
   g. **Follow up on delinquent accounts by tracing denied, adjusted, or unpaid claims.**
3. List the duties of a claims assistance professional.
   a. **Help patients organize, file, and negotiate health insurance claims of all types**
   b. **Assist the consumer in obtaining maximum benefits from insurance companies**
   c. **Tell the patient what checks to write to providers to eliminate overpayment**
4. Skills required for an insurance billing specialist are: (*Some or all of these may be mentioned by the student*).
   a. **knowledge of medical terminology**
   b. **knowledge of insurance terminology**
   c. **proficiency in completing insurance claims**
   d. **knowledge of procedural and diagnostic coding**
   e. **knowledge of anatomy and physiology, disease, and treatment (surgical, drug, and laboratory) terms**
   f. **computer skills; basic typing and/or keyboarding**
   g. **medicolegal knowledge**
   h. **knowledge of insurance carriers and Medicare policies and regulations**
   i. **basic math and use of calculator**
   j. **billing and collection techniques**
   k. **precise reading skills**
   l. **proficiency in accessing information via the Internet**
   m. **expert in legalities of collection on accounts**
   n. **use of photocopy and facsimile equipment**
5. Standards of conduct by which an insurance billing specialist determines the propriety of his or her behavior in a relationship are known as **medical ethics.**
6. Complete these statements with either the words *illegal* or *unethical.*
   a. To report incorrect information to the Aetna Casualty Company is **unethical.**
   b. To report incorrect information to a Medicare fiscal intermediary is **illegal.**
   c. It is **unethical** for two physicians to treat the same patient for the same condition.
7. A confidential communication that may be disclosed only with the patient's permission is known as **privileged communication.**
8. Exceptions to the right of privacy are those records involving:
   a. **industrial accidents (physician employed by insurance company)**
   b. **communicable diseases**
   c. **child abuse**
   d. **gunshot wounds**
   e. **stabbing from criminal actions**
   f. **diseases and ailments of newborns and infants**
   g. **medical information obtained by Medicare insurance carriers**

9. When a physician is legally responsible for an employee's conduct performed during employment, this is known as **vicarious liability (respondeat superior)**.
10. Indicate whether the situation is one of *fraud* or *abuse* in the following situations.
    a. Billing a claim for services not medically necessary. **abuse**
    b. Changing a figure on an insurance claim form to get increased payment. **fraud**
    c. Dismissing the copayment owed by a Medicare patient. **fraud**
    d. Neglecting to refund an overpayment to the patient. **abuse**
    e. Billing for a complex fracture when the patient suffered a simple break. **fraud**
11. A claims assistance professional neglects to submit an insurance claim to a Medicare supplemental insurance carrier within the proper time limit. What type of insurance is needed for protection against this loss for the client? **Errors and omissions insurance**.
12. State three bonding methods.
    a. **position-schedule bond**
    b. **blanket-position bond**
    c. **personal bond**

Self-Study 2–1 Review Questions

1. A/an **insurance contract (policy)** is a legally enforceable agreement or contract.
2. List five health insurance policy renewal provisions.
    a. **cancelable**
    b. **optionally renewable**
    c. **conditionally renewable**
    d. **guaranteed renewable**
    e. **noncancelable**
3. Insurance reimbursement or payment is also called **indemnity**.
4. Name two general health insurance policy limitations.
    a. **exclusions**
    b. **waiver or rider**
5. The act of finding out whether treatment is covered under an individual's health insurance policy is called **precertification**.
6. The procedure to obtain permission for a procedure before it is done to see whether the insurance program agrees it is medically necessary is termed **preauthorization**.
7. Determining the maximum dollar amount the insurance company will pay for a procedure before it is done is known as **predetermination**.
8. Name three ways an individual may obtain health insurance.
    a. **take out insurance through a group plan (contract or policy)**
    b. **pay the premium on an individual basis**
    c. **enroll in a prepaid health plan**
9. List four ways a physician's practice may use to submit insurance claims to insurance companies.
    a. **manual claims submission**
    b. **in-office electronic filing by fax or computer**
    c. **contracting with an outside service bureau to submit claims manually or electronically**
    d. **telecommunications networking system via modem/telephone line/computer**
10. A patient service slip personalized to the practice of the physician and used as a communications/billing tool during routing of the patient is also known as a/an *(answers may vary but may consist of any four of the following)*:
    a. **encounter or routing form**
    b. **transaction slip**
    c. **charge slip**
    d. **fee ticket**
    e. **communicator**
    f. **multipurpose billing form**
    g. **patient service slip**
    h. **superbill**
11. Match the insurance terms in the first column with the definitions in the second column. Write the correct letters in the blanks.

Term	Answer		Definition
adjuster	**e**	a.	An insurance company takes into account benefits payable by another carrier in determining its own liability.
assignment	**c**	b.	Benefits paid by an insurance company to an insured person.
carrier	**j**	c.	Transfer of one's right to collect an amount payable under an insurance contact.
coordination of benefits	**a**	d.	Time that must elapse before an indemnity is paid.
deductible	**g**	e.	Acts for insurance company or insured in settlement of claims.
exclusions	**i**	f.	Periodic payment to keep insurance policy in force.
indemnity	**b**	g.	Amount insured person must pay before policy will pay.
premium	**f**	h.	Period of time in which a claim must be filed.
subscriber	**k**	i.	Certain illnesses or injuries listed in a policy that the insurance company will not cover.
time limit	**h**	j.	Insurance company that carries the insurance.
waiting period	**d**	k.	One who belongs to an insurance plan.

12. An individual promising to pay for medical services rendered is known as a/an **guarantor**.
13. A document signed by the insured directing the insurance company to pay benefits directly to the physician is known as a/an **assignment of benefits**.
14. Electronic access to computer data may consist of the following verification or access methods.
    a. **series of numbers**
    b. **series of letters**
    c. **electronic writing (signatures or initials)**
    d. **voice**
    e. **fingerprint transmission**
    f. **computer key**
15. Guidelines for avoiding unauthorized use and preventing problems when a medical practice uses a fasimile signature stamp are:
    a. **Make only one stamp.**
    b. **Allow only long-term, trusted, bonded staff members to have access to the stamp.**

c. **Keep the stamp in a location with a secure lock.**
d. **Limit access to the stamp.**

Self-Study 3-1 Review Questions

1. Written or graphic information about patient care is termed a/an **medical record**.
2. **Documentation** is written or dictated to record chronologic facts and observations about a patient's health.
3. Match the terms in the first column with the definitions in the second column. Write the correct letters on the blanks.

attending physician	**c**	a. renders a service to a patient.
consulting physician	**d**	b. Directs selection, preparation, and administration of tests, medication, or treatment.
ordering physician	**b**	c. Legally responsible for the care and treatment given to a patient.
referring physician	**e**	d. Gives an opinion regarding a specific problem that is requested by another doctor.
treating or performing physician	**a**	e. Sends the patient for tests or treatment or to another doctor for consultation.

4. Performance of services or procedures consistent with the diagnosis, done with standards of good medical practice and a proper level of care given in the appropriate setting is known as **medical necessity**.
5. If a medical practice is audited by Medicare officials and intentional miscoding is discovered, **fines and penalties** may be levied and providers may be **excluded from the program**.
6. A list of all staff members' names, job titles, signatures, and their initials is known as a/an **signature log**.
7. How should an insurance billing specialist correct an error on a patient's record? **Use legal copy pen, cross out wrong entry with a single line, write the correct entry, date, and initial entry. Never erase or use white-out or self-adhesive paper over error.**
8. Name the five documentation components of a patient's history.
   a. **chief complaint**
   b. **history of present illness**
   c. **past history**
   d. **family history**
   e. **social history**
9. An inventory of body systems by documenting responses to questions about symptoms that a patient has experienced is called a/an **review of systems**.
10. Define the following terms in relationship to billing.
    a. New patient—**one who has not received any professional services from the physician or another physician of the same specialty who belongs to the same group practice, within the past 3 years.**
    b. Established patient—**one who has received professional services from the physician or another physician of the same specialty who belongs to the same group practice, within the past 3 years.**
11. Explain the difference between a consultation and the referral of a patient.
    a. Consultation **Services rendered by a physician whose opinion or advice is requested by another physician or agency in the evaluation or treatment of a patient's illness or a suspected problem.**
    b. Referral **Transfer of the total or specific care of a patient from one physician to another for known problems.**
12. Medical care for a patient who has received treatment for an illness and is referred to a second physician for treatment of the same condition is a situation called **continuity of care**.
13. If two doctors see the same patient on the same day, one for the patient's heart condition and the other for a diabetic situation, this medical care situation is called **concurrent care**.
14. What is (are) the exception(s) to the Right of Privacy and Privileged Communication?
    a. **when the physician examines a patient at the request of a third party who is paying the bill as in workers' compensation cases**
    b. **when the patient is suing someone, such as an employer, who must protect himself**
    c. **when the patient's records are subpoenaed or there is a search warrant**
    d. **when the patient is a member of a managed care organization (MCO) and the physician has signed a contract with the MCO that has a clause that allows the MCO access to the medical records of their patients**
15. When faxing a patient's medical records, a signed document for **authorizing release of information via the fax machine** must be obtained from the patient.
16. Action to take when a faxed medical document is misdirected is **telephone or fax a request to destroy the information erroneously sent**.
17. What must the former physician have from the patient before a record can be given to a new physician? **A written request from the patient or a signed authorization or release of information form.**
18. What must an insurance billing specialist do if he or she receives a request from another physician for certain records? **Obtain a written request from the patient or a signed authorization or release of information form.**
19. What must a physician have from the patient before he or she can give information to an attorney? **An authorization or release of information form signed by the patient or a subpoena.**
20. Indicate either *indefinite retention* or *number of years* for keeping records in the following situations.

a. Computerized payroll records	**7 years**
b. Insurance claim for Medicare patient	**7 years**
c. Medical record of a deceased patient	**5 years**
d. Active patient medical records	**indefinite retention**
e. Letter to a patient about balance due after insurance paid	**1–5 years**

21. Can an insurance billing specialist receive a subpoena for his or her physician? **Yes, if the physician gives him or her this authority.**
22. Can a physician terminate a contract with a patient? **Yes.** If so, how? **By sending a letter of withdrawal of care, registered or certified with return signature.**
23. This question is presented for critical thinking. A patient comes into the office for treatment. He does not return, because he is dissatisfied with Dr. Practon's treatment. Is it necessary to keep his records when he obviously will not return? **Yes.** Why? **Records must be kept as required by state law for a certain period of time. (Note: Records of a dissatisfied patient should be kept indefinitely because of the possibility of a lawsuit at a later date or to prevent a lawsuit.)**

Self-Study 3–2 Review Questions

1. Match the terms in the first column with the definitions in the second column. Write the correct letters on the blanks.

acute	**c**	a. Pertaining to both sides
chronic	**f**	b. Decubitus ucler
menopause	**d**	c. Condition that runs a short but severe course
bilateral	**a**	d. Change of life
bed sore	**b**	e. Tinnitus
ringing of ears	**e**	f. Condition persisting over a long period of time

2. Write in the meaning for these abbreviations and/or symbols commonly encountered in a patient's medical record.

RLQ	**right lower quadrant**
DC	**discharge**
WNL	**within normal limits**
R/O	**rule out**
UPI	**upper respiratory infection**
C	**with**
+	**positive**

3. When documenting incisions, the unit of measure length should be listed in **centimeters (cm).**
4. If a physician called and asked for a patient's medical record STAT, what would he or she mean?
   a. The physician wants a statistic from a patient's record.
   b. The physician wants the record delivered on Tuesday.
   c. The physician wants the record delivered immediately.
5. If a physician asks you to locate the results of the last UA, what would you be searching for?
   a. a urinalysis report
   b. an x-ray report of the ulna
   c. uric acid test results
6. If a physician telephoned and asked for a copy of the last H&P to be faxed, what is he requesting?
   a. heart and pulmonary findings
   b. H_2 antagonist test results
   c. a history and physical
7. If a hospital nurse telephoned and asked you to read the results of the patient's last CBC, what would you be searching for?
   a. carcinoma basal cell report
   b. complete blood count
   c. congenital blindness, complete report
8. If you were asked to make a photocopy of the patient's last CT, what would you be searching for?
   a. chemotherapy record
   b. connective tissue report
   c. computed tomography scan

Self-Study 4–1 *ICD-9-CM* Review Questions

1. The system for coding and billing diagnoses is found in a book entitled ***International Classification of Diseases, 9th Revision, Clinical Modification.***
2. For retrieving types of diagnoses related to pathology by an institution within an institution, the coding system is found in a book entitled ***Systematized Nomenclature of Human and Veterinary Medicine (SNOMED International)***
3. Why is it important that diagnostic *ICD-9-CM* coding become routinely used in the physician's office? **Diagnostic coding should be routinely used in the physician's office to assure accuracy of reporting patient's diagnosis and so the physician's future profiles reflect more realistic payments.**
4. The abbreviation *ICD-9-CM* means **International Classification of Diseases, Ninth Revision, Clinical Modification.**
5. The coding in *ICD-9-CM* varies from **3** to **5** characters.
6. Volume 1, Diseases, is **a/an tabular or numerical** listing of code numbers.
7. Volume 2, Diseases, is **a/an alphabetic** index or listing of code numbers.
8. The abbreviation NEC appearing in the *ICD-9-CM* code books means **not elsewhere classifiable.**
9. To code using Volume 2, the Alphabetic Index, the **condition** is looked up rather than the anatomic part.
10. E codes are a supplementary classification of coding for **external causes of injury** rather than disease and of coding for **adverse reactions to medications**.

Self-Study 4–2 *ICD-10* Review Questions

1. *ICD-10* was created by:
   a. National Center for Health Statistics
   b. World Health Organization
   c. Centers for Disease Control
   d. Health Care Financing Administration
2. *ICD-10-CM* was developed by:
   a. National Center for Health Statistics
   b. World Health Organization
   c. Centers for Disease Control
   d. Health Care Financing Administration
3. *ICD-10-PCS* (Procedure Coding System) was created by:
   a. National Center for Health Statistics
   b. World Health Organization
   c. Centers for Disease Control
   d. Health Care Financing Administration
4. The disease codes in *ICD-10-CM* have a maximum of:
   a. 3 digits
   b. 4 digits
   c. 5 digits
   d. 6 digits
5. Reason(s) the Clinical Modification was developed is/are:
   a. Removal of procedural codes
   b. Removal of unique mortality codes
   c. Removal of multiple codes

d. Only a and c
e. Only b
f. All of the above

6. *ICD-10-PCS* procedure codes have:
   a. 4 digits
   b. 5 digits
   c. 6 digits
   d. 7 digits
7. The first 3 digits of a 7-digit *ICD-10-PCS* code are the:
   a. Code category
   b. Surgical approach
   c. Specific anatomic body part
   d. Type of medical and/or prosthetic device used
8. One of the reasons for *ICD-10-PCS* is that:
   a. *ICD-9-CM* was not capable of necessary expansion
   b. *ICD-9-CM* was not as comprehensive as it should be
   c. *ICD-9-CM* included diagnostic information
   d. All of the above
9. The letters "I" and "O" are (were) used in:
   a. *ICD-9-CM*
   b. *ICD-10-CM* Diseases
   c. *ICD-10-PCS*
   d. None of the above

Self-Study 5-1 Review Questions

1. The coding system used for billing professional medical services and procedures is found in a book entitled ***Current Procedural Terminology.***
2. The Medicare program uses a system of coding composed of three levels, and this is called **Health Care Financing Administration Common Procedure Coding System (HCPCS).**
3. Complications or special circumstances about a medical service or procedure may be shown by using a CPT code with a/an **modifier.**
4. A relative value scale or schedule is a listing of procedure codes indicating the relative value of services performed, which is shown by **unit values.**
5. Name three methods for basing payments adopted by insurance companies and state and federal programs.
   a. **Fee schedule**
   b. **Relative Value Schedule (RVS)**
   c. **Usual, customary, and reasonable (UCR)**
6. List four programs or plans when a medical practice may elect to use more than one fee schedule.
   a. **Providers participating in the Medicare program typically have a fee schedule for Medicare patients and one for non-Medicare patients.**
   b. **Providers not participating in the Medicare program typically have two fee schedules, one based on limiting charges for each service set by the Medicare program, and one used for non-Medicare patients.**
   c. **Providers having a contractual arrangement with a managed care plan probably have additional fee schedules in use.**
   d. **Providers rendering services to those who have sustained industrial injuries use a separate workers' compensation fee schedule.**
7. Name the six main sections of *CPT.*
   a. **Evaluation and Management**
   b. **Anesthesia**
   c. **Surgery**
   d. **Radiology, Nuclear Medicine, and Diagnostic Ultrasound**
   e. **Pathology and Laboratory**
   f. **Medicine**
8. Match the symbol in the first column with the definitions in the second column. Write the correct letters on the blanks.

▶◀	**d**	a. New code
●	**a**	b. Modifier -51 exempt
*	**f**	c. Add-on code
⃠	**b**	d. New or revised text
+	**c**	e. Revised code
▲	**e**	f. Service includes surgical procedure only

9. Name four hospital departments where critical care of a patient may take place.
   a. **coronary care unit (CCU)**
   b. **intensive care unit (ICU)**
   c. **respiratory care unit (RCU)**
   d. **emergency department (ED) or emergency room (ER)**
10. A surgical package includes
    a. **surgical procedure**
    b. **infiltration, digital block, or topical anesthesia**
    c. **normal uncomplicated postoperative care (follow-up hospital visits, discharge, and/or follow-up office visits)**
11. Medicare global surgery policy includes
    a. **preoperative visit (1 day before or day of surgery)**
    b. **intraoperative services that are a usual and necessary part of the surgical procedure**
    c. **complications after surgery that do not require additional trips to the operating room**
    d. **postoperative visits, including hospital visits, discharge, and office visit for variable postoperative period (0, 10, or 90 days)**
12. A function of computer software that performs online checking of codes on an insurance claim to detect improper code submission is called a/an **code edit.**
13. A single code that describes two or more component codes bundled together as one unit is known as a/an **comprehensive code.**
14. Codes grouped together that are related to a procedure are referred to as **bundled.**
15. Use of many procedural codes to identify procedures that may be described by one code is termed **unbundling, also known as "exploding" or "á la carte" medicine.**
16. A code used on a claim that does not match the code system used by the insurance carrier and is converted to the closest code rendering less payment is termed **downcoding.**
17. Intentional manipulation of procedural codes to generate increased reimbursement is called **upcoding.**
18. Give eight reasons for using modifiers on insurance claims.
    a. **A service or procedure has professional and technical components.**
    b. **A service or procedure was performed by more than one physician and/or in more than one location.**

c. **A service or procedure has been increased or reduced.**
d. **A service or procedure was provided more than once.**
e. **Only part of a service was performed.**
f. **An adjunctive service was performed.**
g. **A bilateral procedure was performed.**
h. **Unusual events occurred.**

19. Match the symbol in the first column with the definitions in the second column. Write the correct letters on the blanks.

-21	**f**	a. Unusual procedural services
-22	**a**	b. Multiple procedures
-25	**e**	c. Staged or related procedure
-26	**h**	d. Decision for surgery
-51	**b**	e. Significant, separately identifiable E/M service by the same physician on the same day of the procedure or other service
-52	**g**	f. Prolonged evaluation and management services
-57	**d**	g. Reduced services
-58	**c**	h. Professional component

20. What modifier is usually used when billing for an assistant surgeon? **-80**
21. Explain when to use the -99 or 09999 modifier code.* **If a procedure requires more than one modifier code, a multiple two-digit code (-99) after the usual five-digit code number, is typed on one line, or a separate five-digit code (09999) is typed on a separate line.**

Self-Study 5-2 Define Medical Abbreviations

I & D	**incision and drainage**
IM	**intramuscular**
Pap	**Papanicolaou (smear, stain)**
ER	**emergency room**
EEG	**electroencephalograph (gram)**
DPT	**diphtheria, pertussis, tetanus**
ECG	**electrocardiogram(graph)**
IUD	**intrauterine device**
OB	**obstetrics**
D & C	**dilatation & curettage**
OV	**office visit**
KUB	**kidneys, ureters, bladder**
GI	**gastrointestinal**
Hgb	**hemoglobin**
new pt	**new patient**
rt	**right**
UA	**urinalysis**
est pt	**established patient**
ASHD	**arteriosclerotic heart disease**
tet. tox.	**tetanus toxoid**
CBC	**complete blood count**
E/M	**Evaluation & Management (code)**
CPT	**Current Procedural Terminology**
Ob-Gyn	**obstetrics & gynecology**
TURP	**transurethral resection of prostate**
cm	**centimeter**
T & A	**tonsillectomy & adenoidectomy**
mL	**milliliter**
inj	**injection**
hx	**history**
NC	**no charge**

Self-Study 6-1 Review Quesitons

1. Who developed the Standard Form? **Health Insurance Association of America and American Medical Association.**
2. State the name of the insurance form approved by the American Medical Association. **Health Insurance Claim Form (HCFA-1500).**
3. Does Medicare accept the HCFA-1500 claim form? **Yes.**
4. What important document must you have before an insurance company can photocopy a patient's chart? **Release of information form signed by the patient.**
5. What is dual coverage? **When the patient has two insurance policies and one is considered primary and the other secondary.**
6. The insurance company with the first responsibility for payment of a bill for medical services is known as the **primary payer.**
7. Match the word from the left column with its definition in the right column.

clean claim	**g**	a. Insurance carrier is unable to process a claim for a certain service and claim is held until system changes are made.
paper claim	**c**	b. A phrase used when a claim is held back from payment.
invalid claim	**h**	c. Claim submitted and then optically scanned by the insurance carrier and converted to electronic form.
dirty claim	**d**	d. Claim that needs manual processing because of errors or to solve a problem.
electronic claim	**f**	e. Claim needing clarification and answers to questions.
suspense claim	**b**	f. Claim submitted via telephone, fax, or computer modem.
rejected claim	**e**	g. Claim submitted within the time limit and correctly completed.
dingy claim	**a**	h. Medicare claim that contains complete, necessary information but is illogical or incorrect.

8. If the patient brings in a private insurance form that is not group insurance, where do you send the form after completion? **To the insurance company.**
9. Match the phrase in the first column with the definitions in the second column. Write the correct letters on the blanks.

State license number	**f**	a. A number issued by the federal government to each individual for personal use.
Employer identification number	**i**	b. A number issued by the Medicare program to
Social Security number	**a**	
Provider identification number	**j**	

*_Current Procedural Terminology_ codes, descriptions, and two-digit numeric modifiers only are from _CPT 2001_. Copyright © 2000, American Medical Association. All rights reserved.

Unique provider identification number	e	a. Issued to each member of a group at each specific site of medical practice.
Performing provider identification number	b	
		c. A Medicare lifetime provider number.
Group provider number	d	
National Provider Identifier	c	d. A number listed on a claim when submitting insurance claims to insurance companies under a group name.
Durable Medical Equipment number	g	
Facility provider number	h	
		e. A number issued by the Medicare program to each physician who treats and submits claims to this program.
		f. A number a physician must obtain to practice in a state.
		g. A number used when billing for supplies and equipment.
		h. A number issued to a hospital.
		i. An individual physician's federal tax identification number issued by the Internal Revenue Service.
		j. A number issued by the insurance carrier to every physician who renders services to patients.

10. An insurance claim is returned for the reason "diagnosis incomplete." State solution(s) to this problem on how you would try to obtain reimbursement. **Verify and submit correct diagnostic codes by referring to an updated diagnostic code book and reviewing the patient record. Check with the physician if diagnosis code listed does not go with the procedure code shown.**
11. Indicate whether the following statements are True (T) or False (F).
    a. A photocopy of a claim form may be optically scanned. **F**
    b. Handwriting is permitted on optically scanned insurance claims. **F**
    c. Do not fold or crease an insurance form that will be optically scanned. **T**
    d. Never strike over errors when making a correction on a claim form that is to be optically scanned. **T**
12. When preparing a claim that is to be optically scanned, birth dates are keyed in using **8** digits.
13. Define this abbreviation: MG/MCD. **Medigap and Medicaid coverage.**
14. A HCFA-assigned National Provider Identifier (NPI), number consists of **10** characters.

Self-Study 6-6 Review Patient Record Abbreviations

1. What do these abbreviations mean?

a. PTR	**patient to return**
b. TURP	**transurethral resection of prostate**
c. HX	**history**
d. IVP	**intravenous pyelogrm**
e c̄	**with**
f. Dx	**diagnosis**
g. BP	**blood pressure**
h. CC	**chief complaint**
i. UA	**urinalysis**
j. PE	**physical examination**

2. Give the abbreviations for the following terms.

a. return	**RTN or rtn**
b. cancer, carcinoma	**CA or Ca**
c. patient	**Pt**
d. established	**est**
e. discharged	**DC or disch**
f. gallbladder	**gb or GB**
g. initial	**init**

Self-Study 7-1 Review Questions

1. Insurance claims prepared on a computer and submitted via modem (telephone lines) to the insurance carrier's computer system is known as **electronic claim submission**.
2. The process by which understandable data items are sent back and forth via computer linkages between two or more entities functioning as sender and receiver is known as **electronic data interchange**.
3. Match the terms below with the definitions that follow:

a. batch	k. local area network (LAN)
b. software	l. keypad
c. clearinghouse	m. soft copy
d. hardware	n. input
e. RAM	o. file
f. ROM	p. hard copy
g. CPU	q. modem
h. smart card	r. memory
i. swipe card	s. disk
j. back up	

1. **e** Memory into which the user can enter information and instructions and from which the user can call up data.
2. **l** A device that contains keys to control mathematical functions.
3. **p** A printout.
4. **k** Two or more interconnected computers.
5. **g** The brains of a computer device controlling the internal memory, which directs the flow and processing of information.
6. **j** A duplicate data file.
7. **n** Data that go into a computer memory bank.
8. **o** A single, stored unit of information assigned a file name.
9. **q** A device that converts data into signals for telephone transmission.
10. **m** That which is displayed on a CRT screen.
11. **s** A magnetic storage device.
12. **r** Storage in a computer.
13. **b** Instructions required to make hardware perform a certain task.
14. **d** Physical components of a computer system.
15. **a** Group of claims for many patients submitted in one computer transmission from one office.

16. **f** Computer memory permanently programmed with a group of frequently used instructions.
17. **h** Card containing a computer chip allowing storage of a variety of information.
18. **c** Third-party administrator who receives transmission of claims, separates them, and sends each one to the correct insurance payer.
19. **i** Card with a magnetic stripe containing a small-capacity microchip that holds small amounts of information.

4. When electronically transmitting a claim directly to an insurance carrier, insurance billing specialists may be made aware of errors immediately and can make corrections using a process called **error-edit process. Optional answers: front-end edit process or on-line error checking**.
5. To maintain confidentiality and enhance security, **passwords** or **access codes** should be developed and changed at regular intervals.
6. To prevent computer and data file damage caused by electric power spikes, computer equipment may be plugged into a/an **surge suppressor**.
7. Two types of computer claim systems that may be used when transmitting insurance claims via modem to insurance carriers are **carrier-direct** and **clearing-house**.
8. An individual who converts insurance claims to standardized electronic formats and transmits them to the insurance carrier is known as a/an **electronic claims processor or professional (ECP)**.
9. For electronic insurance claims, an assignment of benefits agreement requires that each patient's signature be obtained either **once a month, once a year**, or **on a one-time basis**.
10. Forms used for verifying data regarding services rendered to each patient during a visit are called **multipurpose billing form. Optional answers: charge slip, communicator, encounter form, fee ticket, patient service slip, routing form, superbill or transaction slip**.
11. Mrs. James comes in for an office visit to see Dr. Doe on March 12. She returns again on March 14, 15, and 16. Abbreviated routing slips for E & M procedural codes used by Dr. Doe's office are called **crib sheets or charge slips**.
12. Codes required when electronically transmitting claims are:
    a. **Medicare HCPCS national and regional codes for services, supplies, and procedures**
    b. **CPT codes with modifiers**
    c. **ICD-9-CM diagnostic codes**
13. After receiving a faxed insurance claim, some insurance carriers send a **faxback** report.
14. State the definition of an electronic remittance notice. **An on-line transaction about the status of a claim**.
15. Various limiting conditions and guidelines that tell the computer to deny, review, or pay transmitted insurance claims are known as **screens or parameters**.

Self-Study 7–5 Review Patient Record Abbreviations

Abbreviations pertinent to the record of Brad E. Diehl:

abt	**about**	AP	**anteroposterior**
adv	**advise**	BP	**blood pressure**
CBC	**complete blood count**	neg	**negative**
cm	**centimeter**	Pt	**patient**
Dx	**diagnosis**	WBC	**white blood [cell] count**
ECG	**electrocardiogram**	WNL	**within normal limits**
hr	**hour**	wk	**week**
lat	**lateral**	$\bar{c}$	**with**
mo	**month**		

Abbreviations pertinent to the record of Evert I. Strain:

adv	**advise**	hosp	**hospital**
ASHD	**arteriosclerotic heart disease**	ltd	**limited**
BP	**blood pressure**	PE	**physical examination**
DC	**discharge**	pt	**patient**
Dx	**diagnosis**	SGOT	**serum glutamic oxaloacetic transaminase**
est	**established**		

Self-Study 8–1 Review Questions

1. Name provisions seen in health insurance policies.
    a. **The claimant is obligated to notify the insurance company of a loss within a certain period of time or the insurance company can deny benefits.**
    b. **If the insured is in disagreement with the insurer for settlement of a claim, a suit must begin within 3 years after the claim was submitted.**
    c. **An insured person cannot bring legal action against an insurance company until 60 days after a claim is submitted to the insurance company.**
    d. **The insurance company is obligated to pay benefits promptly when a claim is submitted.**
2. After an insurance claim is processed by the insurance carrier (paid, suspended, rejected, or denied), a document known as a/an **explanation of benefits** is sent to the patient and to the provider of professional medical services.

3. Name other items that indicate the patient's responsibility to pay that may appear on the document explaining the payment and check issued by the insurance carrier.
   a. **amount not covered**
   b. **copayment amount**
   c. **deductible**
   d. **coinsurance**
   e. **other insurance payment**
   f. **patient's total responsibility**
4. After receiving an explanation of benefits document and posting insurance payment, the copy of the insurance claim form is put into a file marked **closed claims**.
5. A state department or agency that helps resolve insurance conflicts and verifies that insurance contracts are carried out in good faith is known as a/an **insurance commission of the state**.
6. When an insurance company continually pays slow on insurance claims, it may help speed up payments if a formal written complaint is made to the **insurance commissioner**.
7. To locate delinquent insurance claims on an insurance claim register quickly, which column should be looked at first? **Data claim paid column**. Would it appear blank or completed? **Blank**.
8. When no payment has been received from an insurance company, what follow-up should take place? **A tracer**.
9. Name some of the principal procedures that should be followed in good bookkeeping and record-keeping practice when a payment has been received from an insurance company. **Pull out copies of the insurance claims that correspond with the payments and dispose of them, post payment to the patient's ledger and to the day sheet, and deposit the payment check in the bank.**
10. In good office management, to track submitted pending or resubmitted insurance claims, a/an **tickler, suspense, or follow-up file** is used.
11. Two routine procedures to include in a reminder system to track pending claims are
    a. **divide active claims by month**.
    b. **file active claims in chronologic order by date of service**.
12. It is reasonable to assume that a private insurance claim would become delinquent after **4 to 6** weeks and a TRICARE claim after **8 to 12** weeks.
13. When making an inquiry about a claim by telephone, efficient secretarial procedure would be to **document the date, time of the call, name of the person spoken to and their telephone extension, and outline or briefly note the conversation**.
14. Two categories of claim denials are **technical errors** and **medical coverage policy issues**.
15. State the solution if a claim has been denied because the professional service rendered was for an injury that is being considered as compensable under workers' compensation. **Locate the insurance carrier for the industrial injury and send them a report of the case with a bill. Notify the patient's health insurance carrier monthly to let them know the status of the case**.
16. The best solution to prevent downcoding is to **monitor reimbursements and monitor downcodes to discover which codes are affected. Ask the insurance carrier which code system is in use and obtain the code book.**
17. This question is presented to enhance your skill in critical thinking. Using your diagnostic code book, look up the *ICD-9-CM* diagnostic code for a patient being treated for a perforated and hemorrhaging gastric ulcer, with no mention of whether it was acute or chronic. To code such a case, what would you do and why? **Use code 531.5 or ask the physician if the condition was acute 531.2 or chronic 531.6. Since there are fourth and fifth digits with this code category, try not to list the diagnosis as unspecified 531.9, because use of many unspecified codes may result in downcoding or denial of the claim**.
18. At the time of his first office visit, Mr. Doi signed an Assignment of Benefits, and Dr. James' office submitted a claim to ABC Insurance Company. Mr. Doi received, in error, a check from the insurance company and cashed it. What step(s) should be taken by Dr. James' office after this error is discovered?
    a. **Call the insurance company**.
    b. **Call the patient or send a letter by certified mail.**
    c. **File a complaint with the state insurance commissioner**.
19. If an appeal of an insurance claim is not successful, the next step to proceed with is a/an **peer review**.
20. Name the six levels for appealing a Medicare claim.
    a. **inquiry**
    b. **review**
    c. **fair hearing**
    d. **administrative law judge hearing**
    e. **appeals council review**
    f. **federal district court hearing**
21. Medicare reviews by the insurance carrier are usually completed within **30** to **45** days.
22. A Medicare patient has insurance with United American (a Medigap policy), and payment has not been received from the Medigap insurer within a reasonable length of time. State the action to take in this case. **Contact the insurance company and state that if you do not receive payment you will contact the state insurance commissioner**.
23. A TRICARE explanation of benefits is received stating that the allowable charge for Mrs. Dayton's office visit is $30. Is it possible to appeal this for additional payment? **Generally, when the TRICARE contractor determines the allowable charge for a certain medical service, it is nonappealable**.

Self-Study 9–1 Review Questions

1. Third party payers are composed of
   a. **private insurance**
   b. **government plans**
   c. **managed care contracts**
   d. **workers' compensation**
2. The unpaid balance due from patients for professional services rendered is known as a/an **accounts receivable**.
3. Write the formula for calculating the office A/R ratio: **divide the month-end accounts receivable balance by the monthly average of the medical practice charge for the prior 12-month period.**

4. What is the collection rate if a total of $40,300 was collected for the month and the total of the accounts receivable is $50,670? **80%**
5. An important document that provides identifying data for each patient and assists in billing and collection is called a/an **patient registration form or patient information sheet**.
6. A preferable term for "write-off" when used in a medical practice is **courtesy adjustment**.
7. To verify a check, ask the patient for a/an **driver's license** and **one other form of identification**.
8. The procedure of systematically arranging the accounts receivable by age from the date of service is called **age analysis**.
9. A system of billing accounts at spaced intervals during the month based on breakdown of accounts by alphabet, account number, insurance type, or date of service is known as **cycle billing**.
10. Are physicians' patient accounts single-entry accounts, open book accounts, or written contract accounts? **Open book accounts**.
11. Match the terms with the definitions.

1. **d**	Reductions of the normal fee based on a specific amount of money or a percentage of the charge	a. debtor
2. **g**	Phrase to remind a patient about a delinquent account	b. itemized statement
3. **h**	Item that permits bank customers to withdraw cash at any hour from an automated teller machine	c. fee schedule
4. **a**	Individual owing money	d. discounts
5. **i**	Claim on the property of another as security for a debt	e. ledger card
6. **e**	Individual record indicating charges, payments, adjustments, and balances owed for services rendered	f. creditor
7. **b**	Detailed summary of all transactions of a creditor's account	g. dun message
8. **f**	Person to whom money is owed	h. debit card
9. **c**	Listing of accepted charges or established allowances for specific medical procedures	i. lien

12. A court order attaching a debtor's property or wages to pay off a debt is known as **garnishment**.
13. Match the terms with the definitions.
    a. Equal Credit Opportunity Act
    b. Fair Credit Reporting Act
    c. Fair Credit Billing Act
    d. Truth in Lending Act
    e. Fair Debt Collection Practices Act
    1. **c** Law stating that a person has 60 days from the date that a statement is mailed to complain about an error
    2. **d** Consumer protection act that applies to anyone who charges interest or agrees on payment of a bill in more than four installments, excluding a down payment
    3. **e** Regulates collection practices of third party debt collectors and attorneys who collect debts for others
    4. **a** Federal law prohibiting discrimination in all areas of granting credit
    5. **b** Regulates agencies who issue or use credit reports on consumers
14. An individual who owes on an account and moves, leaving no forwarding address, is called a/an **skip**.
15. A straight petition in bankruptcy or absolute bankruptcy is also known as a/an **Chapter 7**.
16. A wage earner's bankruptcy is sometimes referred to as a/an **Chapter 13**.
17. Translate these credit and collection abbreviations.

NSF	**not sufficient funds**	T	**telephoned**
WCO	**will call office**	SK	**skip or skipped**
PIF	**payment in full**	FN	**final notice**
NLE	**no longer employed**	UE	**unemployed**

Self-Study 10-1 Review Questions

1. If a physician or hospital in a managed care plan is paid a fixed, per capita amount for each patient enrolled regardless of the type and number of services rendered, this is a payment system known as **capitation**.
2. When a prepaid group practice plan limits the patient's choice of personal physicians, this is termed a/an **closed panel** program.
3. In a managed care setting, a physician who controls patient access to specialists and diagnostic testing services is known as a/an **gatekeeper**.
4. Systems that allow for better negotiations for contracts with large employers are
   a. **managed care organizations (MCOs)**
   b. **physician–hospital organizations**
   c. **group practices accepting a variety of MCOs and fee for service patients**
5. The oldest of the prepaid health plans is **health maintenance organizations (HMOs)**.
6. Name three types of HMOs.
   a. **prepaid group practice model**
   b. **staff model**
   c. **network HMO**
7. What is a foundation for medical care? **An organization of physicians sponsored by a state or local medical association concerned with the development and delivery of medical services and the cost of health care.**
8. Name two types of operations used by foundations for medical care and explain the main feature of each.
   a. **comprehensive type: Designs and sponsors prepaid health programs or sets minimum benefits of coverage.**
   b. **claims-review type: Provides evaluation of the quality and efficiency of services by a panel of physicians to the numerous fiscal agents involved in its area, including the ones processing Medicare and Medicaid.**
9. A health benefit program in which enrollees may choose any physician or hospital for services but obtain a higher level of benefits if preferred providers are used is known as a/an **preferred provider organization (PPO)**.

10. HMOs and PPOs consisting of a network of physicians and hospitals that provide an insurance company or employer with discounts on their services are referred to as a/an **point-of-service (POS) plan**.
11. Professional review organizations are established to determine and assure **quality and operation of health care through a process called peer review**.
12. Name the three responsibilities and/or tasks of the PROs.
    a. **one or more physicians working with the federal government under federal guidelines evaluate another physician in regard to quality and efficiency of professional care**
    b. **examines evidence for admission and discharge of a patient from the hospital**
    c. **settles disputes on fees**
13. To control health care costs, the process of reviewing and establishing medical necessity for services and providers' use of medical care resources is termed **utilization review**.
14. Explain the meaning of a "stop-loss" provision that might appear in a managed care contract. **If the patient's services go over a certain amount, then the physician may ask the patient to pay.**
15. When a certain percentage of the premium fund is set aside to operate an individual practice association, this is known as a/an **withhold**.
16. Mark the following statements as True (T) or False (F).
    a. An HMO can be sponsored and operated by a foundation. **T**
    b. Peer review determines the quality and operation of health care. **T**
    c. An employer may offer the services of an HMO clinic if he or she has five or more employees. **F**
    d. Medicare and Medicaid beneficiaries may not join an HMO. **F**
    e. Managed care withheld amounts that are not yet received from the managed care plan by the medical practice should be shown as a write-off in an accounts journal. **F**

Self-Study 11-1 Review Questions

1. An individual becomes eligible for Medicare Parts A and B at age **65**.
2. Medicare Part A is **hospital** coverage and Medicare Part B is **outpatient** coverage.
3. An eligibility requirement for aliens to receive Medicare benefits is that a/an **applicant must have lived in the United States as a permanent resident for 5 consecutive years**.
4. Funding for the Medicare Part A program is obtained from **special contributions from employees and self-employed persons, with employers matching contributions**, and for the Medicare Part B program funding is obtained equally from **those who sign up for Medicare and from the federal government**.
5. Define a Medicare Part A hospital benefit period. **Begins the day a patient enters a hospital and ends when the patient has not been a bed patient in any hospital or skilled nursing facility for 60 consecutive days. It also ends if a patient has been in a nursing facility but has not received skilled nursing care there for 60 consecutive days.**
6. A program designed to provide pain relief, symptom management, and supportive services to terminally ill individuals and their families is known as **hospice**.
7. Short-term inpatient medical care for terminally ill individuals to give temporary relief to the caregiver is known as **respite care**.
8. The frequency of Pap tests for Medicare patients is **once every 3 years** and for mammograms, **annual for women aged 40 years and older, plus a one-time baseline mammogram for women aged 35 to 39**.
9. Policies offered by third party payers that fall under guidelines issued by the federal government and cover prescription costs, Medicare deductibles, and copayments are known as **Medigap or Medifill** insurance policies.
10. Name two types of policies for Medicare supplemental insurance.
    a. **service benefit or incurred type**
    b. **indemnity benefit type**
11. If an individual is 65 years of age and a Medicare beneficiary but is working and has a group insurance policy, where is the insurance claim form sent initially? **To the employer's sponsored plan.**
12. If a person on Medicare is injured in an automobile accident, the physician submits the claim form to **the automobile or liability insurance company**.
13. Name two types of HMO plans that may have Medicare Part B contracts.
    a. **HMO risk plans**
    b. **HMO cost plans**
14. The federal laws that prohibit a physician from referring a patient to a laboratory in which he or she has a financial interest are known as **Stark I and II regulations**.
15. The federal laws establishing standards of quality control and safety measures in clinical laboratories are known as **the Clinical Laboratory Improvement Amendment of 1988**.
16. A participating physician who accepts assignment means he or she agrees to **accept payment from Medicare (80% of the approved charges) plus payment from the patient (20% of the approved charges)** after the **$100** deductible has been met.
17. Philip Lenz is seen by Dr. Doe, who schedules an operative procedure in 1 month. This type of surgery is known as **elective** since it does not have to be performed immediately.
18. A Medicare insurance claim form showed a number, J0540, for an injection of 600,000 units of penicillin G. This number is referred to as a/an **HCFA Common Procedure Coding System (HCPCS) Level II code number**.
19. Organizations or claims processors under contract to the federal government that handle insurance claims and payments for hospitals under Medicare Part A are known as **fiscal intermediaries** and those that process claims for physicians and other suppliers of services under Medicare Part B are called **carriers or fiscal agents**.

20. An HCFA-assigned provider identification number is known as a/an **PIN, UPIN, PPIN, or National Provider Identifier (NPI)**. Physicians who supply durable medical equipment must have a/an **DME supplier** number.
21. If circumstances make it impossible to obtain a signature on an insurance claim from a Medicare patient, physicians may obtain a/an **lifetime beneficiary claim authorization and information release form**.
22. The time limit for sending in a Medicare insurance claim is **the end of the calendar year following the fiscal year in which services were used. Example: Oct. 1, 2001, to Sept. 30, 2002, bill by December 31, 2002**.
23. Mrs. Davis, a Medi-Medi patient, has a cholecystectomy. In completing the insurance claim form, the assignment portion is left blank in error. What will happen in this case? **Only Medicare processing will occur and the payment check will go directly to the patient. Medicaid will not pay**.

Self-Study 12-1 Review Questions

1. Medicaid is administered by **state governments** with partial **federal** funding.
2. Medicaid is not an insurance program. It is a/an **assistance** program.
3. In all other states the program is known as Medicaid but in California the program is called **Medi-Cal**.
4. Because the federal government sets minimum requirements, states are free to enhance the Medicaid program. Name two ways Medicaid programs vary from state to state.
   a. **coverage**
   b. **benefits**
5. MCHP means **Maternal and Child Health Programs** and covers children of what age group? **Under 21 years of age**.
6. What people might be eligible for Medicaid?
   a. **certain needy and low-income people**
   b. **the aged (65 years or older)**
   c. **the blind**
   d. **the disabled**
   e. **members of families with dependent children (one parent) financially eligible**
7. Name two broad classifications of people eligible for Medicaid assistance.
   a. **categorically needy**
   b. **medically needy**
8. When professional services are rendered, the Medicaid identification card or electronic verification must show eligibility for (circle one):
   a. day of service c. **month of service**
   b. year of service d. week of service
9. The name of the program for the prevention, early detection, and treatment of conditions of welfare children is known as **Early and Periodic Screening, Diagnosis, and Treatment**. It is abbreviated as **EPSDT. Optional answer for California: Child Health and Disability Prevention (CHDP) program**.
10. Define these abbreviations.
    a. MCD **Medicaid**
    b. SSI **Supplemental Security Income**
    c. AFDC **Aid to Families with Dependent Children**
    d. MI **Medically indigent**
11. Mrs. Ho suddenly experiences a pain in her right lower abdominal area and rushes to a local hospital for emergency care. Laboratory work verifies that she has a ruptured appendix and immediate surgery is recommended. Is prior authorization required in a bona fide emergency situation like this? **No.** What two blocks on the HCFA-1500 claim form need to be completed for emergency services? **Block 24I and in Block 19 enter an emergency certification statement or include an attachment to the claim with this data.**
12. Your Medicaid patient seen today needs chronic hemodialysis services. You telephone for authorization to get verbal approval. Four important items to obtain are:
    a. **date of authorization**
    b. **name of the person who authorized**
    c. **approximate time of day authorization is given**
    d. **verbal number given by field office**
13. The time limit for submitting a Medicaid claim varies from **2 months** to **1 year** from the date the service is rendered. In your state, the time limit is (**answer will vary depending on state laws)**.
14. The insurance claim form for submitting Medicaid claims in all states is **Health Insurance Claim Form HCFA-1500**.
15. Your Medicaid patient also has TRICARE. What billing procedure do you follow? Be exact in your steps for a dependent of an active military person.
    a. **Bill TRICARE first**
    b. **Bill Medicaid second and attach an Explanation of Benefits from TRICARE to the billing form**
16. When a Medicaid patient is injured in an automobile accident and the car has liability insurance, the insurance claim is sent to the (circle one):
    a. patient
    b. **automobile insurance carrier**
    c. Medicaid fiscal agent
17. Five categories of adjudicated claims that may appear on a Medicaid Remittance Advice document are
    a. **adjustments**
    b. **approvals**
    c. **denials**
    d. **suspends**
    e. **audit/refund transactions**
18. Name three levels of Medicaid appeals.
    a. **regional fiscal intermediary or Medicaid bureau**
    b. **Department of Welfare**
    c. **appellate court**

Self-Study 13-1 Review Questions

1. CHAMPUS, the acronym for Civilian Health and Medical Program of the Uniformed Services, is now called **TRICARE** and was organized to control escalating medical costs and to standardize benefits for active-duty families and military retirees.
2. An active duty service member is known as a/an **sponsor;** once retired, this former member is called a/an **service or military retiree**.
3. Individuals who qualify for TRICARE are known as **beneficiaries**.

4. A system for verifying an individual's TRICARE eligibility is called **Defense Enrollment Eligibility Reporting System (DEERS)**.
5. Mrs. Hancock, a TRICARE beneficiary, lives 2 miles from a Uniformed Services Medical Treatment Facility and wishes to be hospitalized for surgery at Orlando Medical Center, a civilian hospital. What type of authorization does she require? **Inpatient nonavailability statement (INAS)**.
6. TRICARE Standard and CHAMPVA beneficiary identification cards are issued to **dependents 10 years of age and older** and **retirees**. Information must be obtained from **front** and **back** of the card and placed on the health insurance claim form.
7. Programs that allow TRICARE Standard beneficiaries to receive treatment, services, or supplies from civilian providers are called **cooperative care** and **partnership**.
8. The TRICARE Standard deductible for outpatient care is how much per patient? **$150**. Per family? **$300**.
9. What percentage does TRICARE Standard pay on outpatient services after the deductible has been met for dependents of active duty members? **80%**. For retired members or their dependents? **75%**.
10. For retired members or their dependents on TRICARE Standard, what is their responsibility for outpatient service? **$150 deductible plus 25% of TRICARE allowable**.
11. A voluntary TRICARE health maintenance organization type of option is known as **TRICARE Prime**.
12. CHAMPVA is the acronym for **Civilian Health and Medical Program of the Veterans Administration**, now known as the **Department of Veterans Affairs**.
13. Those individuals that serve in the United States Armed Forces, finish their service, and are honorably discharged are known as a/an **veteran**.
14. CHAMPVA is not an insurance program but is considered as a/an **service benefit** program.
15. Name those individuals entitled to CHAMPVA medical benefits.
    a. **husband, wife, or unmarried child of a veteran with a total disability, permanent in nature, from a service-connected disability**
    b. **husband, wife, or unmarried child of a veteran who died because of service-connected disability or who, at the time of death, had a total disability, permanent in nature, resulting from a service-connected injury**
    c. **husband, wife, or unmarried child of an individual who died in the line of duty while on active service**
16. The public law establishing a person's right to review and contest inaccuracies in personal medical records is known as **Privacy Act of 1974**.
17. An organization that contracts with the government to process TRICARE and CHAMPVA health insurance claims is known as a/an **fiscal intermediary**.
18. The time limit for submitting a TRICARE Standard or CHAMPVA claim for Outpatient service is **within 1 year from date service is provided**. For inpatient service it is **1 year from patient's discharge from hospital**.
19. If a patient has other insurance besides TRICARE and is the dependent of an active military person, whom do you bill first? **Other insurance**.
20. If Jason Williams, a TRICARE beneficiary who became disabled at age 10 years and is also receiving Medicare Part A benefits, is seen for a consultation, whom do you bill first? **Medicare**.
21. A patient is seen as an emergency in the office who is a CHAMPVA and Medicaid beneficiary. Whom do you bill first? **CHAMPVA**.

Self-Study 14–1 Review Questions

1. Name two kinds of statutes under workers' compensation.
    a. **federal compensation laws**
    b. **state compensation laws**
2. An unforeseen, unexpected, unintended event that occurs at a particular time and place, causing injury to an individual not of his or her own making, is called a/an **accident**.
3. Maria Cardoza works in a plastics manufacturing company and inhales some fumes that cause bronchitis. Since this condition is associated with her employment, it is called a/an **occupational illness. Optional answer: industrial or workers' compensation illness.**
4. Name the federal workers' compensation acts that cover workers.
    a. **Workmen's Compensation Law of the District of Columbia**
    b. **Federal Coal Mine Health and Safety Act**
    c. **Federal Employees' Compensation Act**
    d. **Longshoremen's and Harbor Workers' Compensation Act**
5. State compensation laws that *require* each employer to accept its provisions and provide for specialized benefits for employees who are injured at work are called **compulsory laws**.
6. State compensation laws that *may be accepted or rejected* by the employer are known as **elective laws**.
7. State five methods used for funding workers' compensation.
    a. **monopolistic state or provincial fund**
    b. **employers may qualify as self-insurers**
    c. **territorial fund**
    d. **competitive state fund**
    e. **private insurance companies**
8. Who pays workers' compensation insurance premiums? **Employers**.
9. What is the time limit in your state for submitting the employer's and/or physician's report of an industrial accident? **Answers will vary; see *Handbook* Table 14–1.**
10. When an employee with a pre-existing condition is injured at work and the injury produces a disability greater than that caused by the second injury alone, the benefits are derived from a/an **subsequent or second-injury fund**.
11. Name jobs that may not be covered by workers' compensation insurance.
    a. **domestic or casual employees**
    b. **laborers**
    c. **babysitters**
    d. **charity workers**

e. **gardeners**
f. **newspaper vendors or distributors**

12. What are the minimum number of employees needed in your state before workers' compensation statutes become effective? **Answers will vary; see *Handbook* Table 14–2.**
13. What waiting period must elapse in your state before workers' compensation payments begin? **Answers will vary; see *Handbook* Table 14–3.**
14. List five types of workers' compensation benefits.
    a. **medical treatment**
    b. **temporary disability indemnity**
    c. **permanent disability indemnity**
    d. **death benefits**
    e. **rehabilitation benefits**
15. Who can treat an industrial injury? **Licensed physician, osteopath, dentist, or chiropractor.**
16. Three types of workers' compensation claims are
    a. **nondisability**
    b. **temporary disability**
    c. **permanent disability**
17. Explain the differences between these three types of claims.
    a. Nondisability claim: **Person is injured or ill, treated, and goes back to work. No disability from his or her job.**
    b. Temporary disability claim: **Person is injured or ill and cannot work at his or her job and is off work for a period of time.**
    c. Permanent disability claim: **Person is injured or ill, cannot work, and the problem results in permanent injury or illness.**
18. After suffering an industrial injury, Mr. Fields is in a treatment program in which he is given real work tasks for building strength and endurance. This form of therapy is called **work hardening.**
19. Define these abbreviations.
    a. **TD temporary disability**
    b. **PD permanent disability**
    c. **P & S permanent and stationary**
    d. **C & R compromise and release**
20. Weekly temporary disability payments are based on **the employees' earnings at the time of the injury or illness.**
21. When an industrial case reaches the time for rating the disability, this is accomplished by **the state's industrial accident commission or workers' compensation board.**
22. May an injured person appeal his or her case if not satisfied with the rating? **Yes.** If so, to whom does he or she appeal? **Workers' Compensation Appeals Board or Industrial Accident Commission.**
23. When a case of fraud or abuse is suspected in a workers' compensation case, the physician should report the situation to the **insurance carrier.**
24. Employers are required to meet health and safety standards for their employees under federal and state statutes known as the **Occupational Safety and Health Administration (OSHA) Act of 1970.**
25. A man takes his girlfriend to a roofing job and she is injured. Is she covered under workers' compensation insurance? **No.**
26. A proceeding during which an attorney questions a witness who answers under oath but not in open court is called a/an **deposition.**
27. The legal promise of a patient to satisfy a debt to the physician from proceeds received from a litigated case is termed a/an **lien.**
28. The process of carrying on a lawsuit is called **litigation.**
29. Explain third-party subrogation. **A third party is responsible for the injury (person is injured by an outside party).**
30. What is the first thing an employee should do after he or she is injured? **Notify his or her employer or immediate supervisor.**
31. When an individual suffers a work-related injury or illness, the employer must complete and send a form to the insurance company and workers' compensation state offices called a/an **Employer's Report of Occupational Injury or Illness**, and if the employee is sent to a physician's office for medical care, the employer must complete a form that authorizes the physician to treat the employee, called a/an **Medical Service Order.**
32. When a physician treats an industrial injury, he or she must complete a/an **First Treatment Medical Report or Doctor's First Report of Occupational Injury or Illness** and send it to the following:
    a. **insurance carrier**
    b. **employer**
    c. **state workers' compensation office**
    d. **retain a copy for the physician's files.**

    Is a stamped physician's signature acceptable on the form? **No, each copy must be signed in ink because it is a legal document.**
33. If the physician feels the injured employee is capable of returning to work after having been on temporary disability, what does the physician do? **Sends in a report to the insurance company giving the date for return to work.**
34. In a workers' compensation case, bills should be submitted **monthly** or **at the time of termination of treatment**, and a claim becomes delinquent after a time frame of **45 days.**
35. If an individual seeks medical care for a workers' compensation injury from another state, which state's regulations are followed? **The state (jurisdiction) where the claim originated and the accident or injury occurred.**

Self-Study 15-1 Review Questions

1. Health insurance that provides monthly or weekly income when an individual is unable to work because of a nonindustrial illness or injury is called **disability income insurance.**
2. Another insurance term for benefits is **indemnity.**
3. Some insurance contracts that pay twice the face amount of the policy if accidental death occurs may have a provision entitled **double indemnity.**
4. When an individual who is insured under a disability income insurance policy cannot perform one or more of his or her regular job duties, this is known as **residual** or **partial** disability.

5. When a person insured under a disability income insurance policy cannot perform all functions of his or her regular job duties for a limited period of time, this is known as **temporary** disability.
6. When investigating the purchase of insurance, the word(s) to look for in the insurance contract that mean the premium cannot be increased at renewal time is/are **noncancelable clause**.
7. When an individual becomes permanently disabled and cannot pay the insurance premium, a desirable provision in an insurance contract is **waiver of premium**.
8. Provisions that limit the scope of insurance coverage are known as **exclusions**.
9. Ezra Jackson has disability income insurance under a group policy paid for by his employer. One evening he goes roller blading and suffers a complex fracture of the patella requiring several months off work. Are his monthly disability benefits taxable? **Yes.** Why? **Because he has not made any contribution toward the premiums.**
10. Two federal programs for individuals under 65 years of age who suffer from a severe disability are:
    a. **Social Security Disability Insurance (SSDI)**
    b. **Supplemental Security Income (SSI)**
11. To be eligible to apply for disability benefits under Social Security, an individual must be unable to do any type of work for a period of **not less than 12 months.**
12. Social Security may hire a physician to evaluate an applicant's disability. A physician's role may be any one of the following:
    a. **physician treating the patient**
    b. **consultative examiner (CE)**
    c. **full- or part-time medical or psychologic consultant**
13. A Social Security division that determines an individual's eligibility to be placed under the federal disability program is called **Disability Determination Services.**
14. Jamie Woods, a Navy petty officer, suffers an accident aboard the USS *Denebola* just before his honorable discharge. To receive veteran's benefits for this injury, the time limit in which a claim must be filed is **within 1 year from date of sustaining the injury.**
15. Name the states and territory that have nonindustrial state disability programs.
    a. **California**
    b. **Hawaii**
    c. **New Jersey**
    d. **New York**
    e. **Puerto Rico**
    f. **Rhode Island**
16. List two states where hospital benefits may be paid for nonoccupational illness or injury under a state's temporary disability benefit program.
    a. **Hawaii under a prepaid health care program**
    b. **Puerto Rico under a prepaid health care program**
17. Temporary disability insurance claims must be filed within how many days in your state? **Answers will vary. See Table 15-1 in *Handbook*.**
18. How long can a person continue to draw temporary disability insurance benefits? **Answers will vary. See Table 15-1 in *Handbook*.**
19. After a claim begins, when do basic state disability benefits become payable if the patient is confined at home? **On the eighth day of consecutive disability or the first day of hospital confinement. In California, if disability extends to 22 days or beyond, benefits are paid from first day of disability.** If the patient is hospitalized? **First day of hospital confinement only in Hawaii and Puerto Rico.**
20. Nick Tyson has recovered from a previous temporary disability and becomes ill again with the same ailment. Is he entitled to state disability benefits? **Yes, if 15 days have elapsed.**
21. John S. Thatcher stubbed his toe as he was leaving work. Since the injury was only slightly uncomfortable, he thought no more about it. The next morning he found that his foot was too swollen to fit in his shoe, so he stayed home. When the swelling did not subside after 3 days, John went to the doctor. X-rays showed a broken toe, which kept John home for 2 weeks. After 1 week he applied for temporary state disability benefits. Will he be paid? **Yes** Why? **Benefits become payable on the eighth day of consecutive disability. (This also may depend on whether the injury is declared a work-related or industrial injury and whether the rate of workers' compensation is less than state disability benefits.)**
22. Peggy Jonson has an ectopic pregnancy and is unable to work because of this complication of her pregnancy. Can she receive state temporary disability benefits? **Yes.**
23. If a woman has an abnormal condition that arises out of her pregnancy (such as diabetes or varicose veins) and is unable to work because of the condition, can she receive state disability benefits? **Yes.** Four states that allow for maternity benefits in normal pregnancy are:
    a. **California**
    b. **Hawaii**
    c. **New Jersey**
    d. **Rhode Island**
24. Betty T. Kraft had to stay home from her job because her 10-year-old daughter had measles. She applied for temporary state disability benefits. Will she be paid? **No.** Why? **Betty must be ill or injured to collect benefits.**
25. Vincent P. Michael was ill with a bad cold for 1 week. Will he receive temporary state disability benefits? **No.** Why? **He must be ill more than 1 week to collect state disability.**
26. Betsy C. Palm had an emergency appendectomy and was hospitalized for 3 days. Will she receive state disability benefits? **Yes.** Why? **Because payment begins on the first day of hospital confinement.**
27. Frank E. Thompson is a boxboy at a supermarket on Saturdays and Sundays while a full-time student at college. He broke his leg while skiing so he cannot work at the market, but he is able to attend classes with his leg in a cast. Can he collect state disability benefits for his part-time job? **Yes.** Why? **As long as he has met the quarterly amount that is required to be put into the fund in the state, he is eligible.**
28. Jerry L. Slate is out of a job and is receiving unemployment insurance benefits. He is now suffering from a se-

vere case of intestinal flu. The employment office calls him to interview for a job but he is too ill to go. Can he collect temporary state disability benefits for this illness when he might have been given a job? **Yes.** Why? **Because at the time he gets the flu he can go on state disability as he is not able to go for a job interview.**

29. Joan T. Corman has diabetes, which sometimes makes her weak so that she has to leave work early in the afternoon. She loses pay for each hour she cannot work. Can she collect temporary state disability benefits? **No.** Why? **Because she has not been off work continuously for 7 days.**
30. While walking the picket line with other employees on strike, Gene J. Berry came down with pneumonia and was ill for 2 weeks. Can he collect temporary state disability benefits? **Yes.** Why? **Because he might have become ill whether the strike was on or not.** Gene went back to work for 3 weeks and then developed a slight cold and cough, which again was diagnosed as pneumonia. The doctor told him to stay home from work. Would he be able to collect temporary disability benefits again? **Yes.** Why? **Because more than 15 days had elapsed since his return to work and the recurrence of the illness.**
31. A month after he retired, Roger Reagan had a gallbladder operation. Can he receive temporary state disability benefits? **No.** Why? **Because he is retired and has no state disability insurance.**
32. Jane M. Lambert fell in the backyard of her home and fractured her left ankle. She had a nonunion fracture and was out of work for 28 weeks. For how long will she collect temporary state disability benefits? **Answers will vary. See Table 15–1 in *Handbook*.**
33. Dr. Kay examines Ben Yates and completes a claim form for state disability income due to a prolonged illness. On receiving the information, the insurance adjuster notices some conflicting data. Name other documents that may be requested to justify payment of benefits.
    a. **employer's records**
    b. **employee's wage statements and/or tax forms**
    c. **medical records of attending physician**
34. Trent Walters, a permanently disabled individual, applies for federal disability benefits. To establish eligibility for benefits under this program, data allowed must be **no more than 1** year(s) old.
35. A Veterans' Affairs patient is seen as an emergency by Dr. Onion. Name the two methods or options for billing this case.
    a. **physician may bill VA outpatient clinic**
    b. **patient may pay physician and get reimbursed by the VA by following the instructions on the VA outpatient clinic card**
36. When submitting a claim form for a patient applying for state disability benefits, the most important item required on the form is **claimant's Social Security number.**

Self-Study 16–1 Review Questions

1. You are reviewing a computer-generated insurance claim before it is sent to the insurance carrier and notice the patient's name as being an old friend. You quickly read the code for the diagnosis. Is this a breach of confidentiality? **No. Comment: No breach of confidentiality has occurred. However, the insurance billing specialist or coding clerk must never reveal to anyone anything appearing on the insurance claim without the patient's permission.**
2. You are coding in a medical records department when an agent from the Federal Bureau of Investigation walks in and asks for a patient's address. You ask, "Why do you need Mrs. Doe's address? Do you have a signed authorization from Mrs. Doe for release of information from our facility?" The FBI agent responds, "I'm trying to locate this person because of counterfeiting charges. No, I don't have a signed authorization form." Would there be any breach of confidentiality if you release the patient's address? Explain. **Yes. With no signed authorization, no information may be released.**
3. List three instances of breaching confidentiality in a hospital setting.
   Answers may vary and may be any three responses of the following:
   a. **Discussing patient information with coworkers or other hospital employees**
   b. **Talking about patient's information with your spouse or children**
   c. **Giving copies of a patient's medical reports to family members**
   d. **Relaying confidential information via cellular telephone**
   e. **Using samples of typed insurance claims with identifying data on the documents in one's job-seeking portfolio**
4. Name five different payment types under managed care contracts.
   Answers will vary and may be any five of the following or a combination of some of those listed.
   a. **ambulatory payment classifications**
   b. **bed leasing**
   c. **capitation or percentage of revenue**
   d. **case rate**
   e. **diagnostic-related groups**
   f. **differential by day in hospital**
   g. **differential by service type**
   h. **fee schedule—e.g., fee maximums schedule, fee allowance schedule, workers' compensation fee schedule**
   i. **flat rate**
   j. **per diem**
   k. **periodic interim payments and cash advances**
   l. **withholds**
   m. **managed care stop loss**
   n. **charges (not many of these contracts exist)**
   o. **discounts in the form of sliding scale (percentages)**
   p. **sliding scales for discounts and per diems**
5. What is the purpose of appropriateness evaluation protocols (AEP)? **These criteria are used by the review agency for admission screening. The Medicare PPS (prospective payment system) requires that all patients meet at least one severity of illness or one intensity of service to be certified for reimbursement.**

6. If a patient under a managed care plan goes to a hospital that is under contract with the plan for admission, what is necessary for inpatient admission? **Patient must be referred by a primary care physician and must obtain authorization for length of hospital stay.**
7. In what type of situation would a patient not have an insurance identification card? **Workers' compensation or industrial case.**
8. When a patient receives diagnostic tests and hospital outpatient services prior to admission to the hospital and these charges are combined with inpatient services becoming part of the diagnostic-related group payment, this regulation in hospital billing is known as **the 72-hour rule.**
9. The diagnosis established after study and listed for admission to the hospital for an illness or injury is called a/an **principal** diagnosis.
10. When reviewing an inpatient medical record, terminology and/or phrases to look for that relate to uncertain diagnoses are **"rule out," "suspected," "likely," "questionable," "possible," "still to be ruled out."**
11. From the list of *ICD-9-CM* descriptions shown, place in correct sequential order (1, 2, 3) for billing purposes. In this case, the medical procedure is a repair of other hernia of the anterior abdominal wall, incisional hernia repair with prosthesis, *ICD-9-CM* code 53.61.

	Diagnosis	*ICD-9-CM Code*
3	Chronic liver disease, liver damage unspecified	571.3
2	Alcohol dependence syndrome (other and unspecified)	303.9
1	Other hernia of abdominal cavity without mention of obstruction or gangrene (incisional hernia)	553.21

12. Mrs. Benson, a Medicare patient, is admitted by Dr. Dalton to the hospital on January 4 and is seen in consultation by Dr. Frank on January 5. On January 6, Mrs. Benson is discharged with a diagnosis of coronary atherosclerosis. State some of the problems regarding payment and Medicare policies that would affect this case. **The diagnosis of coronary atherosclerosis is subject to review by the review agency. If a patient is admitted for consultation only, the entire payment for hospital admission will be denied as well as any physician's fees involved.**
13. Match the words or phrases used for managed care reimbursement methods in the first column with the definitions in the second column. Write the correct letters in the blanks.

sliding scales for discount and per diems	**f**
discounts in the form of sliding scale	**n**
reinsurance stop loss	**k**
charges	**o**
withhold	**l**
ambulatory payment classifications	**j**
case rate	**i**
diagnostic-related groups	**g**
differential by service type	**h**
periodic interim payments	**c**
bed leasing	**m**
differential by day in hospital	**a**
capitation	**b**
per diem	**e**
percentage of revenue	**d**

a. Reimbursement method that pays more for the first day in the hospital than subsequent days.
b. Reimbursement to the hospital on a per member per month basis.
c. Plan advances cash to cover expected claims to the hospital.
d. Fixed percentage paid to the hospital to cover charges.
e. Single charge for a day in the hospital regardless of actual cost.
f. Interim per diem paid for each day in the hospital; based on total volume of business generated.
g. Classification system categorizing patients who are medically related with respect to diagnosis and treatment and statistically similar in lengths of hospital stay.
h. Hospital receives a flat per-admission payment for the particular service to which the patient is admitted.
i. An averaging after a flat rate is given to certain categories of procedures.
j. Outpatient classification based on procedures rather than on diagnoses.
k. Hospital buys insurance to protect against lost revenue and receives less of a capitation fee.
l. Method in which part of plan's payment to the hospital may be withheld and paid at the end of the year.
m. When a managed care plan leases beds from a hospital and pays per bed whether used or not.
n. A percentage reduction in charges for total bed days per year.
o. Dollar amount a hospital bills a case for services rendered.

14. Define the term *outpatient*. **An individual who receives medical service from the hospital and goes home the same day.**
15. Define the term *elective surgery*. **A surgical procedure that may be scheduled in advance, is not an emergency, and is discretionary on the part of the physician and patient.**
16. Baby Stephens falls from a high stool, cutting his head. His mother rushes him to St. Joseph's Medical Center for emergency care. The physician examines the baby, takes two stitches closing the laceration, sends the child for skull x-rays, and then discharges him to home. Will the emergency room care be billed as an inpatient or outpatient? **Outpatient since**

patient was not admitted to stay overnight in the hospital.

17. The inpatient and outpatient hospital billing department uses a summary form for submitting an insurance claim to an insurance plan called **Uniform Bill Claim Form, UB-92**
18. You can determine whether a UB-92 claim form is for an inpatient or an outpatient by the following observations:
    a. When the inpatient block number 4 shows three-digit billing code **111**
    b. When the outpatient block number 4 shows three-digit billing code **131**
    c. When revenue codes and block numbers **42, 43, 44, 45, and 46** indicate type of service rendered
19. Describe the significance of Blocks 42, 43, 44, 46, and 47 of the UB-92 claim form.
    a. Block 42 **is the Revenue Code that determines which per diem, case rate, flat rate, *CPT*, and so on applies per contract.**
    b. Block 43 **states the descriptive category of service rendered.**
    c. Block 44 **shows room rates, HCPCS and *CPT* code numbers.**
    d. Block 46 **shows the number of times (units) a single procedure or service was performed.**
    e. Block 47 **is the total charges by department revenue code, total for this bill, and its purpose is to collect statistics for comparisons or to set limits for reimbursement, i.e., reimbursement maximums or stop loss.**
20. Why did Medicare implement the DRG-based system of reimbursement? **To hold down rising health care costs.**
21. Name the six variables that affect Medicare reimbursement under the DRG system.
    a. **the patient's principal diagnosis**
    b. **the patient's secondary diagnosis**
    c. **surgical procedures**
    d. **comorbidity and complications**
    e. **age and sex**
    f. **discharge status**
22. Define the following abbreviations.

AEP	**appropriateness evaluation protocol**
PAT	**preadmission testing**
MDC	**major diagnostic categories**
PPS	**prospective payment system**
TEFRA	**Tax Equity and Fiscal Responsibility Act of 1982**
UR	**utilization review**
IS	**intensity of service**
SI	**severity of illness**
APC	**ambulatory payment classification**

23. Define cost outliers. **Cases that cannot be assigned to an appropriate DRG because of atypical situations.**
24. Define comorbidity. **A pre-existing condition that will, because of its effect on the specific principal diagnosis, require more intensive therapy or cause an increase in length of stay (LOS) by at least 1 day in approximately 75 per cent of cases.**

Self-Study 17-1 Review Questions

1. Read the job descriptions in Chapter 17. An ability to read handwritten and transcribed documents in the medical record, interpret information, and enter accurate code data into the computer system are technical skills required in the job of a/an **coder and specialist for an acute and/or ambulatory care setting; Health Information/Medical Record Technician.**
2. You have just completed a 1-year medical insurance course at a college. Name some preliminary job search contacts to make on campus.
    a. **school placement personnel**
    b. **classmates**
    c. **instructors**
    d. **school counselors**
3. Name skills that may be listed on an application form or in a résumé when seeking a position as an insurance billing specialist.
    a. **Procedural coding**
    b. **Diagnostic coding**
    c. **Knowledge of insurance programs**
    d. **Completing the HCFA-1500 insurance claim form**
    e. **Typing or keying and number of words per minute**
    f. **Optional: second language, if an individual has that skill; knowledge of medical terminology; knowledge and use of computer**
4. A question appears on a job application form about salary. Two ways in which to handle this question are:
    a. **write "negotiable" or "flexible" on the form**
    b. **discuss the topic during the interview**
5. State the chief purpose of a cover letter when sending a résumé to a prospective employer. **To get the employer to schedule an appointment for an interview.**
6. A résumé style that emphasizes work experience dates is known as a/an **chronologic** format; the **functional** format stresses job skills or qualifications.
7. When job applicants have similar skills and education, surveys have shown that hiring by employers has been based on **physical appearance at the interview.**
8. List the items to be compiled in a portfolio.
    a. **letters of recommendation**
    b. **school diplomas or degrees**
    c. **transcripts**
    d. **certificates**
    e. **names and addresses of references**
    f. **copies of résumé**
    g. **Social Security card**
    h. **timed typing tests certified by instructor**
    i. **samples of typed insurance claim forms with evidence of coding skills**
    j. **other items related to education and work experience**
9. You are being interviewed for a job and the interviewer asks this question, "What is your religious preference?" What would you respond? **This is an illegal question and may be either ignored, answered with "I think the question is not relevant to the requirements of this position," or refuse to answer and contact the**

Equal Employment Opportunity Commission office.

10. If a short period of time elapses after an interview and the applicant has received no word from the prospective employer, what follow-up steps may be taken?
    a. **place a telephone call**
    b. **write a thank-you letter**
11. When planning to start an insurance reimbursement business, enough funds to operate the business for a period of **one year or more** is vital.
12. Once an individual has begun his or her own business, the most common reason that a business might fail is **running out of money to keep the business going.**
13. In regard to the Internal Revenue Service, estimated tax payments must be made **quarterly** when the net income is **$500** or more.
14. Hugh Beason was the owner of XYZ Medical Reimbursement Service. A fire occurred, damaging some of the equipment and part of the office premises, requiring him to stop his work for a month so that repairs could be made. What type(s) of insurance would be helpful for this type of problem? **Business interruption insurance and property insurance.**
15. Name three situations in which an established insurance reimbursement service may require additional help.
    a. **work overload**
    b. **vacation needs**
    c. **occurrence of illness**
16. Jerry Hahn is pursuing a career as a claims assistance professional. When marketing his business, the target audience should be **consumers** and **Medicare recipients.**
17. Jennifer Inouye has been hired as a coding specialist by a hospital and needs to keep documentation when working. This may consist of
    a. **number of hours worked**
    b. **quantity of work done each day**
    c. **corrections applied to her work by officials in the contracting hospital**
18. List various methods used for pricing services as a self-employed insurance billing specialist.
    a. **percentage of reimbursement**
    b. **annual, hourly, or per claim fee**
19. A statement issued by a board or association verifying that an individual meets professional standards is called **certification.**
20. Professional registration may be done in either of two ways. They are:
    a. **an entry in an official registry or record that lists names of persons in an occupation who have satisfied specific requirements**
    b. **by attaining a certain level of education and paying a registration fee**
21. Define the following abbreviations that stand for validations of professionalism.

CCAP	**Certified Claims Assistance Professional**
CPC	**Certified Professional Coder**
CCS	**Certified Coding Specialist**
HRS	**Healthcare Reimbursement Specialist**
CMB	**Certified Medical Biller**
NCICS	**Nationally Certified Insurance Coding Specialist**

22. Read each statement and indicate whether True (T) or False (F).
    T a. Enhancing knowledge and keeping up to date are responsibilities of an insurance billing specialist.
    T b. Professional status of an insurance billing specialist may be obtained by passing a national examination for an HRS.
    F c. Professional status of a claims assistance professional may be obtained by passing a national examination as a CCS.
23. Name some ways an insurance billing specialist may seek to keep knowledge current.
    a. **become a member of a professional organization.**
    b. **find a mentor for advice, criticism, wisdom, and guidance.**
    c. **network with members of a professional organization as well as those working in the field**
    d. **if not a member, subscribe to newsletters and journals published by professional organizations**
24. Give the names of two national organizations that certify coders.
    a. **American Academy of Professional Coders**
    b. **American Health Information Management Association**

Self-Study Appendix C Review Questions

1. List the Medi-Cal program managed care plan models.
   a. **MCP: County-Organized Health System (COHS)**
   b. **MCP: Fee-for-Service/Managed Care (FFS/MC)**
   c. **MCP: Geographic Managed Care (GMC)**
   d. **MCP: Prepaid Health Plans (PHP)**
   e. **MCP: Primary Care Case Management (PCCM)**
   f. **MCP: Special Projects**
   g. **MCP: Two-Plan Model**
2. Mrs. Benson is a Medi-Cal recipient and injures her right leg in a fall. She is taken by ambulance to the emergency department of a local hospital. Must she seek treatment from a facility contracted under the Medi-Cal managed care plan or can she be treated wherever the ambulance takes her? **Since this case is an emergency, she can receive treatment from any facility regardless of whether it is contracted or not.**
3. If a Medi-Cal patient receives services from outside of his or her Medi-Cal managed care plan, what must the out-of-plan physician submit with the claim form for services? **A denial letter from the Medi-Cal managed care plan.**
4. Medically indigent individuals who are unable to provide mainstream medical care for themselves and whose incomes are above the assistance level are classified under a group called **medically needy**.
5. Name the entity that issues an identification card to each Medi-Cal recipient who is eligible for benefits. **State of California, Department of Health Services**
6. Name the two most important verifications that are the provider's responsibilities to obtain.
   a. **Patient receiving care is eligible for the month service is rendered**

b. **Patient is the individual to whom the Medi-Cal card was issued**

7. List four methods used to verify eligibility.
   a. **Point of service device**
   b. **Claims and eligibility real-time software**
   c. **Computer software**
   d. **Automated eligibility verification system**
8. Medical services to pregnant Medi-Cal recipients are available through the **Comprehensive Perinatal Services** program.
9. The name of the program that offers temporary coverage for prenatal care before a woman is officially a Medi-Cal recipient is called **presumptive eligibility**.
10. Medi-Cal recipients may receive **two** Medi-Services per calendar month.
11. An automated voice-response system for a provider to obtain prior authorization for a Medi-Cal service is called **Provider Telecommunications Network**.
12. Name two additional methods for obtaining prior approval for a Medi-Cal service.
    a. **Complete a Treatment Authorization Request (TAR) Form 50-1**
    b. **Access the Medi-Cal web site and electronically transmit an e-TAR**
13. To track a submitted Treatment Authorization Request, complete a/an **TAR Transmittal Form MC3020**.
14. A Medi-Cal patient seen today needs chronic hemodialysis services. You telephone for a TAR to get verbal approval. What four important items must you obtain to complete the written TAR?
    a. **Date of authorization**
    b. **Name of person who authorized**
    c. **Time authorization given**
    d. **Log number**
15. A Medi-Cal patient came in for an office visit and the physician said the patient needed to have a cholecystectomy within the next 6 weeks to 2 months and that it needed to be scheduled when convenient (aka elective surgery). Before scheduling surgery, what do you do? **Complete a Treatment Authorization Request (TAR) form and submit it for approval**. After you have completed this procedure, the patient is scheduled for the cholecystectomy. After surgery, you bill Medi-Cal, **noting the TAR control number** and **eligibility verification** on the claim form. Do you need to send any information to the hospital? **If the hospital does not have the TAR, you may have to fax or send a photocopy**.
16. The Medi-Cal copayment fee when a Medi-Cal patient seeks professional medical services from a physician is **$1.00**.
17. The Medi-Cal copayment fee when a patient has a prescription refilled is **$1.00**.
18. The time limit for submission of a Medi-Cal claim to receive 100% of the maximum allowable is **6 months from the end of the month of service**. A claim submitted within 8 months after service is rendered is reimbursed at **75%**. A claim sent within 12 months after service is given is paid at **50%**. A claim submitted over 1 year from the month service is received is paid **0%**.
19. State the difference in policy between the Medi-Cal global fee and the Medicare global package. **The Medi-Cal global fee includes the preoperative visit 7 days prior to surgery, and the Medicare global package includes preoperative visit or hospital visit 1 day prior to admission to the hospital.**
20. When a Medi-Cal patient has a private health insurance policy, who do you submit the initial claim to? **private insurance company**
21. Claims for patients who are recipients of Medicare and Medi-Cal are referred to as **crossover** claims, and the claim **must be** assigned.
22. A Medi-Cal patient also has TRICARE. What billing procedure do you follow? Be exact in your steps for a dependent of an active military man.
    a. **Bill TRICARE first**
    b. **Bill Medi-Cal and attach a TRICARE Summary Payment Voucher to the claim form**
23. Name the five categories of Medi-Cal adjudicated (resolution process) claims that appear on a Remittance Advice Details document.
    a. **Adjustments**
    b. **Payments or approvals**
    c. **Denials**
    d. **Suspends**
    e. **Accounts receivable transactions**
24. When posting dollar amounts from a Remittance Advice Details document to the patient's ledger, payments are shown as **credits** and negative adjustments are posted as **debits**.
25. When the Medi-Cal fiscal intermediary makes a direct deposit into a provider's bank account, this is known as **electronic funds transfer**.
26. If a provider feels a claim was denied in error, he or she should submit a/an **Claims Inquiry Form** for reconsideration.
27. On a Resubmission Turnaround Document, correct data are inserted into **Part B** of the form.
28. Dr. Practon requests an adjustment for an underpaid claim by submitting a/an **Claims Inquiry Form**.
29. A complaint about a Medi-Cal payment must be directed to the fiscal intermediary within **90 days** of the action that caused the complaint.
30. Define these Medi-Cal abbreviations.
    a. PE **Presumptive eligibility**
    b. RAD **Remittance Advice Details**
    c. BIC **Benefits identification card**
    d. TAR **Treatment Authorization Request**
    e. MN **Medically needy**
    f. POS **Point of service**
    g. CIF **Claims Inquiry Form**
    h. RTD **Resubmission Turnaround Document**
    i. SOC **Share of cost**
    j. AEVS **Automated eligibility verification system**